D1558630

Zondervan Illustrated Bible Backgrounds Commentary

Volume 1

Genesis, Exodus, Leviticus, Numbers, Deuteronomy

Contributors to Volume 1

General Editor and Genesis • John H. Walton (PhD, Hebrew Union College), Professor of Old Testament, Wheaton College and Graduate School, Wheaton, Illinois

Exodus • Bruce Wells (PhD, Johns Hopkins University), Assistant Professor of Hebrew Bible, Saint Joseph's University, Philadelphia, Pennsylvania

Leviticus • Roy E. Gane (PhD, University of California, Berkeley), Professor of Hebrew Bible and Ancient Near Eastern Languages, Andrews University, Berrien Springs, Michigan

Numbers • R. Dennis Cole (PhD, New Orleans Baptist Theological Seminary), Professor of Old Testament and Archaeology, McFarland Chair of Archaeology, New Orleans Baptist Theological Seminary, New Orleans, Louisiana

Deuteronomy • Eugene E. Carpenter (PhD, Fuller Theological Seminary), Professor of Old Testament and Hebrew, Scholar in Residence, Bethel College, Mishawaka, Indiana

Zondervan Illustrated Bible Backgrounds Commentary

Volume 1

Genesis, Exodus, Leviticus, Numbers, Deuteronomy

John H. Walton

GENERAL EDITOR

ZONDERVAN®

ZONDERVAN.com/
AUTHORTRACKER
follow your favorite authors

ZONDERVAN

Zondervan Illustrated Bible Backgrounds Commentary: Old Testament: Volume 1, *Genesis, Exodus, Leviticus, Numbers, Deuteronomy*

Genesis—Copyright © 2009 by John H. Walton
Exodus—Copyright © 2009 by Bruce Wells
Leviticus—Copyright © 2009 by Roy E. Gane
Numbers—Copyright © 2009 by R. Dennis Cole
Deuteronomy—Copyright © 2009 by Eugene E. Carpenter

Requests for information should be addressed to:

Zondervan, *Grand Rapids, Michigan 49530*

Library of Congress Cataloging-in-Publication Data

    Genesis, Exodus, Leviticus, Numbers, Deuteronomy / John H. Walton, general editor.
        p. cm.–(Zondervan illustrated Bible backgrounds commentary ; v. 1)
    Includes index.
    ISBN 978-0-310-25573-4 (hardcover)
    1. Bible. O.T. Pentateuch—Criticism, interpretation, etc. I. Walton, John H., 1952-
BS1225.52.G46 2009
222'.107–dc22   2009002197

Interior design by Mark Sheeres

Printed in China

09 10 11 12 13 14 15 16 17 18 19 20 • 20 19 18 17 16 15 14 13 12 11 10 9 8 7 6 5 4 3 2 1

Table of Contents

Acknowledgments

We are grateful for so many who have provided us photographs, some at reduced prices and others free of charge, to help make this work a visual resource on the ancient world. Credits appear by each photograph, but we would especially recognize the following:

Wikimedia Commons makes photographs available through commons.wiki media.org under a variety of licenses. We have benefited greatly from those that have been released into public domain and have sought out appropriate permission for those that have creative commons licensing (cc-by or cc-by-sa). These photographs are not copyright protected in this set but are available for use under the same terms that we used them.

In connection to Wikimedia, we have used a number of photographs from the Yorck Project, whose images are indicated as being in the public domain, but with compilation protected under the GNU Free Documentation License.

We would like especially to thank Marie-Lan Nguyen, who provided so many photos in public domain on Wikimedia, as well as Rama, who even went and took specific photos that we wanted. Others who provided numerous photographs through Wikimedia include Guillaume Blanchard and Keith Schengili-Roberts.

We are grateful to so many who posted their photographs on Flickr and made them available to us when we requested them. Lenka Peacock, Manfred Nader, and Peter White were particularly generous and gracious as they allowed us to use many of their photographs.

The Schøyen Collection supplied many photographs at no charge, and we are grateful to Elizabeth Sorenssen for her capable help.

Edward Loring, Research Fellow and Network Administrator Russian Academy of Sciences Centre for Egyptological Studies, Moscow (CESRAS), Russian Institute of Egyptology in Cairo (RIEC), provided photographs we could not have otherwise gotten.

Photography Suppliers were very helpful in our endless searches for photographs and we would especially like to acknowledge Todd Bolen (www.bibleplaces.com), Zev Radovan (www.biblelandpictures.com), Art Resource (www.artres.com, with thanks to Ann and Jennifer), Werner Forman (www.werner-forman-archive.com, with thanks to Themis), Jim Martin, Jack Hazut (www.israelimage.net), Richard Cleave (Rohr Productions), and Neal Bierling (www.phoenixdatasystems.com).

Thanks also to my colleagues who provided photographs: Fred Mabie, Steven Voth, John Monson, Jim Monson, Rami Arav, Scott Noegel, Aren Maier, Daniel Master, the Leon Levy Foundation, Alan Millard, Stephen Bourke, Constance Gane, and Randall Younker.

We are also grateful to those who supplied photographs from their personal collections: Michael Greenhalgh, Tim Bulkeley (eBibleTools.com/israel), Caryn Reeder, Christina Beblavi, Lisa Jean Winbolt, Brian McMorrow, Kim Walton, David

Hall, and the late Maurice Thompson (photographer of the Bible Scene Set), his sons Peter and Andrew, and Geoff Tucker, who scanned the slides for us.

Our gratitude also goes to Patti Ricotta, who provided helpful financing for Song of Songs pictures.

For artwork we are grateful to Susanna Vagt, Alva Steffler, and Jonathan Walton.

For help with the maps, we are most grateful to Carl Rasmussen, the author of the *Zondervan NIV Atlas of the Bible*.

Thanks also goes to Charlie Trimm for the preparation of the visuals index.

We would like to thank the always helpful staff at Zondervan whose hard work made this project possible: Katya Covrett, Verlyn Verbrugge, and Kim Zeilstra deserve special mention, as well as Jack Kuhatschek, who got the project started while he was still at Zondervan.

Finally, my entire family was involved in the project. Jill and Josh provided photos and Jonathan provided artwork. But far beyond those contributions, words cannot express the gratitude I owe to my wife, Kim, who for three years served as my research assistant in tracking down pictures with her consummate research skills. Without her perseverance, creativity, and companionship, the product here provided could not have been achieved. Through countless hours working by my side, going through the manuscript entry by entry to decide what visuals to provide and then painstakingly researching where they could be found, she became expert in iconography and art from the ancient world. But more than that, she stepped into my world as a cherished partner in my work and ministry, making every day "a day for a daydream." To her these volumes are dedicated with love, respect, and admiration.

John H. Walton
General Editor

Methodology: An Introductory Essay

John H. Walton

Comparative Studies

For over a century, studies comparing the OT and the ancient Near East have hovered on the fringe of hermeneutics and exegesis. Since these studies were at times exploited by critical scholars for polemical attacks against the biblical text, evangelicals were long inclined to avoid or even vilify them. They viewed the idea that the OT borrowed or adapted ancient Near Eastern ideas or literature as incompatible with Scripture's inspiration. Even as evangelicals in recent decades have grown more interested in tapping into the gold mine of comparative data, the results have often been considered tangential to the ultimate theological task. The influence from the ancient world has been identified with all that Israel was supposed to reject as they received the revelation from God that would purge their worldview from its pagan characteristics. Comparative studies served only as a foil to the theological interpretation of the text.

Consequently, comparative studies have been viewed as a component of historical-critical analysis at best, and more often as a threat to the uniqueness of the literature of the Bible. In contrast, today more and more biblical scholars are exploring the positive uses of comparative studies. As a result of half a century of the persistent scholarship of Assyriologists, Hittitologists, Egyptologists, and Sumerologists, we are now in a position to add significant nuances to the paradigms for studying the impact of the ancient Near East on the authors and editors of the Hebrew Bible. The end result is a more thorough and comprehensive understanding of the text.

Ever since the discovery of the Babylonian flood and creation accounts, critical scholarship has been attempting to demonstrate that the OT is derivative literature, a disadvantaged step-sister to the dominant cultures of the ancient Near East. These scholars have attempted to reduce the OT to converted mythology, whose dependency exposes its humanity. For confessing orthodoxy, however, there is no room for the conclusion that the OT is man-made theology. If the Flood is simply a human legend invented by people and borrowed into Israelite thinking, if the covenant is merely Israel's way of expressing their optimism that God has specially favored them through a treaty agreement with them, if the prophets never heard the voice of God but simply mimicked their ancient Near Eastern counterparts, then Christians are greatly to be pitied for having been duped in what would have to be considered the greatest hoax in history. It is no surprise, then, that evangelicals have often rejected the claims of these critical schools of thought.

There is, however, nothing inherently damaging to orthodox theology and beliefs about the Bible *if its authors were interacting at various levels with the literature current in the culture.* All literature is dependent on the culture in which it arises—it must be, if it intends to communicate effectively. Even when a text engages in polemic and correction of culture, it must be aware of and interact with current thinking and literature.

If we think about the example of creation texts, we realize that if God were to reveal his work of creation in our modern culture, he would have to explain how it related to the Big Bang theory or to evolution. His revelation would focus on the origins of the physical structure of the universe because that is what is important in our cultural perspective. In the ancient world, though, physical structure was relatively insignificant. People at that time were much more interested in the aspect of bringing order out of chaos and the divine exercise of jurisdiction demonstrated in giving everything a role and a purpose. In this context, any account of origins would of necessity have to be presented with these ancient ideas in mind.

The biblical text, in other words, formulated its discussion in relation to the thinking found in the ancient literature. It should be no surprise, then, if areas of similarity are found. This is far different from the contention that Israelite literature is simply derivative mythology. There is a great distance between borrowing from a particular piece of literature (as has been claimed in critical circles) and resonating with the larger culture that has itself been influenced by its literatures. When Americans speak of the philosophy of "eat, drink, and be merry, for tomorrow we die," they are resonating with an idea that has penetrated society rather than borrowing from the writings of Epicurus.

Another area where we must be sensitive to cultural issues is in the way we understand literary genres. It should be no surprise that OT genres need to be compared to genres in the larger culture. Whether we are looking at wisdom literature, hymnic literature, historical literature, or legal literature, we find generous doses of both similarities and differences. Understanding the genre of a piece of literature is necessary if we desire to perceive the author's intentions. Since perceiving such intentions is essential to our theological interpretation of a text, we recognize that understanding genre contributes to legitimate theological interpretation. Some genres will operate differently in the ancient world than they do in our own culture, so we must become familiar with the mechanics of the genres represented in the ancient Near East.

Where there are similarities, they help us to understand the genre parameters and characteristics as they existed in the ancient mind. What defined historical writing in the ancient world? How close was it to the journalistic approach of today, which relies heavily on eyewitness accounts? How did genealogies function in OT times? Were they compiled for the same purpose that we compile them for?

Occasionally comparisons within genres reveal close similarities between the biblical and ancient Near Eastern literatures on the level of content. Such similarities do not jeopardize inspiration. Even if the OT had the very same law or the very same proverb that was found in the ancient Near East, inspiration would be involved in the author choosing to incorporate that law or proverb into the canonical collection and to nuance it properly in appropriate context.

Where there are differences, it is still important to understand the ancient Near Eastern genres because the theological points will often be made by means of contrast. The theology behind the book of Job, for example, is built primarily on the distinctives of the ancient Near Eastern view (represented in the arguments of Job's friends), which was based on an appeasement mentality. The book's message is accomplished in counterpoint. If we are unaware of the contrasts, we will miss some of the nuances.

In fact, then, we must go beyond the simple identification of similarities and differences to articulate the relationships on a functional level. Similarities could exist because Israel adapted something from ancient Near Eastern culture or literature, or, as previously mentioned, because they simply resonated with the culture. Differences could reflect the Israelites' rejection of the ancient Near Eastern perspective, or they might emerge in explicit Israelite polemics against the views of their neighbors. In all such cases, the theology of the text may be nuanced by the cultural context.

In light of all of this, it may be logically concluded that without the guidance of comparative studies, we are bound to misinterpret the text at some points. A text is a complex of ideas linked by threads of writing. Each phrase and each word communicates by the ideas and thoughts that they will trigger in the reader or hearer. We can then speak of these underlying ideas as gaps that need to be filled with meaning by the audience. The writer or speaker assumes that those gaps will be filled in particular ways based on the common worldview he shares with his audience. Interpreters have the task of filling in those gaps, and when interpreting authoritative texts, it is theologically essential that we fill them appropriately.

For example, the Tower of Babel is described as being built "with its head in the heavens." Without the benefit of ancient Near Eastern backgrounds, early interpreters were inclined to provide the theological explanation that the builders were trying to build a structure that would allow them to launch an attack on the heavens. Comparative studies have allowed modern interpreters to recognize that this is an expression used to describe the ziggurats of Mesopotamia, which were intended to serve as a bridge or portal between heavens and earth. Such an understanding leads to an alternative, and arguably more accurate, interpretation of the text. In conclusion, then, as our interpretation of the text requires us to fill in the gaps, we have to be careful to consider the option of filling those gaps from the cultural context before we leap to fill them with theological significance.

As we make this transition in our thinking, we must expand the focus of our comparative studies. Too often in the past, comparative studies have been limited either to individual features (e.g., birds sent out from the ark) or to the literary preservation of traditions (e.g., creation accounts, vassal treaties) and have been conducted with either apologetics (from confessional circles) or polemics (against confessional traditions) in mind. As those interested in the interpretation of the text, we should recognize in addition the importance of comparative studies that focus on conceptual issues, conducted with illumination of the cultural dynamics behind the text in mind.

We can now create a spectrum to define the varieties of differences and similarities that can classify these nuances. The spectrum extends from differences to similarities while the matrix takes account of three categories: individual elements, worldview concepts, and literary preservation. This is represented in the following chart:

Relationships	Elements	Concepts	Literature
Totally ignores and presents different view	Sexual activity of gods	Theogony	Apotropaic rituals
Hazy familiarity leading to caricature and ridicule	Napping gods	Making of idols	Tammuz literature
Accurate knowledge resulting in rejection	Monogenesis/ polygenesis	Divine needs	Omen texts
Disagreement resulting in polemics, debate, or contention	Ziggurats	Theomachy; Flood	Cosmology texts
Awareness leading to adaptation or transformation	Circumcision	Kingship ideology; Classical prophecy	Words of the wise; Song of Songs
Conscious imitation or borrowing	Covenant-treaty format	Calf/bull image	Psalm 29
Subconscious shared heritage	Use of lots	Netherworld conditions; temple ideology	Proverbs

In conclusion, there are ten important principles that must be kept in mind when doing comparative studies:

1. Both similarities and differences must be considered.
2. Similarities may suggest a common cultural heritage rather than borrowing.
3. It is common to find **similarities** at the surface but differences at the conceptual level and vice versa.
4. All elements must be understood in their own context as accurately as possible before crosscultural comparisons are made.
5. Proximity in time, geography, and spheres of cultural contact all increase the possibility of interaction leading to influence.
6. A case for literary borrowing requires identification of likely channels of transmission.
7. The significance of differences between two pieces of literature is minimized if the works are not the same genre.
8. Similar functions may be performed by different genres in different cultures.
9. When literary or cultural elements are borrowed, they may in turn be transformed into something quite different.
10. A single culture will rarely be monolithic, either in a contemporary cross-section or in consideration of a passage of time.[1]

Successful interpreters must try to understand the cultural background of the ancient Near East just as successful missionaries must learn the culture, language, and worldview of the people they are trying to reach. This is the rationale for us to study the Bible in light of the ancient Near East. What we contend, then, is that comparative studies has three goals in mind:

1. We study the *history* of the ancient Near East as a means of recovering knowledge of the events that shaped the lives of people in the ancient world.
2. We study *archaeology* as a means of recovering the lifestyle reflected in the material culture of the ancient world.
3. We study the *literature* of the ancient Near East as a means of penetrating the heart and soul of the people who inhabited the ancient world that Israel shared.

These goals are at the heart of comparative studies and will help us understand the OT better.

Comparative Studies in the Pentateuch

A wide array of literature from the ancient Near East provides information that is helpful for interpreting the Pentateuch. Ancient Near Eastern mythology reflects ideas about creation.[2] Though they provide accounts of creation from Mesopotamia[3] and Egypt[4] and in the process provide insight into the creator deities and their roles, they also provide important information concerning how the ancients thought about the cosmos.[5] Consequently, in addition to talking about cosmic and human origins, we learn about their perspectives on cosmic geography,[6] on what is entailed in bringing something into existence (i.e., creation), and what constitutes creative acts.[7]

The patriarchal narratives can be read against the background of family archives from the ancient Near East that explain customs and legal traditions[8] and the religious practice and beliefs of the patriarchs.[9] Ritual descriptions can be illuminated by ritual texts available in wide variety.[10] Covenant documents can be read in light of treaties between countries.[11] Laws can be compared to a variety of law collections from the second millennium. Such comparison can focus on the form[12] or content[13] of the individual laws, but more importantly expands to a study of the source of law and the literary functions of law collections.[14]

Historical and archaeological studies can provide background information to help understand the situation in Canaan during the patriarchal period and try to resolve basic questions such as the historical setting of Israel's slavery in Egypt and the date of the Exodus.[15] Of particular importance are all of the archaeological studies that try to bring further understanding to the Egyptian backdrop of these events.[16] Geographical studies continue to address issues such as the identification of the body of water that the Israelites crossed and the location of Mount Sinai.[17]

Sociological studies can comment on the concept of sacred space and the variety of institutions that exist in a society to manage sacred space, from priests to sanctuaries to rituals.[18] Additional studies in religion also help us to understand some of the ways that Israel was to be distinct from the people around them. As we learn about the perception of deity and the way that perception is reflected in ancient Near Eastern ideas about pantheons, images, divination, and magic, we can understand more clearly some of what Israel is to guard against.[19] This general survey indicates just a few of the ways that comparative and cultural studies will be seen to impact and illuminate our study of the Pentateuch in this volume.

Bibliography on Comparative Studies Methodology

Finkelstein, J. J. "Bible and Babel: A Comparative Study of the Hebrew and Babylonian Religious Spirit." Pages 355–80 in *Essential Papers on Israel and the Ancient Near East*, ed. F. E. Greenspahn. New York: New York Univ. Press, 1991.

Hallo, W. W. "New Moons and Sabbaths: A Case Study in the Contrastive Approach." *HUCA* 48 (1977): 1–18.

_____. "Biblical History in Its Near Eastern Setting: The Contextual Approach." Pages 1–26 in *Scripture in Context*, ed. C. Evans, et al. Pittsburgh: Pickwick, 1980.

_____. "Compare and Contrast: The Contextual Approach to Biblical Literature." Pages 1–19 in *The Bible In Light of Cuneiform Literature: Scripture in Context III*, ed. W. W. Hallo, B. Jones, and G. Mattingly. Lewiston, NY: Edwin Mellen, 1990.

Huffmon, H. B. "Babel und Bibel: The Encounter between Babylon and the Bible." Pages 309–20 in *The Bible and Its Traditions*, ed. M. P. O'Connor and D. N. Freedman. Ann Arbor: Univ. of Michigan Press, 1983.

Loewenstamm, S. E. "Biblical Studies in the Light of Akkadian Texts." Pages 256–67 in *From Babylon to Canaan*. Jerusalem: Magnes, 1992.

Longman, Tremper III. *Fictional Akkadian Autobiography*. Winona Lake: Eisenbrauns, 1991.

Machinist, P. "The Question of Distinctiveness in Ancient Israel." Pages 420–42 in *Essential Papers on Israel and the Ancient Near East*, ed. F. E. Greenspahn. New York: New York Univ. Press, 1991.

Malamat, A. "The Proto-History of Israel: A Study in Method." Pages 303–13 in *The Word of the Lord Shall Go Forth*, ed. C. L. Meyers and M. O'Connor. Winona Lake: Eisenbrauns: 1983.

Malul, M. *The Comparative Method in Ancient Near Eastern and Biblical Legal Studies*, AOAT 227. Kevelaer: Butzon und Bercker; Neukirchen-Vluyn: Neukirchener, 1990.

Millard, A. R. "Methods of Studying the Patriarchal Narratives As Ancient Texts." Pages 35–51 in *Essays on the Patriarchal Narratives*, ed. A. R. Millard and D. J. Wiseman. Winona Lake: Eisenbrauns, 1983.

Ringgren, H. "The Impact of the Ancient Near East on the Israelite Tradition." Pages 31–46 in *Tradition and Theology in the Old Testament*, ed. D. A. Knight. Sheffield: Sheffield Academic Press, 1977/1990.

Roberts, J. J. M. "The Ancient Near Eastern Environment." Pages 3–43 in *The Bible and the Ancient Near East*. Winona Lake: Eisenbrauns, 2002.

_____. "The Bible and the Literature of the Ancient Near East." Pages 44–58 in *The Bible and the Ancient Near East*. Winona Lake: Eisenbrauns, 2002.

_____. "Myth Versus History: Relaying the Comparative Foundations." *CBQ* 38 (1976): 1–13.

Rodriguez, A. M. "Ancient Near Eastern Parallels to the Bible and the Question of Revelation and Inspiration." *Journal of the Adventist Theological Society* 12 (2001): 43–64.

Saggs, H. W. F. *The Encounter with the Divine in Mesopotamia and Israel*. London: Athlone, 1978.

Selman, M. J. "Comparative Customs and the Patriarchal Age." Pages 93–138 in *Essays on the Patriarchal Narratives*, ed. A. R. Millard and D. J. Wiseman. Winona Lake: Eisenbrauns, 1983.

Talmon, S. "The Comparative Method in Biblical Interpretation: Principles and Problems." *VTSup* 29 (1977): 320–56.

Tigay, J. "On Evaluating Claims of Literary Borrowing." Pages 250–55 in *The Tablet and the Scroll*, ed. M. Cohen et al. Bethesda: CDL, 1993.

Toorn, K. van der. *Sin and Sanction in Israel and Mesopotamia*. Assen: Van Gorcum, 1985.

Notes

1. J. Walton, "Cultural Background of the Old Testament," in *Foundations for Biblical Interpretation*, ed. D. Dockery, K. Mathews, and R. Sloan (Nashville: Broadman & Holman, 1994), 256. See also J. Tigay, "On Evaluating Claims of Literary Borrowing," in *The Tablet and the Scroll*, ed. M. Cohen et al. (Bethesda, MD: CDL, 1993), 250–55.
2. R. J. Clifford, *Creation Accounts in the Ancient Near East and the Bible* (Washington, D.C.: Catholic Biblical Association, 1994); J. H. Walton, *Genesis* (NIVAC; Grand Rapids: Zondervan, 2001); J. P. Allen, *Genesis in Egypt: The Philosophy of Ancient Egyptian Creation Accounts* (New Haven, Conn.: Yale Univ. Press, 1988).
3. Such as *Enuma Elish* (COS 1.111) and *Atrahasis* (COS 1.130).
4. Such as the Memphite Theology (COS 1.15)
5. W. G. Lambert, "The Cosmology of Sumer and Babylon," *Ancient Cosmologies*, ed. C. Blacker and M. Loewe (London: George Allen and Unwin Ltd., 1975), 42–65; D. T. Tsumura, "Genesis and Ancient Near Eastern Stories of Creation and Flood: An Introduction," *I Studied Inscriptions Before the Flood*, ed. R. S. Hess and D. T. Tsumura (Winona Lake: Eisenbrauns, 1994), 27–57.
6. W. Horowitz, *Mesopotamian Cosmic Geography* (Winona Lake: Eisenbrauns, 1998); I. Cornelius, "The Visual Representation of the World in the Ancient Near East and the Hebrew Bible," *JNSL* 20 (1994): 193–218.
7. Walton, *Genesis*, 70–72.
8. M. J. Selman, "Comparative Customs and the Patriarchal Age," *Essays on the Patriarchal Narratives*, ed. A. R. Millard and D. J. Wiseman (Winona Lake: Eisenbrauns, 1983), 91–140.
9. Augustine Pagolu, *The Religion of the Patriarchs* (JSOTSup 277; Sheffield: Sheffield Academic Press, 1998).
10. Access through various articles in *CANE*, vol. 3. See also D. Pardee, *Ritual and Cult at Ugarit* (SBLWAW 10; Atlanta: SBL, 2002).
11. D. J. McCarthy, *Treaty and Covenant* (Rome: Pontifical, 1978); Gary Beckman, *Hittite Diplomatic Texts* (SBLWAW 7; Atlanta: SBL, 1996); D. W. Baker, "The Mosaic Covenant against its Environment," *ATJ* 20 (1988): 9–18.
12. R. A. F. MacKenzie, "The Formal Aspect of Ancient Near Eastern Law," *The Seed of Wisdom*, ed. W. S. McCullough (Toronto: Univ. of Toronto Press, 1964), 31–44.
13. W. J. Doorly, *The Laws of Yahweh: A Handbook of Biblical Law* (Mahwah, NJ: Paulist, 2002), 119–22.
14. M. Roth, *Law Collections from Mesopotamia and Asia Minor* (SBLWAW 6; Atlanta: SBL, 1995); S. Paul, *Studies in the Book of the Covenant in the Light of Cuneiform and Biblical Law* (Leiden: Brill, 1970); A. Phillips, *Ancient Israel's Criminal Law* (New York: Schocken, 1970); J. J. Finkelstein, *The Ox That Gored* (Philadelphia: American Philosophical Society, 1981); H. J. Boecker, *Law and the Administration of Justice in the Old Testament and Ancient Near East* (Minneapolis: Augsburg, 1980); R. Westbrook, ed., *Studies in Ancient Near Eastern Law* (Leiden: Brill: 2004); D. Patrick, *Old Testament Law* (Atlanta: John Knox, 1985).
15. J. Hoffmeier, *Israel in Egypt* (New York: Oxford Univ. Press, 1997); J. Currid, *Ancient Egypt and the Old Testament* (Grand Rapids: Baker, 1997); G. Kelm, *Escape to Conflict* (Fort Worth: IAR, 1991).
16. Manfred Bietak, "Dab'a, Tell Ed-," in *Oxford Encyclopedia of Ancient Egypt*, ed. D. B. Redford (New York: Oxford Univ. Press, 2001), 1:351–54. See also Hoffmeier, *Israel in Egypt*, and E. S. Frerichs and L. Lesko, *Exodus: The Egyptian Evidence* (Winona Lake: Eisenbrauns, 1997).

17. J. Huddlestun, "Red Sea," *ABD*, 5:633–42; I. Beit-Arieh, "The Route Through Sinai—Why Israelites Fleeing Egypt Went South," *Archaeology and the Bible: Early Israel*, ed. H. Shanks and D. P. Cole (Washington, D.C.: Biblical Archaeology Society, 1990), 50–59.
18. F. H. Gorman, *The Ideology of Ritual* (Sheffield: Sheffield Academic Press, 1990); R. Gane, *Leviticus and Numbers* (NIVAC; Grand Rapids: Zondervan, 2004); J. Milgrom, *Leviticus*, 3 vols (AB; New York: Doubleday, 1991–2001); J. D. Levenson, "The Temple and the World," *JR* 64 (1984): 275–98; J. M. Lundquist, "Temple, Covenant, and Law in Ancient Near East and in the Hebrew Bible," *Israel's Apostasy and Restoration*, ed. A. Gileadi (Grand Rapids: Baker, 1988), 293–306; J. M. Lundquist, "What Is a Temple? A Preliminary Typology," *The Quest for the Kingdom of God*, ed. H. B. Huffmon, F. A. Spina, and A. R. W. Green (Winona Lake: Eisenbrauns, 1983), 205–20.
19. W. W. Hallo, "Cult Statue and Divine Image: A Preliminary Study," *Scripture in Context II*, ed. W. W. Hallo, J. C. Moyer, and L. G. Perdue (Winona Lake: Eisenbrauns, 1983), 1–18; V. Hurowitz, "Picturing Imageless Deities: Iconography in the Ancient Near East," *BAR* 23 (1997): 46–48, 51. T. Jacobsen, "The Graven Image," *Ancient Israelite Religion*, ed. P. D. Miller, P. D. Hanson, and S. D. McBride (Philadelphia: Fortress, 1987), 15–32; J. J. M. Roberts, "Divine Freedom and Cultic Manipulation in Israel and Mesopotamia," *Unity and Diversity*, ed. H. Goedicke, and J. J. M. Roberts (Baltimore: Johns Hopkins Univ. Press, 1975), 181–90; M. C. A. Korpel, *A Rift in the Clouds: Ugaritic and Hebrew Descriptions of the Divine* (UBL 8; Münster: Ugarit-Verlag, 1990).

General Bibliography

Reference

Anchor Bible Dictionary. Ed. D. N. Freedman. New York: Doubleday, 1992.

Ancient Near East in Pictures. Ed. J. B. Pritchard. Princeton: Princeton Univ. Press, 1954.

Cambridge Ancient History. Ed. J. Boardman et. al. Cambridge: Cambridge Univ. Press, 1970–.

Civilizations of the Ancient Near East. Ed. J. Sasson. New York: Scribners, 1995.

Companion to the Ancient Near East. Ed. Daniel Snell. Oxford: Blackwell, 2005.

Dictionary of Deities and Demons in the Bible. Ed. K. van der Toorn et al. Leiden: Brill, 1995.

Dictionary of the Ancient Near East. Ed. P. Bienkowski and A. R. Millard. Philadelphia: Univ. of Pennsylvania Press, 2000.

Handbook to Life in Ancient Mesopotamia. Ed. S. Bertman. New York: Facts on File, 2003.

IVP Dictionaries of the Old Testament. Downers Grove, Ill.: InterVarsity Press, 2003–.

New Encyclopedia of Archaeological Excavations in the Holy Land. Ed. E. Stern. New York: Simon and Schuster, 1993.

Oxford Encyclopedia of Ancient Egypt. Ed. D. B. Redford. New York: Oxford Univ. Press, 2001.

Oxford Encyclopedia of Archaeology in the Near East. Ed. E. M. Meyers. New York: Oxford Univ. Press, 1997.

Tübinger Bibelatlas. Ed. S. Mittmann and G. Schmitt. Stuttgart: Deutsche Bibelgesellschaft, 2001.

Theological Dictionary of the Old Testament. Ed. G. J. Botterweck and H. Ringgren. Trans. J. T. Willis, et al. Grand Rapids: Eerdmans, 1974–.

Views of the Biblical World. Ed. B. Mazar. Jerusalem: International, 1959.

World History of the Jewish People. Ed. B. Mazar. Jerusalem: Massada, 1963–1979.

Translations of Texts

Amarna Letters. W. L. Moran. Baltimore: Johns Hopkins Univ. Press, 1992.

Ancient Egyptian Literature. 3 vols. M. Lichtheim. Berkeley: Univ. of California Press, 1973–80.

The Ancient Near East: Historical Sources in Translation. Ed. M. Chavalas. Oxford: Blackwell, 2006.

Ancient Near Eastern Texts. Ed. J. B. Pritchard. Princeton: Princeton Univ. Press, 1969.

Babylonian Gilgamesh Epic. 2 vols. A. R. George. Oxford: Oxford Univ. Press, 2003.

Babylonian Wisdom Literature. W. G. Lambert. Oxford: Clarendon, 1960.

Before the Muses. Ed. B. Foster. 3rd ed. Bethesda, Md.: CDL, 2005.

The Context of Scripture. 3 vols. Ed. W. W. Hallo and K. L. Younger. Leiden: Brill, 1997.

Harps That Once ... T. Jacobsen. New Haven, Conn.: Yale Univ. Press, 1987.

Literature of Ancient Sumer. J. Black et al. Oxford: Oxford Univ. Press, 2004 (see www-etcsl. orient.ox.ac.uk).

Myths of Mesopotamia. Ed. S. Dalley. New York: Oxford Univ. Press, 1991.

Near Eastern Religious Texts Relating to the Old Testament. Ed. W. Beyerlin. Philadelphia: Westminster, 1978.

Old Testament Parallels. Ed. V. Matthews and D. Benjamin. 2nd ed. New York: Paulist, 1997.

Proverbs of Ancient Sumer. 2 vols. B. Alster. Bethesda, Md.: CDL, 1997.

Readings from the Ancient Near East. Ed. B. Arnold and B. Beyer. Grand Rapids: Baker, 2002.

SBL Writings from the Ancient World Series. Ed. T. Lewis. Atlanta: SBL, 1990–.
    SBLWAW 2: H. A. Hoffner. *Hittite Myths*.
    SBLWAW 4: J. M. Lindenberger. *Ancient Aramaic and Hebrew Letters*.
    SBLWAW 6: M. Roth. *Law Collections from Mesopotamia and Asia Minor*.
    SBLWAW 7: G. Beckman. *Hittite Diplomatic Texts*.
    SBLWAW 9: S. Parker. *Ugaritic Narrative Poetry*.
    SBLWAW 11: I. Singer. *Hittite Prayers*.
    SBLWAW 12: M. Nissinen. *Prophets and Prophecy in the Ancient Near East*.
    SBLWAW 16: N. C. Strudwick. *Texts from the Pyramid Age*.
    SBLWAW 19: J.-J. Glassner. *Mesopotamian Chronicles*.
    SBLWAW 20: H. Vanstiphout. *Epics of Sumerian Kings: The Matter of Aratta*.
    SBLWAW 23: J. P. Allen. *The Ancient Egyptian Pyramid Texts*.

Wisdom of Ancient Sumer. B. Alster. Bethesda, Md.: CDL, 2005.

Books on Bible Backgrounds

Assmann, J. *The Search for God in Ancient Egypt*. Ithaca, N.Y.: Cornell Univ. Press, 2001.

Baines, J., and J. Málek. *Atlas of Ancient Egypt*. New York: Facts on File, 1980.

Bottéro, J. *Religion in Ancient Mesopotamia*. Chicago: Univ. of Chicago Press, 2001.

_____. *Everyday Life in Ancient Mesopotamia*. Baltimore: Johns Hopkins Univ. Press, 2001.

Braun, J. *Music in Ancient Israel/Palestine*. Grand Rapids: Eerdmans, 2002.

Bryce, T. *The Kingdom of the Hittites*. New York: Oxford Univ. Press, 1998.

Coogan, M. D. *The Oxford History of the Biblical World*. New York: Oxford Univ. Press, 1998.

Day, J. *Yahweh and the Gods and Goddesses of Canaan*. Sheffield: Sheffield Academic Press, 2000.

Dearman, A. *Religion and Culture in Ancient Israel*. Peabody, Mass.: Hendrickson, 1992.

Dorsey, D. A. *The Roads and Highways of Ancient Israel*. Baltimore: Johns Hopkins Univ. Press, 1991.

Forbes, R. J. *Studies in Ancient Technology*. 9 vols. Leiden: Brill, 1964–.

Frankfort, H., et al. *The Intellectual Adventure of Ancient Man*. Chicago: Univ. of Chicago Press, 1946.

Green, A. R. W. *The Storm-God in the Ancient Near East*. Winona Lake, Ind.: Eisenbrauns, 2003.

Hoerth, A. *Archaeology and the Old Testament*. Grand Rapids: Baker, 1998.

Hoerth, A., G. Mattingly, and E. Yamauchi. *Peoples of the Old Testament World*. Grand Rapids: Baker, 1994.

Jacobsen, T. *Treasures of Darkness*. New Haven, Conn.: Yale Univ. Press, 1976.

Keel, O. *The Symbolism of the Biblical World*. New York: Seabury, 1978.

Keel, O., and C. Uehlinger. *Gods, Goddesses and Images of God in Ancient Israel*. Minneapolis: Fortress, 1998.

King, P., and L. Stager. *Life in Biblical Israel*. Louisville: Westminster John Knox, 2002.

Kitchen, K. A. *On the Reliability of the Old Testament*. Grand Rapids: Eerdmans, 2003.

Kuhrt, A. *The Ancient Near East, 3000–330 B.C.* London: Routledge, 1997.

Marsman, H. J. *Women in Ugarit and Israel.* Leiden: Brill, 2003.

Matthews, Victor. *Manners and Customs in the Bible.* Peabody, Mass.: Hendrickson, 1988.

Matthews, V., and D. Benjamin. *The Social World of the Old Testament.* Peabody, Mass.: Hendrickson, 1993.

Mazar, A. *Archaeology of the Land of the Bible.* New York: Doubleday, 1990.

Miller, J. M., and J. Hayes. *A History of Ancient Israel and Judah.* Philadelphia: Westminster, 1986.

Miller, P. D. *The Religion of Ancient Israel.* Louisville: Westminster John Knox, 2000.

Moorey, P. R. S. *Ancient Mesopotamian Materials and Industries.* Winona Lake, Ind.: Eisenbrauns, 1999.

Morenz, S. *Egyptian Religion.* Ithaca, N.Y.: Cornell Univ. Press, 1973.

Nakhai, B. A. *Archaeology and the Religions of Canaan and Israel.* Boston: ASOR, 2001.

Nemet-Nejat, K. R. *Daily Life in Ancient Mesopotamia.* Westport, Conn.: Greenwood, 1998.

Olmo Lete, G., del. *Canaanite Religion.* Winona Lake, Ind.: Eisenbrauns, 2004.

Provan, I, V. P. Long, and T. Longman. *A Biblical History of Israel.* Louisville: Westminster John Knox, 2003.

Rainey, A., and R. S. Notley. *The Sacred Bridge.* Jerusalem: Carta, 2006.

Redford, D. B. *Egypt, Canaan, and Israel in Ancient Times.* Princeton: Princeton Univ. Press, 1992.

Roaf, M. *Cultural Atlas of Mesopotamia and the Ancient Near East.* New York: Facts on File, 1990.

Saggs, H. W. F. *The Greatness That Was Babylon.* New York: Mentor, 1962.

_____. *Encounter with the Divine in Mesopotamia and Israel.* London: Athlone, 1978.

_____. *The Might That Was Assyria.* London: Sidgwick & Jackson, 1984.

Snell, D. *Life in the Ancient Near East.* New Haven, Conn.: Yale Univ. Press, 1997.

Sparks, K. L. *Ancient Texts for the Study of the Hebrew Bible.* Peabody, Mass.: Hendrickson, 2005.

Stern, E. *Archaeology of the Land of the Bible,* Vol. 2. New York: Doubleday, 2001.

Thompson, J. A. *Handbook of Life in Bible Times.* Downers Grove, Ill.: InterVarsity Press, 1986.

Toorn, K. van der. *Family Religion in Babylonia, Syria and Israel: Continuity and Change in the Forms of Religious Life.* Leiden: Brill, 1996.

Van de Mieroop, M. *The Ancient Mesopotamian City.* New York: Oxford Univ. Press, 1999.

_____. *Cuneiform Texts and the Writing of History.* London: Routledge, 1999.

_____. *A History of the Ancient Near East: ca. 3000–323 B.C.* London: Blackwell, 2003.

Walton, J. H. *Ancient Israelite Literature in Its Cultural Context.* Grand Rapids: Zondervan, 1989.

_____. *Ancient Near Eastern Thought and the Old Testament: Introducing the Conceptual World of the Hebrew Bible.* Grand Rapids: Baker, 2006.

Walton, J. H., V. Matthews, and M. Chavalas. *IVP Bible Background Commentary: Old Testament.* Downers Grove, Ill.: InterVarsity Press, 2000.

Westbrook, R. *A History of Ancient Near Eastern Law.* 2 vols. Leiden: Brill, 2003.

Wiseman, D. J. *Peoples of Old Testament Times.* Oxford: Clarendon, 1973.

Yadin, Y. *The Art of Warfare in Biblical Lands.* London: Weidenfeld & Nicolson, 1963.

Yamauchi, E. *Persia and the Bible.* Grand Rapids: Baker, 1990.

Zevit, Z. *Religions of Ancient Israel.* New York: Continuum, 2001.

AAA . . . . *Annals of Archaeology and Anthropology*

AASOR . . . . Annual of the American Schools of Oriental Research

AB . . . . Anchor Bible

AB . . . . *Assyriologische Bibliothek*

ABC . . . . *Assyrian and Babylonian Chronicles.* A. K. Grayson. TCS 5. Locust Valley, New York, 1975

ABD . . . . *Anchor Bible Dictionary.* D. N. Freedman. 6 vols. New York, 1992

ABL . . . . *Assyrian and Babylonian Letters Belonging to the Kouyunjik Collections of the British Museum.* R. F. Harper. 14 vols. Chicago, 1892–1914

ABR . . . . *Australian Biblical Review*

ABRL . . . . . . Anchor Bible Reference Library

AbrN . . . . *Abr-Nahrain*

ABS . . . . Arab Background Series

ACCS . . . . . . Ancient Christian Commentary on Scripture

ACEBT . . . . . *Amsterdamse Cahiers voor Exegese en bijbelse Theologie*

ADD . . . . *Assyrian Deeds and Documents.* C. H. W. Johns. 4 vols. Cambridge, 1898–1923

AEL . . . . *Ancient Egyptian Literature.* M. Lichtheim. 3 vols. Berkeley, 1971–1980

AfO . . . . *Archiv für Orientforschung*

AfOB . . . . . . Archiv für Orientforschung: Beiheft

ÄgAbh . . . . . . Ägyptologische Abhandlungen

AHw . . . . *Akkadisches Handwörterbuch.* W. von Soden. 3 vols. Wiesbaden, 1965–81

AJA . . . . *American Journal of Archeology*

AJBA . . . . . . *Australian Journal of Biblical Archaeology*

AJSLL . . . . . . *American Journal of Semitic Languages and Literature*

AMD . . . . . . Ancient Magic and Divination

AnBib . . . . . . Analecta biblica

ANEP . . . . . . *The Ancient Near East in Pictures Relating to the Old Testament.* J. B. Pritchard. Princeton, 1954

ANET . . . . . . *Ancient Near Eastern Texts Relating to the Old Testament.* J. B. Pritchard. 3rd ed. Princeton, 1969

ANF . . . . *Ante-Nicene Fathers*

AnOr . . . . . . Analecta orientalia

AnSt . . . . *Anatolian Studies*

AO . . . . Antiquités orientales

AO . . . . *Der Alte Orient*

AOAT . . . . . Alter Orient und Altes Testament

AOB . . . . *Altorientalische Bilder zum Alten Testament*

AOS . . . . . . American Oriental Series

AOTC . . . . . Abingdon Old Testament Commentary

AOTS . . . . . . *Archaeology and Old Testament Study.* D. W. Thomas. Oxford, 1967

APOT . . . . . . *Apocrypha and Pseudepigrapha of the Old Testament.* Ed. R. H. Charles. 2 vols. Oxford: Oxford University Press, 1913

ARAB . . . . . . *Ancient Records of Assyria and Babylonia.* Daniel David Luckenbill. 2 vols. Chicago, 1926–1927

Arch . . . . *Archaeology*

ARI . . . . *Assyrian Royal Inscriptions.* A. K. Grayson. 2 vols. RANE. Wiesbaden, 1972–1976

ARM . . . . . . Archives royales de Mari

ARMT . . . . . Archives royales de Mari, transcrite et traduite

ArtH . . . . *Art History*

ARW . . . . *Archiv für Religionswissenschaft*

AS . . . . Assyriological Studies

ASJ . . . . *Acta Sumerologica (Japan)*

ASOR . . . . . . American Schools of Oriental Research

ASORDS . . . American Schools of Oriental Research Dissertation Series

ASTI . . . . *Annual of the Swedish Theological Institute*

ATJ . . . . *Ashland Theological Journal*

AThR . . . . . . *Anglican Theological Review*

ATSDS . . . . Andrews Theological Seminary Dissertation Series

AuOr . . . . . . *Aula orientalis*

AUSDS . . . . Andrews University Seminary Dissertation Series

AUSS. . . . . . . *Andrews University Seminary Studies*

AUU . . . . Acta Universitatis Upsaliensis

BA . . . . *Biblical Archaeologist*

BAIAS . . . . . *Bulletin of the Anglo-Israel Archeological Society*

BAR . . . . *Biblical Archaeology Review*

BARead . . . . *Biblical Archaeologist Reader*

BASOR . . . . . *Bulletin of the American Schools of Oriental Research*

BASORSup . Bulletin of the American Schools of Oriental Research: Supplement Series

BAW . . . . Bayerischen Akademie der Wissen

BBB . . . . Bonner biblische Beiträge

BBET. . . . . . . Beiträge zur biblischen Exegese und Theologie

BBR . . . . *Bulletin for Biblical Research*

BBVO . . . . . . Berliner Beiträge zum Vorderen Orient

BCOTWP . . . Baker Commentary on the Old Testament Wisdom and Psalms

BDB. . . . . Brown, F., S. R. Driver, and C. A. Briggs. *A Hebrew and English Lexicon of the Old Testament.* Oxford, 1907

BeO . . . . *Bibbia e oriente*

BES . . . . *Bes*

BETL. . . . . . . Bibliotheca epheremidum theologicarum lovaniensium

BETS . . . . *Bulletin of the Evangelical Society*

BHH . . . . *Biblisch-historisches Handwörterbuch.* B. Reicke and L. Rost. Göttingen, 1962-1966

Bib . . . . *Biblica*

BibOr . . . . . . Biblica et orientalia

BibSem . . . . . Biblical Seminar

BibRes . . . . . . *Biblical Research*

BiOr. . . . . *Biblioteca Orientalis*

BJRL . . . . *Bulletin of the John Rylands University Library of Manchester*

BJS . . . . Brown Judaic Studies

BM. . . . . British Museum

BN . . . . *Biblische Notizen*

BO. . . . . *Bibliotheca orientalis*

BR . . . . *Biblical Research*

BRev . . . . *Bible Review*

BRM . . . . . . Babylonian Religion and Mythology

BSac . . . . *Bibliotheca sacra*

BSC. . . . . Bible Student's Commentary

BSOAS . . . . *Bulletin of the School of Oriental and African Studies*

BT . . . . *Bible Translator*

BTB . . . . *Biblical Theology Bulletin*

BWL . . . . *Babylonian Wisdom Literature.* W. G. Lambert. Oxford, 1960; reprinted Eisenbrauns, 1996

BZ . . . . *Biblische Zeitschrift*

BZABR . . . . . Beihefte zur Zeitschrift für altorientalische und biblische Rechtsgeschichte

BZAW . . . . . Beihefte zur Zeitschrift für die alttestamentliche Wissenschaft

CAD . . . . *The Assyrian Dictionary of the Oriental Institute of the University of Chicago.* Chicago, 1956–

CAH . . . . *Cambridge Ancient History*

CahRB. . . . . . Cahiers de la Revue biblique

CANE . . . . . . *Civilizations of the Ancient Near East.* J. Sasson. 4 vols. New York, 1995

CAT. . . . . Commentaire de l'Ancien Testament

CAT . . . . *Cuneiform Alphabetic Texts from Ugarit, Ras Ibn Hani and Other Places.* M. Dietrich, O. Loretz, and J. Sanmartin. Munster, 1997

CBC . . . . Cambridge Bible Commentary

CBET . . . . . . Contributions to Biblical Exegesis and Theology

CBQ . . . . *Catholic Biblical Quarterly*

CBQMS . . . . Catholic Biblical Quarterly Monograph Series

CH . . . . Code of Hammurabi

CHANE . . . . Culture and History of the Ancient Near East

CHI . . . . Cambridge History of Iran. 7 vols. 1968-91

CIS . . . . Corpus inscriptionum semiticarum

CIS . . . . *Corpus inscriptionum semiticarum*

CJ . . . . *Classical Journal*

CL . . . . Code of Lipit-Ishtar

CML . . . . *Canaanite Myths and Legends.* G. R. Driver. Edinburgh, 1956. J. C. L. Gibson, 1978²

CNI . . . . Carsten Niebuhr Institute

ConBOT . . . . Coniectanea biblica: Old Testament Series

COS . . . . *The Context of Scripture.* W. W. Hallo. 3 vols. Leiden, 1997–2002

CT . . . . *Cuneiform Texts from Babylonian Tablets in the British Museum*

CTA . . . . *Corpus des tablettes en cunéiformes alphabétiques découvertes à Ras Shamra-Ugarit de 1929 à 1939.* A. Herdner. Mission de Ras Shamra 10. Paris, 1963

CTH . . . . Catalogue des textes hittites

CTU . . . . *The Cuneiform Alphabetic Texts from Ugarit, Ras Ibn Hani, and Other Places.* M. Dietrich, O. Loretz, and J. Sanmartín. Münster, 1995

CU . . . . Code of Ur-Nammu

CurTM . . . . . *Currents in Theology and Mission*

DANE . . . . . . *Dictionary of the Ancient Near East*

DBAT . . . . . . *Dielheimer Blätter zum Alten Testament*

DBI . . . . *Dictionary of Biblical Imagery.* T. Longman and L. Ryken. Downers Grove, 1998

DCH . . . . *Dictionary of Classical Hebrew.* D. J. A. Clines. Sheffield, 1993–

DDD . . . . *Dictionary of Deities and Demons in the Bible.* K. van der Toorn, B. Becking, and P. W. van der Horst. Leiden, 1995. 2nd ed., Grand Rapids, 1998

DISO . . . . . . Dictionnaire des inscriptions sémitiques de l'ouest. Ch. F. Jean and J. Hoftijzer. Leiden, 1965

DNWSI . . . . . Dictionary of the North-West Semitic Inscriptions. J. Hoftijzer and K. Jongeling. 2 vols. Leiden, 1995

DOTHB . . . . *Dictionary of the Old Testament: Historical Books*

DOTP . . . . . . *Dictionary of the Old Testament: Pentateuch.* T. D. Alexander and D. W. Baker. Downers Grove, 2003

DOTT . . . . . . *Documents from Old Testament Times.* D. W. Thomas, London, 1958

DSB . . . . Daily Study Bible

EA . . . . El-Amarna tablets. According to the edition of J. A. Knudtzon. *Die el-Amarna-Tafeln.* Leipzig, 1908–1915. Reprint, Aalen, 1964. Continued in A. F. Rainey, *El-Amarna Tablets, 359–379.* 2nd revised ed. Kevelaer, 1978

EA . . . . *Epigraphica anatolica*

EAEHL . . . . Encyclopedia of Archaeological Excavations in the Holy Land. M. Avi-Yonah. 4 vols. Jerusalem, 1975

GENESIS

by John H. Walton

Introduction

Inferences drawn from the whole of the biblical text suggest that Moses was considered responsible for the shape and content of Genesis from earliest times. The Israelites in the wilderness, in roughly the third quarter of the second millennium B.C., are then the initial audience of the book. Many scholars unconvinced of the connection to Moses are more inclined to view the book against a mid-first millennium B.C. backdrop. The discussion is not without significance, but its impact on background issues will not often be felt. It is more important to become aware of how ancient culture

Composite creature between sacred tree Syro-Phoenician ivory carving, seventh century B.C. from Hadatu (Arslan Tash), Syria. Giraudon/Art Resource, NY, courtesy of the National Museum

▲

differed in general from our own and to assess how the literature of the ancient Near East offers us understanding of that ancient culture.

Historical Setting[1]

Mesopotamia: Sumer through Old Babylonia

Sumerians. It is not possible at this time to put Genesis 1–11 into a specific place in the historical record. Our history of the ancient Near East begins in earnest after writing has been invented, and the earliest civilization known to us in the historical record is that of the Sumerians. This culture dominated southern Mesopotamia for over five hundred years during the first half of the third millennium B.C. (2900–2350), known as the Early Dynastic Period. The Sumerians have become known through the excavation of several of their principal cities, which include Eridu, Uruk, and Ur. They are credited with many of the important developments in civilization, including the foundations of mathematics, astronomy, law, and medicine. Urbanization is also first witnessed among the Sumerians.

By the time of Abraham, the Sumerians no longer dominate the ancient Near East politically, but their culture continues to influence the region. Other cultures replace them in the political arena, but benefit from the advances they made.

Dynasty of Akkad. In the middle of the twenty-fourth century,[2] the Sumerian culture was overrun by the formation of an empire under the kingship of Sargon I, who established his capital at Akkad. He ruled all of southern Mesopotamia and ranged eastward into Elam and northwest to the Mediterranean on campaigns of a military and economic nature. The empire lasted for almost 150 years before being apparently overthrown by the Gutians (a barbaric people from the Zagros Mountains east of the Tigris), though other factors, including internal dissent, may have contributed to the downfall.

Ur III. Of the next century little is known as more than twenty Gutian kings succeeded one another. Just before 2100 B.C., the city of Ur took control of southern Mesopotamia under the kingship of Ur-Nammu, and for the next century there was a Sumerian renaissance in what has been called the Ur III period. It is difficult to ascertain the limits of the territorial control of the Ur III kings, though their territory does not seem to have been as extensive as that of the dynasty of Akkad. Under Ur-Nammu's son Shulgi, the region enjoyed almost a half-century of peace. Shulgi exercised absolute rule through provincial governors and distinguished himself in sportsmanship, music, and literature. He himself was reputed to have composed a hymn and was trained in scribal arts. Decline and fall came late in the twenty-first century through the infiltration of the Amorites and the increased aggression of the Elamites to the east, who finally overthrew the city.

It is against this backdrop of history that the Old Testament patriarchs emerge. Some have pictured Abraham as leaving the sophisticated Ur that was the center of the powerful Ur III period to settle in the unknown wilderness of Canaan, but that involves both chronological and geographical speculation. By the highest chronology (i.e., the earliest dates attributed to him) Abraham probably would have traveled from Ur to Haran during the reign of Ur-Nammu, but many scholars are inclined to place Abraham in

▶ Eras of Mesopotamian History

	Mesopotamian Eras	Levant Ages
2400	Early Dynastic III	Early Bronze III
2350	Dynasty of Akkad	
2300		EB IV / MB I
2250		
2200	Gutians	
2150	Ur III	
2100		
2050	Isin-Larsa	
2000		Middle Bronze II A
1950		
1900	Old Babylonian	
1850		
1800		
1750		
1700		
1650		
1600		

the later Isin-Larsa period or even the Old Babylonian period. From a geographical standpoint it is difficult to be sure that the Ur mentioned in the Bible is the famous city in southern Mesopotamia (see comment on 11:31). All this makes it impossible to give a precise background of Abraham.

The Ur III period ended in southern Mesopotamia as the last king of Ur, Ibbi-Sin, lost the support of one city after another and was finally overthrown by the Elamites, who lived just east of the Tigris. In the ensuing two centuries (roughly 2000–1800 B.C.), power was again returned to city-states that controlled more local areas. Isin, Larsa, Eshnunna, Lagash, Mari, Assur, and Babylon all served as major political centers.

Old Babylonian Period. Thanks substantially to the royal archives from the town of Mari, the eighteenth century has become thoroughly documented.[3] As the century opened there was an uneasy balance of power among four cities: Larsa ruled by Rim-Sin, Mari ruled by Yahdun-Lim

(and later, Zimri-Lim), Assur ruled by Shamshi-Adad I, and Babylon ruled by Hammurabi. Through a generation of political intrigue and diplomatic strategy, Hammurabi eventually emerged to establish the prominence of the first dynasty of Babylon.

The Old Babylonian period covered the time from the fall of the Ur III dynasty about 2000 B.C. to the fall of the first dynasty of Babylon just after 1600 B.C. This is the period during which most of the narratives in Genesis 12–50 occur. The rulers of the first dynasty of Babylon were Amorites. The Amorites had been coming into Mesopotamia as early as the Ur III period, at first being fought as enemies, then gradually taking their place within the society of the Near East. With the accession of Hammurabi to the throne, they reached the height of success. Despite his impressive military accomplishments, Hammurabi is most widely known today for his collection of laws.

The first dynasty of Babylon extends for more than a century beyond the time of Hammurabi, though decline began soon after his death and continued unabated, culminating in the Hittite sack of Babylon in 1595 B.C. This was nothing more than an incursion on the part of the Hittites, but it dealt the final blow to the Amorite dynasty, opening the doors of power for another group, the Kassites.

Canaan: Middle Bronze Age

Abraham entered Canaan during the Middle Bronze Age (2200–1550 B.C.), which was dominated by scattered city-states much as Mesopotamia had been, though it was not as densely populated or as extensively urbanized. The period began about the time of the fall of the dynasty of Akkad in Mesopotamia (ca. 2200) and extended until about 1500 B.C. (plus or

This statuette of a kneeling man, known as the "worshipper of Larsa," has sometimes been identified as Hammurabi. It was dedicated by an inhabitant of Larsa to the god Amurru for the life of Hammurabi. Bronze and gold, early second millennium B.C.
Marie-Lan Nguyen/Wikimedia Commons, courtesy of the Louvre
◀

minus fifty years, depending on the theories followed). In Syria there were power centers at Yamhad, Qatna, Alalakh, and Mari, and the coastal centers of Ugarit and Byblos seemed to be already thriving.

In Palestine only Hazor is mentioned in prominence. Contemporary records from Palestine are scarce, though the Egyptian story of Sinuhe has Middle Bronze Age Palestine as a backdrop and therefore offers general information. Lists of cities in Palestine are also given in the Egyptian texts. Most are otherwise unknown, though Jerusalem and Shechem are mentioned. As the period progresses there is more and more contact with Egypt and extensive caravan travel between Egypt and Palestine.

Egypt: Old and Middle Kingdoms

Roughly concurrent to the Early Dynastic Period in Mesopotamia was the formative Old Kingdom in Egypt that permanently shaped Egypt both politically and culturally. This was the age of the great pyramids. During Egypt's Sixth Dynasty, contemporary with the dynasty of Akkad in Mesopotamia, disintegration became evident. From the mid-twenty-second century until about 2000 B.C., Egypt was plunged into a dark period known as the First Intermediate Period, which was characterized by disunity and at times by practical anarchy. Order was finally restored when Mentuhotep reunited Egypt, and Amenemhet I founded the Twelfth Dynasty, beginning a period of more than two centuries of prosperous growth and development.

The Twelfth Dynasty developed extensive trade relations with Syro-Palestine and is the most likely period for initial contacts between Egypt and the Hebrew patriarchs. By the most conservative estimates, Sesostris III would have been the pharaoh who elevated Joseph to his high administrative post. Others are more inclined to place the emigration of the Israelites to Egypt during the time of the Hyksos. The Hyksos were Semitic peoples who began moving into Egypt (particularly the Delta region in the north) as early as the First Intermediate Period. As the Thirteenth Dynasty ushered in a gradual decline, the reins of power eventually fell to the Hyksos (whether by conquest, coup, or consent is still indeterminable), who then controlled Egypt from about the middle of the eighteenth century to the middle of the sixteenth century. It was during this time that the Israelites began to prosper and multiply in the Delta region, waiting for the covenant promises to be fulfilled.

Geographical Setting

Genesis 1–11 is set in the area of Mesopotamia, mostly in modern Iraq. Though two of the rivers of Eden remain unidentified, the Tigris and Euphrates are well known throughout history. We are not told where Noah's home is, but the mountains of Ararat, where the ark came to rest, are in the region from which the Tigris and Euphrates flow. The kingdoms mentioned in connection with Nimrod (10:10) and the location of the tower of Babel both demonstrate the Mesopotamian backdrop.

The Table of Nations (Gen. 10) expands its view to include the settlement of peoples throughout the known world. With Abraham the focus moves across Mesopotamia and into Canaan. The ancestors spend most of their lives in the southern regions of the land, notably Hebron and Beersheba. Additionally there are occasional journeys outside the region, for instance, to Gerar, or even to Egypt. Jacob spends twenty years back in

▶ Eras of Egyptian History

	Egyptian Kingdoms	Egyptian Dynasties	Levant Ages
2400	Old Kingdom		Early Bronze III
2350		6th Dynasty	
2300			EB IV / MB I
2250			
2200	First Intermediate	8th Dynasty	
2150		9th-10th Dynasty	
2100	Middle Kingdom	9th-10th-11th Dynasty	
2050		11th Dynasty	
2000		12th Dynasty	Middle Bronze II A
1950			
1900			
1850			
1800		13th-14th Dynasty	Middle Bronze II B
1750			
1700	Second Intermediate	15th-16th Dynasty	Middle Bronze II C
1650			
1600		15th & 17th Dynasty	

northern Mesopotamia in the area of Haran. By the end of the book, the whole family has moved to Egypt to join Joseph.

Literary Setting

Literary genres have rules and conventions by which they operate. Communication is jeopardized if we do not understand the parameters of the genre of the literature we are reading. How confusing it would be if we were reading a mystery in which the author gave every appearance of writing a biography! But at the same time, the features that indicate whether a literary work is a mystery or biography are to some extent culturally determined. The reason that genre categories work is that they represent a consensus of expectation among the readers.

When we approach a book like Genesis, we must be aware of what genres we will be encountering. But just as important, we must adjust our expectations so that we will come to those genres understanding the

Geography of the
Ancient Near East

◀

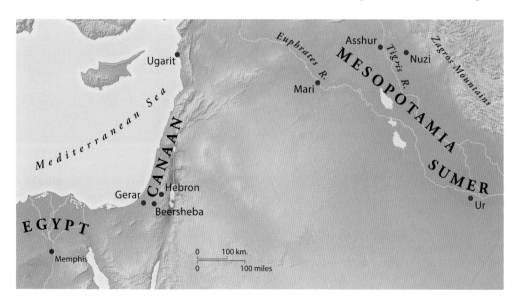

This modern artistic representation of classic Egyptian views of the cosmos uses a variety of ancient scenes. The air god Shu kneels on the earth god Geb while holding up the sky god Nut. Seth fights Apophis, the serpent representative of chaos, while the sun god Re sails in his barque into the heavens accompanied by Maat and Thoth. Osiris, the god of the netherworld, is in the west.
Jonathan Walton

▶

ancient conventions attached to that genre rather than imposing our own genre conventions on their literature.

Genesis contains cosmogony texts, that is, texts that deal with the origins of key aspects of the cosmos. It also contains genealogies (e.g., chs. 5; 11; 36), founders' or ancestors' narratives (e.g., chs. 12–35), destiny proclamations (i.e., formal blessings and/or curses from father to son, e.g., chs. 9; 27; 49), conflict tales (e.g., chs. 4; 6–7; 11; 19; 34), battle accounts (e.g., ch. 14), and a narrative about the rise of a courtier from humble beginnings to a position of power (chs. 40–45).[4] Some of these are unparalleled in the ancient world, and even when possible parallels exist, significant differences lead us to proceed with caution.

Genesis and Mythology

Some people who take their Bibles seriously are uncomfortable with using the literature from the ancient Near East in their Bible study. Often this is a defensive reaction. If the Bible is associated too closely to other ancient literature, its unique status as the Word of God might be tarnished. Ancient Near Eastern literature is viewed as pagan, mythological, depraved, fictional … human. The Bible's reputation, so they maintain, must be guarded against being viewed as similar in any way lest it attract similar labels.

Reactions such as these are understandable, but we cannot afford to lose the benefit of comparative studies as we protect our convictions. Therefore we must be willing to come to the ancient Near Eastern literature with solid methods and firm convictions to learn what there is to learn. With these caveats in mind, we can approach the mythology of the ancient Near East.

Defining the term *mythology* is treacherous. Many formal definitions have been offered, and beyond those, one can find a wide variety of popular conceptions that impede fruitful discussion. Rather than offer yet another definition, it is more productive to identify the function of mythological literature. The mythology of the ancient world encapsulated contemporary thinking about how the world worked and how it came to work that way. It features the gods prominently because the ancients found the answers to their questions about the world in the divine realm. If we describe mythology functionally in this way, we can conclude that our modern mythology is what we call science. That is our culture's way of encapsulating how the world works and how it came to work that way. Contrary to the divine orientation of the ancients, our scientific worldview is naturalistic and empiricist.

Genesis functions in Israelite society the same way that science functions in our culture and the same way that mythology functioned in the rest of the ancient world. Genesis offers an alternative encapsulation of how the world worked and how it came to work that way. Like the rest of the ancient world, it has a divine orientation rather than a naturalistic/

Egyptian Cosmology text, Papyrus Leiden I 350
Courtesy of the Leiden Museum
▼

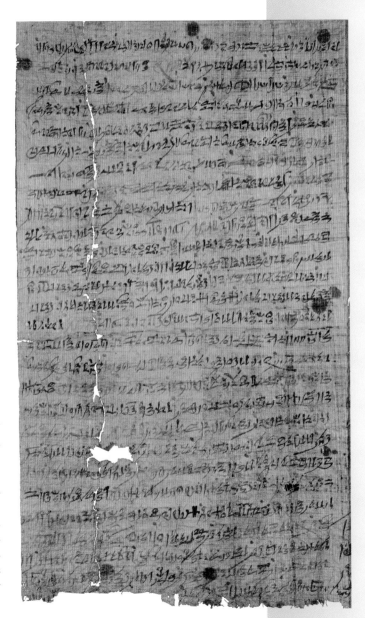

▶ Creation of the Cosmos in the Ancient Near East[A-1]

Creation and cosmology are familiar topics in a number of different sorts of texts, but especially in the mythological literature of the ancient world. Few texts (maybe none) can actually be called "creation texts," but they nevertheless provide considerable information concerning ancient beliefs. The following offers a brief summary of the major sources.

Egypt. The Memphite Theology (focusing on the god Ptah) is known from a single copy dated to about 700 B.C., though it is believed to have originated in the thirteenth century at the latest.[A-2] Texts are found in afterlife literature (i.e., Pyramid Texts, Coffin Texts, and Book of the Dead) from Heliopolis (featuring Atum)[A-3] and Hermopolis (featuring Amun).[A-4] Allusions also occur in wisdom pieces such as The Instructions of Merikare.[A-5] Cosmological depictions such as those found on the Cenotaph of Seti I (13th century) can also be instructive.

Mesopotamia. The Epic of Atrahasis (17th century) contains an account of the creation of man.[A-6] *Enuma Elish* (12th century at the latest) is the most important ancient text for cosmology.[A-7] The Eridu Genesis is a Sumerian text, copied from about 1600 B.C.[A-8]

Many other Sumerian texts contain statements about creation, from myths or rituals to disputation texts or dedicatory inscriptions, and including even genealogical lists of the gods. Traditions from Nippur feature Enlil and traditions from Eridu feature Enki.

empiricist one as is common today. But its view of the situation in the divine realm also makes it distinct from the mythology of the ancient world.

Consequently, studying the mythological literature of the ancient world can help us, whose cultural worldview tends toward empiricism, to make adjustments as we try to understand how a nonempiricist worldview works. The result is that we can be drawn out of the restricted perspectives that come most naturally to us. This is the value of mythological literature for the study of the Bible.

Creation and the Fall (1:1–3:24)

In the beginning (1:1). Whereas we may be inclined to ask, "The beginning of what?" information from the Bible and the ancient Near East leads us in another direction. In the Old Testament "beginning" (*rēʾšît*) refers to a preliminary period of time rather than the first in a series of events.[5] This is comparable to the Akkadian *reštu*, which means the first part or the first installment,[6] and the Egyptian *sp tpy*, rendered the "first time" or the "first occasion."[7] In English, we might refer to such an initial period as "the primordial period."[8]

Egyptian texts use this phrase with various prepositions to refer to the period during which creation took place. Since Egyptians believed that creation was reenacted every day with the rising of the sun, they used this word to differentiate the first time that creation took place from the endless daily repetitions of creation. The Egyptian phrase then refers to "when the pattern of existence was established and first enacted."[9] All of this information leads us to conclude that the "beginning" is a way of talking about the seven-day *period* rather than a *point* in time prior to the seven days.

Created (1:1). If creation is the act of bringing something into existence, we must ask what constituted existence in the ancient world. In our culture, we consider existence to be either material (i.e., having molecules/taking up space and extending to energy and subatomic particles) or experiential (e.g., abstractions such as love or time). Those definitions, however, are culturally determined. By contrast, in the ancient world something existed when it had a function—a role to play.[10]

In Mesopotamia one way to accomplish this was to name something, because a name designated a thing's function or role. Thus, in the Babylonian Creation account, bringing the cosmos into existence begins "when on high no name was given in heaven, nor below was the netherworld called by name … When no gods at all had been brought forth, none called by names, no destinies ordained, then were the gods formed."[11] In the earlier Gilgamesh, Enkidu, and the Netherworld, the first couple of lines read: "After heaven had been moved away from earth, After earth had been separated from heaven, After the name of man had been fixed…."[12]

In Egyptian accounts existence was associated with something having been differentiated. The god Atum is conceptualized as the primordial monad—the singularity embodying all the potential of the cosmos, from whom all things were separated and thereby created.[13] The Genesis account includes both of these concepts as God separates and names.

The actual Hebrew verb "create" (*bārāʾ*) also focuses our attention in this direction. In the Bible, only God can perform this action of bringing something into existence. What is even more intriguing is that the objects of this verb point consistently toward its connection to functional existence rather than material existence.[14] This is much like the ancient Near Eastern way of thinking that it was more important to determine who controlled functions rather than who/what gave something its physical form. In the ancient world something was created when it was given a function. Allen captures this common ancient perspective when he summarizes Egyptian thinking by observing that "the Egyptian explanations are more *metaphysical* than physical."[15] In the ancient world, the cosmos is less like a machine, more like a kingdom.

Formless and empty (1:2). Prior to creation the Egyptian texts talk about the "nonexistent." In their thinking this nonexistent realm continues to be present in the sea, in the dark night sky, and even in the desert—places without role or function. In the Egyptian precreation state of nonexistence there are two elements: primeval waters and total darkness.[16] In Hebrew, "formless" (*tōhû*) is also used to refer to the desert (e.g., Deut. 32:10). In general it designates a situation in which positive values such as purpose and worth are lacking. As a result, it is more appropriate to translate "without function" rather than "without form" and can be seen to be similar in ways to the Egyptian "nonexistent."

This is also apparent in Jeremiah 4:23, where the same pair of Hebrew terms

▶ Cosmic Geography in the Ancient World[A-9]

When people in the ancient world thought about the shape of the cosmos, they thought in far different terms than we do today. It does not surprise us to see that they thought of the sun moving across the sky rather than the earth rotating and revolving around the sun. Likewise the recognition that the earth is a globe rather than a flat surface is a relatively recent development. But the cosmic geography of the ancient world expressed a system that involved much more than a flat earth and a moving sun. As we might expect, their cosmic geography was the result of two influences: the perspective of observation and beliefs about the role of the gods in the cosmos.

Observation. What the ancients observed led them to conclude that the sun and the moon moved in roughly the same spheres and in similar ways. They thought of the sky as somewhat solid (whether like a tent or like a solid dome), resting on the mountaintops. The stars were engraved on the sky and moved in tracks through their ordained stations. Precipitation originated in waters held back by the sky and fell to the earth through openings in the sky. The earth was conceived of as supported on pillars. The heavens (where deity dwelt) were above the sky, and the netherworld was beneath the earth. Cosmic waters, often connected with precosmic disorder, surrounded a single landmass. These were not mathematically deduced realities, but the reality of how things appeared to them.

Theology. A second influence on their cosmology related to how they thought about the role of deity in the cosmos. So, for example, in Mesopotamian thinking, cables held by the gods connected the heaven and earth and held the sun in the sky.[A-10] In Egypt the sun god sailed in his barque across the heavens during the day and through the netherworld at night. The stars of the Egyptian sky were portrayed as emblazoned across the arched body of the sky goddess, who was held up by the god of the air.

Israel's cosmic geography was likewise the result of their observations and their theology. Their observations would have been no different than those of their neighbors, but their theology deviated sharply. God did not reveal to them the details of the cosmic geography of the post-Enlightenment period (which is mathematically deduced and naturalistic). He rather communicated to them about his role from the context of their own perceptions of cosmic geography. Where revelation offered no revisions, the

---

is used. There they refer to a return to a nonfunctional, nonproductive state, and the text further describes this situation by delineating the various areas of the cosmos that are becoming nonfunctional or where order and productivity are threatened.[17] All of this fits nicely with the explanation given in the previous comment. The text will soon describe God's activity in bringing the cosmos into existence (understood in terms of function, not form); thus, the account

begins with a nonfunctional condition, which, similar to Egyptian thinking, consists of primordial waters and darkness—the nonexistent.

In Mesopotamian traditions there is not as much discussion of the precreation state. A Sumerian text from Nippur speaks of darkness on the earth,[18] and *Enuma Elish* refers to the watery existence.[19] This is nevertheless sufficient to see that all ancient Near Eastern cultures believed that there was a precreation

Israelites thought about the world in terms similar to those of the cultures around them. The terminology of the Old Testament reflects this cosmic geography, and discussions of creation are based on this understanding.

▲

Image depicts modern artistic reconstruction of an ancient Israelite view of the cosmos. The sky, supported by mountains at the edges, holds back the waters above as it arches over the flat, disk-shaped earth, which is upheld by pillars. Numerous graves lead to the nether-world, Sheol, and the cosmic waters surround the earth on the horizontal plane, as well as the entire cosmos on the vertical plane. Lurking in the depths is mighty Leviathan (here more in medieval design). The temple on earth is matched by the temple in heaven, the dwelling place of God. The skies are inhabited by birds as well as celestial bodies and rain is let through windows of heaven. Stars are engraved on the underside of the sky.
John H. Walton, drawing by Alva Steffler

condition of nonfunctionality characterized by water and darkness, which was remedied by the creative acts that assigned functions by giving names, separating, and bringing functional order to the cosmos.

Deep (1:2). The deep (Heb. *t^ehôm*) refers to the primordial or primeval sea. In the pre-creation period it covered everything.[20] In creation it was pushed out to the edges of the cosmos, where it was restrained by God's power. There it is identified as the cosmic waters of chaos that can be brought back at any moment if deity requires its services. Although the Hebrew word is the cognate of the Babylonian *tamtu/Tiamat*, it is not personi- fied as a being associated with chaos, nor can it be considered a

▶ Control Attributes in the Ancient Near East

The most important reflection of the way the world worked in Mesopotamian thinking is embodied in the conceptual spectrum framed by the Akkadian terms *parṣu* and *šimtu* (ME and NAM [TAR] in Sumerian).[A-11] The concepts expressed by these terms are at the heart of the functional cosmos and play a major role in the establishment and operation of both the cosmos and the temple. A *parṣu* is a "control attribute," a defining feature of the cosmos, deity, temple, or city. Ninety-four of them associated with Uruk and its patron deity, Inanna, are listed in Inanna and Enki.[A-12] These control attributes did not originate with the gods but are entrusted to the main gods—Anu, Enlil and Enki—who administer them, but are also bound by them.

The term *šimtu* is represented in a tablet held by the gods, usually referred to as the Tablet of Destinies. These are used to assign the semipermanent roles and functions of gods, temples, and cities. Kings and people have their destinies proclaimed annually at the Akitu festival.[A-13]

Though there is no recognized Hebrew *term* coinciding to the Akkadian ones, some have already recognized the *concept* at least tangentially in the biblical material.[A-14] It is possible that Genesis 1 should be understood in light of the concepts behind the *parṣu/šimtu* complex, such that God's creative activities would be seen as establishing and maintaining order just as the *parṣi* do. In such a comparison we find that the role of the spoken word in Genesis 1 takes on a new level of comparison since the *parṣi* were also established by the spoken word.[A-15]

We find, in addition, that the *parṣi* were considered "good"—the best possible expression of world order.[A-16]

Days 1–3 would consequently be viewed as not just activating, but establishing, the *parṣi* of the cosmos, while days 4–6 could be seen as determining the destinies of the functionaries within the cosmos. When the destinies of the gods were determined in the ancient Near East, powers and responsibilities could be delegated. As a result, other gods became "working Enlils" as the *parṣi* were given to them.[A-17] This bears some resemblance to people being created in God's image and becoming Elohim operatives. Following the concept that Genesis 1 concerns the assigning of functions (= *parṣi*) to the cosmic temple, days 4–6 can be seen as bearing some similarity to the temple inaugurations in which the functionaries are installed in the temple and their *šimati* declared prior to the deity taking up his rest.[A-18]

In distinct contrast to Mesopotamian beliefs, however, Genesis 1, if it deals with the *parṣi*, positions them differently. Rather than positing deity as guardian of the cosmic *parṣi*, Genesis portrays God as the one who initiates the cosmic *parṣi*. This is similar to the idea that in Israel Yahweh is considered the source of law whereas in Mesopotamia Shamash is the guardian of law. Moving from the *parṣi* to the *šimati*, Yahweh does not need his own *šimati* to be decreed, nor does he decree the *šimati* of other deities. Predictably, Israel's God does not delegate powers out to other gods, but brings order to the cosmos by determining the destinies of the inhabitants of the cosmos. Along the same line of logic, there is no tablet of destinies. Yahweh needs no emblem because he does not have to protect his power from usurpation by gods such as Anzu or Kingu.

depersonification or demythologization that is dependent on the ancient Near Eastern texts.[21] It is simply used to describe the "pre-cosmic condition."[22]

It is not easy to specify the term as referring to salt water rather than sweet water, nor to attach it to subterranean waters rather than the seas. In Akkadian texts it can be used of the Persian Gulf, Indian Ocean, or Mediterranean, as well as Lake Van and Lake Urmia.[23] Perhaps it is best understood as referring to cosmic waters in whatever form they are found.[24] In Egyptian thinking these waters had both a negative significance (being functionless and chaotic) and a positive significance (holding all the potential of creation within them).[25] The Israelite portrayal does not see chaos as negative or personal—it is rather a neutral, functionless ambiguity.[26]

Spirit of God (1:2). In Genesis, the potentiality in the primeval condition is represented in the presence of the spirit of God. Since Mesopotamian sources often feature a wind that stirs up or roils the primeval waters as a prelude to creative acts,[27] many interpreters have translated this phrase as "mighty wind." Note how in this verse the

wind/spirit stands in parallelism to the darkness and is therefore part of the chaotic landscape. Although it is true that the Hebrew word *rûaḥ* can refer to either "spirit" or "wind," whenever the word appears with "God" it refers to "spirit." In this case, then, the potentiality motif from Egypt is more significant than the stirring waters motif from Mesopotamia. Having said that, we must also note that the potentiality in Egyptian traditions is within the primeval waters.[28]

More important is the Egyptian concept of the *ka*, which is the vital force (i.e., "spirit") of either humans or gods and is associated with regenerative concepts.[29] It was their belief that "the totality of creation ... constituted the sum of the creator-god's vital force."[30] The divine *ka* may be closest to the Israelite "spirit of God"; there is no element of "wind" in the Egyptian *ka*.

No "spirit of God" concept is attested elsewhere in the ancient Near East.[31] In some late Egyptian texts the wind is a manifestation of the creator god, Amun, and serves as a catalyst for creation.[32] Most important, it is involved in the emergence of the primeval hillock from which all Egyptian creation developed.[33] The main parallel in this verse, then, is the implication of creative potentiality in the interaction between the wind/spirit that proceeds from God and the primeval waters.

Egyptian god Amun
Frederick J. Mabie
▲

Detail of the inscription known as the Memphite Theology
Lenka Peacock, courtesy of the British Museum
◀

The Shabako stone is inscribed with the creation myth known as the Memphite Theology. Its poor condition results from the fact that it was used as a grinding stone.
Lenka Peacock, courtesy of the British Museum
◀

Stone bowl from Khafajeh, Iraq, Early Dynastic period, 2600–2400 B.C. A man in a net skirt kneels on two zebus and grasps streams watering vegetation and a palm tree; above are a crescent moon and a rosette sun. The design is probably linked to Iranian mythology.
Erich Lessing/Art Resource, NY, courtesy of the British Museum
▲

to deliver the rain.[59] The Old Testament refers to the gates in the sky through which precipitation comes as "windows" (ʾ*arubôt*),[60] where they are only for rain, not for the celestial bodies (e.g., Gen. 7:11; 8:2; 2 Kings 7:2, 19). Job 38:22 also poetically speaks of storehouses for snow and hail. All precipitation (including dew, see Prov. 3:19–20) comes from above, and thus weather is regulated by the sky. Seely collects the evidence to demonstrate that the church fathers, from Basil, Augustine, and Chrysostom to Luther, all accepted, on the basis of Genesis, that there was a body of water above the sun.[61]

Let dry ground appear (1:9). Nonexistence for the Egyptians was not wiped out in the acts of creation, but was pushed to the outer limits of the cosmos. Existence and nonexistence are balanced in the cosmos (much like our equilibrium between matter and antimatter).[62] Consequently their literature speaks of the primeval hillock that emerged from the primeval waters. Temples were sometimes understood as containing the original primeval hillock in the center of their sacred space. Mesopotamian literature does not speak much of the emergence of the land, but there is discussion of the collection of the waters to their appropriate place.[63]

In this feature, then, Genesis shows more similarity to Egypt. It was common in the ancient world to think of the earth as a single continent in the shape of a flat disc.[64] Likewise in Genesis, the waters are all gathered into one place, and land appears, presumably in one place.

Vegetation (1:11). The indication that the land is producing vegetation is not a statement about the land being involved in creation. What is being created by God is a function whereby the land regularly and characteristically produces vegetation—the principle of fecundity whereby agriculture can exist and food can be grown. This principle also requires the land and the water that were mentioned in the previous verses. Thus Day 3 does not consist of two separate acts of creation as much as it pulls together all the different elements necessary for the function of fecundity: God created the world with all of the necessary ingredients for things to grow—water, soil, and the principle of seeds yielding plants with more seeds.

One Sumerian-Akkadian bilingual text also puts similar elements together portraying the gods determining the courses of the Tigris and Euphrates, preparing irrigation systems, fixing the boundaries for fields, making all kinds of plants grow, and so on.[65] In a text of the Eridu tradition, Enki, the god of fresh waters, "collected all the waters, established their dwelling places, let flow at his side the life-giving waters that begat the fecund seed."[66] In Akkadian texts Marduk creates the green herb of the field, marshes, and canebrakes.[67] In other words, setting up the functional system whereby things grow is also part of the Mesopotamian understanding of the creation process.

Signs … seasons … days … years (1:14). Egyptian hymns often praise the sun god, and similar emphasis is placed on aspects of time. One Hymn to Amun-Re refers to him as "you who create the years, join months together—days, night, and hours occur according to your footsteps."[68] In a prologue to a Sumerian astrological treatise, the major gods An, Enlil, and Enki put the moon and stars in place to regulate days, months, and omens (translation in sidebar, p. 19).[69] In the famous Babylonian Hymn to Shamash, the sun god, reference is also made to his role in regulating the seasons and the calendar in general. It is intriguing that he is also the patron of divination.[70]

The Hebrew word used for "sign" (ʾ*ôt*) has a cognate in Akkadian that is used for omens, but ʾ*ôt* has a more neutral sense. Again the author has emptied the elements

Thus the idea of setting the heavenly bodies in a solid background is the common perception. Some Mesopotamian texts refer to the stars as "cattle of heaven,"[75] suggesting the living quality of the stars as a manifestation of deities. Typically in literature from Mesopotamia the heavenly bodies are not created but are set in their place and given their role.[76]

Great creatures of the sea (1:21). In the mythologies of the ancient Near East a variety of terrible creatures inhabited the sea.[77] At times they are associated with the threatening forces of chaos that need to be defeated and harnessed by creator deities. In *Enuma Elish* the leader of the rebellion is Tiamat,

of the cosmos of their more personal traits, as he did with the description of the pre-cosmic condition (see comments on 1:2). W. Vogels has convincingly argued that the word translated "seasons" here never refers to seasons of the year (e.g., summer) in its 160 occurrences in the Pentateuch. It refers rather to a fixed time, usually for an announced event or for the celebration of a liturgical festival.[71] In this verse the functional aspect of creation is more evident than anywhere else and the functions are relative to human existence and use. The functionaries here have their destinies decreed and operate in relation to the function of time established in Day 1.

Stars (1:16). In Mesopotamian understanding, the stars were engraved on the jasper surface of the middle heavens, and the entire surface moved. In astronomical texts (Mul-Apin series) the thirty-six principal stars were divided into three segments known as the paths of Anu, Enlil, and Ea. These fixed stellar paths occupied the northern, southern, and equatorial bands of the sky.[72] In the omen series known as *Enuma Anu Enlil*, these gods established the positions, locations, and paths of the stars.[73] In *Enuma Elish*, Marduk sets up the stations of the stars.[74]

Babylonian boundary marker depicts chaos creature in the depths among the pillars that support the earth.
Rama/Wikimedia Commons, courtesy of the Louvre
◀

▶ **Sumerian Creation of Living Creatures**

The lord Enki organized the marshes, made grow there reeds young and old, brought fish and birds into the marshes, swamps and lakes, filled the steppe with breathing creatures as [mankind's] food and drink, charged them with supplying the abundance of the gods.... He filled the canebrake and marsh with fish and bird, assigned them to their stations.[A-20]

goddess of the primeval waters, and she is aided by eleven composite creatures.[78]

The Old Testament refers to a number of different cosmic sea creatures (see Ps. 74:13–15; Isa. 27:1). The Hebrew word *tannîn*, is usually considered to be related to the Ugaritic noun *tunnanu*, a great sea monster defeated by Anat/Baal.[79] In Job 7:12 *tannîn* occurs parallel to *yam* (either the sea generically or, because of the parallel here, the creature representing the sea as in Ugaritic Literature, Yamm). In Psalm 74:13–14 the *tannîn* is portrayed with multiple heads and is parallel to Leviathan. This depiction of battle is also seen in Isaiah 51:9 where *tannîn*, like *Rahab*, is defeated. Genesis shows no indication of a battle—only that *tannîn* is created.

This is the first use of the verb *bārā'* since verse 1, perhaps emphasizing that *tannîn* is not some primeval chaos monster that must be overcome, but a creature being given its role (see comment on 1:1) just like everything else in creation. Yet it ought to be viewed as a cosmic creature rather than a marine specimen. The passages in which the word may refer to zoological specimens (Ex. 7:9–10; Deut. 32:33; Ps. 91:13) indicate a land creature or amphibian, not a sea creature as here.

Living creatures (1:24–25). Classification of animals was not as technical as today's systems. Instead, size, domestication, eating habits, dwelling places, or mode of locomotion were used as convenient categories. A Babylonian piece entitled "Two Insects" talks about the gods meeting in assembly after they had created heaven and earth: "They brought into being the animals ... large wild animals, wild animals, small wild animals ... they allotted their respective domains to the cattle and the small domestic animals."[80] In the Sumerian Eridu Genesis Jacobsen's translation makes it appear that the animals are coming forth from the ground as in Genesis,[81] but the translation on the Oxford Sumerian literature site differs.[82]

Image ... likeness (1:26). Throughout the ancient Near East, an image was believed to contain the essence of that which it represented. That essence equipped the image to carry out its function.[83] In Egyptian literature, there is one occurrence of people in general having been created in the image of deity in the Instructions of Merikare, dated to about 2000 B.C. (see sidebar on "Instruction of Merikare" in the introduction), but it is generally the king who is spoken of in such terms.[84] The image is the source of his power and prerogative.

In Mesopotamia there are three categories of significance. (1) As in Egypt, the king is occasionally described as being in the image of deity.[85] (2) An idol contained the image of the deity.[86] (3) The image of a king was present in monuments set up in territories he had conquered.[87] I. Winter concludes in a study of royal images that the representations of the king did not intend to capture the features of

> ### ▶ Instruction of Merikare

Well tended is mankind—god's cattle He made sky and earth for their sake ... He made breath for their noses to live. They are his images, who came from his body ...	He made for them plants and cattle, Fowl and fish to feed them ... When they weep he hears ... For god knows every name.[A-21]

"his own historically particular physiognomy, but those aspects of his features/appearance that had been molded by the gods and that resembled (or could be attributed to) the gods, such that the ruler's features convey qualities of ideal, divinely-sanctioned rulership, not just personhood."[88]

Thus in an image, it was not physical likeness that was important, but a more abstract, idealized representation of identity relating to the office/role and the value connected to the image.[89] When Assyrian king Esarhaddon is referred to as "the perfect likeness of the god," it is his qualities and his attributes that are under discussion.[90] The image of god did the god's work on the earth.

The biblical view is similar as people are in the image of God, embodying his qualities and doing his work. They are symbols of his presence and act on his behalf as his representatives. The two words used in the text differ in nuance, with "image" referring to the something that contains the "essence" of something else, while "likeness" is more connected to "substance," expressing a resemblance at some level. The Aramaic portion of the bilingual inscription from Tell Fekheriye uses cognates of both of these terms to indicate that the statue both contains the essence and represents the substance of Hadad-Yith'i, King of Guzan.[91]

Be fruitful and increase (1:28). Contrary to concerns about overpopulation that are evident in early Mesopotamian literature,[92] in Genesis God desires people to multiply without restriction—they may fill the earth. In the Atrahasis Epic, the gods are distressed because with the multiplication of people, problems and "noise" also increase.[93] The gods therefore send plagues, famine, and drought to counteract the population explosion.

Subdue ... rule (1:28). The characterization of humans as being in the image of God and the functions listed here reflect a royal role for people since these descriptions would most frequently be applied to kings. They are given the responsibility of bringing order to their world. Again, this is in stark contrast to the role of humanity in the ancient Near East, where they are created to serve. Here we see the attribution to all people what was the sole prerogative of the king in the rest of the ancient Near East.

They will be yours for food (1:29). When people are created in the rest of the ancient Near East, it is for the purpose of performing all the menial tasks necessary for providing food for the gods. Both aspects are seen in the disputation Bird and Fish (see excerpt in sidebar, above), in which Enki provides living creatures as food for humankind, which is in turn charged with providing food for the gods.[94] God as the one

▶ The Temple and the Cosmos

The temple on earth was considered only a type of the larger, archetypal cosmic temple, and there are many images and symbols that evoke the relationship between temple and cosmos.[A-22] The temple was considered the center of the cosmos[A-23] and in itself, a microcosmos.[A-24]

In Egypt the temple contained within its sacred precincts a representation of the original primeval hillock that emerges from the cosmic waters.[A-25] In short, the temple was considered deity's cosmic domain. This concept is represented even in the design of temples.[A-26]

In Mesopotamia, the primary imagery of the temple was that it was the center of the cosmos. This perspective can be seen in Gudea's temple building text from early in the second millennium, in which the temple's cosmic qualities are enumerated and show little change in the middle of the first millennium in Neo-Assyrian texts.[A-27]

In Syro-Palestine, the temple is the architectural embodiment of the cosmic mountain.[A-28] This concept is represented in Ugaritic literature[A-29] as well as in the Bible, where Mount Zion is understood as the mountain of the Lord (e.g., Ps. 48) and the place where his temple, a representation of Eden, was built.[A-30]

In Isaiah 66:1 the Lord indicates: "Heaven is my throne and the earth is my footstool? Where is the house you will build for me? Where will my resting place be?" Here God explains that the manmade temple cannot be considered the true temple (cf. 1 Kings 8:27). It is only a micro-scale representation of the cos-

mic temple. Psalm 78:69 communicates a similar idea by indicating that the temple was built on the model of the cosmos. Ideas like these are also found in literature from Mesopotamia that compares temples to the heavens and the earth and gives them a cosmic location and function.[A-31] It is evident, then, that Israel and her neighbors shared an ideology that understood the cosmos in temple terms and viewed the temple as a model of the cosmos or the cosmic temple.

Cylinder B describes Gudea's dedication of the Temple of Ningirsu in Lagash.
Rama/Wikimedia Commons, courtesy of the Louvre

▶

providing food for people rather than other way around is not absent from the ancient Near East, but the concept occupies a more central role here (cf. also 2:8–9, where God planted a garden for food).

On the seventh day he rested (2:2). The concept of divine rest is prominent in ancient Near Eastern literature. Deity's rest is achieved in a temple, generally as a result of order having been established. The rest, while it represents *disengagement* from any process of establishing order (whether through conflict with other deities or not), is more importantly an expression of *engagement* as the deity takes his place at the helm to maintain an ordered, secure, and stable cosmos. The following aspects of divine rest can be found in literature of the ancient Near East:

1. The divine rest can be disturbed by rebellion.[95]
2. The divine rest is achieved after conflict.[96]
3. The divine rest is achieved after order-bringing acts of creation.[97]
4. The divine rest is achieved in the temple.[98]
5. The divine rest is achieved in part by creating people to work in the gods' place and on their behalf.
6. The divine rest is characterized by ongoing control and stability.[99]

Commenting on this last point, N-E. Andreasen concludes, "We can say then that the gods seek rest, and that their rest implies stability for the world order. The gods rest because they want to see the world ordered."[100]

Only Point 3 is transparent in Genesis, though Points 4 and 6 can also be defended. Given the connection between temple and rest in the ancient Near East, it becomes natural to see the biblical creation of the cosmos as being configured in temple building, inauguration, and dedication terms. As Levenson puts it, the seven-day creation account culminating in the divine rest

should be understood as somehow parallel to the building of temples for divine rest.[101] This course of analogy and logic results in the understanding that Genesis 1 is framed in terms of the creation of a cosmic temple in which Yahweh takes up his repose.[102] The seven days are comparable to seven-day temple dedications at the end of which deity takes up his rest in the temple.

Seventh day ... holy (2:3). No precedent in the ancient Near East exists for a seven-day cycle with the seventh day consistently set aside as a holy day. Seven-day cycles were logical enough as approximations of the cycles of the moon, but Israel's Sabbath is clearly not tied to lunar cycles—it is just every seventh day. As a recognition of God's rest and therefore his control and rule of the ordered cosmos, it has its closest functional parallel in the ancient Near Eastern New Year festivals commemorating and reenacting the enthronement of the deity. Israel's commemoration takes place weekly rather than annually.

No plant ... had yet sprung up (2:5). The description of an inchoate condition on the earth is paralleled in part by descriptions of a primeval condition in some ancient Near Eastern texts. A text from Nippur speaks of a time when the earth was in darkness and the lower world invisible. At that time "the waters did not flow through the opening (in the earth), nothing was produced, on the vast earth, the furrow had not been made."[103] Similarly, the cosmogonic introduction to the dispute entitled Ewe and Wheat speaks of a time when there was no wheat, no yarn, no ewe or goat (their names were unknown), and no cloth to wear. "The people of those distant days, they knew no bread to eat, they knew no cloth to wear; they went about with naked limbs in the land, and like sheep they ate grass with their mouth, drinking water from the ditches."[104]

Unlike Genesis, these texts consider the primeval condition of humans to be primitive and uncivilized. Like ancient Near Eastern literature, however, Genesis begins with

Gudea, governor
of Lagash, with
the diagram plan
for the temple on
his lap
Christina Beblavi,
courtesy of the
Louvre

▼

▶ Genesis 1 and Temple Building[A-32]

If the cosmos is viewed as a temple, then it is possible that a cosmological text could adopt the language of temple building, inauguration, and dedication. A fresh look at the Gudea temple building and dedication text offers some intriguing comparisons that might commend seeing Genesis 1 in similar terms.

First, we encounter what we have found to be the common idea that the sanctuary is being constructed in order to provide a resting place—in Gudea's case, for Ningirsu and his consort, Bau. Genesis 1 likewise finds its conclusion in Yahweh's taking up his rest.[A-33] Throughout the account he is making a place of rest for himself, a rest provided for by the completed cosmos. Inhabiting his resting place is the equivalent to being enthroned—it is connected to taking up his role as sovereign ruler of the cosmos. This explains the presence of the ark in the most sacred area of the temple representing the footstool of God's throne.[A-34]

Second, numerous aspects of temple inauguration, consecration, and dedication last seven days.[A-35] This element in Gudea can also be seen in various biblical accounts that have to do with sanctuary building, inauguration, and dedication.[A-36]

In Genesis 1 we have the provision of rest for the deity occurring after a seven-day period, during which we have argued functions are established and functionaries installed through a procedure that has striking similarities to the decreeing of destinies, itself deeply imbedded in temple inaugurations. The focus on decrees for functions and functionaries constitutes the third item of significance.

The inauguration of the temple in Gudea cylinder B vi-xii touches on many of the pertinent elements that we recognize from Genesis 1. The Sabbath element in Genesis not only helps us to recognize the temple-cosmos equation in Genesis, but also to realize the contextual significance of the functions (Days 1–3) and functionaries (Days 4–6) in the creation narrative. Just as Gudea's account established functions for the temple and then supplied functionaries that operate in it, the Genesis account set up functions (Days 1–3) and functionaries (Days 4–6) for the cosmic temple. Genesis 2:1 indicates this by referring to the creation of "the heavens and the earth" (the cosmos with its functions) and "all their vast array [hosts]" (the functionaries in the various realms of the cosmos).

In a temple construction project, the structure would be built, and the furniture and trappings would be made in preparation for the moment when all was ready for the inauguration of the temple. On this occasion, the functions of the temple were declared, the furniture and hangings were put in place, the priests installed, and the appropriate sacrifices made to initiate the temple's operation. Somewhere in the process, the image of the deity was brought into the temple to take up his repose. On the basis of all of this, Genesis 1 can be viewed as using the metaphor of temple inauguration as it portrays God's creation (= making functional/operational) of his cosmos (which is his temple, Isa. 66:1). The main connection, however, is the rest motif, for rest is the principal function of a temple, and a temple is always where deity finds rest.[A-37]

a time when no irrigation or planting strategies were being carried out by people (see "Eridu Genesis" sidebar). In the ancient Near East this resulted in no offerings for the gods. In Genesis God plants the garden and puts people in it. The similarities show the common idea that creation accounts proceed from an unordered, nonfunctional beginning through an ordering process.

Streams (2:6). Much dispute surrounds the meaning of this word (ʾēd), as is obvious by comparing English translations. It occurs only one other time in the Old Testament (Job 36:27) and is equally unclear there. In contrast to the rain, which comes down from above, these waters come up from the earth. In ancient Mesopotamia, the realm of the subterranean waters (the ABZU) is of great cosmic significance and is the home of the god Enki (=Ea). The Hebrew word ʾēd is similar to a Sumerian and Babylonian word used in connection with these waters. Careful analysis of its use in Mesopotamian literature suggests that it refers to the annual inundation in the major water systems, which were known to bring fertility.[105]

Tsumura concludes that it is "not the lack of water but the lack of adequate control of water by man for tilling purposes" that is the identified problem here.[106]

In the Sumerian myth of Enki and Ninhursag, Ninhursag complains to Enki that he has provided no water supply for Dilmun. Enki replies that "from the mouth of the waters running underground sweet waters run out of the ground for you."[107] The text then proceeds to talk about all of the fertility that will result.

Formed the man from dust (2:7). The Sumerian Hymn to E-engura begins: "When humans broke through earth's surface like

Cylinder seal depicting Enki, the Sumerian god of the waters
Scala/Art Resource, NY, courtesy of the Iraq Museum

The Egyptian god Khnum fashions the pharoah on his potter's wheel.
Brian J. McMorrow

▼

▶ Eridu Genesis

In those days no canals were opened,
   no dredging was done at dikes and
   ditches on dike tops
The seeder plough and ploughing had
   not yet been instituted
No one of all the countries was planting in furrows.[A-38]

▶ Creation of Humankind in the Ancient Near East

It is common that some part of deity is used in the creation of humankind. Although there is little information on the creation of humankind in Egyptian literature, the breath of the deity[A-39] or his tears[A-40] represents the endowment from the deity.[A-41]

More information is available from Mesopotamia, where physical elements from the gods such as blood or flesh are used to create humans, thus requiring the death of a deity. The Mesopotamian presentation in the Atrahasis Epic suggests that the elements used to create people correspond to the various parts of the being (e.g., soul, spirit).[A-42] T. Abusch has proposed that Babylonians believed that man's ghost (*eṭemmu*) derives from the flesh of the god, while the blood (Akk. *damu*) of the god provides the human intellect (*ṭemu*), self, or soul.[A-43] "The blood is the dynamic quality of intelligence, and the flesh is the form of the body that is imposed on the clay."[A-44]

Genesis, by contrast, represents the divine element in human beings as seen in the image of God and the breath of life (closer to Egyptian than Mesopotamian thinking). Regarding the latter, God breathes the breath of life into man's nostrils and he becomes a living soul (*nepeš*). If it is true, as some have suggested,[A-45] that the Hebrew *nepeš* is equivalent to the Akkadian *eṭemmu*, we see the breath of God in Genesis functioning the same way as the flesh of the god functions in Atrahasis.

One of the distinctives of the biblical account of the creation of humankind is that only one human pair is created (= monogenesis). In the ancient Near East people are created as a group; that is, Egyptian and Mesopotamian sources are overwhelmingly polygenistic. The ancient Near Eastern texts typically speak of human origins in collective terms. The only extant text that has been suspected of depicting an original human pair is KAR 4. This idiosyncratic text has both Akkadian and Sumerian versions, with the main exemplar from Asshur dated to about 1100 B.C.[A-46] The most important lines (19–49) describe all the intended functions of the human beings that the gods are planning to create (the text never reports their actual creation, only the plan to create them). Line 39 says, "They will be named Ullegarra and Annegarra."

The problem is that these names, which seem as if they ought to be the names of the first humans, are preceded by the divine determinative, suggesting they belong to the divine realm. This text still has many uncertainties connected to its reading and interpretation. The text then sees people multiplying (line 40) and anticipates that "learned person after learned

person, unlearned after unlearned will spring up like the grain" (line 44). This is still far from the Israelite view of Adam (or Noah for that matter) as the progenitor of the race.

Finally, in Mesopotamian traditions people are created to serve the gods by doing the work that the gods are tired of doing. Turning again to KAR 4, "the corvée of the gods will be their corvée: They will fix the boundaries of the fields once and for all, and take in their hands hoes and baskets, to benefit the House of the great gods."[A-47] The labor that had been required for the gods to meet their own needs was drudgery, so people were expected to fill that gap and work to meet those needs.

In Israel, people were created to serve God, but not as slave labor to meet his needs. They served in a priestly role in sacred space.[A-48] God planted the garden to provide food for people rather than people providing food for the gods.[A-49] All of this demonstrates that though the Israelites viewed some issues differently from their neighbors, they operated in the same thought world. All were interested in exploring the divine component of humankind and the relationship between the human and divine. Those questions gave direction to the discussion. Whether similarities or differences emerge, the biblical perspective can be clarified by investigating the larger ancient Near Eastern worldview.

---

plants."[108] It is interesting to compare Genesis to the rest of the ancient Near Eastern literature regarding what ingredients were used to form humans (see sidebar on "Creation of Humankind in the Ancient Near East"). In the rest of the ancient Near East the creation of people focuses on archetypal and often corporate elements. Genesis 1:26–27 could be viewed as corporate and generic rather than individual. Here in Genesis 2 there are archetypal elements that are identifiable. Man is made from the dust, but since "dust he is and to dust he will return," all people can be seen as created from the dust. The creation of Eve from Adam's side likewise expresses a relationship between man and woman that permeates the race.

In these verses Adam and Eve are archetypes representing all of humanity in their creation, just as they do in their sin and their destiny (death). Their function as archetypes does not suggest that they are not historical individuals, it only suggests that they function more importantly as representatives of the race. Archetypes in the ancient Near East can be found in the Myth Enki and Ninmaḫ, in which Ninmaḫ undertakes the challenge of creating archetypes of certain handicapped classes of humans that Enki, the god of wisdom, has to find a role for.[109] Though these are individuals, they function as archetypes and are textually significant only as archetypes.

Breath of life (2:7). This idea occurs in early Egyptian literature, where the god Re puts breath into the nostrils of man,[110] and in a late Egyptian text (second century A.D.), in which the breath of life causes all things to exist.[111] The latter is similar to Israelite thinking, where people and animals both have the breath of life (Gen. 7:22).

In Eden (2:8). Early comparative Semitic studies suggested that the Hebrew word should be considered a cognate to the Sumerian *edin* ("steppe country"), but more recent data attest a link to an Aramaic cognate that means "to enrich, make abundant."[112] This semantic range is confirmed in Ugaritic occurrences and yields the idea of "garden of abundance," specifically to an abundance of water supply (cf. 13:10).[113] Gods such as Mesopotamian Enki/Ea and Canaanite El are understood to dwell in a watery abode.[114]

Genesis 2:10 indicates that we should understand the garden as adjoining Eden because the water flows from Eden and waters the garden. The garden adjoins God's residence in the same way that a garden of the palace adjoins the palace. Eden is the source of the waters and the residence of God. The text describes a situation that was well known in the ancient world: a sacred spot featuring a spring with an adjoining, well-watered park, stocked with specimens of trees and animals.[115]

Tree of life (2:9). The tree of life occurs in Proverbs 3:16–18 as offering extension of life, which suggests rejuvenating qualities. In the Gilgamesh Epic there is a rejuvenating plant that grows at the bottom of the cosmic river.[116] In the Story of Adapa, the hero is offered food by the god Anu that is eventually identified as "food of life" and "water of life."[117] He refuses to partake, having been told it was food of death. Thus humankind is prevented from joining the gods in immortality.[118] Additionally trees often figure prominently in ancient Near Eastern art and on cylinder seals. These have often been interpreted as depicting a tree of life, but more support from the literature is necessary to confirm such interpretations.[119] In Egyptian literature, Amun-Re is the god who created the tree of life, but no further information is given.[120]

Tree of the knowledge of good and evil (2:9). No such tree is known from any of the traditions of the ancient Near East. In the Gilgamesh Epic, the primitive Enkidu becomes wise (possessing reason) not by eating the fruit of a tree but by engaging in sexual intercourse with the prostitute Šamḫat, who was sent to entice and capture him.[121]

Four headwaters (2:10). In Egyptian depictions two or four rivers flow out of the mouth of Nun, who represents the cosmic abyss.[122] A cylinder seal from Mari depicts a high god, perhaps El, sitting on the top of a mountain, and from the base of the mountain the cosmic rivers flow forth from the mouths of serpents.[123] Also at Mari, the fresco from the wall of Zimri-Lim's palace portrays two deities holding pots from each of which flow four streams of water.[124] From the Middle Assyrian period (13th century, period of the judges) an ivory inlaid plaque shows a central divine figure with four rivers flowing from him in four directions. He is flanked by two trees, and standing next to each tree is a winged guardian.[125] It should also be noted that the idea of rivers flowing from the holy place is found not only in Gen-

▸ Garden Parks in the Ancient Near East

The word "garden" here should not make us think of vegetables or even necessarily flowers. Public gardens or a "country garden" convey the idea more accurately as indicating a park with careful landscaping, pools, watercourses, and paths winding among fruit trees and shade trees. Such arboretums, sometimes even containing animals of various sorts, were a common feature of palace complexes in the ancient world.

Kings boasted of large parts of cities devoted to these parks, of the great irrigation works that fed them, and of the distant lands from which the plants and animals were gathered. Tiglath-pileser I (1114–1076 B.C.) created a combined zoological park and arboretum of exotic animals and trees. Ashurnasirpal II (883–859) created a garden/park at Nimrud (Kalhu) by diverting water from the Upper Zab River through a rock-cut channel for his impressive collection of foreign plants and animals. Sennacherib (704–681) makes a similar claim for Nineveh. Parks are beautifully represented on the reliefs from Sargon II's (721–705) palace at Khorsabad, in which a variety of trees and a small pavilion with proto-Doric columns are depicted. Other reliefs depict lion hunts and falconry in the parks. A clay tablet from Babylon names and locates vegetables and herbs in the garden of Merodach-Baladan II (721–710).[A-50]

Temple complexes also sometimes featured gardens that symbolized the fertility provided for by the deity.[A-51] The produce of these temple gardens was used in offerings to the deity, just as the temple flocks and herds were used for sacrificial purposes.

Stone panel from the North Palace of Ashurbanipal shows Ashurbanipal's garden park with waters flowing through it and a prominently featured shrine.
Werner Forman Archive

▼

esis 2 (which portrays Eden as the Holy of Holies)[126] but also in Ezekiel's temple (Ezek. 47:1).[127]

All of this indicates that Genesis uses a familiar picture of fertile waters flowing from the seat of deity. The picture here is of a mighty spring that gushes out from Eden and is channeled through the garden for irrigation purposes. All of these channels then serve as headwaters, for the four rivers flow out in various directions as the waters exit the garden.

Pishon as a major river that dried up in antiquity. This possibility emerges from the analysis of sand patterns and satellite photography, which have revealed an old riverbed running northeast through Saudi Arabia from the Hijaz mountains near Medina to the Persian Gulf in Kuwait, near the mouth of the Tigris and Euphrates.[128] It is estimated that the river dried up between 3500–2000 B.C.[129]

Pishon … Gihon (2:11–13). Attempts to identify these two rivers include: canals, other rivers of Mesopotamia (Balikh, Diyala, Zab, etc.), other rivers outside of Mesopotamia (e.g., Nile, Indus, Ganges), or larger bodies such as the Persian Gulf or the Red Sea. Recent investigation attempts to identify the One of the richest gold mines in the region is found in the Hijaz Mountains.[130] The area it runs through near the Red Sea produces spices and precious stones as well. A final suggestion is that the Pishon and Gihon refer to the encircling cosmic waters.[131] None of these options may be adopted with any confidence.

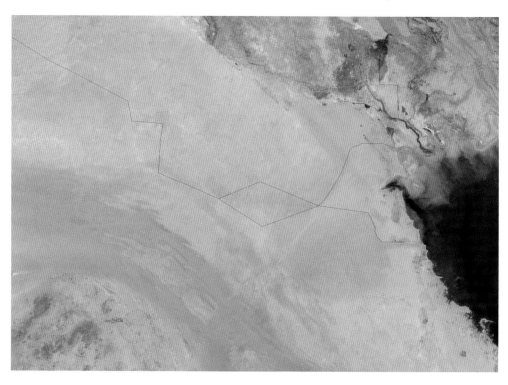

> ▶ **From Gilgamesh Epic**

> Ur-shanabi, this plant is the "plant of
> the heartbeat"
> By which means a man can recapture
> his vitality.
> I will take it to Uruk, the Sheepfold,
> I will feed some to an old man and put
> the plant to the test.
> Its (or his) name will be "The Old Man
> Has Grown Young,"
> I will eat some myself and go back to
> how I was in my youth.[A-52]

To work it and take care of it (2:15). In the rest of the ancient world it was believed that humans had been created to serve the needs of the gods. The gods had grown tired of the drudgery of providing for themselves (see sidebar on "Creation of Humankind in the Ancient Near East" at 2:7). In Genesis people also serve God, but not by meeting his needs.

When people are assigned their function here, priestly terms (*ᶜbd* and *šmr*) are used.[132] Note the contrast to the royal functions given in 1:28–29. In the rest of the ancient Near East, caring for the needs of the gods was also a priestly function. In the Old Testament, the priestly function involved maintaining the status of sacred space and providing for the proper worship and obedience to God's requirements.

Helper suitable for him (2:18). In the Gilgamesh Epic, the tyrant king has no equal to occupy his attention and distract him from oppressing the people, so the gods ordain the creation of his counterpart, Enkidu.[133] Gilgamesh had been singular and alone, and he looks among the animals (where Enkidu dwelt) to find a counterpart for himself. Though vague similarities can be seen here (because Gilgamesh and Adam are both archetypal humans in need of a social equal to share their functions), the context is entirely different. The value in this parallel is its demonstration that the ancient world recognized that a social

context had to be established by deity for humanity to function properly. Adam recognizes that need and God supplies it.

The man gave names (2:20). Names are not given randomly in the ancient world. A name may identify the essential nature of the creature, so that giving a name may be an act of assigning the function that creature will have.

The Egyptian theory of the name was based on the principle that an essential relationship existed between the name and the named.... The relationship between name and essence ran in both directions:

everything that can be gathered from a name says something about the essence of the named, and everything that can be said about the essence of a person can be ascribed to that person as a name.[134]

In Mesopotamia the assigning of function is referred to as the decreeing of destiny. Decreeing destiny by giving a name is an act of authority. In the ancient world, when a king conquered another country, the king he put on the throne was given a new name.[135] In other cases, the giving of a name is an act of discernment in which the name is determined by the circumstances.[136] In either case, Adam's naming of the animals is his first step in subduing and ruling. He is fulfilling the role that he had by virtue of being in God's image, but it also leads him to realize that among the animals there is no social equal to share his function and place.

When we give explanation of names, we usually talk about lexical history—the constituent parts of a name and the words they are derived from. In the ancient world, that was only one level of connection, and not necessarily the most important. Mesopotamian lexical lists connect words and find significance in them based on phonemic and semantic elements as well—a connection that we treat less seriously as we call it "word*play*." In Egypt these obtuse relationships were taken seriously and suggest a greater appreciation of the power of language.

> They testify to a belief in the possibilities of language, a consciousness of language that is foreign to us, for we have come to understand the conventional nature of the signs of language. We speak of "plays" on words because we experience such a use of language, which undermines the conventionality of signs in a cunning and usually amusing manner, as playful. In Egypt, however, wordplay was regarded as a highly serious and controlled use of language, for language was understood to be a dimension of divine presence.[137]

One of the man's ribs (2:21). In Genesis the woman is built from the side (Heb. ṣēlāʿ) of the man. The word is usually architectural,[138] and is used anatomically only here in the Old Testament. In Akkadian, the cognate term ṣelu is also both architectural and anatomical. Its anatomical uses generally refer not just to bone, but to bones and flesh.[139] The Sumerian equivalent is TI, which intriguingly also means "life."[140] These two meanings are both applicable to Eve, since she is made from Adam's side and her name identifies her as the mother of all living (Gen. 3:20). Hebrew as a language developed relatively late (mid-second millennium). Any traditions preserved from the patriarchal period or earlier would likely have been transmitted in the languages of Mesopotamia (Sumerian, Akkadian, Amorite).

In light of this observation, it is interesting to note the potential for wordplay here. This makes it tempting to view the use of Adam's side as metaphorical (indicating the social connectivity that is intrinsic, see 2:23–24). Adam is made from dust, but we would equally claim that dust continues to represent what we all are (for "dust we are and to dust we shall return"). One can then ask whether it is also true that all men and women are to be viewed as two sides of an original whole.[141] While this archetypal identification may be an important element, we cannot ignore that the text also makes the anatomical comment that after God had taken the side from Adam, he "closed up the place with flesh." This remains enigmatic.

Cylinder seal showing the motif referred to as "Lord of the Animals"
Bildarchiv Preussischer Kulturbesitz/Art Resource, NY, courtesy of the Vorderasiatisches Museum, Staatliche Museen zu Berlin, Berlin, Germany ▼

Made a woman (2:22). The verb used for the creation of Eve is one that has not been seen previously in the narrative: "to build" (Heb. *bānâ*). In a late Akkadian text from the Seleucid period, a cognate verb (Akk. *banu*) is used line after line describing how Ea created various gods from pinched-off clay.[142] The Akkadian verb can be used to refer to construction, but also to procreation.[143] This is also true in Hebrew (Deut. 25:9; Ruth 4:11).[144]

A man will leave his father and mother (2:24). In Israelite society, the woman became part of the man's tribe, so one would expect that she would be the one leaving her parents. In their marriage procedures, however, the woman often continued to live in the house of her father and mother for some months after the marriage was initially consummated and received conjugal visits from her husband with the expectation that once she had conceived, she would move to her husband's house. Thus, the reason the man leaves his home is for conception.

But the narrator's comment need not be sociologically based. The text establishes a "flesh-line" that was stronger than a bloodline and causes the man to seek her out. In a sense, a part of him was missing and is, in effect, beckoning him. This is what makes the blessing from Genesis 1 functional—everything is now in place for people to be fruitful and multiply.

Naked (2:25). In Genesis the nakedness of the humans does not appear to be a negative comment, though it is contrasted through wordplay to the craftiness of the serpent in the next verse, so it may refer to a relative naïveté. In contrast, ancient Near Eastern texts indicate that the primeval nakedness of people is a sign of a primitive, uncivilized condition. When Enkidu is civilized in the Gilgamesh Epic, he is clothed by the woman who civilizes him.[145] In the Sumerian text Ewe and Wheat, the text opens with a description of primeval humans that is clearly primitive and negative (see sidebar "Ewe and Wheat").[146] In this way there are

> ### ▶ Ewe and Wheat
>
> The people of those distant days,
> They knew no cloth to wear;
> They went about with naked limbs in the land,
> And like sheep they ate grass with their mouth,
> Drinking water from the ditches.[A-53]

similarities in how Genesis and the Mesopotamian texts describe early humankind, but there is a contrasting assessment of how their condition should be interpreted.

Serpent (3:1). In the Gilgamesh Epic, after Gilgamesh acquires the magical plant that will rejuvenate him, it is stolen by a snake. In the Story of Adapa, one of the guardians of Anu's palace, where Adapa is offered the food of life, is Gizzida (= Ningishzida, "Lord of the Productive Tree"). Ningishzida is serpent shaped or accompanied by horned serpents (Akk. *bašmu)*, and he is the guardian of the demons who live in the netherworld.[147] In Egypt, the serpent was associated with both death and wisdom. The Genesis account draws on both aspects in the wisdom dialogue between the serpent and Eve and with the introduction of death after the expulsion from Eden.

Apophis, the serpent who represented chaos in Egyptian thinking
Frederick J. Mabie

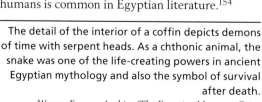

Libation vase of king Gudea, ca. 2100 B.C., dedicated to Ninghishzidda: with this god's acolytes, entwined serpents and winged dragon-snakes. From Girsu, Mesopotamia.

Jill Walton, courtesy of the Louvre

▲

Even when not related to a god, the serpent represented wisdom (occult), fertility, health, chaos, and immortality, and was often worshiped. The snake god Apophis was considered the enemy of order.[148] Snakes were also sometimes considered beneficial or protective. So Wadjet, a lower Egyptian deity, was considered the protector of the pharaoh and is represented by the *uraeus* on his crown. J. Currid summarizes this paradox:

> The Egyptians revered the serpent because they feared it for its power and danger, but they also honored the serpent because at times it offered protection. Thus they regarded the snake as both friend and fiend, protector and enemy, and the personification of the sacred and the profane. Some snakes were to be worshiped, others were to be considered incarnations of evil.[149]

Serpents in Egypt are also connected with occult wisdom. The *ureaus* is sometimes invoked as a magician.[150] In this regard it may be no coincidence that the Hebrew word used for snake here (*nāḥāš*) evokes the similar sounding and perhaps etymologically related verb (*nḥš*), meaning "to give omens."[151] "Many gods, especially the primeval gods, were represented in serpent form. The earth-god Geb had a serpent's head; the 'serpent who created the earth' was worshiped at Thebes. Serpent deities controlled human life and the passage of time."[152]

In the literature of Canaan, the serpent is a fertility figure, and charming of serpents is addressed in the context of sacral marriage.[153] The idea that animals in general, and serpents in particular, could communicate with humans is common in Egyptian literature.[154]

The detail of the interior of a coffin depicts demons of time with serpent heads. As a chthonic animal, the snake was one of the life-creating powers in ancient Egyptian mythology and also the symbol of survival after death.

Werner Forman Archive/The Egyptian Museum, Cairo

▶

What does all of this information from the ancient Near East tell us about Genesis 3? Because of the New Testament and the development of Christian theology, it is most common for people today immediately to think of Satan as the serpent in Genesis 3, but the Israelites never make that connection. We cannot recover what Adam and Eve would have thought about the serpent, but the ancient Near Eastern literature gives us an idea of some of the images that came to mind for the Israelites living in their time and culture. Foremost is the association of the serpent with life and death. Likewise the serpent is wise, is connected with disorder, and can be the enemy of God—perspectives that are meaningful in this context.

You will be like God (3:5). One can imagine a variety of ways in which people might desire or strive to "be like God"—some commendable, others inappropriately ambitious or subversive. The aspiration targeted here is in the category of wisdom, a defensibly laudable pursuit. In the ancient Near East godlikeness pertains to the categories of splendor (Enkidu became handsome like a god) or immortality (Gilgamesh, Adapa). It is interesting that Gilgamesh and Adapa both encounter a snake figure and Enkidu

achieves his godlikeness through a woman (who also gives him understanding). Gilgamesh and Adapa fail to achieve immortality, both through not being able to eat the necessary food.[155]

These examples show that in the ancient world it was common for people to meditate on ways in which people succeeded and failed in becoming like deity. At the same time the differences are significant. In Genesis disobedience figures prominently, and the category of godlikeness is distinct. Furthermore, the consequences of the attempt differ. Adam and Eve do achieve a level of godlikeness (like Enkidu), but with significant negative repercussions. At the same time they lose their access to immortality (like Gilgamesh and Adapa) and also suffer in their lost relationship with God, which is not an issue in any of the others. This is then an excellent example of how the comparison between the Bible and ancient Near Eastern literature shows a similar landscape but with important variations in the essential nature of the issue.

Cool of the day (3:8). This traditional translation is problematic. No precedent exists for interpreting the word for "wind" (*rûaḥ*) as "cool." An alternative using comparative information is that the phrase should be translated "wind of the storm."[156] The basis of this alternative is the claim that the word usually translated "day" (*yôm*) could possibly be translated as "storm." Support is drawn from an Akkadian cognate *umu* and the existence of two other biblical contexts where this alternate meaning might apply (Isa. 27:8; Zeph. 2:2). The resulting interpretation is that Adam and Eve heard the (terrifying) sound of God going through the garden with a storm wind. If so, then God is coming in judgment rather than for a daily conversation, which explains Adam and Eve's desire to hide.

The problem is that though this Akkadian word is connected with the storm, it is more often a "storm demon" or a deified personification of the storm.[157] Thus, it is difficult to argue that the Akkadian word means "storm," and one cannot therefore carry it over to a few ambiguous Hebrew occurrences.

The verb that expresses "walking" in the garden means "to circulate about" and can be used in judgment contexts (Zech. 6:7). Yet in Genesis Adam claims that he hid, not because he was afraid but because he was naked. The meaning of the text therefore remains obscure and the proposed alternative interpretation offered on the strength of ancient Near Eastern information should be judged inadequate. The insufficiency of the alternative does not tacitly support the traditional translation, since that has no support either.

Crawl on your belly (3:14). The Egyptian Pyramid Texts were designed to aid the pharaohs of the Old Kingdom (end of the third millennium) on their journey to the afterlife. Among the over 700 utterances are several dozen spells and curses on snakes that may impede the king's progress. These utterances contain phrases that are reminiscent of the curse on the serpent in Genesis 3. For instance, the biblical statement that the serpent will "crawl on your belly" is paralleled by frequent spells that call on the snake to lie down, fall down, get down, or crawl away (Pyramid Texts 226, 233, 234, 298, 386).[158] Another says that he should "go with your face on the path" (PT 288).

These suggest that when God tells the serpent that he will crawl on his belly, there is no suggestion that the serpent had legs that he now will lose. Instead, he is going to be docile rather than in an attack position. The serpent on its belly is nonthreatening, while the one reared up is protecting or attacking. Notice that on the pharaoh's crown, the serpent (*uraeus*) is pictured as upright and in an attack position. Nevertheless, I should also note that there are occasional depictions of serpent creatures with legs.[159] There is no indication, however, of an occasion in which serpents lost their legs.

▶

Eat dust (3:14). Eating dust is not a comment about the actual diet of a snake. It is more likely a reference to their habitat. Again the Pyramid Texts show some similarity as they attempt to banish the serpent to the dust.[160] The serpent is a creature of the netherworld (that is why the pharaoh encounters it on his journey), and denizens of the netherworld were typically portrayed as eating dust. So in the Descent of Ishtar, the netherworld is described as a place where their food is dust and their bread is clay.[161]

Crush your head (3:15). Treading on the serpent is used in Pyramid Texts 299 as an expression of overcoming or defeating it. Specific statements indicate that the "Sandal of Horus tramples the snake underfoot" (PT 378), and "Horus has shattered [the snake's] mouth with the sole of his foot" (PT 388). This reflects a potentially mortal blow to this deadly enemy. There is no suggestion that the Israelites are borrowing from the Pyramid Texts, only that these texts help us to determine how someone in the ancient Near East might understand such words and phrases.

Strike his heel (3:15). It is true that the ancients were aware that many snakes were not poisonous.[162] But since harmless snakes usually were not seen as aggressive, if someone were bitten by a snake, it was assumed that the snake might be poisonous. Thus the strike to the heel is a potentially mortal blow.

Garments of skin (3:21). In the Tale of Adapa, after Adapa loses the opportunity to eat from the bread and water of life, he is given clothing by Anu before being sent from his presence. But the context is entirely different. In Adapa, food, drink, anointing, and a garment are all offered together, but only the latter two are accepted. These four represent the most basic of human needs. Izreʾel observes that garments and anointing oil represent human wisdom because they distinguish humans from animals.[163] Here in Genesis this reference comes just before the observation that the human pair has gained wisdom. Some have concluded that the divine clothing of an individual is symbolic of rebirth or renewal, but the evidence is scant.[164]

Banished from the garden (3:23). In the ancient Near East there is no time when "sin" begins, no point when humanity moves from a positive relationship with deity into a worse position, no sense of people once being in sacred space but then banished. Perhaps in the Atrahasis Epic there is a time when there is no death for humanity, but then it is instituted.[165] According to Abusch, human death initially comes through violence because there is no illness or old age.[166]

▶ **Pyramid Texts, Utterance 378**

O Snake in the sky! O Centipede on earth! The Sandal of Horus is what tramples the *nhi*-snake underfoot.... It is dangerous for me so I have trodden on you; be wise about me (?) and I will not tread on you, for you are the mysterious and invisible one of whom the gods speak; because you are the one who has no legs, because you are the one who has no arms, with which you could walk after your brethren the gods ... beware of me and I will beware of you.[A-54]

Common motif shows winged creatures guarding a sacred tree. Gold leaf tablet is from 14th-12th century B.C., Syria.
Z. Radovan/www. BibleLand Pictures.com

◄

Thus, it was common in the ancient world to portray "before" and "after" pictures with regard to human death and the relationship between God and humanity, but Genesis identifies different elements in the portrayal and reflects a different theology.

Cherubim (3:24). Cherubs are a class of supernatural creature generally functioning as guardians. They are typically portrayed in beast form rather than human form. They can be four-footed or upright. In cases where it can be determined, they appear to

Cylinder seal impression depicting the sun god in the winged disk that appears above the sacred tree. On each side a winged human figure holds a bucket and stands upon the back of a winged, bearded sphinx.
Werner Forman Archive/The British Museum

◄

be composite (i.e., having characteristics of various beasts the way griffins or sphinxes did in other literatures).[167]

Cain and Abel (4:1–16)

Abel kept flocks, and Cain worked the soil (4:2). This portrays the earliest human vocations. Abel is a pastoralist and Cain a farmer. Both provide food necessary for survival, yet the inherent nature of each creates the potential for conflict with the other. This conflict is likewise reflected in some of the earliest literature from Mesopotamia, namely, the Sumerian tale of Dumuzi and Enkimdu.[168] Here their occupations do not cause their conflict. Instead, both deities (representing shepherds and farmers) are interested in gaining the favor of the same deity (the goddess Inanna). Both talk about the gifts they can offer, and, it can be deduced, both anticipate benefiting from the relationship (since Inanna is associated with fertility).

Likewise in Genesis 4 the conflict is not inherent in the occupations. The occupations explain the offerings, and the divine response to the offerings is the source of the conflict. If one is interested in trying to date the events of Genesis anthropologically, according to archaeologists, the domestication of plants and animals both become evident about 9000 B.C.[169]

Fruits of the soil (4:3). There is intrinsically no problem for Cain to bring produce as a gift to God. The word used for his sacrifice (*minḥâ*) is one that describes the kind of offering outlined in Leviticus 2, which is regularly something other than animal sacrifice. It was likewise common throughout the rest of the ancient world to offer food offerings from what was grown.

Fat portions (4:4). Mention of the fat portions would contrast in the audience's mind to whole burnt offerings, in which the whole animal is consumed. The description of Abel's offering also contrasts to a blood offering. Usually if blood were offered, it was to deal with some offense, and the whole animal was also offered, not just the fat parts. Blood rites were not common in the ancient world[170] and do not appear in the Bible until the period of the Exodus and Sinai. The fat parts (=suet)[171] were inedible and were typically offered as a gift before the meat was eaten in a ritual meal. Offering of the suet is not attested in Mesopotamia, but Milgrom finds it among the Hittites, Canaanites, and Phoenicians.[172]

Sin is crouching at your door (4:7). Recent commentators have preferred repointing the participle "crouching" (Heb. *rōbēṣ*) to *rābiṣ* and seeing it as a reference to a well-known Mesopotamian demon (*rabiṣu*) who lingers around doorways. "Sin" is then portrayed as a doorway demon waiting for its victim to cross the threshold. From the Old Babylonian period on in Mesopotamia, such demons were considered evil and were thought to ambush their victims.

An alternative is available if we access earlier Akkadian texts where the *rabiṣu* is not a demon but an important administrator who served a judicial function. In Ur III texts he was responsible for preliminary examination at trials. By the mid-second millennium, texts from Amarna and Ugarit showed the role of the *rabiṣu* respectively as local ruler and important witness of documents or at trials.[173] The fact that the text mentions the desire to master Cain favors *rabiṣu* as a demon.[174]

▶ The Eridu Genesis

This Sumerian work dates from early in the second millennium B.C., thus is contemporary with the patriarchs. It has been pieced together from various fragments and, as reconstructed, contains the story of creation, the development from nomadic to urban living, and the flood. It includes political developments (king-ship descending from heaven), economic development (redistribution of goods), and technological development (irrigation techniques). Like its near contemporary, the Atrahasis Epic, it therefore contains the three elements that also characterize the early chapters of Genesis: Creation, population growth, and the flood.[A-55]

Cain attacked his brother (4:8). The motif of conflict between brothers is not widespread in the ancient literature. Perhaps the most well-known is the Egyptian story known as the Tale of Two Brothers (see sidebar on "The Tale of Two Brothers" at 39:2).[175] In this case the conflict is over the wife of the older brother, who tries to seduce the younger. Consequently, there are no close parallels to Cain and Abel in the extant literature from the ancient Near East.

Restless wanderer (4:12). In Mesopotamian thinking the ideal lifestyle is urban. Civilized life in the city is the gift of the gods and is highly valued.[176] Agricultural and pastoral activities are part of the urban landscape and are foundational to the success of the city. In this way of thinking, the more nomadic groups are considered uncivilized and a threat to society. The motif of the wild man living out in the steppe country among the animals is represented by Enkidu in the Gilgamesh Epic and is an archetype for these despised and feared people.[177]

An interesting contrast here in Genesis is that the categories are set up differently. As in Mesopotamia, Cain's status as a wanderer marks him as undesirable. But this wandering is in contrast to being a farmer rather than to being a city-dweller. In fact, it is in his line that the arts of civilization are developed (4:17–22).

▶ The Foundation of Eridu

A holy house, a house of the gods, had not been built in (its) holy place;
   A reed had not come forth, a tree had not been produced;
   A brick had not been laid, a brick mold had not been built;
   A house had not been made, a city had not been built;
   A city had not been made, a living creature had not been placed (in it);
   Nippur had not been made, Ekur had not been built;

Uruk had not been made, Eanna had not been built;
   The *apsu* had not been made, Eridu had not been built;
   A holy house, a house of the gods (and) its foundations, had not been made.
   All the lands were sea,
   The spring in the midst of the sea was only a channel.
   Then Eridu was made, Esagil was built.[A-56]

Whoever finds me will kill me (4:14). Blood feuding between clans is not a foreign concept. In the ancient world it was typically the business of the clan to avenge the death of one of its members. This concept is represented in biblical law (cities of refuge, avenger of blood) as well as in the ancient Near East. For example, the Middle Assyrian Laws stipulate as follows: "If a man, who has not yet received his inheritance share, takes a life, they shall hand him over to the next-of-kin. Should the next-of-kin so choose, he shall kill him, or, if he chooses to come to an accommodation, then he shall take his inheritance share."[178]

Lines of Cain and Seth (4:17 – 5:32)

Building a city (4:17). According to Mesopotamian tradition, the first city built was Eridu (remarkably similar to the name Irad, see next entry). City building and urbanization began in the middle of the fourth millennium B.C., though the earliest archaeologically known settlement in the world, Jericho, existed several millennia earlier. Early Jericho, however, cannot even be considered a town[179] and does not possess the characteristics of urbanized life. In Mesopotamian literature, civilized urban life developed from the arts of civilization brought by the renowned sages, the *apkallu*, who were sent by the gods:

Uanna, who completed the plans of
    heaven and earth
Uannedugga, who was endowed with
    comprehensive intelligence
Enmedugga, who was allotted a good fate
Enmegalamma, who was born in a house
Enmebulugga, who grew up on pasture land
Anenlilda, the exorcist of Eridu
Utuabzu, who ascended to heaven
Total of seven brilliant puradu fish born
    in the river, who direct the plans of
    heaven and earth.[180]

In the end, city building was a divine enterprise.[181] Within this tradition, city building was related to, and a part of, creation, because creation involved the establishment of the world as the Mesopotamians knew it—not only in terms of the physical cosmos, but also including the civilized aspect of the social and economic world. In contrast, Genesis sees city building in purely human terms.

Irad (4:18). Eridu (note similar sound to Irad)[182] was considered the first city in the Sumerian King List when kingship first descended from heaven,[183] though Uruk (cf. Erech, 10:10) was by far the largest of the early cities and arguably the one with the greatest influence.[184] The point has been made that the Sumerian King List is, in the end, not a king list after all, but a city list—again emphasizing the importance of cities in the way that Mesopotamians understood the world and creation.[185] Eridu was

▶ Metalworking in History

Forging bronze and iron are developments that take place at different times in history. The earliest use of metal is attested about 8000 B.C. Bronze smelting has been identified in the sixth millennium B.C., and metal workshops appear in the fifth millennium. Much of the bronze of the "Bronze Age" (3400–1200 B.C.) was actually an alloy of copper and arsenic, and only from the Middle Bronze and into the Late Bronze does it show the increased use of copper alloyed with tin, as the latter, with rare deposits in the Near East, became available with the development of trade routes (particularly through Afghanistan).

Though the Iron Age begins at 1200 B.C., evidencing extensive use of iron in Cyprus and Palestine, it is not until about 1000 B.C. that it becomes dominant in the Near East. Worked iron (usually meteoric rather than mined) is in evidence much earlier in the seventeenth century B.C. Iron has a much higher melting point and, though it had long been worked in solid state, the technology for smelting and forging it did not develop until the end of the second millennium as the techniques of carburization, quenching, and tempering were mastered. These techniques developed in the eastern Mediterranean, though the evidence does not support the idea that either the Hittites or the Philistines held a monopoly on the technology.[A-57]

Copper awl set in bone handle, from Beersheba, Israel. Chalcolithic, fourth millennium B.C.
Erich Lessing/ Art Resource, NY, courtesy of the Israel Museum (IDAM)
◀

the city associated with the god Enki and is located in southeastern Mesopotamia.

Married two women (4:19). Polygamy in the ancient Near East was common enough and not outlawed in any context known. It was practiced largely among royalty and the wealthy upper class. Among common people monogamy was the norm[186] except in cases where the first wife was childless, sick, or ill-behaved.[187]

Raise livestock (4:20). Living in tents and raising livestock describe the pastoralist, who had to keep herds and flocks moving to a variety of water sources and grazing lands. This refers not to an achievement (e.g., domestication) but to a lifestyle. Just as Mesopotamians believed cities and kingship to have originated with the gods, so did pastoralism, agriculture, and other lifestyles. Again, in contrast, Genesis sees them as human developments.

Harp and flute (4:21). Earliest examples of these musical instruments identified archaeologically date to the third and fourth millennia B.C. The first flutes were made of bone, but by the fourth millennium examples in silver are attested. Stringed instruments are attested in tombs and musicians in action are portrayed in art.[188]

Forged ... bronze and iron (4:22). The emphasis in Genesis is on development of technology prior to the Flood (since none of Cain's line survives it) that is ultimately used on these named metals. The Hebrew word refers only to "sharpening" and therefore applies to tools and weapons (as opposed to ornamental use). It does not imply melting (casting or

Harp found in the royal cemetery at Ur
Scala/Art Resource, NY, courtesy of the Iraq Museum
▼

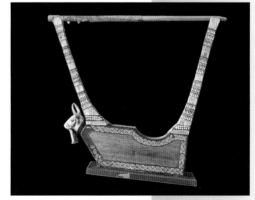

▶ Sumerian King List and Long Lives

If the long lives in the antediluvian world (cf. Methuselah, 969 years) seem amazing to us, we will be utterly astounded by the length of reign credited to antediluvian kings in the Sumerian King List:

Alulim	28,800 years
Alalgar	36,000 years
Enmenluanna	43,200 years
Enmengalanna	28,800 years
Dumuzi	36,000 years
Ensipazianna	28,800 years
Enmeduranna	21,000 years
Uburtutu	18,600 years

It is possible that these large numbers relate to an early scribal confusion between the Sumerian sexagesimal system and the Semitic decimal system. The symbol that stands for 36,000 in the sexagesimal system

stands for 1000 in the earliest decimal notation. In a piece designated "The Rulers of Lagash," the writer comments on what life was like when people were so long-lived: "In those days a child spent a hundred years in diapers; after he had grown up he spent a hundred years without being given any task to do."[A-58]

smelting) since both copper and iron can be worked to an edge by cold-hammering (forging) and by low temperature heating (annealing). The earliest sharpened copper artifact is an awl dating to the seventh millennium B.C.[189] Early iron developed as a by-product of smelted copper.[190] Only one artifact of sharpened iron is known from before 2500 B.C.—a smelted chisel from a grave in Samarra from about 5000 B.C.[191] Most sharpened iron dates to the first millennium.

Call on the name of the LORD (4:26). About a dozen times in the Old Testament people are said to call on the name of the Lord, and in these passages they are generally either calling for help in connection with a ritual or invoking God's presence at a cultic site (see esp. Gen. 12:8; 13:4; 21:33; 26:25; see also 1 Kings 18:24 and as a point of interest, Matt. 18:20. For another connection between the name, a cultic place, and ritual

practices, see Deut. 12:5–6, 11). Eventually humans sought to procure the presence of God through establishing cultic places and performing rituals there, but in Genesis 4:26 there is no indication of these trappings. Thus it seems that people have begun to invoke the Lord's presence (the presence that was lost at the fall). This passage, then, represents the beginning of religion.

As with the other beginnings in this chapter, in the ancient Near East the beginning of religion is not associated with humans but with the gods (oddly enough). That is, the gods establish cultic sites for themselves (since the temples were their dwelling places). When humans are created, they are to serve the gods—the implication being that sacred space existed before humans.

Son in his own likeness (5:3). In the Babylonian creation epic *Enuma Elish*, when the generations of the gods are presented, this same sort of language is used: "Anshar made his son Anu like himself, and Anu begot Nudimmud in his likeness."[192] This idea, so routine to our understanding of heredity, was looked upon with wonder, not unlike how plants produce seeds that grow into the same kinds of plants. These reflect the order that was built into creation.

Took him away (5:24). The idea of humans being taken to heaven is known in the ancient world, but not in the way that Christian theology often understands it. First is the example of Utuabzu, the seventh of the renowned sages (just as Enoch is the seventh from Adam; see comment on 4:17).[193] Second are characters such as Etana and Adapa,[194] who both ascend to heaven under different circumstances. Notable is the fact that their ascensions are passing experiences rather than changes in status and therefore are not in the same category as Enoch.

As a further observation, we should note that Genesis does not indicate where Enoch was taken, so it is possible that we should not assume ascension to heaven. Utnapishtim (the survivor of the flood in the Gilgamesh Epic) was a favorite of the gods and was also "taken" so that he did not experience death. But he was taken neither to heaven nor to the netherworld, but to a faraway, inaccessible place "at the mouth of the rivers."[195]

A final intriguing parallel comes from Egyptian literature in the Pyramid Texts, in which the god Shu takes the king to heaven so that he doesn't die on earth.[196] This must be understood in the context of Egyptian ideas about the afterlife, where death is essential for the transition of states to be made. The action of Shu, therefore, perhaps at best changes the locale of death. At other times it represents the hopes after death. None of these offer transparent explanation of Enoch's experience, but they show a variety of possibilities

to be considered that otherwise would not be recognized.

Comfort us (5:29). Noah's name is related to the Hebrew word for "rest," yet the explanation given for it depends on an entirely different word (*nāḥam*, NIV: "comfort"). The flood brings "rest," but the traditions differ regarding to whom it brings rest. Here in Genesis it brings rest/comfort for humans in relation to the curse on the ground. Mesopotamian literature knows of no curse on the ground, but sees the flood as bringing rest to the gods, who find their lives and their sleep disrupted by humans.[197]

Sons of God, Daughters of Men (6:1–4)

Sons of God (6:2). The royal titulary of the ancient Near East regularly suggested the divine descent of kings, even outside Egypt's context of deified kings. This idea of divine descent was a rhetorical expression of the divine election and legitimization of the king that is typical in royal inscriptions. Throughout the biblical period it was part of the royal prerogative to claim divine heritage (see sidebar). Thus the title "son of God" can be identified as a royal motif both in the Bible and outside of it.

Gilgamesh is portrayed as two-thirds god and one-third man (1.48) and "flesh of the gods" (9.49). Nevertheless, though it is common for kings to be portrayed as having divine parentage, there is no precedent for ancient kings as a group being referred to as "sons of god." This keeps open the possibility that this title could refer to royal elites, though a reference to members of the heavenly council certainly cannot be ruled out.

Married any of them they chose (6:2). There are no examples from Akkadian or Northwest Semitic mythological texts of

▶ Genealogies in the Ancient World

Mesopotamian genealogies are mostly royal, mostly linear (one line of descent, such as Gen. 5, as opposed to segmented, containing more than one line of descent, such as Gen. 10), and rarely more than three or four generations deep. Fluidity occurs primarily in telescoping (i.e., eliminating names), though some rearrangement of the order of the ancestors may be detected in the king lists. Most notably, the genealogy of Ammiṣaduqa (a descendant of Hammurabi in the first dynasty of Babylon) evidences shuffling of the sequence of kings and garbling of some names when compared with the Assyrian king list.

Egyptian sources (mostly from the Persian and Hellenistic periods) preserve long linear genealogies, sometimes extending fifteen to twenty generations, often connecting to priestly lines. Fluidity is also evident only in telescoping within these genealogies. Compar-ing biblical genealogies to one another shows that often several generations are skipped. Thus, a genealogy's purpose is apparently not to represent every generation, as our modern family trees attempt to do.

Some additional ideas the ancients had about genealogies can be inferred from how they continually reorganize the genealogies of the gods. Since such genealogies are occasionally rearranged and grouped to serve a particular function, it seems logical that human genealogies could be treated in similar ways.

Genealogies represent continuity and relationship and are often used for purposes of power and prestige. Genealogies are sometimes formatted to suit a literary purpose. Thus, for instance, the genealogies between Adam and Noah, and Noah and Abraham, are each set up to contain ten members with the last having three sons.[A-59]

divine beings marrying or cohabiting with human women, so it is difficult to make the claim that this account is a vestige of ancient mythology. There are examples of kings claiming mixed ancestry of gods and humans (see previous entry), but that is a different concept.

If the "sons of God" are viewed as kings, the question remains as to what offense they are committing here.[198] Polygamy has always been a weak candidate since the Old Testament does not condemn it. Promiscuity is likewise an unlikely explanation since the Hebrew text describes the situation using the standard idiom for marriage ("taking wives"). An alternate understanding may be found in a practice noted in the Gilgamesh Epic as the prime example of Gilgamesh's tyranny, namely, his exercising the right of the first night with a new bride: "He will couple with the wife-to-be, he first of all, the bridegroom after."[199] This practice accommodates the marriage terminology, and in Gilgamesh it is clearly both oppressive and offensive behavior. The remaining problem is that this practice is infrequently attested in ancient literature. Nonetheless, in the Gilgamesh Epic it is clear.[200]

A hundred and twenty years (6:3). The Sumerian folktale Enlil and Namzitarra, found in a bilingual version at Emar, speaks of 120 years as an ideal human lifespan.[201] Speculation suggests that this number derives not from observation but from abstraction within the Sumerian mathematical system.[202] The idea that deity governs lifespan is reflected in Mesopotamia in the Gilgamesh Epic as the hero continues his quest for immortality. There it is indicated that the Anunnaki (netherworld gods) fix

▶ Examples of Kings Claiming Divine Sonship

Eannatum (Vulture Stele): "Ningirsu inserted the germ of Eannatum into the womb. Baba gave birth to him ... Ninhursaga fed him at her right breast."

Ur-Nammu: "The son born of the goddess Ninsuna."

Gudea: "For me who has no mother, you are my mother; for me who has no father, you are my father. You implanted my semen in the womb, gave birth to me in the sanctuary, Gatumdug, sweet is your holy name."

Samsuiluna (Old Baylonian): "O Samsuiluna, eternal seed of the gods."

Tukulti-Ninurta Epic (Middle Assyrian): "Through the destiny of Nudimmud, he is reckoned as flesh godly in his limbs, by fiat of the lord of the world, he was cast sublimely from the womb of the gods."[A-60]

---

the fates and have established death and life (10.319–22).

In the Egyptian Book of the Dead, the god Thoth reports to the creator god Atum: "You shall not witness wrongdoing, you shall not suffer it! Shorten their years, cut short their months, because they have done hidden damage to all that you have made."[203] This is the same Atum who in the beginning floated in Nun, the primeval ocean.[204] In this way the first two references to the spirit of God in Genesis (1:2; 6:3) both have parallels to the role of Atum in Egyptian texts. One key difference is that Atum is identified as the creator God in the Egyptian texts.

Nephilim ... heroes (6:4). The Nephilim occur only here and in Numbers 13:33. The text presents them not as the offspring of the union, but as contemporaries. The fact that they are also around after the flood indicates that the label is not ethnic. Analysis of the meaning of the designation has been unsuccessful in identifying this group. The latter part of the verse indicates that they are heroic figures, perhaps of the sort exemplified by Gilgamesh, who is described as possessing heroism (1.30) and as being tall,

magnificent, and terrible (1.37). He has a six-cubit stride (1.57) and is eleven cubits tall (Hittite version, 1.8).

A more specific interpretation has been proposed by A. D. Kilmer, who suggested that the Nephilim ought to be identified as the ancient sages (the *apkallu*).[205] The *apkallu* are semidivine (one of their number, Adapa, is called the "son of [the god] Ea"). They likewise marry human women, creating mixed classes. After the flood, the sages are considered of human descent and are called the *ummianu*. These individuals, unlike their predecessors, are more infamous than famous (though only in general terms, e.g., "angered Adad").

Book of the Dead, spell 175
Mary Evans Picture Library
▼

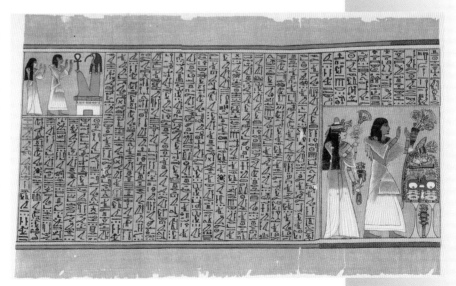

Relief of ancient hero sometimes identified as Gilgamesh

Marie-Lan Nguyen/ Wikimedia Commons, courtesy of the Louvre

▲

Protective figures such as this recall the *apkallu* sages who brought civilization to humankind.

Mark Borisuk/www. BiblePlaces.com

▶

The *apkallu* and the *ummianu* were indeed heroic figures of old. This makes sense of the terminology in verse 4. This view is additionally attractive in that in Genesis this section is in close proximity to the account of the flood, which is also recorded the context of the *apkallu*. Though some similarities are evident, the term "Nephilim" remains unexplained,[206] as does their connection to the inhabitants of the land in Numbers 13:33.

Flood (6:5–9:17)

Make yourself an ark (6:14). Earliest boats were made of skin, reeds, or dugout logs. These were small rivercraft. A boat of the size of the ark would have to be made of planks throughout (rather than using a dugout foundation as the earliest planked boats did).[207] Planks in the earliest ships were not joined by nails (much later technology). Rather, they often used wooden pegs to join planks, which were then sewn together with cords of some sort.[208] The plank skin was built first, then the frame was built inside, and finally the decks were added.

The earliest evidence of even basic plank ships with decks is from Egypt in the middle of the third millennium. In Mesopotamia, larger planked ships appear in the latter half of the third millennium, but the largest known would have only had a capacity of 11 tons.[209] The dimensions of the ark (figuring eighteen inches to a cubit) measured 450 feet by 75 feet by 45 feet. It would have had a displacement of approximately 43,000 tons and a capacity of about 15,000 tons. The largest ships known from the last half of the first

millennium B.C. from Alexandria carried no more than 4,000 tons and were considered of remarkable size—wonders of the classical world and testimony to their technological advancement.

Among the Roman vessels of the first few centuries A.D., the most famous for its incredible size was the Isis. It sailed between Alexandria and Rome in the second century A.D. and was 180 feet by 45 feet by 44 feet—less than a quarter of the size of the ark.[210] It is common to find assertions today on the internet that wooden boats cannot exceed 300 feet and remain seaworthy. Even with iron support strapping, boats of 300 feet require continual bailing. Others refute such statistics, and it is difficult to find unbiased experts to support one view or another. Needless to say, regardless of the date assigned to the flood, the construction of the ark required technologies millennia ahead of their time.

Solar boat show-
ing technique of
sewing planks
together
Frederick J. Mabie
◀

Seven of every kind of clean animal (7:2). This is the only hint that the category of "clean" animals existed prior to Sinai. Here it is not a designation pertaining to diet since eating of meat was ostensibly not permitted until after the flood. No distinction between clean and unclean animals is made anywhere else in the ancient Near East (particularly as it refers to diet). Nevertheless, the designation "clean" could refer to the acceptability of the animal for sacrifice (one could infer that this is how Noah used them). On this count, every temple and culture had its regulations about animals that could be offered and those that could not.

When we remember that in the rest of the ancient Near East sacrifices were considered meals for the nourishment of the gods, the decision about acceptable and unacceptable animals would have been based on what was considered edible or delectable. In Egypt, wild animals such as wild cattle, antelope, gazelle, and ibex were favored for sacrifice, with sheep and goats being largely avoided.[211] Other cultures favored domesticated animals in their sacrificial practices, mostly ungulates such

as sheep, goats, and cattle. Pigs and dogs were used by some in rituals of elimination, but rarely to be fed to gods. Among the equids, donkeys were used in some ritual contexts, but again, not for feeding to the gods. Finally, among the birds, doves and pigeons are the most widely attested sacrificial types. Many of these were recognized as appropriate in the broader ancient Near Eastern world if "clean" refers to being acceptable for sacrifice.[212]

In the Mesopotamian flood stories, the Gilgamesh Epic indicates that Utnapishtim put on board the "seed of all living creatures" (11.27), later detailed as "animals of the wild, creatures of the wild" (11.86).[213] The pertinent section in the Atrahasis Epic is fragmentary, but Lambert and Millard's edition identifies "clean [animals] ... fat [animals] and winged [birds] of the heavens." Then two broken lines refer to cattle and wild creatures.[214] In the Sumerian Eridu Genesis, the section about building and loading the boat are not preserved.

Springs of the great deep ... floodgates (7:11). These are terms from the contemporary understanding of cosmic geography

▶ # Ancient Near Eastern Flood Accounts[A-61]

Comparison of Biblical and Babylonian Flood Accounts

Theme	Bible	Babylonian Accounts
Flood divinely planned	Planned by God	Planned at council of gods Anu, Enlil, Ninurta, Ennugi, Ea, Ishtar
Divine revelation of plan to hero	God wanted to spare Noah because of his righteousness	Ea warned hero, Utnapishtim, in a dream
Reason for flood	Sin of man	Noise of man disturbed the gods' rest
Punishment	Highly ethical and just	Ethically ambiguous and later regretted
Salvation of hero	Included in God's plan	Done secretly
Life saved	8 persons (family), representatives of each animal	Representatives of all living things, beasts, several families, craftsmen, and technicians
Building of boat	Flat-bottomed, rectangular, 300 x 50 x 30 cubits, 3 levels, door, window, pitch coating	Ziggurat-shaped, 120 x 120 x 120 cubits, 7 levels, 9 sections, door, window, pitch coating
Physical causes of flood	More comprehensive: land upheavals, subterranean waters, heavy rains	Rains, winds, breaking of dikes
Duration of flood	40 days, 40 nights	6 days and nights
Landing of boat	Mountains of Ararat	Mount Nisir
Sending of birds	Raven, dove (3 times)	Dove, swallow, raven
Acts of worship	Sacrifice of worship	Sacrifice for appeasement
Blessing of hero	Earthly covenant	Divinity, immortality

Tablet contain-
ing the Sumerian
flood story with
its hero, Ziusudra
The Schøyen Collec-
tion MS 3026, Oslo
and London

▶

Beginning centuries before the book of Genesis took shape, the story of a massive, destructive flood was circulating in written form in Mesopotamia. As the tale was read—or more often, recounted through long centuries of family and community gatherings—transformations occurred that shaped the details of its telling to the culture of the audience. Like Nathaniel Hawthorne adapting the myths of classical Greece to his nineteenth-century A.D. audience in the *Wonder Book*, or Walt Disney reshaping the *Arabian Nights* in *Aladdin*, ancient audiences interpreted the epic event to reflect their own particular worldview.

Comparing the versions is more important for telling us about the cultures in which they were preserved than for helping us reconstruct a trail of literary evolution. Whether the Bible is related to the ancient Near Eastern material through exchange of literary or oral traditions, the similarities make it difficult to dissociate them. Most telling is the fact that both include the episode of sending out the birds to determine when it was safe to leave the ark.

The earliest flood account is in Sumerian and recounts the story of Ziusudra.[A-62] The oldest Babylonian account is found in the Epic of Atrahasis, dating to early in the second millennium.[A-63] The most well-known version from Mesopotamia is imbedded in the famous Gilgamesh Epic. There it is presented as the explanation for how Utnapishtim (the flood hero) gained eternal life (which Gilgamesh was seeking).[A-64] These three are stages in a single tradition as the similarities clearly indicate.

In the biblical flood story, God is distressed with the behavior of the people whom he has created. In the monotheistic setting of Genesis, it is his decision alone to send the flood and to preserve Noah and his family alive. He is portrayed as resigned to this course of action, which is sadly the only appropriate response. The Mesopotamian versions derive from a polytheistic culture and therefore portray the gods deliberating in a council. The decision to send the flood is portrayed as a reaction of angry frustration. As the story progresses the gods are duplicitous, shortsighted, and absorbed in petty squabbles.

Genesis documents the downward slide of humanity from the idyllic garden to the chaotic anarchy that introduces the flood story. Violence has become an incorrigible way of life, and the waters are sent as an act of justice. The Atrahasis Epic preserves most clearly the reasons for the flood in the Mesopotamian tradition. People had been created to do the work that the gods were tired of doing. But the growing population and the inevitable internal strife that resulted had made even more work for the gods, for people were constantly disturbing them with their troubles, demands, and requests. All of this is captured as the "noise" of humankind led the gods to embark on a course of total destruction.[A-65]

Noah attracts God's attention as one who should not share in the fate of the rest of the population. Special provision is therefore made for him to be spared. Mesopotamian accounts agree among themselves that the plan of the gods was that no one should survive. Despite

the fact that they were sworn to secrecy concerning the plans of the assembly, one of their number, Ea, successfully carried out a scheme so that his favorite human would learn of the coming flood. He then instructed him secretly how to keep his knowledge hidden from the gods and the rest of the people and survive the seven days of the flood. His boat resembled a temple[A-66] and saved not just his family, but various skilled workmen so that the arts of civilization could be preserved.

When Noah disembarked from the ark, he offered a sacrifice of thanksgiving and received covenant promises that God would preserve a certain order in the cosmos rather than oppose the chaos of human sin by means of flooding waters. When the Mesopotamian flood heroes emerged, they offered a sacrifice of appeasement to calm the anger of the gods. The gods had forgotten how much they were dependent on humans to supply them food (sacrifices) and gathered around hungrily, wondering how such a foolish decision (the flood) could have been made. The hero is grudgingly granted eternal life by the head of the gods, who remains miffed that word of the flood leaked out.

The flood stories from the ancient Near East and from around the world offer persuasive evidence that a flood of significant magnitude occurred and was remembered. The accounts from ancient Near East are closest to the biblical account and help us to see how the Israelites would have understood the whole event differently from their neighbors.

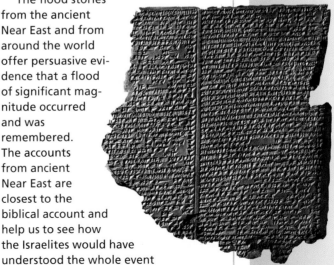

Tablet 11 of the Gilgamesh Epic, recounting the story of the flood
Z. Radovan/www.BibleLand Pictures.com

▼

Mount Ararat

Henry Nissen, courtesy of Noah's Ark
Uncovered

▶

▶ Archaeological Evidences of the Flood

Mount Ararat

Henry Nissen, courtesy of Noah's Ark
Uncovered

No convincing archaeological evidence of anything approaching the size of the biblical flood has been uncovered. Significant silt levels have been discovered at the Sumerian cities of Ur, Kish, Shuruppak, Lagash, and Uruk (all of which have occupation levels at least as early as 2800 B.C.), but since their respective silt layers date to different periods, they cannot reflect a single inundation.[A-67] Other cities whose occupation spans this time period (such as Jericho, continuously occupied from 7000 B.C.) contain no flood deposits whatsoever.

Climate studies have indicated that the period from 4500–3500 B.C. was significantly wetter in this region, but that offers little to go on.[A-68] The search for the remains of Noah's ark have centered on the Turkish peak of Agri Dagh (17,000 feet) near Lake Van, even though the biblical text refers only to the Ararat range. Fragments of wood, which have been carbon–14 dated from this mountain, have proven to come from no earlier than the 5th century A.D.[A-69] A number of sightings have been claimed, but the evidence remains elusive.[A-70]

(see sidebar on "Cosmic Geography in the Ancient World" in the introduction). The Hebrew word translated "deep" ($t^e h \hat{o} m$) is the same one used in 1:2. It refers to the great cosmic ocean that not only surrounds the land, but is that on which the land floats (cf. Ps. 24:1–2). This is what 1:7 calls "the water under the expanse." The "springs" were considered the entry points of these waters to the earth.

The "floodgates," or the windows of heaven, were the comparable entry points for the waters above the earth that are held back by the sky. These allow rain to fall. In Genesis 1 the initial watery condition was remedied by separating these waters and then inserting the dry land between them. In the flood, the restraints on these cosmic waters are lifted and the cosmos is returned to its nonfunctional watery state.

The springs of the deep are well known in ancient cosmic geography. Akkadian uses *tamtu* (cognate to Hebrew $t^e h \hat{o} m$) to refer to the large visible bodies of water and *apsu* to refer to the large body of water believed to flow under the earth.[215] But there is no precedent for the "windows" (*$^{\supset a} rubb \bar{o} t$*) of heaven. When Sumerian speaks of the source of rain it refers to the "teat (UBUR) of heaven."[216] The Mesopotamian flood stories focus not on an onslaught of the cosmic waters but on the terror of the storm and the devastation it brings.

Forty days and forty nights (7:12). In Genesis the flood is much more protracted than in the Mesopotamian accounts. The actual rain lasts forty days and nights rather than seven, and when all of the numbers are added up, Noah and his family are in the ark for about a year. The number forty is often used in schematic ways in the biblical text, so it cannot easily be used for precise reckoning. As frequently as it occurs in the Bible, forty is not used as a schematic number in the ancient Near East.

Mountains of Ararat (8:4). The mountains of Ararat are located in the Lake Van region of eastern Turkey in the area of Armenia (known as Urartu in Assyrian inscriptions), with its highest peak reaching 17,000 feet. In contrast to a range of mountains, the Gilgamesh Epic describes the flood hero's ark coming to rest on a specific mountaintop, Mount Nimush (formerly rendered Nisir) in southern Kurdistan. The only hint to its location is that it is said to be in the land of the Gutium, which is in the Zagros Mountains east of the Tigris and near the Diyala. The modern-day Pir Omar Gudrun is generally considered the strongest candidate.[217] This would place it about four hundred miles south-southeast of Ararat.[218]

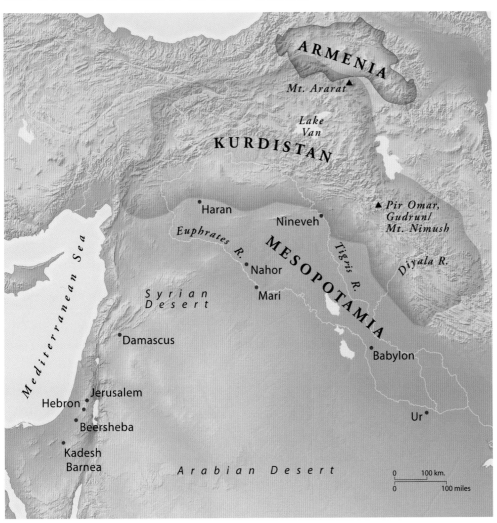

Location of Ararat

◀

▶ The Atrahasis Epic and Genesis

Though the Atrahasis Epic is best known for its account of the flood, there is also great significance in the way that the epic is structured to recount primeval history. The epic deals first with creation (only the creation of humans is preserved), then treats the growth of human population, and finally concludes with the flood account. In this three-part approach it shows a basic similarity to the way Genesis 1–9 proceeds.[A-71] Though some have suggested that this general similarity demonstrates that the author of Genesis was reshaping known mythology, the connections are not firm enough to draw that conclusion. The similarities, however, do suggest that the general outline that governed how people thought about origins was common across ancient Near Eastern cultures.

Sent out a dove (8:8). A number of incantations in recognition of Shamash as the judge of the heavens and the underworld feature the release of two doves (male to the east, female to the west) in an attempt to win the deity's favor.[219] In this sort of ritual context, the idea is that the evil that offends the deity is transferred to the birds, which carry it away (characteristic of *namburbi* rituals). The Babylonian Almanac also indicates that the release of a captive bird on certain days can bring favorable results.[220]

Despite these intriguing texts, the biblical text offers no suggestion that the birds carry away offenses or bring luck. In fact, the purpose of their release is stated in relation to drawing conclusions about the conditions outside the ark. In the Mesopotamian flood story, birds are also used for this same purpose. In Gilgamesh neither the dove nor the swallow is able to find a perch, but the raven does not return (11.148–56).[221] Insufficient data concerning the use of birds in ancient Near Eastern maritime practices cautions against further explanation being offered in this direction.[222]

Olive leaf (8:11). Olive trees are difficult to kill, and they resprout easily. They do not mind rocky soil and grow best on hillsides, but not in high elevations.[223] The olive leaf brought by the dove gives Noah an indication that the lower elevations have drained and that vegetation is once again sprouting.

Smelled the pleasing aroma (8:21). The contrast between the biblical and ancient Near Eastern accounts is more distinct on this point than on any other. In the Gilgamesh Epic the gods have apparently neglected to realize that with all humans destroyed, no one will be left to give them sacrifices. Without sacrifices they are deprived of their sustenance. Consequently, when the sacrifice is offered after the survivors disembark from the boat, "the gods smelled the sweet savour, the gods gathered like flies around the sacrificer."[224]

Both Gilgamesh and Genesis refer to the aroma/savor of the sacrifice, but the portrayal offered of deity is far different. In Gilgamesh this represents the gods' needs and exposes their shortsightedness. It functions to appease their anger. In Genesis it represents God's pleasure in the creatures he has made and his resulting commitment not to destroy them.

Olive branch
Júlio Reis/Wikimedia Commons

▶

Fear and dread (9:2). The divide between the animal world and the human world is seen differently in Mesopotamian literature. In the Gilgamesh Epic, when Enkidu, the uncivilized man of the steppe regions, lived in the wild, the animals were his friends. Once he becomes civilized, they run away from him (1.196–200). In Enmerkar and the Lord of Aratta and in an Ur cosmology text, humanity is understood to be in fear and trembling from wild beasts.[225]

Everything ... will be food for you (9:3). In Mesopotamia the motif of the wild man includes that he lives in the wild with the animals and eats grass.[226] This is also part of the description of human existence in general before they become civilized.[227] Here in Genesis the provision for eating meat is not connected with the development of civilization (Gen. 4) but with the restatement of the blessing. In general in the ancient world meat was a delicacy, eaten only on special occasions in connection with cultic activities. Meat was more regularly part of the palace fare, and Egyptian reliefs and paintings portray the butchering process.[228]

Meat that has its lifeblood still in it (9:4). The draining of the blood was presumably a reflection of the belief that the blood contained the life force of the animal.[229] Whether this was a way of ensuring that the animal was dead or symbolized the return of the life force to God cannot be

ascertained. Ritual draining of blood is not attested in ancient Near Eastern literature.

By man shall his blood be shed (9:6). Exacting punishment for murder is not reserved for deity but is placed under the purview of human judicial systems here, whether they are located in courts or in clans. This verse may well mark the beginning of judicial responsibility that is eventually evidenced in the compilations of sample verdicts (such as those found on the Hammurabi Stele) throughout the ancient Near East. These compendia demonstrate that the kings and societies of the ancient world took their judicial responsibilities seriously. Many of these indicate that capital punishment was common in cases of homicide, though often lesser penalties were exacted depending on the social status of both the perpetrator and the victim.[230]

Rainbow (9:13). In the Gilgamesh Epic the goddess Ishtar identifies the lapis lazuli of her necklace as the basis of an oath by which she will never forget the days of the flood. The beads of the necklace are in the shape of flies and thus reminiscent of the way the gods swarmed like flies around the sacrifice offered by Utnapishtim.[231] A. D. Kilmer suggests that a connection exists between Ishtar's necklace and the rainbow is the iridescence of the flies' wings.[232] An eleventh-century Assyrian relief shows two hands reaching out of the clouds, one hand offering blessing, the other holding a bow.[233] Since the word for "rainbow" (*qešet*) is the same word as that used for the weapon, this is an interesting image. This comparison and ones like it suggest the possibility that these two traditions diverged from a common core.

Noah and his Sons (9:18–29)

Planted a vineyard (9:20). Archaeobotanists have determined that the domestication of grapes (the beginning

Egyptian necklace worn as an amulet features flies of gold.
HIP/Art Resource, NY, courtesy of the British Museum

Painting from the tomb of Ity depicting the slaughtering of an ox
Werner Forman Archive/Egyptian Museum, Turin

of viticulture) occurred in the Levant in the Early Bronze Age (late fourth millennium) and at about the same time in Egypt. The earliest evidence of wine dates to the second half of the fourth millennium in western Iran.[234]

Saw his father's nakedness (9:22). In the history of interpretation of this passage, a number of alternatives have been suggested for explaining the offense committed by Ham, especially in light of the severe curse (on Canaan!) that results. The options of "voyeurism" and paternal (homosexual) incest have little support from the ancient Near East regardless of the case that might be made for them in the biblical text.[235] The option of castration was offered in rabbinic literature and has one supporting text from ancient mythology that portrays a son castrating his father (both deities) in an attempt to usurp his position.[236]

Another option that can be supported conceptually from the ancient Near East is that Ham committed incest with his mother in an attempt to usurp the authority of the family from his father (cf. Reuben in Gen. 35:22 and Absalom in 2 Sam. 16:21–22), or an attempt to provide for additional offspring in a depopulated world (cf. Lot's daughters in Gen. 19:30–38).[237] Bergsma and Hahn even suggest that a resulting illicit union between Ham and his mother eventuated in the birth of Canaan,[238] though if that were the case it would be unusual for the text not to note that fact. The idea of usurping someone's authority

▶ Table of Nations[A-72]

The list of the sons of Shem, Ham, and Japheth contains seventy names, a number that stood for totality and completion.[A-73] More important, the concept of seventy nations is offered as the design of God.[A-74] Nevertheless, the list is certainly not complete in its presentation of the descendants of Noah and his sons. The author penetrated selectively into various lines in order to achieve that final number.

We must therefore conclude that this list of seventy is schematically representative of the totality. Of the seventy names, sixteen are second generation, thirty-five are third generation, three are fourth generation, two are fifth generation, and thirteen are sixth generation (the sons of Joktan).

Nimrod, of undesignated generation, fills out the seventy. Divided by lineage, fourteen are from the line of Japheth, thirty from the line of Ham, and twenty-six from the line of Shem.

The division between the three does not represent language groups (e.g., Canaanite is Semitic). It should also be noticed that not all seventy are names of individuals. A number of them clearly name people groups (esp. in Canaan's list, 10:15–17). Others are well known as city names (e.g., Sidon) or geographic designations (e.g., Mizraim, Tarshish, Sheba), but possibly the list considers these to be the patronymic ancestors of those places. In Hammurabi's genealogy a number of the

Hammurabi's genealogy
Todd Bolen/www.BiblePlaces.com
◀

Egyptian painting showing defeated peoples of many nations
Frederick J. Mabie
◀

continued

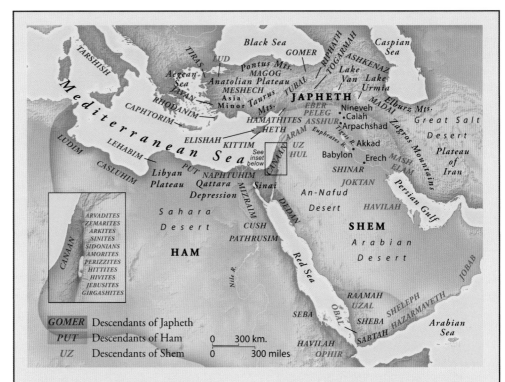

GOMER — Descendants of Japheth
PUT — Descendants of Ham
UZ — Descendants of Shem

0   300 km.
0   300 miles

names are tribal or geographical names, so this is not unusual in an ancient document.[A-75] But kinship language is sometimes used in the Bible to reflect political associations (cf. 1 Kings 9:13).

This group of seventy does not reflect the perspective of Noah's descendants in the third or fourth generation; rather, it is Israel's perspective at the time of the author, Moses. Note that there is no discussion of anyone outside the known world of the ancient Near East in the middle of the second millennium. The text only seeks to account for the groups the Israelites were aware of and does not hint at a world beyond the ancient Near East. In other words, the author has not attempted to provide a comprehensive list of all people(s) descended from the sons of Noah. Instead, he has addressed how all the known peoples and nations of his day are related to the sons of Noah.

by taking his wife is attested in royal contexts in an Akkadian text from Ugarit.[2391] None of this information offers clarification of Canaan's behavior, but it does alert us to a number of alternatives that we otherwise might not have recognized.

Table of Nations (10:1–32)

Sons of Japheth (10:2–5). Most of Japheth's descendants can be defined from an Israelite perspective as coming from across the sea (cf. "maritime peoples" in v. 5). A Babylonian world map from the eighth or seventh century B.C. illustrated the geographical worldview that there were many peoples considered on the outskirts of civilization beyond the sea. Many of the names in Japheth's line are connected with the Mediterranean region (Dodanim, Elishah, and Kittim). Tarshish has generally been identified as a port in Spain, but that is still in the Mediterranean shipping lanes. Others are identified with sections or peoples in Asia Minor (Magog,

Tubal, Meshech, Tiras, Togarmah) and even extending to the area to the east in the region of the Black Sea and the Caspian Sea—Cimmerians (Gomer), Scythians (Ashkenaz), Medes (Madai), and Paphlagonians (Riphath).

Sons of Ham (10:6–20). As the Japhethites stretch east and west across the northern latitudes, Ham's descendants line the southern coast of the Mediterranean and both sides of the Red Sea. Through the "Canaanites" this line also extends partway up the eastern coast of the Mediterranean.

Nimrod (10:8–12). Attempts to identify Nimrod with some historical or literary figure from the ancient world have been many.[240] Speiser identified him as an Assyrian king (Tukulti-Ninurta I, end of the thirteenth century), while van der Toorn, protesting that no known human king fits the description, identified him with the Assyrian god Ninurta, a warrior and hunter of a myriad of mythical creatures. An Assyrian poem from the end of the second millennium epitomizes an Assyrian king (thought to be Tigiath-pileser I) as a great hunter, but the piece is an extended metaphor using the language of hunting to describe the conquests of the king.[241]

It cannot be ruled out that this is also the case in the description of Nimrod, since hunting is a metaphor for royal conquest from earliest times. For example, the royal mace head of Mesilim, king of Kish in the twenty-sixth century B.C., is decorated with six intertwined lions around its circumference.[242] The identification of the hunter as a royal metaphor would offer an explanation of why Genesis 10:9 includes

"before the LORD"—it would indicate that his conquests had divine support. The royal lion hunt was considered a cultic act.[243] "King of Kish" (notice the similarity between Kish and Cush) was a title that indicated some level of rule over a hegemony in the Early Dynastic period.[244]

The description of Nimrod positions him at the head of an empire. Only three major empires are known prior to the time of Moses: the Old Akkadian Empire (2335–2218 B.C.), the Third Dynasty of Ur (2112–2004), and the Old Babylonian Empire ruled by Hammurabi (1792–1750). If Nimrod is to be identified as a historical individual of early history, he must be connected to one of these. Scholars have argued for the following:

(1) Sargon (dynasty of Akkad): Some records indicate military activity on the upper Tigris (Gasur = Nuzi and Aššur, and his son built a temple at Nineveh), but little associates Sargon with the cities named in

Earliest known lion hunting scene from fourth-millennium Uruk
Scala/Art Resource, NY, courtesy of the Iraq Museum

◀

Ancient Mesopotamia
▼

Factors to Identify Names in Genesis 10:8–12						
(3 = strong correspondence, 0 = none)						
	"Nimrod"	"Cush"	Hero	Hunter	Babylon	Assyria
Sargon	0	2	2	0	0	1
Shulgi	0	0	3	3	0	1
Hammurabi	1	1	1	0	3	2

Genesis. Sargon built up Akkad and made it his capital city. Nothing in contemporary records connects him with Babylon. Levin suggests that Nimrod is a composite of the Sargonic kings Sargon I and Naram-Sin.[245] The only evidence he offers is that they established the first empire and referred to themselves as kings of Kish (which he relates to "Cush was the father of Nimrod," 10:8). The Akkadian empire, however, did not include Assyria, there is no mention of these kings as hunters, and nothing in their titulary offers an explanation of the name Nimrod.

(2) Shulgi (Ur III dynasty): Shulgi praises himself as a hunter in his poems,[246] and in his inscriptions he regularly refers to himself as the mighty man or mighty hero.[247] The core area of his political control was in southern Mesopotamia, but his capital was at Ur, not Babylon. His records make no mention of Babylon, though a late chronicle suggests that he despoiled Esagila, the temple of Marduk in Babylon.[248] If this were true, there is even more distinction between him and Nimrod since the latter rules at Babylon. Shulgi also extended his empire from the south to the north, including some cities of Assyria. Extension to the upper Tigris involved cities that paid taxes (as far north as Assur) and allied cities, which included Nineveh, but there was little military control of these regions. There is no name for Shulgi that makes sense of Nimrod.

(3) Hammurabi (Old Babylonian Dynasty): Here we finally find a ruler of an empire whose center is Babylon. When he came to the throne, southern Mesopotamia was united under the rule of Rim-Sin from Larsa and the upper Tigris was united under the control of Shamshi-Adad I from his capital of Shubat-Enlil. The southern

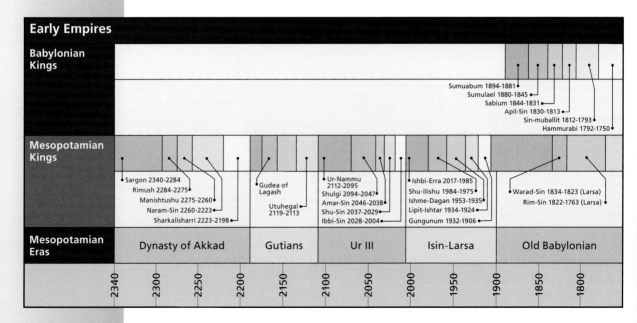

Early Empires

Babylonian Kings

Sumuabum 1894-1881
Sumulael 1880-1845
Sabium 1844-1831
Apil-Sin 1830-1813
Sin-muballit 1812-1793
Hammurabi 1792-1750

Mesopotamian Kings

Sargon 2340-2284
Rimush 2284-2275
Manishtushu 2275-2260
Naram-Sin 2260-2223
Sharkalisharri 2223-2198

Gudea of Lagash
Utuhegal 2119-2113

Ur-Nammu 2112-2095
Shulgi 2094-2047
Amar-Sin 2046-2038
Shu-Sin 2037-2029
Ibbi-Sin 2028-2004

Ishbi-Erra 2017-1985
Shu-Ilishu 1984-1975
Ishme-Dagan 1953-1935
Lipit-Ishtar 1934-1924
Gungunum 1932-1906

Warad-Sin 1834-1823 (Larsa)
Rim-Sin 1822-1763 (Larsa)

Mesopotamian Eras

Dynasty of Akkad	Gutians	Ur III	Isin-Larsa	Old Babylonian

2340 2300 2250 2200 2150 2100 2050 2000 1950 1900 1850 1800

cities were taken from Larsa in 1763 B.C. Then Hammurabi expanded east into Elam, up the Euphrates to Mari, and up the Tigris to Eshnunna in the Diyala region. He campaigned further north on the Tigris, but did not control the region. Nineveh is not among the cities he controls. The fact that he often identified himself as "king of the MARDU" gives a possible connection to the name Nimrod, since a variety of prefixes or determinatives could combine an N with MARDU, though none of them is attested in his inscriptions.[249]

As seems obvious, none of these names offers a close match to the description of Nimrod. Perhaps future finds will reveal an earlier empire and king that will better fit the data.

Babylon (10:10). Babylon is first mentioned (in passing) in contemporary records in the time of Šar-kali-šarri (last king of Akkad, twenty-third century B.C.). References to it remain occasional and suggest no great significance until the First Dynasty of Babylon, when the predecessors to Hammurabi make it their capital. From that time on it becomes legendary as the seat of culture and religion in Mesopotamia. Archaeologically, excavations can only recover data as far back as the First Dynasty of Babylon because the water table shifted and destroyed all earlier layers. We therefore know nothing of the history of Babylon's founding from either literary or archaeological records.

Erech (10:10). This is the Hebrew spelling for the great ancient city of Uruk, the largest city of the third millennium (six miles in circumference) and the home of Gilgamesh. This city of the goddess Inanna was legendary for its great walls and beautiful temples. Archaeological strata suggest that the city was founded in the fifth millennium B.C. Sargon (twenty-fourth century) claims to have conquered the city and destroyed its walls.[250] The kings of the Ur III dynasty continued building on the site, as did the kings of the Old Babylonian period.

Akkad (10:10). The location of the city of Akkad remains unknown archaeologically, though it is well known in the literature. First mention of the city occurs just prior to the time of Sargon, who made it his capital city in the middle of the twenty-fourth century B.C. It continued to exist into the first millennium and was even excavated to some extent by Nabonidus, the last Neo-Babylonian king, who had antiquarian interests. The last reference to it is in the early fifth century in an inscription of Darius.[251]

Calneh (10:10). Though there is a significant city named Kalno in Assyrian records (see also Isa. 10:9), it is located in northern Syria, not in southern Mesopotamia. As a result, the city referred to here in Genesis is unknown.

Nineveh (10:11). Excavations at Nineveh (contiguous with modern Mosul in northern Iraq) indicate that the site was settled in prehistoric times. It shows up briefly in the historical record in the time of Manishtushu, son of Sargon, in the latter part of the third millennium. It was apparently an important city in the kingdom of Shamshi-Adad I around 1800 B.C., and retained some prominence throughout the second and first millennia. Its fortunes rose and fell with Assyrian successes, with its greatest period coming with the building projects of Sennacherib around 700 B.C., who made the city his capital.

Rehoboth Ir (10:11). This unusual name simply means "city squares," which makes it difficult to identify. Some have considered it simply an alternate designation of Nineveh or perhaps a section of Nineveh.[252]

Royal head, perhaps depicting Hammurabi
Rama/Wikimedia Commons, courtesy of the Louvre

Calah (10:11). This appears to be a reference to the well-known Assyrian city of Kalḫu, modern Nimrud, twenty-five miles south of Nineveh. The problem is that the evidence suggests this city was not founded until the thirteenth century and did not become prominent until the ninth century.[253]

Resen (10:12). This city has not been identified. It is said to be between Nineveh and Calah (=Kalḫu), which are only about twenty-five miles apart with no major cities between them. There is a small village called Reš-eni in the other direction, about fifteen miles north of Nineveh, which would hardly seem to qualify. P. Machinist notes the similarity of the name to the Akkadian word *risnu* ("canal") and indicates that such canals were built for both Nineveh and Calah, though only in the Neo-Assyrian period.[254]

Sons of Shem (10:21–31). The descendants of Shem settle along the Arabian Sea, the Persian Gulf, and the Tigris and Euphrates, and stretch west across the Syrian desert (Aram and his descendants).

Tower of Babel (11:1–9)

Moved eastward (11:2). Geological and hydrological studies and migration patterns discernible from the fourth and third millennia B.C. suggest that there was a drying out of the southern alluvial plain as the Gulf receded and a corresponding population movement into that plain toward the end of the fourth millennium.[255]

> The results of studies of the ancient climate and of the changes in the amount of water in the Mesopotamian river system and in the Gulf … now present us with a clearer picture of the developments in southern Babylonia. The climatic changes documented for the middle of the fourth millennium seem, within a space of two to three hundred years, to have stemmed the floods that regularly covered large tracts of land and to have drained such large areas that in a relatively short period of

time large parts of Babylonia, particularly throughout the south, became attractive for new permanent settlements.[256]

This period, known as the Uruk Phase, features technological advances in urbanization, architecture, technology, and language that correspond to elements referred to in this biblical text.[257]

Shinar (11:2). The Hebrew term for Shinar (*šin'ār*) refers to the area that ancient Near Eastern texts refer to as Sumer. It covered the southern part of the Tigris-Euphrates river basin as far north as Sippar, where the rivers converge in the area of modern southern Iraq. Major cities of the region included Kish, Nippur, Shuruppak, Girsu, Uruk, Eridu, and Ur. This is the area where urbanization developed and is the heartland of Mesopotamian civilization.

Let's make bricks and bake them (11:3). Stone is not readily available in the alluvial plain of southern Mesopotamia, so a logical economical choice is to use brick—there is plenty of mud. Mudbrick, however, is not durable, so it was a great technological development to discover that baking the brick made it as durable as stone.[258] This was still an expensive process, since the kilns had to be fueled. As a result, mudbrick was used as much as possible, with baked brick used only for outer shells of important buildings or where waterproofing was desirable.[259]

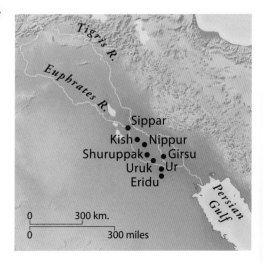

Sumer ▶

Ziggurat in Ur as
it looks today,
partially recon-
structed
Josh McFall
◀

No baked bricks have been found earlier than the Uruk period (latter part of the fourth millennium).[260] In the same general time period, bitumen came to be used as mastic and for additional waterproofing, but it was also expensive because it had to be heated. Consequently, it was used primarily in public projects.[261] The bitumen was absorbed into the bricks (baked or not), creating a product as durable as stone.[262]

City and a tower (11:4). One single architectural feature dominated the landscape of early Mesopotamian cities: towers known as ziggurats. In the earliest stages of urbanization, the city was not designed for the private sector. People did not live in the city. Instead, it was comprised of the public buildings, such as administrative buildings, and granaries, which were mostly connected with the temple. Consequently, the city was, in effect, a temple complex.

What do we know about ziggurats? (1) Though they may resemble pyramids in appearance, they are nothing like them in function. Ziggurats have no inside. The structure was framed in mudbrick, and then the core was packed with fill dirt. The façade was then completed with kiln-fired brick. (2) Ziggurats were dedicated to particular deities. Any given deity could have several ziggurats dedicated to him or her in differ-

ent cities. Furthermore, a given city could have several ziggurats, though the main one was associated with the patron deity of the city. (3) Archaeologists have discovered nearly thirty ziggurats in the general region, and texts mention several others. The main architectural feature is the stairway or ramp that leads to the top. There was a small room at the top where a bed was made and a table set for the deity.[263] Ziggurats ranged in size from sixty feet per side to almost two hundred feet per side.

Most important is the function of the ziggurat. The ziggurat did not play a role in any of the rituals known to us from Mesopotamia. If known literature were our only guide, we would conclude that common people did not use the ziggurat for anything. It was sacred space and was strictly off-limits to profane use. Though the structure at the

Etemenanki, means "temple of the foundation of heaven and earth." One at Larsa means "temple that links heaven and earth." Most significant is the name of the ziggurat at Sippar, "temple of the stairway to pure heaven." The word translated "stairway" in this last example is used in the mythology as the means by which the messenger of the gods moved between heaven, earth, and the netherworld.[264] As a result of these data, we can conclude that the ziggurat was a structure built to support the stairway. This stairway was a visual representation of that which was believed to be used by the gods to travel from one realm to another. It was solely for the convenience of the gods and was maintained in order to provide the deity with amenities and to make possible his descent into his temple.

At the top of the ziggurat was the gate of the gods, the entrance into their heavenly abode. At the bottom was the temple, where hopefully the god would descend to receive the gifts and worship of his people. A similar mentality can be seen among the people of the American West, who picked up their towns and moved them into proximity with the newly laid railroad tracks, then erected a train station so that the train would stop there and bring economic benefits.

In summary, the project the Bible describes is a temple complex featuring a ziggurat, which was designed to make it convenient

top was designed to accommodate the god, it was not a temple where people would go to worship. In fact, the ziggurat was typically accompanied by an adjoining temple near its base, where the worship did take place.

The best indication of the function of the ziggurats comes from the names that are given to them. For instance, the name of the ziggurat at Babylon,

for the god to come down to his temple, receive worship, and bless his people. The key for this passage is to realize that the tower was not built so that people could ascend to heaven, but so that deity could descend to earth.

Reaches to the heavens (11:4). Throughout Mesopotamian literature, almost every occurrence of the expression describing a building "with its head in the heavens" refers to a temple with a ziggurat.[265] As a sample, here is the description by Warad-Sin, king of Larsa, who built the temple É-eš-ki-te:

> He made it as high as a mountain and made its head touch heaven. On account of this deed the gods Nanna and Ningal rejoiced. May they grant to him a destiny of life, a long reign, and a firm foundation.[266]

It is this language, along with the indication that God "came down," that gives textual confirmation that the tower is a ziggurat. This would have been transparent to the ancient reader.

In contrast to this positive assessment and more in keeping with the negative results of the project here, the reader of Genesis will find a few of the omens in the *Šumma Ālu* series remarkable: "If a city lifts its head to the midst of heaven, that city will be abandoned" (1.15), and "If a city rises like a mountain peak to the midst of heaven, that city will be turned to a ruin" (1.16). Yet Mesopotamian cities were regularly built on high ground, with the temple on the highest ground. Guinan argues that the wording of these omens understood in the context of the omen series is essentially about exceeding natural boundaries: "A city which reaches for the preeminence reserved for sacred structures assures its own downfall."[267]

Make a name (11:4). The ancient world placed immense value on the sense of continuity from one generation to another.[268] In some cultures a person's continued comfort in the afterlife was dependent on care from descendants in the land of the living. The details often involved memorial meals (*kispu*) and various regular mortuary rites. But more basi-

cally, and more importantly for this passage, all of those rituals provided opportunity for the name of the deceased to be spoken. There is continued life and vitality as long as one is remembered. Descendants took on themselves this responsibility more than any others, and thus the most reliable way to make a name for oneself was to have children. The living thus form a bridge of continuity between the past ancestors and the future descendants—the cord must not be broken.

The building of monuments could also contribute to the desirable end result, as could achievements and adventures of various sorts. The important point here is that the desire to make a name in the ancient world is common to all; it is not generally motivated by pride,

Painting of a reconstruction of the ziggurat within its temple complex in Babylon
Courtesy of the Oriental Institute of the University of Chicago

▶ **Enmerkar and the Lord of Aratta: Ancient Near Eastern Confusion of Tongues Account?**

The account of Enmerkar and the Lord of Aratta probably dates to the Ur III period, but takes its literary form in the Old Babylonian period a few centuries later,[A-76] so it is roughly contemporary to the patriarchal period. A segment of this epic entitled "Nudimmud's Spell" has occasioned a lot of controversy. It speaks of a time when there are no predators and there is peace between nations and rulers. The section ends with a statement about people speaking the same language.

The dispute is whether this refers to a time in the distant past or a time in the anticipated future. Vanstiphout, following Alster, translates: "For on that day ... shall Enki ... change the tongues in their mouth, as many as he once placed there, and the speech of mankind shall be truly one."[A-77] This indicates an ideal situation in the future. Jacobsen, in contrast, translated it as referring back to a past event: "In those days ... did Enki ... estrange the tongues in their mouths as many as were put there. The tongues of men which were one."[A-78] B. Batto agrees with the translation in the past, but considers it a description of an inchoate, primitive, uncivilized condition rather than an idyllic or paradisiacal one.

If Jacobsen is correct, this section of the epic may stand as a parallel to the Babel account in providing an account of the disruption of languages. It would not be out of character, however, for Genesis to have a far different assessment of language diversity than that encountered in the rest of the ancient Near East. Just as paradise was a negative condition in the ancient Near East and a positive one in the Bible, so the unified language is positive in the Bible and negative in the ancient Near East. In Mesopotamia people had pride in their bilingual character. At this stage, however, we must exercise patience and caution until the literature becomes more transparent.

Enmerkar and the Lord of Aratta
University of Pennsylvania Museum (neg. #B2150)
▶

but by the desire to vouchsafe one's survival beyond death through the memory of others, particularly family members. The more people who remember one's name, the more secure is one's existence in the afterlife.

Scattered (11:4). The fear of scattering is directly related (both syntactically and conceptually) to the previously stated desire to make a name. Remembrance takes place in the vicinity of the burial ground. Descendants who move away (as Abraham does in ch. 12) cut the ties of continuity between the past and the present. When sons move away, no one remains to care for the elderly parents, to provide for proper burial, and to arrange for remembrance.

Should the ties between the ancestor and his offspring dissolve, the family is doomed to dispersion and annihilation. Old Babylonian family religion, in its aspect of the cult of the ancestors, produced and maintained in its participants a sense of historical identity: they belonged to a close-knit social group firmly anchored in the past. When this sense of identity is put in jeopardy, the very existence of the family becomes problematic.[269]

Though some have considered this desire not to scatter as disobedience to the blessing, it must be recognized that the blessing does not relate to scattering, only to filling—far different issues.[270]

The LORD came down (11:5). As mentioned above, this is precisely the reason the tower was built—for God to come down. Unfortunately, rather than being pleased to take up his residence among the people, he finds it an occasion for counteraction.

In the literature of the ancient Near East, one other remarkable example discusses an unauthorized undertaking of construction of sacred space. The Curse of Agade recounts the story of Naram-Sin, the last great king of the Dynasty of Akkad.[271] He desired to rebuild the Ekur shrine of Enlil at Nippur and sought omens granting divine approval for seven years. When he did not receive them, he proceeded anyway. The renovation required tearing down, and he is therefore accused of desecrating the temple. As a result, the gods abandoned their sanctuaries and left the land defenseless against the

invading Gutians—the barbarian hordes who destroyed the empire. This story has little in common with the Tower of Babel story outside of the underlying premise that construction of sacred space does not always bring the favor of deity—sometimes just the opposite.

Babel (11:9). Any third-millennium history of Babylon is inaccessible (see comment on 10:10). The fact that only one or two passing references can be found in the fairly extensive literature suggests it was not an important city, and the archaeological remains are lost in the water table. Consequently, nothing in history, literature, or archaeology can illuminate the role of the city of Babylon in this incident.

Line of Shem (11:10–32)

Ur of the Chaldeans (11:28). The city of Ur in southern Mesopotamia is well known in the literature of the ancient Near East, particularly prominent over the latter half of the third millennium B.C. The excavations on the site of Tell el-Muqayyar (its modern name), begun by Leonard Woolley in 1922, reveal the grandeur of its civilization. A temple already

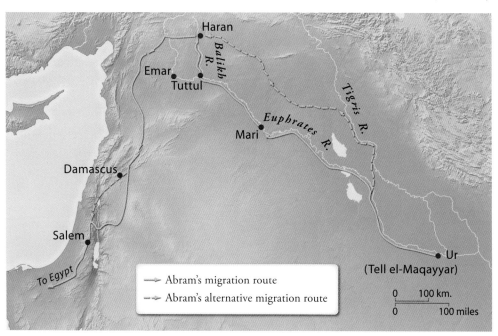

Area of Abram's Travels

◀

Abram's migration route
Abram's alternative migration route

0   100 km.
0   100 miles

Remains of Ur as
seen from the top
of the ziggurat
scottpigeon
▶

stood there in the late fourth millennium and its ziggurat (completed later) is the best preserved from ancient Mesopotamia. An early empire with Ur as its capital existed for about a century at the end of the third millennium founded by Ur-Nammu and solidified by his successor, Shulgi.

By some chronological schemes Abraham's time in Ur and Haran coincide with the empire phase.[272] Some

have deduced that Abraham was an urban socialite in this grand center of civilization and that Yahweh's call required a substantial change in lifestyle. Even if it were true that Abraham was born in this highly civilized city, however, we cannot necessarily conclude that he was a city dweller. Ur had its share of herdsmen and farmers as any city did.

All of the above discussion is based on the premise that Tell el-Muqayyar is to be equated with the biblical Ur of the Chaldeans, but that is not the only option. Tell el-Muqayyar is the most famous Ur and the one we know best, but it is not the only Ur, and controversy still remains as to why Genesis adds "of the Chaldeans." Unfortunately, we know little about the history of the Chaldeans at this period. During the mid-first millennium B.C. the Chaldeans ruled in southern Mesopotamia (Nebuchadnezzar), and consequently the Chaldeans are associated with Babylon by the prophets Isaiah, Jeremiah, and Ezekiel. But prior to this period, the earliest substantial reference to the Chaldeans is in the ninth-century inscriptions of Shalmaneser III, when they are located southeast of Babylon near Elam.[273]

A vague, earlier reference is in the campaign inscriptions of Ashurnasirpal II (883–859 B.C.), inscribed on stone reliefs in the Ninurta temple at Calah, where the Chaldeans are referred to in passing in connection with a campaign along the middle Euphrates east of Mari.[274] Their mention in Job 1:17 suggests that they were nomadic raiders at some point earlier in their history, but it does not help locate them geographically.

Suspicion arises concerning identifying the Ur of Abraham as the famous city in the south because the move to Haran does not seem a logical one from there. The distance is at least seven hundred miles, and Haran is well off the beaten track for someone traveling up the Euphrates. Genesis 11:31 indicates that they were setting out for Canaan when they arrived at Haran and settled there. The route to Canaan from southern Ur would logically follow the Euphrates through Mari to Emar, where the Euphrates turned north.[275] From there the caravan routes left the Euphrates and went west into Syria and then south into Canaan. To get to Haran one would have to turn away from the Euphrates to follow the Balikh River from its confluence with the Euphrates at Tuttul, about seventy miles east of Emar. With this turn, the traveler would no longer be heading toward Canaan, but an eighty-mile trek north would lead to Haran.[276] If a town were eighty miles out of the way (especially

traveling on foot), it would hardly be considered on the way.

This geographical problem leads some to consider alternatives, and the literature of the ancient Near East preserves numerous other town names with some similarity to Ur:[277]

Ura and Uru in the Ebla tablets (mid-third millennium)
Urê and Ura in the Alalakh tablets, ca. 1600 B.C.
Uri in the Nuzi tablets, ca. 1400 B.C.
Ura in the Ugaritic texts, thirteenth century B.C.
Modern Urfa (Orhai in Syriac) north of Haran
Ura'u near the Habur River, west of the Tigris, almost directly west of Haran

So why should Tell el-Muqayyar be preferred over these other candidates? Primarily because of the sure connection to the Chaldeans. Until one or the other of the alternatives is found to have some relationship to the Chaldeans, the case for any of them will be weak.[278] Since the only Chaldeans we know of are from the south, the designation "of the Chaldeans" in relationship to Ur must be considered a later explanation placed in the text to help readers who were no longer familiar with the location of the town.

Sarai was barren (11:30). Barrenness was considered a judgment from God in the ancient world.[279] Ancient peoples did not yet understand the physiology associated with fertilization. They viewed the woman as a receptacle for male seed. Rather than supplying an egg to be fertilized, the woman was seen simply as an incubator for the child.[280] Therefore, if a man provided the seed at the proper time (they understood that timing was in relation to menstruation) and nothing came of it, the

Fertility figure from Mesopotamia in the early second millennium
Kim Walton, courtesy of the Oriental Institute Museum

woman was seen to be a faulty incubator. But this defect would not be seen as simply a physical problem, since no illness, symptom, or condition was simply physical. Deity was responsible for creation in the womb, and deity was the one who opened the womb. Note an Akkadian Prayer to the moon god, Sin:

> Without you scattered people are not
>   brought together.
> Where you command so the scorned one
>   gives birth to children....
> Whoever has no son you give him an heir.
> Without you the childless one can receive
>   neither seed nor impregnation.[281]

Nevertheless, ancient medical texts indicate various remedies for infertility (charms, recitations, and medications),[282] though ritual solutions were foremost. Note the following prayer to Ishtar:

> I have strewn for you a mixture of [pure]
>   aromatic herbs and [fra]grant incense.
> Eat what is good, drink what is [sweet]!
> May your heart calm down, your mind
>   [relax].
> I am So-and-so, descendant of so-and-so.
> Something dreadful has befallen me....
> You are the judge, procure me justice!
> You bring order, inform me of a ruling!

> May my god who is endangered with me
>   turn back to me.
> May my transgression be forgiven and my
>   guilt be remitted.
> May the disease be snatched out of my
>   body
> And the sluggishness be expelled from
>   my blood!
> May the worries disappear from my heart.
> Give me a name and a descendant!
> May my womb be fruitful.[283]

Sarai's barrenness would have potentially resulted in a fragile marriage (since failure to deliver children to the family was the most common cause of divorce), in shame in society (since her condition was seemingly the result of having angered a god and she was therefore unable to fulfill her societal role), and in an uncertainty for the afterlife (since descendants were believed to sustain the deceased in the netherworld). In Abraham and Sarai's case, it also presented quite an obstacle to the covenant promise of having many descendants.

Haran (11:31). As noted in the entry on Ur of the Chaldeans above, Haran was located on the Balikh River, some eighty miles upstream from its confluence with the Euphrates, as well as on an east-west highway from Nineveh to the Orontes near Alalakh. It is mentioned in texts in the early second millennium and was the site of a major temple to the moon god, Sin. It has not been extensively excavated, though some surveys and soundings have been carried out.

Call of Abraham (12:1–9)

Leave your country, your people and your father's household (12:1). Why does God ask Abram to leave these behind? One reason may be that it is by these three connections that one related to deity. The gods one worshiped tended to be national or city gods (country), the clan god

▶ Personal God in Mesopotamia[A-79]

Around 2000 B.C., when the Abraham stories should probably be placed, an interesting development was taking place in Mesopotamia—the rise of the concept of a "personal God."[A-80] In this period people began to see themselves in a personal relationship with a family god who undertook the divine sponsorship of the family. As a result, most family worship was directed to this god with the expectation that protection and guidance would be provided. When someone senses that a god has taken his family under his protective wing, the expression used is that they have "acquired a god."

In some texts this seems merely an expression of personified luck (Jacobsen)[A-81] or a personification of self (Abusch).[A-82] Terminology used to express this relationship was that of a parent who had created or engendered the indi-vidual. Given this background, it can be considered likely that when God began interacting with Abram, the patriarch would have thought of himself as "acquiring a god"—entering a relationship with a divine being who would become the family patron deity.

In Mesopotamia this god came to be known as the "god of the father(s)"[A-83]—a description also used in Genesis (26:24; 28:13; 31:5, 29, 42, 53; 32:9; 43:23; 46:1–3; 50:17; cf. the plural in Ex. 3:13–16). A personal god was not viewed as the only god, but was the god most directly involved with the family and the one that was the focus of most of the routine religious activity. Devotion to this deity was extended in the family from generation to generation, and as such was inherited rather than chosen.[A-84] Though the major gods could on occasion serve as personal gods, more typically a personal god was a lower echelon deity in terms of rank within the pantheon. Only in Israel did a personal God eventually become the God of a nation.[A-85]

Mesopotamian Lama goddess associated with personal protection
Kim Walton, courtesy of the Oriental Institute Museum

◀

(family), or ancestral gods, that is, ancestors who have taken a place in the divine world (father's household). As Yahweh severed the ties Abram would have had with other deities, he then filled the resulting void as the only God Abram would need.

Great nation (12:2). This offer is unique in the ancient world. One can certainly find offers by deities to make someone king and to prosper their line—or even a promise that a particular individual would have many offspring. But the prospect that an individual would grow into a great nation is not broached in any other literature from the ancient world.

I will make your name great (12:2). This offer stands in contrast to the desire of the city and tower builders in Genesis 11 (see comment on 11:4). They had embarked on an initiative to establish their name, whereas here it is Yahweh's initiative that will result in Abram's name being magnified. Every aspect of this offer explains the ways that Abram's name will be magnified because a person's name is exalted through remembrance. All peoples will call Abram their ancestor and will recognize him as the one through whom their blessing has come.

Canaan (12:5). Canaan is a broad geographical description whose boundary,

▶ The Covenant

Though the agreement between the Lord and Abram is not termed a "covenant" until 15:18, the first articulation of the general terms of the covenant occurs in 12:1–3. Though the monotheistic worship of Yahweh is a clear distinctive for Israel in contrast to the peoples of the ancient world, more distinctive yet is the covenant relationship between God and people. Israel's self-identity, her view of history, her belief in her destiny, her understanding of the attributes of God (e.g., as holy and faithful), her understanding of her obligations to God (articulated in the *torah*), and the basis of the prophetic institution all derive directly from the covenant.

In each of those areas, despite the existence of similarities with the rest of the ancient world, the covenant marks the departure and underlies the uniqueness of Israel. Gods in the ancient world may have been viewed as personal gods who undertook the protection of the family, but they did not make covenants.

The covenant targets the most essential elements of identity in the value system of the ancient Near East. Land was connected to one's survival, livelihood, and political identity. Family linked the past, present, and future, offering one's most basic sense of identity (more so than self).[A-86] Inheritance fixed one's place in the family and ensured that the generations past would be remembered in the present and future. When Abram gave up his place in his father's household, he forfeited his security. He was putting his survival, his identity, his future, and his security in the hands of the Lord.

Canaan

▼

through the middle of the second millennium, is roughly designated on the south as extending from the Wadi el-Arish (brook of Egypt), dipping south to include Kadesh, then northeast to the bottom tip of the Dead Sea. On the north it follows a line from the coast just north of Byblos to the Syrian desert. Its eastern boundary encompasses most of what eventually became Aramaean territory under the control of Damascus as well as the area known as Gilead east of the Sea of Galilee. South of the Sea of Galilee, the Jordan River and Dead Sea become the eastern boundary.[284]

In Egyptian and Hittite texts of the mid-second millennium, the area of Canaan (*kinaḫḫi*) is similar (with the inclusion of Transjordan) and is used in contrast to the land of Amurru, just to the north.[285] The specifics of territorial identification get much more complex.[286]

Tree of Moreh (12:6). No hint is given that the trees themselves were worshiped,

Shechem
Bible Scene Multimedia/Maurice
Thompson
◀

but notable trees became places where various sacred rituals were performed. The significance given to certain trees in the biblical text suggests that they designated sacred space (cf. 13:18; 35:4, 8; Deut. 11:30; Judg. 4:5; 6:11; 9:37).[287] Note the eventual indictment of the Israelites that they set up sacred stones and Asherah poles "under every spreading tree" (2 Kings 17:10).

The name given to the oak here has been interpreted as suggesting that oracular information was gained here ("Diviner's Oak").[288] Of all of the divination procedures known from the ancient world, there is no suggestion of trees used as divinatory mechanisms; thus, we conclude that the tree had significance as a locale rather than as a mechanism.

Shechem (12:6). Shechem has been identified with modern Tell Balatah, just east of modern Nablus and thirty-five miles north of Jerusalem. It is strategically located at the east entrance to the pass between the twin hills, Mount Ebal and Mount Gerizim. Its proximity to these mountains and its location on a trade route both contributed to its nearly continuous occupation in the second and first millennia. As early as the Middle Bronze I period, Shechem is mentioned in the Egyptian texts of Pharaoh Sesostris III (1880–1840 B.C.). Excavations have revealed an

Sacred stone at
Shechem
Z. Radovan/www.
BibleLand
Pictures.com
◀

apparently unwalled settlement in Middle Bronze IIA (about 1900 B.C.) with the development of fortifications in Middle Bronze IIB, about 1750 B.C. No settlement is referred to here in Genesis, though one is mentioned in Genesis 35.

Canaanites were in the land (12:6). This verse has at times been interpreted as suggesting that at the time of the author or editor of Genesis, Canaanites were no longer living in the land. The Hebrew particle used here, however, is not usually used to indicate a situation that existed at one point but not any longer. The background question here, nevertheless, is through which periods Canaanites were in the land.

It must first be noted that there is some question whether "Canaanite" is more properly understood as an ethnic designation or as a geographical designation. Recent studies have leaned toward the latter, understanding the term as referring to the multiethnic people living in the region at this time who shared a common culture and were the ancestors of first millennium peoples such as the Phoenicians.[289] Though that may offer an adequate reflection of the material culture, it is problematic in regard to the biblical text. When the Pentateuch and Joshua refer to the inhabitants of the land, many groups are mentioned alongside the Canaanites (see, e.g., 15:21; Ex. 3:8; Deut. 7:1; Josh. 9:1); thus "Canaanites" does not appear as a word for just anyone living within the geographical boundaries of Canaan.

Nevertheless, assuming an ethnic identification, we have no information about where they may have come from or when they entered the land. The earliest clear reference to Canaanites is in the Mari letters of the mid-eighteenth century B.C.[290] Archaeologically, most of the material remains of the Middle and Late Bronze periods in this region are associated with Canaanite populations. The Iron Age (beginning about 1200) evidences early the disappearance of the Canaanites from both the written and archaeological records. They are displaced

by the Philistines as the great enemy of Israel and are not among the enemies fought by Saul or David, and there is only a brief mention of them in the reign of Solomon (1 Kings 9:16). As a result, the time "when the Canaanites were in the land" is roughly equivalent to the second millennium B.C.

Built an altar (12:8). We usually think of altars in terms of raised platforms used for offering sacrifices. Here, however, there is no mention of sacrifices. Furthermore, sacrifices usually (though admittedly not always) took place in the vicinity of a temple and were serviced by a priesthood. No ancient Near Eastern document refers to altars used for anything other than sacrifices in the presence of deity; they were pointless if not offered where a deity was believed to be present.[291] In fact, the only sacrifice by Abram described in the text is the near-sacrifice of Isaac.

If Abram is not using the altar for sacrifice in a place where God's presence was established, what is he using it for? One option is for a land claim marker. This use of "altar" is attested in the Old Testament in Joshua 22:26–28, but nothing in Genesis indicates this function. The only activity that Abram is involved in at altars is to "call on the name of the LORD" (12:8; 13:4). This phrase can be understood as invoking God's presence, thus anticipating his presence rather than assuming it. Support for this interpretation is that several of the altars are built at potentially sacred sites (trees, 12:7; 13:18; hills, 12:8).

Bethel (12:8). Bethel is usually identified with Tell Beitin just over ten miles north of Jerusalem, about a mile and a half west of et-Tell, the traditional site of Ai. There was a major fortified city on the site during the Middle Bronze Age that was built up through the first half of the second millennium. Kelso reported a destruction at the end of Middle Bronze (about 1550 B.C.), but the evidence is sketchy, and opinions vary.[292] After an apparent occupation gap in Late Bronze I, it was grandly

Beitin, commonly
believed to be
Bethel, with mod-
ern town built on
ancient site
Todd Bolen/www.
BiblePlaces.com

rebuilt in the Late Bronze II (about 1400).
Another destruction level is identified by
Kelso at the end of the Late Bronze period
(1200), though, again, the reports offer
little help for those who want to assess his
findings.[293] Some have questioned whether
Beitin is Bethel because it has been difficult to find a satisfactory adjoining site for
Ai (cf. Josh. 7:2).[294]

Negev (12:9). The Negev is the geographical area located south of the hill
country of Judah. It is bordered on the
south by a steppe region called the "wilderness." The focal point of the Negev is
the valley to the east of Beersheba over
to Arad. The region in biblical terms
extends about ten miles north and south
of Beersheba.[295]

Abram in Egypt (12:10–20)

Famine (12:10). In the Negev, rainfall
is minimal (averaging between four and
twelve inches per year), thus making the
availability of grazing lands and subsistence agriculture fragile and vulnerable to
climatic whims. Water is supplied to the

region by wells, and even the rain that does fall
does not easily support agriculture because the
loess soil hardens when it rains and the water
runs off rather than soaks in. Ten to twelve
inches in a year can allow for wheat and barley
to be grown, but a yield is realized in only one
out of every three or four years.[296]

Modern archaeologists and geologists
have found evidence of a massive three hun-
dred-year drought cycle that occurred during the end of the third millennium and the

Negev east of
Beersheba
Z. Radovan/www.
BibleLand
Pictures.com

beginning of the second millennium—one of the time periods to which Abraham is dated.[297] Egyptian Papyrus Anastasi VI reports of an entire clan of Shasu Bedouin going down into Egypt during a drought toward the end of the second millennium.[298]

Travel was frequent between Canaan and Egypt for the purpose of trade. Tomb paintings from the nineteenth century B.C. during the Twelfth Dynasty in the Middle Kingdom period portray caravans of "Asiatics" with their trade goods.[299] From these we can see the sorts of clothing Abram may have worn and the sorts of goods being traded.

Egypt (12:10). Recourse to Egypt in time of famine in Canaan was not unusual because the food supply in Canaan depended on rainfall, while the food supply in Egypt depended on the flooding of the Nile—thus two different ecological systems. The text offers no identification of the pharaoh at this time. Politically Egypt was ruled by the Middle Kingdom pharaohs from the end of the twenty-first century until the end of the eighteenth century. By the earliest chronology for Abraham, the pharaoh of Genesis 21 would have been one of the kings of the "First Intermediate Period" that preceded the Middle Kingdom (perhaps Inyotef II). Many are more comfortable locating Abram and his immediate descendants in the first quarter of the second millennium, which coincides with the Middle Kingdom. Little is known of this period in Egyptian history, and it is difficult to date the patriarchs with any precision or confidence.

Beautiful woman (12:11). Sarai was sixty-five when she and Abram left Haran; perhaps several years have gone by, so we can estimate her age at seventy. The compliment cannot be simply attributed to a doting husband, for the text indicates that the Egyptians share this opinion (12:14–15). What is not clear is which features lead to this assessment. In Genesis 41:2 the cows of pharaoh's dream are described by this same Hebrew term (NIV translates it "sleek"), where it conveys robust healthiness—fine specimens.

Our culture has persuaded us that beauty is connected with sensuality, nubility, youth, and particular facial and bodily features. We need not think that every culture is so superficial in its assessment of beauty. A woman in the ancient world could be attractive either as showing good potential for childbearing or as a tool for political alliance.[300] Neither of these seems appropriate for Sarai, however, for she is clearly not entering childbearing years, and there is no political alliance that makes it attractive to marry her.

Say you are my sister (12:13). This is the first of three narratives in which a patriarch attempts to identify his wife as his sister to avoid problems with the power establishment of the region (see also 20:1–18; 26:1–11). Interpreters have proposed many ingenious explanations for this behavior. One that was popular for several decades suggested that the wife's status would be elevated if her husband also adopted her as a sister. In this explanation, the patriarch was trying to provide extra social protection for his wife. The problem with this is that the

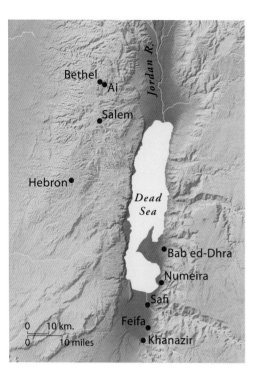

Nuzi texts used to illustrate this sister status were eventually read in other ways, and the proposed social gain was lost.[301]

Others have argued that if the wife posed as a sister, the patriarch would be viewed as a party to negotiate with rather than as an obstacle to be eliminated. This put him in a position to drive a hard bargain that eventually would result in no deal, and they could go on their way. This view is difficult to sustain since it looks as if Abram capitulated and sold her after all (12:16).

Many of the proposed theories have the underlying motivation to save Abram's reputation. Unfortunately at present we remain ignorant of what sociological realities commended this course of action to Abram. The Israelite audience undoubtedly knew what advantage was to be gained from the ruse, so there was no need for the author to explain it. For our part, we accomplish nothing by devising solutions designed to either vindicate or vitiate Abram.

Serious diseases (12:17). The terminology here is as general as it can possibly be. With no symptoms being given, it is impos-sible to speculate on what these diseases may have been. In the ancient world, with no knowledge of epidemiology, parasites, viruses, bacteria, or any of the diagnostic tools of modern medicine, people believed disease had its source in the supernatural realm.[302] Treatment focused on the symptoms and combined herbal remedies with magical potions and incantation rituals. Prognoses could offer hope for healing most confidently if an offense against deity could be identified and appeasement effected. Extensive catalogs of symptoms and treatments are available in medical texts from Mesopotamia.[303]

Abram and Lot (13:1–18)

Went up from Egypt (13:1). This journey that ends at Bethel covered several hundred miles. Herders of livestock were used to constant traveling as they sought out grazing land and water sources.

Quarreling arose (13:7). The provision for the health of their herds was not just their livelihood; it determined their prospects for survival. It is understandable, then, that given the scarcity of grazing land and water sources, tempers were short. There were limits as to the size of herds that the land could support. This way of life (i.e., pastoral nomadism) was common in the ancient Near East, especially in this region where agriculture was more challenging.

Plain of the Jordan (13:10). The Jordan Valley is at a considerably lower elevation than the hill country and has a more stable climate. The area features lush vegetation and therefore is attractive. It is difficult to determine how the plain of the Jordan relates to the "cities of the plain" since we still do not have firm identification of the location of those cities.

Zoar ... Sodom and Gomorrah (13:10). The association of Sodom and Gomorrah

Diagnoses of medical conditions with prognoses of the outcomes
The Schøyen Collection MS 2670, Oslo and London
▲

Madaba map
with Zoar, sur-
rounded by trees,
visible in the bot-
tom right hand
corner
Todd Bolen/www.
BiblePlaces.com

▶

Tablet granting
restoration of
land by King
Nabu-apla-iddina,
ninth century B.C.
Michael Greenhalgh/
ArtServe, courtesy of
the British Museum

▼

with Zoar (Zoara on the sixth-century A.D. Madeba map) and the bitumen pits "in the valley of Siddim" (14:10) both point to the southern end of the Dead Sea as the most likely location of these cities. Arguments for their identification with the north end are based on the distance to travel from Hebron (eighteen miles versus forty miles to the southern location) and the mention of the "plain of the Jordan" here. The southern location enjoys stronger biblical support as well as the support of the earliest extrabiblical traditions.[304]

There are five sites of Early Bronze Age cities on the southeast plain of the Dead Sea; these demonstrate that fairly large populations existed here in the third millennium. From north to south they are Bab edh-Dhraᶜ (Sodom?), Numeira (Gomorrah?), Safi (Zoar), Feifa, and Khanazir, with the last being about twenty miles from the first. At the north end of the east side of the Dead Sea, the hills of Moab come right up to the shore. But along the southern half of the east coast there is a stretch of plains before the hills rise up. These cities were located one each along five perennial freshwater streams that traveled through this stretch of plains and fed into the Dead Sea. Only Bab edh-Dhra and Numeira have been excavated extensively, and the destruction of these cities (by fire) has been set by archaeologists at about 2350 B.C., seemingly too early for Abraham, though chronological reckoning of this period is difficult.

Walk through ... the land, for I am giving it to you (13:17). It is common for the biblical covenants to be compared to political treaties in the ancient Near East. These treaties formed relationships between political entities that required loyalty from the vassal and offered protection from the suzerain. The formal documents that articulate the covenant between Yahweh and Israel compare favorably in form and function to these treaties.

The covenant with Abram, however, seems different. Rather, it is better to compare this covenant with ancient land grants.[305] In the ancient Near East, ruling elites commonly made land grants to their faithful vassals. This phenomenon is attested from the mid-second millennium through the mid-first millennium. Weinfeld points out that while the form of treaties and land grants overlap considerably, the important difference is that the treaty is a document that imposes obligation on the vassal, while the royal grant represents an obligation of the suzerain.

In the grant the curse is directed towards the one who will violate the rights of the king's vassal, while in the treaty the curse is directed towards the vassal who will violate the rights of his king. In other words, the "grant" serves mainly to protect the rights of the *servant*, while the treaty comes to protect the rights of the *master*. What is more, while the grant is a reward for loyalty and good deeds already performed, the treaty is an inducement for future loyalty.[306]

Abram would have easily recognized what is transpiring here, and it will be formally confirmed and ratified in Genesis 15.

Hebron (13:18). Hebron is located in the Judean hill country about halfway between Jerusalem and Beersheba. A major roadway from the coastal plain and Lachish passes through the Shephelah and meets here with a road that goes north to Jerusalem or south to Beersheba or Arad. The site is at the southern end of the Hebron hills (about 3,300 feet above sea level), an area about ten miles wide and fifteen miles long (with Bethlehem at the north end of it).

The higher elevation provides a greater amount of rainfall (twenty to twenty-eight inches annually), and vineyards were common in the region.[307] Twenty-five springs there provided additional water supply.[308] Terrace farming allowed the inhabitants to take advantage even of the hillsides, providing for rain to nourish crops rather than just to flow down the hillsides, taking all the soil with it. Thus, Hebron was an ideal location both ecologically and strategically.

The archaeology of Hebron is complex. The ancient site is on the flanks of Jebel er-Rumeida across the valley from the modern el-Khalil. Excavation of the fifteen-acre site has been limited because of continuing occupation in the area. A Middle Bronze wall, presumably Canaanite, dates perhaps to the eighteenth century B.C. (beneath the wall is an Early Bronze stratum from an occupation level destroyed about half a millennium earlier). It is made of huge, uncut stones, and remains of its towers are twenty feet high.[309]

The Middle Bronze finds also include an Akkadian cuneiform tablet listing animals for sacrifice and perhaps naming a king. A scarab was also found from the Twelfth Dynasty of Egypt (Middle Kingdom).[310] These provide ample evidence of settlement during the first half of the second millennium. Little evidence remains of the Late Bronze settlement identified in Joshua 10, but a topographical list of Ramesses II at Karnak includes Hebron on its itinerary, so its continued settlement is confirmed.[311]

Abram and the Kings (14:1–24)

Amraphel king of Shinar (14:1). Amraphel is a Semitic name that has many possible connections to names known from the ancient Near East.[312] Both the "Amar" element

The area of Mamre is just a couple of miles north of Hebron. The ruins on the site range from the Iron Age paving to the Herodian walls to the fourth century A.D. basilica.
Z. Radovan/
www.BibleLand
Pictures.com

and the "a-p-l" element occur in personal names.[313] Shinar refers to the southern Mesopotamian plains (see comment on 11:2). During the early part of the second millennium southern Mesopotamia was characterized by independent city states with cities such as Isin or Larsa at times enjoying prominence. By the eighteenth century this gave way to the Old Babylonian period.

Arioch king of Ellasar (14:1). One name from the second millennium similar to this one is that of Zimri-Lim's subordinate Arriwuk, from the eighteenth-century Mari archives. A city named Ilan-ṣura is also known from those texts in the vicinity of Shubat-Enlil north of Mari, though it does not seem prominent enough to figure here. Others have noticed the vague similarity to Larsa, a prominent city-state in Mesopotamia during the first half of the second millennium.[314]

Kedorlaomer king of Elam (14:1). Elam is the usual name for the region that in this period comprised all the land east of Mesopotamia from the Caspian Sea to the Persian Gulf (modern Iran). Only in the first several centuries of the second millennium was Elam involved in international politics in Mesopotamia and the West,[315] largely because of its role as supplier of tin, which

was alloyed with copper to make bronze.[316] During the first two centuries of the second millennium, Elam is ruled by the Šimaški dynasty (2050–1860).[317] In the middle of the second millennium the Mari texts make it clear that Elam was attempting to extend its control throughout Mesopotamia, but no information suggests Elamite control of sections of Palestine.

Kedorlaomer appears to be the head of the coalition. The first part of the name is a common element in Elamite royal names (compare Kutir-Nahhunte, who ruled during the Old Babylonian period, the Elamite *sukkalmah* period). Nahhunte is the name of an Elamite deity, as is Lagamar (represented in the Hebrew *laʿōmer*). Though the two elements of Kedorlaomer (=*Kutir-Lagamar) are thus attested as authentic, so far that combination is not known among Elamite royal names.[318]

Tidal king of Goiim (14:1). Goiim (Heb. "nations") is the most vague, but is generally associated by commentators with the Hittites (located in the eastern section of present-day Turkey), mostly because the king's name, Tidal, is easily associated with the common Hittite royal name, Tudhaliya. The earliest occurrence of this name for a ruler, however, is about 1400 B.C.,[319] far too late to match this context. Furthermore, the names of the Hittite kings as early as the mid-eighteenth century are known, and none of them bears any resemblance to Tidal.

The history of Anatolia prior to that time is sketchy. As a reference to a group of people, Goiim could be handled in a number of different ways. One option is that it reflects how the population of Anatolia called themselves. They do not use a gentilic (e.g., "Hittite") but refer to themselves as "peoples" from the land of Hatti.[320]

A second option is that it should be considered a way to refer to a coalition of "barbaric" peoples, like the Akkadian designation *Umman Manda*, a term associated with the Gutians who overran Mesopotamia at the

Regions of the Kings of the East

▼

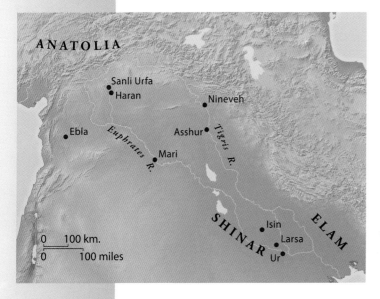

ANATOLIA

Sanli Urfa
Haran
Nineveh

Ebla
Euphrates R.
Asshur
Tigris R.
Mari

SHINAR
Isin
Larsa
Ur
ELAM

0   100 km.
0   100 miles

▶ Genesis 14 and Ancient History

Genesis 14 theoretically offers the best chance of placing the patriarchal narratives in the framework of the ancient Near East historically and chronologically. Unfortunately, as can be seen from comments on 14:1, details continue to give a mixed picture and connections elude us. None of the kings of the East is attested in ancient literature. In fact, even the cities of the plain themselves are not yet attested.[A-87]

While there were many periods in the first half of the second millennium when the Elamites were closely associated with powers in Mesopotamia, it is more difficult to bring the Hittites into the picture (and, it should be noted, we are not even sure the Hittites are involved here). We do know that Assyrian merchants had a trading colony in the Hittite region, and one of the key trade items was tin from Elam. But there is no indication of joint military ventures.

Early Hittite history is sketchy as well, and we have little information about where they came from or precisely when they moved into Anatolia. None of the known empires or major military coalitions from Mesopotamia is known to have made forays into the southern Levant (Canaan) at any time during the second millennium. Consequently, though many authentic features characterize this narrative, no ready links to the known history are currently possible.

---

end of the Dynasty of Akkad toward the end of the third millennium.[321] The Gutians came from Anatolia and swept southeast all the way to Elam. The term *Umman Manda* continues to be used as a reference to enemies of the Hittites and the Babylonians in the mid-second millennium.[322] The trouble with this interpretation is that the *Umman Manda* would not likely be involved in a large, formal coalition of nations. None of these options offers clarification of this king's identity.

Rephaites in Ashteroth Karnaim ... Hazazon Tamar (14:5–7). Ancient Near Eastern campaign reports throughout the biblical period regularly preserve the itinerary of the armies. The route described in Genesis 14 represents a straightforward march through the land going south on the main route through Transjordan, the King's Highway, to where it cuts west at Bozrah. This international artery runs across the top of the plateau about ten to fifteen miles east of the Jordan River and the rift valley. From Bozrah they depart from the King's Highway (which cuts west) and follow the south-

ern branch (Way of the Wilderness) to the tip of the Gulf of Aqaba. From there they come north on the "Way of the Red Sea" to

Army Routes from Genesis 14

▼

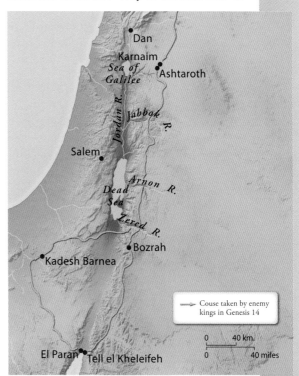

Course taken by enemy kings in Genesis 14

▶

Kadesh Barnea, where they rejoin the King's Highway, taking it east to Tamar and from there north to the cities of the plain in the vicinity of the Dead Sea.

Ashtaroth was the capital of the region just east of the Sea of Galilee near the site of Karnaim, a later capital. This area provided some of the sources of the Yarmuk River and was the home to people known as the Rephaim. Little is known of the Rephaim as an ethnic group, though the same term is used in other places both in and out of the Bible as a reference to the heroic dead. Zuzites, Emites, and Horites, judging by the cities identified with them, are the inhabitants of Transjordan in the regions eventually occupied respectively by the Ammonites, Moabites, and Edomites. Ham is located in northern Gilead, and Shaveh, also known as Kiriathaim, was in Reubenite territory when the land was divided among the tribes.

El Paran should probably be equated with Elath at the tip of the Gulf of Aqaba.[323] Some have tentatively suggested that Elath is Tell el Kheleifeh, though no remains on the site predate the Iron Age.[324] The Amalekites are engaged at Kadesh Barnea (En Mishpat), located in the northeastern Sinai near the southwestern extremity of Canaan (about fifty miles southwest of Beersheba). It is identified with Wadi el-ʿAin near ʿAin el-Qudeirat. It boasts one of the most productive water sources in the region in its oasis.

Finally, the Amorites are met at Hazazon Tamar. Rainey and Aharoni identify the site as located some forty miles southwest of the southern tip of the Dead Sea,[325] whereas 2 Chronicles 20:2 identifies it with En Gedi, halfway up the western shore of the Dead Sea. The association with En Gedi is problematic if the cities of the plain are along the southeastern rim of the Dead Sea, since the itinerary then requires significant retracing of steps. No known routes travel

the western bank of the Dead Sea to En Gedi.[326]

Tar pits (14:10). Bitumen was used as a mastic in the ancient world, generally as an adhesive or for waterproofing. The Dead Sea is one of the source zones for bitumen since it was available there close to the surface, both on the water and on the land.[327] The procurement of bitumen by digging created the tar pits referred to in the text. These would have been more the size of wells than of large stone quarries. The language of the text allows for the possibility that the kings went down into these pits intentionally for the purpose of hiding.

Abram the Hebrew (14:13). The designation of Abram as a "Hebrew" may reflect a social status more than an ethnic identity. The term is usually used in the Bible to identify Israelites to foreigners (Gen. 39:14–17; Ex. 2:11; 1 Sam. 4:6; Jon. 1:9). As a social status it seems to have referred to dispossessed or disenfranchised peoples. This is the usage of a similar sounding term throughout a wide range of ancient texts (often transliterated *ḫabiru*, more accurately, *ʿapiru*) referring to various people groups throughout the second millennium.[328]

They are documented through eight hundred years of history from Ur III down to the XXth Dynasty in Egypt. They are never mentioned as pastoralists, and the preserved personal names of people bearing this designation are from no single linguistic group. There are Semites, Hurrians and others. They never belong to tribes. They may worship various deities. Geographically they are known from east of the Tigris, to Anatolia, to Egypt, in short, over the entire Ancient Near East.[329]

This label gives someone an "outsider" status and at times implies that the people are unsettled or even lawless renegades. Other times they are refugees or political opponents. In the Amarna texts they sometimes serve as mercenaries. The term cannot be considered as a reference to ethnic Israelites, but it is possible that ethnic Israelites (and here, Abram) are being classified socially as ʿapiru.

318 trained men (14:14). The word translated "trained" (ḥānîk) occurs nowhere else in the Old Testament, but does occur in an Akkadian letter of the fifteenth century B.C. from Taʿanach, referring to military retainers.[330] Canaan in this period was predominantly occupied by herdsmen and villagers, and even within the later Middle Bronze Age when there were more fortified settlements, this army would have been a match for any other armed force in the region. Even as late as the Amarna period the armies of any particular city-state were not much larger.

Despite this comparison, we have no information about the size of the invading force in order to ascertain whether Abram was outnumbered. We would expect international coalitions to have fielded armies in the thousands rather than in the hundreds. One text from early in the second millennium has the marauder, Ashduni-iarim king of Kish, lamenting that his army has been reduced to only three hundred.[331] In the Mari letters, a force of three hundred is considered optimum for foray expeditions.[332]

Dan (14:14). It is difficult to imagine what route would have taken the armies of the east through Dan if they were traveling from the cities of the plain. If these cities are on the eastern side of the Dead Sea (as they are by anyone's assessment), it makes the most sense for the armies to rejoin the King's Highway straight up to Damascus, which does not bring them within twenty-five miles of Dan. The only route that would take them through Dan proceeds north along the spine of hills through Jerusalem, Shechem, and Hazor—and there is no indication that they went that far west or had any reason to do so.

Thus, most likely the route through Dan is not traveled by the armies but by Abram and his allies as they try to cut off the armies traveling by the King's Highway. Dan is mentioned not as the place where he catches them, but as a marker that he is leaving the land. The only other alternative is to maintain that the whole region was different at this time before the destruction in the region in Genesis 19.

Valley of Shaveh (14:17). The text indicates that this is also called the "King's Valley," which locates it with some degree of probability (based on 2 Sam. 18:18) at the confluence of the Kidron and Hinnom Valleys at the base of the south end of the ridge that became the City of David in Jerusalem.

Melchizedek, king of Salem (14:18). If we base our analysis solely on information

Mosaic known as the Madaba Map shows Salem in a location near Shechem near building in top left quadrant.
Z. Radovan/
www.BibleLand
Pictures.com

▶ Melchizedek in Later Traditions

Little is known about Melchizedek from ancient Near Eastern literature. But as we look at the scope of the whole canon of Scripture, we may wonder whether there is more going on. Melchizedek next makes a brief appearance in Psalm 110:4, where the idealized Davidic king is identified as also having priestly credentials "in the order of Melchizedek." Once we get to the intertestamental period, Melchizedek becomes a much more intriguing figure. The Hasmoneans, seeking to establish a messianic dimension to their rule in the second century B.C., justified their priestly-royal prerogatives by reference to Melchizedek. This practice was continued by the Sadducees.[A-88]

In the Dead Sea Scrolls 11QMelchizedek and 4QAmram both show that he has become the subject of much speculative interpretation. The former assigns him a judging function in heaven and associates Psalm 7:8–9 and 82:1 with him. The latter identifies him as Michael and calls him "the Prince of Light." He is depicted as a heavenly redeemer figure, a leader of the forces of light, who brings release to the captives and reigns during the messianic age. He is the heavenly high priest to whom archangels make expiation for the sins of ignorance of the righteous.[A-89]

In the Talmud (*b. Ned.* 32b) and Targum Neofiti, Melchizedek is identified as Shem. The former attributes irreverence to him and thereby transfers his priesthood to Abraham. In the apologetic works of Justin Martyr (*Trypho* 19, 33), Melchizedek is portrayed as a representative of the Gentiles, who is seen as superior to the Jewish representative, Abraham. Philo of Alexandria (*Leg. alleg.* 3.79–82) considers him the eternal Logos.[A-90]

When we get to Hebrews 7, all of this Jewish tradition is mixed into consideration of Melchizedek. The author of Hebrews is not drawing his information on Melchizedek solely from the Old Testament; he is also interacting with the traditions known to his audience. It is the Jewish profile of Melchizedek, not just the canonical profile, that informs his comparison.

As a result, there is nothing in Hebrews or anywhere else to suggest that we need to believe that Melchizedek was anything other than the Canaanite king he is depicted as in Genesis 14. The fact that he combined the roles of priest and king (as many did in the ancient world) in Jerusalem was sufficient to establish the precedent of a royal priesthood in Jerusalem that was adopted by the Davidic dynasty and therefore came into the messianic profile.[A-91]

from Genesis 14, Melchizedek is a city-state king of Canaanite, Amorite, or Hurrian extraction, and apparently one of the chief petty kings of the region. His city is Salem, generally considered to be Jerusalem (cf. Ps. 76:2), though early Christian evidence and the Madeba map associate it with Shechem.[333] Archaeological finds, though scant, attest to the fact that Jerusalem was settled at this period. The city

is mentioned in extrabiblical literature as early as the Egyptian execration texts from around 1900 B.C.

Bread and wine (14:18). It is unclear whether the bread and wine are shared by all of Abram's men or just in council between Melchizedek and the victorious commander(s). It would seem to be meager fare if the latter were the case. Abram's success has signaled the possibility of a major shift of power in the region, and it appears that Melchizedek is taking the opportunity of the army's return to explore what ambitions or loyalties Abram might have. It was common for a meal to be shared when treaty negotiations were being finalized, but generally meat was part of the meal as sacrifices were made in association with oaths to the respective deities.

Priest of God Most High (14:18). "God Most High" is a translation of El Elyon, a compound divine name/title. El is well known as the chief Canaanite god in Ugaritic and Phoenician literature, but it is sufficiently generic to use for any high God. Though Hebrew regularly uses the plural form Elohim for the God of Israel, El is also sometimes used. Consequently, El could refer to either a Canaanite deity or to Abram's.

The epithet Elyon (ʿelyôn) is used parallel to the Canaanite El as well as of Baal, but El Elyon never occurs as a compound in Ugaritic texts.[334] No evidence of Elyon as an independent deity is found until the writings of Philo.[335] Since El Elyon can designate a Canaanite god, we have no reason to think of Melchizedek as a worshiper of Yahweh or

even as monotheistic. It is Abram who identifies El Elyon as Yahweh.

Tenth of everything (14:20). Tithing is known in the ancient Near East and the Old Testament in a variety of contexts.[336] Evidence from the ancient Near East occurs as early as about 2000 B.C. in Sumerian Ur III texts, where the obligatory tithe is in goods given to the temples. Akkadian texts referring to tithes appear in both Old Assyrian texts and Old Babylonian texts.[337] In some of these, the tithe is paid annually to the temples from the barley harvest.

In this period there is also reference to a tithe of the palace. Ugaritic texts attest to grain payment tithes to the royal storehouses being made from villages rather than individuals. No texts suggest a tithe of booty taken in battle,[338] though Pagolu attempts to include this in a larger category that he labels "tithe following an expedition."[339]

The question, then, is whether this tithe was paid to Melchizedek in his role as priest (thereby indirectly to the god El Elyon) or in his role as king (tribute and acknowledgment of his political position). Hittite treaties did not require vassals fighting on the suzerain's behalf to give the suzerain a share of their "take," but allowed them to keep captives and booty (though the land remained in the possession of the suzerain).[340] In light of all of this information, Abraham's payment of a tithe to Melchizedek stands as unique both in the Bible and the ancient Near East.

I will accept nothing (14:23). Though it seems likely that the armies of the east did not traverse the territory west of the Jordan, they had come into possession of much land in the region by virtue of conquest. Abram's defeat of them would have theoretically given him possession of that land, however its boundaries would be drawn. This right has suddenly made him a political power to be reckoned with and explains Melchizedek's overtures. Abram, instead of exerting his newfound political leverage, relinquishes any and all claims to the land.

Covenant with Abram (15:1–21)

Vision (15:1). Visions may be either visual or auditory and are not the same as dreams in that one does not have to be asleep to experience a vision. God used visions to communicate to people; they constitute a more aggressive form of communication than dreams. In contrast to this one, visions in the Old Testament were typically given to prophets in order to communicate oracles to be delivered to the people. They may involve natural or supernatural settings, and the individual having the vision may be either an observer or a participant.

Besides the category of "dream" in the ancient Near East, there are "waking dreams,"[341] but these are the dreams one has when half awake in the morning, not like biblical visions. The closest thing to biblical visions are the oracular decisions seen when a person was in a semicomatose state or trance.[342] The idea of "seeing an oracular decision" makes sense both in the context of Genesis 15 (where Abram asks an oracular question, 15:8) and in the context of the prophets (where oracles emerge from the vision). As in the Old Testament, these visions are distinct from dreams but can be communicated in dreams.

Inherit my estate (15:2). Besides today's practice in which children are adopted to provide for the child, ancient Near Eastern practice sometimes involved adopting an adult for the purpose of providing for the parents. Through adoption the parents vouchsafed an heir to keep property and possessions intact and procured someone to care for them in old age. In these cases at

times a trusted slave was adopted as a son.[343] One Old Babylonian letter from Larsa says, "This judgment has never been delivered in Larsa. A father does not adopt his slave if he has sons."[344] Despite the attestation of this practice, information is lacking in Genesis 15 to suggest that Abram has actually adopted Eliezer.[345] Another possibility is that he simply sees this as his only option at the moment.

Count the stars (15:5). Skilled astrologers in ancient Mesopotamia catalogued and tracked the stars (both constellations and individual stars). They recognized three paths: the paths of Anu, Enlil, and Ea (three of the major cosmic deities; see comment on 1:14). They calculated the extent of the heavens and the distances between stars.[346] It should be remembered, however, that in the ancient world the stars were considered engraved on the underside of the stone pavement that constituted the heavens, and, therefore, were confined in a finite space. Despite all of this, they did not believe that

they could number the stars. In fact, a quantity that was considered innumerable was compared to the numbers of the stars of the heavens.[347]

Cut them in two and arranged the halves (15:10). Controversy remains about what kind of ceremony is carried out here. What/whom do the pieces represent (possibilities: sacrifice for oath, God if he reneges, nations already as good as dead, Israelites in slavery)? Whom do the birds of prey represent (nations seeking to seize available land, e.g., Gen. 14, or to plunder Israel)? Whom do the implements represent (God and/or Abram)?

These issues cannot currently be resolved, but a few observations can help identify some of the possible connections with the ancient world. Before we look at the options, a word is in order about what this is not. It is *not a sacrifice*. There is no altar, no offering of the animals to deity, and no ritual with the carcasses, the meat, or the blood. It is *not divination*. The entrails are not examined and no meal is offered to deity. It is *not an incantation*. No words are spoken to accompany the ritual and no efficacy is sought — Abram is asleep. The remaining options are based on instances where animals are ritually slaughtered in the ancient world not for the purposes of sacrifice, divination, or incantation.

Option 1: This is a covenant ceremony, or more specifically, royal land grant ceremony. In this case the animals typically are understood as substituting for the participants or proclaiming a self-curse if the stipulations are violated. Examples of the slaughter of animals in such ceremonies but not for sacrificial purposes are numerous. In tablets from Alalakh, the throat of a lamb is slit in connection to a deed executed between Abba-El and Yarimlim.[348] In a Mari text, the head of a donkey is cut off when sealing a formal agreement.[349] In an Aramaic treaty of Sefire, a calf is cut in two with explicit statement that such will be the fate of the one who breaks the treaty.[350] In Neo-Assyrian literature, the

head of a spring lamb is cut off in a treaty between Ashurnirari V and Mati'ilu, not for sacrifice but explicitly as an example of punishment.[351]

The strength of these examples lies in the contextual connection to covenant. The weakness is that only one animal is killed in these examples, and there is no passing through the pieces and no torch and firepot. Furthermore, there are significant limitations regarding the efficacy of a divine self-curse.

Option 2: Purification. This option is more associated with the torch and firepot (see below) and offers no explanation for the cutting up of the animals. Further weakness is in the fact that Yahweh doesn't need purification and Abram is a spectator, not a participant, so neither does he. In the Mesopotamian Hymn to Gibil (the torch), the god purifies the objects used in the ritual, but the only objects in the ritual in Genesis 15 are the dead animals, and it is difficult to understand why they would need to be purified.[352]

Option 3: Confirming signs related to the promise of what will be done to the nations. In incantations seeking to rid a person of the consequences of offense (*šurpu*), the torch and oven are two in a series of objects that can serve as confirmatory signs.[353] This same incantation series also occasionally speaks of the person who is swearing an oath in connection with their participation in the incantation as holding an implement of light and/or heat.[354] The strength of this option is that it fits best the context of land promise. The problem is that it offers little connection to the cutting up of the animals. The ten parts of the animals would refer to the ten nations to be dispossessed.[355]

The following entries will explore the elements in relation to these three options.

Smoking firepot with a blazing torch (15:17). The "torch" is a portable, hand-held object for bringing light. The "smoking firepot" can refer to a number of different vessels used to heat things (e.g., oven for food, kiln

Pottery kiln (fire-pot)
Kim Guess/www.
BiblePlaces.com
▶

for pottery). Here the two items are generally assumed to be associated with God, but need not be symbolic representations of him. These implements are occasionally used symbolically to represent deities in ancient Near Eastern literature, but usually sun gods (e.g., Shamash) or fire gods (e.g., Girru/Gibil). Gibil and Kusu are often invoked together as divine torch and censer in a wide range of cultic ceremonies for purification.[356]

Abram would have probably been familiar with the role of Gibil and Kusu in purification rituals, so that function would be plausibly communicated to him by the presence of these implements. Yet in a purification role, neither the torch nor the censer ever passes between the pieces of cut-up animals in the literature available to us. As mentioned above, implements of heat and/or light also at times play a role in oath rituals.[357] By the translation "firepot," the NIV shows that it infers that the object is portable; but everywhere else the term (*tannûr*) is used, it refers to a large stationary oven. This fact leaves open the possibility that in the vision, only the torch passes through the pieces, while the oven is a stationary prop.[358]

Passed between the pieces (15:17). The only example of ritual participants passing between the pieces of several cut-up animals occurs in a Hittite military ritual.[359] In response to their army's defeat, several animals are cut in half (goat, puppy, piglet—as well as a human), and the army passes through the parts on their way to sprinkling themselves with water from the river to purify themselves with the idea that this will ensure a better outcome next time. As with Achan's story in Joshua 7, they fear that some offense of the soldiers has caused them to be defeated. The obvious problem is that the context of the Hittite ritual has no similarity to the context in Genesis 15.

In summary, torch and censer figure frequently in a variety of Mesopotamian ritual contexts, and multiple examples can be found of rituals that involve passing through the pieces of a single animal—but these two elements never occur together. There are plenty of examples of oaths with division of animals, but never passing through the pieces. There are plenty of examples with self-curse, but never by a deity. It is therefore difficult to combine all of the elements from the context of Genesis 15 into a bona fide ritual assemblage.

The context refers to a "covenant" (15:18), and therefore an oath (by Yahweh) could easily be involved. If there is purification, it would have to be purification of the ritual or its setting, for neither Abram nor Yahweh requires purification. Since the pieces cannot represent self-curse, the only other ready option is that they represent the nations, but it is hard to imagine in that case what the force of the ritual is.

River of Egypt (15:18). This is the only reference to the "river of Egypt." Usually Israel's southwestern border is designated the "Wadi [brook] of Egypt" (e.g., Josh. 15:4, 47), which is identified as the Wadi el 'Arish in northeastern Sinai. It is unlikely that the reference in this verse is to the Nile River, though it could conceivably refer to the easternmost Delta tributary of the Nile that emptied into Lake Sirbonis.

Hagar and Ishmael (16:1–16)

Perhaps I can build a family through her (16:2). The solution proposed by Sarai is not as shocking or outlandish as it would seem to us today. In the ancient world, barrenness was a catastrophe (see comment on

▶ Religion of Abram

In general, patriarchal religious practice can be identified as informal, having no cultic place or personnel and no prescribed sacrifices, procedures, or festivals.[A-92] The biblical text is clear on the point that Abraham came from a family that is not monotheistic (see Josh. 24:2, 14). We must assume that he was brought up sharing the polytheistic beliefs of the ancient world. These gods did not reveal their natures or give any idea of what would bring their favor or wrath.

The Lord, Yahweh, is not portrayed as a God whom Abraham already worshiped. It is interesting, then, that when he appears to Abraham, he does not give him a doctrinal statement or require rituals or issue demands; rather, he makes an offer. Yahweh does not tell Abraham that he is the only God there is, and he does not ask him to stop worshiping whatever gods his family was worshiping.

11:30) because one of the primary roles of the family was to produce the next generation. The survival of the family line was of the highest value, and it depended on producing progeny. Whatever threat a second wife might pose to harmony in the family paled in comparison to the necessity of an heir being produced.

Marriage contracts of the ancient world, therefore, anticipated the possibility of barrenness and at times specifically dictated a course of action. Solutions ranged from serial monogamy (divorcing the barren wife to take another, presumably fertile one),[360] to polygyny (taking a second wife of equal status), to polycoity (the addition of handmaids or concubines for the purpose of producing an heir), to adoption.[361] The third option is the one pursued here; this attempted remedy is consistent with contemporary practice as a strategy for heirship. This option was often more attractive because if the wife were divorced, there would be an economic impact on the family (she took her marriage fund/dowry with her). Concubines bring no dowry, only their fertility to the family.[362]

A marriage contract from the town of Nuzi a few centuries after the patriarchal period illustrates the practice: "If Gilimninu bears children, Shennima shall not take another wife. But if Gilimninu fails to bear children, Gilimninu shall get for Shennima a

woman from the Lullu country (a slave girl) as concubine. In that case, Gilimninu herself shall have authority over the offspring."[363] An Old Assyrian marriage contract closer to the time of the patriarchs reflects a similar solution to infertility:

> Laqipum took (in marriage) Hatala, the daughter of Enishru. In the country Laqipum shall not take (in marriage) another (woman), (but) in the city (of Ashshur) he may take (in marriage) a priestess. If within two years she has not procured offspring for him, only she may buy a maid-servant and even later on, after she procures somehow an infant for him, she may sell her wherever she pleases.[364]

It is therefore plausible that Sarai is simply invoking the terms of her marriage contract.

Angel of the Lord (16:7). In the ancient world direct communication between important parties was a

Laqipum and Hatala marriage contract
Istanbul Archaeological Museum; © Dr. James C. Martin

▼

rarity. Diplomatic and political exchange normally required the use of an intermediary, a function that our ambassadors exercise today. The messenger who served as the intermediary was a fully vested representative of the party he represented. He spoke for that party and with the authority of that party.[365] He was accorded the same treatment as that party would enjoy were he there in person. While this was standard protocol, there was no confusion about the person's identity.

This explains how the angel in this chapter can comfortably use the first person to convey what God will do (16:10).[366] When official words are spoken by the representative, everyone understands that he is not speaking for himself but is merely conveying the words, opinions, policies, and decisions of his liege.[367] So in Ugaritic literature, when Baal sends messengers to Mot, the messengers use first person forms of speech. E. T. Mullen concludes that such usage "signifies that the messengers not only are envoys of the god, but actually embody the power of their sender."[368]

Sign of Circumcision (17:1–27)

God Almighty (17:1). Much controversy surrounds the meaning of the name El Shaddai ("God Almighty").[369] One Ugaritic text refers to "El of the field" (*il šd*),[370] while Akkadian refers to the "Lord of the Mountain/Steppe" (*belu šadu*),[371] though these may be descriptions rather than divine epithets. The only extrabiblical use of the divine epithet occurs in the Balaam text of Deir 'Alla, where the *šdyn* are the beings of the heavenly council.[372]

Your name will be Abraham (17:5). Per-

sonal names in the ancient world provided much more than a moniker.[373] Sometimes they preserved recognition of a distinguishing characteristic or reflected circumstances at the time of the person's birth. Often they made statements about deity (e.g., Isaiah = Yahweh saves).[374] Names generally offered information at some level about the person's identity and in a variety of ways were believed to be intertwined with a person's destiny (see comment on 2:20).

Knowing a person's name created a relationship with that person—that is, the person was further known by knowing the name. A person's name also provided potential power over that person, most radically when used in spells or hexes. The naming of a person was one of the most dramatic impositions of authority over another individual. Since the name of a person was believed to be intertwined with their destiny, to name a person meant that you controlled their identity and directed their destiny.

In this passage, it is not that God is demonstrating his authority over Abram (though the fact that he can change his name is not insignificant), but more important he is designating his destiny—to be the father of a multitude. The name Abram meant "the father is exalted." Reference to "father" (*ʾab*)

in personal names usually indicated veneration of an ancestor, so this name looked to the past. His new name designates Abraham as the significant ancestor as it looks to future generations yet to be born.

Every male among you shall be circumcised (17:10). Circumcision is well known in the ancient Near East from as early as the fourth millennium, though the details of its practice and its significance vary from culture to culture.[375] Anthropological studies have suggested that the rite always has to do with at least one of four basic themes: fertility, virility, maturity, and genealogy.[376] Study of Egyptian mummies demonstrates that the surgical technique in Egypt differed from that used by the Israelites. Egyptians were not circumcised as children, but in either prenuptial or puberty rites. The common denominator, however, is that circumcision appears to have been a rite of passage, giving new identity to the one circumcised and incorporating him into a particular group.[377]

Evidence from the Levant comes as early as bronze figurines from the ʿAmuq Valley (Tell el-Judeideh) from the early third millennium. An ivory figurine from Megiddo from the mid-second millennium shows Canaanite prisoners who are circumcised.[378] Southern Mesopotamia shows no evidence of the practice, nor is any Akkadian term known for the practice. The absence of such evidence is significant since Assyrian and Babylonian medical texts are available in abundance. Abram was therefore aware of the practice from living in Canaan and visiting Egypt rather than from his roots in Mesopotamia. Since Ishmael is thirteen at this time, Abram may even have been wondering whether it was a practice that would characterize this new family of his. In Genesis 17 circumcision is retained as a rite of passage, but one associated with identity in the covenant.

In light of today's concerns with gender issues, some have wondered why the sign of the covenant should be something that marks only males. Two cultural issues may offer an explanation: patrilineal descent and identity in the community. (1) The concept of patrilineal descent resulted in males being considered the representatives of the clan and the ones through whom clan identity was preserved (as, e.g., the wife took on the tribal and clan identity of her husband).

(2) Individuals found their identity more in the clan and the community than in a concept of self. Decisions and commitments were made at the level of the family and clan more than at the individual level. The rite of passage represented in circumcision marked each male as entering a clan committed to the covenant, a commitment that he would then have the responsibility to maintain. If this logic holds, circumcision would not focus on individual participation in the covenant as much as on continuing communal participation. The community is structured around patrilineal descent, so the sign on the males marks the corporate commitment of the clan generation to generation.

Your wife Sarah will bear you a son (17:19). Since procuring an heir was so essential in the ancient Near East, and deity was considered to provide the heir, it is not unusual to record divine announcements of an impending birth to significant individuals. A few examples will suffice. In Ugaritic literature from the mid-second millennium, King Danʾel has no sons and prays to his gods that they may remedy his situation. In response, El, the chief Canaanite deity, announces that he will have a son even in his old age.[379]

In Hittite literature the childless and wealthy Appu requests children, and the sun god tells him to get drunk and go home and sleep with his wife, and he will have a son.[380] In Mesopotamian literature, Etana, the Sumerian king of Kish, offers repeated sacrifices and prays to the sun god Shamash that he might remove his shame by providing a son by means of the "plant of birth." Shamash advises him where to find an eagle that needs his help, who will, in return, find the plant of birth for him.[381] These last two

Bab-edh Dhra
(Sodom?)
Todd Bolen/www.
BiblePlaces.com
▶

the gods, and whoever is not respectful to the gods, let not the good ones perish with the evil ones. Whether it is a single town, a single house, or a single person, O gods, destroy only that one!"[389] Likewise in the Gilgamesh Epic, after the flood, the god Ea reprimands the god Enlil with the exhortation that in the future he "punish the sinner for his sin, punish the criminal for his crime" rather than bringing widespread destruction.[390] Abraham is making a similar plea on behalf of the cities of the plain.

Beersheba gate
with benches
Kim Walton
▶

Sodom (19:1). For the possible identification of the cities of the plain and their locations, see comment on 13:10.

Lot was sitting in the gateway of the city (19:1). Lot's presence at the gate is neither casual nor incidental. At the gate formal activities took place. Public decisions were made, cases heard, business transacted, and visitors processed or registered according to the conventions of the city.[391] Lot's presence in the gate is undoubtedly related to some of these activities. We have no reason to think that Lot is alone in the gate, yet he is the one who interacts with the messengers. Perhaps security in the city has been heightened in the aftermath of the invasion in Genesis 14 so that they are on the watch for the infiltration of possible spies reconnoitering the city (cf. the spies who go to Jericho in Josh. 2).[392] In this view Lot's intention in taking the visitors in not only fulfills the obligations of hospitality, but also places them under guard.

Surrounded the house (19:4). The intentions of the men of the city have traditionally seemed clear enough, but recent interpreters have suggested various alternatives. Perhaps the most developed is Morschauser's contention that when the men say they want to "know" the visitors, they are expressing distrust in Lot's ability to protect the city from spies and they want to "interrogate" the men. Lot identifies this intention as "wicked" because interrogations in the ancient world were typically not gentle. In this view Lot offers his daughters as hostages to be held as warranty that he has the situation well in hand.[393] The most devastating problem to this position is that in Hebrew, when the verb "to know" (*yāda*) has a personal direct object (i.e., to know someone), it always has a sexual innuendo.[394]

Struck ... with blindness (19:11). The word for blindness here is used elsewhere only for the Aramean army at Dothan (2 Kings 6:18). It is a term related to an Akkadian word for day or night blindness.[395] This rare word is used only in medical texts apparently referring to a corneal disease. As a judgment of God blindness can be found in the Ugaritic Legend of ʾAqhat. Danʾel curses three towns near to where his son ʾAqhat has been slain with the words, "May Baal strike you blind" (cf. Deut. 28:28).[396]

Pillar of salt (19:26). Lot's wife becoming a pillar of salt need not be seen as an arbitrary and instantaneous transformation. The destruction is described in terms of sulfur (brimstone) and fire "raining down" on the cities. The scene is one of divine retribution, and brimstone appears here and elsewhere as an agent of purification and divine wrath on the wicked (Ps. 11:6; Ezek. 38:22).

One can only speculate about the actual manner of this destruction, but perhaps the combustion of natural tars and sulfur deposits and the release of noxious gases during an earthquake form part of the story (Deut. 29:23). The mineral salts of

the region include sodium, potash, magnesium, calcium chloride, and bromide. An earthquake in the area could easily have ignited these chemicals, causing them to rain down on the victims of the destruction. Since the destruction does not begin until Lot and his daughters have reached Zoar (Gen. 19:23–24), we should assume that Lot's wife does not simply glance back, but returns to the city and is swept up in the destruction like everyone else in the cities (cf. Luke 17:28–32). Many "pillars of salt" would have littered the streets.

Father of the Moabites ... father of the Ammonites (19:37–38). The Moabites and Ammonites historically occupied the regions east of the Jordan River from the Jabbok River in the north to the Wadi Zered (= el-Hesa) in the south. The latter is the wadi by which Zoar is located. The northern border of Moab was traditionally the Arnon, but they frequently extended their border north to the Wadi Heshban. If the

Moabites and
Ammonites
◀

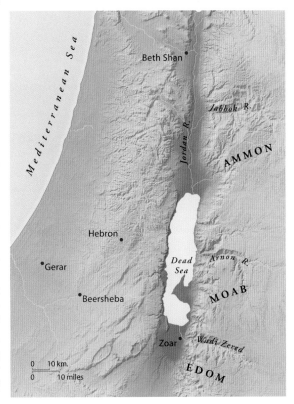

southern locations of the cities are correct, the three northernmost cities of the plain are then in traditionally Moabite territory, while the two southern ones are in what was to become Edomite territory. The fact that it would be more expected to find the cities of the plain closer to Ammonite territory would be another point in favor of a more northern location for the cities.

Archaeologists in Transjordan have been uncovering increasing amounts of evidence pointing to a developed urban civilization (though still oriented toward pastoralism) in the region as early as the Late Bronze Age (1550–1200 B.C.), though the evidence is still sketchy.[397] There is every indication that these peoples are indigenous to the region rather than immigrants, though their historical identification as Ammonites or Moabites is not possible until later.[398] The only Transjordanian city mentioned in the Amarna texts is Pella, across the Jordan from Beth-Shean; this shows that even in the Late Bronze Age southern Transjordan was sparsely settled. The occupants of this territory were designated *shasu* by the Egyptians, a social label (pastoral nomads) rather than an ethnic or national one.[399]

Tel Haror
Todd Bolen/www.
BiblePlaces.com

Abraham and Abimelek (20:1–18)

Kadesh and Shur (20:1). Kadesh is an oasis nearly fifty miles south of Beersheba in the northeastern Sinai. "Shur" has been commonly thought to refer to the "wall" of Egyptian fortresses in the eastern Delta region. The Egyptian story of Sinuhe (twentieth century B.C.) mentions such a "Wall of the Ruler" as a barrier to the incursions of Asiatics into Egypt. More recently it has been identified as lying further south along a mountain ridge.[400]

Gerar (20:1). The location of Gerar remains speculative, though not a matter of great controversy. Most archaeologists identify it with Tell Haror (Tell Abu Hureireh), about fifteen miles west-northwest of Beersheba on the road from there to Gaza. It is never mentioned outside of the Bible. A major town existed there in the Middle Bronze period with a smaller settlement in the Late Bronze.[401]

She is my sister (20:2). See comments on 12:13.

He is a prophet and he will pray for you (20:7). The connection between prayer and prophets is not transparent. In the ancient world, prophets gave messages from deity because they putatively had a seat in the heavenly council where decisions of judgment and destiny were made. This privileged seat also gave a prophet the ability to effectuate a curse or remove it (cf. 1 Kings 13:4–6, which included prayer as part of the prophet's procedure). Their messages comprised the announcement of the decisions of the heavenly council. The intercessory role of the prophet was therefore found in the opportunity he or she had to bring issues to the council table for discussion and to serve as advocate for the earthly party.[402] Then, as spokesperson for the council and deity, he or she would announce the verdict in the form of a prophetic message. Such information was typically given by prophetic oracle, usually derived from a divination setting (note Balaam's procedures in Num. 22–24).

The verbs describing Abraham's anticipated action are modal ("he *may* pray for you, so that you *may* live"). No guarantee is offered of either, though if there is no restoration, the death sentence is certain. In this context, however, there is no hint of divination.

A thousand shekels of silver (20:16). Abimelech's payment to Abraham and Sarah is like a reverse bride price. A bride price was paid by the groom to the family of the bride as surety that the marriage would take place. Here the payment moves the same direction, but the woman is moving the opposite direction—from the would-be husband back to the family. Rather than a bride price, it is a restitution payment restoring the woman to her family intact.

The text is clear, however, that this is more than a social transaction when Abimelech indicates that by this payment she is vindicated. A thousand shekels of silver is exorbitant. We encounter the same number in the Ugaritic poem The Betrothal of Yarikh and Nikkal-Ib, in which a thousand shekels of silver is part of the bride price paid among the gods, along with ten thousand shekels of gold and precious stones.[403] In weight it equals about twenty-five pounds of silver; in value it is more than a worker could expect to make in a lifetime (common wage earners were paid ten shekels per year). The king's generous payment is multifunctional. It is his guarantee that Sarah has been untouched, a fee to Abraham for his intercessory role, and an appeasement of the deity who has virtually cut off all fertility in his family.

Birth of Isaac and Departure of Hagar and Ishmael (21:1–21)

Get rid of that slave woman (21:10). Hagar's status in the household of Abraham now creates friction. Her initial status as Sarah's handmaiden was altered when Sarah chose her as the one to give an heir to Abraham—that is, when she became not just a concubine (whose children would not have the status of legitimate heir) but a wife.[404] A concubine had no dowry and her children were slaves in the household, not legitimate heirs. As Westbrook asserts, "The child was reckoned to be the offspring of its mother; it had no father."[405] She could be sold and did not have to be divorced.

But with a handmaiden given as a wife, as Hagar was, all this changed. Consequently a dual claim of authority was established. A woman of Hagar's status could be expelled, but not by either husband or wife alone, and she could not be sold. Her son had the status of legitimate heir, and she would generally have to be divorced. By sending Hagar away, both Sarah's and Abraham's claims are being dissolved. This means that she is being given her freedom as well as being divorced.[406] The verb used in 21:14 ("sent her away") is the verb for divorce (cf. Mal. 3:16).

Desert of Beersheba (21:14). Though Abraham later dug wells in the area of Beersheba (21:25), it is possible that when the events of Genesis 21 take place he is still living closer to Gerar (26:17–18). The southern

Nahal Zin mountains
Todd Bolen/www.
BiblePlaces.com

Negev region around Beersheba where Hagar wanders is inhospitable and barren steppe land. Eventually Hagar and Ishmael settle in the arid desert of the northeastern Sinai near Kadesh Barnea in a region called Paran (see 21:21).

Treaty at Beersheba (21:22–34)

Well of water (21:25). The region of Beersheba had limited rainfall, so water supply was largely provided through wells. Water rights in such ecological situations were established by contracts, as here. That such discussion could become important for international relations is evidenced by some correspondence between Rim-Sin of Larsa and the king of Eshnunna in the Old Babylonian period, where water rights are under dispute and negotiations take place.[407]

Well technology required sufficient knowledge of hydrology to identify the location of aquifers and the ability to dig down to them, but also sufficient knowledge of well-building technology, including the construction of lining to stabilize the shaft and prevent seepage from the sides. The significant amount of labor necessary for such an undertaking makes it obvious why the rights to this water supply would be worth fighting over. Urban wells have been found in the excavations of major cities such as Ebla, Ugarit, and Nimrud.[408]

Land of the Philistines (21:32). The Philistines known from the time of the Judges and the early monarchy did not come into the

region and occupy this territory until around 1200 B.C.—much later than the time of Abraham and likewise later than the time of Moses. The first known mention of the Philistines outside the Bible is in the records of Ramesses III (1182–1151 B.C.).[409] They were one of the tribes of the Sea Peoples who eventually settled in five city-states along the southern coast of Canaan. Abimelech is a Semitic name, and as "king of Gerar" he matches nothing that is known of the Philistine profile. While it is not impossible that this story represents contact with an earlier group of Philistines who settled the area prior to the Sea Peoples, most likely this is simply an anachronistic use of the name "Philistines" for the area rather than an ethnic identification of the people whom Abraham encounters.[410]

Eternal God (21:33). The title used here (Heb. *ʾēl ʿôlām*) occurs also in the proto-Sinaitic inscriptions found in western Sinai.[411]

Binding of Isaac (22:1–19)

Region of Moriah (22:2). Since the journey is two to three days, we can look for the location of Moriah in a forty-mile radius from Beersheba. This circle reaches from Kadesh Barnea in the south to Jerusalem in the north, and from the Dead Sea to the Mediterranean coast. The only other reference to Moriah is in 2 Chronicles 3:1, which identifies it as the site of the temple in Jerusalem, but it makes no mention of Abraham or this incident.[412] Abraham appears to be familiar with the place, and since he takes firewood with him, presumably he knows that wood

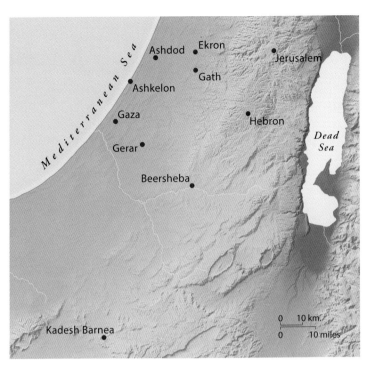

is not available in the region. In contrast, the wooded hills around Jerusalem would have provided ample firewood for the sacrifice. Furthermore, if the site were Jerusalem, we would expect it to be designated "Salem" (as in Gen. 14). Consequently we cannot be certain that Genesis 22 and 2 Chronicles 3 refer to the same place.

Sacrifice him (22:2). God's demand that Abraham offer Isaac is unlike anything in the ancient world (see sidebar on "Child Sacrifice in the Ancient

▶ Child Sacrifice in the Ancient Near East

Determination of the role that child sacrifice had in the ancient Near East is difficult. The four major sources of information are archaeological excavations, iconography (such as cylinder seals), biblical sources, and extrabiblical written sources. Much of the archaeo-

logical information admits to a variety of interpretations because infant burials are usually ambiguous with regard to the cause of death. Infant mortality was high in the ancient world and could explain various subfloor burials or the Gezer infant jar burials.[A-93] Nevertheless, Green believes that the evidence supports some foundation sacrifices in early Mesopotamia.[A-94]

Portrayals of what some have considered as human/child sacrifice on cylinder seals from the late third and early second millennia are likewise interpreted variously.[A-95] Contemporary literary sources outside of the Bible that refer to child sacrifice or even human sacrifice are virtually nonexistent.[A-96]

Infant burial jar
from Ashkelon
Joshua Walton,
courtesy of the Leon
Levy Expedition to
Ashkelon

Near East"). Child sacrifices would have been carried out soon after birth and would have been associated either with fertility rituals or foundation offerings to secure protection for the home. The prohibition of child sacrifice in the Pentateuch demonstrates that it was sometimes practiced, but none of the potential ritual contexts are pertinent to Genesis 22. Human sacrifice may have been carried out in extreme circumstances, but there are no dire conditions here. Undoubtedly in Genesis 22 Abraham would not have considered this command of God commonplace.

Took the knife (22:10). Excavations of a Middle Bronze II tomb (about 1700 B.C.) at Hebron discovered next to a skeleton the ten-inch long bronze blade of a wide, two-edged dagger with a limestone pommel.[413] This is a good example of the type of knife Abraham may be using.

Sacrificed it as a burnt offering instead of his son (22:13). Though animal substitution is clear enough in the Old Testament (e.g., firstborn substitution, Passover), the idea of an animal being sacrificed as a substitute for a human being is not as common in the ancient

world as might be expected. In the cultures in which animal sacrifice was practiced, the people often simply provide a lavish meal for the deity, at times with the participation of the officiates and the worshipers.

The theory that the animal takes the place of the person whose offenses are thereby vicariously expiated is a different matter (and it should be noted that even in Gen. 22 no offense is identified as a reason for the sacrifice). When rituals from the ancient world do involve animal substitution, it is typically in the context of magic—that is, that through ritual the disease, impurity, evil spirit, or spell might be transferred to the animal, which was then slaughtered, thus bringing relief to the human.[414]

Beersheba (22:19). Beersheba is a town in the Negev that marks the traditional southern limit of Israel's territory (Judg. 20:1; 1 Sam. 3:20). The modern city

is about three miles west of an ancient tell, Tell es-Sebaᶜ (or Tell Beersheba). Since this site lacks evidence of occupation prior to the Iron Age, others favor identification of the ancient town with Bir es-Saba.⁴¹⁵ The absence of remains from the period of Abraham is not a problem since the text does not suggest there is a settlement there.

Family Matters and the Burial of Sarah (22:20–23:20)

Hittites (23:3). The terminology in this chapter identifies these people as the "sons of Heth" throughout except for the gentilic "the Hitti" in 23:10. In 10:15 Heth is listed as a son of Canaan among largely Semitic peoples. Outside of the Bible, the most well-known Hittites were Indo-European peoples who inhabited central Anatolia in the middle of the second millennium B.C. After the collapse of that empire around 1200, remnants of the civilization persevered in northern Syria.

The term "Hittites" for the Anatolian peoples derives from their association with the land of Hatti, not only in their own texts but also in Ugaritic, Egyptian, and Akkadian texts. The Indo-European "Hittites" (speaking Nesite) gained prominence over the original Hattian inhabitants beginning

about 2000 B.C.⁴¹⁶ The Old Testament probably makes no reference to the Nesite Hittites of the empire age. The term with the i/e vowel designating Ephron and his kin is used in no other designation of any of the Anatolian peoples. The Anatolian people referred to as "Hittites" should more precisely be referred to as "Hattians" or "Nesites" (referring to land and language respectively); these should not be confused with the Semitic Hethites/Hittites of Genesis.

Property for a burial site (23:4). The negotiations here are not concerned with the rights to dig a hole and mark a grave. Contemporary burial practices favored rock-cut or cave tombs, which were meant to accommodate the clan through generations. Bodies would be laid out on rock shelves until nothing remained but the bones, at which point the bones would either be cleared to the back of the tomb or relocated into a container of some sort to make room for another body. The use of family tombs may partially explain the use of the phrase "gathered to his people" (25:8).⁴¹⁷ Deceased ancestors were honored through a variety of practices that

did not stop after burial. These practices made it desirable for tombs to be in proximity to somewhat permanent settlements.[418]

Sell it to me for the full price (23:9). Abraham negotiates for the long term. If he had been willing to accept the land on a grant basis, the land could have been reclaimed in a later generation or in hard times.[419] In contrast, Abraham wants to "acquire an inheritable estate."[420]

Four hundred shekels (23:15). Four hundred shekels is a significant amount of money. It equals about seven and a half pounds of silver, but its value can be assessed by the fact that the average wage was ten shekels per year. Having said this, it is still not determinable whether the price is fair, exorbitant, or a bargain because the text does not indicate the size of the parcel of land. It is much less than what Omri paid for the much larger site of Samaria (six thousand shekels; 1 Kings 16:24), nor is it comparable to what David paid for the site of the temple (six hundred *gold* shekels; 1 Chron. 21:25).

Mamre (23:17). Mamre is clearly in the vicinity of Hebron and has been identified as Ramet el-Khalil, about two miles north of Tell Rumeideh (Hebron). Excavations on the site have discovered monumental buildings from the Roman-Byzantine period, but there is little to illuminate the earlier history of the site.[421] Already in the second temple period a wall surrounded an ancient terebinth there.

Machpelah in modern Hebron has long been considered a sacred site. The monumental construction

around the area visible today is Herodian. Explorations of the "tomb of the patriarchs" area have taken place from time to time. In A.D. 1119, one group claimed to have found the bones of the patriarchs. But no physical remains or artifacts have ever been subjected to scientific analysis, and nothing from the patriarchs or their age has been attested.

Isaac and Rebekah (24:1–67)

Put your hand under my thigh (24:2). It is possible that the oath is sworn on the genitals of Abraham, which would then be understood to be binding even if Abraham should die.[422] None of this can be confirmed, however, because the text offers no explanation and no parallels have been found in the ancient Near East.

Go to my country and my own relatives and get a wife for my son Isaac (24:4). In the ancient world it was common to restrict or at least prefer marriage within the social group, a practice called endogamy. Endogamy is particularly significant in social contexts that emphasize inheritance. In this way the lineage is isolated for purposes of social status and property ownership.[423] Though in our modern context endogamy has a religious context related to orthodoxy, in the ancient world this was not the case because in large measure the wife simply adopted the gods and religious practices of the family into which she was marrying.

In Israel the concerns are ethnic because the land was promised to Abraham and his family and he is avoiding assimilation with the people in the land. At this point in history, no one else shares Abraham's beliefs or worships "the God of Abraham" (at least as far as we know)—certainly Laban and his family do not, so this is not a matter of "marrying within the faith."

Camels (24:10). Though the biblical text portrays camels being used for long-distance travel in a number of places in Genesis, the evidence for camel domestication is somewhat sketchy. Kitchen gives a complete

One of the earliest depictions of a camel, ninth century, Tell Halaf

David Q. Hall, courtesy of the Baltimore Walters Museum

▼

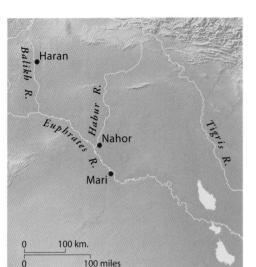

listing of the data—zoological, textual, and iconographic—from the period between 2000 and 1200 B.C.[424]

Aram Naharaim (24:10). This is alternative terminology for the area elsewhere referred to as Paddan Aram (see comment on 28:2). The phrase is translated "Aram of the two rivers," but it does not clarify which two rivers. Rivers flowing south through northern Mesopotamia from west to east are the Euphrates, Balikh, Habur, and Tigris (the middle two are major tributaries to the Euphrates once it turns east). Theoretically, any combination of two rivers that includes the central area between the Balikh and the Habur (where Haran is located) could work. The area between the Euphrates and the Habur is most likely, though a few locations west of the Euphrates are sometimes included. The Egyptian term *naharina* is as early as Thutmose I, and the Amarna letters' reference to *na-aḫ-ri-ma* may represent similar geographic designations.[425]

May it be that when I say (24:14). In seeking guidance from God, the servant uses a strategy much like that used for seeking oracles in the ancient world. In an oracle a binary question (i.e., yes/no) was put to deity and then a device of some sort was used as a means by which the deity could give an answer. In the ancient world the device that was often used entailed either casting lots or employing a divination priest to perform extispicy (the investigation of the entrails of sacrificed animals for positive or negative signs). In Israel the high priest used the Urim and Thummim as a way of conducting such an oracular procedure.

Since Abraham's servant has no lots to cast and has no immediate access to specialized professionals, he has to improvise. He therefore resorts to using his current surroundings to devise an oracle. When this procedure is used, it is typical that a highly irregular occurrence designates "yes" and the normal turn of events designates "no," with the expectation that God will thereby communicate his answer. Here the question is whether the girl whom the servant approaches is the chosen mate for Isaac. The designated indicator of a "yes" answer is if the girl offers to do far beyond what human nature or the conventions of hospitality would dictate, specifically, to water all his camels when he asked only for a drink for himself. Such an unusual offer would serve as evidence that deity was overriding all natural instinct and social etiquette. For similar mechanistic oracles, see Judges 6:36–40 and 1 Samuel 6:7–12.

I'll draw water for your camels (24:19). If the servant's camels had gone several days without water, they could potentially drink up to twenty-five gallons each. Given the standard size of the vessels used to draw water, this would mean that Rebekah would have to draw eight to ten jars for each camel, thus requiring nearly a hundred trips from the well—several hours of work. Since it is already almost evening when the scene opens (24:11), it is sensible to conclude that the camels may have been watered more recently and would have required considerably less water than that. But Rebekah would not have known the current needs of the camels, so the offer remains impressive and extraordinary.

Gold nose ring (24:22). The small gold ring described here could be worn either in the nose or in the ear. Near the nose of a skeleton in a Middle Bronze tomb at

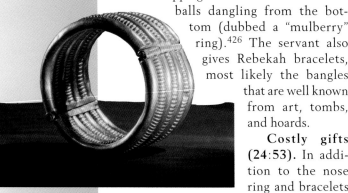

Gold bracelet
from the tomb
of Psusennes I,
dedicated to the
king by his wife
Werner Forman
Archive/Egyptian
Museum, Cairo
▲

Megiddo one was found that was tubular with overlapping ends and a cluster of little balls dangling from the bottom (dubbed a "mulberry" ring).[426] The servant also gives Rebekah bracelets, most likely the bangles that are well known from art, tombs, and hoards.

Costly gifts (24:53). In addition to the nose ring and bracelets initially presented in 24:22, the remainder of the bride price is summarized here. Marriage customs included an exchange of wealth between the families with several purposes.[427] The *marriage price* indicated here is given from the groom's family to the bride's family. This transfer is part of the socioeconomic system of provision and should not be thought of as purchase of chattel.[428] In Sumerian sources, one form of bride-wealth (*nigmussa*) is made up primarily of foodstuffs presented just before the wedding feast. A less common form (*nigdea*) sometimes includes precious objects and is presented when the agreement is made between the families.[429] The latter is more likely represented here.

The transfer often took place in two parts: a small "down payment" offered as surety that the wedding would take place, with the remainder changing hands shortly before the wedding.[430] These two stages are approximated in 24:22 and 24:53. In the Nuzi texts of the mid-second millennium, bride prices averaged thirty to forty shekels of silver.[431] At times, this property was "rolled over" into the dowry (and therefore referred to as an "indirect dowry"), which is the other transfer associated with marriage.

The *dowry* was given by the bride's family to the bride (a transaction from father to daughter, not between families per se[432]) and represented her inheritance from the family since she typically did not inherit land. Moveable property and valuables were common dowry items.[433] Its function was to provide for the support of the woman should the husband die, desert her, or divorce her. At times, part of the dowry remained the personal property of the wife, but whatever its disposition, it could not be sold without her consent.[434] In like manner, however, she was not free to dispose of it. If it were not used to support her at some stage in life, it would become part of the inheritance of her children. The dowry of Rebekah is not detailed, though her nurse (24:59) may have been part of it.

Let's call the girl and ask her about it (24:57). It is neither typical nor necessary for the woman to be consulted with regard to marriage arrangements by the family, though certainly the ones to be married were known to express their opinions or even exercise choice through various legitimate and less-than-legitimate options.[435] It should be noted here, however, that it is possible that Rebekah's opinion is only asked when the question concerns the unusual circumstance of her being so quickly and completely removed from the potential protection provided by her family. Until a woman conceived and bore a child to her new family, her status within the family was tenuous, and the proximity of her father's family would have been a strong motivator for her husband not to mistreat her or discard her.

Veil (24:65). Veils were used in a variety of ways in different cultures and different times, but they always signified something of the woman's status.[436] Some veils might cover only the hair (scarf or turban) while others covered the lower part of the face. More commonly, the veil in the ancient Near East covered both hair and lower face. These were not sheer or gauzy. In the Middle Assyrian Laws, married women or concubines were not to appear in public without face and head veiled, whereas veils were prohibited to prostitutes and slave girls.[437]

In the Code of Hammurabi, the betrothed wears a veil.[438]

In texts from the ancient Near East, veils are most often mentioned in connection with marriage, as here in Genesis.[439] It is more usual, however, that the *husband* veils the wife-to-be in a legal act. In a Mari text from about the time of the patriarchs, when the king's legal emissaries bring a bride from her country to be presented to the king, her future husband, it is the emissaries who cover her with a particular garment.[440]

Death of Abraham (25:1–11)

Concubines (25:6). The children of concubines did not have the status of legitimate heirs.[441] A concubine typically brought no dowry and her children had the status of servants or slaves in the household. They were part of the inheritance rather than recipients of it. Here Abraham sends these children away, thus removing them from any presumed position of privilege; yet at the same time he gives them freedom and gifts. Giving gifts of moveable property (rather than land) would be a typical procedure used to consolidate the chief heir's inheritance.[442] For Abraham to provide this for these sons is unusual generosity.

Gathered to his people (25:8). This expression finds its roots in ancient views about burial and afterlife. Both the practice of burials in family tombs and the view of continuing social relationships in the afterlife retain the concept of the ancestors as a distinguishable group.[443] One's place in the family of deceased ancestors was just as central to one's identity as one's place in the family in the land of the living. The living family honored the deceased both individually and corporately through a variety of practices that did not stop after burial.

Sons of Ishmael (25:12–18)

Sons of Ishmael (25:13). The Ishmaelites—that is, the peoples descended from Ishmael—are mentioned infrequently in Scripture and are absent entirely from ancient Near Eastern literature. Besides the genealogical listing (here and in 1 Chron. 1:29–31) and the reference to groups associated with the Midianites (Gen. 37:25–28; 39:1; Judg. 8:24) and with a wide array of Israel's enemies (Ps. 83:6), individual Ishmaelites are only mentioned in connection with Esau's wives (Gen. 28:9; 36:3) and David's administration (1 Chron. 2:17; 27:30).

The Ishmaelites are never identified with a group designated in the Old Testament as the "Arabs"—a term that refers to various tribes who inhabit the area of the Arabian Peninsula. The term "Arab" is not a gentilic term.[444] "Arab" takes on its modern sense only after the rise of Islam in the seventh century A.D., at which point it is still not a gentilic, but a combination of geographical, linguistic, and religious identity. Modern Muslims are not descended from Ishmael, nor do they share common biological descent from Muhammad. Moreover, even the prophet of Islam himself did not claim descent from Ishmael. We have no

Traditional site of Abram's tomb in Hebron
Copyright 1995–2009 Phoenix Data Systems

▼

record of what became of the Ishmaelites after the time of David and have no basis for seeing their survival in any known group in the later Old Testament period, and certainly not today.

Jacob and Esau (25:19–34)

She went to inquire of the LORD (25:22). At times this phrase can refer to depending on the Lord rather than on other entities for aid (e.g., gods or foreign nations, as in Isa. 31:1; Jer. 10:21). At other times it refers to the formal act of asking for an oracle from Yahweh through an official prophet (e.g., 1 Kings 22:8; 2 Kings 22:13, 18). Here the former initially commends itself since the patriarchs never encounter any such official cult personnel. Nevertheless, the latter must be the preferred option here because the result of her inquiry is an oracle (Gen. 25:23).

Usually an oracle is delivered by a prophet or priest, and in the ancient world at large is mediated by a diviner. The statement that "she went" suggests travel to a sanctuary, though if she intends to visit a prophet, they are not always associated with a sanctuary. Whatever the source of the oracle, this statement features the same laconic silence about the details as about Laban's divination (30:27) and the role of the household gods (31:34). All of these elements of divination derive from Laban's family and indicate the continuation of standard ancient Near Eastern religious practices that are preserved by that side of the family. Yet Yahweh shows some level of tolerance for the slow progress

Collection of Nuzi texts
Courtesy of the Semitic Museum, Harvard University ▶

and here is willing to communicate through whatever specialist Rebekah consults. During the time of Moses, he likewise communicated through the foreign prophet Balaam.

Named him (25:25–26). See comment on 2:20 that names are at times connected to destiny since they somehow capture the essence of the person.[445] In other cases, the giving of a name is an act of discernment in which the name is determined by certain circumstances.[446] In this context the immediate significance of the names relates to the circumstances at birth. But significance is not necessarily exhausted by the initial setting. It is not strange, then, to find other significances tumbling out of these names as the narrative unfolds. The extrapolation of additional meanings inherent in the form and content of names is evident in the internal exegesis of the fifty names of Marduk within the text of *Enuma Elish*.[447]

Sell me your birthright (25:31). The privilege of the firstborn in inheritance is referred to as primogeniture. Primogeniture was not universally practiced in the ancient world, but it was a sort of default position.[448] Sufficient numbers of examples exist of either a younger son having the privileges or

of the estate being equally divided to demonstrate that a variety of arrangements was possible.

The birthright consists of the material inheritance. The firstborn usually received a double share from the father because he was expected to become the paterfamilias, having ultimate responsibility for all of the members of the extended family (e.g., mother, unwed sisters) as well as for the continuing care of the deceased.[449] With this greater responsibility came greater resources.[450] When Jacob negotiates to purchase the birthright, it is not clear whether the additional responsibilities come along with that or not. It is likely that this incident involves only the extra share of the inheritance while leadership in the clan is given in Genesis 27 (see comment there).

Isaac and Abimelech (26:1–35)

King of the Philistines (26:1). For discussion about the Philistines, see the comment on 21:32. In 20:2 Abimelech is referred to only as the "king of Gerar," but he is located in "the land of the Philistines" (21:32). The term "king" is not as lofty a title as may be assumed since even the rulers of small cities in a city-state system (as this is) are referred to in that way.

Well of fresh water (26:19). See comment on 21:25.

Beersheba (26:23). See comment on 22:19.

Isaac's Blessing (27:1–46)

Give you my blessing (27:4). This blessing is one that transfers the leadership of the clan to the next generation.[451] If the inheritance remained undivided for some time (which was common), the privileged son (usually the firstborn) was designated the administrator of the estate.[452] The administrator had significant control of the estate. His roles included presiding at sacrificial meals celebrated by the family, supervising burials and funerary rites, and serving as kinsman-redeemer.[453] Jacob (and Rebekah on his behalf) would desire this because it was also in the administrator's hands to approve the timing for the division of the inheritance. If Esau were the administrator, he could presumably delay the division indefinitely and thus deprive

Journey from Beersheba to Bethel and Haran
▼

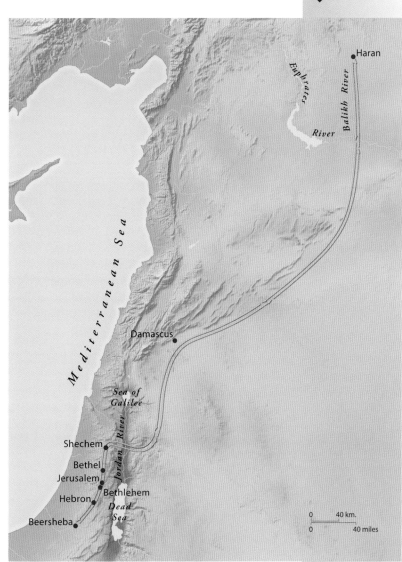

Jacob of the advantage of the double share of the inheritance.[454]

The blessing also served as a proclamation of the destiny of the sons. It was not accorded the same status as a prophecy from God (note Isaac's use of the first person, "I have made him . . ." in 27:37), but it still was an exercise of authority believed to be binding through the very speaking of the words. This is why Isaac could not "take it back" even though it became clear that he had been tricked.

It is clearly a celebratory occasion since Isaac asks for the preparation of a special meal, but as such it is odd that the whole household is not asked to be present, both as cocelebrants and as witnesses to the legal transaction. It is not hard to imagine, however, that when political issues of favoritism are involved, there is an inclination to be secretive.

Jacob Travels to Haran (28:1–22)

Paddan Aram (28:2). See comment on 24:10 for the variant, Aram Naharaim. While the two designations may be variants, it is also possible that Paddan Aram refers to a much more limited area. This would be the case if the word Paddan is related to the Akkadian word *padānu/paddānu*, meaning "road, highway." Some suggest that Paddan is an Aramaic term synonymous with the Akkadian *ḥarrānu*, meaning the same thing, in which case Paddan Aram is the Aramaic equivalent of Haran in Aram.[455] Until other occurrences are attested, further clarification is not possible.

Isaac sent Jacob on his way (28:5). Why was Isaac prohibited from leaving the land, yet Jacob was encouraged to do so? The difference lies in the fact that if Isaac left and Abraham subsequently died, no heir of the family would be left to safeguard the land by his presence. But when Jacob leaves, Isaac and Esau are still there to maintain the claim.[456]

Aramean (28:5). The term "Aramean" first occurs in a topographical list on a funer-ary temple of Amenophis III at Thebes.[457] The first appearance of this term in Mesopotamian historical records are in the annals of the Assyrian king Tiglath-pileser I about 1100 B.C., where they are equated to the *Aḥlamû*. By means of this corresponding designation the early history of the Arameans can be traced in the literary record. The *Aḥlamû* first appear in northern Babylonia in the mid-eighteenth century during the reign of Rim-Anum.[458] The consensus is that they occupied the regions of the upper Euphrates throughout the second millennium, eventually developing a national identity early in the first millennium.[459]

Set out for Haran (28:10). From Beersheba Jacob likely travels north along the ridge of the hills passing just west of Hebron, Bethlehem, and Jerusalem to Bethel.[460] The distance covered is about fifty-five miles. Jacob probably arrives at Bethel on the third night.

Stairway (28:12). From the fact that the messengers of God appear passing between the realms in Jacob's dream, it is clear that he is viewing a portal to heaven.[461] Such portals are envisioned as stairways (as opposed to ladders) in ancient mythology (see comments on 11:4). They are also architecturally represented in the ziggurats of ancient Mesopotamia, which were built to provide the stairway for the gods to come down and be worshiped in their temples. Jacob is not seeing a ziggurat, but he is seeing the stairway portal between heaven and earth that ziggurats were designed to provide.

We should not imagine that the angels he sees are marching in procession down and up the stairway as often pictured in art. Rather he sees messengers (= angels) going off on missions and returning from delivering their messages.

House of God . . . gate of heaven (28:17). The portals mentioned in the previous comment were considered sacred space. The link between heaven and earth provided passage for the deity from the gate of his heavenly temple-palace to the sacred space marked

▶ A Temple and the Gate of Heaven

When kings sought to build temples to particular deities, they sought the deity's direction to identify such a sacred place.[A-97] Thus, the "house of God," usually referring to a temple (in 28:17 Jacob identifies a sacred space, but there is no temple built yet to mark the spot), is linked with the "gate of heaven" to the entry to the heavenly abode of deity.

There is a continuum in space between the heavenly dwelling and the earthly one such that they are not simply considered mirror images or paired structures, but in the sense that they are more like the upstairs and downstairs of the same building. Yet it is even more than that, as the earthly

temple can be thought of as actually existing in the heavenly realm. The temple is a place in both worlds,[A-98] just as the grave is a place both on earth and in the netherworld. One might compare it to the wardrobe in the Chronicles of Narnia, which exists in both worlds.

Some temples featured a stairway from the antechamber up to the central cella where the deity dwelt,[A-99] indicating perhaps that the deity's heavenly dwelling was there in the middle of the earthly temple. If this is so, the "gate of heaven" could be considered the entryway to the temple's inner sanctum (whether at the bottom of the stairway or at the top[A-100]).

out on earth for his presence and worship. Such places were marked with temples once their location had been revealed to people living in the area. See sidebar on "A Temple and the Gate of Heaven."

Set it up as a pillar and poured oil on top of it (28:18). In the ancient world, cult symbols (such as the pillar set up here) are abundantly observable.[462] For example, U. Avner has documented 142 independent sites featuring standing stones in the Negev and eastern Sinai alone.[463] An additional thirty-six have been identified in Iron Age Israel.[464] These standing stones could at times be deified (i.e., considered to contain the essence of a deity),[465] probably the function of the two found in the vicinity of the Iron Age temple unearthed at Israelite Arad. Others were believed to represent ancestral spirits,[466] whereas others could simply stand as memorials of treaties or special events (notice the twelve set up by Moses in Ex. 24:4–8).[467]

In early Israelite history such stones were acceptable, but as time progressed and they were more inclined to serve the same function as images, they were rejected along with the idea that deity can inhere in a physical

Stairway of restored Ziggurat at Ur
Bible Scene Multimedia/Maurice Thompson
◀

Standing stone at
Gezer
Dr. Tim Bulkeley,
www.eBibleTools.com
▲

object.[468] This explains why some pillars were innocent enough and legitimate, while others represented apostasy. Most standing stones were unhewn, though some had minimal adornment (e.g., carved hands reaching upward) and a few had intricate reliefs (e.g., the stele of Baal from Ugarit).

In this context the standing stone may well be intended to mark where the presence of God is manifest in Jacob's vision.[469] Jacob has slept in what is in effect the antechamber of a temple, has seen the stairway leading to the gate of heaven (the inner chamber) with the messengers coming and going from the Lord's presence, and has set up a standing stone either to mark the "Holy of Holies" (at the top of the stairway) or the place where Yahweh stood ("beside"[470] the stairway). In an Aramaic treaty text found in Sefire from the eighth century B.C., when the gods are called to witness the agreement, the stone pillars on which the treaty is engraved is inscribed as the "house of God."[471] Alternatively it could function as commemorating the covenant agreement and Jacob's response in a vow.

Made a vow (28:20). Vows in the ancient world generally involved a request made of deity with a promise of a gift in return when the request is fulfilled.[472] The request often concerned protection or provision, and the gift was typically a sacrifice or a donation to the sanctuary of the deity. The details in this chapter conform to that pattern. God has promised protection, provision, and return to the land, so Jacob makes those the condition of his proffered gift: a tithe of all that he acquires during his absence.

Wealth and possession in the ancient world were not based on money, so Jacob expects to gain flocks and herds. Though tithes could at times be a form of taxation, this tithe is not imposed on Jacob. Gifts related to vows were usually given to the temple (whether by means of sacrifice or donation), but in this case it will have to be by sacrifice because donations must be handed over to temple administrators, and there is no formal temple here. Jacob returns to Bethel to fulfill his vow in Genesis 35, and presumably animals are sacrificed at that time (though the text does not say so). Jacob builds an altar (35:1), but no further information is given.

Jacob in Haran (29:1–30:43)

We can't ... until all the flocks are gathered (29:8). Herding contracts in the ancient world were critical to assure the fair distribution of resources that were the foundation for survival. Grazing land and water were often in limited supply.[473] Legal agreements existed between herdsmen and the livestock owners whose animals they cared for since they all shared responsibility for the welfare of the herds and flocks,[474] as well as presumably among livestock owners who shared resources. The latter sort of contract is not well represented in the extant literature, and it is that sort that is probably the basis for this scene at the well, though there may have been more of an informal agreement here.

Herdsmen typically operated outside of urban areas, but often in symbiosis with the sedentary population. It is not unusual to find groups that are farmers part-time and herdsmen part-time. In this passage the herds are being kept in close proximity to the settlement. These groups are not nomadic in lifestyle, but do their herding in an orbit around the settled areas.

You are my own flesh and blood (29:14–15). This initial statement by Laban shows some similarity to terminology used in adoption literature. It is possible that in verse 14 Laban is proposing taking Jacob into partnership, which suggests that Jacob will have some prospects for inheritance. A month later, however, Laban acts as if no such deal has ever been made (or he legally repudiates the arrangement, which he can do) and asks Jacob, "Are you my brother that you should work for nothing?" In this proposal the entire relationship is restructured in that Jacob is considered as doing "work-for-hire" as an employee rather than enjoying a share in the property as a family partner.[475]

Seven years (29:18). The groom and his family traditionally provided a contribution to the bridewealth often referred to as the bride price (see comment on 24:53 and the footnotes). Jacob has brought no wealth with him (the inheritance he will eventually gain has not yet been divided), so the agreement is reached that his seven years labor will serve in lieu of a bride price. Since bride prices averaged thirty to forty shekels of silver in mid-second millennium Nuzi,[476] and since Jacob's work would normally pay about a shekel per month, the substitution of seven years of Jacob's labor for the bride price results in about twice the normal going rate for brides. Perhaps Laban can take advantage of Jacob because Jacob, being penniless and moonstruck, is in a poor bargaining position.

Gave a feast (29:22). According to ancient customs marriage was celebrated as a joyful business transaction between families rather than as a civil or sacred ceremony.[477] Though the personal feelings of the couple were not immaterial, legal, economic, and social issues were predominant in the institution.[478] The marriage did not take place in the vicinity of sacred space, nor did religious personnel officiate. No vows were made in the name of deity and there was certainly no sacramental aspect to the institution. The agreement was often struck years before the marriage took place and initiated a period termed "inchoate marriage."[479]

When the agreed time came, a feast marked the culmination of the agreement after which the marriage was consummated (often within the family compound of the bride's parents).[480] It was not unusual for the wife to continue living with her family as the husband made conjugal visits for several months until the woman conceived.[481] K. van der Toorn observes that "to the ancients a childless marriage is not a full-fledged marriage."[482] Her pregnancy was the signal that the time was right for her to move into the household of her new husband.

It is not our custom (29:26). Hammurabi's law 160 stipulates a penalty for failing to deliver the bride for whom the pride price has been received. The very existence of the law indicates that this breach sometimes occurred, though there it specifies that the woman was given to another man. Laban deflects any accusation of breach of contract by claiming custom as support for his action. Little evidence can substantiate Laban's claim of custom on the basis of ancient Near Eastern documents.[483]

Bridal week (29:27). The marriage was generally consummated on the first night of the feast, but it was not unusual for the marriage feast to last a week or more.[484]

She named him ... (29:32 and passim). For the naming of children with significant names and the importance of a name, see comments on 2:20 and 25:25–26.

So she gave him her servant (30:4, 9). For the practice of giving a handmaiden as a surrogate wife, see comment on 16:2.

Mandrake plants (30:14). The usual identification of this plant is *Mandragora*, frequently believed in the ancient and classical world to possess magical properties, primarily as an aphrodisiac (see Song 7:13)

Mandrake (Mandragora)
Bible Scene Multimedia/Maurice Thompson

with the power to make a barren woman conceive.[485] In Egypt it appears to be the aroma that had the erotic powers.[486] Modern study has confirmed that the fruit is a sedative, narcotic, and purgative.[487] Unusual characteristics include that the shape of its roots is often reminiscent of the human form and that the plant shines in the dark. The plant is a Mediterranean genus of the nightshade family and its physical appearance is described as follows:

> It is a stemless perennial herb with thick, bizarrely branched roots and large, ovate or oblong, very wrinkled leaves growing in a rosette. In winter it bears bluish, bell-shaped flowers on long stalks. The fragrant plum-like, yellowish-red fruits ripen in spring.[488]

Yet there remains some question whether the identification of the fruit in this passage as *Mandragora* is correct since that plant is not known to grow in Mesopotamia.[489] Furthermore, in a pseudepigraphal expansion of this passage (*T. Issachar* 1:3–5, second century B.C.) they are described as apple-like and found by the riverbank, neither of which are true of the *Mandragora*, though from the same period the LXX translators rendered it *mandragorou*. The association continues to be made in later Greek, Arabic, and rabbinic sources.

After Rachel gave birth (30:25). A woman's status in the marriage was not fully attained until she bore a son. In some contracts from the second millennium, a time limit is set after which she can be divorced should an heir not be provided.[490] Prior to Joseph's birth, it would have been inappropriate for Jacob to leave with Rachel since her status would be more secure with family in the area.

Learned by divination (30:27). The details of the divination are not given here, so we do not know what sort of specialist Laban consulted (if any) or what class of divination was used. Divination is divided into categories labeled "inspired"

(divine communication using a human intermediary, e.g., prophecy, dreams) or "deductive" (divine communication through events and phenomena—either provoked situations, such as lots or extispicy using animal entrails, or passive, such as celestial observation).[491] Given Laban's report of the result of the divination, it is most likely that he consulted an expert in extispicy. In this procedure, a binary (yes/no) question is posed and then the specialist slaughters an animal and examines the entrails (usually the liver) for indications that their experience dictates as being positive or negative. To get the information Laban conveys, he must have asked whether Jacob's God was the one bringing prosperity.

They will be my wages (30:32). Shepherds' wages in the ancient Near East were usually the byproducts of the herd (mostly a percentage of the wool and milk). Sometimes the shepherd would also get to keep a percentage of the new births.[492] The percentage is not often stated in the texts, but one text from Ischali indicates that the shepherd was allowed to keep twenty percent.[493] Rather than using a percentage, Jacob requests that his share be those that are marked in their coloring. The Awassi fat-tailed sheep was most common in the region and was usually white. Goats were typically black. Deviations from these norms were relatively uncommon and would certainly have been less than twenty percent in normal circumstances.

111

Genesis

Rams and sheep
at feeding
troughs
Frederick J. Mabie

Placed the peeled branches in all the watering troughs (30:38). In verses 41–42 Jacob shows some knowledge of breeding by favoring the stronger animals. The principle of "like breeds like" is common in pastoral societies worldwide.[494] But his use of the visual aids in the water troughs indicates, unsurprisingly, that he also is bound to the superstitions of the day. No evidences have yet been found in the ancient Near East of the procedure used by Jacob or similar ones based on the premise that what the animal sees will influence the lambs.

Jacob Leaves Haran (31:1–55)

Does he not regard us as foreigners? (31:15). The bride price paid by the groom was often transferred to the bride as an indirect dowry. As such it became part of a financial reserve for her that served as an insurance policy of sorts.[495] This claim of Leah and Rachel suggests that they have neither direct nor indirect dowry (their share of the inheritance), and therefore no financial security would be provided by staying in the region of their family. The value of Jacob's fourteen years of labor have apparently never been assigned to their present or future holdings.

According to Westbrook, if Leah and Rachel remain in their father's household, they will not receive this inheritance share until his death, "but at the same time they despair of receiving it even then, if their father, as his conduct hitherto has indicated, has no intention of making a formal assignment."[496] Without such an assignment, Laban alone has profited from Jacob's labor, meaning that he has, in effect, simply sold his daughters. Van Seters suggests that the absence of resources available to the daughters may simply be the result of Jacob's continued success,[497] but this does not explain their declaration that their father has sold them.

Household gods (31:19). The household gods (*terāpîm*) were images that represented deceased ancestors in order to venerate them.[498] See sidebar on "Teraphim and Family Gods."

Pursued Jacob for seven days (31:23). The site of Mizpah (where Laban catches up to Jacob) is not known, but from Haran to the northern end of the hill country of Gilead is approximately 350 miles. To reach there in ten days (Jacob's three-day head start plus seven days for Laban's travel, 31:22–23), Jacob must travel thirty-five miles a day, an incredible rate; caravans usually managed twenty-three at most. Sheep and goats could neither achieve nor maintain that pace (see 33:13), and women and children would likewise slow down the speed of travel. Given the circumstances, Jacob could not expect to cover more than ten miles per day.

This has led even conservative commentators to suspect that we are reading something wrong.[499] Whenever the biblical text refers to a journey (Heb. *derek*) of a particular number of days, the number is one, three, or seven,[500] suggesting the possibility that the expression is idiomatic rather than precise.[501] Yet that does not solve all the problems, because if Jacob travels at a rate of only ten miles per day, one would expect Laban to catch him long before he arrives at the hill country of Gilead. Laban can perhaps travel twenty miles per day, in

▶ Teraphim and Family Gods

There are a variety of opinions about the *tᵉrāpîm*, and there probably were various practices with regard to whether these ancestors were worshiped or considered to have even quasi-divine status. Minimally, ancestor images provided a focus for rites related to the care of the dead and also were at times used in divination.

In some of the archives from the mid-second millennium B.C., legal documents allow us to see how the family gods figured in the inheritance. At Nuzi, several texts indicate that the principal heir received the family gods.[A-101] In texts from Emar, one document suggests that the household gods were not to be given to a man outside the family.[A-102] Rachel would have no right to this portion of the inheritance, nor would Jacob. Laban is logically distressed over this breach of inheritance practices as well as concerned that the care of the ancestors will be jeopardized by the loss of the images. "The family gods were not only the tie between the family unit and its property but also the very heart of the family."[A-103]

We can therefore conclude that Rachel's interest in the *tᵉrāpîm* has more to do with family and inheritance than with the issue of worshiping other gods. The spirits of the ancestors were not substitute deities, though some uses of them were certainly proscribed in ideal Yahwism as it eventually took shape.

When women married, it was customary for them to transfer their loyalty to the gods of their husband.[A-104] "Women were not free to choose the god they would worship," but were automatically by marriage bound to the god of the husband.[A-105] In most cases, because of endogamy, the god of her fathers would be the same as the god of her husband, because people in the same geographical location, and especially people in the same clan, tended to worship the same deities.

Ancestor images
Z. Radovan/www.
BibleLand
Pictures.com

▶

Gilead mountains
west of Gerasa
Todd Bolen/www.
BiblePlaces.com

which case he could have caught Jacob after only three days, about sixty-five miles from Haran, soon after he crossed the Euphrates at Til-Barsib.

Certainly the results will be different if one assumes that Jacob is traveling faster or Laban slower, but the numbers we have used (ten and twenty miles per day respectively) are the most defensible. If Jacob is traveling twelve or thirteen miles per day, and Laban is traveling seventeen, Laban would catch Jacob after about seven days (as the text seems to suggest), but they would only be about 110 miles from Haran. That would put them somewhere near Ebla, still only one third of the way to the hill country of Gilead. The only conceivable solution at the moment that explains Laban's not catching up to Jacob before the hill country of Gilead is to assume that it takes Laban a week or ten days to prepare for the trip before he can set out and that he cannot travel very fast (after all, he is over 150 years old at this point).[502]

Having my period (31:35). In the ancient world menstruation was a mysterious thing. Blood was often connected to impurity, and since impurity was contagious, menstruating women were typically isolated, and there was some reluctance to touch them or even be near them.[503] In some cultures, the monthly bleeding made a woman vulnerable to demonic attack—she was considered a woman under taboo (see comment on 18:9).[504] Any of these aspects of belief would have made Laban reticent to search Rachel's tent too carefully.

Your sheep and goats (31:38–39). The claims of Jacob match up well with the normal sorts of arrangements that were made between shepherds and sheep owners.[505]

The terms of the contract reflect the inescapable fact that the shepherd is beyond the control of the owner: the accounts were drawn up at the spring shearing when the wool was weighed and the main lambing season was over, and a

▶

heap of stones is gathered. The agreement is then marked ceremonially by a communal meal and the formal proclamation of stipulations and an oath. The pillar has been discussed previously (see 28:18) and serves two purposes here: to commemorate the covenant and to mark a territorial boundary (31:52).

Jacob's obligation concerns the treatment of his wives, Laban's daughters. He agrees not to take other wives (an act that would potentially lower the status of Leah and Rachel in Jacob's family). This sort of clause is also found in marriage contracts from the town of Nuzi in the mid-second millennium.[508] There it appears that marriage contracts were typically drawn up only when there were unusual circumstances that called for a document to protect the rights of the groom, the legal status of the wife, or the property rights of children.[509]

Jacob's Entry into Canaan (32:1–32)

Mahanaim (32:2). The name means "two camps," referring to Jacob's camp and the camp of the angels. When he left the land, he encountered angels (28:12); now they encounter him as he reenters. The precise

▶

new agreement was made for the coming year. This used the annual productivity ratio in respect of birth of new animals set against expected deaths. The shepherd normally kept all the milk products, and a fixed amount of wool per adult animal plus any animals in excess of the agreed ratio, while tradition also allowed him a food ration and a clothing allowance, as well as the pay of a subordinate.[506]

Typical agreements assumed there would be a 15 percent natural loss and an 80 percent birth rate.[507]

Heap is a witness (31:48). In verse 45 Jacob responds to the suggestion of a covenant by setting up a pillar, after which a

location of Mahanaim is unconfirmed, but assessing the valley of the Jabbok River for major sites, the consensus opinion associates it with Tell edh-Dhahab el Gharbi,[510] which stands by a natural ford of the river. The site has not been excavated.

Land of Seir (32:3). This land is identified with the mountainous central region of Edom (elevations mostly over 5,000 feet) that runs along the eastern side of the Arabah from the Brook Zered at the south end of the Dead Sea to the Gulf of Aqaba.[511]

Selected a gift (32:13). Jacob's gifts serve several functions,[512] but above all are to indicate to Esau that Jacob is not interested in taking anything that Esau may have inherited. The gift of 220 goats, 220 sheep, 30 camels (plus their young), 50 cows/bulls, and 30 donkeys is generous. It is larger than many towns would have been able to pay in tribute to conquering kings even at later dates. If Esau or his men had plunder on their mind, it saves them the trouble

and makes the trip worth their time and effort. Assyrian sources contain numerous lists of booty collected in their conquests. A list of tribute collected by Tukulti-Ninurta II, a ninth-century Assyrian king from the town of Hindanu (near Mari on the Middle Euphrates), is given in the sidebar on "Tribute List from Hindanu."[513]

> ▶ **Tribute List from Hindanu**

10 minas gold	10 minas silver
2 talents tin	30 dromedaries
50 oxen	30 asses
14 ducks	200 sheep

Let me go, for it is daybreak (32:26). This encounter takes place by a river, the stranger can be interpreted as fearing daylight, and Jacob clearly believes the wrestler is a supernatural being. These factors together led to a multitude of ingenious mythological explanations, based on literature from much later times.[514] On the basis of anthropological folklore and Greco-Roman literature, it has been proposed that it is a river demon or a guardian of the fords, a creature of the night who attacks Jacob. The data relevant to comparative studies, however, should not be sought in such literature. It is much more difficult to find in the literature of the ancient Near East examples of river gods and supernatural beings who cannot be seen in the light of day. There is no shortage of river gods in ancient Mesopotamia and Syria and they can be antagonistic,[515] but the idea of these gods attacking humans to prevent their crossing is not attested in the ancient Near East.[516]

One tale from Hittite literature has some intriguing features in the context of a ritual to honor the gods Teshub and Ḥebat.[517] The goddess speaks something to the king and begins to depart or at least states an intention to do so. The next section has some familiarity:

[62]The king (answers), "Come back!"

The goddess (says) as follows: [63]"If I come back, will you in whatever manner—(such as) with horses and chariots—[64](strive to) prevail over me?"

The king (says) as follows, "I shall (strive to) prevail over you."

The goddess (says) as follows, [65]["Make (then) a wish"]

The king (says) as follows, "Give me life, health, sons (and) daughters in the future, [[(strong weapons)]], and put my enemies under my feet."[518]

Clearly, there is no actual combat here. Common features include only that the human being detains the deity, conveys his intention to prevail, and requests a blessing. The most important common motif to be recognized here is the human risk in initiating a confrontation (though it never becomes physical) with a divine representative in order to gain audience and receive a blessing. Jacob and the Hittite king are both pursuing the same sort of goal. The Hittite text has been identified as a rite designed to ensure that the gods give powers to the king.[519]

Jacob and Esau Meet (33:1–20)

Bowed down to the ground seven times (33:3). This practice is attested protocol used when a vassal has an audience with his superior. Most notably, the petty city-state kings of Canaan speak of themselves acting this way toward the Egyptian pharaoh in the Amarna letters (mid-second millennium).[520]

Succoth (33:17). Tell Deir 'Alla is now commonly identified as biblical Succoth. It is located east of the Jordan near the confluence of the Jordan

and Jabbok Rivers. It is on the north side of the Jabbok, about seven miles west of Mahanaim. Excavations at the site have identified occupation levels from nearly three millennia, from the Chalcolithic period into the Iron Age.[521]

Shechem (33:18). See comment on 12:6. Shechem is about thirty-five miles from Succoth—perhaps a weeklong journey with the herds and families. Though there is no mention of a settlement when Abraham first passes through on his journey into the land, nearly two centuries have passed, and now there is a city here built and settled by the Hivites.

Little is known of the Hivites, but they are thought to be associated with the Hurrians, and in Joshua's time they occupied the city of Gibeon (Josh. 9). Archaeological excavation at the site coincides with the biblical information to the extent that the site was not settled at the end of the Early Bronze Period but was resettled sometime in the Middle Bronze

I period after 1900 B.C.[522] The city is also named in the Egyptian execration texts from the Twelfth Dynasty (19th century B.C.). Evidence for a city wall dates to the Middle Bronze II period.[523]

Hundred pieces of silver (33:19). The monetary unit referred to here (*qeśîṭâ*) has not been identified. It occurs elsewhere only in Joshua 24:32 (a reference back to this passage) and Job 42:11. Neither archaeology nor extrabiblical literature provides further information. One possibility is that these pieces are not shaped like coins but take some other form. In Egypt at this time

rings of silver (known as *šᶜat*) were used for exchange.[524] The richest mining zone for silver in the ancient world was in Anatolia.[525]

Altar (33:20). See comment on 12:8.

Jacob's Family and the Shechemites (34:1–31)

Took her and violated her (34:2). In societies in which marriages were arranged with economic and sociological goals in mind, the couple did not always have an opportunity to pursue their love interests. One way around the problem of parents unwilling to indulge their children's desires was to bypass the process and engage in sex. Whether this was only the expression of interest on the part of the would-be husband, in which case it would be termed "rape," or involved a mutual decision of engaging in consensual sex, the result is similar—the parents would generally have to go ahead with concluding the marriage.

Exodus 22:16–17 and Deuteronomy 22:28–29 both include regulations to address this situation. It is also regulated in ancient Near Eastern law.[526] Frymer-Kensky's evaluation is that what took place in Genesis 34 should be considered "wrongful intercourse."

> To use contemporary American terminology, sleeping with Dinah was statutory rape. In our society, girls below a certain age (the "age of consent") are not free to arrange sexual liaisons, and men are not free to sleep with them. Dinah was very young, a *yalda* (v. 4). Even today, when a Congressman sleeps with a high school girl, when a cult leader has "consensual" sex with the young girls of the cult, our society is outraged, and the man can be considered a felon. In ancient society, unmarried girls never acquired the right of consent. Only the prostitute owned her own sexuality. By sleeping with [Dinah], Shechem was acting as if she had no family to protect, guard and marry her. As the

brothers say, "should our sister be treated as a whore?" He has disgraced her, and through her, the whole family.[527]

Frymer-Kensky further points out that whether Dinah has been raped or virtually "eloped," the family is shamed by the incident. A rape would be demeaning to Dinah and the family. But if Dinah were in any way involved in the decision, the family would be shamed not only by Shechem's act, but by Dinah's lack of respect for the family.[528]

Price for the bride (34:12). See comments on 20:16; 24:53; 29:18.

Circumcised (34:14). See comment on 17:10.

City gate (34:24). The city gate is the place where business was conducted (see comment on 19:10), and Shechem had a city gate as early as Middle Bronze II. In addition, the text refers to those who "went out of the city gate"—a possible reference to the army.[529]

Jacob Returns to Bethel (35:1–29)

Get rid of the foreign gods (35:2). In order to fulfill the vow made to Yahweh in Genesis 28, Jacob commands several activities, each with ritual significance. Jacob's vow had included not only the payment of a tithe, but the promise that Yahweh would be his God. Consequently, he instructs his household to bury their foreign gods (v. 4), whose presence is indicative of divided loyalty. Burial is one of the approved methods of discarding images.[530] These are not the household gods Rachel brought with her, for those were not strictly divine images but images of the ancestors (see comment on 31:19). Instead, the buried images are most likely ones plundered from the town of Shechem.

Purify yourselves and change your clothes (35:2). Purification is a normal preparation for ritual activity. Those officiating in rituals often have outfits befitting their position, from the elaborate garments of priests and kings to the linen of assistants. But here the celebrants are directed to change clothes. Some ritual texts, especially those involving the king, portray him putting on clean garments for a ritual.[531] For many celebrants, however, the issue may not be what they are changing into, but what they are changing out of. When work or other activity has sullied one's clothing, it is appropriate to change clothes in order to avoid ritual impurity. For Jacob's entourage, this may be necessitated simply to eliminate the dirt and grime of travel with all the animals, but it could also refer to the residue of the recent massacre at Shechem.

Rings in their ears (35:4). The earrings referred to are closely related to the images. Commentators commonly suggest tentatively that earrings in their shape or symbolism may be quasi-representations of deity themselves. Keel, however, has pointed out that archaeology thus far attests no earrings in the shape of deity,[532] though it is speculated that crescent shaped earrings may be symbolic representations of the moon god.

V. Hurowitz points out that many images in the ancient Near East were adorned with earrings,[533] a fact that leads him to suggest that the phrase "the rings in their ears" in this verse, the pronoun "their" points to the gods, not to Jacob's household. That is, as they dispose of the images, they should not hold back the earrings from the images for themselves. N. Fox makes the case that the earrings in the images indicated their willingness to hear supplicants, while the worshipers wore earrings to indicate their willingness to obey.[534]

Oak at Shechem (34:4). For discussion of the importance of trees, see comment on 12:6.

Set up a stone pillar (35:14). Here again the standing stone is intended to mark the place where God's presence is manifest, but it also serves as a testimony to the covenant agreement that is communicated. For more on this, see comment on 28:18.

Rachel's tomb (35:20). The text, geography, and traditions all complicate precise location here.[535] Jacob is traveling south from Bethel (35:16) to arrive eventually in Hebron (35:27). Specifically they are on the way to Ephrath/Bethlehem (cf. 48:7) and have not yet arrived at Migdal Eder (35:19–21). They are therefore following the main north-south road through the central hill country. From Bethel to Bethlehem is just under twenty miles (going through Jerusalem). In 1 Samuel 10:2 Rachel's tomb is identified as being at Zelzah on the border of Benjamin (cf. Jer. 31:15, which has

This ear-stele was dedicated by Bai, citizen of Deir el-Medineh (lower left) to the "good ram Amun." Ears signify the god who listens to the petitioner.
Erich Lessing/Art Resource, NY, courtesy of the Egyptian Museum, Cairo

Traditional site of Rachel's tomb in Bethlehem
Jack Hazut

been interpreted to suggest it is near Ramah, just east of Gibeon, more in the middle of Benjaminite territory).[536] Jerusalem is on Benjamin's southern border with Judah. Zelzah is unknown other than this reference.[537]

Part of the confusion occurs because the term "Ephrath" has multiple references (cf. 1 Chron. 2:50–51). Besides its association with Bethlehem (see Mic. 5:2), it can refer to people from the tribe of Ephraim. The traditional tomb of Rachel today located outside Bethlehem does not fit these details. One last wild card is the location of Migdal Eder, which unfortunately is unknown, but it may not have helped since it could be some distance from Rachel's tomb, just not as far as Hebron. Given all of this information, it is most logical to locate Rachel's tomb somewhere along the road from Bethel to Jerusalem, but it is difficult to be more precise.

Slept with his father's concubine (35:22). Though this is technically an incestuous act, the offense here is treated more as social usurpation than as sexual immorality. Possession of the concubines that belonged to the head of the clan was presumably a sign of leadership in the clan.[538] When the father died, the care and ownership of the concubines (as part of his property) passed to the next head of the clan. To seize ownership of the concubines prior to the father's death would then be seen as an act of subversion and disrespect (comparable to seizing land or herds), but would not be unusual if succession to clan leadership were contested.

In this context, Reuben's offense against his father circumvents proper succession procedures and implies that the father is powerless. Beyond clan leadership, Wenham suggests that Reuben's act is not necessarily to secure his own position in the clan, but by treating Bilhah this way, it assures that Leah will assume the place of principal wife (since Rachel has just died).[539] In this sense it is an offense against Bilhah, but again, not just in a sexual sense, but by an act intended to undermine her status in the clan.

Line of Esau (36:1–43)

Esau, the father of the Edomites (36:9). The earliest mention of the Edomites outside of the Bible is in the fifteenth-century campaign list of Thutmose III. In records from Egypt during this period, the territory is inhabited by nomads (*Shasu*). Archaeologists have found no Edomite records or literature. Material remains from the Middle and Late Bronze Age are scarce, but this would be expected given the type of society represented by Esau and his descendants.

Joseph and His Brothers (37:1–36)

Richly ornamented robe (37:3). An Egyptian tomb painting from the nineteenth century B.C. depicts a troupe of Semitic merchants coming down to Egypt. Some of the men are wearing knee-length, sleeveless garments that are colorful. We do not know whether this was the type of garment Jacob gave Joseph, but it gives an idea of the fashions of the general period. A fresco from Mari (eighteenth century B.C.) portrays priests dressed in garments made of rectangular pieces of cloth of various colors sewn together into a long strip that is then wrapped around the body seven or eight turns from the ankles up to the chest and then draped over one shoulder.

Various types of clothing communicated rank and status in society. In the ancient world the fabrics, ornamentation, colors, length, and hem all played a role in indicating the position of the wearer. Undoubtedly Joseph's coat designated authority as well as favor, but little more can be said because the Hebrew word occurs only here and in the passage describing Tamar's cloak (2 Sam. 13:19). No cognates from comparative Semitic languages offer any confident clarification.[540] The traditional interpretation of a "coat of many colors" goes back to the Greek and Latin translations of the Old Testament (though now abandoned in many scholarly circles). Most commentators favor something more along the line of a full-length coat or a long-sleeved coat,[541] reflected in Aquila's Greek translation in the second century A.D.

Joseph had a dream (37:5). The ancients believed dreams derived from the divine realm and were therefore taken seriously. The ordinary dreams of common people were believed to contain omens that communicated information about what the gods were doing, though they usually made no reference to deity. Dreams were often filled with symbolism necessitating an interpreter, though at times the symbols were reasonably self-evident. The information that came through dreams was not believed to be irreversible.

Dreams of a rise to power, like the ones Joseph had, are known in the ancient Near East, notably one by Sargon, king of Akkad, half a millennium earlier than Joseph. Sargon, cupbearer to King Urzababa, recounts his dream to the king as follows:

> There was a single young woman [the goddess Inanna],
> she was high as the heavens, she was broad as the earth,
> She was firmly set as the base of a wall.
> For me, she drowned you in a great [river] of blood. [542]

Urzababa's advisors reinterpreted the dream to suggest that it was Sargon who was going to die rather than the king. This demonstrates how even fairly transparent dreams could be reinterpreted to suit the desires of one party or another. Joseph's dream does not indicate the death of his brothers, simply their subordination to him. There is nothing in the dream that leads them to consider

Head which has long been believed to be representation of Sargon now commonly thought to represent his successor Naram-Sin
Erich Lessing/ Art Resource, NY, courtesy of the Iraq Museum

◀

Image from the tomb of Beni Hassan shows troupe of Semitic merchants coming down to Egypt.
Lepsius Denkmaler

▼

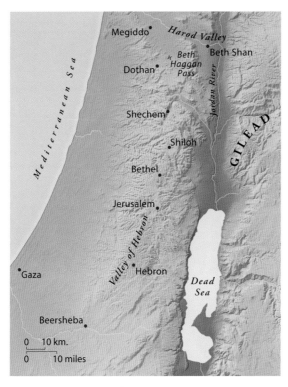

Joseph will be first among his brothers (in which case it would be similar to the patriarchal blessings found in 9:26 and 27:29), but that Joseph rises to prominence in the entire ancestral line, superseding his parents in significance. This justifies the inclusion of family members living or dead. Another option is that, since Joseph was still less than ten years old when his mother died, Rachel's handmaid, Bilhah, had been a surrogate mother to Joseph and Benjamin, so that the dream perhaps refers to her.[543]

Dothan (37:17). From Jacob's home base in the Valley of Hebron, Shechem is just over fifty miles, and Dothan is about fourteen more. The journey would therefore take Joseph four to five days. Dothan was a site of significant size and was occupied during this period. It is by a valley that cuts through the Carmel range joining the coastal plains and the Jezreel Valley.

It is no surprise that a caravan passed by since Dothan is on the usual caravan route from Gilead to Egypt. The route crossed the Jordan at Beth Shan and then passed through the Harod Valley to the town of Jezreel. From there a caravan could follow the International Coastal Highway either by proceeding west toward Megiddo and going through the Iron Pass in the Carmel range, or by going south toward the Dothan Valley and taking the route that ran along the north side of the valley and through the Hadera Pass to the coast. Alternatively, some caravans followed the National Highway through the Beth Haggan Pass (= modern Jenin) to Dothan, and from there through Samaria to Shechem, Shiloh, Bethel, Jerusalem, Hebron, and Beersheba.[544]

Excavations were conducted at Dothan in the mid-twentieth century B.C. and have recently been published.[545] The site was abandoned at the end of Early Bronze III and resettled and fortified in Middle Bronze IIB; it was therefore occupied from 1750 to

that Joseph's eventual prominence will extend beyond the confines of the family, for only his family members bow down to him. It would not have occurred to any of them that Joseph would rise to the position of second in command of a dominant world power.

Both in Sargon's and Joseph's dreams the dreamer's life is put in jeopardy as those who would be supplanted in his rise to authority seek to prevent the fulfillment of that dream by eliminating the one marked for ascendancy. Of course, there is no reason to think of literary dependence here, only to observe the common motifs that reflect widespread human experience.

A curious feature of the second dream (37:9–10) is the symbolic presence of Joseph's mother and all eleven brothers. This is odd in that his mother had previously died giving birth to her second son. The inclusion of Joseph's parents is of significance here, because it indicates that the message of the dream does not just suggest that

Dothan
Bible Scene Multimedia/Maurice Thompson

about 1450 in Late Bronze I. This story does not indicate whether there was a town at Dothan or not.

Cisterns (37:20). Where wells could not be dug and precipitation was sufficient, cisterns were constructed to catch rain and runoff during the wet season to provide some supply for the dry season.[546] The area of Dothan averages twenty-four to twenty-eight inches of rainfall annually; thus, if 20 percent of the runoff from a one hectare field could be caught and stored, about 5,000 sheep could be supplied with water for the year.[547]

As one can imagine, water collected in cisterns easily became stagnant. It was not unusual for dry cisterns to be miry at the bottom because the runoff would carry sediment. But if it were maintained for constant use, it would have been cleaned out regularly. The region of Dothan features limestone, which is porous, and thus cisterns were coated on the inside with plaster (a procedure documented in the Early Bronze and Middle Bronze periods [e.g., at Taanach and Megiddo respectively]) to prevent absorption of the water.

Caravan of Ishmaelites (37:25). The text refers to both Ishmaelites and Midianites, kinfolk both descended from Abraham (Midianites through Keturah, 25:2; Ishmaelites through Hagar). The forebears of these two peoples were then half-brothers to one another (and to Isaac) and uncles to Jacob; thus, these traders are second or third cousins to Joseph and his brothers. Both clans occupied the Arabian desert region. One recent study sees the two terms as alternative ways of referring to the same group.[548]

Cistern at Arad
Dr. Tim Bulkeley, eBibleTools.com

We might add that such a variation may be explained if both groups are operating together at this period of history. For example, perhaps Midianite merchants are serving as middlemen for the Ishmaelite businessmen. The Midianites are the negotiators and buyers fronting for their Ishmaelite bosses, who provide them with the capital (like floor traders for investment companies). So the Midianites do the business (37:28, 36), but the goods belong to the Ishmaelites, who are financing the caravan (37:25–28; 39:1).

The goods that the caravan is transporting are common commodities for trade. Myrrh was imported from southern Arabia and must have come by caravan up the Incense Road, which traversed the west coast of Arabia, to the King's Highway, which led north-south through Transjordan (east of the Jordan Valley) to Damascus. Perhaps the Ishmaelites purchased this myrrh and other spices from the Arabian caravans passing through Gilead on the King's Highway and then added to their shipment some of the balm that was native to that region to make their trip down to Egypt.[549]

Sold him for twenty shekels of silver (37:28). Kitchen has done an extensive study of slave prices in the ancient Near East. His findings confirmed that twenty shekels was the going rate in the mid-second millennium. Examples from Hammurabi's Code (§§116, 214, and 252), Mari, and a variety of Old Babylonian documents support this. In contrast, prices in southern Mesopotamia about 2000 B.C. were ten shekels and by the time of Nuzi and Ugarit (fourteenth and thirteenth centuries) the price was more like thirty shekels. By the time we get into the first millennium, the going rate was fifty shekels, and by the Persian period, eighty to a hundred shekels was common.[550]

Sackcloth (37:34). The Akkadian term for sackcloth is *bašāmu*. The most relevant usage of it is in an Esarhaddon inscription in which he is said to have "wrapped his body in sackcloth befitting a penitent sinner."[551]

Note also the Adad-Guppi autobiography in which the mother of Nabonidus says: "In order to appease the heart of my god and my goddess, I did not put on a garment of excellent wool, silver, gold, a fresh garment; I did not allow perfumes (or) fresh oil to touch my body. I was clothed in a torn garment. My fabric was sackcloth."[552] See sidebar on "Mourning in the Baal Epic."

Judah and Tamar (38:1–30)

Fulfill your duty to her as a brother-in-law (38:8). The custom of levirate marriage mandated that if a man died without a male heir, a relative was to sire a son with the widow on his behalf.[553] A number of possible motives or anticipated results may underlie this custom, and the issue is still disputed. Alternative and not unrelated possibilities include provision of an heir, protection of the family holdings and/or dowry, or caring for the widow. Information from the ancient Near East comes from family documents from Emar as well as Hittite laws and Middle Assyrian laws.[554]

Westbrook points out that care for the widow cannot be seen as the sole motive, for then the legislation would simply mandate that the dead husband's family care for her.[555] He also points out that it is unlikely for the retention and benefit of the dowry to be the motivation, for then the new husband would have much to gain and would hardly view the task as unpleasant duty.[556] The primary beneficiary of the practice must therefore be considered to be the dead husband rather than the surviving family. But as Westbrook concludes, it is not simply for the memory of the dead father that an heir must be born, but so that the deceased might be provided with an heir to his estate. If the land has been forfeited, the relative must redeem it for the widow and then produce an heir to whom to pass it.[557]

It should be pointed out that the law pertains when brothers are living together (cf. Deut. 25:5). Westbrook concludes that

▶ Mourning in the Baal Epic

The Baal Epic from Ugarit contains an extensive description of mourning:

Then Beneficent El the Benign
Descends from his seat, sits on the footstool,
[And] from the footstool, sits on the earth.
  He pours dirt on his head for mourning,
  Dust on his crown for lamenting;
  For clothing he puts on sackcloth.
  With a stone he scrapes his skin,
  Double-slits with a blade.
    He cuts cheeks and chin,
    Furrows the length of his arm.
    He plows his chest like a garden,
    Like a valley he furrows the back
    He raises his voice and cries.[A-106]

Some of the key words here have alternative translations. For instance, instead of referring to sackcloth, some translators refer to a loincloth.[A-107] But this does demonstrate that Israelite mourning practices had much in common with those in the rest of the ancient Near East.

this refers to a situation in which the inheritance has not yet been divided. In such a case, if one brother dies, each of the others would receive a larger share.[558] Three circumstances call for the invoking of the levirate rule:[559]

  father is alive and brothers are still living in his house

  father is dead but the inheritance has not yet been divided

  land has been alienated and levir must redeem it

None of the ancient Near Eastern material reflects identical circumstances, but shows that concern for the central issues was shared across the ancient world. The specific

▶ Middle Assyrian Laws A43

If a man wither pours oil on her head or brings (dishes for) the banquet, (after which) the son to whom he assigned the wife either dies or flees, he shall give her in marriage to whichever of his remaining sons he wishes, from the oldest to the youngest of at least ten years of age.[A-108]

▶ **Hittite Law 193**

If a man has a wife, and the man dies, his brother shall take his widow as wife. (If the brother dies,) his father shall take her. When afterwards his father dies, his (i.e., the father's) brother shall take the woman whom he had.[A-108]

Hittite Laws
Istanbul Archaeological Museum; © Dr. James C. Martin
▲

wording of the most pertinent documents can be found in the accompanying sidebar.[560]

Live as a widow (38:11). A widow without children was a woman without legal, economic, or social status—a woman without a household.[561] Judah here relegates Tamar (through his continuing authority over her)[562] to the protection of her father's household. This is unusual in that a dowry would have been initially paid by her father precisely for the purpose of supporting her in situations such as this. It is unlikely that her father would have had any legal obligation to support her. Her widow's clothes (38:14) would be sufficiently distinctive to mark her station, but our sources are inadequate for determining what these clothes looked like.

Prostitute (38:15). Sheep-shearing time was payday, and the income windfall, the celebratory atmosphere, and the isolation of the men from the family compound all were conducive to the activity of prostitutes. Prostitution in the ancient world can be divided into a number of different categories, and there is some dispute concerning the labels and descriptions.

Particularly debatable is what is called "sacred prostitution" (in which the proceeds go the temple) and "cultic prostitution" (which is performed as a rite of fertility).[563]

The latter is only attested in relation to the tightly regulated sacred marriage rites and was not engaged in by the public at large. It is not legitimately labeled "prostitution." With regard to the former, though undoubtedly secular prostitutes might congregate around the temple (especially at feast times), evidence is lacking for the temples profiting from or organizing prostitution (though Deut. 23:18 makes it clear that such a practice did exist).[564]

Westenholz identifies some groups of women in the Old Babylonian period (e.g., *naditu, qadištu*) who were regulated by codes and identified with male deities, and whose sexuality was controlled by either celibacy or marriage.[565] These were often associated with temples. Other groups (e.g., the *ḥarimtu*) were associated with female deities, had no regulating codes, and were uncontrolled sexually.[566] The latter typically operated from the tavern and acted for pay.

Tamar is referred to by two separate terms in this passage. In verse 15 Judah considers her a *zōnâ*, the normal Hebrew word for "prostitute" (used also in 38:24). He reaches this conclusion not because her face is veiled (that detail is given to explain why he did not recognize her—usually prostitutes were unveiled),[567] but because she has stationed herself by the road as a prostitute would. But when Judah sends his friend to look for her, the friend inquires concerning the *qᵉdēšâ* (38:21–22; NIV: "shrine prostitute").[568]

This latter term is used only two other times in the Old Testament (Deut. 23:18; Hos. 4:14).[569] Ugaritic texts list women similarly labeled (*qdš*) among the temple personnel, and Akkadian literature attests those who were dedicated for life to serve the temple with a cognate term (*qadištu*).[570] These shrine functionaries were not by definition prostitutes—they had other, legitimate roles. But in practice, it may not have been uncommon for them to engage in prostitution. By inquiring after the *qᵉdēšâ* Judah's friend has concealed the specifics in ambiguity—there may be a number of reasons a gift would be brought to a shrine functionary.

Have her burned to death (38:24). It was a fact of life and society that sometimes widows were forced into prostitution (either regular or occasional) in order to live. Yet it was still unacceptable behavior and was treated severely. The punishment of burning is rare and reserved for the most serious of sexual crimes (cf. Lev. 20:14; 21:9 for the only other biblical occurrences). In ancient Near Eastern legal texts, burning is likewise a rare punishment, but used in similar circumstances: for a *naditu* (see previous comment) who opens a tavern or enters a tavern to drink beer, and for incest with one's mother.[571] This was a most serious punishment since it probably precluded proper burial.

Seal ... cord ... staff (38:18). In the ancient world legal identification was not by signature or specially assigned numbers as today. The seal was the most common form of identification.[572] In Mesopotamia inscribed cylinders were used (and often worn around the neck), whereas in the rest of the ancient world scarab or stamp seals were carved in intaglio on disk-shaped bits of stone (the size of a small coin), usually decorated with some sort of simple picture and occasionally with the individual's name and/or position.[573] These were often pierced so as to be worn some-

where on the body, often around the neck on a cord, probably referred to in this verse. Stamp seals are attested as early as the seventh millennium B.C. Neolithic period. Cylinder seals made their appearance in the early fourth millennium.

The staff that Judah leaves with Tamar must have also been distinctive and capable of identifying the owner. One possibility is that it was a staff that designated the head of the family (cf. Num. 17:2). Akkadian *ḫaṭṭu* is used for the scepter of a king, but also for the shepherd's staff and the staff that serves as the insignia of office for important people. It seems that the top of the staff was often engraved.

Joseph in Egypt (39:1–45:28)

Where the king's prisoners were confined (39:20). Jails were not common in the ancient world since imprisonment was not a standard punishment for crimes. If Potiphar truly believed that Joseph, his slave, was guilty of sexually assaulting his wife, execution would have been the swift and normal response. Instead, Joseph is confined where political prisoners were kept to await trial, judgment, or execution.[574]

Since Potiphar is referred to as the "captain of the guard" (39:1) and later Joseph meets Pharaoh's other officials in the house of the captain of the guard (40:3), it appears that Joseph is detained under Potiphar's supervision and is there again given authority. In other words, he is transferred to another part of Potiphar's house. That does not mean that his imprisonment is a farce, but it suggests that Potiphar's anger may well have been directed toward his wife and that after an adequate show of indignation, Joseph is gradually again moved into a position of authority.[575]

Middle Bronze
II scarabs from
Lachish
Todd Bolen/www.
BiblePlaces.com

◄

▶ Egyptian Tale of Two Brothers

An Egyptian tale from the thirteenth century B.C. recounts the story of the brothers Anubis and Bata. Anubis's wife seduces Bata and when refused, accuses him to her husband of rape.[A-109] The husband acts on the testimony of his wife and seeks to punish the innocent victim. From here the story goes an entirely different direction than the Joseph story, so the only real parallel is the false accusation of sexual advances by the woman spurned against the virtuous trusted companion of her husband. This is hardly sufficient to consider borrowing, and the motif would seem common enough in human experience to relegate this to the realm of idle curiosity.[A-110]

Chief cupbearer and chief baker (40:2). Though these titles may in part be ceremonial, these two men had overall responsibility for what was served to the king. The potential for assassination attempts through the king's food was real and constant, so these officials not only needed to be incorruptible themselves, but also had to be able to hire people above reproach and to identify attempts at infiltration of the staff by enemies of the king. The text is silent concerning their offense, but since both were responsible for meals, it seems logical to speculate that the king may have gotten sick from a meal.

Each dream had a meaning of its own (40:5). Dreams were considered important vehicles of divine communication in the ancient world (see comments on 37:5).[576] Trained specialists interpreted the dreams of important people and paying customers using "dream books," compiled both in Egypt and Mesopotamia.[577] These books were consulted for the meaning of symbols in dreams. The Egyptian books typically indicate that a particular element in the dream is good or bad. Mesopotamian dream books offer ritual remedies. The specialists depended on this literature because the gods did not reveal the interpretation of the dreams.

Joseph, however, has no knowledge of the "science" and no access to the literature; he relies on God for the interpretation of the dream. The interpretation he offers nevertheless uses principles well known from the

literature. For instance, the idea that the number of items indicates the number of days/years has precedent in the literature.[578] The symbols in these dreams are similar to some of those found in the dream books. A full goblet, for instance, is indicative of having a name and offspring. Carrying fruit on one's head is indicative of sorrow.[579]

Pharaoh's birthday (40:20). Hoffmeier points out that no evidence for celebrations surrounding the birthday of Pharaoh are known until the first millennium B.C.[580] He suggests alternatively that the day of birth may refer to the anniversary of his accession or coronation as king (cf. Ps. 2:7), for which there is evidence as early as the Sixth Dynasty.[581]

Hanged the chief baker (40:22). Hanging in the ancient world was generally not a means of execution, but an additional indignity in the treatment of a corpse. The corpse would be hung in some way (often impaled on a stick, cf. NIV note) to be devoured by insects, birds, and animals of prey. Here the execution was carried out by beheading (Gen. 40:19; cf. 1 Sam. 31:9–10) and then the body was hung out to be devoured.

Pharaoh (41:1). It is impossible (given the paucity of data) to identify the pharaoh of the Joseph story, who throughout is simply called "Pharaoh." The term "Pharaoh" (= "great house") originally referred to the palace and is not attested as a designation for the king of Egypt until the fifteenth century B.C. Even then, for the next five hundred years or so it was not used with the name of the king, but stood alone as here and in Exodus. It is not until the tenth century that it is used in combination with a personal name.[582]

The general chronology locates Joseph in the period known as the Middle Kingdom (first quarter of the second millennium) or the Second Intermediate period (second quarter of the second millennium). Those who feel that a precise chronology can be derived from the biblical record place Joseph in the reign of Amenemhet II or Senusret (Sesostris) II or III.[583]

Had a dream (41:1). A king's dream is always of special import, and he customarily employed dream specialists to interpret the dream and offer advice as to how to proceed. It was of particular importance if a dream were repeated, and a number of examples are known from the literature.[584]

Just as Pharaoh has a double dream here, Gudea king of Lagash (around 2000 B.C.)

Painting in the tomb of Qe-namun, West Thebes shows bakers mixing and kneading dough and filling bread molds.
Werner Forman Archive/E. Strouhal

◀

Egyptian dream book
Lenka Peacock, courtesy of the British Museum

▼

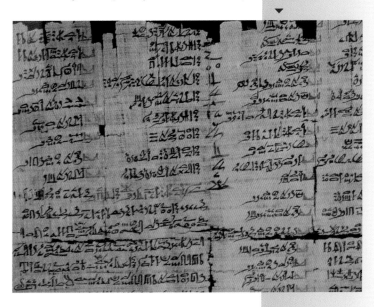

had a double dream concerning the building of a temple. In a Mari letter, the king is warned twice (given to someone else on consecutive nights) that he should not rebuild a temple in Terqa.[585] In the Gilgamesh Epic at the end of tablet 1, Gilgamesh has a double dream about his upcoming encounter with Enkidu. In tablet 4, he has a sequence of five dreams concerning the upcoming encounter with the guardian, Huwawa.[586] In the Babylonian Poem of the Righteous Sufferer (*Ludlul bel Nemeqi*), the sufferer receives three dreams informing him that he has been cleansed from his offense.[587] In these examples, multiple dreams give warning (Mari), inform concerning the future (Gilgamesh), and offer absolution (Sufferer). Pharaoh's dreams contain the first two of these.

Magicians and wise men (41:8). "Magicians" (*ḥarṭummim*) refer to the specialists centered in the "House of Life," where the dream interpretation manuals were stored and studied.[588] This term is constructed from an Egyptian title referring to a chief lector priest (*ḥry-tp ḥry-ḥb*).[589] This same term is used in late literature to describe the famous Egyptian architect from the Third Dynasty, Imhotep,[590] who was also the high priest of Heliopolis. A stele on Sehel Island, purporting to be a decree by King Djoser but is actually a product of the Ptolemaic period (second century B.C.), is where the term is applied to Imhotep.[591]

Another famous Egyptian lector priest was the prophet Neferti, who rehearses the troubled times of the first intermediate period at the end of the third millennium B.C. Lector priests were those who recited

spells and rituals. They were experts in the literature of ritual and were considered to have access to mysteries. They play a major role in the Tales of King Khufu and the Magicians, a cycle of five stories where they perform miracles and can see the future.[592]

Shaved (41:14). As Egyptian monuments certify, male Egyptians were characteristically clean-shaven and at times shaved their heads as well (bald or close-cropped), though they would then at times wear wigs made of human hair.[593] The text here is unclear concerning the extent to which Joseph was shaved.

Seven years of famine (41:27). The Famine Inscription on Sehel Island mentioned above (see comment on 41:8) is of interest also because the setting is a seven-year famine. The king consults Imhotep, who, after research, advises the king that the famine can be ended by acknowledging the role of Khnum (whose temple was at Elephantine) in controlling the inundation of the Nile. The only parallel here is the existence of a seven-year famine—nothing else shows similarity to the Joseph story; there is no reason to think of the two pieces as being related or referring to the same event. It only shows that extended famines were known in Egypt.

Tablet recording Gilgamesh's dreams
The Schøyen Collection MS 3025, Oslo and London
▲

Chief lector-priest
Werner Forman Archive/The Egyptian Museum, Cairo
▶

Famine inscription on Sehel Island
Markh/Wikimedia Commons

system suggested and administered by Joseph, though there is no evidence to support such a connection.

Appoint commissioners (41:34). In Egypt as well as in the rest of the ancient Near East, incantations were generally used to avoid the negative consequences portended by dreams. Here, in contrast, Joseph offers a strategy to counteract the effect of the dream. In the nineteenth century, Senusret III is known for reducing the power of the nomarchs (provincial governors) to restore a more centralized government.[596] In the process a new "bureau of the vizier" and a new bureaucracy were established, involving new commissioners.

Two bureaus (*waret*) were created, one each for the northern and southern areas of Egypt, operated by a hierarchy of officials. Other departments, such as the "treasury," the "bureau of the people's giving," and the "organization of labour," were also inaugurated.[597]

Again, there is no evidence to associate this with Joseph, but it demonstrates that periodic modifications in the bureaucracy were not uncommon.

In charge of my palace (41:40). Pharaoh's initial appointment gives Joseph authority in the palace based on the recognition of the spirit of God in Joseph (41:38). The combination of insight (indicated by the dream interpretation) and wisdom (indicated by the proposed strategy) were sufficient to conclude that Joseph

If the nineteenth century B.C. is the time period of Joseph, it may be of interest that there is evidence of massive irrigation projects in the Faiyum area designed to reclaim additional land for farming (probably during the reign of Senusret II).[594] It might also be noted that during the reign of Amenemhet III around 1800 B.C., a number of years show record high levels of the Nile during the inundation (reaching as high as sixteen feet), but in succeeding years the Nile declined markedly so that ten years later it was only one and a half feet high.[595] Either of these events could conceivably be related to the

Senusret III
Werner Forman Archive/The Egyptian Museum, Berlin

enjoyed divine favor—a good reason to keep him close to the throne.

In Egyptian documents, the administrative second-in-command over Egypt is the vizier, known as the "Overseer of the Royal Estates." Joseph's new role, however, may not be quite as lofty as that.[598] There are other posts that could make the claim of being second-in-command in the area of their responsibility. This is similar to a company today that has a President and CEO, and a staff of vice presidents: Vice President of Production, Vice President of Marketing, Vice President of Legal, etc. Each of these individuals could legitimately claim to be second-in-command in his or her particular area and to be set in charge of the entire company in the area of his or her jurisdiction. Similarly, numerous Egyptian nobles could serve in offices and bear titles that identified them as second only to Pharaoh. Such titles include "Great Favorite of the Lord of the Two Lands" and "Foremost among his Courtiers."

One of the most appropriate known titles that describes Joseph's duties is "Overseer of the Granaries of Upper and Lower Egypt."[599] It is not unusual to find accounts of officials who were elevated from lowly status to high positions of authority.[600]

In charge of the whole land of Egypt (41:43). Joseph is given authority that is not regional or just in one city. The signet ring allows him to make decisions and authorize them in the name of Pharaoh. The clothing, jewelry, and transportation all designate his high station.[601] His renaming and his marriage into a priestly family give him a new identity as an Egyptian noble. The city of On (reflecting Egyptian *Iunu*) is later known as Heliopolis and is one of the most revered of Egypt's ancient cities (along with Memphis and Thebes). It is located just north of modern Cairo at the base of the Delta.

You are spies! (42:9). Semites/Asiatics were often distrusted by the Egyptians, so this is not an unusual charge. The Egyptians referred to them by various epithets such as "sand dwellers" and "throat slitters" and considered them wild and uncivilized.

But for what purpose would they be spying on Egypt? It is not likely that the Egyptians feared invasion from Canaan, though they may have been wary of limited raids (razzias). Since we use the word "spy" mostly for military intelligence, a better translation here might be "scouts." Economic motives would be more logical than military ones. Fields and storehouses could be plundered. What might ostensibly be a request for grain could serve as a guise for discovering what supplies of grain existed and how they might be ransacked. Reflections on the First Intermediate period in works such as the Instructions of Merikare and the Prophecy of Neferti[602] reveal the social unrest caused by unruly foreign elements infiltrating Egyptian society. The result was increased attention to fortification of the Delta during the Middle Kingdom period.[603]

Each man's silver (42:25). The very fact that the brothers have both the grain and their silver potentially confirms the accusation that they are scouts intent on stealing grain. Frequently we might see trade in grain or herds, but Jacob's family has no grain, and the herds are difficult to transport. It is no

surprise, then, that they have brought silver with which to trade.

Cup ... for divination (44:5). The idea that a cup was used for divination suggests that divination took place by observing liquids poured into the cup (either the shapes of oil on water or the ripples of the water, to name a few techniques known from Mesopotamia). Little is known of these techniques in Egyptian practice. Divination was a means of acquiring information. It is of interest that Joseph acquires information by means of the cup—not by pouring liquid into it, but by using it to test his brothers, thus using observation at a different level.

Father to Pharaoh (45:8). The Egyptian title *it-ntr* ("father of the god") refers to a variety of officials and priests. Since the pharaoh was considered divine, it is likely that "father of Pharaoh" carries a similar connotation of "advisor."

Region of Goshen (45:10). In Egyptian texts the heaviest concentrations of Semites occurs in the eastern Delta region closest to Canaan. This corresponds to the biblical texts in which the region of Goshen is equated to the district of Ramesses (47:11), which is certainly in the Delta region. In the early chapters of Exodus, this is the location of the Israelite labors and towns such as Pithom and Ramesses. The region is bounded by the branches of the Nile Delta on the west and the series of lakes from the

Mediterranean down to the Red Sea on the east. Crossing east to west through the center of it is the Wadi Tumilat.

Jacob in Egypt (46:1–47:31)

All shepherds are detestable to the Egyptians (46:34). By identifying themselves as shepherds Jacob's clan offer assurance that they are not coming to take Egyptian farmland or to get involved in politics. Flocks and herds were kept by Egyptians during all periods and were used for meat, milk, and wool or hides, as well as for some sacrifices (more cattle than sheep and goats).[604] They are depicted in reliefs, models, and tomb paintings, remains are found in excavation, and deities were associated with the ram and the cow (but not the sheep or the goat)—all demonstrating the pervasive penetration of these animals into Egyptian culture. In contrast, sheep and goats do not figure prominently in fables, metaphors, or

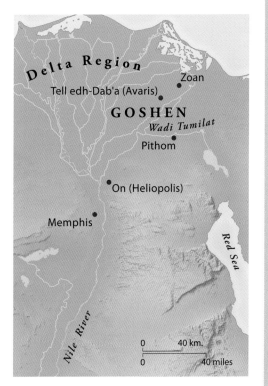

◀

Tell ed-Dab'a Region

◀

personal names, which indicates that they were considered rather common.

It is difficult to ascertain whether shepherds were detested because of associations of shepherds with foreigners, with a low status in society, or with sheep and goats as inferior animals that threatened farmland. Extant Egyptian records offer no insight on this comment.

District of Rames(s)es (47:11). At this period Ramesses was not a common name and no city was yet so named. The pharaohs with the name "Ramesses" do not come along until the thirteenth century. It is logical to conclude that this geographical name is supplied at a later period. The city of Ramesses, Piramesse, is eventually going to be located at Qantir/Avaris (Tell ed-Dabʾa). It was the capital of the Hyksos in the sixteenth century and was rebuilt as the capital of Ramesses the Great in the thirteenth century. In the twelfth century it was dismantled to build Tanis (Tell San el-Hagar, about twelve miles to the north), which in turn became the capital city.

Tell ed-Dabʾa has been extensively excavated by M. Bietak and has provided much evidence of the Semitic population that lived there. The site was founded in the Twelfth Dynasty, the most likely setting for Joseph. "A community of Canaanites (carriers of the Syrian-Palestinian Middle Bronze Age culture IIA) settled there in the late Twelfth Dynasty, which led to a considerable enlargement of the town."[605]

Despite the growing Syro-Palestinian population of this town over the next centuries, no remains permit the identification of descendants of Abraham. The material culture is Canaanite and the religious practices show a syncretism between Canaanite and Egyptian elements.

Buy us and our land (47:19). Joseph's policy suggests a shift from privately owned property to centralized ownership of property worked by tenant farmers. The socioeconomic situation of the Middle Kingdom as it pertains to land ownership remains vague. The Middle Kingdom and Early New Kingdom evidence large tracts of crown property administered by government officials.[606] In this way centralization is in evidence as is the state-run redistributive economy.[607] In the New Kingdom, much land gradually comes under the control of the temples. In that period, there was no longer any private property, but only per-

sonal rights to the use of property granted in trust for a land-owning institution such as the crown or temple.[608]

Priests ... received a regular allotment from Pharaoh (47:22). Priests did not need to grow their own food, and therefore shortages did not drive them to sell their land. Instead, temples, like the kings, were owners of land and benefited from renting out the land to be farmed by laborers. Temple ownership of land is well documented in Egypt in all periods, but became extensive in the New Kingdom period.

Do not bury me in Egypt (47:29). Jacob's sentiment reflects the extent to which he is tied to the land of Canaan as it looks to both past and future. Since the ancestral burial ground is in Canaan, he "sleeps with his fathers" by being buried with them, thus actualizing his solidarity with them. One's burial place also serves as the focus for any ongoing care and remembrance after death. The request to be buried in Canaan thus serves as an indication that he sees the future of his descendants as connected to the covenant land—a statement of faith in God's promise to bring his family back there.

Manasseh and Ephraim (48:1–22)

Israel reached out his right hand and put it on Ephraim's head, though he was the younger (48:14). For patriarchal blessings see comment on 27:4. For discussion of primogeniture, see comment on 25:31.

Ridge of land I took from the Amorites with my sword and bow (48:22). This verse provides two difficulties: (1) How do we handle the Hebrew word šᵉkām (NIV: ridge of land; NIV margin: portion; LXX and NRSV margin: Shechem) and the word "one" that follows it; and (2) how can we explain this claimed conquest historically? In terms of translation, I am inclined to follow De Hoop: "And I, I give Shechem to you—O one above your brothers—which I took from the hand of the Amorites with my sword and my bow."[609] Historically, this refers to the conquest of

Shechem (or should we call it the slaughter of the Shechemites?) by Simeon and Levi. Jacob did not approve of this act and was not proud of it, but it was irreversible and undeniable. The land was therefore his to give, since it was taken in his name and by his clan. This justifies Jacob's use of the first person ("I took").[610]

Jacob's Blessing (49:1–33)

What will happen to you in days to come (49:1). As was typical of patriarchal pronouncements, Jacob makes statements concerning the future destiny of his sons. These are not prophecy, for they are not given in the name of deity. They forecast the future. Like a weather forecaster or an economic forecaster, Jacob identifies expectations derived from observed indicators that are considered reliable and thus can be interpreted with a high level of probability. Words had power in the ancient world, and the very speaking of them, especially by someone in authority, was taken seriously.

I will scatter them in Jacob and disperse them in Israel (49:7). The tribes of Simeon and Levi are to be dispersed (not the individuals, of course), deprived of clearly identified land as a consequence of their violence in Shechem (Gen. 34). This represents virtual disinheritance.[611] Simeon is eventually assigned villages scattered in Judah's territory (Josh. 19:1–9), and Levi, though having no claim to land, serves its priestly function from the bases known as the levitical cities, which were distributed among the tribal territories (Num. 35).

Your father's sons will bow down to you (49:8). Westbrook identifies this as the legal transfer of clan leadership to Judah. Though Joseph has received the double portion of the inheritance (since Ephraim and Manasseh both inherited shares among Jacob's sons, Gen. 48), Judah will be the administrator of the undivided inheritance.[612]

Like a lion (49:9). Lion imagery is common in the ancient Near East.[613] There are lion/lioness cults in Egypt, particularly

A god, probably Nergal, carrying lion-headed scepters
Ashmolean Museum, University of Oxford
▲

Murex snail, one ancient source of purple dye, engraved with the name of Rimush, one of the kings of the Empire of Akkad
Marie-Lan Nguyen/ Wikimedia Commons, courtesy of the Louvre
▼

associated with On, where Joseph's in-laws were from.[614] More important, the lion is used in Egypt as the symbol of the king.[615]

In Mesopotamia the lion is most often associated with the goddess Ishtar. The god Nergal carries a lion scepter,[616] and numerous other gods are described using lion metaphors.[617] The lion as a royal metaphor as well as an animal for the royal hunt is more familiar in Mesopotamia from the later Neo-Assyrian period, though it is not absent from the earlier periods.[618] In these contexts, the image that the metaphor presents is one of fierceness, cruelty, and power. In contrast, the imagery with Judah tends to invoke the image of quiet power at rest but is not to be trifled with, rather than representing an immediate threat. Another point of interest is that the cub and lioness are mentioned here along with the lion, but art from Syria-Palestine portrays only the male.[619]

Wash his garments in wine (49:11). This imagery is suggestive of Judah's descendants having the blue/purple/red clothing often associated with royalty, though that coloring is usually achieved through the processing of murex snails (an expensive process because of the number of snails needed to produce the dye).[620]

The dyeing industry has been reconstructed to some extent by archaeologists and with the help of ancient and classical literary sources. Fabrics as well as threads (for color patterns) were dyed through soaking them in a bath. For the color to last, the dye had to be "fixed," usually through the use of a chemical mordant such as alum. Though several of the more desired and expensive dyes were "self-fixing" (purple from snail shells, the indigo from the woad plant, and the red from insects),[621] once the fixing process was discovered early in the second millennium, many more plant products became usable.

An Assyrian manual containing recipes for dyes shows the complexity of the industry.[622] The earliest written records concerning dyeing are from Nuzi in the mid-second millennium. The earliest evidence of the use of the snail for purple dye comes from seventeenth-century B.C. Crete.[623] That suggests that at the time of the patriarchs, that technology for dyeing is unknown, yet dyeing itself was known because Egyptian tomb paintings show clothing with color patterns.

Prior to the discovery of murex-snail purple, might wine have been used for dyeing? Would red/purple have been associated with royalty? Royal women in the tomb of Ur from the end of the third millennium wore red-colored clothing, but no evidence suggests that wine was used for dyeing, though its staining effect would have been well-recognized since wine was filtered through linen cloth.

Haven for ships (49:13). Seafaring took place primarily from the north, where there were natural harbors. The difficulty with this verse is that Zebulun, to our knowledge, never had territory adjacent to the sea. The tribal allotment given him was in western Lower Galilee, entirely landlocked and sixty-five miles from Sidon. This would actually be a more appropriate description of the territory allotted to Asher, which stretched along the coast from Acco to

▶ Embalming

Embalming served to preserve the body of the deceased, but in Egypt the reason for doing so involved a lot of theology. They preserved the body so that it could be reinhabited by the spirit (*ka*) in the afterlife. Nothing in the text suggests that Joseph or his family had adopted the complex afterlife theology of ancient Egypt with its emphasis on rituals, spells, and other sorts of magic.

The physicians referred to are probably mortuary priests, who were the experts in the techniques of embalming as they prepared the body not only physically for the grave, but spiritually for the afterlife. Evidence of embalming goes back to about 2600 B.C. The principal agent used in the embalming process is natron, which served to dry out the body after the important viscera were removed.[A-111] This dehydration process took about forty days. The viscera were packed in natron individually and eventually replaced in the body.

Meanwhile, the body was washed out with spiced wine, and after the process was over, it was anointed with oils and gum resins. As the body was wrapped in linen, protective amulets were included at various places. As a final step, a liquid resin was poured over the whole body.[A-112]

A painting in the tomb of Sennedjem shows a priest wearing the mask of Anubis, the jackal-headed god of embalming. The priest is leaning over a mummy in its anthropoid coffin to perform the ritual of Osiris prior to burial.
Werner Forman Archive/E. Strouhal
◀

Tyre. These apparent discrepancies suggest that we cannot treat this blessing as simply reflecting a description of the territories as they existed after the conquest. There is no known period when Zebulun controlled the coastal regions.

Death of Jacob and Joseph (50:1–26)

Directed the physicians ... to embalm his father (50:2). Jacob was embalmed for forty days (see sidebar on "Embalming") and mourned for seventy (50:3). Herodotus also indicates a seventy-day period, though the

Egyptians were well aware that forty days was the optimum period for the preparation of the body.[624]

Threshing floor of Atad ... Abel Mizraim (50:11). The location of Abel Mizraim is unknown, and it is difficult to understand why a procession from Egypt to Hebron should bring them anywhere near the Jordan.

He lived a hundred and ten years (50:22). One hundred ten was considered the ideal age in Egypt. As early as 1950 J. M. A. Janssen collected some thirty references to Egyptian individuals living this ideal lifespan over two thousand years of Egyptian history.[625]

Main Text Notes

1. This section is adapted from J. Walton and A. Hill, *Old Testament Today* (Grand Rapids: Zondervan, 2004), 41–51. The details of Mesopotamian history are available in works such as A. Kuhrt, *The Ancient Near East, 3000–330 B.C.* (London: Routledge, 1995), and M. Van de Mieroop, *History of the Ancient Near East, ca. 3000–323 B.C.* (London: Blackwell, 2003).

2. Students should note that labeling of centuries in B.C. works the same as in A.D., so the 24th century is the years 2399–2300. Additionally, since the numbers are going backward, "late" in the century would be the lower 2300 numbers, e.g., 2315.

3. See a detailed history of the period in W. Heimpel, *Letters to the King of Mari* (Winona Lake, Ind.: Eisenbrauns, 2003), 37–163.

4. I have used functional descriptions to label all of these genres rather than some sort of ancient category titles or even currently circulating labels.

5. J. Sailhamer, *Genesis Unbound* (Sisters, Ore.: Multnomah, 1996), 38. Detailed discussion may be found in idem, "Genesis," in *The Expositor's Bible Commentary*, ed. F. E. Gaebelein (Grand Rapids: Zondervan, 1990), 2:20–23, and a summary by B. Arnold, "רֵאשִׁית," *NIDOTTE*, 3:1025–26. Differentiation between *rēʾšit* and *tᵉḥillâ* can be found in S. Rattray and J. Milgrom, "רֵאשִׁית," *TDOT*, 13:269–70.

6. *CAD*, 14:272.

7. S. Morenz, *Egyptian Religion* (Ithaca, N.Y.: Cornel Univ. Press, 1973), 168–71. For use in an Egyptian creation text see *COS*, 1.16, the 100th chapter of Papyrus Leiden 1 350.

8. It would be opposite to "eschaton" or the "latter days" (Heb. *ʾaḥᵃrît*).

9. J. Allen, *Genesis in Egypt* (New Haven, Conn.: Yale Univ. Press, 1988), 57.

10. See extensive discussion of this and other elements of cosmology in the ancient world in J. Walton, *Genesis One as Ancient Cosmology* (Winona Lake, Ind.: Eisenbrauns, forthcoming).

11. *Enuma Elish* 1:1–2, 7–9, *COS*, 1.111. This perspective is also present in Egyptian texts such as Papyrus Berlin 3055, 16.3–4 (see E. Hornung, *Conceptions of God in Ancient Egypt* [Ithaca, N.Y.: Cornell Univ. Press, 1982], 175). Notice also the biblical statements that Yahweh gave an individual a name while yet in the womb (e.g., Isa. 49:1; cf. Jer. 1:5, which speaks of function in other ways besides naming).

12. S. N. Kramer, *Sumerian Mythology* (Philadelphia: Univ. of Pennsylvania Press, 1972), 37.

13. Allen, *Genesis in Egypt*, 57–58: "Creation is the process through which the One became the Many."

14. For example, God "creates" fire, cloud, destruction, calamity, darkness, righteousness, and purity. For fuller discussion see J. Walton, *Genesis* (NIVAC: Grand Rapids: Zondervan, 2001), 70–71.

15. Allen, *Genesis in Egypt*, 56. See also V. A. Tobin, "Creation Myths," *OEAE*, 2:469.

16. Hornung, *Conceptions*, 176–77.

17. D. Tsumura, *Creation and Destruction* (Winona Lake, Ind.: Eisenbrauns, 2005), 22–35.

18. Clifford, *Creation Accounts*, 28 (from NBC 11108).

19. "Primeval Apsu was their progenitor, and matrix-Tiamat was she who bore them all, They were mingling their waters together" (*COS*, 1.111.3–5). Cf. the bilingual Foundation of Eridu: "All the lands were sea," in Clifford, *Creation Accounts*, 63.

20. Cf. previous note.

21. For thorough treatment see Tsumura, *Earth and Waters*, 45–65; Horowitz, *Mesopotamian Cosmic Geography*, 301–6.

22. "Precosmic" is appropriate, for the Greek word *kosmos* implies order. It is also a more neutral description than "chaos."

23. Horowitz, *Mesopotamian Cosmic Geography*, 303.

24. Gilgamesh crosses the *tamtu* when he reaches the waters of death at the end of the world. In later texts, the Babylonian word *marratu* comes alongside *tamtu* as a synonym and represents the cosmic waters on the Babylonian world map. See Horowitz, *Mesopotamian Cosmic Geography*, 304–5, 332–33.

25. Tobin, "Creation Myths," *OEAE*, 2:469.

26. C. Hyers, *The Meaning of Creation* (Atlanta: John Knox, 1984), 67.

27. *Enuma Elish* 1.105–10.

28. Allen, *Genesis in Egypt*, 57. He points out that by the Ptolemaic period, a concept developed of a dialectic between nonexistence and potentiality.

29. See A. Bolshakov, "Ka," *OEAE*, 2:215–17, for this element in the human *ka*, and D. Meeks and C. Favard-Meeks, *Daily Life of the Egyptian Gods* (Ithaca, N.Y.: Cornell Univ. Press, 1996), 71, for the divine *ka*.

30. Meeks and Meeks, *Daily Life*, 71.

31. Akkadian has protective spirits (*lamassu, šedu*) as well as the *melammu* of the gods ("shining glory") that might be recognizable in a king. Ugaritic has a cognate to Hebrew *rûaḥ* but it is only attested as "wind," not "spirit."

32. M. Smith, *On the Primaeval Ocean: Carlsberg Papyri 5* (CNI 26; Copenhagen: Museum Tusculanum Press, Univ. of Copenhagen, 2002), 194.

33. Morenz, *Egyptian Religion*, 176, quoting K. Sethe, *Amun*.

34. Hornung, *Conceptions*, 209.

35. Morenz, *Egyptian Religion*, 163–66.

36. *COS*, 1.15:22.

37. Rosengarten, *Sumer et le Sacré*, 219 20.

38. Walton, *Genesis*, 79.

39. G. Kadish, "Time," *OEAE*, 3:408.

40. *Enuma Elish* 5.39–40. See Horowitz, *Mesopotamian Cosmic Geography*, 117–18. It is also worth

noting that in one of the Babylonian god lists, the first deity to exist was Duri ("Ever and Ever"), referring to time. See W. G. Lambert, "The Cosmology of Sumer and Babylon," in *Ancient Cosmologies*, ed. C. Blacker and M. Loewe (London: George Allen & Unwin, 1975), 53.

41. Allen, *Genesis in Egypt*, 4.

42. Ibid., 57–58 (see comment on 1:1).

43. H. Hoffner, "Song of Ullikummi," in *Hittite Myths* (SBLWAW 2; Atlanta: SBL Press, 1990), 59 § 61.

44. *Enuma Elish* 4.135–38; also note the concept in Hittite, "Song of Ullikummi," ibid., 59 § 61, 63).

45. Lines 1–5 (Clifford, *Creation Accounts*, 31); the poem Enki and Ninmah has fates decreed after heavens and earth were split (ibid., 40).

46. P. Seely, "The Firmament and the Water Above, Part 1: The Meaning of *raqiaᶜ* in Gen 1:6–8," *WTJ* 53 (1991): 233; see PT 1040c; 299a. If wordplays are to be taken seriously, the Egyptians may have believed that the heavens were made of meteoric iron, since pieces of it occasionally fell to earth; see L. Lesko, "Ancient Egyptian Cosmogonies and Cosmology," in *Religion in Ancient Egypt*, ed. B. Shafer (Ithaca, N.Y.: Cornell Univ. Press, 1991), 117.

47. *Enuma Elish* 4.139–40, cf. Horowitz, *Mesopotamian Cosmic Geography*, 262, with support of *CAD*, 17/1:22a but against *CAD*, 10/1:342a.

48. Horowitz, *Mesopotamian Cosmic Geography*, 263.

49. Ibid., 120, 265; Lambert, "Cosmology of Sumer and Babylon," 62; see *Enuma Elish* 5.59–68.

50. Seely, "The Firmament and the Water Above, Part 1," 236.

51. Ibid.

52. Ibid.

53. O. Keel, *The Symbolism of the Biblical World* (New York: Seabury, 1978), 35–47.

54. *Enuma Elish* 4.139–40; see Horowitz, *Mesopotamian Cosmic Geography*, 262.

55. Keel, *Symbolism*, 37.

56. Ps. 104:13 and 148:4 both refer to waters above but do not use *mabbûl*.

57. Horowitz, *Mesopotamian Cosmic Geography*, 262.

58. Ibid., 262–63.

59. Stadelmann, *Hebrew Conception of the World*, 132.

60. Gen. 7:11; 8:2; 2 Kings 7:2, 19; Isa. 24:18; Mal. 3:10. See extensive discussion in Stadelmann, *Hebrew Conception of the World*, 120–26. For similar terminology in Ugaritic, see M. Weinfeld, "Gen. 7:11, 8:1, 2 Against the Background of Ancient Near Eastern Tradition," *Die Welt des Orients* 9 (1978): 242–48.

61. Seely, "The Firmament and the Water Above, Part 2," 37–38.

62. Hornung, *Conceptions*, 182–83.

63. Clifford, *Creation Accounts*, 39; found in the cosmogonic introduction to the disputation Bird and Fish—a Sumerian piece from the Ur III period.

64. Seely, "The Geographical Meaning of 'Earth' and 'Seas,'" 236–37.

65. KAR 4; see Clifford, *Creation Accounts*, 49–51.

66. Bird and Fish; see ibid., 38–39.

67. Ibid., 63.

68. Papyrus Leiden 1 350; translation in John L. Foster, *Hymns, Prayers, and Songs: An Anthology of Ancient Egyptian Lyric Poetry* (SBLWAW 8; Atlanta: SBL Press, 1995), 71.

69. Clifford, *Creation Accounts*, 67; Horowitz, *Mesopotamian Cosmic Geography*, 147. A variation occurs in the last lines in the celestial omen series *Enuma Anu Enlil*, where it says, "They saw Shamash in his gate, they made him appear regularly in heaven and earth"; see U. Koch-Westenholz, *Mesopotamian Astrology* (CNI 19; Copenhagen: Museum Tusculanum, Univ. of Copenhagen, 1995), 77.

70. Lines 150–154 specifically mention the omens; see translation in COS, 1.117.

71. W. Vogels, "The Cultic and Civil Calendars of the Fourth Day of Creation (Gen 1,14b)," *SJOT* 11 (1997): 163–80.

72. Horowitz, *Mesopotamian Cosmic Geography*, 170.

73. Ibid., 146–47. For additional studies on astronomy and astrology in the ancient world see H. Hunger and D. Pingree, *Astral Sciences in Mesopotamia* (Leiden: Brill, 1999); U. Koch-Westenholz, *Mesopotamian Astrology* (CNI 19; Copenhagen: Museum Tusculanum, Univ. of Copenhagen, 1995); F. Rochberg, *Heavenly Writing* (Cambridge: Cambridge Univ. Press, 2005).

74. Horowitz, *Mesopotamian Cosmic Geography*, 114–15.

75. Ibid., 255.

76. Clifford, *Creation Accounts*, 68.

77. For a helpful introduction to all of these, see J. Westenholz, *Dragons, Monsters and Fabulous Beasts* (Jerusalem: Bible Lands Museum, 2004).

78. *Enuma Elish* 1.133–143. See discussion in W. G. Lambert, "Ninurta Mythology in the Babylonian Epic of Creation," in *Keilschriftliche Literaturen: Ausgewälte Vorträge der XXXII. Rencontre assyriologique internationale*, ed. K. Hecker and W. Sommerfeld (Berliner Beiträge zum Vorderen Orient 6; Berlin: Reimer, 1986), 56–58.

79. G. C. Heider, "Tanin," *DDD*², 835; see S. B. Parker, *Ugaritic Narrative Poetry* (SBLWAW 9; Atlanta: SBL Press, 1997), 111 line 40.

80. Clifford, *Creation Accounts*, 65.

81. COS, 1.158 line 14.

82. http://etcsl.orinst.ox.ac.uk 1.7.4, 14.

83. W. W. Hallo, "Cult Statue and Divine Image: A Preliminary Study," in *Scripture in Context II*, ed. W. W. Hallo, J. C. Moyer and L. G. Perdue (Winona Lake, Ind.: Eisenbrauns, 1983), 1–18; I. J. Winter, "Art in Empire: The Royal Image and the Visual Dimensions of Assyrian Ideology," in *Assyria 1995*, ed. S. Parpola and R. M. Whiting (Helsinki: Neo-Assyrian Text Corpus Project, 1997), 359–81; B. F. Batto, "The Divine Sovereign: The Image of God in the Priestly Creation Account," in *David and Zion*, ed. B. Batto and K. L. Roberts (Winona Lake, Ind.: Eisenbrauns, 2004), 143–86; E. M. Curtis, *Man as the Image of God in Genesis in Light of Ancient Near Eastern Parallels* (Ann Arbor,

160. "May your poison fangs be in the earth, your ribs in the hole" (230); "spittle in the dust" (237).

161. COS, 1.108 (line 8). This is a stock description also found in the Gilgamesh Epic and Nergal and Ereshkigal.

162. Ancient Egyptian texts list thirty-seven types of snakes along with the symptoms of bites and believed remedies. See N. Hansen, "Snakes," OEAE, 3:296. Cf. Fabry, "נָחָשׁ," 9:359 for the Old Testament.

163. Izre'el, Adapa, 122.

164. R. Schärf Kluger, The Archetypal Significance of Gilgamesh: A Modern Ancient Hero (Einsiedeln, Switzerland: Daimon, 1991), 202.

165. Abusch, "Ghost and God," 367.

166. Ibid., 364.

167. For discussion of the variety of composite beasts in the ancient world, see Westenholz, Dragons; Black and Green, Gods, Demons and Symbols; for discussion of cherubim see Keel, Symbolism, 167–71; T. N. D. Mettinger, "Cherubim," DDD², 189–92

168. J. Black et al., The Literature of Ancient Sumer (Oxford: Oxford Univ. Press, 2004), 86–88.

169. OEANE, 1:23, 140–41.

170. T. Abusch, "Blood in Israel and Mesopotamia," in Emanuel: Studies in Hebrew Bible, Septuagint, and Dead Sea Scrolls in Honor of Emanuel Tov, ed. S. M. Paul et al. (VTSup 94; Leiden: Brill, 2003), 675–84.

171. J. Milgrom, Leviticus 1–16 (AB; New York: Doubleday), 205–7.

172. Ibid., 205; though his citation suggests that the suet was used along with the meat offering rather than as an independent gift.

173. M. L. Barré, "Rabiṣu," DDD², 682–83; see M. J. Geller, "Freud and Mesopotamian Magic," in Mesopotamian Magic, ed. T. Abusch and K. van der Toorn (AMD 1; Groningen: Styx, 1999), 50.

174. Adapted from Walton, Genesis, 264.

175. AEL, 2:203–11, New Kingdom period.

176. M. van de Mieroop, The Ancient Mesopotamian City (Oxford: Oxford Univ. Press, 1999).

177. G. Mobley, "The Wild Man in the Bible and the Ancient Near East," JBL 116 (1997): 217–33.

178. MAL B2, translation from M. Roth, Law Collections from Mesopotamia and Asia Minor (SBLWAW 6; Atlanta: Scholars Press, 1995), 176.

179. H. Nissen, The Early History of the Ancient Near East, 9000–2000 B.C. (Chicago: Univ. of Chicago Press, 1988), 35–38.

180. Conflated from a variety of sources by A. D. Kilmer, "The Mesopotamian Counterparts of the Biblical Nepilim," in Perspectives on Language and Text, ed. E. Conrad and E. Newing (Winona Lake, Ind.: Eisenbrauns, 1987), 39–44. See also E. Reiner, "Etiological Myth of the 'Seven Sages,'" Or 30 (1961): 1–11.

181. P. D. Miller, "Eridu, Dunnu, and Babel: A Study in Comparative Mythology," HAR 9 (1985): 239–40.

182. There has been long discussion whether the first city is built by Cain and named after Enoch, or built by Enoch and named after Irad. For summary and citations see R. A. Wilson, Genealogy and History in the Biblical World (New Haven, Conn.: Yale Univ. Press, 1977), 139–41; Miller, "Eridu, Dunnu, and Babel," 241, n.9.

183. ANET, 265–66; see also OEANE, 2:258–60; cf. the Eridu Genesis, COS, 1.158, line 41.

184. OEANE, 5:294–98.

185. Miller, "Eridu, Dunnu, and Babel," 227–51; W. W. Hallo, "Antediluvian Cities," JCS 23 (1970): 57–67; Wilson, Genealogy and History, 80–83.

186. Evident in most studies that have surveyed entire societies. See H. Marsman, Women in Ugarit (Leiden: Brill, 2003), 129. See throughout R. Westbrook, HANEL.

187. Marsman, Women in Ugarit, 126–28.

188. J. Braun, Music in Ancient Israel/Palestine (Grand Rapids: Eerdmans, 2002), 59–64.

189. Moorey, Ancient Mesopotamian Materials, 255.

190. Ibid., 287.

191. P. McNutt, Forging of Israel, 118.

192. Enuma Elish 1:15–16, trans. by S. Dalley, Myths from Mesopotamia: Creation, Flood, Gilgamesh, and Others, rev. ed. (Oxford: Oxford Univ. Press, 2000), 233.

193. For comprehensive treatment of the motif see R. Borger, "The Incantation Series Bit Meseri and Enoch's Ascension to Heaven," in I Studied Inscriptions before the Flood, ed. R. S. Hess and D. T. Tsumura (Winona Lake, Ind.: Eisenbrauns, 1994), 224–33.

194. COS, 1.129, 131. Adapa is identified as "the purification priest of Eridu, who ascended to heaven."

195. Gilgamesh Epic 11.205–6.

196. Location in Faulkner, The Ancient Egyptian Pyramid Texts, Utterance 361 and many others.

197. Atrahasis 1.352–59; 2.I, 1–8

198. For discussion of all of the possibilities with their pros and cons see J. Walton, "Sons of God, Daughters of Man," in Dictionary of the Old Testament: Pentateuch, ed. T. D. Alexander and D. W. Baker (Downers Grove, Ill.: InterVarsity Press, 2003), 793–98, or idem., Genesis, 290–97.

199. This practice is indicated clearly in the Old Babylonian version (=P) of the epic only, on line 160. See George, The Babylonian Gilgamesh Epic, translation on 179, and footnote on lines 196–99 on 190.

200. See discussion in W. G. Lambert, "Morals in Ancient Mesopotamia," JEOL 15 (1958): 195–96.

201. J. Klein, "The 'Bane' of Humanity: A Lifespan of One Hundred and Twenty Years," Acta Sumerologica 12 (1990): 57–70.

202. The Sumerian sexagesimal system features 60 as its most central number. Accordingly, the ideal age could be understood as 60x2. See R. Harris, Gender and Aging in Mesopotamia (Norman, Okla.: Univ. of Oklahoma Press, 2000), 30–31.

203. R. Faulkner, The Egyptian Book of the Dead: The Book of Going Forth by Day (San Francisco: Chronicle Books, 1998), plate 29, spell 175.

204. Assmann, Mind of Egypt, 206.

205. Kilmer, "The Mesopotamian Counterparts of the Biblical Nepilim," 39–44.

206. Kilmer (ibid., 43 n. 14) tentatively suggests a possible link to Hebrew use of the root npl in a noun

referring to miscarriage or those stillborn extended to beings considered "anomalies" (comparable to Akk. *izbu*).

207. L. Casson, *Ships and Seamanship in the Ancient World* (Baltimore, Md.: Johns Hopkins Univ. Press, 1995), 8.

208. Ibid., 9–10; R. K. Pedersen, "Was Noah's Ark a Sewn Boat?" *BAR* 31 (2005): 18–23, 55–56.

209. Casson, *Ships and Seamanship in the Ancient World*, 23.

210. Ibid., 186–89.

211. E. Firmage, "Zoology," *ABD*, 6:1113.

212. Such would seem to be the case judging from the occasional use of Akk. *ellu* ("pure, clean") as an adjective for animals in cultic use (*CAD* E, 103).

213. Translations are from George, *The Babylonian Gilgamesh Epic*.

214. Lambert and Millard, *Atrahasis*, 93 (3.2.32–37). In the translation in *COS*, 1.130 by B. Foster, the clean and fat animals are being sacrificed prior to the flood rather than taken on board.

215. Extensive discussion and documentation in Horowitz, *Mesopotamian Cosmic Geography*, 301–17.

216. Ibid., 262–63.

217. Discussion and bibliography in George, *Babylonian Gilgamesh Epic*, 516.

218. *COS*, 1:460, n.5.

219. A. Livingstone, "On the Organized Release of Doves to Secure Compliance of a Higher Authority," in *Wisdom, Gods and Literature: Studies in Assyriology in Honour of W. G. Lambert*, ed. A. R. George and I. L. Finkel (Winona Lake, Ind.: Eisenbrauns, 2000), 375–87.

220. Ibid., 385–86.

221. The Atrahasis Epic is broken where the section concerning the birds would have been.

222. Discussion and bibliography in George, *Babylonian Gilgamesh Epic*, 517.

223. F. N. Hepper, *Baker Encyclopedia of Bible Plants* (Grand Rapids: Baker, 1992), 104.

224. 11.162–3.

225. There is still discussion whether these texts refer to a past time or a future time (or both). Texts and discussion may be found in B. Batto, "Paradise Reexamined," in *The Biblical Canon in Comparative Perspective: Scripture in Context IV*, ed. K. L. Younger, W. W. Hallo, and B. F. Batto (Lewiston, N.Y.: Mellen, 1991), 33–66.

226. See esp. the description of Enkidu in the Gilgamesh Epic, Tablet 1.110, and compare the description of Nebuchadnezzar who reverts to the uncultured wild man in Dan. 4. See G. Mobley, "The Wild Man in the Bible and the Ancient Near East," *JBL* 116 (1997): 217–33.

227. In Ewe and Wheat (see sidebar "Ewe and What" at 2:25), see B. Batto, "Paradise Reexamined."

228. D. Brewer, "Hunting, Husbandry and Diet in Ancient Egypt," in *A History of the Animal World in the Ancient Near East*, ed. B. J. Collins (Leiden: Brill, 2002), 436–43.

229. M. Vervenne, " 'The Blood Is the Life and the Life Is the Blood': Blood as Symbol of Life and Death in Biblical Tradition (Gen. 9,4)," in *Ritual and Sacrifice in the Ancient Near East*, ed. J. Quaegebeur (Belgium: Peeters, 1993): 451–70; F. H. Gorman, *The Ideology of Ritual* (Sheffield: Sheffield Academic Press, 1990), 181–89.

230. H. A. Hoffner, "On Homicide in Hittite Law," in *Crossing Boundaries and Linking Horizons*, ed. G. Young, M. Chavalas and R. Averbeck (Bethesda, Md.: CDL, 1997), 293–314; P. Barmash, *Homicide in the Biblical World* (Cambridge: Cambridge Univ. Press, 2005); M. Roth, "Homicide in the Neo-Assyrian Period," in *Language, Literature, and History*, ed. F. Rochberg-Halton (New Haven, Conn.: American Oriental Society, 1987), 351–66. Full discussion can be found in the various sections throughout R. Westbrook, *HANEL*.

231. George, *Babylonian Gilgamesh Epic*, 518.

232. A. D. Kilmer, "The Symbolism of the Flies in the Mesopotamian Flood Myth and Some Further Implications," in *Language, Literature, and History*, ed. F. Rochberg-Halton (New Haven, Conn.: American Oriental Society, 1987), 175–80.

233. *ANEP*, 440 on the so-called broken obelisk from Nineveh.

234. *OEANE*, 5:305.

235. See the thorough treatment by J. S. Bergsma and S. W. Hahn, "Noah's Nakedness and the Curse on Canaan (Genesis 9:20–27)," *JBL* 124 (2005): 25–40, for discussion of many of the issues connected to these verses.

236. See the Hittite Song of Kumarbi in Hoffner, *Hittite Myths*, 40; Bergsma and Hahn (see previous note) indicate also a Canaanite example (p. 38), but their reference is to U. Oldenburg, *The Conflict Between El and Baʿal in Canaanite Religion* (Leiden: Brill, 1969), who unfortunately inferred that Baal had castrated El from a reconstruction of an extremely broken portion of the myth. Most today have rejected that interpretation; see N. Wyatt, *Religious Texts from Ugarit* (Sheffield: Sheffield Academic Press, 1998), 51.

237. Though the mother is not mentioned in the text, to see or uncover the nakedness of the father is equated with incest with the mother, see Lev. 18:7–8.

238. Bergsma and Hahn, "Noah's Nakedness," 39.

239. PRU 3 76a = RS 16.144. See M. Tsevat, "Marriage and Monarchical Legitimacy in Ugarit and Israel," *JSS* 3 (1958): 237–43. In the Annals of Sennacherib he reports taking the wives and harem of kings as spoil—but it doesn't go so far as to suggest that he made them his wives or added them to his own harem; see D. D. Luckenbill, *The Annals of Sennacherib* (Chicago: Univ. of Chicago Press, 1924), campaign one, lines 32–33 (p.52) and campaign two, line 9 (p.56).

240. E. A. Speiser, "In Search of Nimrod," in *Oriental and Biblical Studies*, ed. J. J. Finkelstein and M. Greenberg (Philadelphia: Univ. of Pennsylvania Press, 1967), 41–52; W. H. Gispen, "Who Was Nimrod," in *The Law and the Prophets*, ed. J. H. Skilton (Philadelphia: Presbyterian & Reformed, 1974), 207–14; K. van der Toorn and P. W. van der Horst, "Nimrod before and after the Bible,"

HTR 83 (1990): 1–29. The latter article includes references to additional articles in French, German, and Hebrew.

241. V. Hurowitz and J. Westenholz, "LKA 63: A Heroic Poem in Celebration of Tiglath-pileser I's Muṣru-Qumanu Campaign," *JCS* 42 (1990): 46–49, translated in B. Foster, *Before the Muses*, 3rd ed. (Bethesda, Md.: CDL, 2005), 336.

242. AO 2340. See discussion of this metaphor and its significance in M. B. Dick, "The Neo-Assyrian Royal Lion Hunt and Yahweh's Answer to Job," *JBL* 125 (2006): 243–70, esp. 245.

243. Ibid., 249-51, with most of the data from the Neo-Assyrian period.

244. See brief discussion in M. van de Mieroop, *A History of the Ancient Near East ca. 3000-323 BC* (Oxford: Blackwell, 2004), 48-49.

245. Y. Levin, "Nimrod the Mighty, King of Kish, King of Sumer and Akkad," *VT* 52 (2002): 350–66.

246. Šulgi B (see www.etcsl.orient.ox.ac.uk, t.2.4.2.02), lines 56–113 describe in detail his hunting prowess. This is one of the few texts that present a king as hunter prior to the late second millennium B.C. The earliest iconographic representation of a possibly royal personage hunting a lion is in the "Lion-Hunt Stele" from Uruk, see C. Watanabe, *Animal Symbolism in Mesopotamia* (Weiner Offene Orientalistik 1; Wien: Universität Wien, 2002), 42, fig. 1.

247. D. Frayne, *Ur III Period (2112–2004)* (RIME 3/2; Toronto: Univ. of Toronto, 1997).

248. See J. Glassner, *Mesopotamian Chronicles* (SBLWAW 19; Atlanta: SBL Press, 2004), 271.

249. For example, Sumerian *nè* means "chief" (J. Bottéro, *La Religion babylonienne* [Paris: Presses universitaires de France, 1952], 108; the Sumerian sign, Deimal/Labat #444 can also have the value "nim"). It can be seen in the etymology of the divine name Nergal = *nè.iri.gal* "chief of the Netherworld" (see W. G. Lambert, "Studies in Nergal" *BO* 30/5–6 [1973]: 355–63, esp. 356). Thus, *nè.mardu* would presumably mean "chief of the Mardu" (Amorites)—but again the caution—this title is not attested.

250. D. Frayne, *Sargonic and Gutian Periods (2334–2113 B.C.)* (RIME 2; Toronto: Univ. of Toronto Press, 1993), 10; cf. *OEANE*, 5:294–97.

251. *OEANE*, 1:41–43.

252. J. R. Davila, "Rehoboth-Ir," *ABD*, 5:664.

253. P. Machinist, "Nimrod," *ABD*, 4:1117.

254. See also V. A. Hurowitz, "In Search of Resen (Genesis 10:12): Dūr-Šarrukin²" in *Birkat Shalom*, ed. C. Cohen et al. (Winona Lake, Ind.: Eisenbrauns, 2008), 511–24, who identifies the city as Dur-Sharrukin.

255. Nissen, *The Early History of the Ancient Near East*, 56.

256. Ibid., 67.

257. J. Walton, "The Mesopotamian Background of the Tower of Babel Account and Its Implications," *BBR* 5 (1995): 155–75.

258. As the text indicates, this is different from Palestine, where stone is plentiful and where no baked brick is yet attested.

259. P. R. S. Moorey, *Ancient Mesopotamian Materials and Industries* (Winona Lake, Ind.: Eisenbrauns, 1994), 302, 306.

260. Ibid., 307.

261. Ibid., 332–33.

262. Ibid., 335.

263. For more details of ziggurat architecture and use see T. Jacobsen, "Notes on Ekur," *ErIsr* 21 (1990): 40–47.

264. See the Myth of Nergal and Ereshkigal. The Hebrew cognate of this word is also used in the story of Jacob's "ladder," which serves the same purpose as the stairways of the ziggurat.

265. The NIV's "tower that reaches to the heavens" can be misleading. The Hebrew expression "with its head in the heavens" is idiomatic, just like our English "skyscraper." This is not a siege tower as the early rabbis suggested.

266. D. Frayne, *Royal Inscriptions of Mesopotamia: Old Babylonian Period* (Toronto: University of Toronto Press, 1990), 208.

267. A. Guinan, "The Perils of High Living: Divinatory Rhetoric in *Šumma Ālu*," in *DUMU-E2-DUB-BA-A: Studies in Honor of Ake W. Sjöberg*, ed. H. Behrens, D. Loding, and M. Roth (Philadelphia: Occasional Publications of the Samuel Noah Kramer Fund, 1989), 234.

268. D. Sheriffs, "The Human Need for Continuity: Some ANE and OT Perspectives," *TynBul* 55 (2004): 1–16.

269. K. van der Toorn, *Family Religion in Babylonia, Syria and Israel: Continuity and Change in the Forms of Religious Life* (Leiden: Brill, 1996), 127.

270. See extensive discussion in Walton, *Genesis*, 375.

271. J. S. Cooper, *The Curse of Agade* (Baltimore, Md.: Johns Hopkins Univ. Press, 1983).

272. That is, if he were born in 2166, his departure from Haran at age seventy-five would be in 2091; this makes him a contemporary of Ur-Nammu.

273. *CAH*³, 3/2, 287, 289–90 (Brinkman).

274. See A. K. Grayson, *Assyrian Rulers of the Early First Millennium B.C. (to 1114–859 B.C.)* (RIMA 2; Toronto: Univ. of Toronto Press, 1991), 214, iii.24.

275. It should be noted that in times of political difficulties along the middle Euphrates, caravans might instead travel up the Tigris to Nineveh and from there take a road west across to Syria, bypassing the Euphrates altogether (crossing it at Til Barsib). This was a royal road during the Neo-Assyrian period and went right through Haran (see S. Parpola and M. Porter, *Helsinki Atlas of the Near East in the Neo-Assyrian Period* [Helsinki: Neo-Assyrian Text Corpus Project, 2001], 3–4).

276. Travel from Tuttul to Haran was considered a three-day journey in the Mari literature, see B. Beitzel, "From Harran to Imar along the Old Babylonian Itinerary: The Evidence from the *Archives Royales de Mari*," in *Biblical and Near Eastern Studies*, ed. G. Tuttle (Grand Rapids: Eerdmans, 1978), 214–15.

277. A. Millard, "Where Was Abraham's Ur?" *BAR* 27/3 (2001): 52–53, 57.

278. For the strongest case for an alternative northern location, see B. Beitzel, *The Moody Atlas of Bible Lands* (Chicago: Moody, 1985), 80.

279. Marsman, *Women in Ugarit*, 196–98, 712–13.

280. Marsman sees a more active role for women in the process at Ugarit, ibid., 214–15, but it still has nothing to do with providing an egg to be fertilized.

281. Cited in K. van der Toorn, *From Her Cradle to Her Grave* (Sheffield: Sheffield Academic Press, 1994), 78.

282. J. Scurlock and B. Andersen, *Diagnoses in Assyrian and Babylonian Medicine* (Urbana, Ill.: University of Illinois Press, 2005), 260–61. Of course they were familiar with many genitourinary problems that males could have, but the absence of any such symptoms would generally suggest that the problem was with the woman.

283. Cited in van der Toorn, *From Her Cradle to Her Grave*, 79–80.

284. A. Rainey and R. S. Notley, *The Sacred Bridge* (Jerusalem: Carta, 2006), 34–35.

285. S. Mittmann and G. Schmitt, *Tübinger Bibelatlas* (Stuttgart: Deutsche Bibelgesellschaft, 2001), Map B III 3.

286. N. Naʾaman, "The Canaanites and Their Land," in *Canaan in the Second Millennium B.C.E.* (Winona Lake, Ind.: Eisenbrauns, 2005), 110–33.

287. A. Pagolu, *The Religion of the Patriarchs* (JSOTSup 277; Sheffield: Sheffield Academic Press, 1998), 57–59; K. Nielsen, "Oak," *DDD*², 637–38; and "Terebinth," 850–51. Note that not all of these use the same terminology.

288. Nielsen, "Oak," 637–38.

289. A. E. Killebrew, *Biblical Peoples and Ethnicity* (Atlanta: SBL Press, 2005), 94.

290. Ibid., 95.

291. Rare exceptions can be seen in the slaughter of the Passover lamb, where it anticipates God's presence.

292. See W. Dever's cautious assessment in both "Beitin, Tell," *ABD*, 1:651; "Bethel," *OEANE*, 1:300.

293. It is of some interest that Kelso's excavation reports claim evidence of this destruction, but his summary of the excavations in *NEAEHL*, 1:192–94, says nothing about it.

294. The search for an alternative has been led by D. Livingston; see his "Location of Bethel and Ai Reconsidered," *WTJ* 33 (1970–71): 20–44; "Traditional Site of Bethel Questioned," *WTJ* 34 (1971): 39–50; and "The Last Word on Bethel and Ai," *BAR* 15/1 (1989): 11. He suggests the site of El-Bireh. See A. Rainey's refutation and defense of Tell Beitin in "Bethel is Still BEITIN," *WTJ* 33 (1971): 175–88; and *The Sacred Bridge*, 116–18.

295. C. Rasmussen, *NIV Atlas of the Bible* (Grand Rapids: Zondervan, 1989), 49–51.

296. Ibid., 50.

297. This was even reported in the *New York Times* (Aug. 24, 1993) in the "Science Times" section (interview of Harvey Weiss of Yale University).

298. *COS*, 3.5.

299. Particularly the painting in the tomb of Khnumhotep III at Beni-Hasan.

300. Compare Penelope's plight in Homer's *Odyssey*, who is probably forty-five or even fifty years old when the suitors line up for her hand. Besides being queen, she is also considered attractive and in possession of many other qualities that make her desirable to the suitors (2.115); she is described as excelling all women "in comeliness and stature, and in the wise heart within" (18.248–49).

301. S. Greengus, "Sisterhood Adoption at Nuzi and the 'Wife-Sister' in Genesis," *HUCA* 46 (1975): 5–31.

302. Thus an external personal cause rather than the internal "humor" of Hippocrates. See the excellent discussion in Scurlock and Andersen, *Diagnoses in Assyrian and Babylonian Medicine*, 10–12.

303. Ibid.

304. Here we refer to sources such as Philo, Strabo, Josephus, and Eusebius rather than ancient Near Eastern sources. There is as yet no verified reference to these cities in extrabiblical documents contemporary to the Old Testament. For an excellent summary of the data concerning the location of the cities see D. M. Howard, "Sodom and Gomorrah Revisited," *JETS* 27 (1984): 385–400; M. J. Mulder, "Sodom and Gomorrah," *ABD*, 6:99–103.

305. M. Weinfeld, "The Covenant of Grant in the Old Testament and the Ancient Near East," *JAOS* 90 (1970): 184–203; reprinted in F. E. Greenspahn, ed., *Essential Papers on Israel and the Ancient Near East* (New York: New York Univ. Press, 1991), 69–102 (pages cited in following footnotes will be from the latter).

306. Weinfeld, "Covenant of Grant," 70.

307. Rasmussen, *NIV Atlas of the Bible*, 42.

308. P. Hammond, "Hebron," *OEANE*, 3:13.

309. J. Chadwick, "Discovering Hebron," *BAR* 31/5 (2005): 25–33, 70–71.

310. A. Ofer, "Hebron," *NEAEHL*, 2:607–9.

311. C. Krahmalkov, "Exodus Itinerary Confirmed by Egyptian Evidence," *BAR* 20/5 (1994): 58.

312. It should be noted that the well-known Hammurabi is *not* one of them since it does not account for the ending of the biblical name.

313. See discussion by K. Kitchen, *On the Reliability of the Old Testament* (Grand Rapids: Eerdmans, 2003), 568, n. 21.

314. None of these city names are perfect matches, see ibid., 568, n. 22.

315. K. Kitchen, "Genesis 12–50 in the Near Eastern World," in *He Swore an Oath: Biblical Themes from Genesis 12–50* (Cambridge: Tyndale, 1993), 73.

316. Heimpel, *Letters to the King of Mari*, 56.

317. F. Vallat, "Elam," *ABD*, 2:425.

318. Three tablets from the late Babylonian period (ca. 600 B.C.) have been traditionally referred to as the "Kedorlaomer tablets" and have been related by some scholars to Genesis 14 (see M. Astour, "Political and Cosmic Symbolism in Genesis 14

and in its Babylonian Sources," in *Biblical Motifs*, ed. A. Altmann [Cambridge, Mass.: Harvard Univ. Press, 1966], 65–112). This is a spurious designation since there is no mention of this king in the tablets, properly referred to as the Spartoli tablets. Instead they refer to the Elamite king of the Kassite period, Kudu-Nahhunte. See discussion in C. R. Cohen, "Genesis 14:1–11—An Early Israelite Chronographic Source," in *The Biblical Canon in Comparative Perspective*: *Scripture in Context IV*, ed. K. Lawson Younger, W. W. Hallo, and B. F. Batto (Lewiston, N.Y.: Edwin Mellen, 1991), 67–108, append. 2 (85–86).

319. T. Bryce, *The Kingdom of the Hittites* (Oxford: Clarendon, 1998), 131.

320. Ibid., 19.

321. *CAH*, I/2, 454. This would appear to be far too early for Abram.

322. *CAH*, II/1, 38–9.

323. J. Zorn, "Elath," *ABD*, 2:429.

324. G. Pratico, "Tell el-Kheleifeh," *NEAEHL*, 3:870.

325. Rainey and Notley, *Sacred Bridge*, 15; Y. Aharoni, *Land of the Bible* (Philadelphia: Westminster, 1979), 140.

326. D. Dorsey, *The Roads and Highways of Ancient Israel* (Baltimore, Md.: Johns Hopkins Univ. Press, 1991), 147.

327. Moorey, *Ancient Mesopotamian Materials*, 332–35.

328. In the Amarna letters, see, e.g., 286, 288. Discussion can be found in N. Na°aman, "Habiru and Hebrews: The Transfer of a Social Term to the Literary Sphere," in *Canaan in the Second Millennium B.C.E.* (Winona Lake, Ind.: Eisenbrauns, 2005), 252–74; A. F. Rainey, "Unruly Elements in Late Bronze Canaanite Society," in *Pomegranates and Golden Bells*, ed. D. P. Wright, D. N. Freedman, and A. Hurvitz (Winona Lake, Ind.: Eisenbrauns, 1995), 481–96; Rainey and Notley, *Sacred Bridge*, 88–89.

329. Rainey and Notley, *Sacred Bridge*, 89.

330. *CAD*, Ḥ, 76; J. A. Naudé, "חנך," *NIDOTTE*, 2:200; for complete discussion see Cohen, "Genesis 14:1–11—An Early Israelite Chronographic Source," 67–108, append. 1 (82–84). Some earlier discussions suggested an Egyptian cognate from the execration texts, but Cohen has provided the argument and documentation that refutes this connection.

331. Frayne, *Royal Inscriptions of Mesopotamia*, 654–55.

332. Y. Yadin, "Warfare in the Second Millennium B.C.E.," in *Patriarchs: The World History of the Jewish People*, ed. B. Mazar (Jerusalem: Massada, 1970), 138.

333. The Madeba map is the earliest map of Palestine. It is a mosaic on the floor of a sixth century A.D. church. See V. R. Gold, "The Mosaic Map of Madeba," in *The Biblical Archaeologist Reader 3*, ed. E. F. Campbell and D. N. Freedman (New York: Doubleday, 1970), 366–89.

334. The most complete summary of the information concerning Elyon is in H.-J. Zobel, "עֶלְיוֹן," *TDOT*,

11:121–39. See other treatments in J. Reiling, "Melchizedek," *DDD²*, 560–63; E. E. Elnes and P. D. Miller, "Elyon," *DDD²*, 293–99; T. Mettinger, *In Search of God* (Philadelphia: Fortress, 1988), 122; F. M. Cross, *Canaanite Myth and Hebrew Epic* (Cambridge, Mass.: Harvard Univ. Press, 1973), 50–52.

335. Elnes and Miller, "Elyon," 294, though some have thought that the wording of the Sefire I treaty between Bir-Ga°yah and Matiel, which has a conjunction between El and Elyon, supports independent status.

336. Pagolu, *The Religion of the Patriarchs*, 171–91; G. Anderson, *Sacrifices and Offerings in Ancient Israel* (Atlanta: Scholars Press, 1987), 77–82.

337. See Akkadian *ešretu*, *CAD* E, 368. For an assemblage of the variety of texts where there is a 10 percent assessment (usually in animals or produce to the state or temple) see E. Salonen, "Über den Aehnten im alten Mesopotamien," *Studia Orientalia* 43 (1972): 3–65; M. DeJ. Ellis, "Taxation in Ancient Mesopotamia: The History of the Term *miksu*," *JCS* 26 (1974): 211–50.

338. This is true even of the rest of the Old Testament. In Num. 31 a portion of the booty is given to the Lord, but clearly not as a tithe.

339. Unfortunately, the only example of this is in a text from Larsa, where it followed a trade expedition (Pagolu, *Religion of the Patriarchs*, 174, 183).

340. Cf. G. Beckman, *Hittite Diplomatic Texts* (Atlanta: Scholars Press, 1996), 17, Treaty #2, §§ 23, 26, 30, 33.

341. Akk. *munattu*, *CAD* M/2, 200; cf. discussion in S. A. L. Butler, *Mesopotamian Conceptions of Dreams and Dream Rituals* (Münster: Ugarit-Verlag, 1998), 34–35.

342. Akk. *purussu amaru*, *CAD* P, 534; cf. Butler, *Mesopotamian Conceptions of Dreams*, 36–37.

343. F. Knobloch, "Adoption," *ABD*, 1:76–79. Nuzi texts are in E. Lacheman, ed., *Excavations at Nuzi VIII: Family Law Documents* (HSS 19; Cambridge, Mass.: Harvard Univ. Press, 1962); and *Joint Expedition with the Iraq Museum at Nuzi*, 595 (often abbreviated *JEN*).

344. *Textes cunéiformes du Louvre* 18, 153:20, see *CAD* A/2, 244.

345. See discussions in M. J. Selman, "Comparative Customs and the Patriarchal Age," in *Essays on the Patriarchal Narratives*, ed. A. R. Millard and D. J. Wiseman (Winona Lake, Ind.: Eisenbrauns, 1983), 114; M. J. Selman, "The Social Environment of the Patriarchs," *TynBul* 27 (1976): 114–36 (see 125–27); T. Thompson, *The Historicity of the Patriarchal Narratives* (Berlin: de Gruyter, 1974), 203–30; J. van Seters, *Abraham in History and Tradition* (New Haven, Conn.: Yale Univ. Press, 1975), 85–87.

346. Discussion and full presentation of data in Horowitz, *Mesopotamian Cosmic Geography*, 151–92, 252–56.

347. *CAD* K, 47a, 48b (*kakkabu*)

348. AT 456; R. S. Hess, "The Slaughter of the Animals in Genesis 15: Genesis 15:8–21 and Its

Ancient Near Eastern Context," in *He Swore an Oath*, ed. R. S. Hess, P. E. Satterthwaite, and G. J. Wenham (Cambridge: Tyndale, 1993), 55–65 (see 60); Weinfeld, "Covenant of Grant," 79–80.

349. ARM II, 37: 6, 11; Weinfeld, "Covenant of Grant," 80.

350. 1.A, 39–40; Hess, "Slaughter of Animals," 61–62.

351. Hess, "Slaughter of Animals," 62; Weinfeld, "Covenant of Grant," 81. Note also the treaty between Bir-Gaʾyah and Matiᶜilu where a calf is cut in two, again explicitly indicating that this would be the punishment for violating the terms of the treaty.

352. P. Michalowski, "The Torch and the Censer," in *The Tablet and the Scroll*, ed. M. E. Cohen, D. C. Snell, and D. B. Weisberg (Bethesda, Md.: CDL, 1993), 152–62 (see 156).

353. E. Reiner, *Šurpu: A Collection of Sumerian and Akkadian Incantations* (AfO 11; Graz: Selbstverlag des Herausgebers, 1958), 2.109–10; "he has asked for a sign through the lit stove, he has asked for a sign through the torch."

354. Ibid., 3.15, 17, 32, 93, 145; Weinfeld, "Covenant of Grant," 91–92.

355. In some translations it appears that there are only eight parts since the birds are not divided. The verbs in 15:10, however, more likely indicate that the larger animals are cut in half whereas the two birds are not, but instead, just have their heads pinched off according to standard practice. I owe this observation to G. Johnston from a yet unpublished paper.

356. Michalowski, "Torch and Censer," 159.

357. See *šurpu* 8.75: "together with the oath of furnace, grill, kiln, stove, brazier or bellows"; or 3.145: "oath of lamp and stove"; see Weinfeld, "Covenant Grant," 97–98 n. 118.

358. The verb "passed" (ᶜābar) is singular, thus perhaps even favoring this interpretation, though not requiring it. I owe this observation to G. Johnston from an unpublished paper.

359. COS, 1.61.

360. After adultery, childlessness was probably the primary reason for divorce. See Marsman, *Women in Ugarit*, 176.

361. N. Steinberg, *Kinship and Marriage in Genesis: A Household Economics Perspective* (Minneapolis: Fortress, 1993), 15.

362. Ibid., 16–17.

363. HSS 5, 67 (AASOR 10, 2); see *ANET*, 220.

364. *Inscriptions cunéiformes du Kultépé* 3.34, translated in J. Lewy, "On Some Institutions of the Old Assyrian Empire," *HUCA* 27 (1956): 9–10; see *ANET*, 543; A. K. Grayson and J. van Seters, "The Childless Wife in Assyria and the Stories of Genesis," *Or* 44 (1975): 485–86. J. Van Seters, "The Problem of Childlessness in Near Eastern Law and the Patriarchs of Israel," *JBL* 87 (1968): 401–8, also makes reference to a Neo-Assyrian text from Nimrud (*Nimrud Documents* 2307), which features polycoity, though here the wife does not take initiative, nor is it her handmaiden,

see B. Parker, "The Nimrud Tablets 1952—Business Documents," *Iraq* 16 (1954): 37–39; Selman, "Comparative Customs," 129.

365. J. F. Ross, "The Prophet as Yahweh's Messenger," in *Israel's Prophetic Heritage*, ed. B. W. Anderson and W. Harrelson (New York: Harper, 1962), 101–2.

366. Cf. how Moses adopts the first person formula though he is reporting what God did (Deut. 29:2–6); see also Gen. 44:5, 10 where Joseph's messenger adopts a first person formula.

367. For discussion of the role of royal messenger in Assyria see J. S. Holladay, "Assyrian Statecraft and the Prophets of Israel," *HTR* 63 (1970): 29–51.

368. E. T. Mullen, *The Assembly of the Gods* (Atlanta: Scholars Press, 1980), 144. It may also be noted in passing that the Ugaritic literature uses the same type of designation for the messenger, e.g., *malʾaka yammi*, "messengers/angels of [the god] Yam"; see ibid., 210.

369. H. Niehr and G. Steins, "שַׁדַּי," *TDOT*, 14.418–46; E. A. Knauf, "Shadday," *DDD²*, 749–53.

370. Niehr and Steins, "שַׁדַּי," 14:420–21, referring to *KTU* 1.108, 10–13.

371. *CAD* Š/1, 57.

372. COS, 2.27; see discussion in ibid., 14:422–23.

373. See *TLOT*, 3:1348–67 (S. van der Woude), for a carefully nuanced and comprehensive treatment of naming. See also Ramsey, "Is Name-Giving an Act of Domination?" 24–35.

374. Most biblical names that begin or end with El, begin with Jo- or Jeho-, or end in -iah contain statements about God. These are called "theophoric" names.

375. J. M. Sasson, "Circumcision in the Ancient Near East," *JBL* 85 (1966): 473–76; P. J. King, "Circumcision: Who Did it, Who Didn't, and Why," *BAR* 32/4 (2006): 48–55. The earliest evidence is in art (in a tomb relief from Egypt, about 2340 B.C.; see picture in King, "Circumcision," 48)—written texts refer to it a few centuries later (Egyptian stele from Naga-ed-Dar, ibid., 49).

376. M. Eilberg-Schwartz, *The Savage in Judaism: An Anthropology of Israelite Religion and Ancient Judaism* (Bloomington, Ind.: Indiana Univ. Press, 1990); see summary and critique in M. Malul, *Knowledge, Control and Sex* (Tel Aviv-Jaffa: Archaeological Center, 2002), 396–97.

377. Malul, *Knowledge*, 395.

378. *ANEP*, 332.

379. Legend of ʾAqhat, Tablet 1, column 1, lines 42–43. The following lines describe the role of the heir. COS, 1.103.

380. Appu and His Two Sons, COS, 1.58.

381. *Etana*, COS, 1.131.

382. V. Matthews, "Hospitality and Hostility in Genesis 19 and Judges 19," *BTB* 22 (1992): 3–11; W. Fields, *Sodom and Gomorrah* (Sheffield: Sheffield Academic Press, 1997), 54–64.

383. S. Meier, *The Messenger in the Ancient Semitic World* (HSM 45; Atlanta: Scholars Press, 1988), 93–96.

384. COS, 1.103.

385. P. J. King and L. Stager, *Life in Biblical Israel* (Louisville: Westminster John Knox, 2002), 65–66.

386. Marsman, *Women in Ugarit*, 488, 540.

387. Van der Toorn, *From Her Cradle to Her Grave*, 52.

388. Ibid., 51; discussed also under the entry for *harištu*, *CAD* 6:103–4.

389. I. Singer, *Hittite Prayers* (SBLWAW 11; Atlanta: SBL Press, 2002), 53 par. 10.

390. Gilgamesh 11.185–86.

391. King and Stager, *Life in Biblical Israel*, 234.

392. S. Morschauser, "'Hospitality,' Hostiles and Hostages: On the Legal Background to Genesis 19:1–9," *JSOT* 27:4 (2003): 461–85 (see esp. 465–67).

393. Ibid., 472–76.

394. Morschauser attempts to support his proposed interpretation in n. 39 on 472, but though they convey investigation, none of the five examples he cites have personal direct objects despite how English translations make it sound. For instance, Ps. 139:2 reads, "You have searched me and you know (= have investigated)." Likewise in the single example from Amarna (*EA* 60) of the verb with a personal direct object cited by Morschauser, "knowing" does not indicate interrogation or even investigation, but showing concern, care and trust; see W. Moran, *The Amarna Letters* (Baltimore, Md.: Johns Hopkins Univ. Press, 1992), 132, n.8.

395. Akk. *sinlurmâ* (*CAD* S, 285, occurring in two medical diagnosis texts and related form, *sinnuru*; cf. M. Stol, "Blindness and Night-Blindness in Akkadian," *JNES* 45 (1986): 295–99; Scurlock and Andersen. *Diagnoses in Assyrian and Babylonian Medicine*, 195–96.

396. *CTA*, 19, iv.167, transl. in Parker, *Ugaritic Narrative Poetry*, 75, column IV line 5.

397. R. W. Younker, "Ammonites," in *Peoples of the Old Testament World*, ed. A. Hoerth, G. Mattingly, and E. Yamauchi (Grand Rapids: Baker, 1995), 300–304; see also G. Mattingly, "Moabites," 321–26.

398. The first reference to Moab in extrabiblical literature occurs in the thirteenth century inscriptions of Ramesses II (Mattingly, "Moabites," 324). See discussion in B. Routledge, *Moab in the Iron Age* (Philadelphia: Univ. of Pennsylvania Press, 2004), 58–60.

399. Routledge, *Moab in the Iron Age*, 77–78. Pages 78–82 contain his assessment of Late Bronze settlement patterns in southern Transjordan.

400. J. Hoffmeier, *Ancient Israel in Sinai* (Oxford: Oxford Univ. Press, 2005), 159–61; idem, *Israel in Egypt*, 188; see also Rainey and Notley, *Sacred Bridge*, 120 (map).

401. E. D. Oren, "Gerar," *OEANE*, 1:474–76; idem, "Gerar," *ABD*, 2:989–91.

402. Compare Moses' successful intercession on behalf of Israel (Ex. 32:31–35) and Jeremiah's being told not to try to intercede (Jer. 7:16; 11:14; 14:11).

403. *KTU* 1.24; Parker, *Ugaritic Narrative Poetry*, 215–18.

404. Marsman, *Women in Ugarit*, 143–44; R. Westbrook, "The Female Slave," in *Gender and Law in the Hebrew Bible and the Ancient Near East*, ed. V. Matthews, B. Levinson, and T. Frymer-Kensky (New York/London: T. & T. Clark, 2004), 214–38.

405. Westbrook, "Female Slave," 220.

406. Marsman, *Women in Ugarit*, 188.

407. M. B. Rowton, "Watercourses and Water Rights in the Official Correspondence from Larsa and Isin," *JCS* 21 (1969): 267–74.

408. Much of this is drawn from the excellent article by J. P. Oleson, "Water Works," *ABD*, 6:883–93.

409. Killebrew, *Biblical Peoples and Ethnicity*, 202–8.

410. See, however, "king of the Philistines" in 26:1, which might lead to consideration of Kitchen's suggestion that Abimelech and his kin represent an ethnic group that originated in Kaphtor as the later Philistines also did (*Reliability*, 339–41).

411. Inscriptions have been discovered in ancient mines at Serabit Khadim. This particular inscription was found in Mine M. See J. Hoffmeier, *Ancient Israel in Sinai* (Oxford: Oxford Univ. Press, 2005), 178–79; F. M. Cross, *Canaanite Myth and Hebrew Epic* (Harvard, Mass.: Cambridge Univ. Press, 1973), 18–19. These inscriptions are from the eighteenth to seventeenth centuries B.C. and represent some of the earliest examples of alphabetic script in the ancient world. The site is not far from the route that the Israelites would have taken to Sinai, though the inscriptions are from several centuries earlier.

412. Note also that in 2 Chronicles it is called Mount Moriah, whereas here it is referred to as "the region [land] of Moriah."

413. J. Chadwick, "Discovering Hebron," *BAR* 31/5 (2005): 25–33, 70–71.

414. Hittite rituals are clearly expiatory and defensibly substitutionary, See Milgrom, *Leviticus 1–16*, 174–75; D. P. Wright, *The Disposal of Impurity* (Atlanta: Scholars Press, 1987).

415. See discussion in Herzog, "Beersheba," *OEANE*, 1:287–91.

416. H. A. Hoffner, "The Hittites and Hurrians," in *Peoples of the Old Testament Times*, ed. D. J. Wiseman (Oxford: Clarendon, 1973), 197–228; idem, "Hittites," in *Peoples of the Old Testament World*, ed. A. J. Hoerth, G. L. Mattingly, and E. M. Yamauchi (Grand Rapids: Baker, 1994), 127–56.

417. S. M. Olyan, "Some Neglected Aspects of Israelite Interment Ideology," *JBL* 124 (2005): 601–16.

418. E. Bloch-Smith, "Burials," *ABD*, 1:785.

419. R. Westbrook, *Property and the Family in Biblical Law* (Sheffield: Sheffield Academic Press, 1991), 24–35.

420. Ibid., 27.

421. *NEAEHL*, 3:938–42.

422. M. Malul, "More on *paḥad yiṣḥāq* (Genesis XXXI 42, 53) and the Oath by the Thigh," *VT* 35 (1985): 192–200.

423. Steinberg, *Kinship and Marriage*, 12.

424. Kitchen, *Reliability*, 339; see also the brief discussion of zoological finds in C. Grigson, "Plough and Pasture in the Early Economy of the Southern Levant," in *The Archaeology of Society in the Holy Land*, ed. T. Levy (New York: Facts on File, 1995),

259; Wapnish, "Camel," *OEANE*, 1:407–8; Hesse, "Camel," *CANE*, 1:217. Some generally reliable sources still sometimes indicate a date for camel domestication at the end of the second millennium (e.g., *CANE*, 3:1402) and judge the references in the patriarchal narratives as anachronistic (King and Stager, *Life in Biblical Israel*, 117). See the more nuanced and complete discussion in Firmage, "Zoology," *ABD*, 5:1138–40.

425. W. T. Pitard, "Aram-Naharaim," *ABD*, 1:341.

426. E. E. Platt, "Jewelry, Ancient Israelite," *ABD*, 3:825–26.

427. For a good summary of the various aspects of marriage negotiations see V. H. Matthews, "Marriage and Family in the Ancient Near East," in *Marriage and Family in the Biblical World*, ed. K. M. Campbell (Downers Grove, Ill.: InterVarsity Press, 2003), 1–32; for discussion of the financial arrangements at Nuzi, see K. Grosz, "Dowry and Brideprice in Nuzi," in *Studies on the Civilization and Culture of Nuzi and the Hurrians*, ed. M. A. Morrison and D. I. Owen (Winona Lake, Ind.: Eisenbrauns, 1981), 161–82.

428. Steinberg, *Kinship and Marriage*, 28. In early (Sumerian) practice, the gifts usually took the form of foodstuffs provided for the feast to celebrate the marriage, see S. Greengus, "Bridewealth in Sumerian Sources," *HUCA* 61 (1990): 25–88. This type of gift would have been an impractical option for Abraham's servant because of the long trip. Provision of foodstuff by the family brings to mind our modern practice of the groom's parents bearing the responsibility for the rehearsal dinner and the bride's family bearing the responsibility for the reception.

429. Greengus, "Bridewealth," 78.

430. Marsman, *Women in Ugarit*, 90.

431. Grosz, "Dowry and Brideprice in Nuzi," 176–77.

432. Ibid., 162.

433. Westbrook, *Property and the Family*, 142–64. A text with a dowry list from the Old Babylonian Period may be found on 143.

434. Marsman, *Women in Ugarit*, 94.

435. Van der Toorn, *From Her Cradle to Her Grave*, 64–65.

436. K. van der Toorn, "The Significance of the Veil in the Ancient Near East," in *Pomegranates and Golden Bells*, ed. D. P. Wright, D. N. Freedman, and A. Hurvitz (Winona Lake, Ind.: Eisenbrauns, 1995), 327–40; M. Tsevat, "The Husband Veils a Wife (Hittite Laws, §§ 197–98)," *JCS* 27 (1975): 235–40.

437. MAL A § 40. See Isa. 47:1–3.

438. CH 156.

439. Van der Toorn, "Significance of the Veil," 330–31.

440. Ibid., 333 (ARM 26.10:13–15).

441. Marsman, *Women in Ugarit*, 143–44; Westbrook, "The Female Slave," 214–38.

442. Westbrook, *Property and the Family*, 123 n.2.

443. Olyan, "Some Neglected Aspects of Israelite Interment Ideology," 601–16.

444. K. Kitchen, "Ancient Arabia and the Bible," *Archaeology in the Biblical World* 3/1 (1995):

26–34; R. H. Smith, "Arabia," *ABD*, 1:324–27; A. K. Irvine, "Arabs and Ethiopians," in *Peoples of Old Testament Times*, ed. D. J. Wiseman (Oxford: Oxford Univ. Press, 1973), 287–311.

445. Assmann, *Search for God*, 83–84. Critique of the relationship between name and essence is offered in Ramsey, "Is Name-Giving an Act of Domination?" 24–35.

446. Ramsey, "Is Name-Giving an Act of Domination?" 24–35.

447. The names of Marduk represent a complex exegetical analysis of the attributes and nature of the god based on scribal hermeneutics both in semantics and orthography. J. Bottéro, "Les Noms de Marduk, l'écriture et la logique en Mesopotamie ancienne," in *Essays on the Ancient Near East in the memory of Jacob Joel Finkelstein*, ed. M. de Jong Ellis (Hamden, Conn: Archon, 1977), 5–28.

448. F. E. Greenspahn, "Primogeniture in Ancient Israel," in *Go to the Land I Will Show You*, ed. J. Coleson and V. Matthews (Winona Lake, Ind.: Eisenbrauns, 1996), 69–80; B. J. Beitzel, "The Right of the Firstborn in the Old Testament (Deut.21:15–17)," in *A Tribute to Gleason Archer*, ed. W. C. Kaiser Jr. and R. F. Youngblood (Chicago: Moody Press, 1986), 179–90.

449. Van der Toorn, *Family Religion*, 223, enumerates the responsibilities of the paterfamilias to care for the deceased in the town of Nuzi. The particulars may have differed from culture to culture, and the specifics of what the patriarchs would have included in the care for the dead cannot be reconstructed. But whatever the responsibilities were, the paterfamilias was entrusted with them.

450. Beitzel, "The Right of the Firstborn," 180.

451. Westbrook, *Property and the Family*, 137.

452. Ibid., 125.

453. Van der Toorn, *Family Religion*, 198, 223.

454. Westbrook, *Property and the Family*, 138.

455. W. Pitard, "Paddan Aram," *ABD*, 5:55.

456. Steinberg, *Kinship and Marriage*, 84, n.106.

457. W. Schniedewind, "The Rise of the Aramean States," in *Mesopotamia and the Bible*, ed. M. W. Chavalas and K. L. Younger (Grand Rapids: Baker, 2002), 276–87. Zadok (see next note) mentions a place name *Aramu* as early as the Ebla texts, but believes it to be an unrelated Hurrian term (106).

458. R. Zadok, "Elements of Aramean Pre-history," in *Ah, Assyria*, ed. M. Cogan and I. Eph'al (ScrHier 33; Jerusalem: Magnes, 1991), 104–20 (see 105).

459. W. Pitard, "Aramaeans," in *Peoples of the Old Testament World*, ed. A. J. Hoerth, G. L. Mattingly, and E. M. Yamauchi (Grand Rapids: Baker, 1994), 207–30.

460. Dorsey, *The Roads and Highways of Ancient Israel*, 119–46.

461. A. R. Millard, "The Celestial Ladder and the Gate of Heaven," *ET* 78 (1966): 86–87; for full discussion of the lexical background of *sullām* (= "stairway"), see C. Houtman, "What Did Jacob See in His Dream at Bethel?" *VT* 27 (1977): 337–51. Houtman is more inclined to interpret the *sullām* as the ascent to the high place at Bethel (see 347).

462. For discussion of the standing stones (*maṣṣēbôt*) see the following: U. Avner, "Sacred Stones in the Desert," *BAR* 27/3 (2001): 31–41; V. Hurowitz, "Picturing Imageless Deities," *BA* 23/3 (1997): 46–48, 51, 68; K. van der Toorn, "Worshipping Stones: On the Deification of Cult Symbols," *JNSL* 23 (1997): 1–14; E. C. LaRocca-Pitts, *Of Wood and Stone* (HSM 61; Winona Lake, Ind.: Eisenbrauns, 2001), 205–28; T. N. D. Mettinger, *No Graven Image?* (Stockholm: Almqvist & Wiksell, 1995), 140–91; Pagolu, *The Religion of the Patriarchs*, 135–70; Z. Zevit, *The Religions of Ancient Israel* (New York: Continuum, 2001), 256–62; E. Bloch-Smith, "*Maṣṣēbôt* in the Israelite Cult: An Argument for Rendering Implicit Cultic Criteria Explicit," in *Temple and Worship in Biblical Israel*, ed. J. Day (New York/London: Continuum/T. & T. Clark, 2005), 28–39; T. N. D. Mettinger, "Israelite Aniconism: Developments and Origins," in *The Image and the Book*, ed. K. van der Toorn (Leuven: Peeters, 1997), 173–204.

463. U. Avner, "Sacred Stones in the Desert," 31–41. He dates the earliest to the eleventh to tenth millennium B.C.

464. Bronze age finds include Megiddo, Hazor, Gezer, and Shechem; Iron Age finds include Arad, Lachish, Beth Shemesh, Megiddo, Taanach, and Dan (see complete list in Mettinger, "Israelite Aniconism," 197). Bloch-Smith, "*Maṣṣēbôt* in the Israelite Cult," calls into question many of these based on a narrower definition, e.g., Iron Age Megiddo Shrine 2081, 31–35 (see her complete list of questioned sites on 36). She concludes that only the Arad fortress temple is indisputable among the proposed Iron Age Israelite *maṣṣēbôt*.

465. Van der Toorn, "Worshipping Stones."

466. Cf. the one referred to in the Ugaritic Epic of ʾAqhat, *COS*, 1.103.

467. Pagolu, *Religion of the Patriarchs*, 147–51, identifies four categories: legal stones, memorial stones, commemorative stones, and cultic stones, a classification system first set up by C. Graesser's unpublished Harvard dissertation in 1969. See also LaRocca-Pitts' summary classification, *Of Wood and Stone*, 227. Bloch-Smith, "*Maṣṣēbôt* in the Israelite Cult," offers a reassessment and criteria for some controls for identifying *maṣṣēbôt*.

468. Hurowitz, "Picturing Imageless," 68. See Deut. 12:3–4; 16:22.

469. Houtman, "What Did Jacob See?" 343.

470. This translation is contrary to NIV, "above it." This combination of verb and preposition always means "beside" (see Walton, *Genesis*, 571, n. 6). For examples in Genesis see 18:2; 24:13; 45:1; see also the discussion in Houtman, "What Did Jacob See?" 348–49.

471. Avner, "Sacred Stones," 33; See *ANET*, 660, Sefire IIC.

472. See T. W. Cartledge, *Vows in the Hebrew Bible and the Ancient Near East* (JSOTSup 147; Sheffield: Sheffield Academic Press, 1992), for a complete study of vows.

473. For a good summary discussion of pastoral nomadism in the ancient world, see G. Schwartz, "Pastoral Nomadism in Ancient Western Asia," in *CANE*, 1:249–58. For information on herders in the ancient world, see V. Matthews and D. C. Benjamin, *Social World of Ancient Israel* (Peabody, Mass.: Hendrickson, 1993), 52–66; M. A. Morrison, "Evidence for Herdsmen and Animal Husbandry in the Nuzi Documents," in *Studies on the Civilization and Culture of Nuzi and the Hurrians*, ed. M. A. Morrison and D. I. Owen (Winona Lake, Ind.: Eisenbrauns, 1981), 257–96.

474. For an Old Babylonian example see J. J. Finkelstein, "An Old Babylonian Herding Contract and Genesis 31.38f.," in *Essays in Memory of E. A. Speiser*, ed. W. W. Hallo (American Oriental Series 53; New Haven, Conn.: American Oriental Society, 1968), 30–36.

475. This interpretation was initially proposed by D. Daube and R. Yaron, "Jacob's Reception by Laban," *JSS* 1 (1956): 60–62, and is accepted by Westbrook, *Property and the Family*, 133–34.

476. Grosz, "Dowry and Brideprice in Nuzi," 176–77.

477. This is not to suggest that marriage was "secular," for nothing was truly secular in the ancient world. K. van der Toorn (*From Her Cradle to Her Grave*, 59–69), while acknowledging the lack of data to demonstrate a sacral element to the ceremony, nevertheless rightly contends that the wedding context does not signal the absence of a religious aspect to their views of marriage. The gods instituted marriage and are interested in fidelity within marriage. Cf. the discussion in Marsman, *Women in Ugarit*, 107–22, for a persuasive presentation of the elements that commend considering marriage a religious institution in the ancient world.

478. Matthews, "Marriage and Family in the Ancient Near East," 1–32 (esp. 6–14).

479. Marsman, *Women in Ugarit*, 84–122 (esp. 87).

480. Van der Toorn, *From Her Cradle to Her Grave*, 61, 65–66.

481. Ibid., 73–74.

482. Ibid., 70.

483. J. Van Seters, "Jacob's Marriages and Ancient Near East Customs: A Reexamination," *HTR* 62 (1969): 377–95, engages in an extensive discussion the marriage customs reflected in this section of Genesis and in the ancient Near East and has nothing to offer on this point.

484. Van der Toorn, *From Her Cradle to Her Grave*, 66.

485. For a full treatment of the lore see M. Pope, *Song of Songs* (AB; Garden City, N.Y.: Doubleday, 1977), 648–50.

486. O. Keel, *The Song of Songs* (Minneapolis: Fortress, 1994), 257. In the Cairo love poetry, the Egyptian term *rrmt*, referring to an erotic stimulant is sometimes rendered "mandragora" or "mandrake," though the identification is not certain. See M. Fox, *The Song of Songs and the Ancient Egyptian Love Songs* (Madison, Wisc.: Univ. of Wisconsin Press, 1985), 9.

487. M. Zohary, *Plants of the Bible* (Cambridge: Cambridge Univ. Press, 1982), 188–89; Hepper, *Baker Encyclopedia of Bible Plants*, 151.

488. Zohary, *Plants of the Bible*, 189.

489. Ibid., 189; for a possible cognate in the literature of Ugarit, see Pope, *Song of Songs*, 648, who refers to the Anat section of the Baal cycle; also J. C. L. Gibson, *Canaanite Myths and Legends* (Edinburgh: T. & T. Clark, 1978), 49 (line 12) and 51 (line 68). For a different interpretation ("love") see Parker, *Ugaritic Narrative Poetry*, 110 (line 15) and 112 (line 9).

490. Anywhere from two to seven years, see Beitzel, "The Right of the Firstborn," 180, referring to texts from Kultepe and Alalakh respectively.

491. The categories "inspired" and "deductive" are introduced by J. Bottéro, *Religion in Ancient Mesopotamia* (Chicago: Univ. of Chicago Press, 2001), 170–71. M. Nissinen uses "noninductive" rather than "inspired," in *Prophets and Prophecy in the Ancient Near East* (SBLWAW 12; Atlanta: SBL Press, 2003), 1.

492. M. Morrison, "The Jacob and Laban Narrative in Light of Near Eastern Sources," *BA* 46 (1983): 155–64 (see 156–57).

493. Finkelstein, "An Old Babylonian Herding Contract," 33.

494. B. Hesse, "Animal Husbandry and Human Diet in the Ancient Near East," in *CANE*, 1:209.

495. See Marsman, *Women in Ugarit*, 103.

496. Westbrook, *Property and the Family*, 158; Morrison, "The Jacob and Laban Narrative," 160–61.

497. Van Seters, "Jacob's Marriages," 391–94.

498. K. van der Toorn, "The Nature of the Biblical *Teraphim* in the Light of the Cuneiform Evidence," *CBQ* 52 (1990): 203–22; idem, *Family Religion in Babylonia, Syria and Israel*, 218–25; T. J. Lewis, "Teraphim," *DDD²*, 844–50; H. Hoffner, "Hittite Tarpiš and Hebrew Teraphim," *JNES* 27 (1968): 61–68.

499. Hamilton, *Genesis 18–50*, "nonliteral," 299; Wenham, *Genesis 12–36*, "rough approximation," 274.

500. One (Num. 11:31; 1 Kings 19:4); three (Gen. 30:36; Ex. 3:18; 5:3; 8:27; Num. 10:33; 33:8); seven (Gen. 31:23; 2 Kings 3:9).

501. In English we might speak of a cross-country trip or a weekend trip. No useful information is gained by asking the person how big is the country you are crossing or calculating how many days are counted as a weekend and how far could one go on each day. The idioms communicate clearly as they stand.

502. Entry taken from Walton, *Genesis*, 590–91.

503. Cf. Middle Assyrian Palace Decrees #7; see Roth, *Law Collections from Mesopotamia and Asia Minor*, 200.

504. Van der Toorn, *From Her Cradle to Her Grave*, 52; cf. Akk. *musukkatu*, *CAD* M/2, 239.

505. M. A. Morrison, "Evidence for Herdsmen and Animal Husbandry in the Nuzi Documents," in *Studies on the Civilization and Culture of Nuzi and the Hurrians*, ed. M. A. Morrison and D. I. Owen (Winona Lake, Ind.: Eisenbrauns, 1981), 257–96.

506. J. N. Postgate, *Early Mesopotamia* (New York: Routledge, 1994), 160; cf. also idem, "Some Old Babylonian Shepherds and Their Flocks," *JSS* 20 (1975): 1–20.

507. Postgate, *Early Mesopotamia*, 161.

508. HSS V, 67:17–18; G 51; see discussion in Thompson, *The Historicity of the Patriarchal Narratives*, 269–80, who demonstrates that the motivation for the clause in the Nuzi contracts differs considerably from that represented in Genesis. J. Paradise, "Marriage Contracts of Free Persons at Nuzi," *JCS* 39 (1987): 1–36 (see 11, n. 31), points out that there are only two texts (AASOR 16:55 and HSS 9:24) that forbid the groom to take another wife under any circumstances, and in both of them there are already children, as here in Gen. 31.

509. Paradise, "Marriage Contracts of Free Persons at Nuzi," 1–36.

510. Rainey and Notley, *Sacred Bridge*, 115.

511. Ibid., 41 (map on 38).

512. Walton, *Genesis*, 603–5.

513. M. De Odorico, *The Use of Numbers and Quantifications in the Assyrian Royal Inscriptions* (SAAS III; Helsinki: Neo-Assyrian Text Corpus Project, 1995), 200; see RIMA 2.A.0.100.5: 76–78.

514. Cf. Westermann, *Genesis 12–36*, 516–18; H. Gunkel, *Genesis*, trans. M. Biddle (Macon, Ga.: Mercer Univ. Press, 1997), 349–53; J. Skinner, *Genesis* (Edinburgh: T. & T. Clark, 1930), 411; T. Gaster, *Myth, Legend and Custom in the Old Testament* (New York: Harper & Row, 1975), 205–12; J. G. Frazer, *Folklore in the Old Testament* (New York: Hart, 1975), 251–58; R. Graves and R. Patai, *Hebrew Myths: The Book of Genesis* (New York: McGraw-Hill, 1964), 226–30.

515. Mesopotamia, Enki/Ea; Ugarit, Judge Nahar.

516. Their battles are typically with other deities, not with humans. See discussion in Westenholz, *Dragons*, 20–24.

517. M. Tsevat, "Two Old Testament Stories and Their Hittite Analogues," in *Studies in Literature from the Ancient Near East*, ed. J. M. Sasson (New Haven, Conn.: AOS, 1984), 321–26.

518. Tsevat, "Two Old Testament Stories," 321. H. Hoffner (personal correspondence) indicates a few minor changes to this translation, including that line 65 more precisely says "Ask (something) for yourself" rather than the more idiomatic, "Make a wish." The king's request involves imperfectives rather than imperatives, "Keep giving…" and "Keep putting.…"

519. V. Haas, *Geschichte der hethitischen Religion* (HO I/15; Leiden: Brill, 1994), 215–16, with n. 195. I am grateful to Professor Hoffner for directing me to this book.

520. Dozens of occurrences in the Amarna letters, e.g. ## 52–53, 74–76, 83–85, 88–92, 103–109, 116–119, 121–126 in Moran, *The Amarna Letters*.

521. H. J. Franken, "Deir ʿAllah, Tell," *OEANE*, 2:137–38.

522. J. Seger, "Shechem," *OEANE*, 5:19–23.

523. Ibid., 21.

524. D. Lorton, "Legal and Social Institutions of Pharaonic Egypt," *CANE*, 1:352–53; Moorey, *Ancient Mesopotamian Materials*, 237. See pictures of a variety of shapes in *OEANE*, 2:43.

525. Moorey, *Ancient Mesopotamian Materials*, 235.

526. In Roth, *Law Collections from Mesopotamia and Asia Minor*, Middle Assyrian Laws A.55–56 (pp. 174–75); for similar issues in Hittite law see Hittite Laws 28, 35–37, 197 (pp. 221–22, 237); Sumerian Laws #7 (p. 44). See additional discussion in T. Frymer-Kensky, "Virginity in the Bible," in *Gender and Law in the Hebrew Bible and the Ancient Near East*, ed. V. Matthews, B. Levinson, and T. Frymer-Kensky (New York/London: T. & T. Clark, 2004), 79–96 (esp. 86–93); Walton, *Genesis*, 628–29; K. Mathews, *Genesis 11:27–50:26* (NAC; Nashville: Broadman & Holman, 2005), 591–92.

527. Frymer-Kensky, "Virginity," 89.

528. Ibid., 90.

529. See A. Schmutzer, "'All Those Going Out of the Gate of His City': Have the Translations Got It Yet?" *BBR* 16 (2006): 37–52.

530. W. W. Hallo, "Cult Statue and Divine Image: A Preliminary Study," in *Scripture in Context II*, ed. W. W. Hallo, J. C. Moyer, and L. G. Perdue (Winona Lake, Ind.: Eisenbrauns, 1983), 1–18, esp. 15–16; cf. O. Keel, "Das Vergraben der 'fremden Götter' in Genesis XXXV 4b," *VT* 23 (1973): 305–36, who catalogs buried caches of images found by archaeologists.

531. Note the *bit rimki* (= "house of purification") rituals. See *ebubu*, *CAD* E, 3; *rimku*, R, 355–58; see J. Læssøe, *Studies on the Assyrian Ritual* bit rimki (Copenhagen: Munksgaard, 1955).

532. Ibid., 306–7, n. 4.

533. V. Hurowitz, "Who Lost an Earring? Genesis 35:4 Reconsidered," *CBQ* 62 (2001): 28–32; cf. Hallo, "Cult Statue," 16. Hurowitz traces the textual evidence for gods wearing earrings (e.g., Ishtar gives up her earrings at one of the gates in the Descent of Ishtar) as well as the archaeological evidence from Canaan (particularly the finds at Megiddo and Tel Judeideh), 30–31.

534. N. Fox, "Holy Piercing? The Connection Between Earrings and Cult Images," unpublished paper.

535. L. Luker, "Rachel's Tomb," *ABD*, 5:608–9, attempts to sort it all out and includes much helpful information, but in the end is not able to offer a satisfying resolution.

536. See refutation and alternative reading in M. Tsevat, "Studies in the Book of Samuel II: Interpretation of 1 Sam. 10.2, Saul at Rachel's Tomb," *HUCA* 33 (1962): 107–18.

537. Ibid., 113–15, Tsevat finds reason in the LXX to emend it *ṣlḥ* and associates it with Kiriath Jearim (about ten miles northwest of Jerusalem and off the route being traveled), which he indicates as one of the alternates for Ephrath. The reasoning is complex and speculative and will seem convoluted to many.

538. Little evidence exists in the ancient Near East to illustrate this on the clan level, but the principle is amply attested in the context of kingdom rule (cf. in biblical texts, 2 Sam. 3:7; 12:8; 16:21–22; 1 Kings 2:13–25). For an example in literature from Ugarit see M. Tsevat, "Marriage and Monarchical Legitimacy in Ugarit and Israel," *JSS* 3

(1958): 237–43; T. Ishida, "Solomon's Succession to the Throne of David," in *History and Historical Writing in Ancient Israel* (Leiden: Brill, 1999), 102–36 (esp. 131).

539. G. Wenham, *Genesis 16–50* (WBC; Dallas: Word, 1994), 327. The strongest support for this is the fact that it takes place so shortly after Rachel's death.

540. V. Hamilton, *Genesis 18–50* (NICOT; Grand Rapids: Eerdmans, 1995), 408, summarizes a few of the suggestions that have been made: "Speiser links *keⁿtonet passim* [from this passage] with Akk. *kitu pišannu*, a ceremonial robe draped about statues of goddesses and studded with gold ornaments.... Also possibly related is Phoenician *ps*, 'tablet, piece,' suggesting a garment made of pieces sewn together. Finally we note the possible connection with Akk. *paspasu*, 'brightly colored bird.'"

541. Cf. Westermann's "tunic reaching to the extremities," 37, in agreement with KB³.

542. J. Cooper, "Sargon and Joseph: Dreams Come True," in *Biblical and Related Studies Presented to Samuel Iwry*, ed. A. Kort and S. Morschauser (Winona Lake, Ind.: Eisenbrauns, 1985), 33–39.

543. See Walton, *Genesis*, 663–64.

544. Dorsey, *Roads and Highways*, 140–43.

545. D. M. Master et al., *Dothan I: Remains from the Tell (1953–1964)* (Winona Lake, Ind.: Eisenbrauns, 2005).

546. Oleson, "Water Works," *ABD*, 6:887–88.

547. Calculated from ibid., 6:887.

548. E. J. Revell, "Midian and Ishmael in Genesis 37: Synonyms in the Joseph Story," in *World of the Aramaeans*, ed. P. M. M. Daviau, J. Wevers, and M. Weigl (JSOTSup 324–26; Sheffield: Sheffield Academic Press, 2001), 70–91. For example, perhaps "Ishmaelite" had already become less an ethnic designation and more a word like "gypsy" or "Bedouin" that describes a way of life; cf. Hamilton, *Genesis 18–50*, 423; Wenham, *Genesis 16–50*, 355. This may find support in Judg. 8:24. Critical scholars are inclined to see different sources behind the two names.

549. See Walton, *Genesis*, 665.

550. K. Kitchen, *Reliability*, 344–45 (and notes on 576). R. Hendel contested Kitchen's finds in "Finding Historical Memories in the Patriarchal Narratives," *BAR* 21/4 (1995): 52–59, 70–71, slave price discussion on 56, but only with regard to how significant the data were for dating the narratives.

551. Quoted in *CAD*, 2:137, from R. Borger's publication of Esarhaddon's inscriptions, *Die Inschriften Asarhaddons, Königs von Assyrien* (AfO 9; Osnabruck: Biblio-Verlag, 1967), 102. II.i.3.

552. COS, 1.147:478.

553. For a legal study of levirate marriage see Westbrook, *Property and the Family*, 69–89. For the necessity of a son, not just any child, see 81–82.

554. Little evidence exists in the family documents from Nuzi, and in Ugaritic literature there is just one passing reference to the practice, but it offers no detail for comparison (ibid., 89, in reference to *PRU*

3:16.144). A text from Emar indicates that a widow was abandoned by her husband's brothers and had to devise other means of support. This suggests that there were certain duties that were expected of the brothers without further specification, see H. Marsman, *Women in Ugarit*, 296. For additional studies see C. Pressler, *The View of Women Found in the Deuteronomic Family Laws* (BZAW 216; Berlin: deGruyter, 1993); G. Beckman, "Family Values on the Middle Euphrates in the Thirteenth Century B.C.E.," in *Emar: The History, Religion and Culture of a Syrian Town in the Late Bronze Age*, ed. M. Chavalas (Bethesda, Md.: CDL, 1996), 57–79.

555. Westbrook, *Property and Family*, 72.

556. Ibid.

557. Ibid., 74.

558. Ibid., 78. He points to MAL A25, Eshnunna 15–16, and CH 165 for situations of the undivided inheritance.

559. Ibid., 78–79.

560. Additional information may be found in MAL A30 and A33.

561. Matthews and Benjamin, *Social World of Ancient Israel*, 132–41. See also lengthy discussion in Marsman, *Women in Ugarit*, 291–320; van der Toorn, *From Her Cradle to Her Grave*, 134–40.

562. Marsman, *Women in Ugarit*, 292. She points to this as the result of the fact that a marriage was an arrangement between families, so that the marriage bond was not dependent on the husband alone.

563. K. van der Toorn, "Cultic Prostitution," *ABD*, 5:510–13; E. J. Fisher, "Cultic Prostitution in the Ancient Near East? A Reassessment," *BTB* 6 (1976): 225–36; J. G. Westenholz, "Tamar, q{dec63}dçðà, qadištu, and Sacred Prostitution in Mesopotamia," *HTR* 82 (1989): 245–65 (see her n. 1 for additional bibliography).

564. Van der Toorn, *ABD*, 5:512, points out that Neo-Babylonian records from Uruk indicate that the temple hired out some of its lower level personnel as concubines to private citizens.

565. Westenholz, "Tamar," 251.

566. Ibid.

567. For the significance of the veil see comment on 24:65. In the Middle Assyrian Laws, married women or concubines were not to appear in public without face and head veiled, whereas veils were prohibited to prostitutes and slave girls. MAL A40; see Isa. 47:1–3.

568. The term is etymologically related to the root expressing holiness and would logically convey that such a person has been set apart, consecrated, sequestered, or perhaps even cloistered.

569. There are also six occurrences of the corresponding masculine form usually translated "male shrine prostitutes" (Deut. 23:17; 1 Kings 14:24; 15:12; 22:47; 2 Kings 23:7; Job 36:14), but disputed in meaning; see P. Bird, "The End of the Male Cult Prostitute: A Literary Historical and Sociological Analysis of Hebrew qades-qedesim," in *Congress Volume: Cambridge 1995 (VTS:LXVI)*, ed. J. A. Emerton (Leiden: Brill, 1997), 37–80. She makes the valid observation that male (homosexual) prostitutes would have little logical role in any fertility rite, since such activity is antifertility by nature. Cf. W. Cornfeld and H. Ringgren, "קדש," *TDOT*, 12:542–43.

570. Bird, "End of the Male Cult Prostitute," 43–45. See CH, 181; *CAD* Q, 48–50.

571. CH, §§110, 157; cf. *qalu*, *CAD* Q, 70. These are the only cases in the law codes.

572. H. Pittman, "Cylinder Seals and Scarabs in the Ancient Near East," *CANE*, 3:1589–603; M. Stol, "Private Life in Ancient Mesopotamia," *CANE*, 1:485–501, esp. the section on "Identification" on 487–88; see also the variety of articles in W. W. Hallo and I. J. Winter, *Seals and Seal Impressions* (RAI 45, Part II; Bethesda, Md.: CDL, 2001).

573. Many of these are pictured and discussed in O. Keel and C. Uehlinger, *Gods, Goddesses and Images of God in Ancient Israel* (Minneapolis: Fortress, 1998).

574. The word translated "prison" is literally "house of confinement." Joseph describes his situation in 40:15 as being in a pit (NIV: "dungeon"), the same word used for the cistern in 37:22 and thus relates his two situations of confinement.

575. Notice in 40:6 that Joseph "came to them" in the morning, suggesting some freedom of movement, though in 40:15 he still speaks of being confined. For more information see Walton, *Genesis*, 671–72.

576. S. A. L. Butler, *Mesopotamian Conceptions of Dreams and Dream Rituals* (AOAT 258; Münster: Ugarit-Verlag, 1998), 217–240; J-M. Husser, *Dreams and Dream Narratives in the Biblical World* (Sheffield: Sheffield Academic Press, 1999); A. L. Oppenheim, *The Interpretation of Dreams in the Ancient Near East* (Transactions of the American Philosophical Society 46/3; Philadelphia: American Philosophical Society, 1956).

577. For Mesopotamia see Oppenheim, *Interpretation of Dreams*; for Egypt see R. Ritner, "Dream Books," *OEAE*, 1:410–11; cf. *COS*, 1.33. The earliest Egyptian dream book dates to the Twelfth Dynasty, the time of Joseph.

578. At least in the broader diviner's interpretation; see F. H. Cryer, *Divination in Ancient Israel and its Near Eastern Environment* (JSOTSup 142; Sheffield: Sheffield Academic Press, 1994), 270.

579. Ibid., drawn from Oppenheim, *Interpretation of Dreams*, 279, 288–89.

580. Hoffmeier, *Israel in Egypt*, 89.

581. Ibid., 89–91.

582. Ibid., 87–88.

583. The precise chronology of ancient Egypt is still disputed with several competing systems promulgated by various Egyptologists. Thus even if we could propose an exact date from the biblical record, there would still be differences of opinon regarding which pharaoh was on the throne at that time.

584. Oppenheim, *Interpretation of Dreams*, 208.

585. ARM 13.112; A. L. Oppenheim, *Letters from Mesopotamia* (Chicago: Univ. of Chicago, 1967), 110.

586. George, *The Babylonian Gilgamesh Epic*, 463–65.

587. Lambert, *Babylonian Wisdom Literature*, 49 (Tablet 3).

588. Hoffmeier, *Israel in Egypt*, 88. Cf. H. te Velde, "Theology, Priests, and Worship in Ancient Egypt," *CANE*, 3:1747–48.

589. Hoffmeier, *Israel in Egypt*, 88.

590. He built the step pyramid at Saqqara for King Djoser in the third millennium B.C. His reputation grew as the millennia passed and by the Ptolemaic period he was deified and was considered a healer.

591. *AEL*, 3:94–103.

592. D. Doxey, "Priesthood," *OEAE*, 3:69. These tales are found in the Westcar Papyrus (Papyrus Berlin 3033), dated to the mid-second millennium B.C.

593. L. Green, "Hairstyles," *OEAE*, 2:73–76.

594. G. Callender, "The Middle Kingdom Renaissance," in *The Oxford History of Ancient Egypt*, ed. I. Shaw (New York: Oxford Univ. Press, 2000), 164.

595. Ibid., 169.

596. Ibid., 167.

597. Ibid., 175.

598. W. Ward, "The Egyptian Office of Joseph," *JSS* 5 (1960): 144–50; G. van den Boorn, *The Duties of the Vizier: Civil Administration in the Early New Kingdom* (London: Kegan Paul, 1988).

599. Ward, ibid., lists other titles as well that may be appropriate.

600. Adapted from Walton, *Genesis*, 676–77.

601. For a study of investiture scenes in Egypt (of which most date to the New Kingdom period), see D. Redford, *The Biblical Story of Joseph* (VTSup 20; Leiden: Brill, 1970), 208–24. Kitchen reviewed Redford's work at length in *Oriens Antiquus* 12 (1973): 223–42, and Hoffmeier summarizes their respective positions in *Israel in Egypt*, 91–93. Another analysis of the background of Joseph's elevation can be found in W. L. Humphreys, *Joseph and His Family* (Columbia, S.C.: Univ. of South Carolina Press, 1988), 154–75.

602. *COS*, 1.35 and 1.45 respectively.

603. A. Leahy, "Foreign Incursions," *OEAE*, 1:549.

604. See the several articles on various aspects of animals in Egypt in B. J. Collins, ed., *History of the Animal World in the Ancient Near East* (Leiden: Brill, 2002).

605. M. Bietak, "Dab'a, Tell ed-," *OEAE*, 1:351–54 (quote on 351). Lest we draw too hasty a conclusion, note that Bietak indicates that the majority of these settlers appear to have been soldiers and craftsmen employed by the Egyptians.

606. M. Römer, "Landholding," *OEAE*, 2:256–57.

607. D. O'Connor, "The Social and Economic Organization of Ancient Egyptian Temples," *CANE*, 1:325.

608. Römer, "Landholding," 257.

609. R. De Hoop, *Genesis 49 in its Literary and Historical Context* (Leiden: Brill, 1999), 346–47.

610. Adapted from Walton, *Genesis*, 712.

611. J. Fleishman, "Towards Understanding the Legal Significance of Jacob's Statement: 'I Will divide Them in Jacob and Scatter Them in Israel' (Gen 49, 7b)," in *Studies in the Book of Genesis Literature, Redaction, and History*, ed. A. Wénin (Leuven: Peeters, 2001), 541–60.

612. Westbrook, *Property and the Family*, 136.

613. See G. J. Botterweck, "אֲרִי," *TDOT*, 1:378–82; C. Watanabe, *Animal Symbolism in Mesopotamia* (Weiner Offene Orientalistik 1; Wien: Universität Wien, 2002), esp. 42–56; Collins, ed., *History of the Animal World*.

614. Botterweck, "אֲרִי," 1:378. See here also the various epithets of the gods that refer to them as lions.

615. Ibid.; see also E. Teeter, "Animals in Egyptian Literature," in Collins, ed., *History of the Animal World*, 267, for many examples; Watanabe, *Animal Symbolism*, 42 makes the point that while it is common to see kings described as lions, the lion is never described as king in Sumerian or Akkadian literature.

616. Botterweck, "אֲרִי," 1:379.

617. Ibid., 379–80.

618. Watanabe, *Animal Symbolism*, 45–46.

619. A. Caubet, "Animals in Syro-Palestinian Art" in Collins (ed.), *History of the Animal World*, 223.

620. I. Ziderman, "Seashells and Ancient Purple Dyeing," *BA* 53 (1990): 98–101; idem, "First Identification of Authentic *Tekelet*," *BASOR* 265 (1987): 25–33; R. J. Forbes, *Studies in Ancient Technology* (Leiden: Brill, 1964), 4:99–150.

621. E. J. W. Barber, "Textiles," *OEANE*, 5:192.

622. A fragment from Ashurbanipal's library, seventh century B.C.

623. Ziderman, "Seashells and Ancient Purple Dyeing," 98.

624. A. R. David, "Mummification," *OEAE*, 2:439–44.

625. "On the Ideal Lifetime of the Egyptians," *Oudheidkundige Mededelingen uit het Rijksmuseum van Oudheden te Leiden* 31 (1950): 33–41.

Sidebar and Chart Notes

A-1. The best detailed discussion may be found in R. Clifford, *Creation Accounts in the Ancient Near East and the Bible* (CBQMS 26; Washington, D.C.: Catholic Biblical Association, 1994).

A-2. Found on the Shabako Stone; *COS*, 1.15; *ANET*, 4–6.

A-3. *ANET*, 3.

A-4. Leiden Papyrus I.350 (*COS*, 1.16).

A-5. *COS*, 1.35.

A-6. *COS*, 1.130.

A-7. *COS*, 1.111.

A-8. *COS*, 1.158; *ANET*, 42–44.

A-9. The most important sources for this study are: W. Horowitz, *Mesopotamian Cosmic Geography* (Winona Lake, Ind.: Eisenbrauns, 1998); B. Janowski and B. Ego, *Das biblische Weltbild und seine altorientalischen Kontexte* (Tübingen: Mohr Siebeck, 2001); L. Stadelmann, *The Hebrew Conception of the World* (AnBib 39; Rome: Biblical Institute Press, 1970); P. Seely, "The Firmament and the Water Above, Part 2: The Meaning of 'The Water above the Firmament,'" *WTJ* 54 (1992): 31–46; idem, "The Geographical Meaning of 'Earth' and 'Seas' in Genesis 1:10," *WTJ* 59 (1997): 231–55; I. Cornelius, "The Visual Representation of the World in the Ancient Near East and the Hebrew Bible," *JNSL* 20/2 (1994): 193–218; J. E. Wright, "Biblical

Versus Israelite Images of the Heavenly Realm," *JSOT* 93 (2001): 59–75; F. E. Deist, "Genesis 1:1–2:4A: World Picture and World View," *Scriptura* 22 (1987): 1–17.

A-10. Horowitz, *Mesopotamian Cosmic Geography*, 265.

A-11. These concepts have been clarified by the following studies: W. G. Lambert, "Destiny and Divine Intervention in Babylon and Israel," *OtSt* 17 (1972): 65–72; J. Lawson, *The Concept of Fate in Ancient Mesopotamia of the First Millennium* (Wiesbaden: Harrassowitz, 1994); Y. Rosengarten, *Sumer et le Sacré* (Paris: Boccard, 1977); A. R. George, "Sennacherib and the Tablet of Destinies," *Iraq* 48 (1986): 133–46.

A-12. G. Farber-Flugge, *Der Mythos "Inanna und Enki" unter besonderer Berücksichtigung der Liste der me* (Studia Pohl, Dissertationes scientificae de rebus orientis antiqui 10; Rome: Biblical Institute Press, 1973).

A-13. J. Bidmead, *The Akitu Festival* (Piscataway, N.J.: Gorgias, 2002), 92.

A-14. Gen. 8:21 is connected with ME/NAM. by H. W. F. Saggs, *Encounter with the Divine in Mesopotamia and Israel* (London: Athlone, 1978), 74.

A-15. Rosengarten, *Sumer et le Sacré*, 219–20.

A-16. Ibid., 12, 74.

A-17. Ibid., 120, *Enliluti* ("l'Enlillité")

A-18. Gudea B vi–xii.

A-19. Translation from Clifford, *Creation Accounts*, 67.

A-20 "Bird and Fish" translation from Clifford, *Creation Accounts*, 39.

A-21. Instruction of Merikare, ca. 2050 B.C., trans. M. Lichtheim, *AEL*, 1:106.

A-22. B. Janowski, "Der Himmel auf Erden: Zur kosmologischen Bedeutung des Tempels in der Umwelt Israels," in *Das biblische Weltbild und seine altorientalischen Kontexte*, ed. B. Janowski and B. Ego (FAT 32; Tübingen: Mohr Siebeck, 2001), 229–60.

A-23. Levenson, "Temple and the World," 283–84, drawing from M. Eliade, *The Sacred and the Profane* (New York: Harper & Row, 1961), 36–47.

A-24. Levenson, "Temple and the World," 284–88. See also his citation of G. Ahlström's statement that Syro-Palestinian temples were meant to be heaven on earth, 295; G. Ahlström, *The History of Ancient Palestine* (Minneapolis: Fortress, 1993), 256–57; cf. Hornung, *Conception*, 229. As an example from Mesopotamia, part of the temple of Nippur was called *ki-ùr* and bore the epithet "the great land" (Clifford, *Creation Accounts*, 26); cf. L. R. Fisher, "Creation at Ugarit and in the Old Testament," *VT* 15 (1965): 318–19.

A-25. Lundquist, "What Is a Temple?" 208.

A-26. R. Gundlach, "Temples," *OEAE*, 3:372.

A-27. Gudea Cylinder B I 1–7, COS, 2.155; Esarhaddon's description of Esarra quoted from Hurowitz, *I Have Built*, 245.

A-28. Lundquist, "What Is a Temple?" 207.

A-29. R. Clifford, *The Cosmic Mountain in Canaan and the Old Testament* (HSM 4; Cambridge, Mass.: Harvard Univ. Press, 1972).

A-30. L. Stager, "Jerusalem as Eden," *BAR* 26/3 (2000): 37; M. S. Smith, "Like Deities, Like Temples (Like People)," in *Temple and Worship in Biblical Israel*, ed. J. Day (New York/London: Continuum/T. & T. Clark, 2005), 3–27; E. Bloch-Smith, "'Who Is the King of Glory?' Solomon's Temple and Its Symbolism," in *Scripture and Other Artifacts*, ed. M. Coogan, J. C. Exum, and L. E. Stager (Louisville: Westminster, 1994), 18–31.

A-31. Hurowitz, *I Have Built*, 335–37

A-32. Much of this can be seen worked out in detail and placed within the context of biblical theology in G. Beale, *The Temple and the Church's Mission* (Downers Grove, Ill.: InterVarsity Press, 2004). See esp. his extensive treatment of the cosmic symbolism of temples, 29–80.

A-33. A comprehensive treatment of rest as a theme in biblical theology can be found in J. Laansma, *"I Will Give You Rest"* (Tübingen: Mohr, 1997). See esp. his thorough treatment of Old Testament and ancient Near Eastern texts, 17–76.

A-34. See also 1 Sam. 4:4; 2 Sam. 6:2; Ps. 132:7–8; Isa. 6:1.

A-35. Gudea Cylinder B xvii.18–19; see Hurowitz, *I Have Built*, 271.

A-36. Levenson, "The Temple and the World," 288–89; see Hurowitz, *I Have Built*, 275–76.

A-37. Ps. 132:13–14.

A-38. T. Jacobsen, "The Eridu Genesis," *JBL* 100 (1981): 516, n. 7.

A-39. In The Instructions of Merikare, COS, 1.35, 65, people are additionally called the "god's cattle" and "images who came from his body."

A-40. In Egyptian the word for tears (*rmwt*) is similar to the word for people (*rmt*); J. van Dijk, "Myth and Mythmaking in Ancient Egypt," *CANE*, 1707. In text see Coffin Text spell 1130 in COS, 1.17, 27.

A-41. Other traditions speak of people being formed on the potter's wheel of Khnum (S. Morenz, *Egyptian Religion* (Ithaca, N.Y.: Cornell Univ. Press, 1973), 183–84; R. A. Simkins, *Creator and Creation* (Peabody, Mass.: Hendrickson, 1994), 70–71.

A-42. COS, 1.130:210–230.

A-43. T. Abusch, "Ghost and God: Some Observations on a Babylonian Understanding of Human Nature," in *Self, Soul and Body in Religious Experience*, ed. A. Baumgarten, J. Assmann, and G. Stroumsa (Leiden: Brill, 1998), 363–83.

A-44. Ibid., 371.

A-45. J. C. Greenfield, "Un rite religieux araméen et ses parallèles," *RB* 80 (1973): 46–50.

A-46 *KAR* 28, 34. Text and discussion in G. Pettinato, *Das altorientalische Menschenbild und die sumerischen und akkadischen Schöpfungsmythen* (Heidelberg: Carl Winter Universitätsverlag, 1971); translation of the text and a limited commentary (no discussion of monogenism/polygenism) in Clifford, *Creation Accounts*, 49–51.

A-47. Clifford, *Creation Accounts*, 50 (lines 21–23).

A-48. J. Walton, *Genesis*, 172–74.

A-49. Note the combination of digging ditches and caring for sacred space in *KAR* 4, where people are doing manual labor in the care of sacred space (lines 27–51). See D. Callender, *Adam in Myth and History* (HSS 48; Winona Lake, Ind.: Eisenbrauns, 2000), 57.

A-50. K. Gleason, "Gardens in Preclassical Times," *OEANE*, 2:383. Another has been excavated at Cyrus's capital city, Pasargadae. For an excellent summary of the use of gardens including many photographs of the relevant data see Stager, "Jerusalem as Eden," 36–47.

A-51. Gleason, "Gardens in Preclassical Times," 2:383. All of these elements are also discussed in I. Cornelius, "גן," *NIDOTTE*, 1:875–78.

A-52. George, *The Babylonian Gilgamesh Epic*, 723.

A-53. Clifford, *Creation Accounts*, 45.

A-54. Faulkner, *The Ancient Egyptian Pyramid Texts*.

A-55. See T. Jacobsen, "The Eridu Genesis" *JBL* 100/4 (1981): 513–29; P. D. Miller, "Eridu, Dunnu, and Babel: A Study in Comparative Mythology," *HAR* 9 (1985): 227–51.

A-56. Translation by Clifford, *Creation Accounts*, 62–63.

A-57. On this, see J. Muhly, "Metals," in *OEANE*, 4:1–15; P. McNutt, *The Forging of Israel* (JSOT-Sup 108; Sheffield: Sheffield Academic Press, 1990); P. R. S. Moorey, *Ancient Mesopotamian Materials and Industries* (Winona Lake, Ind.: Eisenbrauns, 1999); J. Muhly, "How Iron Technology Changed the Ancient World," *BAR* 8 (1982): 42–54.

A-58. There are several versions of this list; this one represents WB 444 published by T. Jacobsen, *The Sumerian King List* (Chicago: Univ. of Chicago Press, 1939). For discussion of the number systems relative to long lives, see J. Walton, "The Antediluvian Section of the Sumerian King List and Genesis 5," *BA* 44 (1981): 207–8. The translation of the "Rulers of Lagash" is from B. Batto, "Paradise Reexamined," in *The Biblical Canon in Comparative Perspective: Scripture in Context IV*, ed. K. L. Younger, W. W. Hallo, and B. F. Batto (Lewiston, N.Y.: Mellen, 1991), 33–66.

A-59. Sources for this sidebar are R. R. Wilson, *Genealogy and History in the Biblical World* (New Haven, Conn.: Yale Univ. Press, 1977); J. J. Finkelstein, "The Genealogy of the Hammurabi Dynasty," *JCS* 20 (1966): 95–118; R. S. Hess, "The Genealogies of Genesis 1–11 and Comparative Literature," *Bib* 70 (1989): 241–54; J. Klein, "The Genealogy of Nanna-Suen and Its Historical Background," in *Historiography in the Cuneiform World*, ed. T. Abusch et al. (RAI 45; Bethesda, Md.: CDL, 2001), 279–301; A. Malamat, "King Lists of the Old Babylonian Period and Biblical Genealogies," *JAOS* 88 (1968): 163–73.

A-60. Sources for these quotes, in order, are T. Jacobsen, *Samuel Noah Kramer Anniversary Volume* (AOAT 25; Neukirchen: Neukirchen-Vluyn, 1976), 247–59; RIME 3/2, 37–38; Black, *LSA*, 46; RIME 4, 386, line 64; Foster, *FDD*, 181, lines 63–34.

A-61. L. R. Bailey, *Noah: The Person and the Story in History and Tradition* (Columbia, S.C.: Univ. of South Carolina Press, 1989), 11–22.

A-62. COS, 1.158; see T. Jacobsen, "The Eridu Genesis," 513–29.

A-63. COS, 1.130.

A-64. COS, 1.132.

A-65. R. A. Oden Jr., "Divine Aspirations in Atrahasis and in Genesis 1–11," *ZAW* 93 (1981): 197–216; Batto, *Slaying the Dragon*, 42, and extensive bibliography is n. 31, p. 196. As Batto points out, this interpretation is confirmed by the allusion to the event in the Poem of Erra.

A-66. S. W. Holloway, "What Ship Goes There: The Flood Narratives in the Gilgamesh Epic and Genesis Considered in Light of Ancient Near Eastern Temple Ideology," *ZAW* 103 (1991): 328–55.

A-67. See discussion in D. Young, *The Biblical Flood* (Grand Rapids: Eerdmans, 1995), 216–25; Bailey, *Noah*, 28–37.

A-68. Nissen, *Early History of the Ancient Near East*, 55–67.

A-69. Young, *Biblical Flood*, 314–19.

A-70. Comprehensive presentation and analysis of evidence see Bailey, *Noah*, 53–115.

A-71. Batto, *Slaying the Dragon*, 44–72, esp. 51–52; I. Kikawada and A. Quinn, *Before Abraham Was* (Nashville: Abingdon, 1985), 46–48.

A-72. Adapted from Walton, *Genesis*, 367–69.

A-73. Seventy descendants of Jacob, Ex. 1:5; seventy elders of Israel, 24:1; seventy disciples sent out, Luke 10:1–16; outside the Bible, seventy sons of the Canaanite goddess Asherah and seventy members of the Sanhedrin.

A-74. This according to a most probable textual variant in Deut. 32:8, where the numbers of the nations are compared to the numbers of the sons of God. In an Ugaritic text, the god El begat seventy sons. This is thoroughly and convincingly discussed by M. Heiser, "Deuteronomy 32:8 and the Sons of God," *BibSac* 158 (2001): 52–74.

A-75. Discussion of this important genealogy can be found in Wilson, *Genealogy and History in the Biblical World*, 107–14.

A-76. See introduction and translation in H. Vanstiphout, *Epics of Sumerian Kings: The Matter of Aratta* (SBLWAW 20; Atlanta: SBL Press, 2003).

A-77. Vanstiphout, *Epics of Sumerian Kings*, 65, and similar rendition in B. Alster, "An Aspect of 'Enmerkar and the Lord of Aratta,'" *RA* 67 (1973): 101–9. For some of Alster's revised thinking see his "Dilmun, Bahrain, and the Alleged Paradise in Sumerian Myth and Literature," in *Dilmun: New Studies in the Archaeology and Early History of Bahrain*, ed. D. Potts (Berlin: Dietrich Reimer, 1983), 39–74.

A-78. Jacobsen, *The Harps That Once . . .*, 290.

A-79. Van der Toorn, *Family Religion in Babylonia, Syria and Israel*, 66–93; Abusch, "Ghost and God," 363–83; T. Abusch, "Witchcraft and the Anger of the Personal God," in *Mesopotamian Magic*, ed. T. Abusch and K. van der Toorn (Groningen: Styx, 1999), 105–7, offers an explanation of the phenomenon in terms of psychological projection.

A-80. This development and the resulting trend in religious thought was recognized and popularized in T. Jacobsen, *Treasures of Darkness* (New Haven, Conn.: Yale Univ. Press, 1976), 147–64.

A-81. Ibid., 155.

A-82. Abusch, "Ghost and God," 378.

A-83. Van der Toorn, *Family Religion*, 73–74.

A-84. Ibid., 78–79.

A-85. Jacobsen, *Treasures of Darkness*, 164.

A-86. C. Meyers, "The Family in Early Israel," in *Families in Ancient Israel*, ed. L. Perdue et al. (Louisville: Westminster John Knox, 1997), 1–47.

A-87. Early translators of the tablets from Ebla claimed that these five cities were mentioned in those tablets, but that claim is no longer accepted.

A-88. *Assumption of Moses* 6.1; Josephus, *Ant.* 16.163.

A-89. Paul Kobelski, *Melchizedek and Melchireša* (CBQMS 10; Washington, D.C.: Catholic Biblical Association, 1981); C. M. Pate, *Communities of the Last Days* (Downers Grove, Ill.: InterVarsity Press, 2000), 121, 209.

A-90. Richard Longenecker, "The Melchizedek Argument of Hebrews: A Study in the Development and Circumstantial Expression of the New Testament Thought," in *Unity and Diversity in New Testament Theology*, ed. R. Guelich (Grand Rapids: Eerdmans, 1978), 161–85.

A-91. Much of this entry was adapted from Walton, *Genesis*, 426–27.

A-92. Pagolu, *Religion of the Patriarchs*, 242.

A-93. A. R. W. Green, *The Role of Human Sacrifice in the Ancient Near East* (ASOR Dissertation 1; Missoula, Mont.: Scholars Press, 1975), 154–55.

A-94. Ibid., 190–91.

A-95. Ibid., 34–46, 157.

A-96. Most of the textual information (and a good deal of the archaeological data) comes from Punic texts from Carthage from the fourth century B.C. on, and a variety of classical sources writing about the Punic world. This is quite removed from the Old Testament both chronologically and geographically, though it is often extrapolated back to the Phoenicians as the parent civilization to the Punic world. For discussion of this material see M. Aubet, *The Phoenicians and the West* (Cambridge: Cambridge Univ. Press, 1993), 207–17; S. Ribichini, "Beliefs and Religious Life," in *The Phoenicians*, ed. S. Moscati (New York: Rizzoli, 1999), 139–41; G. Markoe, *Phoenicians* (Berkeley: Univ. of California, 2000), 132–36; M. Selman, "Sacrifice in the Ancient Near East," in *Sacrifice in the Bible*, ed. R. T. Beckwith and M. J. Selman (Grand Rapids: Baker, 1995), 88–104, esp. 99–100.

A-97. Compare Gudea's requests of Ningirsu about where to build the temple, COS, 2.155.

A-98. Houtman, "What Did Jacob See?" 345: "where heaven and earth melted into one."

A-99. It is uncertain whether such a stairway was characteristic of Solomon's temple, see V. Hurowitz, "Yhwh's Exalted House—Aspects of the Design and Symbolism of Solomon's Temple," *Temple and Worship in Biblical Israel*, ed. J. Day (New York/London: T. & T. Clark, 2005) 63–110; he leans toward the architectural interpretation that there were no steps in Solomon's temple (73–74).

A-100. In the Mesopotamian myth Nergal and Ereshkigal, the gate is at the top of the stairway and is designated the gate of Anu, Enlil, and Ea, the three principal gods.

A-101. E.g., HSS 14, 108:23–25. See M. Heltzer, "New Light from Emar on Genesis 31: The Theft of the Teraphim," in *'Und Mose Schrieb dieses Lied auf': Studien zum Alten Testament und zum Alten Orient*, ed. M. Dietrich and I. Kottsieper (AOAT 250; Münster: 1988), 357–62.

A-102. Heltzer, "New Light," 361, referring to the text designated RE 94.

A-103. M. Morrison, "The Jacob and Laban Narrative in Light of Near Eastern Sources," *BA* 46 (1983): 161.

A-104. V. Matthews, "Family Relationships," *DOTP*, 293; K. van der Toorn, "Torn between Vice and Virtue: Stereotypes of the Widow in Israel and Mesopotamia," in *Female Stereotypes in Religious Traditions*, ed. R. Kloppenborg and W. J. Hanegraaf (Leiden: Brill, 1995), 1–2.

A-105. Van der Toorn, *Family Religion*, 75; cf. idem, *From Her Cradle to Her Grave*, 66.

A-106. *KTU* 1.5 vi 11–23; trans. M. Smith in Parker, *Ugaritic Narrative Poetry*, 149–50.

A-107. X. H. T. Pham, *Mourning in the Ancient Near East and the Hebrew Bible* (Sheffield: Sheffield Academic Press, 1999), quoting G. A. Anderson, *A Time to Mourn, A Time to Dance: The Expression of Grief and Joy in Israelite Religion* (University Park, Pa.: Univ. of Pennsylvania Press, 1991), "His clothing he tears, down to the loincloth," 19; Wyatt, *Religious Texts from Ugarit*, "For clothing he put on a loincloth," 127. J. C. L. Gibson, *Canaanite Myths and Legends* (Edinburgh: T. & T. Clark, 1978), 73, translates it "sackcloth" but in note 12 says that it is literally "loincloth." The disputed Ugaritic word is *mizrt*. For discussion of the significance of mourning practices, see S. M. Olyan, *Biblical Mourning* (Oxford: Oxford Univ. Press, 2004), 28–61.

A-108. Translation by M. Roth, *Law Collections from Mesopotamia and Asia Minor.*

A-109. COS, 1.40.

A-110. See summary discussion in Hoffmeier, *Israel in Egypt*, 81; more detailed analysis in S. Hollis, *The Ancient Egyptian "Tale of Two Brothers": The Oldest Fairy Tale in the World* (Norman, Okla.: Univ. of Oklahoma Press, 1990), 97–99.

A-111. David, "Mummification," 443.

A-112. Ibid.

EXODUS

by Bruce Wells

Introduction

The narratives of Exodus, which describe God's deliverance of the Israelites from Egypt, formed the basis for the Israelites' relationship with God.[1] The book narrates events at Mount Sinai and the establishment of the covenant there that later biblical texts refer back to repeatedly. Moreover, the combination of the exodus from Egypt and the creation of the Sinai covenant served as the paradigm for the people who returned from exile in Babylonia to their homeland in Judah. The ideas and the theological message of this book played an integral role in ancient Israel's identity and self-understanding.

Detail from coffin of Nespawershepi, chief scribe of the Temple of Amun. The scene shows the sun god Ra in his solar barque and the daily killing of the serpent Apophis, representing the sun's victory over the power of darkness.
Werner Forman Archive/ The Fitzwilliam Museum, Cambridge

▲

Historical Setting

The historical setting for the book of Exodus is essentially unknown. It describes events that lead to an escape of ancient Israelites from Egypt, but a specific time period during which events such as these might have taken place cannot be determined with certainty. Suggestions have been made (see below), and some accord better with the available evidence than others. The text of Exodus, however, yields too little information to establish a precise and convincing historical framework. The best one can do is to ascertain a broad time period into which the text attempts to place its narrated events.

Many scholars believe that the book of Exodus places the events it recounts in a time period that fits best within the second half of the second millennium B.C. In Egypt, this is known as the New Kingdom (1550–1069 B.C.). For the area of Syria and Palestine in western Asia, this time period includes the Late Bronze Age (c. 1550–1200) and the first part of the Iron Age (referred to as Iron I, 1200–1000).

It is in Iron I that remains of a distinctly Israelite character begin to appear in Palestine and go on to predominate throughout the Iron II period (1000–586; in 586 Jerusalem and much of Judah were overrun by the Babylonians).[2] Any departure of Israelites from Egypt would presumably have taken place before this settlement process begins, and there are no compelling reasons to consider time periods prior to the New Kingdom in Egypt and the Late Bronze Age in Palestine. Moreover, in Palestine, the transition from the Late Bronze to the Iron Age is primarily one from Egyptian domination to a marked absence of Egyptian control.

It was during the New Kingdom that Egypt's imperialistic ambitions grew.[3] One of its early kings, Amenhotep I, led Egypt to renewed military success in Nubia (modern Sudan) to the south, and his kingdom began to reap economic benefits. Later, during the reign of Thutmose III, Egypt expanded its power into Syria and Palestine, subjecting a number of city-states to its control. This provided Egypt with access to a variety of raw materials, an important source of human labor from prisoners of war, military spoils, and tribute payments from vassal rulers. Such rewards motivated subsequent kings to continue to exert control over Syria and Palestine. An archive of letters from the site of el-Amarna (see comments on 1:15) amply attests to this.

Moreover, while Semitic slaves had been in Egypt for some time, it was during the New Kingdom that their numbers increased significantly. Building projects—tombs, monuments, temples—also grew until they reached unprecedented levels during the reign of Ramesses II. Thus, Egypt's control of Palestine, its increasing numbers of Semitic slaves, and its swiftly growing construction efforts combine to make the New Kingdom an attractive option as a backdrop for the narratives in Exodus.

Notably, Egypt was able to maintain control over Palestine in spite of nearby powers that rivaled Egypt in size and strength. This was the time of the so-called Great Powers' Club, which included, in addition to the Egyptians, the Hittites in Anatolia (Turkey), the Mitannians in northeast Syria, the Assyrians in northern Mesopotamia, and the Babylonians in southern Mesopotamia.[4] The territories in Palestine and western Syria (often referred to as the Levant) were often caught in the vortex

of international struggle. Whenever Egyptian power waned, for instance, the Hittites quickly reasserted domination over portions of the region, and vice versa.

But the end of the Late Bronze Age saw a widespread collapse in civilization across the ancient Near East. For the Levant, an especially critical element was the migration eastward, from the Aegean basin, of many different groups known as the Sea Peoples (see sidebar on "The Philistines" at 15:14).[5] Their arrival coincides with the abandonment—and utter destruction in some cases—of a number of Late Bronze urban centers and the demise of Egyptian power in Syria and Palestine.

Subsequently, no political entity seemed able to project its authority into the Levant, leaving a vacuum of power throughout much of Iron I. It is within this vacuum that the small, fledgling nation of Israel, along with others (Edom, Moab, Ammon), begins to emerge. Therefore, an exodus not far removed from the decline of Egyptian control over Palestine toward the end of the Late Bronze Age seems the most attractive option for a possible Israelite escape from Egyptian domination (see sidebar on "The Timing of the Exodus, Part II" at 12:40).

Types of Literature

Exodus contains an array of literary forms, each of which can be found in other ancient Near Eastern societies. The grand saga describing the Israelites' miraculous escape from enslavement in Egypt is epic narrative. In addition to the Ten Commandments, the book contains a long list of legal provisions; thus, the genre of law must be considered. The section concerning the construction of the tabernacle is an example of the ancient Near Eastern literary form used to describe the building of sacred shrines. There are also ritual instructions, such as the elaborate ceremonies required to consecrate Aaron and his sons as priests. The nature of these genres and how they were used must function as key elements in any background analysis of biblical texts. Thus, literary considerations are, at times, equally important as historical and cultural aspects of the ancient world in shedding light on the text of Exodus.

▶ Egyptian Kings of the New Kingdom

An Egyptian priest named Manetho, who lived during the 200s B.C., divided Egyptian history into sections or dynasties. He did this based on groups of kings who, in his view, shared important kinship, political, or geographical ties. He numbered each dynasty, and the New Kingdom includes the Eighteenth, Nineteenth, and Twentieth Dynasties.[A-1] Overlapping dates can be explained by coregencies (two rulers sharing power).

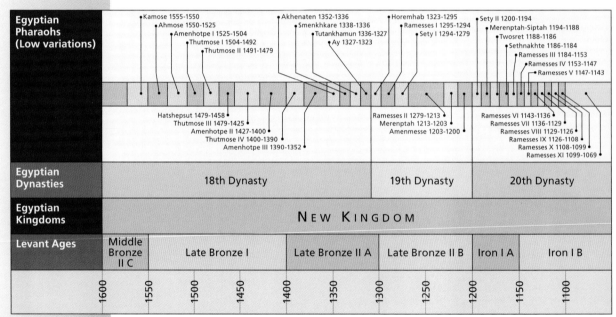

Egyptian Pharaohs (Low variations)				
Kamose 1555-1550	Akhenaten 1352-1336	Horemhab 1323-1295	Sety II 1200-1194	
Ahmose 1550-1525	Smenkhkare 1338-1336	Ramesses I 1295-1294	Merenptah-Siptah 1194-1188	
Amenhotpe I 1525-1504	Tutankhamun 1336-1327	Sety I 1294-1279	Twosret 1188-1186	
Thutmose I 1504-1492	Ay 1327-1323		Sethnakhte 1186-1184	
Thutmose II 1491-1479			Ramesses III 1184-1153	
			Ramesses IV 1153-1147	
			Ramesses V 1147-1143	
Hatshepsut 1479-1458		Ramesses II 1279-1213	Ramesses VI 1143-1136	
Thutmose III 1479-1425		Merenptah 1213-1203	Ramesses VII 1136-1129	
Amenhotpe II 1427-1400		Amenmesse 1203-1200	Ramesses VIII 1129-1126	
Thutmose IV 1400-1390			Ramesses IX 1126-1108	
Amenhotpe III 1390-1352			Ramesses X 1108-1099	
			Ramesses XI 1099-1069	

Egyptian Dynasties	18th Dynasty	19th Dynasty	20th Dynasty

Egyptian Kingdoms	NEW KINGDOM

Levant Ages	Middle Bronze II C	Late Bronze I	Late Bronze II A	Late Bronze II B	Iron I A	Iron I B

1600 1550 1500 1450 1400 1350 1300 1250 1200 1150 1100

Ancient Near Eastern Comparative Material

In view of the factors set forth above, the study of background material for Exodus requires a wide-ranging look at ancient Near Eastern history, literature, religion, law, social customs, and material culture. It is worth considering a variety of periods, while maintaining a focus on the New Kingdom in Egypt and the Late Bronze and Iron Ages in other parts of the ancient Near East. Helpful information comes not only from Egypt and the land of modern Israel but also from the Hittite territories in modern Turkey, the Assyrian and Babylonian societies of Mesopotamia, and ancient Israel's closer neighbors in western Syria and Transjordanian Palestine.

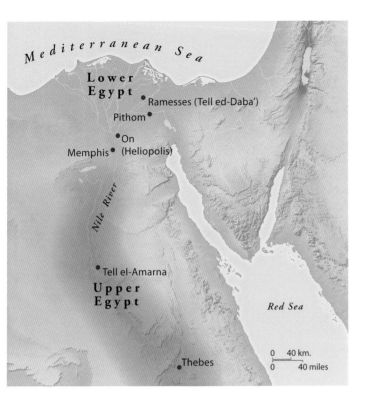

Moreover, since archaeological excavations have produced more data for some locations and time periods than for others, the information sought from a specific place and time may simply be unavailable, and one must look elsewhere. But ancient Near Eastern societies often operated with similar customs and traditions, which tended to change slowly, if at all, during the first three millennia B.C. Thus, in order to obtain an understanding of the ancient perspective regarding a particular issue, material from the first or third millennium may be just as enlightening as that from the late second millennium. Similarly, literature from Mesopotamia can prove just as helpful in understanding a biblical text as that of societies located closer to the land of Israel.

This commentary will use, therefore, a diverse set of literary and archaeological sources in order to explain features and themes of the biblical text, to examine topics of ancient Near Eastern society and culture to which passages in Exodus allude, and to raise questions that are worth assessing in light of the ancient world of the Bible.

The Israelites in Egypt (1:1–14)

Egypt (1:1). Egypt lies in the northeast corner of Africa. Ancient Egypt stretched from the Mediterranean Sea south along the Nile River and was divided—conceptually and sometimes politically—between Upper Egypt in

Nile delta
Courtesy of NASA
◀

▶ Bedouin (*Shasu*) in Egypt

Papyrus Anastasi VI is a well-known Egyptian text from around 1200 B.C. It contains a letter, perhaps used by scribes as a model when learning how to write letters, that mentions a group of Semitic nomads or Bedouin (Egyptian *shasu*) coming into Egypt. These Bedouin were mainly shepherds and their families who periodically roamed along the borders of Egypt looking for better pastures for their herds. The papyrus states:

> Another communication to my [lord], to [wit: We] have finished letting the Bedouin tribes (*shasu*) of Edom pass the Fortress [of] Mer-ne-Ptah Hotep-hir-Maat—life,

prosperity, health!—which is (in) Tjeku, to the pools of Per-Atum (Pithom) [of] Mer-[ne]-Ptah Hotep-hir-Maat, which are (in) Tjeku, to keep them alive and to keep their cattle alive.^A-2

These *shasu* were coming from the Sinai desert, east of Egypt. They entered at one of the border checkpoints set up by the Egyptian military. "The region to which these *shasu* were being admitted is the region in which the Israelites of the sojourn in Egypt are located in Exodus 1–15, to the east of the Nile Delta."^A-3 While the *shasu* mentioned here are probably not Israelites, the text does show is that it was not unusual for nomadic Semites to enter Egypt at this time especially along the eastern border of the Delta.

the south (the Nile Valley) and Lower Egypt (the Nile Delta) in the north (the Nile River flows *down* as it flows north). The Nile Delta, so-called because when viewed from the north its shape looked to the Greeks like their letter *delta* (Δ), had as many as sixteen tributaries running from the Nile into the Mediterranean in ancient times.[6] Its southern base lies close to the modern city of Cairo. This is the part of Egypt that the biblical text probably has in mind. There is ample evidence that Semitic peoples (from Syria and Palestine) entered the Delta for a variety of reasons,[7] such as to obtain food for themselves and their herds.

Who did not know about Joseph (1:8). Scholars have tried to determine what this statement means in terms of Egyptian history.

One idea relates to the people known as the Hyksos (a Greek rendering of the Egyptian word for "ruler of foreign lands").[8] The Hyksos were Semitic foreigners in Egypt who took over and ruled Lower Egypt (see comment on 1:1) for about one hundred years (c. 1630–1530 B.C.). They had gradually been coming into Egypt, and their "assumption of power reveals itself as a peaceful takeover from within by a racial element already in the majority."[9] They were eventually ousted by Egyptians who had retained power over Upper Egypt.

In light of the Hyksos rule in Egypt and their eventual demise, at least two inferences are possible with respect to the biblical text. First, it seems reasonable to identify the period of Hyksos rule as a period of time when a person from, perhaps, another Semitic group could have risen to an extraordinarily high position within the governmental hierarchy, as the story of Joseph in the book of Genesis describes. Presumably, the Hyksos were sympathetic to other

▶ **Semites in Egypt**

Avaris was the capital of the Hyksos (see comments on 1:8). Most archaeologists identify it today with the site of Tell el-Dab'a in the eastern Delta region.[A-4] Many finds from this site are intriguing because they do not represent ancient Egyptian material culture but that of Syria and Palestine. In other words, while there is evidence of an Egyptian presence at this site, Semites were living here for much of the seventeenth and sixteenth centuries B.C.

Inhabitants from Syria and Palestine had been infiltrating this region of Egypt until their numbers were sufficiently large to throw off Egyptian control and establish independent rule. Whether the Hyksos were from one particular Semitic group or from Semites in general is not clear. They were probably the dominant Semitic group who held most of the political power during this period. But leaders from several groups may have joined to form a more centralized political administration, and

the Egyptians simply identified them collectively as "Hyksos."

Features that demonstrate the presence of Syro-Palestinian material culture at this time include: tombs located within residential dwellings (a practice well attested from Middle Bronze Age Megiddo in northern Palestine);[A-5] pottery from a type known as Tell el-Yehudiya ware, which is associated primarily with locations in Palestine;[A-6] and burials of humans that also included the nearby burial of donkeys and sacrificed sheep, a Semitic custom.[A-7]

Inferences regarding the Israelites in particular must remain tentative. If there were Israelites living in or near Avaris (the very region from which the Bible indicates the Israelites left Egypt), their material remains would be indistinguishable from those left by other Semitic groups. Thus, some of the so-called Hyksos archaeological evidence in this region may be Israelite, though there is as yet no reliable means by which to establish this.

Semites and amenable to sharing some political power with them. Second, it is conceivable that the defeat of the Hyksos and the return of indigenous Egyptian rule to Lower Egypt form the background for this verse in Exodus.[10] The Hebrews—and any Semitic persons for that matter—would have come under great suspicion after the Egyptians had just retaken their Nile Delta from the despised Hyksos. Thus, it is likely that a Semitic group that had been shown special favor by the Hyksos would have fallen out of favor under the new Egyptian king.

They built Pithom and Rames(s)es (1:11). These names probably refer to locations near the eastern edge of the Nile Delta. Pithom is likely the Hebrew rendering of the Egyptian phrase "House of (the god) Atum," and it perhaps refers to Tell el-Retabeh. Archaeological finds from there include scarabs from Egypt's Eighteenth Dynasty (1300s and 1400s B.C.), inscriptions praising the god Atum, and a scene with Ramesses II striking a

Ramesses II
Frederick J. Mabie
▼

possible to imag-
ine Semitic slaves,
even Hebrew
slaves, as part of
those conscripted.
Some scholars con-
clude that Exodus
attempts to place
the enslavement
and oppression of
the Israelites in the
reign of Ramesses
II (see sidebar on
"The Timing of the
Exodus, Part II" at
12:40).

Semite while the god Atum looks on; there
may have been a temple (house) of Atum
here.[11] The site was also an important military point on Egypt's eastern border during
the time of Ramesses II, who reigned more
than sixty years in the mid-1200s B.C. It is
this Ramesses who gives his name to the other
location — "Rameses" in Exodus 1:11 but
Piramesse ("House of Ramesses") in Egyptian — identified today as the site of Qantir.[12]

The building projects of Ramesses II sur-
passed those of all other pharaohs.[13] Uphill
suggests this site "was probably the vastest
and most costly royal residence ever erected
by the hand of man. As can now be seen, its
known palace and official
centre covered an area of at
least four square miles, and
its temples were in scale
with this, a colossal assemblage forming perhaps the
largest collection of chapels
built in the pre-classical
world by a single ruler."[14]
This site was clearly a special focus for Ramesses II,
and he moved the Egyptian
capital there shortly after
taking the throne.

The projects under-
taken here required a
massive labor force. It is

Hard labor in brick and mortar

(1:14). Intensive brick-making was needed
to support the large-scale building projects
in Egypt, particularly at sites like Piramesse.
An Egyptian text from early in the reign of
Ramesses II describes an attempt to determine how many bricks were needed for a
ramp — essentially just a piece of construction equipment — over 1000 feet long, 80 feet
wide, and about 90 feet at its highest point.[15]
Another report records that work was moving
along smoothly in one of the royal workshops
and that those responsible for producing bricks
were meeting their daily requirements: "Likewise, people are making bricks in their *bkᶜ* and

bringing them to work in the house. They are making their quota of bricks daily" (for more on brick-making, see comments on 5:11).[16]

Pharaoh's Plan (1:15–22)

Hebrew (1:15). The term "Hebrew" has linguistic connections to the term "Apiru," used in a number of ancient texts. It occurs frequently, for example, in the approximately 380 tablets discovered at the site of el-Amarna, about 150 miles south of Cairo. Most of these tablets come from the mid-1300s B.C. (during the reigns of Amenhotep III and Amenhotep IV) and are letters that were written by local rulers in Syria and Palestine to the Egyptian king who had established his capital at this site. Egypt had loose control of Syria and Palestine during this period.

The letters speak disparagingly of the Apiru people. For example, Abdi-Hepa, the local ruler in Jerusalem, wrote with the dire news: "The land of the king has gone over to the Apiru. And now, in addition to this, a town belonging to Jerusalem, Bit-Ninurta by name, a town belonging to the king, has gone over to the men of Qiltu. May the king listen to Abdi-Hepa, your servant, and send archers to restore the land of the king to the king. If there are no archers, the land of the king will go over to the Apiru!"[17]

The Apiru may refer to groups of people who were social outcasts, did not own property, often resorted to banditry, and threatened the status quo for settled people. Those viewed as outsiders or foreigners were also often labeled as Apiru. Before forming the nation of Israel, most likely the Hebrews were viewed in this way. A Hebrew could certainly have been called an Apiru, though not every Apiru was a Hebrew. Note that while "Hebrew" is primarily an ethnic designation, "Apiru" is strictly a social one.[18]

Shiphrah and Puah (1:15). An Egyptian papyrus from around the year 1700 B.C. presents a list of ninety-five household servants.[19] Over half the names are Semitic. One is Shiphrah, who is designated as a weaver of fine linen. This woman is clearly not the one referred to in the biblical text, but this Semitic name (meaning "fair, beautiful") appears to have been known in Egypt.

Throw into the Nile (1:22). The Nile, the longest river in the world, was the most important physical feature of ancient Egypt. The rainy season caused the river to overflow its banks and spill into much of the land every summer. This deposited fertile sediment on the farmland, so that after the flooding, farmers had remarkably rich soil for their crops. This yearly inundation assured the Egyptians that they and their land would be

Woman on birthing stool
Brian J. McMorrow
▲

Image of the Nile River shows contrast between the fertile green flood plain and the desert.
Bionet/Wikimedia Commons
◄

▶ # Moses and the Legend of Sargon

A number of stories about abandoned children come from the ancient world.[A-8] In most of these stories, one parent (usually the mother) abandons the child out of shame or in an effort to save the child's life. Greek legends tell of a prediction that Paris, the son of King Priam of Troy, will bring ruin on the city. Priam, therefore, abandons the infant Paris on Mount Ida to die. Of course, he does not.

The Legend of Sargon tells of the rise to power of a

Mesopotamian king from around 2300 B.C. The story may have been written well after Sargon's lifetime, though it is nearly impossible to arrive at a precise date for the composition of the text.[A-9] It begins:

Sargon, strong king, king of Agade (Akkad), am I.
My mother was a high priestess, my father I do not know.
My paternal kin inhabit the mountain region.
My city of birth is Azupiranu, which lies on the bank of the Euphrates.
My mother, a high priestess, conceived me, in secret she bore me.
She placed me in a reed basket, with bitumen she caulked my hatch.
She abandoned me to the river from which I could not escape.
The river carried me along; to Aqqi, the water drawer, it brought me.
Aqqi, the water drawer, when immersing his bucket lifted me up.
Aqqi, the water drawer, raised me as his adopted son.[A-10]

prosperous. The Nile was their most precious gift from the gods. Ironically, the pharaoh in Exodus uses this river—the guarantee of Egyptian fertility—in an attempt to squelch the fertility of the Hebrews.

The Birth and Rescue of Moses (2:1–10)

She placed the child in it (2:3). The baby's mother abandons her child in hopes of saving him. This is reminiscent of a theme—the abandoned or exposed child who is rescued and eventually grows up to perform some heroic deed—that turns up in a wide variety of other literature. The story clos-

est to the Exodus account is the Legend of Sargon from Mesopotamia (see sidebar). By means of this traumatic event, the biblical text hints to the reader regarding the kind of future in store for this child. Moses has "hero" written all over him.

Nurse him for me (2:9). Both Egyptian and Mesopotamian records, mostly from the second millennium B.C., indicate that a woman could have the occupation of wet nurse—someone who breast-feeds another woman's child.[20] They were often employed after the adoption of an abandoned child and were typically paid with basic provisions such as food and clothing. The standard period of time for a wet nurse was about three years.

Like Moses' mother, Sargon's mother places her baby in a reed basket, seals it, and sets it adrift on a river. Like Moses, Sargon is then taken from the water by the one who eventually adopts him. Determining the relationship between such accounts is not an easy problem to solve. Could the authors of some of these stories have borrowed the idea from others? Possibly. There is evidence, however, to suggest that it was not uncommon for a child to be abandoned.

Reasons for this practice are not entirely clear, although families often had great difficulties finding enough food for the members they already had. We do know that abandoned children, who were then later adopted, could receive names that referred to their abandonment—for instance, Ha-pi-kalbi ("He-of-the-dog's-mouth") and Naru-eriba ("The-river-has-compensated-me").[A-11] One could conclude, then, that since authors knew this was a very real occurrence, they simply included it, along with other known social practices, in their narratives. This type of conclusion tends to reduce the likelihood—though it does not entirely preclude the possibility—of literary dependence of one story on the other. While the Moses narrative likely does not depend on the Sargon legend, it may well be that the biblical story attempts to describe the events in Moses' life in such a way that an astute reader in the ancient world would recognize the "abandoned child" theme and foresee that great achievements are in store for this lonely infant afloat on the river.

Papyrus basket
Cairo Archaeological Museum; © PBT & Dr. James C. Martin

She named him Moses (2:10). "Moses" was frequently used in Egyptian names, such as Ahmose, Thutmose, and Ramesses. Its basic meaning is "to father" or "to be fathered (born)."[21] For example, Thutmose probably means "the god Thoth is born," or perhaps "the god Thoth has fathered" or "born of the god Thoth." Moses' name, then, is really just a half-name: "born of...." One has to wonder if we are to understand this as his real name, as a truncated name with the half containing an Egyptian god's name eliminated so as not to offend Israelite sensibilities, or as a symbolic name meant to represent Moses as partially influenced by Egypt. In any event, the half-name fits the narrative and is left as it is, probably because it sounds like the Hebrew word for "to pull out, retrieve"—in this case, from the water.

Ramesses cartouche
Frederick J. Mabie

Moses' Crime and Flight to Midian (2:11–25)

Egyptian beating a Hebrew (2:11). Beating slaves was certainly not uncommon or illegal in the ancient world. Was this a fatal beating? The Hebrew word for "beating" here is the same as the one for "killed" in 2:12. The word can have either connotation, depending on the context. Even killing a slave was not a serious crime. When a person caused the death of another's slave—in this case, the taskmaster may have killed one of Pharaoh's slaves—the perpetrator typically only had to pay a fine to compensate the victim's owner for loss of labor.[22] Here the taskmaster would have had Pharaoh's authority to beat the slave and may not, therefore, have been culpable of any wrongdoing. Thus, Moses' reaction is severe—especially if the slave did not die—but, the text implies, understandable in light of his relation to the one beaten.

He tried to kill Moses (2:15). There is virtually no evidence from ancient Egypt regarding the treatment of homicide. Egypt certainly had the death penalty, however, since participants in an unsuccessful coup during the reign of Ramesses III (1186–1155 B.C.) were executed. Apparently, a minor queen and her supporters had wanted to dethrone Ramesses and make her son king.[23] In other words, the Egyptian jus-

tice system had no qualms about imposing the death penalty on those guilty of murder. In this case, the Egyptian king is interested not only in justice but also in revenge. Since one from his own court has violated the system for enforcing his authority, Pharaoh is out to kill Moses not only to ensure that the latter receives his just desserts but also to make clear that violations of Pharaoh's authority will be dealt with severely.

Midian (2:15). This area is probably located in northwestern Arabia, just to the east of the Gulf of Elat (Aqaba). This area raises an interesting possibility when one considers that it is here where Moses for the first time encounters Yahweh (the Israelite name for God; see comments on 3:14). This region is referred to as the "Land of the Shasu"—*shasu* refers to Bedouin shepherds—in two Egyptian texts found in ancient Nubia (modern Sudan) from approximately 1400 B.C. These texts mention "*Yhw* (in) the land of the Shasu."[24] This *Yhw* is most likely a form of Yahweh and represents a location possibly based on the Israelite name for God. This may support the conclusion that some people in that region may have been worshiping Yahweh at this time.

In fact, the biblical text may be trying to depict Moses' eventual father-in-law, called a priest in 2:16, as a worshiper of Yahweh. That he lives in this region and has flocks that need shepherding certainly qualifies him and his family as *shasu*. All that is missing is an explicit reference to his worship of Yahweh, though this may come in 18:10–11.

Encounter with God (3:1–10)

Horeb, the mountain of God (3:1). Horeb (Heb. "wasteland, desert") is specifically referred to as the "mountain of God" only here and in 1 Kings 19:8. Many scholars assume that Horeb and Sinai are two names for the same mountain, though this is not conclusive. In Exodus 24:13–16, for instance, Sinai also seems to be referred to as the "mountain of God."[25] In any case, that

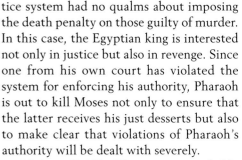

Taskmaster about to beat slave while another looks to be trying to stop the beating
Manfred Näder, Gabana Studios, Germany
▼

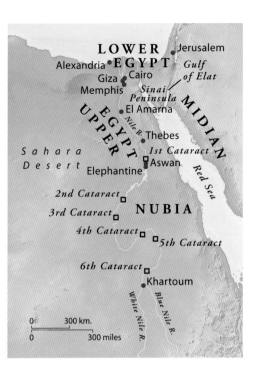

One reason why the people of Israel left Egypt was for them to come to this abode of God and to worship him (3:12). In fact, when they arrive at the mountain, Yahweh states, "I have brought you to myself" (19:4). Yahweh then leaves this dwelling place and travels with the people in the tabernacle—a portable dwelling place (40:34–38).

This understanding accords with the idea that there were already worshipers of Yahweh in the area of Midian (the general vicinity of Horeb) before Moses arrived (see comments on 2:15). It would not be out of place, then, for some Israelites to have believed that *the*, or perhaps *a*, dwelling place of God was in this location. This is not the only interpretive option, however. A somewhat different understanding is that this verse looks ahead to the time when God will reveal himself to the people of Israel from this mountain. It is *his* mountain in the sense that it is his special venue of revelation.[29] In either case, Moses stumbles unknowingly onto God's property, so

one particular mountain is referred to as God's mountain is intriguing. Ancient Near Eastern deities often had their dwelling place on a mountain.[26] In the mythology of Ugarit in Syria, for example, Baal had his palatial abode on Mount Zaphon (Jebel ʾel-Aqraʿ in western Syria), about twenty-five miles north of Ugarit.[27] The Ugaritic literary work known as The Baal Cycle or The Baʿlu Myth (from the 1300s B.C.) has Baal speaking of Mount Zaphon as "my mountain, Divine Sapan / In the holy mount of my heritage, / In the beauty of my might."[28]

Did the ancient Israelites understand God's dwelling place, at least for some period of time, to be at Horeb? Perhaps.

Area around
Mount Sinai near
Wadi ed-Deir
Todd Bolen/www.
BiblePlaces.com

▼

to speak, and is completely taken aback by his encounter.

God called to him (3:4). In 3:2, the "angel of the LORD" appears to Moses "from within a bush." Now we read that "God" speaks to Moses "from within the bush." Who exactly is in the bush—the angel or God?[30] It was not unusual for ancient Near Eastern deities to be thought of as sending "angels" (lit., "messengers"). For instance, in the Babylonian story Nergal and Ereshkigal (600s B.C.), the god Kakka is the messenger of the god Anu, who sends Kakka to carry a message to Ereshkigal, queen of the underworld.[31] Typically, such messengers were gods or goddesses in the service of superior deities.

One theory is that for the ancient Israelites, messengers from God were indeed celestial beings. Because of ancient Israel's monotheism, however, these beings could not be separate gods, and there was thus some merging between the identities of the messengers and the identity of God. The former were not God but could become God—possessed, in a way, by him—and be referred to as God, as happens here.[32] Another theory is that scribes involved in copying biblical texts inserted the word "angel/messenger" in some passages to make the passages more theologically palatable.[33] With respect to this verse, their reasoning may have been this. God, for them, was not to be seen by humans, except in extraordinary circumstances (e.g., 33:21–23). It was almost unimaginable to them that God would have "appeared" to Moses. Speaking is one thing; appearing is another. According to this view, then, it must have been a messenger and not God himself who actually formed the visible entity that captured Moses' attention.

Take off your sandals (3:5). Some depictions of religious rituals from the ancient Near East show worshipers going barefoot before their gods. Also, in ancient Egypt, it seems to have been unacceptable to wear sandals in the presence of the king, even if he should be wearing them. Thus, this act is

probably symbolic for Moses to show respect for sacred space ("holy ground") or subservience to God. Others have suggested that it may simply have been a matter of not tracking dirt—perhaps representative of that which is unclean—into the holy presence of God.[34]

Flowing with milk and honey (3:8). This expression evokes the image of a prosperous land. The Egyptian Story of Sinuhe (from the Twelfth Dynasty, early second millennium B.C.) also describes the land of Canaan as prosperous: "It was a wonderful land called Yaa. There were cultivated figs in it and grapes, and more wine than water. Its honey was abundant, and its olive trees numerous. On its trees were all varieties of fruit. There were barley and emmer, and there was no end to all varieties of cattle."[35] But the land seems not to have been consistently prosperous; several biblical texts refer to famine in Canaan (Gen. 12:10; 26:1; 43:1). Biblical texts describe the blessing of Yahweh as the determining factor. When he wished for there to be prosperity, there was. Ugaritic texts present a similar perspective: When there was divine blessing—in their case, from Baal—then "the heavens rain oil, / the wadis run with honey."[36]

Exactly what kind of prosperity does the biblical expression refer to?[37] It probably does not refer to the most common forms of agriculture, such as the cultivation of grains. Rather, the "milk" most likely refers to animal husbandry and the use of animal byproducts for food and clothing. Sheep were important for their wool and meat, but goats may have been more important. They provide twice as much milk as sheep, and their hair and hides could be used for tents, clothing, carpets, and even satchels for holding liquids.[38] The "honey" refers to horticulture—the cultivation of fruits and vegetables. "Honey" in Israel is more commonly the syrup from grapes and dates than the substance produced by bees.[39]

Given the mountainous and arid landscape of much of Canaan, it would be difficult for a society to rely strictly on agricultural crops. Herding and horticulture were essential. Still, to the casual observer, the lush environs of Egypt's fertile delta appeared far more inviting than Canaan (cf. 16:3; Num. 16:13, where Israelites call *Egypt* a "land flowing with milk and honey"). One can imagine, however, that a bit of "milk and honey" eaten in freedom would feel luxurious compared to the bondage of slavery. Moreover, parts of Canaan were indeed verdant compared to the nearby desert.

Moses' Objections (3:11–22)

I AM WHO I AM (3:14). This statement is essentially in answer to the question, "What is your name?" God's initial answer seems evasive.[40] He is hinting at the real answer, though, since the Hebrew words for "I am" sound a bit like "Yahweh," the name finally revealed in 3:15. Two aspects of how divine names were utilized in ancient Egypt may relate to this revelation of God's name.

First, ancient Egyptians believed in a close relationship between the name of a deity and the deity itself. That is, the name of a god could reveal part of the essential nature of that god. In Egyptian texts that refer to

different but important names for the same deity, the names are often associated with particular actions or characteristics, and the words used tend to sound similar to the names with which they are associated. One can say there is wordplay between the action or characteristic and the name.[41]

For example, one text says, "You are complete [*km*] and great [*wr*] in your name of Bitter Lake [*Km wr*].... See you are great and round [*šn*] in (your name of) Ocean [*Šn wr*]."[42] One can discern a similar wordplay at work in 3:14. The action God refers to is that of being or existing. The wordplay consists in that the statement "I AM" comes from the Hebrew consonants *ʾ-h-y-h*, while the name in 3:15 contains the consonants *y-h-w-h*. Both words come from the same verbal root, and the linguistic connection would be immediately clear to an ancient listener or reader. It is not that God's name is actually "I am" but that "Yahweh" reveals something about the essence of who God is—an essence that relates to the concept of being and to the idea of one who brings others into being (see sidebar). Thus, on the one hand, there really is little more to the statement "I AM WHO I AM" than wordplay. On the other hand, note that in the ancient world "wordplay was regarded

The name Yah-
weh in Kuntillet
ʿAjrud inscription
Z. Radovan/www.
BibleLand
Pictures.com

▶

▶ What Is God's Name

To this day, no one knows for sure how to pronounce the name of God—at least not as the ancient Israelites would have pronounced it. There are four consonants in the name—sometimes called the Tetragrammaton ("four-letter word"): *y-h-w-h*.[A-12] The vowels are the tricky part. Hebrew is generally written without vowels. In the second half of the first millennium A.D., some Jewish scribes began adding small marks to biblical manuscripts in order to indicate how the vowel sounds of each word should be pronounced. They treated the name of God, however, differently from other words. It had long been customary in Jewish tradition *not* to pronounce the name Yahweh. Instead of saying "Yahweh," people would often say "Adonay," which means "my Lord" (and has led to "the LORD" as the traditional rendering of Yahweh in the English Bible). In order to remind readers to say "Adonay" instead of "Yahweh," the scribes added the marks for the vowel sounds of Adonay to the consonants for Yahweh in their manuscripts.

What, then, were the original vowels in God's name? Ultimately, we do not know. During the period of the divided kingdom, the name may have been pronounced something like "Yau," with the "au" forming a diphthong rather than two separate syllables. Evidence from classical Hebrew (found in both biblical and nonbiblical texts) and certain Greek renderings of the name, however, have led scholars generally to believe that "Yahweh" was the way in which the name eventually came to be pronounced.[A-13]

More significant is the meaning of the name Yahweh. For this there has been a wide range of suggestions: "Truly He!"; "My One"; "He Who Is"; "He Who Brings into Being"; "He Who Storms."[A-14] One of the best suggestions is that the name is a shortened form of a longer name,[A-15] Yahweh Sebaoth (often rendered in English as "the LORD of Hosts" or "the LORD Almighty"; see, e.g., 2 Sam. 6:2).[A-16] The word "Yahweh" itself is most likely a verb. Many other shortened names from the ancient Near East are imperfect verb forms, which is exactly what Yahweh appears to be.[A-17] It comes from the Hebrew verb meaning "to be." But if the first vowel really is an *a*-vowel, then the verb likely has a causative sense: "to cause to be." Thus, a fairly literal translation of Yahweh Sebaoth would be, "He Who Causes the Hosts (of Heaven) to Be."[A-18] In general, then, the name refers to the One who creates or brings into being.[A-19]

as a highly serious and controlled use of language, for language was understood to be a dimension of divine presence."[43]

A second aspect of divine names in Egypt may be relevant. Deities sometimes had secret names, and special power was granted to those who knew them.[44] Certain Egyptian magical texts (e.g., the Harris Magical Papyrus) give instructions on how to use the words of a god and thereby wield a degree of that god's power. "It was of course especially effective if instead of using the usual name of the god, the magician could name his *real name*, that special name possessed by each god.... He who knew this name, possessed the power of him who bore it."[45]

In The Legend of Isis and the Name of Re (from the 1200s B.C.), the goddess Isis devises a trick to learn the secret name of the god Re. She fashions a serpent that bites Re. Then she comes to him as he is writhing in agony and says, "Tell me thy name, my divine father, for a person lives with whose name one recites (magic)."[46] Re responds: "I am he who made heaven and earth, who knotted together the mountains, and created what is thereon."[47] Re lists a long series of accomplishments, but, like Yahweh in Exodus, Re is evading the point. Isis answers him: "Thy name is not really among these which thou hast told me."[48] She finally convinces Re to tell her, and he does (though the text does not reveal it). Isis, now that she knows Re's secret name, commands the poison to leave Re and heals him.

It would have been unusual in the ancient Near East for a deity quickly and easily to reveal his name (see, e.g., Gen. 32:29); this may be part of the reason for the delayed answer here in Exodus. Nevertheless, Yahweh's name is not meant to be kept secret, and it is vitally important for Moses to have this knowledge. He is to speak Yahweh's words (6:29), wield his power (7:17), and function like Yahweh to both his brother Aaron (4:16) and to Pharaoh (7:1).

Signs and Reassurance for Moses (4:1–17)

It became a snake (4:3). Tales even from the modern era have been told of an Egyptian magical act in which a snake becomes as stiff as a staff. One account refers to "both a snake and a crocodile thrown by hypnotism into the condition of rigidity in which they could be held up as rods by the tip of the tail."[49] The sign given to Moses is the opposite, which raises the possibility that the sign is an obvious reversal of Egyptian magic.

It was leprous (4:6). Exactly what the Hebrew term for "leprous" means is uncertain (see sidebar). Other biblical texts (e.g., Lev. 13–14) discuss "leprosy" in more detail.

Return to Egypt (4:18–31)

Bridegroom of blood (4:25). The strange events in verses 24–26 are notoriously dif-

ficult to interpret. To begin with, Yahweh appears intent on killing Moses, the one he has just commissioned as the deliverer of the Israelites. One explanation is that Yahweh feels compelled to punish Moses for the latter's murder of an Egyptian taskmaster (2:12).[50] But why would Yahweh wait until now? In other biblical texts, those who are guilty of *accidental* or *unintentional* homicide may flee to so-called cities of refuge or asylum (21:13; Num. 35:9–34; Deut. 19:1–13; Josh. 20:1–9). This affords them protection from the relatives of the victim who are likely to seek revenge, and they must remain in their chosen city of refuge until the death of the high priest (Num. 35:28; Josh. 20:6).

The analogy to Moses' situation is inexact but intriguing. Moses' flight to Midian could be seen as an effort to seek asylum. That there was justification for Moses' killing of the Egyptian is debatable, but it may have counted as a crime of passion or an appropriate act of revenge for the killing of Israelites.[51] In this way, Moses qualifies for leniency and thus for the chance at asylum. He then remains in Midian until he is told that "all the men who wanted to kill you are dead" (4:19). This suggests that Moses is now free to leave his place of asylum and make his return. Yet, Yahweh still attacks him. The idea may be that, even though Moses is free in a legal sense to return, he still carries about on his person a kind of spiritual or religious pollution as a result of the homicide—a pollution that must be purged.[52] In the case of homicide, the pollution is referred to by the Hebrew word *dām* ("blood"); the perpetrator has been contaminated by the victim's blood.

This notion of blood contamination turns

A staff in the form of a coiled serpent was found tangled in a mass of hair, in a chest full of papyri, bearing incantations and prescriptions to secure good health.
Werner Forman Archive/The Fitzwilliam Museum, Cambridge

▶ Biblical Leprosy

Gerhard Henrik Armauer Hansen, a Norwegian physician, in the 1860s discovered the organism that he named *Mycobacterium leprae*—the bacterium that causes what today is known as leprosy or Hansen's disease. There is little evidence, however, that this disease existed to any substantial degree in the ancient Near East. Examinations of skeletal remains from both Egypt and Israel show little evidence of the bone deformities typically caused by leprosy; the earliest indication of true leprosy in Egypt dates to the early Christian period.[A-20] The Hebrew term *ṣāraʿat*, often translated as "leprosy," most likely refers to changes in the skin that result from any number of dermatological conditions (e.g., psoriasis, eczema), fungal infections (e.g., ringworm), or other causes.[A-21]

In Exodus 4:6, Moses' hand is said to be "like snow." This could refer either to color (white) or to texture (flaky), though the latter is more likely in light of other biblical texts referring to *ṣāraʿat*.[A-22] Ancient Mesopotamians also had names for skin diseases (*epqu, sahʿaršubbû*) that have been translated into English as "leprosy." Like the Israelites, they feared these diseases. Some texts use this disease to curse wrongdoers: "May Sîn, great lord, fill him with leprosy and may he bed down like a wild ass outside the city."[A-23] A court case at ancient Nuzi (c. 1400 B.C.) cites testimony of one man to another, "You are filled with 'leprosy' [*epqu*]. Do not come near me."[A-24] Thus, Moses' hand, whatever it was, is meant to startle and repulse any observer and even Moses himself, though he cannot run from this as he had from the snake.

The London Medical Papyrus from Egypt, late Eighteenth Dynasty, 1325 B.C. The text is a combination of recipes and magical spells for various ailments. The main concerns of the papyrus are skin complaints, eye complaints, bleeding (mostly incantations against miscarriage) and burns.

HIP/Art Resource, NY, courtesy of the British Museum

▶

up in ancient Greece and Mesopotamia as well.[53] An Assyrian text from the mid 600s B.C. declares that the perpetrator of a homicide must make a payment (what is really a ransom for his own life) to the victim's family and in so doing "wash the blood away."[54] A text from Mari (c. 1800 B.C.) refers to a "criminal who is polluted with that blood (shed in murder)."[55] In Exodus, Yahweh cannot allow Moses to emerge from his place of asylum unless the contamination is purged.[56]

This is where Zipporah's act of circumcision becomes important. It appears to function as the expiation—purging, atonement—for the guilt, pollution, or "blood" that Moses is still carrying around and on account of which Yahweh attacks him. It is

Ebers Papyrus medical text includes remedies for stopping bleeding of circumcision
Courtesy of the University of Leipzig

Hebrew word for "bridegroom" (ḥātān). The verb form of this word in both Hebrew and Arabic means "to become a relative by means of marriage." But the etymology of this word leads to another verb that means "to circumcise."[60] By the word "bridegroom," then, Zipporah refers both to a bridegroom and to a circumcised one. This suggests that Moses is indeed circumcised, albeit symbolically, by her act. In the end, the circumcision cleanses Moses and thereby appeases Yahweh's anger.

hard to say, however, exactly how circumcision accomplishes this expiation. There is a Phoenician myth in which the god Kronos circumcises himself and thereby seems to halt an impending catastrophe sent by another god. "At the occurrence of a fatal plague, Kronos immolated his only son to his father Ouranos, and circumcised himself, forcing the allies who were with him to do the same."[57] This myth reflects a belief that circumcision could quell divine wrath.

If some such similar belief is at work in Exodus, the problem then becomes why Moses himself is not the one circumcised. In light of both Egyptian and Hebrew customs, though, he likely already is circumcised and thus cannot be physically circumcised again.[58] Thus, the touching of his son's bloody foreskin to Moses' own genitalia (the Hebrew word for "feet" can be euphemistic for male sex organs) may have functioned as a symbolic circumcision and produced the required expiatory effect.[59]

In light of all this, Zipporah's comment about "a bridegroom of blood" probably contains a pair of double meanings. First, Moses is a bridegroom of blood because he still possesses the blood or pollution that resulted from his homicide, but also because of the bloody circumcision that Zipporah performs. The other double meaning comes from the

Confrontation with Pharaoh (5:1–21)

Hold a festival (5:1). To hold a festival meant to hold a specialized religious ceremony. In later biblical texts (23:14–17; 34:18–23; Deut. 16:1–7), three ceremonies are referred to with the Hebrew term for "festival" (ḥag): the Feast of Unleavened Bread/Passover; the Feast of Harvest (Feast of Weeks); and the Feast of Ingathering (Feast of Booths). Whether this verse means to refer to one of these festivals is hard to say; it may simply refer to one like them.

But why could not such a festival be held in Egypt? Why is a trip into the desert necessary? Is this just a ploy to get the Israelites away from Egypt? Perhaps it is, although Moses later explains that the Israelite sacrifices would be "detestable to the Egyptians" (8:26).

But there may have been other, more important reasons. Religious festivals are known from all around the ancient Near East. Mesopotamian and Egyptian society both had numerous feasts tied to particular times of their civil calendar.[61] The Hittites, too, had festivals that "were held monthly or yearly, while others, such as the Festival of the Sickle or the Festival of Cutting Grapes, took place in connection with events of the agricultural year" (civil and agricultural calendars did not always match).[62] In almost every case, a festival connected with a particular deity took place at that deity's place of residence—at its temple or wherever the priests happened to place its statue.[63] Perhaps the Israelites could not hold a festival to their God in Egypt because his place of residence was the "mountain of God" in "the desert" (see comments on 3:1).

I do not know the Lord (5:2). It is not that the Egyptian king is unfamiliar with deities worshiped by Semitic peoples. The Egyptians knew well and even venerated a number of Semitic deities.[64] Baal, for instance, was highly revered. The Egyptian king was at times said to be "great in power like Baal over foreign lands" or to have a "roar like that of Baal in heaven."[65] Perhaps the pharaoh here is saying that he has never heard of Yahweh. But his statement more likely means a refusal to acknowledge Yahweh as one worthy of his attention.

Get your own straw (5:11). Straw was crucial for mud bricks that would hold firmly together. Even in modern Egypt, bricks have often been made of soil, water, and what is known in Arabic as *tibn*—essentially the same term as the Hebrew word for straw (*teben*). Without straw, more bricks would fail, and quotas would be more difficult to meet.

Scientific experiments have shown that the use of chopped straw in mud brick increases its breaking strength over three times. This is partly due to the binding character of the straw, and partly to the action of such products of decaying vegetable matter as humic acid upon the clay, which increases its strength and plasticity. Thus if the mixture of straw and mud is allowed to stand some time before use, it becomes easier to handle and makes a stronger brick.... In ancient Egypt mud brick was the almost universal building material for homes.... The evidence of both ancient and modern methods in the manufacture of mud brick in Egypt indicates that while bricks are occasionally made without straw, this practice is far from common.[66]

Quota of bricks (5:14). The Louvre Leather Scroll, an Egyptian text from the reign of Ramesses II, contains a list of brick quotas assigned to individual workers and how many bricks each worker delivered. The relevant portion of the text begins: "The great Stable of Ramesses II, Life Prosperity and Health! Amenemhat son of Kuroy—bricks, 2000: delivered, 150; delivered, 150; delivered, 165; delivered, 185; delivered, 170; total, 820. Wepwawetmose son of Huy—ditto, 2000: delivered, 100; delivered, 350; delivered, 180; delivered, 320; total, 950."[67] Of the approximately thirty-five workers listed, not one met his quota of bricks. To what degree this caused problems for the building project or to what degree these workers may have been punished is not disclosed.

Lazy (5:17). Literally, "Slackers!" Pharaoh deems them such, of course, because of the request for time off from work. The reason for the request—going into the desert to worship—Pharaoh sees merely as an excuse. But time off from work for worship was not unheard of in Egypt. A collection of texts has been preserved from the New Kingdom site of Deir el-Medina, where many Egyptian workers were stationed in order to construct and decorate royal tombs.

▶ **No Straw and Hard Times**

A New Kingdom text (Papyrus Anastasi 4) records a complaint somewhat reminiscent of the situation in Exodus 5.

I am dwelling in Damnationville with no supplies. There have been no people to knead bricks and no straw in the district. Those supplies I brought are gone, and there are no asses, (since they) have been stolen. I spend the day watching the birds and doing some fishing (all the while), eyeing the road which goes up to Djahy with (homesick) longing. Under trees with no edible foliage do I take my siesta (for) their fruit has perished.... The gnat attacks in sunlight and the mosquito in the (heat of) noon, and the sand-fly stings—they suck at every blood vessel ... if ever a jar filled with Kode wine is opened and people come out to get a cup, there are 200 large dogs and 300 jackals—500 in all—and they stand waiting constantly at the door of the house whenever I go out, since they smell the liquor when the container is opened ... the heat here never lets up.[A-25]

Records list workers who were absent for a variety of reasons, including participation in religious rituals and festivities.[68] Pharaoh does not want to give the Hebrews time off for any reason.

More Revelation from God (6:1–27)

My mighty hand (6:1). This phrase can just as easily be translated, "my strong arm." It appears to have a direct parallel in royal rhetoric from ancient Egypt.[69] For instance, there is an Egyptian account of the epic battle of Qadesh (c. 1275 B.C.), in which Ramesses II led his army against the Hittites near Qadesh in Syria. The Egyptians escaped with a narrow victory but proclaimed their triumph in grandiose terms. Ramesses boasts:

Then, when my troops and my chariotry
    saw me,
that I was like Montu, my arm strong,
Amun my father being with me instantly,
turning all the foreign lands into straw
        before me,
    then they presented
        themselves one by
        one,
    to approach the camp at
        evening time....
Then my army came to
    praise me,
their faces [amazed/
    averted], at seeing
    what I had done.
My officers came to
    extol my strong arm,
and likewise my
    chariotry, boasting of
    my name.[70]

Workers village at valley of kings
Frederick J. Mabie

Beth Shean Stele
of Seti I
Steven Voth,
courtesy of the
Rockefeller Museum,
Jerusalem
▶

▶ Historicity of the Exodus

When historians consider the Israel-ites' flight from Egypt, some are highly skeptical, going so far as to say that the events described in Exodus have no connection to what really happened.[A-26] Others take the biblical text more at face value and find its description of the Israelites' enslavement and eventual escape highly probable.[A-27] It is impor-tant to realize that decisive proof for the historicity of any event is virtually unattainable. Events can be shown to be *possible*, *plausible*, or even *probable*, depending on the nature and amount of evidence supporting them. But they can-not be *proved* in any ultimate sense.

While some dispute this, there is actually little historical evidence that substantially corroborates an escape of slaves from Egypt on the order of the large-scale exodus described in the Bible.[A-28] There is one aspect of the biblical narrative, however, that has a fair amount of circumstantial evidence in its favor: the enslavement of Israelites in Egypt. This evidence is sufficient to argue for the *plausibility* of this event. The Egyptians used a particular term, often translated "Asiatics," to refer to Semitic people groups. This term typi-cally applied to those who hailed from the regions of western Asia, such as Syria and Palestine, and it could easily have been used of Israelites. Asiatics

Ramesses with
outstretched arm
to smite enemies
as a god looks on
Frederick J. Mabie
▼

Other Egyptian texts refer to the Egyptian king as "powerful of arm," "the strong-armed," and "lord of the strong arm."[71] In addition, several Amarna letters (see comment on 1:15) refer to the Egyptian king's "strong arm" or the "power of his arm."[72] The rhetoric in Exodus turns the tables on Egyptian royal ideology. This time Yahweh is the one who possesses the strong arm, and he will defeat the one whom all of Egypt thinks possesses it. Yahweh intends to beat Pharaoh at his own game, and the lines for the ensuing battle have been clearly drawn.

entered Egypt by one of several means: as prisoners of war; as part of tribute payments from Asiatic rulers to the Egyptian king; as victims of slave trade; on business trips to conduct trade and related activities; and in search of food and water for themselves and their flocks.[A-29] The first three ways usually led to enslavement, often at the hands of official institutions, such as the palace, the temple, and the military.

Much of the evidence for Asiatic slaves in Egypt comes from the New Kingdom. Beginning with Thutmose III in the 1400s B.C., Egyptian kings brought back unprecedented numbers of Asiatic slaves from their military campaigns into Syria and Palestine.[A-30] From the 1300s, the Amarna letters (see comment on 1:15) show a fairly active slave trade between Palestine and Egypt. Kings from the 1200s, such as Seti I, continued forays into Palestine, capturing large numbers of prisoners. By the time of Ramesses II, so many Semitic slaves in Egypt make it hard to imagine that no Israelites were among them. Whether they were enslaved in exactly the way that Exodus describes is another question. Unfortunately, there is no extrabib-lical evidence to provide an answer on this particular point.

Note, too, that an examination of the historicity of the Exodus events must take into account the nature of historical understanding in the ancient world. Biblical authors and other ancient writers were often much more interested in making theological points than in convincing their readership of the historical reality of their assertions. This approach typically entailed the inclusion of theological claims and literary artistry in with the historical core to a narrative, and it is not a simple task to sift out that core. As Redmount aptly puts it,

> The biblical Exodus account was never intended to function or to be understood as history in the present-day sense of the word. Traditional history, with its stress on objectivity ... is a modern obsession.... In the end, the Exodus saga is neither pure history nor pure literature, but an inseparable amalgam of both, closest in form to what we would call a docudrama. For the Israelites, the Exodus events were anchored in history, but at the same time rose above it.[A-31]

I am the LORD (6:2). Literally, "I am Yahweh." Is this statement merely to inform Moses as to the identity of his conversation partner? Other ancient Near Eastern texts also record deities speaking in this way, although such statements are not common in Egyptian texts. Part of the "Sphinx Stele" from the time of Thutmose IV states: "See me, look at me, my son Thutmose. I am thy father, Harmakhis-Kepri-Re-Atum, I shall give thee my kingdom upon earth."[73] Assyrian texts from the 600s B.C. ascribe the following statements to the goddess Ishtar: "I am the great divine lady, I am the goddess Ishtar of Arbela, who will destroy your enemies from before your feet.... I am Ishtar of Arbela. I shall lie in wait for your enemies"; "I am Ishtar of Arbela, O Esarhaddon, king of Assyria. In the cities of Ashur, Nineveh, Calah, protracted days ... unto [you] shall I grant."[74]

Such "I am" statements seem mainly associated with assertions of a deity's power and authority. King Esarhaddon of Assyria can rest assured that he will enjoy long life and see his enemies defeated, because Ishtar has confirmed her declaration: "I am Ishtar of Arbela." For its part, the biblical text insists that all involved in this situation in Egypt acknowledge ("know") who Yahweh is and accept his power and authority, even though Pharaoh fails to acknowledge any of

▶ **Egyptian Military Campaigns and Prisoners of War**

Egyptian reports of military victories are prone to exaggerate the results of their army's triumphs. The report of the second military campaign into Syria and Palestine by Amenhotep II is one such text. Toward the end of the document, the text summarizes the people and material captured: "List of the plunder which his majesty carried off: princes of Retenu: 127; brothers of princes: 179; Apiru: 3,600; living Shasu: 15,200; Kharu: 36,300; living Neges: 15,070; the adherents thereof: 30,652; total: 89,600 men."[A-32]

If one adds the numbers listed, the total is over one hundred thousand. Where the number 89,600 comes from is not clear. Even though the numbers seem exaggerated, they indicate deportation on a massive scale. It almost goes without saying that these prisoners of war would have become slaves and been forced to do manual labor in Egypt.

this (see 5:2). Moreover, the driving force behind Israel's deliverance from Egypt is to build in them an unwavering conviction: "Then you will know that I am the LORD

Sphinx of Giza with the granite dream stele of Pharaoh Thutmosis IV between his paws
Erich Lessing/Art Resource, NY
▶

your God" (6:7). The Egyptians, too, are not left out of this equation: "And the Egyptians will know that I am the LORD" (7:5). Exodus repeatedly stresses this kind of knowing (7:17; 8:10; 10:2; 14:4, 18).

I did not make myself known (6:3). God's statement here is puzzling, since previous biblical texts speak clearly of Abraham's knowledge of the name Yahweh. Abraham uses the name himself (Gen. 15:2, 8), and Yahweh declares it to Abraham: "I am the LORD" (15:7). One possible explanation has to do with the promise that seems most closely associated with the name Yahweh—the land of Canaan. When referring to the land that will someday belong to the Israelites, biblical texts most often use Yahweh instead of names such as Elohim ("God") and describe the promise in terms of an oath that Yahweh has made (e.g., Ex. 13:5). For Abraham, Isaac, and Jacob not to have "known" God by the name Yahweh may have meant that the biblical narrative never portrays them as experiencing the fulfillment of the Yahweh-promise. The later Israelites possess the land of Canaan in ways their forefathers would probably never have imagined and thus come to "know" Yahweh in the sense of experiencing the realization of the promise.[75]

expressed by "take" (Akkadian *leqû*, cognate with Hebrew *lāqaḥ*) in conjunction with the expression "as a son" or "as a daughter." For example, Laws of Hammurabi 186 begins: "If a man takes a young child as a son...." In Exodus, Yahweh says that he "takes" the Israelites "as a people." One can say he adopts them.

Adoption functions for at least three purposes: (1) to provide a secure way to care for orphans, abandoned children, and children from families in distress; (2) to provide children for couples with none of their own; and (3) to provide an heir for an individual or a couple.[76] Yahweh's "adoption" of the Israelites fulfills at least two of these purposes. First, biblical texts liken the Israelites to an abandoned child and refer to them, collectively, as Yahweh's son (Ezek. 16:4–5; Hos. 11:1). Second, Israel is called a "people of inheritance," and the land of Canaan is "the land the LORD your God is giving you as an inheritance" (Deut. 4:20–21). The practice of adoption may thus have provided an important context for ancient Israel's understanding of her relationship with Yahweh.[77]

Faltering lips (6:12). The note in the NIV gives the more direct rendering of the Hebrew: "I am uncircumcised of lips." Biblical texts speak of two other body parts that one would not ordinarily think of as being uncircumcised: the ear (Jer. 6:10) and the heart (Lev. 26:41; Deut 10:16; 30:6; Jer. 4:4; 9:26; Ezek. 44:7, 9). "In these passages, at issue is neither deafness

Take you as my own people (6:7). This expression comes from contract law. It is the classical expression of the covenantal (or "contractual," since the Heb. *bᵉrît* can be translated "covenant" or "contract") relationship between Yahweh and the Israelites. They will be his people, and he will be their God. Literally, the statement is, "I take [*lāqaḥ*] you to myself as a people." The forming of a marriage relationship is also expressed in this way: "Aaron took [*lāqaḥ*] Elisheba ... to himself as a wife" (lit. trans. 6:23).

Adoption also provides a helpful analogy. In Mesopotamia, adoption was often

nor a cardiac condition, but moral imperviousness to the divine word."[78] Moses is here no longer speaking of himself as "slow in speech and tongue" (4:10). He is referring to an entirely different idea. It is not a physical disability that he has in mind but a moral one. He is acutely aware of his lack of success so far with both Pharaoh and the Israelites. What other explanation could there be for this but his own moral failings—his "uncircumcised" lips? Moses' statement implies that he believes his mouth is no longer a clean, free, and open channel for Yahweh's words.

This focus on the mouth and lips may relate to the so-called mouth-washing rituals in Mesopotamia, which were to purify a person or object in order to come into contact with a divine presence.[79] Kings, priests, regular citizens, animals, and objects could undergo this ritual. It was especially important for statues that were to receive the presence of a deity and thereby to become a god: "You purify him [the statue] with the *egubbû*-basin and (then) perform the *Mīs Pî* [washing of the mouth] ritual. You set up a libation and the *āšipu*-priest stands to the left of that god. You recite three times the incantation, 'When the god was made.'"[80]

After the washing, the mouth was "opened"—a necessary step in the process of transforming the statue into a god. Clearly, preparing the *mouth* was critical for preparing the entire person or object for divine contact.[81] In Isaiah 6:5, the prophet has been in the presence of Yahweh, but he cries out, "I am ruined! For I am a man of unclean lips, and I live among a people of unclean lips."[82] Moses, too, believes he has moral deficiencies that have stymied his efforts. In the end, the narrative does not reveal how this problem is solved, but it surely must be, since Moses is back on track in short order and does precisely what Yahweh wants (Ex. 7:6).

First Demonstration of Power (6:28–7:13)

Like God to Pharaoh (7:1). The word "like" is not in the Hebrew text. Literally the text reads: "I have made you God to Pharaoh." This kind of statement would not seem odd in the ancient world. In certain situations, a person could be turned into a different class of creature—a class to which he or she does not naturally belong. The transformation is not physical, but the change was still considered valid within its context.

Such a transformation, for example, took place within the world of law. In some ancient Near Eastern societies, a man with no male heirs would pass his estate on to his daughter. Before doing so, however, he would formally declare that his daughter is a son, a change that allowed the daughter to inherit lawfully from the father. This type of situation is known mainly from the Late Bronze Age and particularly from Nuzi and Emar.[83] Some documents from Emar record wills in which two legal transformations take place: A daughter is made "female and male" and thereby becomes a son as well as a daughter; and the testator's wife is made "father and mother."[84] These changes give to the wife full authority over the estate, once the testator has passed away, and to the daughter all the rights and privileges accorded a lawful heir.

A painting in the tomb of Inherkha shows a priest wearing the mask of Horus performing the Opening of the Mouth ritual. The purpose of the ceremonial Opening of the Mouth was to restore to the deceased the use of the senses, thus restoring life in the next world.
Werner Forman Archive/E. Strouhal

▶ The Timing of the Exodus, Part I

One question has been much discussed by historians: If indeed there was an Israelite exodus from Egypt, when did it take place? First, however, is the issue of how long the Israelites lived in Egypt. The ancestral history given for Aaron and Moses in 6:14–25 raises difficulties. The genealogy it constructs for Moses is this: Levi → Kohath → Amram → Moses. This would mean that Moses is in the fourth generation since the Israelites came to Egypt, if one counts Levi's generation as the first. How can we reconcile this ancestral history with verses such as Genesis 15:13 and Exodus 12:40, which place the Israelites' time in Egypt at 400 and 430 years, respectively? Surely four generations takes up much less time than 400 years.

Moreover, Kohath, Levi's son, was already born when Levi and his relatives went to live in Egypt (Gen. 46:11). One could perhaps argue that some children were born when their fathers were quite old. This, however, would still not account for 400 years, and the child-bearing years for parents in the ancient world typically came sooner than they do for many parents today.[A-33]

Another possibility is that the ancestral history here omits several generations.[A-34] The text in 1 Chronicles 7:23–27 lists eleven generations between Jacob and Joshua. Would this not require more generations than four between Levi and Moses? Yet other passages in 1 Chronicles (e.g., 6:1–3; 23:12–15) do not seem to allow for any break between Levi, Kohath, Amram, Aaron, and Moses, and the sons of Aaron and Moses. In addition, Genesis 15:16 appears to say that the return to Canaan will indeed take place in the fourth generation following the move of Jacob's family to Egypt. This is not to say that biblical or other ancient genealogies never skip generations, but there is no clear indication that this is one of those instances. For the time being, there is no obvious solution that makes all the biblical data fit together neatly (see also sidebar on The Timing of the Exodus, Part II," at 12:40).

The transformation of Moses here is no less valid. He is now God to Pharaoh in the sense that he has the rights and privileges of God in his relationship to Pharaoh. He has the authority to command, judge, and punish Pharaoh and the power to perform wonders deemed even by the Egyptian magicians as supernatural in origin (8:19). For the ancient Egyptians, Pharaoh was divine and should have been the one to function as a god to Moses.

Seti I is portrayed here with his son, Ramesses II, receiving offerings from two priests.
Kim Walton, courtesy of the Oriental Institute Museum
◀

Algae blooms offer one explanation of the waters turning to blood.
Adam Fritzler
▶

Upper part of a stone shabti for the lector-priest Pediamenopet
Werner Forman Archive/Sold at Christie's, 1996
▼

This snake standing upright is reminiscent of the staffs that became serpents.
Frederick J. Mabie
▶

It became a snake (7:10). The Hebrew word for "snake" in this verse is different from the one used in 4:3. The word here can refer to a sea-monster, dragon, crocodile, or snake. The purpose of this event is also different. The sign with Moses' staff was for the Israelite elders. They saw it and, initially, believed Moses (4:30–31). The sign with Aaron's staff is for Pharaoh and his officials and demonstrates what appears to be an assault on Egyptian ideology. If Aaron's staff did indeed become a snake, then its devouring of the magicians' snakes, on the one hand, demonstrates an overpowering of the magicians and even a commandeering of their own abilities and expertise.[85] On the other hand, it could also serve as an attack on the snake as a symbol of Egyptian power. It is hard to know, though, whether Aaron's staff was supposed to become a snake that the Egyptians feared and despised or one that they worshiped. In either case, the narrative describes the actions of Moses and Aaron as an emphatic display of power.

Egyptian magicians (7:11). The Hebrew term for "magicians" appears related to an Egyptian word often used to refer to theological specialists in ancient Egypt, who studied their culture's sacred literature and knew an array of secret charms, spells, and rituals.[86] They were often said to be associated with the "House of Life," a special section in some Egyptian temples that housed ritual and magic texts said to be inspired by the sun god.[87] They were the heavy hit-

▶ The Magician and the Crocodile

It is possible that Aaron's staff turns into a crocodile (see comment on 7:10). In an Egyptian document known as the Westcar Papyrus, now housed in Berlin, five tales are preserved. The papyrus was probably written during the period of the Hyksos (c. 1650–1550 B.C.), although scholars tend to think the tales were composed during the Twelfth Dynasty (c. 1950–1750 B.C.).[A-35] The tales themselves are set even further back during the time of King Cheops (c. 2550 B.C.). The second tale recounts how the wife of priest Webaoner is having an affair with a townsman. Webaoner fashions a crocodile of wax and gives it to the caretaker of his estate, with instructions to throw the crocodile after the townsman the next time the latter returns from one of his clandestine visits to the priest's wife. When the caretaker does this, the crocodile becomes alive and grows to a length of twelve feet. It grabs the townsman and takes him under water where it keeps him for seven days.

Webaoner then brings the king to see the crocodile. Webaoner "[called out to the] crocodile and said: Bring back [the]

townsman. [The crocodile] came [out of the water]…. Said His Majesty the King of Upper and Lower Egypt, Nebka, the vindicated: this crocodile is indeed fearful! But Webaoner bent down, and he caught it and it became a crocodile of wax in his hand."[A-36] Later the crocodile is animated again and returns to the depths of the water never to be seen again. The Egyptian magician's ability to manipulate the crocodile was used to punish a man perceived to be a wrongdoer. In the Exodus story, similar manipulation occurs as a blow to the abilities of the Egyptian magicians. In addition to a display of power, the point may be to ask: Who is in the wrong now?

The Westcar Papyri contain ancient Egyptian stories of magic including the story of The Magician and the Crocodile.
Margarete Büsing/ Bildarchiv Preussischer Kulturbesitz/Art Resource, NY, courtesy of the Aegyptisches Museum, Staatliche Museen zu Berlin, Berlin, Germany

ters, so to speak. Magical wands are also known from ancient Egypt, used mainly to ward off evil power and illness.[88] Whether these Egyptian magicians here use such wands ("staffs") is not clear.

The Ten Plagues (7:14–11:10)

Water was changed into blood (7:20). This is usually considered the first of the so-called ten plagues that Yahweh sends against

Goddess Wadjet
as ureaus on
Pharaoh's crown

Frederick J. Mabie

▶

▶ Snakes in Egyptian Thought

In ancient Egypt various preternatural beings (deities, demons, etc.) took the form of a snake.[A-37] For example, Apophis was an evil serpent and a great enemy of the sun god Re. In Egyptian mythology, he regularly attacked the sun god and, unless regularly defeated, could impede or even halt the sun god's orbit and thus bring disaster for human life on earth.[A-38]

Another important snake deity was the goddess Wadjit. She functioned as the protective and representative deity of Lower Egypt, the Delta region. She was normally portrayed as an upreared cobra—referred to as a *uraeus*—ready to strike.[A-39] Wadjit was represented by the uraeus adorning the Egyptian king's headdress. Having the cobra just above the king's forehead was meant to bring protection to Pharaoh and terror to his enemies. An Old Kingdom (c. 2686–2160 B.C.) text states: "Ho Fiery Serpent? Grant that the dread of me be like the dread of you; grant that the fear of me be like the fear of you."[A-40]

The inscription commemorating Ramesses II's victory at Qadesh over the Hittites (c. 1275 B.C.) also refers to Wadjit. Ramesses speaks of how he entered the fray and fought ferociously, with his "uraeus-serpent" beating back his enemies and spitting "fiery flame" into the faces of his enemies.[A-41] The uraeus on the king's head imbued him with the mystical force by which he maintained order in Egypt and even the entire world; no uraeus meant no power.[A-42]

The episode with Aaron's staff makes a more effective attack on Egyptian ideology if the snake is one like the king's uraeus rather than an evil creature like Apophis. If so, this narrative is another instance when the biblical text takes a power symbol, crucial within the Egyptian worldview, and attempts to reverse its power and make it advantageous for the Israelites.

Egypt. (On "plague," see the sidebar "Plague Terminology" at 11:1.) Within ancient Near Eastern societies, this event would have signified national calamity, the invasion of chaos, and even a divine curse on the land. In Egypt, for example, it was Pharaoh's responsibility to maintain a state of proper order and justice, referred to as *ma'at*, which was "the idea of a meaningful, all-pervasive order that embraces the world of humankind, objects, and nature—in short, the meaning of creation, the form in which it was intended by the creator god."[89]

In a sense, Egyptian religion with all its beliefs and practices was designed to restore *ma'at* to Egypt and preserve it as fully as pos-

sible. As titular and functional head of his religion, the Egyptian king was expected to protect his land against the forces of chaos, disorder, and injustice. The Admonitions of Ipuwer (c. 2000 B.C.) uses a variety of verbal imagery to describe what chaos in the land would look like. At one point it speaks of blood:

Verily, [the heart] is horrified,
For affliction pervades the land,
Blood is everywhere....
Verily, the river is blood, but one drinks
   from it;
One may turn away from people, yet one
   will thirst for water.[90]

In the Sumerian myth Inanna and Shu-kale-tuda, the goddess Inanna is sleeping and, unbeknownst to her, is raped by a gardener. Upon awaking and discovering what has happened, Inanna inflicts three plagues on the land; the third is the turning of all water to blood.[91] Another Sumerian myth, The Exaltation of Inanna, refers to a land that has failed to worship Inanna: "In the mountain where homage is withheld from you vegetation is accursed. Its grand entrance you have reduced to ashes. Blood rises in its rivers for you, its people have nought to drink."[92] Thus, for the Nile and its canals to be turned to blood meant that chaos has crossed Egypt's borders, that Pharaoh has failed in his duty, and that a divine power is at work against them.

Nile will teem with frogs (8:3). Some scholars see a direct cause-and-effect relationship between the plague of blood and this plague of frogs. If the Nile, never in short supply of frogs, were to become uninhabitable, where else would the frogs go but up onto the land? This is speculative at best. Another idea is that this plague is one more attack on Egyptian ideology, with the frog goddess Heket as its particular target. Heket was a giver of life. As the consort of Khnum, a creator god, she assisted in the creation of infants.[93] In a Middle Kingdom (c. 2055–1650 B.C.) tale, she and others serve with Isis at the birth of three kings.[94] Later, she develops a special association with childbirth and becomes a kind of patron goddess of midwives.[95]

Egyptians did not, however, associate every common frog with the goddess. If there is symbolic meaning in the account of this plague, it may simply be to point out the inability of Pharaoh and the Egyptian gods to maintain proper order. First the water is ruined, and now the frogs are out of control. The disorder is taking different forms.

Magicians did the same things (8:7). This is the third and final time that the Egyptian magicians are able to duplicate a wonder produced by Moses and Aaron (cf. 7:11, 22). That the magicians are interested in magnifying a plague that has just been released raises the question of motivation. Are they simply attempting to demonstrate that they, too, can conjure blood from water and summon frogs from the depths of the earth? If so, this seems a foolhardy attempt, since they are exacerbating their people's problems rather than solving them. They are, if anything, assisting their enemies.

The magicians' first attempt to demonstrate that their powers are equal to those of Moses and Aaron may have served as a portent of this assistance that they seem unwittingly to offer. The episode where Aaron's staff/snake swallows theirs depicts what can be called "superposition."[96] This refers to the elevation of one entity over another, and "when snakes are directed against snakes, opponents are made to function as allies and 'assistant' means only 'subjected opponent.'"[97] Thus, the triumph of Aaron's staff/snake over those of the magicians signifies the superposition of Moses and Aaron, such that their role in future encounters will, in fact, be that of assistants. This seems to be the role we find them performing in this verse.

He hardened his heart (8:15). In the NIV translation of Exodus, there are seventeen times when a form of the word "hard" (e.g., "hardened") is used to refer to a heart. Two other verses in the NIV speak of a heart being "unyielding."

Fragment of a magic wand with symbol of power and a toad, the sign of the birth goddess Heket

Bildarchiv Preussischer Kulturbesitz/Art Resource, NY, courtesy of the Aegyptisches Museum, Staatliche Museen zu Berlin, Berlin, Germany

▶ The Plagues as Natural Phenomena

In the 1950s, Greta Hort gave the most detailed explanation of the theory that the plagues described in Exodus could have occurred naturally within Egypt, given the right conditions.[A-43] In a sense, they were natural disasters. Hort believed that the first six plagues formed a progression of events, each of which naturally resulted from one of the plagues before it. The next three plagues fit with the general pattern of the Egyptian agricultural and seasonal calendars. The last plague, of course, does not correspond to any natural phenomenon. Here is a more specific overview of this theory.

Blood. The water did not change into actual blood. Instead, it took on the appearance of blood. This could have been caused by flagellates (single-cell organisms living in water) flowing down the Nile from Ethiopia. Certain types of flagellates made the river water appear red and, because they upset the balance of oxygen in the water, killed the fish.

Frogs. Frogs were already abundant along the banks of the Nile, but with the changes in the river due to the flagellates, many more came up onto the land. Their sudden death (Exod. 8:13) was caused by anthrax, contracted from the piles of rotting fish.

Gnats. These came to feast on the rotting fish and frogs and possibly spread one of the diseases mentioned later in Exodus.

Flies. Biting flies appeared for the same reason as the gnats and later spread disease from animals to humans, thereby causing the plague of boils.

Livestock Plague. This would be anthrax, spread by the frogs and possibly the gnats.

Boils. Anthrax has symptoms similar to boils and spread to humans by the flies.

Hail. Violent thunderstorms occur in Egypt during the time when barley and flax are harvested (9:31).

Locusts. Large swarms of invading locusts are not unknown in the Middle East and northern Africa.

Darkness. This plague may have been a desert sandstorm, not uncommon in Egypt during the spring, perhaps about six months after the time when the first plague occurred.

Two aspects of this theory seem somewhat speculative. First, Exodus is silent on any direct connection between the different plagues. It does not, therefore, encourage its reader to identify such connections. Second, the text presents many of the events as of an entirely miraculous nature rather than the intensification of natural phenomena. For instance, does the biblical text want the reader to believe that the "gnats" come to feast on the dead fish or come from "the dust of the ground" (8:16)? Again, was the disease of "boils" spread by the flies or by means of the soot that Moses tossed into the air (9:8)?

Each event is presented as unexpected and unbelievable. Admittedly, Exodus uses hyperbolic language in a number of instances; in light of that, the idea of naturally occurring disasters may have some merit. But there is little in the plagues stories themselves to move the reader in that direction. Ultimately, the plagues are symbolic of chaos, and they overthrow the right ordering of life so prized by the Egyptians.[A-44] Chaos is turning up everywhere in Egypt, and Pharaoh is powerless to stop it.

A depiction
of four of the
plagues is found
in the Golden
Hagada, an il-
lustrated Hebrew
Manuscript of the
Old Testament
from Spain
(A.D. 1320).
Z. Radovan/
www.BibleLand
Pictures.com

All except one refer to the heart of Pharaoh (14:17 speaks of the "hearts of the Egyptians"). In the Hebrew text, three different words lie behind the concepts of hard and unyielding: *ḥzq* ("to be strong"), *kbd* ("to be heavy"), and *qšh* ("to be hard," only in 7:3). Scholars tend to agree that the Exodus texts using *ḥzq* and *kbd* probably find their background in Egyptian terminology and beliefs.[98] But there is disagreement as to which aspect of Egyptian culture provides this background.

One view relates the concept of a hard heart to the judgment that ancient Egyptians believed would take place in the afterlife.[99] Much of this belief is revealed in the document known as The Book of the Dead. A portion of this text describes the judgment scene at which the heart of the deceased is weighed on a scale to determine if it is heavier than the feather that represents the Egyptian conception of what is right and just. If not, the deceased is granted great favor in the afterlife. If it is, the creature Ammit (also known as the "Devouress" or "Swallower") will consume the deceased. The biblical expressions about a hard or strong heart, according to this view, are actually about a heavy heart. Each time the text says that Pharaoh's heart grows hard or strong, it means that his heart grows heavier; that is, he becomes more and more guilty when compared to the standard of what is right. At times, Yahweh is said to be the one to "harden" the heart of Pharaoh, which refers to Yahweh's judging Pharaoh to be guilty of wrongdoing, even though ancient Egyptians believed their king could do no wrong.

There is another view, however,[100] that points to Egyptian expressions that appear to be the functional equivalents of the biblical language. One of these, which literally means "heavy-hearted," is often used of those who have great self-control and are able to refrain from speaking rashly. The expression could be translated as "level-headed."[101] Another expression means "stout-hearted" and refers to those who have great courage and determination.[102] Perhaps, then, the biblical text is attempting to use these expressions in a way that Egyptian texts most certainly would not. Whereas the latter speak positively of a heart that grows hard, heavy, or strong, the Exodus passages use this language to render a severe critique of the Egyptian king. In fact, the biblical text may be offering a caustic satire on the Egyptian ideas.

Both views have some evidence in their favor. The second view connects the Hebrew phrases to Egyptian terminology that is indeed similar. None of this terminology occurs in the accounts of the judgment scene involving the weighing of the heart. Nevertheless, the first view seems able to explain the "hardening" process in a way that fits with the tendency of Exodus to condemn Pharaoh and his actions. One problem with both views is that they fail to distinguish suf-

▶ The Hardening of Pharaoh's Heart

Exodus refers to a heart that is hardened or unyielding nineteen times. In the list below, each of the references is listed, along with the Hebrew verb used and the subject of that verb. At times the text states that the heart itself grows hard, while in other instances there is an agent—Yahweh or Pharaoh—who does the hardening.

Reference	Verb	Subject
4:21	ḥzq	Yahweh
7:3	qšh	Yahweh
7:13	ḥzq	heart
7:14	kbd	heart
7:22	ḥzq	heart
8:15	kbd	Pharaoh
8:19	ḥzq	heart
8:32	kbd	Pharaoh
9:7	kbd	heart
9:12	ḥzq	Yahweh

Reference	Verb	Subject
9:34	kbd	Pharaoh
9:35	ḥzq	heart
10:1	kbd	Yahweh
10:20	ḥzq	Yahweh
10:27	ḥzq	Yahweh
11:10	ḥzq	Yahweh
14:4	ḥzq	Yahweh
14:8	ḥzq	Yahweh
14:17	ḥzq	Yahweh

Interestingly, Yahweh is the subject of *kbd* only once (10:1); all other times it is the heart of Pharaoh or Pharaoh himself. When the verb *ḥzq* is used, Pharaoh is never the subject. Thus, Yahweh tends to be the one to "strengthen" (*ḥzq*) Pharaoh's heart, whereas Pharaoh himself tends to be the one to "make heavy" (*kbd*) his heart. A possible conclusion is that the text uses two different approaches to describe and critique Pharaoh's stubbornness (see comments on 8:15). On the one hand, by strengthening Pharaoh's heart, Yahweh is giving the king exactly what he wants—stoutheartedness, a concept highly prized by the Egyptians. In this case, however, getting what he wants leads Pharaoh and his land straight to disaster. On the other hand, it is generally not Yahweh who "makes heavy" Pharaoh's heart. It is instead Pharaoh himself who heaps the guilt of wrongdoing—assuming this is the import of a heavy heart (see comments on 8:15)—on himself and thereby dooms himself to punishment.

ficiently the differences in meaning between the Hebrew terms *ḥzq* and *kbd*. Both terms are assumed to mean the same thing. A more careful distinction may be able to shed light on what the biblical text is trying to do with these expressions (see sidebar on "The Hardening of Pharaoh's Heart").

Gnats came (8:17). With this plague and that of flies, it is impossible to be precise about the insects named here. Biting gnats, stinging mosquitoes, lice, or any number of other insects could be in view.[103]

Finger of God (8:19). For the ancient Egyptians, the concept of the "finger" of a deity represented something dangerous and powerful that could bring about good or evil. The "finger of Seth" was feared for the harm it had done to the god Horus, while the "finger of Thoth" was praised for the threat it posed to the evil Apophis.[104] By attributing

▶ The Plagues as Attacks against Egyptian Deities

Another popular idea about the plagues is that each one was directed at a particular Egyptian deity.[A-45] Exodus 12:12 states: "I will bring judgment on all the gods of Egypt" (though this refers primarily, and perhaps only, to the last plague). The ancient Egyptians had numerous deities—nearly 1,500 throughout their recorded history.[A-46] Many deities could take the form of more than one animal or creature. If one were to look hard enough, one should eventually be able to find a deity or two whose significance and symbolism could, conceivably, serve as the object of an attack by each plague account.

For example, the god Hapy was associated with the inundation of the Nile, which was crucial

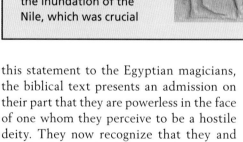

for ensuring good crops.[A-47] Perhaps the first plague was directed at him. It is difficult, though, to find deities for all the plagues that, together, make a convincing case. With the third and fourth plagues, for instance, one suggestion is that the god Khepri, usually portrayed as a scarab beetle, is under attack.[A-48] But there is little consensus on even which insects are in view here, and any correlation with Khepri is inexact. In the end, no consistent linking of the plagues with Egyptian deities is discernible. To be sure, there are a number of points at which the biblical text does seem to be directed at the Egyptian belief system, but each instance must be examined on its own merits.

this statement to the Egyptian magicians, the biblical text presents an admission on their part that they are powerless in the face of one whom they perceive to be a hostile deity. They now recognize that they and their land are under divine attack.

This same phrase occurs in 31:18 but in a different context. There, the two tablets of stone that record God's covenant with the Israelites are said to be "inscribed by the finger of God." The verse clearly does not imply a hostile threat but still seems to invoke the image of a potent and mystical God. Thus, "finger" is probably a symbol for power and ability.

This interpretation finds support from the use of the same type of terminology in a festal song of Thoth for Pharaoh Merenptah (about 1200 B.C.):

> Whoever grants you Everlasting, on them
> shall heaven's lord shine!
> In Thoth's writing, by his own fingers,
> at the right hand of Atum.[105]

This text is particularly intriguing in light of the fact that it refers to a testament between god and king. The reference to the "right hand of Atum" suggests that the context concerns power.

Terrible plague (9:3). One of the words used for the "plagues" is Hebrew *negaʿ* (see comments on 11:1). The term here is *deber*. Rather than meaning general calamity or affliction as *negaʿ* seems to, *deber* can mean "plague" in the medieval sense: a disease of epidemic proportions that is sure to bring death. Jeremiah 21:6 states: "I will strike down those who live in this city—both men

Hathor, Egyptian goddess sometimes portrayed as a cow
Werner Forman Archive/The British Museum

and animals—and they will die of a terrible plague (*deber*)." Some interpret this word to mean bubonic plague.[106] Since ancient Near Eastern texts, including biblical texts, do not differentiate precisely between diseases, this term likely refers to a number of different illnesses. Nevertheless, any disease referred to by this term would probably have been deadly and widespread (Ezek. 14:19). Words from other Semitic languages that are cognate to Hebrew *deber* (e.g., Ugaritic *dbr*, Arabic *dabr*) can mean simply death. The Akkadian *dibiru* often refers to a disaster that has spread through a city or an entire land.[107] Thus, the translation "terrible plague" in the NIV is quite apt.

All the livestock (9:6). This is an example of hyperbole. If the narrative wanted the reader to think that *all* livestock (Heb. *miqnēh*) died in this plague, from where would *miqnēh* have come that are out in the fields when the plague of hail arrives (9:19–21)?

Hyperbole is common in ancient Near Eastern texts. Egyptian accounts of New Kingdom military campaigns frequently speak of the king conquering "every foreign land," even when the battle involved only one city-state or people group.[108] Neo-Assyrian scribes exaggerated the exploits of their army's military campaigns. Sennacherib's attack on Babylonian areas in southern Mesopotamia reports that he defeated and plundered 176 fortified cities and 1,640 villages in the region.[109] He took as spoil, among other things, 208,000 men, 11,073 donkeys, and 800,100 sheep.[110] Based on the size and nature of the settled areas in southern Mesopotamia at that time, these numbers seem much out of proportion.[111] Such numbers were simply a way to emphasize a massive scale.

Festering boils (9:10). Again, it is hard to say what type of condition is meant here. The term *šᵉḥin* is often translated as "boil" or "ulcer." Words from other languages that are related to this term mean "to burn" (Ugaritic *šḥn*) and "to become hot" (Akkadian *šaḥānu*). Some have wondered if this condition is equivalent to "Nile sores," a condition dubbed so by British travelers who contracted them while in the region.[112] A skin disease of this type is representative of divine disapproval and punishment. A number of Neo-Assyrian treaties call for the gods to curse future treaty breakers with a skin disease often translated as "leprosy."[113] This is another of the divinely orchestrated misfortunes for the Egyptians.

His staff toward the sky (9:23). It is when Moses stretches out his staff to the sky that lightning, thunder, and hail come. This is reminiscent of a phrase used of Baal in Ugaritic literature, who sends forth thunder and lightning and wields a "tree of lightning."[114] The word "tree" may be a piece of wood—hence, a staff.

Apis, the sacred bull
Loic Evanno/Wikimedia Commons, courtesy of the Louvre

Perhaps we can compare Moses and Baal, then, since both possess a stick of wood that can produce severe thunderstorms. But there is more to it. Moses' staff seems to have been transformed into something extraordinary; he possesses "the staff of God" (4:20; 17:9).

Up to this point, no mention has yet been made of *Moses'* staff. Aaron certainly has his own staff (e.g., 7:9, 10, 12; 8:5), but the staff that Moses uses is identified differently: "this staff in your hand" (4:17); "the staff that is in my hand" (7:17; cf. 7:20, where the identify of the staff's owner is ambiguous). The only staff in Moses' possession that the text clearly refers to is "the staff of God" (9:23). Here and in 10:13; 14:16, a staff is identified that can be interpreted as Moses' own. What, then, does Moses have in his hand—his own staff or the staff of God?

A variety of ancient Near Eastern texts make use of the idea that a deity can bestow his staff upon a favored individual.[115] For example, the king of Mari (in eastern Syria), Zimri-Lim (c. 1780–1758 B.C.), is said to receive the staff of the god Addu, which Addu used to slay the great enemy Sea.[116] Sennacherib (c. 700 B.C.) says that the god Assur "placed in my hand the just scepter that extends the realm, the merciless staff for the destruction of enemies."[117]

The Egyptian king too received a divine staff that symbolized his power and rule over the land. In the case of Moses, one scholar suggests that Moses' staff has been "transubstantiated" into the staff of God.[118] Whether this is so or not, the staff presents a direct challenge to Pharaoh's rule.[119] One theme running throughout Exodus is that Yahweh, not Pharaoh, is the legitimate ruler, even within

the borders of Egypt. Thus, the staff in Moses' hand is the genuine article; the one in Pharaoh's hand is fake and powerless.

Flax and barley (9:31). According to 13:4, the Israelites leave Egypt in the March-April time frame. This verse probably indicates a time in February for the plague of hail, since flax and barley in Egypt are typically harvested in late February or early March.[120] This text reflects some knowledge of the Egyptian agricultural calendar. In Palestine, barley is not harvested until April.[121] If the narrative had placed the plague at that time, there would not have been enough time left in the narrative to include both the subsequent plagues and the exodus from Egypt.

Wheat (9:32). Locusts tend to begin eating wheat shortly before harvest. In Egypt, this is late March and early April—around the same time proposed by the text for the exodus. But wheat in Palestine is not harvested until later, usually in May—well after the time assigned to the exodus by the narrative.[122]

Locusts (10:4). The translation "locust" is probably correct for *ʾarbeh*. The English word "locust" can refer to a number of different species within the family *Acrididae*. The species most likely to swarm is *Schistocerca gregaria*, more commonly known as the desert locust. Parts of western Asia and northern Africa are particularly prone to swarming desert locusts and have known their devastating effects in both ancient and modern times. The Israelites and the other inhabitants of the ancient Near East were all too aware of these effects. Joel uses the image of a locust swarm as a metaphor for a massive invading army that will leave the land in ruin.

The societies of the ancient Near East viewed invading locusts as a clear sign of divine outrage and punishment (cf. Amos 4:9). A number of texts from Mesopotamia and Syria refer to locusts swarms as a divine curse. For

▶ Pharaoh's Staff

The shepherd's staff was an important sign of the Egyptian king's authority throughout much of Egypt's history. Many Egyptian kings from the Old Kingdom (c. 2686–2160 B.C.) onward are holding a long shepherd's staff or a shortened version. The meaning of the staff lay in the pharaoh's rule and guidance of his subjects. A Middle Kingdom (c. 2055–1650 B.C.) wisdom text, The Teaching for King Merikare, instructs the Egyptian king in poetic fashion:

Shepherd the people, the cattle of God,
For it is for their sake that He created
heaven and earth.
He stilled the raging of the waters,
And created the winds so that their nostrils might live.
They are His images who came forth from His body,
And it is for their sake that He rises in the sky.[A-49]

In Exodus, Pharaoh's ability and even his right to perform his shepherding role are directly challenged.

Pharaoh with staff
Frederick J. Mabie

◀

example, in the vassal treaties of the Neo-Assyrian king Esarhaddon (c. 670 B.C.) comes this curse for those who violate their oath to the gods: "May Adad, the canal inspector of heaven and earth, put an end [to vegetation] in your land, may he avoid your meadows and hit your land with a severe destructive downpour, may locusts, which diminish the [produce] of the land, [devour] your crops."[123]

Egyptian texts are also familiar with locusts. In a New Kingdom letter, for example, one scribe scolds another for leaving his trade for agricultural endeavors: "Have you not recalled the condition of the cultivator faced with the registration of the harvest-tax after the snake has carried off one half and the hippopotamus has eaten up the rest? The mice abound in the field, the locust descends, the cattle devour."[124] Exodus 10 is again stressing how many of Yahweh's actions against the Egyptians come from what are perceived as the standard repertoire of the angry god, who wishes to inflict pain and agony on those who oppose him.

Modern observers might describe the cause of a locust swarm otherwise. Locusts can go through what is known as a gregarious phase. If this goes on for too long, an overcrowding in one

Locust swarm in Morocco
Julio Era

◀

Egyptian relief from the tomb of Mereruka depicts a locust on a papyrus thicket.
Werner Forman Archive

▼

▶ Modern Locust Plagues

Locust infestation is a perennial problem in some parts of the world. The longest locust plague on record took place from 1950–1962 in East Africa. Approximately fifty swarms invaded Kenya in early 1954: "They covered a total area of approximately 1,000 square kilometers and rose to 1,000 to 1,500 meters above the ground, with the largest swarm covering 200 square kilometers, approximately 10 billion locusts."[A-50] The following excerpt from *The Hindu* of August 12, 2004, describes a more recent event:

> The Food and Agriculture Organization (FAO) of the U.N. has described the situation as extremely critical; swarms big enough to

engulf an area as big as London and containing 50 million locusts were monitored to sweep southwards from their breeding grounds in Northwest Africa.... A typical locust weighs 2–5 grams and consumes its own weight of vegetation in a day. A swarm would thus be able to finish off fields and fields of crops and vegetation in a single day—food that would have fed thousands of people for weeks. The last time such a locust swarm hit Africa and deprived its people of their food was in 1986; the invasion lasted a full three years and starved 40 of the 54 countries of the African continent. No wonder they refer to such swarms as locust plagues.[A-51]

place results in a shortage of food. They then migrate elsewhere in search of sustenance. The ancient Israelites, however, are not interested in scientific explanations. The ultimate level of explanation for them is theological. They have little doubt that divine intervention is the cause, that it is the work of Yahweh, and that he is punishing the Egyptians for their disobedience.

West wind (10:19). Literally, this is "a wind of the sea." For ancient Israel, what lay to the west was the Great Sea—the Mediterranean. For the Egyptians, a wind coming from the Mediterranean was a north wind. The author (or perhaps editor) betrays here his geographical bias by designating directions based on the Israelite homeland in Palestine. According to the biblical narrative, however, the Israelites have not yet

Sun god Amun-Re
Frederick J. Mabie

settled there, and it has been centuries since their ancestors lived there. This is one example of how the written form of the narrative seems to come from a perspective well after the time period when the events in the narrative are said to have occurred.

Total darkness (10:22). From the perspective of the Egyptians, the absence of sunlight had profound meaning. They believed that the regular circling of the sun god in the sky meant his blessing on Egypt. Any interruption in that cycle spelled disaster. Thus, this text seems to be targeting the sun god, probably the most venerated deity in Egypt.

But which Egyptian god does the biblical text have in mind? Throughout Egyptian history, the sun was worshiped as a manifestation of various deities, such as Atum, Re, Amun, and Amun-Re. Pharaoh, too, was associated with the sun. Despite this ambiguity, the narrative of Exodus is once again claiming utter powerlessness for the king and the gods of Egypt. Moreover, darkness frequently turns up in biblical texts as a symbol of judgment (Isa. 8:22; Joel 2:2; Zeph. 1:15). Here, the Egyptian life-force

▶ The Egyptian Pantheon and Its Sun Gods

Evidence from ancient Egypt reveals more than one understanding of the Egyptian pantheon and the interrelationships among the gods. Often, one understanding is associated with a particular place. For example, the idea that there were originally eight gods—four males and four females—is said to have come from Hermopolis, about 150 miles south of Cairo. These gods give life to the sun god, who then brings about the remainder of the created order.

The view associated with Heliopolis, just north of Cairo, starts with the sun god Atum. He is essentially self-created and then, by means of masturbating, creates two other gods. These unite sexually to produce another pair, who, in turn, produce four more deities. These nine deities are referred to as the *Ennead*, a Greek term that can refer to other groups of nine gods as well. Together, they formed all substances (e.g., air, earth, sky) essential for creation. The view from Memphis, just south of Cairo, exalts the god Ptah over all others and attributes to him the creation of Atum and the other gods.

A number of other gods were also associated with the sun. Re, perhaps the most important Egyptian deity, is the one most commonly viewed as the sun god. In fact, worship of Re eventually superseded that of Atum, even at Heliopolis, and he became viewed as the supreme creator god. "Son of Re" was an epithet for the Egyptian king, and ruling under Re meant ruling according to *maʾat*, the Egyptian conception of what is right and orderly. Amun was also an important deity, whose worship was centered at Thebes in Upper Egypt.

Over time, conceptions of Amun and Re drew closer and closer together until the two gods merged into one, known as Amun-Re. An Eighteenth Dynasty (c. 1550–1300 B.C.) hymn praises him:

> Hail to thee, Amon-Re,
> Lord of the Thrones of the Two Lands,
>   presiding over Karnak ...
> Lord of what is, enduring in all things ...
> The goodly bull of the Ennead, chief of
>   all gods,
> The lord of truth and father of the gods.[A-52]

During the reign of Amenhotep IV in the mid-1300s B.C., an interesting development took place. The king changed his name from Amenhotep ("Amun is content") to Akhenaten ("the effective form of the Aten"). The Aten was the sun disk, usually portrayed with light rays streaming down from it. For unknown reasons, Akhenaten refused to acknowledge any god but the sun and forbade the worship of all others. He may have believed the sun disk actually to be the god Aten, or the direct manifestation of the god. The so-called Hymn to the Aten reflects his devotion.[A-53] Although the sun god maintained a dominant role for centuries to come, Akhenaten's peculiar beliefs and partiality toward the Aten were rejected as heresy after his rule.

Ennead
Scott Noegel

◀

Satellite photo-
graph of a dust
storm
Courtesy of NASA

▶

The tenth plague
struck not only
Pharaoh's son,
but the "firstborn
son of the slave
girl, who is at
her hand mill"
(Exodus 11:5).
Kim Walton, cour-
tesy of the Oriental
Institute Museum

▼

month comes in the
spring. Second Kings
25:8 concurs, stating
that the destruction of
Jerusalem by the Baby-
lonians took place in the
fifth month (the sum-
mer, probably late July),
again placing the first
month in the spring.[126]

But there are also
hints that the new
year began in the fall.
In 2 Kings 22:3, for
instance, King Josiah
orders repairs on the
temple "in the eigh-
teenth year of his reign."
Subsequent to this
order, a number of events transpire. Then,
23:23 states that Passover was celebrated "in
the eighteenth year of King Josiah." According to Exodus, Passover was to begin on the
tenth day of the first month. The only way
for Josiah's order and this Passover celebration both to occur in his eighteenth year—if
the first day of the year was in the spring and
Passover was celebrated on the tenth day of
the year—is for all of the intervening events
to have occurred within ten days, the first ten
days of Josiah's eighteenth year. This seems
unlikely. Thus, this narrative may be assuming that the new year came in the fall.

Exodus itself has two verses that seem
to assume a change of years in the fall
(23:16; 34:22). In addition, there is the so-
called Gezer Calendar—a small, inscribed
limestone tablet discovered at Gezer and
probably dating to the late tenth century
B.C. It contains what has been described
as a schoolboy's writing exercise.[127] The
inscription is a brief explanation (a bit like
a riddle, since the months are not named)
of the months of the year as they relate to
agricultural production. Its year begins in
the fall.

Even in later Judaism, there is disagreement about the calendar.[128] One way to solve

has been extinguished. For them at this
juncture in the narrative, the favor (or, at
least, efficacy) of their gods has vanished.
The wrath of the Hebrew deity has reached
its most intense stage yet. Creation has been
undone. Chaos has returned.[125]

One more plague (11:1). This is an
intriguing turn of phrase. Previously, Yahweh has tended to refer to his demonstra-
tions of power as either "signs" (7:3; 10:1,
2) or "wonders" (4:21; 7:3; cf. also 11:9).
This raises the questions of what exactly is
a plague and whether there is a difference
between a plague and a sign/wonder (see
sidebar). Most likely the difference is simply
whether one is on the receiving end of one
of these catastrophes.

Instructions for the Passover (12:1–30)

First month of your year (12:2). The
commemoration of Rosh Hashanah,
the Jewish New Year, takes place today
in the fall. Biblical texts, however, are
ambiguous regarding when the new year
begins. This verse places it in the spring.
Jeremiah 36:22 speaks of the ninth month
as being in the winter, indicating that the first

▶ Plague Terminology

The events that Exodus describes as devastating the land of Egypt are typically called plagues, at both the lay and scholarly levels. But what is the biblical terminology for these events? The Hebrew word in 11:1 is *negaᶜ*, which can be translated as "affliction, plague, blow." Given that the death of all Egyptian firstborn is called "one more plague" (11:1), this term can certainly be used of the previous afflictions as well.

A different term shows up in 9:14: *maggēpâ*, which can be translated in ways similar to *negaᶜ*. There Yahweh speaks of "the full force of my plagues." Yet another term (*makkâ*,

"blow, wound") occurs in 1 Samuel 4:8, which refers back to the plagues of Exodus. As noted in the comments on 11:1, the most commonly used terms in Exodus itself for these events are "sign" (*ᵓôt*) and "wonder" (*môpēt*). These terms occur together in Exodus 7:3, but they become a standard way to identify the plagues elsewhere in the Bible (Deut. 4:34; 6:22; 7:19; 26:8; 29:3; 34:11; Neh. 9:10; Ps. 78:43; 105:27; 135:9; Jer. 32:20, 21). Thus, it is more in keeping with the perspective of the Israelites to speak of the "signs and wonders" of Exodus rather than the "plagues."

Cairo calendar
Brian J. McMorrow
◀

the problem is to assume more than one "New Year's Day." Perhaps there was a new year's celebration based on the agricultural calendar and one tied to a religious calendar. Some indication of this dual calendar system comes through in later rabbinic literature.[129]

Blood will be a sign for you (12:13). Blood painted on the doorframes of their houses protects the Israelites. They are protected from a divine executioner, perhaps Yahweh himself ("when I see the blood, I will pass over you" here) or "the destroyer" (12:23), whose identity is not clear. The blood thus functions as an apotropaic symbol—a symbol or object designed to ward off evil.

This belief in the protective capacity of blood is similar to beliefs regarding a variety of objects in ancient Near Eastern societies.[130] Tablets inscribed with a literary work known as the Poem of Erra constitute one such item from Mesopotamia. This poem, probably from the first quarter of the first millennium B.C., tells of divine wrath toward a number of Mesopotamian cities that leads to their destruction.[131] The god Erra uses seven creatures known as the Divine Seven or the "Sebetti." Erra and the Sebetti are bent on destruction, but this destruction can be avoided:

Religious Year	Civil Year	Hebrew Month	Western Correlation	Farm Seasons	Climate	Special Days
1	7	Nisan	March-April	Barley harvest	Latter Rains (Mal-qosh)	14 - Passover 21 - First Fruits
2	8	Iyyar	April-May	General harvest		
3	9	Sivan	May-June	Wheat harvest Vine tending	Dry Season	6 - Pentecost
4	10	Tammuz	June-July	First grapes		
5	11	Ab	July-August	Grapes, figs, olives		9 - Destruction of Temple
6	12	Elul	August-September	Vintage		
7	1	Tishri	Setember-October	Ploughing		1 - New Year 10 - Day of Atonement 15–21 - Feast of Tabernacles
8	2	Marchesvan	October-November	Grain planting	Early Rains (Yoreh) Rainy Season	
9	3	Kislev	November-December			25 - Dedication
10	4	Tebet	December-January	Spring growth		
11	5	Shebat	January-February	Winter figs		
12	6	Adar	February-March	Pulling flax Almonds bloom		13–14 - Purim
		Adar Sheni	Intercalary Month			

To the house in which this tablet is
    placed—
however furious Erra may be,
however murderous the Sebetti may be—
the sword of destruction shall not come
    near:
salvation shall alight on it.[132]

This tablet functions similarly to the blood in Exodus. Divine wrath has led to a divine intent to destroy. Only the object designated by the deity will suffice to avert the coming destruction, and only if it is affixed to or within the house. In both cases, using these objects in the prescribed way reflects a belief in the divine message that is the catalyst behind the warning and the instructions for taking protective measures.

Generations to come (12:14). The earliest reference outside the Bible to an observance of Passover comes from an Aramaic letter addressed to the Jewish commu-

▶ Passover

Any reading of the accounts of the major festivals in the Old Testament suggests that at least some of them were originally harvest festivals that are later historicized—that is, given an association with some historical event and thereafter tied to that event though often retaining some of the original harvest associations. It would therefore not be unusual if the roots to the Passover antedated the connection to the exodus story. If so, the "institution" of Passover refers to its institution in association with an event.[A-54]

Certain elements in the Passover suggest that at its roots may be a nomadic herdsmen's ritual in which they sought both protection from demonic attack as they moved to summer pasture and fertility for the herds in the new breeding season.[A-55] Note how the observance is centered in the family (therefore not necessitating proximity to a sanctuary) and requires no altar (no animal is offered to deity) or priestly personnel. The blood on the doorpost purifies one's house and thus prepares it for Yahweh's presence and protection from the slaughtering angel.[A-56] In this regard, it is evident that the verb psḥ has its meaning of "protect" (as seen clearly in Isa. 31:5) rather than "pass over."[A-57] Blood is used, for instance, in Mesopotamian namburbi rituals, in which it is smeared on the door and keyhole to protect a house from spirit invasion.[A-58]

The existence of such a prehistory is plausible enough, though the details of its practice and function can only be speculated since no specific predecessors are known. Blood as an apotropaic device and ritual animal substitution are both known, but a spring nomadic ritual for protection and fertility of the herd is unattested in the ancient Near East.

Man bringing lamb for sacrifice
Kim Walton, courtesy of the Field Museum, Chicago

nity on the Nile's island of Elephantine in Egypt.[133] It dates to around 420 B.C. and refers to a seven-day observance of what appears to be Passover and the Feast of Unleavened Bread. The letter is badly damaged, but it seems to include a prohibition on particular drinks—perhaps fermented drinks—that would be in addition to the stated regulations in Exodus.

Departure from Egypt (12:31–51)

Plundered the Egyptians (12:36). The silver and gold items taken were some of the most valuable of the Egyptians' possessions. Moreover, these events are set in the spring, when it was customary for Egyptian kings, particularly those of the New Kingdom, to send out messengers (and accompanying armies) in order to collect tribute payments from the smaller political entities (e.g., city-states) outside Egypt.[134] In a sense, then, springtime was the time the Egyptians officially plundered their subject

Hyssop was used
to spread blood
on the doorposts.
Kim Guess/www.
BiblePlaces.com

▶

peoples. Once again, the biblical text turns the tables on an Egyptian custom. This time, the Egyptians are the ones exploited and forced to pay.

From Rames(s)es to Succoth (12:37). Succoth appears to designate a region on Egypt's eastern border with several military outposts.[135] Traveling there suggests a route toward the Sinai Peninsula. Scholars typically imagine the Israelites traveling through what is known as the Wadi Tumilat, a riverbed of sorts that allowed passage from the eastern region of the Delta into the desert regions of the Sinai east of Egypt.[136]

Six hundred thousand men (12:37). If this number of military personnel is taken at face value, the total number of Israelites is easily near or beyond three million. There are several problems with this. First, population estimates for all of New Kingdom Egypt suggest that population was certainly on the rise at this time but reached an apex of about three million people.[137] Second, the Egyptian fighting force at this time probably did not exceed 25,000 and was likely less.[138] It would have been no match for an Israelite army of 600,000. Third, population estimates for ancient Palestine do not support an Israelite group of this size. At the beginning of this same era (middle of the Bronze Age), Palestine had a population of approximately 160,000.[139] It declined somewhat during the Late Bronze Age but rebounded to around 400,000 by the middle (c. 700s B.C.) of the Iron Age.[140]

There are two main explanations for these incongruities. One relates to the Hebrew word for "thousand" (ʾelep), which can also mean a clan or a tribe (Num. 10:4; Josh. 22:30). In other words, ʾelep can refer to a group that is part of a larger whole. Thus, ʾelep here could refer to a military group or division, in which case the narrative is stating that the Israelites had six hundred military divisions (each division with a small number of men). It is hard to say how likely it is that ʾelep carries such a meaning in this verse.

A second possibility is that an epic narrative such as this was expected, by the literati of the ancient world, to use numbers for their rhetorical value—that is, for stylistic effect—rather than to communicate mathematical precision, especially regarding the numbers of the protagonist's army. Consider the Kirta Epic from Ugaritic literature.[141] The main character, Kirta, leads an army of three million men, and many of the epic's features (e.g., religious rituals and sacrifices, a journey interrupted by a stopover at a sacred site) show similarities to those of the Exodus story. This Ugaritic work has clearly put its numbers to use as rhetorical devices. It is certainly plausible to conclude that the biblical text has as well.[142]

430 years (12:40). The Hebrew text of this verse appears to establish the length of the Israelites' time in Egypt. But the evidence on this is mixed. Other important texts (e.g., the LXX and the Samaritan Pentateuch) include in this verse the words "in the land of Canaan" in addition to "in Egypt."[143] This would mean that the 430 years encompasses a period of time from Abraham's entrance into Canaan until the Exodus, considerably reducing the time in Egypt.

Yet some nonbiblical evidence may support the Hebrew text. This comes primarily with an Egyptian monument erected by Ramesses II, which celebrates what he perceived to be the beginning of the rule of the god Seth over the Delta region.[144] The Hyk-

▶ Runaways from Egypt

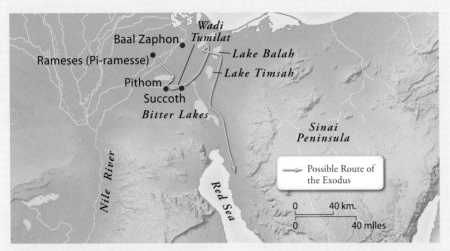

A New Kingdom report details an Egyptian military official's pursuit of two runaway slaves. These slaves seem to have taken a route similar to the presumed route of the Israelites' departure from Egypt. That is, they headed east away from the Delta region by means of the Wadi Tumilat. The official, who failed to overtake them, reports the following:

> I was sent forth from the broad-halls of the palace ... following after these two slaves. Now when I reached the enclosure-wall of Tjeku ... they (those stationed at Tjeku) told [me] ... that they (the slaves) had passed by on the 3rd month of the third season, day 10. [Now] when [I] reached the fortress, they told me ... they (the slaves) had passed the walled place north of the Migdol of Seti Mer-ne-Ptah.... When my letter reaches you, write to me ... about all that has happened to them and how many people you send out after them.[A-59]

The reference to "the palace" probably has the city Piramesse ("Ramesses" in Exodus) in view. The official then travels to Tjeku—probably the area designated by the biblical Succoth, given linguistic connections between the Hebrew term *sukkōt* and the Egyptian word for Tjeku. Thus, the path from "Ramesses to Succoth" (12:37) is the same route traversed by this official in his pursuit of the slaves.

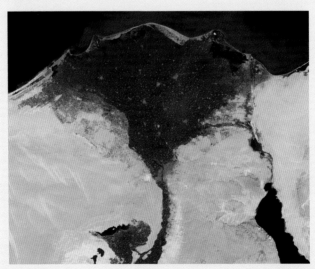

continued

Satellite view
shows the Wadi
Tumilat—iden-
tifiable as the
east-west green
line connecting
the delta to the
canal.
Courtesy of NASA

◀

▶ The Timing of the Exodus, Part II

Historians who accept the idea that there was an exodus from Egypt by a group of Israelites wonder when it happened and under which Egyptian king. The statements in Judges 11:26 and 1 Kings 6:1 provide a starting point. The latter verse states that there were 480 years between the exodus and the building of Solomon's temple in Jerusalem. Judges 11:26 has Jephthah saying that by his time, Israel had been in control of parts of Canaan for 300 years. If one follows only these two verses, then the exodus took place in the middle of the fifteenth century (the 1400s) B.C.

But nonbiblical evidence, both documentary and archaeological, is also important for this issue, and a mid-fifteenth century date for the exodus does not fit well with this evidence. First, Thutmose III ruled Egypt for much of the fifteenth century (c. 1479–1425; initially as a coregent with Hatshepsut, then thirty-two years as the sole ruler). He led numerous military campaigns into Palestine and reestablished Egypt's dominance there.[A-60] In light of this, it is hard to imagine the Israelite escape during this period.

Second, the Egyptian capital at this time was in Thebes, about 400 miles south of the northeastern Delta region that the Israelites presumably occupied. With frequent meetings between Moses and Pharaoh, the biblical narrative seems to assume an Egyptian capital much farther north.[A-61] The capital was moved back to Memphis in the north during the reign of Tutankhamun (c. 1336–1327 B.C.).

Third, the mention of the city of Ramesses (1:11; 12:37) most likely refers to the ancient site known as Piramesse ("House of Ramesses"). It underwent extensive development and expansion during the reign of Ramesses II (c. 1279–1213 B.C.), who became its namesake and made it his chief residence.[A-62] Thus, a number of scholars find the thirteenth century a more appropriate setting for a possible Israelite exodus.

In view of this evidence, perhaps the 480 years in 1 Kings 6:1 is a way of expressing the amount of time required to move through twelve generations. Forty years seems to have been a standard number for one generation in biblical texts. If a more realistic number of years is used to define the length of one generation (e.g., twenty years or so), this reduces the number of years between the exodus and the building of Solomon's temple considerably and favors a thirteenth-century exodus. It is still not clear how to interpret Jephthah's statement in Judges 11:26; he may be exaggerating or simply mistaken.

Another important archaeological artifact is the so-called Merneptah Stele, also referred to as the "Israel Stele." This monument contains an inscription regarding a military campaign that the Egyptian king Merneptah apparently led into Syria and Palestine around 1210 B.C.[A-63] It refers to several sites that Merneptah claims to have conquered, including "Israel." This is the earliest nonbiblical historical reference to Israel:

> Princes are prostrate saying: "Shalom!"
> Not one lifts up his head among the Nine Bows.
> Now that Tjehenu has come to ruin,
> Khatti is pacified;
> The Canaan has been plundered into every sort of woe:
> Ashkelon has been overcome;
> Gezer has been captured;
> Yanoam is made nonexistent.
> Israel is laid waste, his seed is no longer;
> Khor is become a widow because of Egypt.
> All lands combined, they are at peace.
> Whoever roams about gets subdued

by the King of Upper and Lower Egypt, Baenre-miamon;

the Son of Re, Merenptah-hetephimaat, given life like Re every day.[A-64]

The inscription identifies Israel in a particular way. Ancient Egyptian made use of determinatives before particular types of nouns. A determinative is a symbol that identifies to which class of things (e.g., men, gods, cities, months, rivers) a noun belongs. While determinatives for countries and cities generally occur for the other items in the list of what Merneptah conquered, before the word "Israel" comes the determinative for a people group or a tribe—not a geographic location. This may mean that the Egyptians did not perceive this people group, whom they cite as "Israel," to be unified enough politically or even geographically to be considered a political entity such as a city or nation-state. But it also probably means that enough settlement took place by this time for there to be a recognizable group known as "Israel." This suggests that any Israelite departure from Egypt would have had to take place by this time. Others have expressed less optimism regarding the usefulness of the Merneptah Stele for this issue.[A-65]

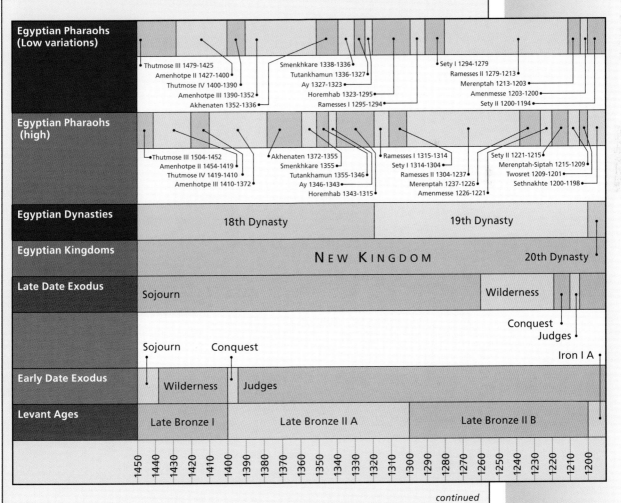

Egyptian Pharaohs (Low variations)		
Thutmose III 1479-1425 Amenhotpe II 1427-1400 Thutmose IV 1400-1390 Amenhotpe III 1390-1352 Akhenaten 1352-1336	Smenkhkare 1338-1336 Tutankhamun 1336-1327 Ay 1327-1323 Horemhab 1323-1295 Ramesses I 1295-1294	Sety I 1294-1279 Ramesses II 1279-1213 Merenptah 1213-1203 Amenmesse 1203-1200 Sety II 1200-1194

Egyptian Pharaohs (high)		
Thutmose III 1504-1452 Amenhotpe II 1454-1419 Thutmose IV 1419-1410 Amenhotpe III 1410-1372	Akhenaten 1372-1355 Smenkhkare 1355 Tutankhamun 1355-1346 Ay 1346-1343 Horemhab 1343-1315	Ramesses I 1315-1314 Sety I 1314-1304 Ramesses II 1304-1237 Merenptah 1237-1226 Amenmesse 1226-1221	Sety II 1221-1215 Merenptah-Siptah 1215-1209 Twosret 1209-1201 Sethnakhte 1200-1198

Egyptian Dynasties: 18th Dynasty / 19th Dynasty

Egyptian Kingdoms: NEW KINGDOM / 20th Dynasty

Late Date Exodus: Sojourn / Wilderness / Conquest / Judges / Iron I A

Early Date Exodus: Sojourn / Conquest / Wilderness / Judges

Levant Ages: Late Bronze I / Late Bronze II A / Late Bronze II B

Timeline: 1450 1440 1430 1420 1410 1400 1390 1380 1370 1360 1350 1340 1330 1320 1310 1300 1290 1280 1270 1260 1250 1240 1230 1220 1210 1200

continued

All of this relates to the question of which pharaoh was ruling at the time of the exodus. He is unnamed in the biblical text. If scholarship can determine who he was, the question of the timing of the exodus might be settled once and for all. Some argue that the reference to the site of Ramesses (1:11), the extensive building projects conducted there, and the slave labor mentioned in the narrative all make Ramesses II the most likely candidate.[A-66] This would make his successor, Merneptah, the king when the Israelites leave Egypt.

In some ways, the Merneptah Stele poses a problem for this view. If the "Israel" in the stele refers to the same "Israel" as the one coming out of Egypt, would not the departure have had to take place before Merneptah's reign? This has led some to opt for the father of Ramesses II, Seti I, as the pharaoh of the oppression in Exodus and for Ramesses II as the pharaoh of the Exodus itself.[A-67] Others, mostly evangelical scholars, also recognize the potential problem posed by the Merneptah Stela and find the fifteenth century as the better time period for the Exodus. Their major contention is that this setting fits more of the biblical data than does a thirteenth-century date.

The issues involved are complex and range from chronological uncertainties in Egyptian history to disputed archaeological findings.[A-68] In the end, it is simply not clear which kings of Egypt

the biblical text has in view, and perhaps a reluctance to name them is meant to leave the reader in the dark. In this way, the nameless pharaohs can function as symbols for any oppressor of the Israelites, and the story thereby broadens its appeal to future generations.

sos (see comments on 1:8) also worshiped Seth and appear to be the ones who began this type of worship in the Delta. The Hyksos were Semites and probably would have been friendly to other Semites, possibly including people such as Joseph and his relatives. From the beginning of their rule to the middle of the reign of Ramesses II is about four hundred years. In fact, the monument commemorates the four-hundredth year of

Seth's rule and has been termed the "Four-Hundred-Year Stela."[145]

Thus, if the biblical text places the arrival of Jacob and his family in Egypt during the Hyksos period, and if it points to Ramesses II as the king during the Egyptian oppression of the Israelites described in Exodus, then this stela provides some evidence that people even back then believed this period covered approximately four hundred years.

Consecration of the Firstborn (13:1–16)

Sign on your hand (13:9). Other biblical texts give instructions that certain words, commands, and directions should be placed on the hands (Deut. 6:8; 11:18; Prov. 7:3). Proverbs 6:21 says to wear parental instructions "around your neck." It is difficult, however, to determine what exactly in this passage is supposed to be the "sign." The subject of the verb "will be" is not explicit in the Hebrew text. The NIV assumes that the referent is "this observance," which may be right. If so, the text is probably speaking metaphorically. No actual object has to be placed on one's hand or forehead.

This is not to say, however, that these texts are not open to a more literal interpretation. It has long been traditional for Jews to wear phylacteries on their arms and foreheads on certain occasions. In the Epic of Gilgamesh, the goddess Ishtar states that she will wear a necklace as a reminder to her of the flood sent to destroy humankind.[146] In any case, the text requires the "sign" to function as a reminder. This is more than a jog of one's memory. It is a visceral reminder because of the extensive physical participation in the ritual.

This is why I … redeem (13:15). Redemption in the ancient Near East usually involved a specific purpose. Often a man who had taken on debt and could not pay it off was forced to sell himself or one of his family members to the creditor as a debt-slave. No actual "sale" took place, but the person was transferred into the possession of the creditor. The "sale price" was understood to be the loan, which the debtor had already received and was now unable to repay. Redemption occurred when the debtor or one of his family members eventually acquired the means to pay off the debt and thereby retrieve the debt-slave from the creditor.[147] To redeem a person was, in a sense, the act of buying the person back from the creditor, often at the same price (the amount of the loan) at which the person was "sold."

How then does the concept of redemption function here in Exodus 13? Perhaps the Israelites believed they owed a debt to Yahweh for their deliverance from Egypt. The means of this deliverance is explicit: "The LORD killed every firstborn in Egypt, both man and animal" (13:15). The Israelites were given, in a sense, all the firstborn of Egypt as the purchase price of their freedom, and they now owed to Yahweh their own firstborn, both "man and animal." The animals they could pay directly through sacrifice. Their sons, too, belonged to Yahweh by right, but the Israelites were offered a way to buy back their sons from Yahweh. By sacrificing a lamb, an Israelite family could "redeem" their firstborn son.

Crossing the Sea (13:17–15:21)

Road through Philistine country (13:17). For quite some time, scholars have considered this road probably to refer to a road that in ancient Egypt was known as the "Ways of Horus" and later as the *Via Maris* ("Way of the Sea").[148] This road ran from the northeastern region of the Delta along the Mediterranean coast in a northeasterly direction into Palestine. It is true that important Philistine settlements came to be located along this route. The reference to the Philistines, though, seems anachronistic since the Philistines settled here later (see sidebar on "The Philistines" at 15:14), and the "war" that might cause the Israelites to turn around was probably war with Egyptian forces stationed along this route rather than with the Philistines.

The ancient site known as Tjaru (probably Tell-Hebua) was one of the most important Egyptian fortresses on this road, where a large New Kingdom fort has been discovered.[149] It was from this fortress that New Kingdom kings typically began their campaigns into Palestine.[150] In fact, a wall relief at Karnak from the time of Seti I shows a series of fortresses running from Egypt's northeastern border (close to Tjaru) to Palestine's southwestern border (near Gaza). Whether or not as many fortresses actually existed as the relief depicts is unknown.

But there is substantial evidence for an Egyptian fortress at Deir el-Balaḥ in the early 1200s B.C. About one mile from the Mediterranean coast and eight miles southwest of modern Gaza, this site has yielded the remains of a large monumental structure—likely an Egyptian fortress dated to the reign of Seti I.[151] One of the main reasons for its dating is the remarkable degree to which it resembles the typical Egyptian fortress represented on the Karnak wall relief. "It proved to be the veritable picture-image of the depictions at Karnak and provided stark evidence for the resurgence of Egyptian military activity in Sinai and Canaan in the 13th century."[152] Tjaru was near the border of Egypt, Deir el-Balaḥ near the border of Palestine, and there were probably smaller

stations in between. Thus, the strength of the Egyptian military presence in this region at this time was well known.

Red Sea (13:18). The Hebrew phrase here is *yam sûp*; it is not clear to what this phrase refers. The term *sûp* in Hebrew means "reed(s)"; it is among the *sûp* that Moses' mother placed the waterproof basket that served as his hiding place shortly after his birth (2:3). Perhaps, then, the *yam sûp* is not the Red Sea but a body of water known as the "Sea of Reeds." The LXX, however, translates *yam sûp* with a Greek phrase that means "Red Sea." Some, appreciating the translational difficulty presented by this phrase, refer to it as the "Re(e)d Sea."[153] Most scholars today believe the Hebrew text intends a body of water around which reeds grew in abundance—perhaps one of the lakes found north of the Gulf of Suez.[154] Others still opt for the Red Sea.[155]

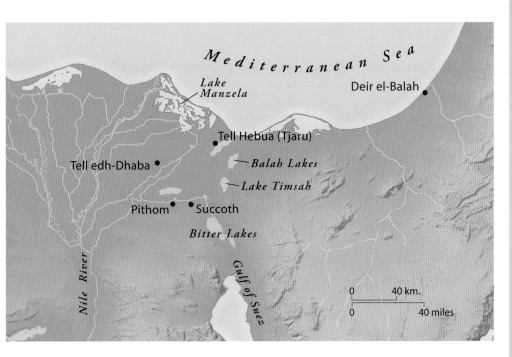

Among those who reject the Red Sea, at least four main possibilities stand out.[156] The first is Lake Manzeleh, located in the northeast corner of the Nile Delta along the Mediterranean coast. About thirty miles to the south were the Ballah Lakes, most of which were drained during the construction of the Suez Canal. A smaller lake south of the Ballah Lakes is Lake Timsah. Finally, the Bitter Lakes are located even further south. All of these bodies of water were situated along ancient Egypt's eastern border, where it meets the Sinai Peninsula, between the Mediterranean Sea in the north and the Gulf of Suez in the south.

One evangelical scholar has recently argued strongly in favor of the Ballah Lakes.[157] He argues that 14:2 indicates that the Israelites made a turn to the north (they were to "turn back") after having traveled in a southeasterly direction. This would have taken them away from Lake Timsah and the Bitter Lakes, since they were still north of both, and toward the Ballah Lakes. Second, Egyptian literary sources seem to indicate that the *yam sûp* lay in fairly close proximity to the site of Tjaru; of the four major possibilities, Tjaru is closest to the Ballah Lakes. Third, Abu Sefêh, the modern Arabic name for a site probably located on the edge of the Ballah Lakes in ancient times, may be related linguistically to the Egyptian term from which Hebrew *yam sûp* comes. Ultimately, the evidence is inconclusive; perhaps the biblical text is intentionally ambiguous on this point.

The LORD went ... in a pillar of cloud (13:21). This verse records a theophany—a visible manifestation of the deity's presence. But why is this manifestation a cloud that takes the form of a large pillar or column and seems to reach all the way to the ground? The reason for the shape of the cloud is not clear, but the reference to a cloud is typical of a theophany of Yahweh. A number of biblical texts ascribe to Yahweh attributes of what ancient Near Eastern societies would have recognized as a storm deity. That is, Yahweh tends to manifest his presence in a storm.[158] Thus, clouds were expected. Psalm 18:9–12 says of Yahweh:

He parted the heavens and came down;
dark clouds were under his feet.
He mounted the cherubim and flew;
he soared on the wings of the wind.

He made darkness his covering, his
canopy around him—
the dark rain clouds of the sky.
Out of the brightness of his presence
clouds advanced,
with hailstones and bolts of lightning.

Similar language is used of the Canaanite god Baal, also viewed as a storm god. One Ugaritic text describes Baal: "He has thundered in the stormclouds / He has blazed his lightning bolts to the earth."[159] Yahweh's presence appearing as a visible cloud is especially important in Exodus (16:10; 34:5; 40:34). The idea of Yahweh's riding on the cloud seems to be behind the statement in 14:24—"the LORD looked down from the pillar of fire and cloud"—and fits the description in Psalm 18: "dark clouds were under his feet." Baal, too, is referred to as a "cloud-rider."[160] Storm imagery is integral to the biblical authors' descriptions of those moments when they believed Yahweh made his presence visible. Moreover, Psalm 18 brings together cloud and "brightness"; Exodus combines cloud and fire in one pillar. The imagery may be that of a burning (lightning?)

in the midst of the cloud that is able to shine through it at night.[161]

Encamp near Pi Hahiroth (14:2). Scholars disagree about where this site is and even about whether there is enough information to allow for an investigation of its location. The "Pi" looks like a typical Egyptian element in place names (as in Piramesse), meaning "house." "Hahiroth" is unknown in Egyptian. Some argue that the name is perhaps Hebrew.[162] Its most likely meaning, then, is "Mouth of the Canals." In the 1970s, archaeologists discovered a canal that ran along Egypt's frontier with the Sinai Peninsula during the New Kingdom.[163] Perhaps Pi Hahiroth is a "Semitic toponym that is descriptive of a particular area; specifically a point where the Frontier Canal emptied into the Sea of Reeds."[164] According to this view, the sea that the Israelites miraculously cross should be associated with one of the lakes serviced by this canal.

Six hundred of the best chariots (14:7). The use of chariotry by the Egyptian military, especially during the New Kingdom, is well attested. Chariots functioned mainly as vehicles for archers, who could spray the enemy with arrows while staying mobile and, therefore, relatively safe.[165] The figure of six hundred chariots may be hyperbole. There is no evidence for such a large chariot force in ancient Egypt; the highest estimates are around 200–250.[166] This would mean that the Egyptians were also wont to inflate such figures. The Egyptian account of their battle against the Hittites at Qadesh lists the Hittite chariot force at 2,500[167]—a much greater exaggeration than the one here.

Cloud brought darkness (14:20). The motif of the warrior deity who aids his people at crucial moments in battle against their enemies occurs frequently in ancient Near Eastern litera-

ture.[168] Here, Yahweh sends a cloud so dense that it functions as an impenetrable—by sight or movement—barrier between the Egyptians and the Israelites. Records of the military exploits of the Hittite king Murshili report a similar phenomenon:

> The mighty Storm-god ([d]U.NIR.GAL) [my lord, helped me] and it continually rained all night, [so that the enemy] did not see the fire of the camp. But when it became light … the mighty Storm-god … and in the morning suddenly a cloud [arose; …] 'put' cloud(s), and as long as […] the cloud [went] before my troops.[169]

It was not uncommon in military reports to speak of advantageous circumstances in terms of divine intervention and aid. If one group found itself on the successful end of a skirmish, it credited its own god or gods and often spoke of the deity as if he had arranged all aspects of the natural order to ensure a triumphant outcome. To what degree, then, the reference to a cloud is to be taken literally is difficult to determine, since the biblical text may be implementing this kind of stylized description of events. That the text intends to affirm the active participation of Yahweh on behalf of the Israelites, though, is certain.

Waters were divided (14:21). There are virtually no ancient Near Eastern paral-lels to the narrative describing the parting of the sea—the *yām sûp*. The closest may be a tale from Middle Kingdom Egypt (c. 2055–1650 B.C.), recorded on the Westcar Papyrus. The Egyptian king is bored. He asks one of his chief priests for help. The priest recommends a boating excursion on the palace lake, with the boat rowed by twenty of the most beautiful palace women. The king calls for such women and has them wear nothing but fishing nets as they row. At one point, one of the women loses a piece of jewelry adorning her hair in the water. She and some of the other women stop rowing:

> I said to her: "Why have you stopped row-ing?" She said to me: "It is a fish-shaped charm of new turquoise which has fallen into the water." I said to her: "Row! I will replace it!" She said to me: "I prefer my own to its look-alike." Then said the chief lector (priest) Djadjaemonkh his magic sayings. He placed one side of the water of the lake upon the other, and lying upon a potsherd he found the fish-shaped charm. Then he brought it back and it was given to its owner. Now as for the water, it was twelve cubits deep, and it amounted to twenty-four cubits after it was folded back. He said his magic sayings, and he brought back the water of the lake to its position.[170]

Westcar Papyrus cols. VI–IX
Bildarchiv Preus-sischer Kulturbesitz/ Art Resource, NY, courtesy of Aegyp-tisches Museum, Staatliche Museen zu Berlin, Berlin, Germany

◀

To be sure, there may be no connection between the two narratives. But if one does exist, this may be yet another attempt by the biblical text to refute Egyptian belief and lore and to show that ultimate power—including power over bodies of water—resides in the hands of Yahweh.

Israelites sang (15:1). The text does not reveal who composed the song, but the distinct possibility exists that it was authored by one or more women. Ancient Israelite culture seems to have developed a significant musical tradition.[171] Rhythm (as opposed to melody) was probably the music's dominant feature, and women may have had a crucial role in creating and performing this type of music. Women are the only ones explicitly mentioned in biblical texts as using the "tambourine" (cf. 15:20).[172] Moreover, clay figurines from Iron Age Israel that depict musicians show all percussionists to be women.[173]

It also stands to reason that victory songs, like the one here, would come from women, since they are the ones who most likely sang songs as the men returned home from battle. Whether the text intends to credit Miriam with the authorship of this song is not clear, but the evidence does point tantalizingly in that direction.

Shattered the enemy (15:6). Significantly, the drowning of the Egyptian army is celebrated in terms of smashing and shat-

tering. This statement is reminiscent of how a particular set of Egyptian inscriptions, known as Execration Texts, was used.[174] These inscriptions were incised on stone, wood, and clay objects, which were often shaped to represent a foreign ruler. Many have been found on pottery bowls as well.[175] The objects and their accompanying inscriptions apparently played an important role in Egyptian curse rituals. Though it is not clear that all such rituals involved the use of objects like these, there is evidence that formal cursing of enemies was practiced in Egypt throughout much of the third and second millennia B.C. Most of the objects bearing inscriptions, however, seem to date to a more narrow period of time—generally the first half of the second millennium.[176]

The inscriptions themselves contain the names of various local rulers in Syria and Palestine and often conclude with a summary reference to anyone "who may rebel, who may plot, who may fight, who may talk of fighting, or who may talk of rebelling."[177] A curse formula was then pronounced over the object, and the object was smashed to depict the fulfillment of the curse and the hoped-for destruction of the targeted enemy. The wording of this verse in Exodus may be alluding to this type of symbolic action. Although the narrative speaks of drowning, the song describes the destruction of Yahweh's enemies in terms that would have offended ancient Egyptian sensibilities, since it reverses the roles and presents Egypt as the shattered enemy.

Who among the gods (15:11). There are parallels between the description of Yahweh's victory in Exodus 15 and the victory of Baal recorded in Ugaritic literature.[178] In the latter, the terrible and monstrous character Sea demands that the high god El hand Baal over to him as a prisoner. El complies. Later, the craftsman god Kothar fashions two mighty clubs with which Baal defeats Sea. El then grants Baal a palatial residence on Mount Zaphon, in part because he has proved his superiority in the divine council with his defeat of Sea. In Exodus, Yahweh too shows his mastery over the sea. By means of the victory won there, Yahweh receives praise as the greatest among the gods.

This verse contains a straightforward rhetorical question with "no one" as the obvious answer. After the victory, Yahweh and the people he has rescued head for the "mountain of God" (3:1), the place where Moses was told that he and the people would worship God (3:12). This may be what is meant by the "mountain of your inheritance, the place, O LORD, you made for your dwelling" (15:17). Baal wins a victory *over* Sea and then settles on his mountain; Yahweh's victory *with* the sea is followed by travel to his.

In light of this, it is interesting to note the combination of the two miraculous crossings for the Israelites: crossing a sea in Exodus and crossing a river in Joshua (Josh. 3). Baal's victory over Sea is described in this fashion:

Sea fell,
He sank to earth
His joints trembled,
His frame collapsed
Ba'l destroyed,
Drank Sea!
He finished off Judge River.[179]

In the Ugaritic poem, "Judge River" is a common nickname for Sea. Any god who claims superiority must surely demonstrate victory over Sea/River. This is also evident in the Babylonian creation myth *Enuma Elish*. Marduk proves his superiority by defeating Tiamat, the watery sea goddess/monster. Yahweh's demonstration of his ability to control deftly both sea and river may be

reminiscent of this idea.[180] He shows their complete submission to him. This line of thinking may also underlie Psalm 114:3–6, which describes the rescue from Egypt:

The sea looked and fled,
    the Jordan turned back;
the mountains skipped like rams,
    the hills like lambs.
Why was it, O sea, that you fled,
    O Jordan, that you turned back,
you mountains, that you skipped like
    rams,
    you hills, like lambs?

Thus, Yahweh's triumph over the combination of sea and river would have held important theological implications for the Israelites and functioned as a significant part of their basis for exalting Yahweh above all other purported deities.

The earth swallowed them (15:12). This statement may refer to the Egyptian conception of the punishment that awaits wrongdoers in the afterlife. Those who are, at the postmortem judgment, found guilty of wrongdoing and thus unworthy of a blissful afterlife are eaten by a beast known as the "Devouress" or "Swallower" (see comments on 8:15). By stating that the Egyptians have been swallowed up, the biblical text may be figuratively dooming them to the one fate every ancient Egyptian hoped to avoid.

People of Philistia (15:14). The reference to Philistia may be an anachronism; that is, it may come from a time later than the purported time of the Exodus. The Philistines probably did

A relief from a tomb at Saqqara depicts a funeral procession with women dancing and playing musical instruments.
Werner Forman Archive/The Egyptian Museum, Cairo

▶ The Philistines

While some aspects regarding Philistine settlement in Palestine are unclear, others are known. The Philistines came from the area of Crete and Greece (i.e., the region around the Aegean Sea). A massive upheaval in that area (the exact causes of which are unknown) seems to have led to large numbers of people, including the Philistines, moving east into Syria and Palestine. They settled in southwest Palestine, along the Mediterranean coast, in the early twelfth century B.C. This can be shown, first, by a pottery type known as Mycenaean IIIC1b, which does not appear in this area until that time.[A-69] (The term Mycenaean describes the civilization in the Aegean region that flourished prior to the aforementioned upheaval.) Mycenaean IIIC1b is strikingly similar to Mycenaean pottery that had previously been imported into Palestine. One of its chief differences, though, is that it was manufactured from materials found in Palestine. The Philistines were making it in their newly claimed territory in Palestine.

Second, an Egyptian inscription from around 1190 B.C. commemorates the Egyptians' victory over "those who came on the sea" (often referred to as the Sea Peoples).[A-70] Included in this category are the "Philistines, Tjeker, Shekelesh, Denye(n), and Weshesh." Although the inscription boasts of a decisive Egyptian victory, most likely the Egyptians did little more than keep the invading Sea Peoples at bay and maintain the security of their borders.

Subsequent to this battle, several of the groups—including the Philistines and Tjeker—retreated from the Egyptian border and settled in Palestine. This time period, based on the date given in the Egyptian text, fits with the time when Mycenaean IIIC1b pottery first appears. Both sets of evidence, then,

not settle in the area until the early twelfth century (see sidebar).

Miriam the prophetess (15:20). Two other women prophets are mentioned in the Old Testament: Deborah (Judg. 4:4) and Huldah (2 Kings 22:14). It is not completely unexpected, then, to encounter a reference here to a "prophetess." Other

The site of Ein Musa is considered by some to be Marah and by others to be Elim. It is most certainly one of the stops made by the Israelites.
Todd Bolen/www.BiblePlaces.com
▶

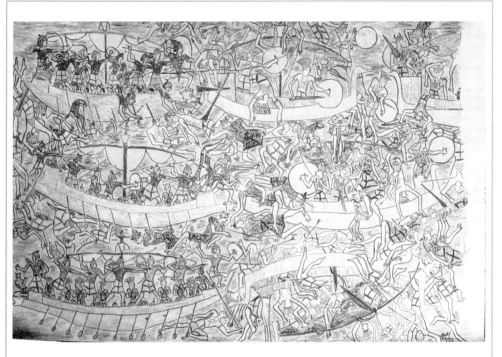

Battle between
Ramesses III and
the Sea Peoples
reconstructed
from wall relief at
Medinet Habu
Copyright
1995–2009 Phoenix
Data Systems

point to the first half of the twelfth century for the Philistine settlement in Palestine. The problem is that this is after the presumed date of the Israelite exodus (see sidebar on "The Timing of the Exodus, Part II," at 12:40).

How can this be explained? One explanation is that the poem in Exodus 15 was not composed until after the Philistines had become a recognizable presence in Palestine. Another explanation is that the song first had a strictly oral form but was not put into written form until the tenth century.[A-71] At that time, there may well have been an updating of geographical place names, which would account for this reference to Philistia.

---

ancient Near Eastern societies also accorded prophetic ability to women. The city-state of Mari, located in eastern Syria along the Euphrates River, provides some of the best examples. A number of the texts from Mari, which date to the first half of the eighteenth century B.C., refer to women who offer prophetic utterances, primarily concerning the king of Mari, Zimri-Lim, and his prospects for the future.[181]

It is not entirely clear why the text refers to Miriam as a prophetess here. Prophets were typically viewed as channels of communication from Yahweh to the people. Perhaps Miriam's song was understood as containing both a hymn of praise and the revelation of a divine message.

Travels in the Desert (15:22–17:16)

Take an omer (16:16). Evidence for volume measurements in early Israel is negligible. In postexilic times, an omer was equal to about 3.6 liters. Based on both Mesopotamian evidence and the writings of Josephus, the omer in earlier times was likely significantly smaller—around 1.75 liters, almost 2 quarts.[182] It is one-tenth of the amount represented by the unit of measurement called an "ephah" (16:36).

Desert of Sin and
Rephidim
▼

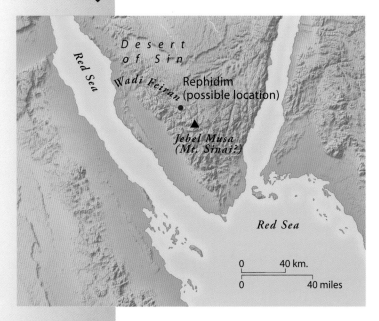

Called the bread manna (16:31). When the Israelites first saw manna, they said to each other, "What is it?" (16:15). The Hebrew for this question is *mān hûʾ*. The *n* in the word *mān* is unusual, since the expected Hebrew word for "what" is *mâ*. It is possible, though, based on comparisons with other Semitic languages, that Hebrew contained the alternative form *mān*.[183] In verse 31, the name the Israelites give to the bread is simply *mān*. From where, then, does our word "manna" come? Some Greek and Aramaic translations of Exodus render *mān* as "manna" (μαννα in Greek and *mannāʾ* in

Aramaic). This appears to have led to the traditional English translation.

Is it possible to determine exactly what manna is? Some scholars point to the secretions of certain insects as underlying the production of the substance.[184] It is physically impossible, however, for these insects to have produced enough secretions to feed the number of people that Exodus envisions. Moreover, the biblical text portrays the appearance of manna as unexpected and miraculous. Perhaps in the minds of ancient Israelites, there was a connection between the sweet substance they knew about from the desert and the food they believed their ancestors ate shortly after departing Egypt. They would have little doubt, however, that the text also wanted them to see in this event one more powerful wonder from the hand of Yahweh.

They quarreled (17:2). The Hebrew word for "quarreled" is *rîb*, which can refer to an ordinary argument but also to bringing a lawsuit (Deut. 25:1). To be sure, its usage here may not necessarily indicate a formal, full-fledged lawsuit.[185] But it may refer to an event that is well known from other ancient Near Eastern societies and that could well lead to a trial. This event has been identified with various terms, such as pretrial confrontation and prejudicial quarrel. It is well documented in Mesopotamia during the Old Babylonian period.[186]

The potential plaintiff approaches the potential defendant, issues a demand, and then waits to see if the latter will acquiesce or force the plaintiff to take the case before a panel of judges and initiate a formal suit. In biblical texts, it can be difficult to distinguish such pretrial events from actual trial proceedings.[187] Here in Exodus, the people issue a demand to Moses: "Give us water to drink" (17:2). They may be threatening to accuse Moses of breaching his agreement with them—the agreement that he will not only deliver them from Egypt but usher them into the Promised Land. They

Sinai Desert area
Copyright
1995–2009 Phoenix
Data Systems

even broach the charge of attempted murder ("to make us ... die" in v. 3). Moses senses the danger and tells Yahweh that the process could lead to a death sentence for him (v. 4). Yahweh vindicates Moses before a group of witnesses, namely, the "elders of Israel" (v. 6).

This entire scene has legal overtones. At another level, though, Moses states that their legal action against him is really a way to put Yahweh to the test (17:2). To test God is a grave matter. Biblical texts allow God to test people (e.g., 15:25) but not vice versa. Thus, while the Israelites may claim that their legal action has sufficient grounds, their underlying motives are without justification.

Rock at Horeb (17:6). It is from this rock or crag that the water flows. Elsewhere, Horeb is called the "mountain of God" (3:1; 18:5). Hence, the water flows from God's mountain. This idea may have religious or even cosmic implications. In Ugaritic literature, the god El is said to reside at "the Sources of the Two Floods / In the midst of the headwaters of the Two Oceans."[188] He is also said to have his abode on a mountain that would appear

to be Mount Amanus.[189] These two places probably refer to the same location.

This combination of the watery and the mountainous also turns up in Exodus. It is the mountain of the deity that serves as the source of flowing water. Perhaps the ancient Israelites believed, similar to their Ugaritic neighbors, that their God was the ultimate source of this life-sustaining commodity that was so vital in their often rain-deprived land. Where else, then, would Moses be more likely to find water than at Horeb?

Battle standards on the Narmer Palette
Keith Schengili-Roberts/Wikimedia Commons, courtesy of the Royal Ontario Museum

▶

Held up his hands (17:11). The reason for Moses' gesture has long puzzled scholars. It could be a smiting or war-like gesture, similar to what Joshua does with his javelin in Joshua 8:18. It could be symbolic of prayer, beseeching Yahweh for victory, although Moses, uncharacteristically, does not explicitly seek help or guidance from Yahweh here. One possible clue comes in the name for the altar in 17:15: "The LORD is my Banner." The word "banner" (*nēs*) refers to a battle standard, flag, or insignia that leads an army into war. If Yahweh is the banner, as it were, how can the Israelites keep the banner aloft without a symbol, such as the ark (25:10–22), to lead them into battle (as in Josh. 6:6–9)? Perhaps Moses' raised arms are symbolic of raising Yahweh, their "banner" of military strength and power. With the banner raised, the army prevails.

Write this (17:14). This is the first reference to literacy in the Bible. Unfortunately, little is known about the extent of literacy among the ancient Israelites and other Near Eastern societies.[190] For the most part, only scribes, certain religious and governmental officials, and some wealthy businessmen, along with other elite persons, could read and write. Possibly those with lower socio-economic standing would have had occasional access to a degree of scribal training, but the evidence for this is small.

The invention of writing appears to have occurred in Egypt and Mesopotamia at about the same time—the late fourth millennium B.C.—but neither of those writing systems is alphabetic like ancient Hebrew.[191] One must presume that some predecessor of ancient Hebrew, a Northwest Semitic language (see sidebar), is the language that the biblical text is referring to, since the writing is to be preserved for future reference. Ancient Hebrew itself and most other alphabetic languages (including modern languages such as English) all appear to derive from the same alphabet—likely a Semitic invention in the first half of the second millennium B.C.[192] Recent discoveries of primitive alphabetic inscriptions in Egypt have raised the possibility that the alphabet was developed by Semitic peoples living there as early as 1800 B.C.[193]

In assessing literacy rates for ancient Israel, one must consider both biblical and epigraphic evidence, and little assessment can be done for periods prior to the Iron Age. Nothing that is rec-

▶

▶ **Biblical Hebrew**

Biblical or classical Hebrew, the language of most of the Old Testament, is part of the Afro-Asiatic family of languages. This chart identifies the place of Hebrew within that family.

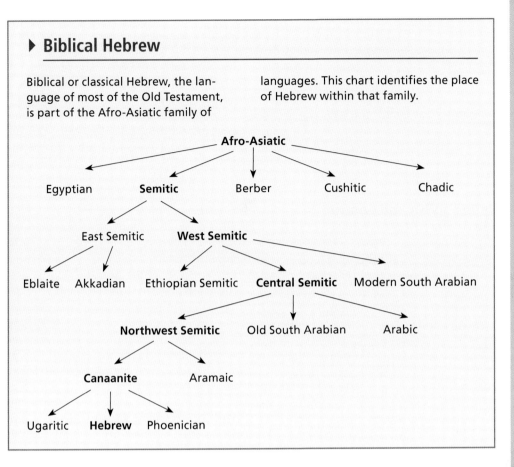

ognizable as Hebrew appears before this time period.[194] From the Late Bronze Age come nearly four hundred Amarna letters, written mostly by scribes living in Syria and Palestine, but these are in Akkadian (an East Semitic language), though they do contain some West Semitic features. Apart from those, however, there are only about twenty texts that have survived from Palestine, that date to the general time period covered by the Late Bronze Age, and that seem to reflect a Northwest Semitic language, but this language is not Hebrew.[195]

It is not until the Iron Age that actual Hebrew inscriptions turn up—just under five hundred by one count.[196] This evidence, in combination with biblical references to writing, however, still does not indicate widespread literacy among ancient Israelites. There is insufficient evidence for the kind of educational and economic systems that typically promote the growth of literacy in human societies.[197] While ancient Israel may have had a higher rate of literacy than some other Near Eastern societies—one estimate for ancient Egypt is a literacy rate of one percent[198]—still only a small percentage of the population could actually read and write.

Someone with the kind of background that the text describes for Moses would probably have been literate, but was he trained in both an Egyptian and a West Semitic language or only in Egyptian? Yet the biblical text attributes to Moses the ability both to read (24:7) and to write (17:11) in a language that the Israelites can understand. One must then wonder what specific language would have been spoken by Israelites coming out of Egypt toward the end of the Late Bronze Age. We simply cannot know. To suppose they spoke some type of Northwest Semitic dialect is not unreasonable, but it almost certainly was not the kind of Hebrew we find in the Bible, a dialect of Northwest Semitic that did not fully develop until later. Thus, anything written down in the Late Bronze or the early Iron Age and preserved in biblical texts has been updated for presentation in the kind of classical Hebrew found in biblical manuscripts.

Jethro's Visit and Counsel (18:1–27)

To seek God's will (18:15). The language used here indicates that this type of seeking involves a specific request on Moses' part for direct revelation from Yahweh. Such revelation from a deity is typically referred to as an oracle. Because Moses has in mind situations that involve his role as a judge in the resolution of legal disputes, the type of oracle at issue is almost certainly a judicial oracle (see comments on 22:8 for discussion of the judicial oracle).

Capable men (18:21). The word "capable" here can mean "brave," "heroic," or even "upper class." In light of the qualifications that follow this one, though, "capable" or "competent" is probably better. The other qualifications literally read, "fearers of God, men of truth, haters of unjust gain." Other societies had similar expectations of those who served as judges. For example, Code of Hammurabi 5 pertains to a judge who reverses a previous decision he himself made.

Shamash was the god of justice in ancient Mesopotamia. Judges answered to the deity, who was understood to provide the wisdom and authority to judges.
Marie-Lan Nguyen/ Wikimedia Commons, courtesy of the Louvre

▼

Whether the judge has been influenced by a bribe or is simply undependable is not made clear. But such a judge is to be fined and to have his adjudicating privileges permanently revoked.

Judges (18:22). Well-ordered societies require a mechanism for resolving disputes. Many of the extant records from the ancient Near East refer to legal disputes and their adjudication. Exodus 18 describes the establishment of a fledgling judicial system for Israel, and the text presents a hierarchically organized system. What is not clear is whether the reader is to imagine that the men chosen to serve in this system could come from any walk of life or had to have a specific social status. Although the text refers only to qualities of piety and trustworthiness, the selection process would likely have focused on those who already held positions of responsibility. In the ancient world, those in such positions formed the pool of acceptable judicial candidates.

The Covenant at Mount Sinai (19:1–25)

Keep my covenant (19:5). One of the most crucial concepts to understanding ancient Israelite religion and the theology of the Old Testament is that of the covenant. The Hebrew word for covenant ($b^e r\hat{\imath}t$) essentially means a binding legal agreement (contract) and can refer to agreements in a wide variety of contexts, including personal (Gen. 31:44), familial (1 Sam. 20:16; Mal. 2:14), business (Jer. 34:8–10), and international settings (Josh. 9:6; 1 Kings 15:19). Other ancient Near Eastern societies utilized the same sorts of agreements, many of which have survived to this day. The covenant established at Sinai between Yahweh and the Israelites is both like and unlike these more ordinary agreements that were necessary for the effective functioning of those societies.

There are several similarities. Like legal agreements of the day, the covenant at Sinai

▶ Judicial Personnel in the Ancient Near East

In the ancient Near East, various people had the authority to judge legal disputes and render verdicts. Much of the evidence for this comes from Mesopotamia, where persons designated as "judges" (Akkadian *dayyānū*) were often the ones who had this authority. Such people most likely had other vocations and served in their judicial capacity only occasionally.

Ample evidence demonstrates that others could also perform the function of a judge, even though they do not have this title. These typically included those who already commanded a significant degree of social respect: the king, other government officials (e.g., mayors, provincial governors), city elders, small groups of free citizens (often referred to as "assemblies"), and religious officials or temple personnel.[A-72] After Israel became established as a nation, their judicial system likely operated similarly.[A-73]

It is not entirely clear what the jurisdictional boundaries were for these various groups who held adjudicative power. There were probably areas of overlap. At times, similar types of cases could be tried by "judges," by government officials, or by city elders. The factors that determined which group heard a given case remain unknown. In addition, some records reveal more than one group presiding over a case. The judicial panels who tried these cases could include combinations such as "judges" and local assemblies, or government officials and temple officials. As for any hierarchy among these groups, the king was the ultimate judicial authority. Whether "judges" had authority over some of the other groups is difficult to determine; in some periods this seems to have been the case.[A-74]

The excerpts below, from Mesopotamian trial records, make explicit reference to those who are judging each case.

- Old Babylonian Period (c. 1770 B.C.): "In the temple of Shamash, the judges rejected their suit."[A-75]
- Old Babylonian Period (uncertain date): "The *pašīšu*-priests, the mayor, and the elders of the city gathered in the courtyard of Ninmarki."[A-76]
- Old Babylonian Period (c. 1770 B.C.): "Before the council of (the cities of) Kullab and Larsa, the ward and the prefect of the ward, the judge Ili-Ippalsam supervisory priest of Nergal, the judge Iddin-Amurrum son of Sanum, the judge Ibbi-Sumukan prefect of the "five," the judge Humbaya son of Lu-Ninsianna, the judge Habil-kinum brother of Iribam-Sin prefect of the merchants, the judge Sin-shamuh son of Ili-Iqisham."[A-77]
- Neo-Babylonian Period (c. 530 B.C.): "Bel-uballiṭ, the temple administrator in the city of Sippar and an *ērib bīti* (important official) of the temple of the god Shamash, and the elders of the city examined the contracts ... deliberated together ... and rendered a verdict against the woman Ayartu."[A-78]
- Neo-Babylonian Period (c. 530 B.C.): "Nabu-mukin-apli, administrator of the Eanna temple, Nabu-aḫ-iddin, representative of the king and overseer of the Eanna temple, and the assembly of the citizens of Babylon and Uruk ... rendered a verdict against [the five defendants]."[A-79]
- Neo-Babylonian Period (c. 535 B.C.): "Kiribtu ... testified before Nidinti-Bel, administrator of the Eanna temple ... and before Nabu-aḫ-iddin, representative of the king and overseer of the Eanna temple."[A-80]

carried with it obligations for both parties. To "keep" the covenant for the Israelites meant obeying the laws—their covenantal obligations—set forth in the next few chapters. In 24:7 we hear of "the Book of the Covenant," a term most likely referring to a written record of these obligations. Yahweh, too, had obligations, namely, to treat the Israelites as his own people, as his "treasured possession."

Another similarity lies in the willingness of both parties to enter the agreement voluntarily. At times, of course, the notion of the inferior party's voluntary commitment to the agreement is strictly a legal fiction. The will of another is being imposed on that party. The world of law and the world of reality can differ. This is made clear by a number of slavery contracts from the site of Emar. These contracts typically speak of the one being sold into slavery as taking on the status of slave "of his/her/their own free will."[199] Two of these refer to sales of infant girls into slavery, and both make mention of the children's "free will," a capacity they could hardly have, considering their age and situation.[200] With respect to the Sinai covenant, Yahweh has clearly initiated the agreement of his own free will. The Israelites, too, seem to accept the agreement and its accompanying obligations voluntarily (19:8), though a logic similar to that in the

aforementioned Emar texts may be at work here.

At a more specific level, many scholars have understood the Sinai covenant to find its closest parallel in one particular type of "contract"—namely, international treaties from the ancient Near East typically called a "suzerainty treaty" or a "vassal treaty," because it was concluded between a superior state (suzerain) and an inferior state (vassal). A number of such treaties have been preserved from the Hittite empire (mid-second millennium B.C.) in Anatolia (modern-day Turkey) and from the Neo-Assyrian empire (early to mid-first millennium B.C.) based in northern Mesopotamia. While both Hittite and Assyrian texts offer parallels to the biblical idea of covenant, the Hittite treaties have often been the focal point of comparison.[201]

A comprehensive analysis of these texts shows that they tend to contain a regular sequence of elements:[202] (1) a preamble, with the name and titles of the suzerain, in this case the Hittite king; (2) a historical introduction that describes any previous relations between the Hittites and the vassal state and points out historical reasons why the latter should be loyal to the Hittite king; (3) provisions and stipulations that impose duties on the vassal; (4) a list of those deities who are to witness the agreement and can enforce punishments if necessary; (5) a collection of curses and blessings, either of which could ensue depending on whether or not the vassal state fulfills its obligations and duties.

The description of the covenant in Exodus does not present a tidy sequence of elements in exactly the same manner as the Hittite treaties, but several of the same elements occur. The statement "I am the LORD your God" in 20:2 serves well as a preamble. References to Yahweh's deliverance of the Israelites from Egypt (19:4; 20:2) constitute an appropriate historical introduction. The laws in Exodus 20–23 form a list of stipulations—and a rather lengthy one at that. Element 4 would have served little purpose for monotheistic Israelites, and a specific counterpart to element 5 in Hittite treaties also seems to be missing from Exodus, though other biblical texts (Lev. 26; Deut. 28) contain blessings and curses related to the Sinai covenant.

Important differences, however, must not be overlooked. Typically, both parties to a contract, treaty, or similar legal agreement could expect to benefit from their commitment. It is not at all clear that the biblical text wants its reader to believe that Yahweh will receive some benefit from this relationship with the Israelites that he would not otherwise be able to obtain. The text speaks of great benefit awaiting the Israelites for their consistent obedience to their covenantal obligations. For Yahweh's part, his actions do not appear to be based in self-interest but in a willingness to be gracious and to extend freely his blessing. It must also be stressed that no treaty or contract from the ancient Near East provides a precise match for the Sinai covenant. There is no evidence of an agreement between a deity and a people group in these terms.

Thus, all parallels are inexact. Israel's relationship with Yahweh—at least in the form it takes—is unique. Exactly why the relationship takes the form of a covenant is difficult to say.[203] Nevertheless, a number of the implications of having a covenantal relationship with their God would have been clear to many Israelites, since it mirrored, at least in some respects, several types of relationships they already knew well.

Mount Sinai (19:11). This is the first use of the exact phrase "Mount Sinai" in the Bible. Its precise geographical location has been the subject of great debate and prob-ably still remains unknown despite a number of attempts since antiquity to identify it (see sidebar).

The Ten Commandments (20:1–26)

These words (20:1). What follows is traditionally called the Ten Commandments.[204] Most of these commandments are brief, negative injunctions. There are no exact parallels to this list from other ancient Near Eastern societies, although a few texts present similarities. Such texts are not legal texts, however. One (the Sumerian wisdom text known as the Instructions of Shuruppak) offers advice on how to conduct a happy and productive life. Its various maxims include the following:

> Don't extend a house too close to a public square; it will cause obstruction....
> Don't steal anything; don't kill yourself!...
> My son, don't commit murder....
> Don't laugh with a girl if she is married; the slander (arising from it) is strong!...
> Don't plan lies; it is discrediting....
> Don't speak fraudulently; in the end it will bind you like a trap.
> Don't have sexual intercourse with your slave girl; she will neglect you.
> Don't drive away a debtor; that man may turn hostile toward you....
> Don't rape a man's daughter; the courtyard will find out about you....[205]

Another text comes from the Egyptian Book of the Dead (spell 125) and describes how a man might obtain a blissful life after death. The deceased is to declare his innocence by naming nearly eighty actions he did not commit. These include actions proscribed by the Ten Commandments: "I have not robbed ... I have not been envious ... I have not killed people ... I have not copulated with a man's wife ... I have not debased the god in my town."[206] They also include an array of other actions: "I have not deprived an orphan ... I have not made suffering for

Possible Locations
for Mount Sinai
▶

▶ The Location of Mount Sinai

Traditionally, Mount Sinai has been identified with a mountain known as Jebel Musa (Arabic for "Mountain of Moses"). Saint Catherine's Monastery sits at the foot of this mountain and has welcomed visitors for centuries who believe they are visiting the very ground that Moses trod. Jebel Musa rises 7,500 feet in the southern part of the Sinai Peninsula, which probably derives its name from the traditions that placed the famous mountain there. Early Christian writings show that Jebel Musa was believed to be Mount Sinai as early as the middle of the fourth century A.D.[A-81] But this means that the earliest evidence for this belief comes over 1,500 years after any possible journey of the Israelites to this mountain. To be sure, the number of years between this belief and the

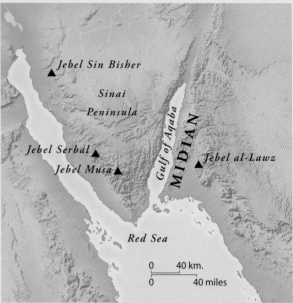

time when the text of Exodus reached the form we have today is somewhat less. Nevertheless, the question must be asked: Is Jebel Musa really Mount Sinai?[A-82]

Older traditions actually point to an entirely different location for Mount

Sinai. There is evidence from biblical and other ancient texts that Mount Sinai was not located anywhere in the Sinai Peninsula but was thought to be in northwest Arabia, slightly to the east of the Gulf of Aqaba. This would place the mountain in the region referred to as Midian. To begin with, Moses was in or near Midian when he came to "Horeb, the mountain of God" (3:1), often identified as Mount Sinai. In addition, Moses was to bring the Israelites back to "this mountain" (3:12) in or near Midian, in order for the people to worship God there. This is what happens in Exodus 19, where the mountain is called "Mount Sinai" (19:11).

Exodus 18 may also suggest that the mountain is in the vicinity of Midian, since Jethro, called the "priest of Midian" (3:1), visits Moses when the latter is camped with the Israelites at Mount Sinai. In light of this, some have speculated that a mountain known as Jebel al-Lawz, the tallest mountain in the region of Midian, may be the correct identification of Mount Sinai.[A-83]

Nonbiblical texts also support Midian as the location of the mountain. The translators of the LXX (done in the last two centuries before Christ) refer to Midian and Mount Sinai in a way that shows they likely believed Mount Sinai was in northwest Arabia rather than in the Sinai Peninsula.[A-84] Other Jewish writers before, during, and after the time of Jesus placed Mount Sinai in the region of Midian, such as Demetrius the Chronographer, Philo of Alexandria, and Josephus.[A-85] Paul himself refers to "Mount Sinai in Arabia" (Gal. 4:25). It is not entirely clear, though,

Wadi Feiran oasis and Jebel Serbal
Todd Bolen/www. BiblePlaces.com

whether Paul's "Arabia" meant only what we know today as the Arabian Peninsula or whether it included a broader region encompassing the Sinai Peninsula as well.[A-86] Still, the evidence for northwest Arabia as the location of Mount Sinai substantially predates the evidence for Jebel Musa.[A-87]

Even if Midian is the region where the biblical authors believed Mount Sinai to be, however, we still do not know whether Jebel al-Lawz is the correct identification. There is no clear evidence on which mountain is the right one. The region of Midian lies in modern Saudi Arabia and is currently closed to archaeological excavation. Whether such work would provide further data to help clarify the issue remains to be seen.

anyone ... I have not added to the weight of the balance ... I have not trapped fish in their marshes ... I have not masturbated ... I have not been impatient."[207] As with the Ten Commandments, such lists summarize a number of basic principles believed to be characteristic of one who has led a just and upright life.

No other gods before me (20:3). The Hebrew wording of this verse is ambiguous. This could be an assertion of either monotheism or henotheism (also termed monolatry). Practitioners of a henotheistic religion believe in and worship one deity, but they do not deny the possible existence of other deities. If this verse reflects a henotheistic perspective, then this call is for the Israelites to devote their worship exclusively to Yahweh, while accepting the possibility that other gods could legitimately be worshiped by non-Israelites.

It is possible for this verse to be understood as proceeding from monotheisitic belief. The reference to "no other gods *before* me" may be an attempt to counteract belief in a divine assembly. To have no other gods in the presence of Yahweh implies that he is, in a sense, an assembly unto himself. He consults with no other divine beings, and since the latter are thus removed from the divine decision-making

process, it makes little sense to consider them as gods.[208] Still, the language does not explicitly refute the existence of other gods. It is later biblical texts (e.g., Isa. 44) that are clearly and dogmatically monotheistic.

Ancient Near Eastern societies were, of course, polytheistic. Throughout Israelite history, this type of religious perspective impacted Israelite religion to varying degrees. One manifestation is the small statues that scholars refer to as Judean pillar figurines, which portray the torso of a woman with her hands supporting unusually large breasts. Over eight hundred have been found in Judah, and most date to the late eighth century and seventh century B.C. Some have interpreted these as goddess icons, while others insist they simply represent a wish for prosperity and fertility.[209] Even if the latter interpretation is more accurate, the figurines may be related in some fashion to the worship of a goddess in ancient Israel.[210]

Other polytheistic tendencies show up in ancient Israel, particularly regarding the god Baal. Baal was an important deity in several societies located near Israel (e.g., Ugarit, Phoenicia), and there is evidence, from the

Bible and elsewhere, that he was worshiped at times by Israelites. Engravings that depict Baal and that come from the period of the divided monarchy have been discovered at several sites in Israel.[211] Clearly, the Israelites did not consistently follow the principle set forth in this command. This is part of what led to the outrage of later biblical prophets and authors.

An idol in the form of anything (20:4). A question arises here: Does this prohibition on images apply to Yahweh, to deities other than Yahweh, or to both? Perhaps, given the reference in 20:5 to Yahweh's being a "jealous God," the verse has other deities primarily in view. Even if this were the case, however, the commandment likely assumes that Yahwistic worship did not involve images.[212] Thus, the attitude expressed here is thoroughly aniconic, that is, opposed to icons and images as representations of any deity whatsoever, even Yahweh.[213] It is understandable that the exclusive worship of Yahweh required a ban on images of other deities. But is it possible to discern a reason for the prohibition on images of Yahweh?

One possible reason was to prevent the Israelites from associating their worship of Yahweh with religions that practiced iconic worship. Most ancient Near Eastern societies were polytheistic and used a variety of divine statues in their worship. Some of these images were anthropomorphic (with human features), some zoomorphic (with animal features), some astral (related to stars and planets), and some utilized plants and vegetation. All types are forbidden here. Perhaps the idea was that entanglement with certain types of religious practice, such as the use of images, would lead to entanglement with the religions in which those practices prevailed.

Second, Yahweh's superiority had to be maintained and consistently reaffirmed. Banning images of Yahweh may have presented him as a deity of

such transcendence that he could not be represented satisfactorily by any image. In the Babylonian creation story known as *Enuma Elish*, the superiority of the god Marduk is proclaimed. Aspects of this superiority come through in an attempt at a physical description of Marduk.

> His limbs were ingeniously made beyond comprehension,
> Impossible to understand, too difficult to perceive.
> Four were his eyes, four were his ears;
> When his lips moved, fire blazed forth.
> The four ears were enormous
> And likewise the eyes; they perceived everything.
> Highest among the gods, his form was outstanding.
> His limbs were very long, his height (?) outstanding.[214]

For the author of this text, the grandeur of much of Marduk's physique was ineffable — "beyond comprehension … too difficult to perceive." This was a way to exalt Marduk over the other gods whose physical descriptions could actually be put into words. The prohibition on images of Yahweh seems

Relief from the tomb of Ankhma-hor shows sculptors working on two statues.
Werner Forman Archive

▼

to portray a similar attitude.[215] It reinforces Yahweh's superiority and demonstrates the futility of trying to place him into the confines of an image. Interestingly, throughout Israel's history, the production of Yahweh images does not appear to have been a widespread phenomenon.[216]

A final possibility has to do with the mediatory function that a divine image was believed to fulfill in societies. The transformation of a newly crafted image into the embodiment of a god's presence entailed lengthy and complex rituals.[217] The purpose of these rites was to make the statue holy and fit for inhabitation by the god—"to become the pure epiphany of its god and to be a fully interacting and communicating partner for the king, the priests and the faithful."[218] It was by means of the image that the deity could appear to, interact with, and communicate to its worshipers. Thus, it served as an intermediary agent for the god's relationships with humans and for the god's revelation of himself and his decrees.

The nature of Yahweh's interactions with the Israelites seems much more direct. While at times some mediation was necessary (cf. the role of Moses and the priests), no image performs this function, and the revelation of the person and message of Yahweh to the Israelites is essentially unmediated, so much so that the people are terror-stricken (20:18–19). This commandment may, therefore, bespeak a directness in Yahweh's relationship with his people that was perceived as uncharacteristic of other ancient Near Eastern deities.[219]

Third and fourth generation (20:5). This statement likely refers to the punishment of an entire household, not to punishment of children yet to be born. There are biblical examples of entire households (including wives, sons and daughters, and young children) receiving punishment for acts of wrongdoing committed primarily by the male heads of those households (e.g., Num. 16:25–33; Josh. 7:24–26). It was not uncommon in the ancient world to have

three or even four generations living in the same household.

A young woman typically entered marriage in her early teens, shortly after she began menstruating, in order to ensure as many productive child-bearing years as possible.[220] If her groom had not yet inherited a portion of his father's estate, she would live with her husband's family and be under her father-in-law's authority. She would likely give birth shortly after the marriage, and, if the infant survived, the three generations lived together for quite some time.

Misuse the name (20:7). Based on this verse, it has been traditional for many Jews to avoid ever saying the name "Yahweh," saying instead "Adonay" ("lord, master") or "ha-Shem" ("the Name"). Complete nonuse of the name precluded any misuse. But in the ancient world, this statement would have carried a clearly legal connotation. A literal rendering is: "You shall not lift the name of Yahweh your God to falsehood." The idiom "lift the name" refers to oath-taking.[221]

The ancient Near East had two types of oaths: promissory oaths and judicial oaths. In the former, a person swore to complete some specified action in the future. The judicial oath was taken more seriously and typically occurred in the context of a trial.[222] When a trial court was unable to reach a verdict because of a lack of clear evidence, it often required one of the parties to take a judicial oath. In this oath, the party swore by one or more gods that his or her version of events was indeed true. If the party followed the court's order and took the oath, that party automatically won the trial. The prohibition in the third commandment likely targets those who might swear false judicial oaths in the name of Yahweh—to lie under oath, as it were.

Remember the Sabbath (20:8). The hallowing of the seventh day—even the use of a seven-day week—was unique in Israel within the broader ancient Near Eastern world. Calendars and most measurements of time were based on the lunar or the solar cycle; the seven-day week is based on neither. Still, a period of seven days seems to have had special significance.

Several examples can be cited.[223] Gudea, the ruler of the Mesopotamian city of Lagash (end of the third millennium), held a seven-day dedicatory feast after completing the temple for his god Ningirsu. In the Epic of Gilgamesh, Utnapishtim (the Noah-like figure in the story), builds his ark in seven days and experiences six straight days of rain, but then it ceases on the seventh. The Ugaritic Baʿlu Myth describes a six-day cleansing by fire of Baal's palace, which ceases on the seventh. Each of these examples has religious significance. While the law in Exodus also carries religious overtones, it includes a humanitarian component, allowing rest for everyone at all levels of society.[224]

Honor your father and your mother (20:12). This verse has been subjected to many interpretations. Most ancient readers would have understood this as an admonition to care for one's elderly parents.[225] There is ample ancient Near Eastern evidence to support this. The Akkadian term *palāḫu*, like the Hebrew verb (*kibbēd*) used here, means "to revere, treat reverently." The term *palāḫu* also designates the responsibility of a son or, less often, a daughter to provide food and other necessary items to one or both parents.[226] Texts from the site of Emar in Syria, for example, use *palāḫu* as a synonym for the term *wabālu*, which means "to carry/support" and frequently occurs in texts that require adult children to support aging parents.[227] Thus, when used in the context of a child-parent relationship, *palāḫu* carries the same connotation as *wabālu*. In such contexts, Hebrew *kibbēd* probably does as well.

What type of support is intended? The Mesopotamian texts typically refer to rations for three items that ancient Near Eastern societies regarded as basic necessities: barley, wool, and oil. Barley was most important. It has been estimated that a "reasonable minimum subsistence level was 2 litres of barley per day, which means 720 litres per year," the equivalent of approximately 540 kilograms of wheat. In PBS 8/1 16, two brothers have come of age and are dividing the estate of their father. The father is still alive, however, and they must provide for him: "W. and N. shall give to A., their father, monthly 60 litres of barley, 1/3 litre of oil each; yearly 3 minas of wool each. By (these) rations of barley, oil and wool they shall support him. Whoever does not support him, shall not exercise his right to the inheritance."[228]

The idea of supporting one's aging parents accords well with the last half of 20:12. If a son, for instance, supports his parents as they grow older and thereby helps to extend their lifetimes, he can reasonably expect to receive similarly beneficent treatment in his twilight years.

Murder (20:13). Explicit prohibitions of homicide occur in a number of other ancient Near Eastern legal texts, and they often distinguish between intentional and unintentional homicide (see comments on 21:12–13). This verse does not make explicit any such distinction, though other biblical texts do (Num. 35:16–28; Deut. 19:4–7).[229] If this verse should be read in light of that distinction, then the command refers only to intentional homicide.

Akhenaten often had himself depicted in intimate family scenes such as this.
Gerbil/Wikimedia Commons, courtesy of the Staatliche Museum, Berlin

▶ Law Codes from the Ancient Near East

Law codes or parts of law codes have been preserved from societies other than ancient Israel. There are essentially seven known codes.

Code	Abbreviation	Place of Origin	Approximate Date
Laws of Ur-Nammu	LU	Ur	2100 B.C.
Laws of Lipit-Ishtar	LI	Isin	1900 B.C.
Laws of Eshnunna	LE	Eshnunna	1800 B.C.
Laws of Hammurabi	LH	Babylon	1750 B.C.
Hittite Laws	HL	Hattusha	1500 B.C.
Middle Assyrian Laws	MAL	Assur	1200 B.C.
Neo-Babylonian Laws	NBL	Sippar	700 B.C.

The term "code" is really a misnomer, since neither these codes nor the ones in the Bible fit the definition of a modern law code. First, all are far from comprehensive in scope and omit a number of expected topics.[A-88] Second, their content sounds much more like case law than legislation. Most of the provisions in the codes present possible cases—usually beginning with "if"—and then give a ruling for that case. Third, scholarship on the codes is now generally agreed that the purpose of these written collections was not to establish law in their respective societies. Rather, their purpose was by and large propagandistic—to justify and legitimize the rule of the king who authorized the compilation of the code.[A-89]

An additional purpose may have been to promote the legal wisdom of the king and to influence the rulings of local judges.[A-90] It is also possible that the individual provisions in each collection tend to reflect law that was being practiced at the time.

Nevertheless, it seems that the primary motivation to compile these codes in written form had more to do with politics than with law. A similar understanding can be applied to biblical law collections, such as the Covenant Code in Exodus 21–23 and the Deuteronomic Code in Deuteronomy 12–26. Primarily religious rather than legal considerations led to the incorporation of these codes into the biblical texts. In this written form, moreover, they represented for the ancient Israelites obligations based more in religious belief than in legislative activity, though it is likely that they also provide important insight into the legal systems of Israel and Judah.

But even within the category of intentional homicide, a distinction can be made between intentional killing deemed lawful and that which is deemed unlawful. According to both biblical and other ancient Near Eastern law codes, the former includes acts of self-defense (22:2; Laws of Eshnunna 12–13; see comments on 22:3), killing in war (Deut. 20:13; see the references to military personnel in LH 26–38), and the execution of certain lawbreakers (kidnappers in Exod. 21:16; murderers in Num. 35:20–21; adulterers in Deut. 22:22; false witnesses in capital cases in LH 1–3; thieves in LH 6–8). Most instances of unlawful killing mentioned in law codes and trial records involve the intentional murder of one's fellow citizen when there is no legal justification for the death.[230]

Adultery (20:14). Biblical texts (e.g., Lev. 20:10; Deut. 22:22) reveal that the death penalty could be imposed on those found guilty of committing adultery. In the ancient Near East, adultery was considered an act of sexual relations between a married woman and any man not her husband.[231] Married men could have sex with single women and either not be subject to any penalty (in the case of prostitutes or their own female slaves) or be subject to a penalty much less severe than those for adultery (Deut. 22:28–29).

It is difficult to identify in the Old Testament or in other ancient Near Eastern literature a well-developed system of sexual ethics.[232] Some passages within wisdom literature (e.g., parts of Prov. 5–7) come closer than the legal material in the Pentateuch to establishing an ethical basis for proper sexual behavior; still, the overriding concerns about sex were primarily social.

There seem to be at least two reasons for an ancient society's desire to control sexual behavior. First, certain sexual acts brought about a change in legal status.[233] It was often the act of sexual consummation that established a couple as fully married. Sleeping with the wives and concubines of a deceased monarch demonstrated that the successor had made the transition from heir apparent to king. Such changes in status had to be regulated. Second, a man needed to know that the offspring of his wife were indeed his own children. He particularly needed to know who his sons were, because they would be his legitimate heirs. It is this concern that is the most likely motivating force behind rules concerning adultery.

Ancient societies viewed acts of adultery as wrongs against the husband of the woman involved. This meant that the husband had the right to determine the penalty for his adulterous wife and her lover. He could not, however, pardon his wife and punish her lover. Provisions from the Laws of Hammurabi and the Middle Assyrian Laws (see sidebar on "Law Codes from the Ancient Near East" at 20:13) make this clear.

> LH 129: If a man's wife should be seized lying with another male, they shall bind them and cast them into the water; if the wife's master allows his wife to live, then the king shall allow his subject (i.e., the other male) to live.[234]

> MAL A 15: If a man should seize another man upon his wife and they prove the charges against him and find him guilty, they shall kill both of them … if the woman's husband kills his wife, then he shall also kill the man … if [he wishes to release] his wife, he shall [release] the man.[235]

The same seems to have been true in ancient Israel.[236] The husband had the right to determine the penalty, and he was free to choose a penalty other than death.[237] For instance, Jeremiah 3:8 indicates that divorce was one of the lesser penalties a husband could impose on his adulterous wife.

Steal (20:15). Theft was a crime in every ancient Near Eastern society. In addition to ordinary theft, it included misappropriation or embezzlement. Such acts might occur when one person was in legal possession of another person's goods but then removed the goods or sold them for personal profit. It also included receiving stolen goods. Those guilty of receiving such goods were typically treated like a convicted thief.[238]

False testimony (20:16). Some have interpreted this as a prohibition on lying in general. This is not the case. The Hebrew terms used here have forensic connotations; that is, they relate to the proceedings of a trial court. Furthermore, the language here points to a particular type of false statement: false accusation. This prohibition is about wrongful prosecution, specifically coming before a court to initiate a trial and wrongfully accuse another person.[239]

Provisions in the Laws of Hammurabi (see sidebar on "Law Codes from the Ancient Near East" at 20:13) also deal with false testimony. Two of these (LH 1–2) address false accusation (the same issue as here). Two others (LH 3–4) address false statements given by third-party witnesses—those who are neither the accuser nor the defendant in the trial. These provisions set forth a particular type of punishment for both types of wrongdoing. They say that the false accuser/ witness should be punished with the same punishment that the defendant in the trial would have received if the court had found him guilty. Other biblical texts (22:7–9; Deut. 19:16–21) call for this same type of punishment for those who falsely accuse another person. There are no biblical texts, however, that explicitly require this punishment for nonparty witnesses.[240]

Covet (20:17). Unlike many of the previous commandments, this injunction has been thought to possess few if any parallels in other ancient Near Eastern legal texts. A discovery in the year 2000 in ancient Anatolia (Turkey), however, of a treaty between Assyrians in that area and their Anatolian trading partners has brought such a parallel to light.[241] The treaty (early second millennium B.C.) is written from an Assyrian perspective and imposes a number of obligations on the other, clearly Anatolian, party. These include requirements to follow certain business practices, to hand over any persons responsible for the death of an Assyrian, and to compensate Assyrian merchants for any thefts they might suffer in Anatolian territory. The treaty goes on to state:

> You shall not covet a fine house, a fine slave, a fine slave woman, a fine field, or a fine orchard belonging to any Assyrian, and you will not take any of these by force and hand them over to your own subjects/ servants.[242]

This treaty seems to confirm that it is not entirely out of place for the issue of coveting to be included in a list of legal stipulations. It also points to the idea that the concern behind coveting is the illegal acts of confiscation that it can motivate. Interestingly, three of the items in the treaty—house, slave, slave woman—also appear in Exodus. The Deuteronomic version of this commandment also includes "field" (Deut. 5:21).

The Rules of the Covenant (21:1–23:33)

These are the laws (21:1). Exodus 21–23 forms what is often called the Book of the Covenant. This phrase comes from 24:7, which says that Moses "took the Book of the Covenant and read it to the people." This

Wallpainting from the tomb of Ounsu, Thebes, Egypt, Eighteenth Dynasty, shows slaves in various activites.
Erich Lessing/Art Resource, NY, courtesy of the Louvre

▼

"book" most likely refers to the laws in Exodus 21–23. Exodus 24:7 also says that the people responded to the reading of the laws by saying, "We will obey." These laws thus contain the principles or values to which the Israelites were to be loyal in order to fulfill their portion of the covenant with Yahweh. Like other collections of laws from the ancient Near East, this set of laws has often been considered a code of law and is sometimes termed the Covenant Code.[243]

If you buy a Hebrew servant (21:2). This refers to the purchase of a debt-slave.[244]

When a man could not repay a debt, he might sell himself or one or more of his family members, even small children, into the service of the creditor. When the man was finally able to repay the debt, along with any interest charges, he could redeem his family member(s) from slavery. If he sold himself into slavery, a relative, such as a brother, would often try to redeem him.[245]

Serve you for six years (21:2). If the family of a debt-slave was unable to redeem their loved one, a time limit of six years was placed on the length of the slavery. In second millennium Babylonia, the time limit appears to have been three years. LH 17 states that the release of a debt-slave should take place in the fourth year. The labor of the debt-slave counts as repayment of the loan.

Only the man shall go free (21:4). When a free man gave a wife to another man who owed him something, certain conditions applied to that marriage. The man in the inferior position was often a pledge (one who worked as a servant, not a slave, and whose services functioned as security or collateral for a debt that was owed) or a debt-slave, as here in Exodus. Typically, the pledge or debt-slave could take his wife—and any children she had borne him—only by satisfying particular requirements.

The record of a contract from the city of Emar (probably thirteenth century B.C.) presents an example of such a situation.[246] The pledge in this case may take his wife and children with him when he leaves the service of his creditor, but only if he abides by the basic agreement set forth in the contract. When this document addresses the possibility that the pledge might renege on his commitment to abide by the contract, then the pledge "will have no claim to his wife and children." This law in Exodus may be establishing what was standard procedure in these types of situations; modifications were probably allowed if clearly established in a contractual agreement.

Let her be redeemed (21:8). It was standard procedure to allow debt-slaves to be redeemed (see 21:2). But in this case, the daughter has been sold into debt-slavery with the understanding that she will become the concubine of her master (the creditor). If the master does makes her his concubine, redemption appears to be disallowed. Why is it resurrected if she displeases him and he decides not to make her his concubine? LH 146–147 indicates that a slave concubine who bore children had certain protections that ordinary slaves (even debt-slaves) did not. If the daughter does not become the master's concubine, she loses the chance to gain these extra protections, and thus the right of redemption is revived.[247]

Marries another woman (21:10). Given the context, this second "marriage" probably means the taking of another concubine. Regardless, the first woman—the daughter in 21:7—must not have her rations diminished. One would expect rations to be mentioned only with respect to slaves and dependents. Wives would automatically get what they needed.[248] The most common set of rations in the ancient Near East was food, wool (for clothing), and oil (for cleaning, cooking, etc.). It is possible that the Hebrew word for "marital rights" means "oil." If not, then the "marital rights" would be the right to sexual relations and the chance to bear children (see comments on 21:8).

Put to death (21:12). The death penalty for those who committed intentional homicide seems uniformly allowed in the ancient Near East. But the death penalty was not usually mandatory; it simply represented the fullest extent of the law. Convicted murderers could, in some cases, make a payment that functioned as a ransom for their life.[249] The text of one Neo-Assyrian document states that the perpetrator will, instead of making a monetary payment, give a person (perhaps from his household) to the son of the victim: He "shall give Amat-adimri, the daughter of Attar-qamu, to Shamash-kenu-uṣur, the son of Samaku [who was killed] in place of blood [money] and wash the blood away. If he does not give the woman, they will kill him on top of Samaku's grave."[250] Here, the ransom takes the place of the death penalty.

Intentionally (21:13). Other ancient Near Eastern societies also had laws against homicide (e.g., LU 1), and some explicitly considered intention a crucial factor. The lack of intention mitigated the perpetrator's punishment (as in LH 207), but intention to kill made the perpetrator liable to the death penalty.

If men quarrel (21:18). LH 206 states that the one who struck the blow must pay the physician, who, presumably, was summoned to help care for the one injured. This may be what is meant by the statement in 21:19, "and see that he is completely healed."

Beats his male or female slave (21:20). LH 116 stipulates a punishment for a man who beats to death a distrainee in his possession—that is, someone forcibly detained by the creditor in order to coerce the debtor to pay. The creditor could treat the distrainee poorly but could not kill or sell the person. If the distrainee dies because of a beating by the creditor, the punishment is as follows: If the distrainee was the debtor's son, then the creditor's son is to be killed; if the distrainee was a slave, then the creditor must pay twenty shekels of silver; in either case, the debt is cancelled. If this law in Exodus has in view a debt-slave, then a punishment similar to LH 116 may be intended here.

Serious injury (21:23). There are two possible understandings of this verse, both having to do with who sustains serious injury—the fetus or the mother.[251] Ancient Near Eastern parallels to this law suggest the mother is in view. Four other law codes (LL, LH, HL, MAL) address the issue of a man's striking a pregnant woman and causing her to miscarry.[252] All stipulate monetary penalties that the assailant must pay in order to compensate the family for the loss of the child. Three of these codes (LL, LH, MAL) go on to consider what to do if the woman is killed by the blow. In two (LL, MAL), the man who struck the blow is to be killed. In LH, the daughter of the man is killed, since the law assumes that he struck the pregnant daughter of another man. Only in MAL 50 is the death of the fetus linked to a death penalty: If the husband of the victimized woman has no sons and the fetus is male, the perpetrator is to be killed.

In light of these provisions of other codes, it seems likely that this law in Exodus follows their general pattern. The law calls for a fine in 21:22, probably as compensation for the fetus. It then addresses possible "serious injury" to the woman. If she dies, the perpetrator dies—"life for life" (21:23). Otherwise, the perpetrator will suffer a punishment similar to that inflicted on the woman (21:24–25).

Eye for eye (21:24). The principle of "eye for eye" also shows up in LH 196–201. This type of punishment, which tries to mirror the injury, is known as talionic retribution, which was a basic principle of ancient Near Eastern law.[253] Part of its purpose was to deter potential wrongdoers and to ensure that they would be punished appropriately, getting what they deserved. Another purpose, though, was to ensure that punishments did not go too far. If a man gouges out the eye of another, his eye can be gouged out, but his ear cannot also be cut off. The system may still seem cruel to modern readers, but this was one way in the ancient world to put limits on punishment.

These talionic penalties thus constituted for ancient Near Eastern legal systems the maximum penalty for a given crime. It was also possible for lesser punishments to be imposed. For instance, in LE 42 the penalty for the loss of an eye does not call for the assailant's eye to be put out; rather, it stipulates a sixty-shekel fine. It is probable that most, if not all, ancient Near Eastern societies allowed for such lesser penalties (usually monetary fines).[254] Statements like "eye for eye" thus declare the most severe punishment allowed by law.

If a bull gores (21:28). The laws in Exodus that deal with an ox (or bull) that gores are remarkably similar to the Laws of Eshnunna (LE 53–55) and Laws of Hammurabi (LH 250–252). The closest parallel between biblical law and other ancient Near Eastern codes occurs with Exodus 21:35 and LE 53. The latter states: "If an ox gores another ox and thus causes its death, the two ox-owners shall divide the value of the living ox and the carcass of the dead ox."

What stands out, however, is that, even though the issue of the goring ox occurs in some detail in several law codes, there is no mention of any such case in the thousands of trial-related records from the ancient Near East.[255] This suggests that ancient Near Eastern law codes were not concerned only with legal issues that might arise in daily life. They also seem to include legal problems and cases that were more academic in nature and that allowed certain legal principles to be expressed, even if the details had little to do with the problems people encountered on a regular basis.[256]

A son or daughter (21:31). An important principle of most ancient Near Eastern legal systems was that of vicarious punishment. For instance, if a man (a free citizen who was the head of his household) were to kill the son of another man (another free citizen and head of household), the man himself—the actual murderer—would not be subject to the death penalty. Rather, it is his son who could be put to death (see, e.g., LH 229–230). Because it was the son within the other household who was the victim, it is the one with the same status or rank in the first household who received the punishment vicariously—as a substitute for the real perpetrator. Scholars disagree as to whether this law in Exodus rejects or accepts the principle of vicarious punishment.[257] The wording in Exodus provides too little clarity to decide. Other biblical texts, however, do indeed appear to reject the principle (Deut. 24:16; Ezek. 18).

After sunrise (22:3). The situation addressed here is that of a thief who breaks into another's house and finds himself confronted by the owner who is ready to defend his property. The owner may use violence and even kill a burglar during the night. But if the burglar is killed in the daytime, the owner is guilty of murder. The same type of legal logic shows up in LE 12–13, where a thief caught in another's field or house at night can lawfully be killed by the latter.[258]

Silver or goods for safekeeping (22:7). The issue here is that of deposit. One person (the depositor) has deposited goods with another

Bull palette from Pre-dynastic Egypt
Erich Lessing/Art Resource, NY, courtesy of the Louvre

(the receiver) until such time as the first person will require the goods again. Other ancient Near Eastern law codes also treat deposit (LE 36–37; LH 120–126).[259] The Laws of Hammurabi consider what to do in a variety of situations: if the receiver lies and claims no deposit was ever made; if the depositor claims a deposit was made but has no witnesses to prove it; if the deposited goods are taken by a thief (the law says the receiver must compensate the depositor for the stolen goods); and if the depositor lies and claims his goods have gone missing when, in fact, they have not.

Apart from the law in LH that requires a depositor to have witnesses who can attest to the deposit, the issues are essentially three: theft, lying by the receiver, and lying by the depositor. This verse deals with theft, and the twofold fine here corresponds to the same fine for theft in 22:4. As the coming verses will show, Exodus addresses the other two issues as well.

Appear before the judges (22:8). The footnote in the NIV indicates that this phrase can also be translated "appear before God." The word translated as "judges/God" is *ʾelōhîm*, a word often rendered in English as Elohim and one of the designations for God. But since this word is used of non-Israelite gods as well as Yahweh, it is best to understand it simply as the generic Hebrew term for a deity. Note that the NIV translates this same term in 22:28 as "God."

While "judges" might be a possible translation for *ʾelōhîm* in 22:8—the term can be understood as either singular or plural—the most natural reading is to understand *ʾelōhîm* at face value as referring to God.[260] What does it mean, then, for the receiver of the goods (the "owner of the house") to appear before God? The text has in view a particular method for resolving the dispute at hand, namely, what scholars call suprarational procedures. These are procedures that go beyond the pale of rational evidence, such as testimony, physical evidence, or documentary evidence, by appealing directly to divinity to settle the matter.

There are three basic categories of suprarational methods used for resolving legal disputes: the judicial oath, the judicial ordeal, and the judicial oracle.[261] Only one party to a trial could take the *judicial oath*. If that party did so, the court granted that party victory in the case and felt confident that divine power would punish the oath-taker, if the latter had sworn falsely, with greater severity than any legal penalty might (see also the comments on 20:7).

The most common version of the *judicial ordeal* was the river ordeal, popular in Mesopotamia.[262] In such cases, Mesopotamian courts allowed the river god to render the verdict. If the party undergoing the ordeal sank, the person was guilty; if not, the person was innocent.

What appears most common in ancient Egypt and Israel was the *judicial oracle*. Here too the case is offered directly to the deity for a verdict, but not by means of an ordeal. A number of such procedures are recorded within the community that lived at Deir el-Medina in Egypt during the New Kingdom.[263] The evidence for the judicial oracle in Mesopotamia is meager. Three Neo-Assyrian trial records state that the god Adad is the one who issued the verdict.[264] Also, the beginning of tablet A of MAL seems to refer to soliciting a judicial decision from a deity.

Thus, this law regarding deposit in 22:8 is calling for a judicial oracle to decide the case (see comment on 18:15). It says that God will decide whether one man "has laid his hands on the other man's property."

▶ A Depositor Found Guilty

One of the possible situations that the law in 22:7–9 addresses actually occurs in a text from the site of Nuzi, probably from the 1300s B.C.[A-91]

> Zigi, son of Aripapu, entered into a dispute with Ilanu, son of Tayauki, before the judges. Zigi said the following: "I placed 30 seahs (c. 300 liters) of my barley in the house of Ilanu, and the seals were rolled. I took 3 seahs of barley from Ilanu, and I demanded the remaining barley from Ilanu. But he will not give it." The judges questioned Ilanu. Ilanu said the following: "Zigi placed these 30 seahs of barley in my house. Zigi (later) took 27 seahs of barley; 3 seahs of barley from it were left over. Afterward, Zigi took the 3 seahs of barley which were left over. Then I dragged my hem before the witnesses." The judges demanded witnesses from Ilanu, and Ilanu brought … (names of the witnesses) … five men before the judges as his witnesses. (They said:) "As for the 3 seahs of Zigi's barley, his hem was lifted. He said before us, 'I placed my barley in the house of Ilanu, and I took my barley. I also took the 3 remaining seahs of barley from Ilanu, and I am satisfied.' Ilanu then dragged his hem before us." Then the judges appointed three men … (names of the men) … as court officers and said: "Go, Zigi, and with respect to Ilanu lift up the gods against his witnesses." Zigi turned back from Ilanu; Ilanu was victorious in the dispute. The judges fined Zigi in the matter of the barley.[A-92]

Clearly, Zigi deposited barley with Ilanu. He then took Ilanu to court and claimed that Ilanu was refusing to return all of the deposited barley. Even though Ilanu had witnesses on his side, the judges resorted to a special supra-rational procedure known only from Nuzi: the lifting-of-the-gods ritual. It may have involved a judicial oath, but the details are not clear.[A-93] In any case, Zigi loses the trial and is fined. He, the depositor, has falsely accused the receiver of failing to return to him the full amount that he had originally deposited.

According to verse 9, the one whom God finds guilty must pay damages.

Pay back double (22:9). This verse establishes the general principle on which the situation in the previous verse is based. Whenever there is disagreement between the depositor and the receiver about goods that may or may not have been deposited, the case is to be decided by a judicial oracle (see comment on v. 8). The word "judges" here ($^{e}l\bar{o}h\hat{\imath}m$) should again be rendered "God": "The one whom God declares guilty must pay back double to his neighbor." If the receiver is declared guilty, he has most likely committed wrongdoing by appropriating the deposited goods for himself, and perhaps he has denied that the depositor ever gave him anything. But if the depositor is declared guilty, what wrong has he done? Either he never deposited any goods in the first place and now claims that certain goods, which actually belong to the receiver, are his, or he has asked to be returned to him more goods than he originally deposited and is accusing the receiver of cheating him.

Interestingly, the penalty for the depositor in Exodus matches that of the receiver, if the latter should be found guilty. The reason is that if the depositor (or would-be depositor) is guilty, what he is guilty of is false accusation. He has brought against the receiver criminal charges, which the judicial oracle has clearly refuted. In much of ancient Near Eastern law and in a later biblical text (Deut. 19:16–21), false accusers are to be punished with the same penalty that the defendant in the trial would have received if the accusation had turned out to be true.[265] Hence, the matching penalty.

An oath before the LORD (22:11). The issue in verses 10–13 is similar to the one discussed in verses 7–9 but is not quite the same. Rather than deposit in general, the issue here is one who has been given an animal for safekeeping—that is, the person has been hired to perform the duties of a shepherd or herdsman. This law establishes the limits on the shepherd's liability for the loss of or any injury to the animal.[266] Verse 12 states that theft of the animal requires the shepherd to compensate the owner for the latter's loss. Verse 13 releases the shepherd from any liability if an animal predator attacks and kills the animal in his keeping.

In other situations—death, injury, loss (with, presumably, no conclusive evidence of theft)—the shepherd is allowed to take an "oath before the LORD." This is the suprarational procedure known as the judicial oath (see comments on 22:8). The shepherd swears, invoking the name of Yahweh, that he is not the cause of the death, injury, or loss. In short, he swears to his innocence.

Taking the oath is decisive here: "The owner is to accept this." Numerous Mesopotamian trial records refer to this type of oath and make clear that the one who takes the court-ordered judicial oath is guaranteed to win the case.[267]

Seduces a virgin (22:16). Deuteronomy 22:28–29 deals with a similar situation. There, however, the man takes the virgin woman by force and rapes her. Here the term "seduces" implies that the woman, though perhaps duped, has given her consent. Admittedly, the ancient concept of consent was not as precise as that used by modern legal systems, which assume that certain types of seduction deprive the woman of her right to give or not to give consent. It is difficult to determine where ancient Near Eastern legal systems drew the line, but it seems fairly clear that this law assumes consent on the part of the woman.

Another important element in this law is the status of the woman. She is not married and is not "pledged to be married." If she were married or pledged to be married, then for a man—other than the one to whom she is pledged—to have sex with her constitutes adultery. Thus, what is mentioned here is what we call premarital sex. The law does not forbid premarital sex but attempts to regulate it. Middle Assyrian Laws (MAL A 56) presents an interesting parallel:

> If a maiden should willingly give herself to a man, the man shall so swear; they shall have no claim to his wife; the fornicator shall pay "triple" the silver as the value of the maiden; the father shall treat his daughter in whatever manner he chooses.

If the maiden had not given herself willingly to the man but had been raped, then the wife of the man would be punished (as described in MAL A 55). But here there is "no claim to his wife." The man must pay three times the amount of a standard bride price. A bride price was typically paid by a potential groom to the father of his future bride at the time of betrothal, and such pay-

Fragment of a painting from the tomb of Nebam-un depicts cattle being brought for inspection.
Werner Forman Archive/The British Museum

Middle Assyrian
Laws, tablet A
Emily Katrencik,
courtesy of the
Vorderasiatisches
Museum, Staatliche
Museen zu Berlin,
Berlin, Germany

Sorceress (22:18). The Old Testament refers to a variety of practices that can all be placed under the rubric of magic (see, e.g., Deut. 18:10–11). It is difficult to determine the precise nature of these activities. Some involve identifying future events through dreams, consultation with the dead, and probably the observation of physical phenomena (e.g., stars, animal behavior).[268] The activity of a sorceress likely involved the casting of spells or curses.

The use of curses in general was not forbidden in ancient Israel. Joshua issued a curse on anyone who might try to rebuild the city of Jericho (Josh. 6:26). Numbers 5:16–28 imposes potential curses on a woman suspected of adultery. Even Yahweh himself is spoken of as bringing curses on the Israelites if they are disobedient (Deut. 28:15–68). In ancient Israel, some curses were legitimate; others were not.

This was also the case in other ancient Near Eastern societies. The clearest evidence comes from Mesopotamia, where different terms were used for legitimate (āšipu ["exorcist"]) and illegitimate (kaššāpu ["sorcerer"]) practitioners of magic.[269] MAL A 47 prescribes death for the latter: "If either a man or a woman should be discovered practicing witchcraft ... they shall kill the practitioner of witchcraft."[270] The word for "witchcraft" (kišpū) is cognate to the Hebrew word translated "sorcery" (kešep, which yields m^ekaššēpâ ["sorceress"]). As in Exodus, it is the female practitioner who comes in for censure in NBL 7. There she is to receive the death penalty, but only if her activity is directed against a person rather than an inanimate object such as a field.

ment established the status of the woman as pledged to be married. It would be significantly harder for a father to obtain a bride price for his daughter if she had already had sexual relations with a man.

Part of the reason for the payment of a monetary fine in the laws in Exodus and MAL is to compensate the father for losing his opportunity to obtain a full bride price for his virgin daughter. But now that the man has paid a bride price (and a rather high one), the father may, if he chooses, allow his daughter to marry him. He can also refuse for this to happen. Even if he refuses, though, he still receives the payment from the man, since he may not be able to marry his daughter off in the future.

For no apparent reason, male practitioners are not specifically mentioned in Exodus. No penalty is prescribed when they are referred to elsewhere (Deut. 18:10; Jer. 27:9; Mal. 3:5), though it is not unreasonable to assume that the biblical authors would have deemed the males worthy of a fate identical to that of the females.

But what distinguished the legitimate practitioner (priest, prophet, or someone else) from the illegitimate? The former might be referred to as a miracle worker. Moses performed wonders with what mere observers might take for a magical staff. As priest, Aaron carried special paraphernalia (the Urim and Thummim; see comments on 28:30), which were the "means for making decisions for the Israelites" and which, presumably, gave him access to special communications from Yahweh. The casting of lots, another activity whose details are rather obscure, was also practiced.[271] Thus, activities of a mystical, miraculous, or magical nature were condoned, encouraged, and even commanded.

In what circumstances, then, would such activities cross the line and become evil? In Mesopotamia, it seems to have been those practices perceived as hurtful to society and its individual members. Magic for purportedly useful purposes—keeping sickness away, hampering military enemies, boosting economic prosperity—was allowed. For ancient Israel, a similar rationale may have held sway. To be sure, one factor would be whether the activity is done in the name of Yahweh. But that alone would be insufficient to ensure that harmful magic is kept at bay. That which is useful socially and religiously would be related to "group practice important for legitimating and sustaining the community as a whole, [but illegitimate] magic, by contrast, is seen as individualistic and often antisocial."[272] Only what is beneficial—either as a blessing or as a disciplinary measure—for the community as a collective entity would be permissible.

Widow or an orphan (22:22). A number of ancient Near Eastern texts refer to widows and orphans as if they must be protected classes within society. In the prologue to LU, the king of Ur states: "I did not deliver the orphan to the rich. I did not deliver the widow to the mighty."[273] In his epilogue, Hammurabi claims to have established his system of laws "in order that the mighty not wrong the weak, to provide just ways for the waif and the widow."[274] Using the terms "widow" and "orphan" together may have been a way of designating disadvantaged classes in general. Lofink argues that "Israel inherited [this phraseology] from its surrounding cultures as a symbolic name for those in need of help."[275]

Numerous biblical texts refer to the widow and orphan and advocate for their support and well-being. While such persons often undoubtedly lacked the means to support themselves, some passages seem to make a distinction between them and "the poor." According to Zechariah 7:9–10, for instance, "Administer true justice; show mercy and compassion to one another. Do not oppress the widow or the fatherless, the alien or the poor." If the widow and the orphan were representative of certain classes within society, they most likely stood for those inherently disadvantaged—whether or not they were actually poor—because of the nature of their situation. Certainly groups other than true widows and orphans fell into this category.

Do not show favoritism (23:3). This statement is reminiscent of sayings that come from ancient Near Eastern wisdom literature.[276] The wisdom text in which these legal statements from Exodus find their closest match is the Egyptian text known as the Instruction of Amenemope (probably a New Kingdom text). The relevant passage states:

> Do not confound a man in the law court,
> In order to brush aside one who is right.
> Do not incline to the well-dressed man,
> And rebuff the one in rags.
> Don't accept the gift of a powerful man,
> And deprive the weak for his sake....
> Do not make for yourself false
>   documents,
> They are a deadly provocation....
> Hand over property to its owners,
> Thus do you seek life for yourself.[277]

The statements from Exodus that this passage seems to parallel include: "Do not spread false reports" (23:1); "do not pervert justice" (23:2); "if you come across your enemy's ox ... be sure to take it back to him" (23:4); "do not deny justice to your poor people" (23:6); and "do not accept a bribe" (23:8). Thus, in addition to the laws that are part of the Sinai covenant, the biblical text includes these statements that, on first glance, appear to be more at home in Proverbs than in Exodus. What this wisdom material can do, however, is to help clarify the nature of the entire block

of stipulations in Exodus 21–23. While the biblical text certainly seems to make the rules in these chapters obligatory for the Israelites, it also points toward a particular interest in the spirit, as well as the letter, of the law.

Wisdom literature is typically interested in general guidelines that individuals should bear in mind and apply as they make daily decisions that affect the direction of their lives. The legal material, too, in Exodus can also point beyond itself to principles of living and decision-making that are about more than simply ensuring that a rule has not been violated. They are about a commitment to live as part of a community that has a special relationship with Yahweh and that pursues a lifestyle in keeping with that relationship.

Celebrate a festival to me (23:14). The three feasts mentioned here are to be held at set times during the Israelite year. These are, presumably, the same three times per year when "all the men are to appear before the Sovereign LORD" (23:17). The times designated for the feasts are tied to agricultural activities and especially to harvest times.[278] The first is the Passover and the Feast of Unleavened Bread, celebrated in the spring at the time of the barley harvest. It is referred to as a seven-day feast here in Exodus. Evidence for regularized, seven-day feasts from other ancient Near Eastern societies is meager, but texts from the Late Bronze Age site of Emar in Syria do attest to such festivals.[279]

The second festival, the Feast of Harvest (also called the Feast of Weeks), occurs in the late spring or early summer, which coincides with the wheat harvest. The third, known either as the Feast of Ingathering or the Feast of Booths, comes when summer fruit is harvested. Thus, each festival, while having its own particular religious focus, also celebrates the material provision of Yahweh for the Israelites.

In its mother's milk (23:19). Various explanations have been offered for this enigmatic command, and various ideas have been put forward regarding how this command ought to be implemented.[280] Early

Jewish rabbis extrapolated from this law the custom—still current among observant practitioners of traditional Judaism—of not combining in one meal milk or milk byproducts together with any form of meat (represented by the "kid"). But how can this verse be understood in its ancient context? One of the more popular notions in the mid-twentieth century was that this command was directed at a particular religious practice of nearby polytheistic societies. A Ugaritic text appears to mention a ritual procedure that entailed cooking a young goat in milk.[281] The Israelites could not, it was thought, participate in this practice because it was too closely associated with illegitimate worship.

More recent work has shown, however, that this Ugaritic text does not say anything about cooking a young goat. To begin with, part of the tablet where the wording in question occurs is damaged, so that the exact meaning of this portion of the text is not clear. Moreover, advances in the study of Ugaritic have led to a rather different understanding of several relevant terms. Thus, while there is mention in the text of milk, there is no reference to a mother, cooking, or a goat.[282]

A more likely theory has to do with the ancient Israelite religious understanding that important opposites must be separated. That which is holy must be separated from that which is ordinary or common; the pure or clean must be kept separate from the impure or unclean; the Israelites must separate themselves from other nations. In this case, life and death must be kept separate. A mother's milk is a life-sustaining force and, by this line of reasoning, must not be used to flavor the younger animal after its death.[283] Along with laws such as those that separated clean from unclean animals, this law, too, is a reminder to the Israelites that they have been set apart from other nations to be Yahweh's special possession.

The Covenant Confirmed (24:1–18)

Sprinkled it on the people (24:8). While the purpose of this sprinkling is not entirely clear, we can infer some aspects of its significance. The blood may have created a connection between the people and the sacrificed animals. In a sense, the people are now part of what has been offered to Yahweh. The blood also seems to make binding the people's commitment to abide by the obligations that the agreement places on them. Their submitting to the sprinkling may be compared to signing a contract today.

That such a use of blood relates to a solemn and binding agreement between two parties is partially confirmed by a letter from Mari that refers to a treaty between Zimri-Lim, the king of Mari, and Sharraya, the king of Razama.[284] This text advises Zimri-Lim not to aid the king of Andarig, who has imperialistic ambitions toward Razama. The primary motivation for Zimri-Lim to refuse to support the king of Andarig and his troops is the pact that Zimri-Lim has made with Sharraya. This pact is referred to when the letter writer instructs Zimri-Lim to say to the king of Andarig: "There is blood between me and Sharraya." The letter also refers to those who are part of the agreement as being "held in blood." Whether or not anyone was actually sprinkled with blood at the creation of this alliance is unknown, but the concept of blood represented the binding nature of what had transpired.

Nursing calf ivory from Arslan Tash
Michael Greenhalgh/ ArtServe, courtesy of the British Museum

Materials for the Tabernacle (25:1–27:21)

Blue, purple and scarlet yarn (25:4). The dyeing of this fabric would have been a costly and labor-intensive process. Blue and purple dyes most likely came from the murex, a type of snail abounding in tropical seas like the Mediterranean. Phoenicia (mainly modern Lebanon) was renowned for its dyeing industry, and large numbers of murex shells have been found there from various time periods.[285] Many thousands of snails would have been required to produce the amount of material described in Exodus. Scarlet dye probably came from the eggs of an insect that fed on oak trees.[286]

I will dwell among them (25:8). Sacred space—space set aside for inhabitation by a deity—was important in all ancient Near Eastern societies. It was the place where heaven met earth and had to be treated accordingly. What we call temples are typically referred to as the "house" of a deity: house of Nabu, house of Shamash, house of Yahweh.[287] These houses served partly as a visible reminder to the members of a society that their patron god or goddess was present with them. Their main purpose, however, was to care for the deity with clothing and food (presenting offerings to the deity), with a focus on the divine statue living inside.[288]

Like the pattern (25:9). There is debate on the Hebrew word for "pattern" (*tabnit*). One possibility is that the item shown to Moses is actually supposed to represent Yahweh's dwelling place in the heavens. This is, then, the pattern for the tabernacle, which becomes the earthly counterpart to the heavenly residence.[289] The other possibility is that the text refers simply to a scale model of the structure that Moses is commanded to build.

Several ancient Near Eastern texts seem to support this second option.[290] These documents refer to instances of divine intervention when models of or plans for religious objects are revealed to those responsible for building them. The models appear to have no connection to heavenly counterparts. In one Middle Babylonian document, a clay model of the statue of the god Shamash was miraculously discovered on the banks of the Euphrates River, which showed how the statue was to look and what clothing was to adorn it. This was important since these items had been missing for many years. With the model in

Mollusks from which purple dye was extracted
Z. Radovan/ www.BibleLand Pictures.com
◀

Assyrian warrior god standing atop winged guardian similar to cherubim
Bildarchiv Preussischer Kulturbesitz/ Art Resource, NY, courtesy of the Vorderasiatisches Museum, Staatliche Museen zu Berlin, Berlin, Germany
▼

hand, the Babylonian king had a new statue and new clothing made.

Ark (25:16). This was the most holy of all the items in the tabernacle, for it marked the location of the divine presence (25:22). It is referred to numerous times in Exodus as the "ark of the Testimony" (25:22; 26:33, 34; 30:6, 26; 31:7; 39:35; 40:3, 5, 21), because of the deposit of "the Testimony" within it. The Hebrew word *ʿēdût* ("testimony") is a synonym of *bᵉrît* and should thus be understood to mean "covenant."[291] What is to be placed within the ark, then, is most likely the written record (perhaps the "tablets of stone" in 24:12) of the covenantal agreement that Yahweh has made with the Israelites.

Disagreement exists, however, about whether the Israelites viewed the ark as Yahweh's throne or as his footstool (with the wings of the cherubim then functioning as his seat or throne). Extrabiblical evidence tends to favor the latter view. For example, the records of some international treaties, similar to the covenant between Yahweh and the Israelites, were deposited into box-like containers, which were then placed at the feet of deities.[292] Support for this latter conception comes from biblical texts such as 1 Chronicles 28:2, where David says, "I had it in my heart to build a house as a place of rest for the ark of the covenant of the LORD, for the footstool of our God."

Two cherubim (25:18). These sculpted creatures are most likely winged sphinxes known from a number of other sites throughout the ancient Near East.[293] Such creatures have been found in temples and shrines and are often arranged as if guarding the entrance. Their purpose seems to have been protective—to prevent, perhaps only symbolically, unauthorized individuals from entering space where they were not allowed. In the Exodus tabernacle, the creatures seem to function as protectors of Yahweh's presence. They are the last barrier between any possible human entrant and the divine presence. It is not out in front of them but "between" them, says Yahweh, that "I will meet with you and give you all my commands for the Israelites" (25:22).

Bread of the Presence (25:30). It is not clear whether this enigmatic phrase symbolizes the presence of Yahweh or whether there must be bread in or near the presence of Yahweh—a presence located within the Most Holy Place. A temple or shrine in the ancient world typically had as one of its chief purposes to feed the deity who was worshiped there. Large quantities of food were thus kept in temples and placed in front of a divine statue; specifically, the laying out of bread before a god is attested in Egypt, Mesopotamia, and Anatolia.[294]

But this seems unlikely as the reason for the "bread of the Presence." Nothing is said here about the bread being for Yahweh's consumption. Moreover, bread used as food for a god or goddess was prepared on a daily basis; but according to Leviticus 24:8–9, new bread for the tabernacle table is set out once per week—every Sabbath—and is eventually to be eaten by Aaron and his sons. It may have been placed "before" Yahweh as a token or symbolic offering and only then used as food by the priests.

Lampstand (25:31). The Hebrew word for "lampstand" is *m^{e}nōrâ*, and the Jewish tradition of lighting a menorah is still with us today. Lampstands with a range of similarities to the one described in Exodus are known from the ancient Near East and the Mediterranean world.[295] Some depictions of such lampstands show them in the presence of deities, who are seated on a winged sphinx as if on a throne, much as the divine presence hovers over the ark in the tabernacle.[296] Evidently, lampstands carried important religious significance. In what ways might this have been true for the tabernacle lampstand?

Despite apparent similarities with other ancient lampstands, the elaborate branches on the menorah give it a unique quality. "Nothing in the realm of stands, cultic or otherwise, can be related to the branched form of the menorah."[297] Many of the terms that describe items on the lampstand (e.g., flowers, buds, blossoms), along with the extended branches described in the text, lead one to believe that the lampstand is meant to represent a tree. Based on artistic representations of trees in the ancient Near East, one can conclude that the lampstand is a symbolic tree of life.[298] As such, it did more than merely provide light within the tabernacle; it represented life and fertility and the life-giving presence of Yahweh.

In fact, there is sufficient reason to suggest that the tabernacle contained much symbolism that relates to the divine garden or the garden of Eden. Typically, this type of connection has been observed between the temple in Jerusalem and the Garden of Eden, but it also applies to the tabernacle.[299] For instance, the Genesis narrative describes the garden of Eden as being entered from the east, as was the tabernacle.[300] Eventually, cherubim were stationed to guard access to the garden, as cherubim are erected in the tabernacle to protect the presence

Sacred tree motif in Assyrian art
Marie-Lan Nguyen/ Wikimedia Commons, courtesy of the Louvre
▲

Menorah on the Arch of Titus
Anthony M./Wikimedia Commons
◄

▶ The Tabernacle and Its Parallels

The instructions in Exodus 27:9–13 for the outer section of the tabernacle specify a structure 50 cubits wide and 100 cubits long (roughly 75 by 150 feet). The inner section is approximately 10 cubits by 30 cubits (15 by 45 feet; see 26:15–23). Twenty wooden frames, each 1½ cubits wide, are to be placed along the south side, and twenty more along the north side. This yields 30 cubits for each of these longer sides. Along the shorter west side (the east side served as the entrance to this section and is thus not enclosed in the same way), six frames are to be placed. This would make the west side 9 cubits in length, but when the corner supports are figured in (26:23–25), that number increases.

One recent calculation attempts to take into account how the corner frames were situated and arrives at a length for this section of 31.15 cubits (north and south sides) and a width of 10.9 cubits (west side).[A-94] If this is correct, then the inner section was closer to 16 by 47 feet. Its height was a remarkable 10 cubits or 15 feet (26:16).[A-95]

The inner section or Holy Place contained yet another room called the "Most Holy Place" (26:33) and is often referred to as the "Holy of Holies." This makes the tabernacle a tripartite structure: the outer section or "courtyard" (27:9), the inner section or "Holy Place" (26:33), and the "Most Holy Place" (26:33). The arrangement of religious structures in this way was probably not unusual in the ancient Near East. For

instance, the temple uncovered at Arad (southern Israel) is dated to the divided monarchy. It consisted of a "forecourt, main hall, and Holy of Holies."[A-96] The most likely purpose of this arrangement was to establish a hierarchy of space, with a progression toward space that was more holy and thus more restricted. This prevented those unfit for direct contact with the divine from trespassing within the space inhabited by the presence of Yahweh.

Another parallel to this three-part division comes from Egyptian reliefs depicting the military encampment of Ramesses II during the battle of Qadesh.[A-97] The main entrance to the Israelite tabernacle (the courtyard area) lay on the east side, one of the shorter sides of the tabernacle. The main entrance to the Egyptian army's camp was also on the east side, one of the short sides of the rectangular-shaped camp. If one followed a basically straight line from this entrance westward into the center of the camp, one eventually entered the king's reception tent, which contained, at the west end, the pharaoh's private area and throne room. This reception tent, like the Holy Place in the tabernacle, was three times

portable tent-shrines for deities existed in several ancient Near Eastern societies,[A-99] and the more important parallels come from the same time period during which the events in Exodus purport to have taken place.

Because of the theophany at Mount Sinai, the tabernacle was critically important for the Israelites. The visible manifestation of Yahweh and the establishment of his covenant with them at the mountain marked that spot as holy—a place where the Israelites had encountered the divine. But this location was not to be their permanent dwelling place. How could they retain the holiness and the sanctity of this location if they left? The construction of the tabernacle answers this dilemma.[A-100] Though small in comparison to Mount Sinai, the tabernacle was portable and, more important, designed by Yahweh himself. It was the place where the encounter with the divine could take place on a regular basis. It would house, as it were, the holiness of the Mount Sinai experience and the very presence of Yahweh as they traveled to the Promised Land.

as long as it was wide. Moreover, the pharaoh's throne had falcon wings on either side, reminiscent of the winged cherubim in the tabernacle's Most Holy Place. As the divine commander of the Egyptian military, Pharaoh was deserving of this specialized tent-shrine for his travels. For the Israelites, the tabernacle was the tent-shrine for Yahweh, their commander and the one who was to lead them to their ultimate destination.

Finally, an important parallel comes from Ugaritic literature. The chief god of the pantheon at Ugarit was El. His dwelling place is frequently said to be a tent, and the Ugaritic term *mškn* occurs in several texts with reference to his abode.[A-98] This term corresponds to the Hebrew *miškān* ("tabernacle"). Thus,

---

of Yahweh. Also, the man in the Genesis story was placed in the garden "to work it and take care of it" (Gen. 2:15). This combination of verbs occurs again in the Pentateuch only with reference to the duties of the Levites who took care of the tabernacle (Num. 3:7–8; 8:26; 18:5–6). The lampstand as a tree of life fits with this garden symbolism as well.

The question, then, is whether the garden was meant to symbolize a shrine or the tabernacle was symbolic of the garden. Given the highly symbolic nature of much of the early Genesis material, it seems best to conclude that the garden of Eden was a type of sanctuary—essentially a place of divine presence and a place of worship.

Make the tabernacle (26:1). This is the portable dwelling place for Yahweh. It consists of two rectangular sections, one inside the other. Both sections are, at times, referred to by *miškān*, usually translated "tabernacle" (see 26:7 for the inner section, 27:9 for the outer section). Here the term refers to the inner section, also called the "Holy Place" (26:33).

Hides of sea cows (26:14). This phrase has baffled scholars for years. Suggestions have included "badgers, seals, porpoises, narwhals, and even unicorns."[301] Some have opted for the dugong, a marine mammal known to live in the Red Sea.[302] The Hebrew terminology here is not clear and may not be referring to any kind of animal. A more plausible suggestion is that this term refers to the color of the material that must cover the inner section of the tabernacle—a color on the order of orange or red.[303]

Upright frames (26:15). These planks of wood formed the supports for the inner tent—that is, the section within the larger tabernacle known as the Holy Place. The Hebrew word for this type of plank is *qereš*. Similar terms (Ugaritic *qrš* and Akkadian *qersum*) turn up in other ancient Near Eastern texts. Two texts from Mari (c. 1800 B.C.) refer to what seem to be rather large tents with similar frames.[304] One document states that it required twenty men to carry ten of these planks, and forty-three men to carry the whole tent and all its parts. The other document mentions a tent erected with these frames, in which sacrifices are made to the gods. In addition, the god El, known from Ugaritic texts, lives in a tent-shrine made of planks.[305]

These structures may not have been entirely similar to the Exodus tabernacle; too little is known about them. Nevertheless, they point to the idea that the ancient Israelites may have known of portable structures of this type, even rather large ones, and that it would have been understandable to them that such a structure could serve as the residence for the divine presence and as the place of interaction between the human and the divine.

An altar of acacia wood (27:1). Most altars discovered by archaeologists are smaller than the one described here.[306] This altar stands approximately 4½ feet tall with a square top roughly 7½ feet by 7½ feet. Moreover, this altar consists primarily of wood. Typically altars in ancient Syria, Palestine, and nearby regions were made of dirt or stone. The shrine at the site of Arad is arranged in much the same way as the Exodus tabernacle, with three sections comprising a court, a main or center section (the Holy Place), and an inner sanctum (the Most Holy Place). Yet the altar in the court is stone.

This passage does not indicate the exact function of the altar, but later texts (e.g., 29:13) suggest that on this altar sacrifices are burned. Would a wood altar work for this purpose? Would not the fire from the sacrifice kindle the wood? The metal coating would do little to prevent this. Perhaps the altar is more symbolic than functional. Although the text does not state this, the idea may have been for the altar to be used once or twice, as a ceremonial shovel might be used at a groundbreaking ceremony today. Subsequently, another altar—one that could endure the rigors of regular fire rituals—could be substituted for it.

Make a horn (27:2). See comments on 30:1.

Model of the
tabernacle at
Timnah
Todd Bolen/www.
BiblePlaces.com

Courtyard (27:9). This passage describes the outer section of the tabernacle, approximately 150 feet by 75 feet, which makes it twice as long as it is wide (a ratio slightly different from that of the inner section of the tabernacle). Most buildings in that part of the ancient world had some open space that was enclosed but unroofed.[307] This made easier certain activities such as cooking large amounts of food and caring for animals. The purpose of this courtyard probably included similar activities, since the altar for burnt offerings is there, but it may also have allowed ordinary Israelites to enter the general precinct of the tabernacle and still be protected, by means of the enclosure around the Holy Place, from any dangers associated with drawing too near the location of the divine presence.

Priests and the Priesthood (28:1–29:46)

Ephod (28:6). This description portrays the ephod as a rather expensive piece of clothing, given the material of which it consists. A similar garment appears to be mentioned in Old Assyrian texts (the term is *epattu*) and in a few documents from Ugarit (*ipd* in Ugaritic). There is some hint that these garments were also costly, though the evidence is inconclusive.[308] Based on the bibli-

cal account, the ephod was like an apron that wrapped around the body from the waist down. Depictions of similar garments on figures that appear to be royal and/or divine have been preserved in artistic representations from New Kingdom Egypt.[309] These garments include shoulder straps, fastened to the main piece by gems in similar fashion to the priestly ephod. Their purpose is unclear, as is any connection to their Israelite counterpart.

Engrave the names (28:11). The exact type of stone involved here is disputed, but engraving a name on a stone is a well-attested practice. It was common for an individual to have his (such persons were typically men) name engraved on a stone, which he then used as his official seal.[310] For example, legal documents frequently have seal impressions. After the document was drawn up, the individual pressed or rolled his stone seal onto a portion of clay affixed to the document, thereby leaving his insignia on the document and making it officially his. With these "memorial stones for the sons of Israel" (28:12) fastened on his garments, the high priest was marked as the official representative of the people and could bring their petitions, gifts, and offerings before Yahweh (cf. also 28:21).

Breastpiece for making decisions (28:15). This covered the pectoral area of the high priest and was also made of costly material. Scholars have attempted to identify parallels to this piece, though there is little consensus.[311] One possible artifact comes from Byblos along the Phoenician coast and dates to the 1700s B.C. It is a type of vest with a frontpiece for the chest and cords to be strapped around the back. It has eleven

precious or semi-precious stones affixed to the outer edge and contains Egyptian artwork or an imitation thereof. This may have been worn by a Phoenician king, who also functioned as a priest. The inclusion of the stones is especially intriguing, although their arrangement differs from those described in Exodus.

While some have dismissed the relevance of this piece from Byblos, it nevertheless points to the idea that the priestly clothing in the Bible was probably not devised from scratch, as it were. Rather, priestly garments were reminiscent of what some Israelites would already have known to be religiously significant apparel. The reference to decision-making is probably an allusion to the Urim and Thummim (see next comment).

The Urim and the Thummim (28:30). Multiple and wide-ranging interpretations have been applied to these objects.[312] They include the ideas that the objects are gems in the shoulder-straps of the ephod or in the breastpiece, that they are other gems or stones besides those in the priestly garments, and that they are letters inscribed on the high priest's breastpiece. The biblical text is not clear on this. What does seem clear is that the objects were used to obtain revelation from Yahweh.

But how? Some scholars suggest that these objects would glow with a "miraculous authenticating light" as a means by which information from Yahweh came in response to an inquiry from the high priest.[313] Another suggestion is that they were cast, as one might roll dice today, and the position in which they came to rest indicated a "yes" or "no" answer to a question from the high priest to Yahweh.[314] Recent excavation work at the Iron Age site of Tel Dan in northern Israel has turned up a small object made of blue faience with white markings on its six sides.[315] The marks on opposite sides of the stone add up to seven, giving it an uncanny resemblance to a modern die. Interestingly, it was discovered next to a room containing an altar.

Perhaps the Urim and Thummim were objects like this. In contrast to rolling them, however, they may have been used in the same manner as objects referred to as "lots." One of the most likely methods for using lots in Israel and elsewhere was to place several of these objects—perhaps stones or pebbles with markings—in a container and then shake the container until one of the objects fell or jumped out.[316] Processes of this nature were believed to be divinely controlled and thus indicators of the divine will.

Linen undergarments (28:42). The wearing of undergarments is not well attested during this time period. Undergarments have been discovered, however, in the tomb of Tutankhamun, which suggests they were not entirely unknown.[317] The purpose of these for the Israelite priests seems to be specialized and not necessarily required for the common person. Verse 43 indicates that the garments somehow protected them from deadly guilt, probably because they covered the parts of their bodies that could emit human waste. Elsewhere, such waste is prohibited from being even within the bounds of an army camp: "For the LORD your God moves about in your camp.... Your camp must be holy, so that he will not see among you anything indecent and turn away from you" (Deut. 23:14). A similar rationale may be at work here in Exodus.

Serve me as priests (29:1). If prophets are individuals who brought messages from God to humans, priests are those who operated in the opposite direction: representing the people before God. While the priests here are said to possess the equipment necessary to receive messages from Yahweh (see comments on 28:30), their primary role was that of an intermediary on behalf of the people. For Yahweh to be their God and for there to be proper worship, the people needed religious officials who could make contact with Yahweh and provide the necessary worship and service to Yahweh within his place of residence—the tabernacle. While prophets were often reformers and individualistic, priests were more institutionalized and associated with long-standing traditions.[318] Here, the biblical text has Aaron and his sons as the first in the institution of the priesthood and as the inaugural keepers of the tradition.

Bring the bull (29:10). This begins a lengthy set of instructions regarding the ceremonies that had

Replica of the high priest's vestments
Z. Radovan/
www.BibleLand
Pictures.com

to be performed in order to "consecrate" (29:1; lit., "make holy") Aaron and his sons as priests. Modern readers may wonder at the elaborate and often bloody details of the rituals described here. Ancient readers would have puzzled much less over the details, in part because of previous experiences with such rites, but also because they understood the nature of what was taking place. In order to serve as a priest, a person had to be prepared for contact with that which was holy—the sacred realm, the world of the divine.

Ancient Israelite society operated on the understanding that there were three distinct categories or states in which persons (and objects) could find themselves: the state of uncleanness, the state of cleanness, and the state of holiness.[319] Yahweh inhabited the last, and animals unfit to eat inhabited the first. Persons could move between being clean and unclean, depending on what they had recently been doing, eating, touching, and so forth. Persons in

Horned altar at Beersheba
Dr. Tim Bulkeley,
eBibleTools.com

▶ **Instructions to Hittite Priests**

A lengthy set of instructions for Hittite temple officials has been preserved from the mid-second millennium B.C. It contains a number of general parallels to instructions found in Exodus and elsewhere in the Bible:

> Furthermore, let those who prepare the daily loaves be clean. Let them be bathed (and) groomed, let their (body) hair and nails be removed. Let them be clothed in clean dresses. [While unclean], let them not prepare (the loaves)....
>
> Further: You who are temple officials, if you do not celebrate the festivals at the time proper for the festivals and (if) you celebrate the festival of spring in the autumn ... the gods will seek to take revenge on you in the future....
>
> Further: You who are temple officials, be very careful with respect to the precinct. At nightfall promptly go to be in (the temple); eat (and drink), and if the desire for a woman [overcom]es anyone, let him sleep with a woman. But as long as [...] let him stay and let e[very one] promptly come up to spend the night in the temple.... Night by night one of the high priests shall be in charge of the patrols. Furthermore, someone of those who are priests shall be in charge of the gate of the temple and guard the temple. A-101

Painting from the tomb of Ity depicting the slaughtering of an ox

Werner Forman Archive/Egyptian Museum, Turin

a state of uncleanness were not allowed to approach anyone or anything deemed holy. Even persons who believed themselves to be in a state of cleanness could suffer dire consequences for coming into contact with that which was holy without authorization (e.g., 2 Sam. 6:6–7).

One of the goals of Yahweh's covenant with the Israelites was to make of them a "holy nation" (19:6). But this would not happen in an instant, and for the time being only the priests were to be made holy. The consecration of priests thus was a process fraught with peril. The transfer of a human being from the world of the ordinary—the world of the profane, where things and people were either only clean or unclean—to the world of the holy was not to be approached carelessly. While the significance of all the ritual actions described is not clear to us, what is clear is that this type of transfer process required time and ritual precision. Similarly elaborate rituals accompanied the installation of religious functionaries in other ancient Near Eastern societies.[320] The Israelites were no exception in the attention they gave to the proper consecration of their priests.

Blood ... and anointing oil (29:21). The placing of blood and oil on Aaron and his sons assists in consecrating them—transferring them into the realm of the sacred and making them fit for service to Yahweh. What is unclear is how blood and oil bring this about. An interesting parallel turns up from Emar in a text about the celebration of the *zukru* festival, which can be characterized as a celebration of the new year. At one point during the ceremonies, a set of stones is to be rubbed with oil and blood.[321] This may also be an act of consecration, but the type of stones involved and the precise nature of the act are obscure. Nevertheless, the combination of oil and blood seems to have held important religious significance in other ancient Near Eastern societies and may relate to ceremonies where people and objects must cross the sometimes dangerous chasm between the sacred and profane.[322]

Ephah ... hin (29:40). For the ephah, see comments on 16:16. As for liquid measurements in preexilic Israel, the evidence is murky. Estimates of modern equivalents for units like the hin have varied among scholars over the years. One of the most detailed studies to date estimates that the hin is equal to approximately six liters, making the amount called for here the equivalent of about 1.5 liters.[323]

Other Instructions Regarding the Tabernacle and Worship (30:1–31:11)

Horns of one piece with it (30:2). Archaeologists have discovered four-horned incense altars at various sites throughout Palestine, including Philistine and Israelite sites. This particular altar style appears to have Late Bronze Age antecedents that take the shape of models of towers made of clay.[324] Some of these clay models are close to four feet tall with a rectangular base slightly over one foot square. At the top of these model towers, the corners slope upward to form points as if on a turret. Offerings were burned on the tops of these models as a way to imitate the longstanding practice, in some ancient Near Eastern societies, of performing religious rituals and presenting burned sacrifices on the rooftops of houses.[325] Perhaps the Israelite horned altar is an offshoot of this tradition, with the top of the altar shaped to represent the roof of a shrine and to accommodate the symbolism of sending up incense to Yahweh from the highest point on the shrine.

Half shekel (30:13). Throughout the ancient world, there were different standards for different types of shekels. This, along with other factors, leads to some uncertainty in trying to identify the modern equivalents of ancient measures for weight. During the Late Bronze Age, for instance, the shekel from Ugarit was about twenty percent heavier than the shekel from Ashdod. Moreover, the Ashdod shekel was probably equivalent to the weight designated by the Hebrew term *pîm* (1 Sam. 13:21), which itself seems to have been equal to about two thirds of an Israelite shekel.[326] This makes the Israelite

Pilgrim flask
Joshua Walton, courtesy of the Joseph P. Free Collection and Wheaton College

◀

Incense altar from the tabernacle model at Timnah
Z. Radovan/ www.BibleLand Pictures.com

◀

the modern equivalent of this shekel.[327] Small artifacts marked with the Hebrew letters *bqʿ* ("beka") are equal in weight to about 6 grams, just over one-fifth of one ounce.[328] That the beka weight is the same as a half shekel (cf. 38:26) indicates that the sanctuary shekel does indeed fall into the range of the 11 – 13 gram standard. In most cases, payments of the type mentioned here were made in silver based on the weight (number of shekels) required.

Finger of God (31:18). See comments on 8:19.

The Golden Calf (32:1 – 32:35)

These are your gods (32:4). At least two questions surface here. Why is there a reference to multiple gods when Aaron fashions only one statue? And is the statue the god(s), or is something else serving as the referent? With respect to the first question, the NIV footnote indicates that the translation "this is your god" is equally justifiable. This is because the Hebrew word for "God/god" is

shekel heavier than other shekel standards in the West Semitic world.

This text makes clear the standard by which it expects the people to operate, namely, "the sanctuary shekel." Does this imply that the sanctuary shekel was different from the ordinary Israelite shekel? Some evidence suggests that they were the same, though many aspects of this issue remain unclear. Some archaeological evidence (mainly small weights) points to a shekel standard in Israel that falls between 11 and 13 grams; some have opted for 11.4 grams as

▶ Weight Measurements in Ancient Israel

Based on biblical texts and archaeological finds, the table below lists the units of measurement for weight used in ancient Israel. They are listed from lightest to heaviest. The modern equivalents are estimates and are not exact. They are based on the assumption that one shekel is approximately 12 grams (see comments on 30:13).

Unit	Texts	Ancient Equivalent	Modern Equivalent
gerah	Ex. 30:13; Lev. 27:25; Num. 3:47; 18:16; Ezek. 45:12		0.6 gram
beka	Gen. 24:22; Ex. 38:26	10 gerahs; half shekel	6 grams
pim	1 Sam. 13:21	two-thirds shekel	8 grams
shekel	e.g., Ex. 21:32; 30:13, 15, 24; 38:24, 25, 26, 29	2 bekas	12 grams (0.42 oz.)
mina	1 Kings 10:17; Ezra 2:69; Neh. 7:70, 71; Ezek. 45:12	50 shekels	0.6 kg (1.32 lbs.)
talent	e.g., Ex. 25:39; 37:24; 38:24, 25, 27, 29	3,000 shekels	36 kg (79.365 lbs.)

same? In light of Aaron's statement in verse 5—"Tomorrow there will be a festival to the LORD"—it seems best to understand the god at issue to be, in fact, none other than Yahweh. Is the golden calf or bull then an image of Yahweh? Perhaps, but perhaps not. From the ancient Near East (mostly from the Late Bronze Age), there are pictures of gods riding on various animals, such as lions, horses, gazelles, and bulls.[329] Moreover, there are depictions of bovines (these are generally from the Iron Age), most likely bulls, that have no rider whatsoever.[330] In the first set of images, the animal clearly functions as the seat or pedestal for the deity. In the second, there is no deity, which may raise possibilities for understanding the use of the golden calf here.

One idea is that the calf is still the pedestal, but this time of an invisible deity. The ark within the tabernacle functioned as a seat or footstool (see comments on 25:16) for the divine presence without any object to represent that presence. Perhaps, then, the golden calf functioned similarly. Or perhaps the calf is more in the nature of an emblem or symbol that stands in for the deity.[331] The worship is still directed toward Yahweh, but it makes use of a representative, one that embodies Yahweh's power and protection and brings reassurance to the people with Moses absent.[332] Regardless of how one interprets the calf, the

Elohim (ʾelōhîm) and can be taken as either singular or plural. The Hebrew pronoun for "these" is indeed plural, but this could simply be the result of grammatical agreement with ʾelōhîm, which is grammatically plural. Thus, this statement may indeed have only one god in view.

But should we understand the god(s) referred to and the statue to be one and the

worship in which the people engage angers Yahweh, in all likelihood because it violates the prohibition on making images, which they are supposed to know and to which they have already agreed.

Indulge in revelry (32:6). This is a notoriously difficult phrase to interpret. The most basic meaning of the Hebrew verbal root used here (ṣḥq) is "to laugh" (e.g., Gen. 17:17). Some forms of this verb can also indicate joking (Gen. 19:14), teasing (39:14), amusement (Judg. 16:25), and perhaps sexual fondling (Gen. 26:8). One suggestion for the way in which the verb is used here is "to amuse oneself wildly," though the precise nature of such amusement is not at all clear.[333] Since the calf may be symbolic of the power that delivered the people from slavery in Egypt, perhaps the term simply refers to the idea of celebration—the kind of celebration that often ensues following a stunning military victory.[334]

The bull as a symbol of military prowess was common throughout ancient Near Eastern societies, including Mesopotamia, Syria, and Egypt.[335] With Moses apparently having disappeared, the people need another tangible sign of their connection to Yahweh, their mighty deliverer. He is their warrior, their conquering hero, and a celebration of him would not be out of place.

Breaking them to pieces (32:19). This text may describe an outburst of anger on Moses' part, but the implications of breaking the tablets go beyond that. To smash tablets recording a legal agreement signifies the annulment of that agreement. The biblical text never makes clear precisely what is written on the tablets. We do know from 24:12 that they contain the "law and commands." The latter were directly related to the covenant established between Yahweh and the Israelites and contained the essence of the Israelites' obligations—what they were required to do to fulfill their end of the contract. For Moses to smash them is to declare unequivocally that the agreement is broken. Israel's recent action constitutes a violation of the agreement.

As mentioned previously (see comments on 19:5), the covenant in Exodus is modeled after the standard legal agreements or contracts of that day. In Mesopotamia, such agreements were typically recorded on clay tablets. The legal act that declared the end or invalidation of the agreement often included breaking the tablet.[336] The Israelites' violation of the covenant and Moses' invalidation of the agreement by breaking the tablets make necessary a renewal of the covenant, which comes in chapter 34.

Ground it to powder (32:20). It is difficult to determine if this text portrays a literal description. The actions of Moses may be patterned after actions considered standard in any description of the destruction of a hated and despised deity or divine symbol. In The Baᶜlu Myth from Ugarit, the goddess Anat sets out to destroy the god Mot. When she finally catches him,

> She seizes Divine Mot,
> With a sword she splits him,
> With a sieve she winnows him.
> With a fire she burns him,
> With millstones she grinds him,
> In a field she sows him.
> The birds eat his flesh,
> Fowl devour his parts,
> Flesh to flesh cries out.[337]

Anat's actions convey, with literary flourish, the complete destruction of Mot. Perhaps Moses' actions are stylized in similar fashion. Anat casts the leftover particles of Mot into a field; Moses strews the dust in the water. The birds, unwittingly, devour the last of Mot; the Israelites drink the last bits of the idol. Literal or not, it is the utter end of the image of the young bull.[338]

This Sumerian land sale document from about 2600 B.C. is one of the oldest stone inscriptions known. The stone is inscribed on both sides and the picture shows how the text went around the edge to the other side.
Kim Walton, courtesy of the Oriental Institute Museum

Book you have written (32:32). The idea that deities kept written records that related to human activity is prevalent throughout the ancient Near East, particularly in Mesopotamia. Such books or records are referred to in both Sumerian and Akkadian texts and fall essentially into two categories: "tablets of destiny" or "tablets of life," and tablets that record human behavior.[339] The former were believed to be kept by the god Nabu, who functioned as the scribe for the divine assembly. In one text from the sixth century B.C., Nebuchadnezzar prays, "On your [Nabu's] unchangeable tablet, which established the boundaries of heaven and earth, proclaim length of days for me, inscribe long life."[340] A Sumerian text (c. 1800 B.C.) offers a prayer for the king Rim-Sin: "Grant to prince Rim-Sin a reign all joyous and length of days! On a tablet of life never to be altered place its [the reign's] name[s]!"[341] The second type could be referred to as a "tablet of misdeeds, errors, crimes" or a "tablet of good deeds."[342]

The book referred to in Moses' statement in 32:32 is most likely one of the first type. In the next verse, Yahweh speaks of blotting "out of my book" those who have sinned against him, and the punishments that occur in verses 28 and 35 are death. Inhabitants of the ancient world hoped that the heavenly books of destiny/life designated long life for them. To be removed from the book would lead to certain death. Thus, Moses is saying that he would prefer to die on the spot if Yahweh refuses to forgive the people as a collective group for their violation of his law.

Tent of meeting (33:7). Apparently, because of the illegitimate worship practiced in chapter 32, a separate tent is erected *outside* the camp. Yahweh will meet with Moses there. He will not come inside the camp because, as the text points out, Yahweh is angry and prone to wreak havoc on the people if he is in their midst (33:5). Here in 33:7, the structure in question goes by the term "tent of meeting," a term used also of the tabernacle (e.g., 40:34). This tent, though, does not perform the equivalent function of the tabernacle. There is no indication that this particular tent will house the presence of Yahweh, since no rituals are performed to purify the tent and make it fit for the divine presence. Instead, this tent may represent a reversion, albeit partial, to Yahweh's earlier mode of interacting with humans—occasional and, at times, unpredictable appearances such as that of the burning bush.

A possible parallel comes from the Mesopotamian celebration of the *akītu* festival.[343] In Babylonia, the celebration of this festival merged with the New Year celebration and was marked by the procession of Marduk outside the city to a small structure where he would dwell for several days. During this time, prayers were offered in the hopes that Marduk would restrain his anger and bless his people. His regular dwelling, the temple, underwent a ritual purification during his absence. The highlight of the festival came with the procession of the god back to the city and to his proper residence.

In somewhat similar fashion, a small (presumably smaller than the tabernacle) structure is erected outside the Israelite camp. Encounters with Yahweh will take place there while a much more proper dwelling is made ready. In addition, the Israelites hope that Yahweh's anger will eventually be appeased and that his blessing will return. The Mesopotamian parallel is imprecise; no revelatory encounters occur while Marduk is outside the city, and his presence does not seem to come and go during his hiatus as does Yahweh's. Yet the removal of the divine presence from the camp or the city was significant in both instances. It undoubtedly meant that the first priority was doing all that was necessary to ensure the deity's return to dwell securely among his people.

Covenant Renewal (34:1–34:35)

The LORD, the LORD (34:6). This repetition of Yahweh's name is followed by a list of attributes that focus on his love and compassion. This was not uncommon in descriptions of deities in the ancient world. Examples abound of gods or goddesses (and even kings) who are described in lengthy lists of epithets or titles that refer to their character traits or special activities. The epilogue to the Laws of Hammurabi, for instance, mentions a dozen deities, after whose names are listed various epithets. It refers, for example, to

> the god Ea, the great prince, whose destinies take precedence, the sage among the gods, all-knowing, who lengthens the days of my life … the god Shamash, the great judge of heaven and earth, who provides just ways for all living creatures, the lord, my trust … the goddess Ishtar, mistress of battle and warfare, who bares my weapon, my benevolent protective spirit, who loves my reign.[344]

With its focus on love, this description of Yahweh seems in contrast with the portrayal of Yahweh in chapters 32–33, when he was ready, at the very least, to sever ties with the disobedient Israelites. This proclamation to Moses, then, may be emphasizing that Yahweh's anger has now subsided and the people may expect to be back on good terms with him again.

Asherah in Kuntillet 'Ajrud graffiti
Z. Radovan/
www.BibleLand
Pictures.com

Asherah poles (34:13). The goddess Asherah was worshiped under various names in ancient Near Eastern societies, and she apparently had followers in some parts of ancient Israel.[345] Other biblical texts condemn Asherah worship (Deut. 7:5; 12:3; 2 Kings 21:7); the goddess may also have been referred to as the "Queen of Heaven" (Jer. 7:18). An eighth-century ink inscription on a pottery jar, discovered at Kuntillet 'Ajrud, a site in the northern Sinai region, refers to a blessing offered in the name of "Yahweh and his Asherah."[346] This may suggest an ancient Israelite belief in a goddess wife of Yahweh, and this type of belief and the practices associated with it may be the target of commands like this one and those in Deuteronomy.

It is unlikely that the "poles" referred to in this verse are images of the goddess; rather, they are probably religious objects used in rituals associated with Asherah worship or perhaps with non-Yahwistic fertility rites in general. Because of their perishable nature, it is difficult to identify any such poles in the archaeological record. One may come from the Judahite site of Lachish. A religious shrine seems to have been located there and was in use at some point during the ninth and eighth centuries B.C. At this spot (locus 81) were found an elongated stone standing erect and a pile of ash, thought to be the remains of a wooden pole.[347] Perhaps the stone is one of the "sacred stones" that the Israelites are commanded here to destroy and the pole may have been one of the forbidden Asherah poles, though this conclusion has to remain tentative.[348]

Ten Commandments (34:28). Literally, "the ten words." This is the first time this phrase occurs in Exodus. The list in Exodus 20 that we normally associate with the Ten Commandments is simply called "these words." Moreover, these two lists differ substantially. The former contains several essentially noncultic provisions (e.g., those commandments related to murder, adultery, theft, false accusation, coveting), which tie it to some degree to the content of the ancient Near Eastern law codes. The provisions in Exodus 34, by contrast, seem to have no connection to the law code tradition since they reflect a much more cultic focus. They center on laws related to proper worship and ritual and, as part of the covenant that must be created because of the annulment of the first, may possess this focus because of the failings in the area of worship, so clearly demonstrated in the episode of the golden calf.

His face was radiant (34:29). Despite the many English translations that refer to radiance or brightness emanating from the face of Moses, it is not clear what the Hebrew text means to say. Literally, the text says, "The skin of his face *qāran*." What does this word mean in this context? The main reason why many English translations refer to brilliance is that several ancient translations do so: the LXX (done two centuries before Christ), the Peshitta (Syriac translation probably completed by the fourth or fifth century A.D.), and the Targummim (Aramaic translations of Old Testament books that originated during the first few centuries B.C. and continued to develop throughout the first millennium A.D.).

It is possible that the understanding of *qāran* represented by these translations is misguided. One potential reason for the confusion is the Hebrew word for "skin" (*ʿôr*) in this verse. Its pronunciation is virtually the same as the Hebrew word for "light" (*ʾôr*). These words differ only in their initial letters, and the two letters have a nearly identical sound; there are other examples where the LXX confuses these two words.[349]

The most basic meaning of the Hebrew word *qāran* is "to have horns." Could this verse mean that Moses' encounter with Yahweh left him with horns protruding from his head? This interpretation is not so farfetched as one might think.[350] Moses has

just experienced an intimate encounter with Yahweh; he has made direct contact with the divine. In this verse, the text seems to indicate that Moses' encounter has left him with an indelible mark of divinity. Horns are in fact a prevalent symbol of divinity throughout Mesopotamian art[351] (the focus of the text, though, is on his face, not the top of his head). Another possibility is that the brilliance of Yahweh's glory has left the skin of Moses' face hardened as skin would be that has been exposed to the sun for long periods of time.[352] His face has become hard *like* a horn.

Somewhat more convincing is an interpretation that attempts to combine the concepts of horns and light.[353] The basis for this comes from a series of astronomical texts from ancient Babylonia known as *Enuma Anu Enlil*, and the way in which these texts use the Sumerian word SI. At one point the text states: "If the sun's horn (SI) fades and the moon is dark, there will be deaths; (*explanation:*) in the evening watch, the moon is having an eclipse (and in this context), SI means 'horn,' and SI means 'shine'...."[354] The Exodus passage may thus be referring to horns of light radiating from Moses face.[355]

What would be the significance of such horns? It is true that the biblical text says that no human can see God's face "and live" (33:20);

Cylinder seal picturing two gods with horns on their helmets and light emanating from their shoulders
Scala/Art Resource, NY, courtesy of the Iraq Museum

▼

yet it also claims that Moses spoke with Yahweh "face to face" (33:11). The passage about Moses' radiant face may help to resolve this apparent contradiction. The radiant horns on Moses would mark him as something no longer fully human, for one cannot experience what Moses did and continue to "live," presumably as a normal, nontransformed human being. Since horns were typically a mark of divinity, it seems that a transformation has occurred—one that has now placed Moses partially within another world, the world of the divine. This is not to say that Moses has been divinized in any way, but that his face-to-face encounter with Yahweh has left him with a visible aura of other-worldliness from which the Israelites now recoil.[356]

Construction and Dedication of the Tabernacle (35:1–40:38)

This is what the LORD has commanded (35:4). Moses has received a series of commands from Yahweh, and now he takes these instructions to the people and delivers them as Yahweh's messenger. This recitation of Yahweh's commands is an integral part of a series of events described in the tabernacle narrative that appears to find a parallel in a set of events from The Baʿlu Myth, which contains an account of the building of a palace for the god Baal.

This portion of the Ugaritic text follows a sequence that also appears in Exodus. (1) There is a set of commands—regarding the building of a dwelling place for a divine presence—given by a deity to a messenger; (2) the messenger goes to the one(s) to receive the commands; (3) the messenger repeats the commands; (4) materials for the building are collected; (5) skilled craftsmen are designated to carry out the work; (6) extra building materials arrive; (7) the construction of the dwelling place is carried out.[357] The biblical narrative has not borrowed this order of events from the Ugaritic text; rather, both appear to be utilizing a sequence that is characteristic of ancient literature describing

the construction of divinely ordained sacred space (see also next comment).

Made the tabernacle (36:8). Exodus 35–40 recounts the fulfillment of the instructions given to Moses in Exodus 25–31. Much of this fulfillment section repeats or restates passages from the instructions section. This may seem odd. Why must there be so much repetition? Is not one version enough? One plausible answer is that the entire section in Exodus devoted to the tabernacle (Exodus 25–31, 35–40) is based, in part, on a particular literary pattern for describing the building of divinely sanctioned shrines in the ancient Near East.[358] One feature of this pattern was its requirement that "the building be described after an account of the preparations and before the dedication ceremonies."[359]

The text of Exodus does indeed describe the tabernacle structure (Exodus 36–38) after it recounts the preparations made (Exodus 35) and before the ceremonies described in Exodus 40. But does Exodus fail to follow the pattern when it describes the tabernacle and its contents both in the instructions section and in the fulfillment section? The biblical text may, in fact, be following a known variation of this literary pattern.

This variation is revealed to some degree in The Baʿlu Myth from Ugarit (see previous comment). It is further revealed by an inscription from the reign of the Old Babylonian king Samsuiluna, the son and successor of Hammurabi. The inscription contains a command, issued by the god Shamash to the king, to rebuild and restore the temple of Shamash known as Ebabbar. It reads in part as follows:[360]

> He commanded me, by his mouth which will not be altered, to build the wall of Sippar, the ancient city, his holy city; to return (the temple) Ebabbar to its place; to raise the head of the *ziqqurrat*, his lofty *gegunû*, like the heavens; to cause the deities Shamash and Aya to enter their abode pure in happiness and joy. (lines 8–24)

I raised the wall of Sippar like a great mountain; I restored Ebabbar. I raised the head of the *ziqqurrat*, his lofty *gegunû*, like the heavens; I caused the deities Shamash, Aya, and Adad to enter their abode pure in happiness and joy. I restored to Ebabbar its good *lamassum*. (lines 79–95)

Like Exodus, this text repeats, in a fulfillment section, much of what was stated earlier in the instructions section. Thus, it is not simply the words of the biblical text but also the literary form adopted by the narrative that conveys the nature of the structure to be built.

Poles ... to carry it (37:5). The practice of carrying statues of deities and other objects related to divinity is known particularly from ancient Egypt (see sidebar). Perhaps some in the Israelite community were familiar with this Egyptian practice.

Women who served at the entrance (38:8). Unlike much of the rest of Exodus 35–40, this verse contains information not already recounted by Exodus 25–31. As described previously (see comments on 36:8), all of the tabernacle passages in Exodus, when taken together, seem to follow a literary pattern known from other ancient Near Eastern texts. Apparently, the latter section can also incorporate information omitted from the instructions. In the Old Babylonian inscription cited above (see 36:8), the section recounting how the king carried out the orders of his god includes the name of an additional deity (Adad) and adds a line regarding the king's restoration of divine protection to the temple. Thus, this verse in Exodus is not out of place. The tabernacle narrative still seems to conform to the pattern.

But what exactly were the women doing at the entrance to the "Tent of Meeting"? Women could serve in a variety of capacities at a sacred shrine. Some temples maintained large estates, operated economic ventures, and thus employed women to provide labor in the form of agricultural and weaving work.[361] Some women served as devotees of a particu-

lar deity and lived, often as celibates, within the precinct of that deity's shrine.[362] Others held what was essentially the status of slave and served the temple to which they were attached; some speculate that such women could have been hired out as prostitutes to generate income for the temple.[363]

Exodus offers no clear indication regarding the precise role these women played in the life of the tabernacle, though it seems unlikely that their service was economic in nature. Since we know that women in other societies were involved in the basic operations and upkeep of religious shrines, it is reasonable to assume that Exodus is speaking of similar functions here, though it may be hinting that they remained at the door of the shrine because they were not allowed to enter within it.

Talents (38:24). On the amount of weight represented by this term, see sidebar "Weight Measurements in Ancient Israel" at 30:13.

Thin sheets of gold (39:3). The Hebrew word *paḥ* ("thin sheets") seems to come from the Egyptian word *pḥ*.[364] The Egyptians were well known for their abilities to cover items of wood in a layer of thin gold. A number of objects from the famous tomb of the Egyptian king Tutankhamun are remarkable attestations to this skill. This verse, then, may be referring to a method of gilding that was derived from an originally Egyptian practice.

Tunics of fine linen (39:27). Linen has already been mentioned a number

Image shows statue of the grand high priest of Osiris, Uennefer. He is clothed in the insignia of his rank and a lion skin and holds the emblem of Abydos in his hands. Uennefer was high priest under Pharaoh Ramses II, Nineteenth Dynasty.
Erich Lessing/ Art Resource, NY, courtesy of the Louvre

▶ Pole-Carrying Priests and Religious Processions

From New Kingdom Egypt come a number of artistic representations of portable shrines being carried by poles typically held by religious functionaries such as priests.[A-102] At the site of Karnak is a shrine that comes from the coregency of the woman Hatshepsut and her eventual successor, Thutmose III. One relief there shows a small boat, known as the barque of the god Amun, being borne upon two poles that rest on the shoulders of priests. Within the boat is what appears to be a wooden box or chest that holds a statue of Amun.

Another building at Karnak shows a relief from the time of Seti I. A group of priests are carrying a shrine by the poles that appear to run to (and perhaps through rings in) the corners of the shrine. Interestingly, "statues of [the gods] Amun and Re are shown in the shrine, with a pair of goddesses extending their wings to protect the deities."[A-103]

A further example comes from a shrine built for Ramesses III. This time it is the king who is seated and being carried, apparently by his sons. Again, two deities have their wings extended over him in a gesture of protection.

Finally, a small and portable box was found in the tomb of Tutankhamun. Atop the box was a statue of the god Anubis. Poles to carry the box were also discovered. The box turns out to be only somewhat smaller than the size given for the Israelite ark.

One probable purpose of the carrying poles was to prevent direct human contact with a most holy object. By using the poles, priests would not have to touch the shrine or, in the case of the Israelites, the chest or ark on which the divine presence rested. A number of later biblical texts speak of the Israelite priests using the carrying poles and bearing the ark in front of the Israelites (e.g., Num. 4:11; Josh. 3:6–8). Whether this method of transporting the ark was one of the practices that the Israelites borrowed from the Egyptians is difficult to say. It is clear, though, that it is a practice with which a number of them were familiar.

Relief from Medinet Habu showing Ramesses III being carried in a shrine on poles by his sons
Manfred Näder, Gabana Studios, Germany

▶

of times in the instructions for and the construction of the tabernacle. The linen here, though, is for the priestly garments. The Hebrew word for linen (šēš) likely comes from the Egyptian word šś, and the linen in view is most likely fine Egyptian linen. This material was considered to be of a high quality and was known for its white color.[365] The art of weaving is well documented and depicted in Egypt, and like the thin sheets of gold, the biblical text may be referring to a method of performing this craft that originated there.

Glory of the LORD (40:34). Several instances throughout Exodus (e.g., 16:10; 34:5) have made clear that the visible manifestation of Yahweh's presence often occurs in the form of a cloud. Since the Israelites conceived of Yahweh as invisible, they needed a visible entity—a reminder or symbol that could be seen by the human eye—to reassure them that Yahweh was indeed present with them. That visible entity is often referred to in the Old Testament as the "glory" of Yahweh. Isaiah 40:5, for instance, states that it is the "glory of the LORD" that "all mankind together will see."

Once the construction and arrangement of the tabernacle in Exodus is complete, the glory of Yahweh, in the form of a cloud, so fills the place that Moses is unable even to enter it (40:35). It seems, therefore, to have been more than something that could merely be seen; it could be sensed in other ways. At one point in Exodus, the "glory" is called a "consuming fire" (24:17). The glory of Yahweh was reassuring and fear-inspiring all at the same time.

This is reminiscent of the Mesopotamian concept of *melammu* ("radiance, supernatural awe-inspiring sheen")—a quality that gods and goddesses possessed and one that they could bestow on humans, typically royalty, and take back again if they so desired. In fact, anything that was imbued with divine power and presence was believed to possess *melammu*.[366] On the one hand, it was a blessing, for it was considered part of what gave legitimacy to a king and his rule; on the other hand, it was a terror that could overwhelm and decimate one who had become the enemy of the gods.

Yahweh's glory was also dual in nature, bringing reassurance to some, terror to some, and probably equal parts of both to most. This recalls Moses' close encounter with Yahweh in

Exodus 34, when Moses asked to see the latter's "glory" (34:18). When he is granted this request, Yahweh descends, stands before him, and proclaims both his love and loyalty and his willingness to punish. Throughout the Exodus narrative, Moses himself has experienced both aspects of Yahweh's presence—the providential deliverance of the Israelites and yet an angry Yahweh threatening to annihilate his people. It is this glory, as both cloud and fire, that, as Exodus comes to a close, is always "in the sight of all the house of Israel" (40:38), ever reminding them of God's presence and their covenantal obligation to obey him.

◀

Carving commemorates the religious action of King Ur-Nanshe, the founder of the First Dynasty of Lagash. He is shown presiding over the ceremonies of the foundation and inauguration of a shrine.
Marie-Lan Nguyen/ Wikimedia Commons, courtesy of the Louvre

Stamp seal; emanating rays may indicate the figure on the right is the sun god or could be the *melammu* (divine glow).
Kim Walton, courtesy of the Oriental Institute Museum

◀

BIBLIOGRAPHY

Halpern, B. "The Exodus from Egypt: Myth or Reality?" Pages 87–117 in *The Rise of Ancient Israel*. Edited by H. Shanks. Washington, D.C.: Biblical Archaeological Society, 1992. This detailed article carefully considers the historical evidence, both literary and archaeological, related to the possibility of an Israelite exodus from Egypt. The author seeks to maintain a balanced perspective and includes a number of references to primary source material. It is written for both general and scholarly audiences.

Hoffmeier, J. K. *Israel in Egypt: The Evidence for the Authenticity of the Exodus Tradition*. New York: Oxford Univ. Press, 1996. Also: *Ancient Israel in Sinai: The Evidence for the Authenticity of the Wilderness Tradition*. Oxford: Oxford Univ. Press, 2005. These two books are written by a scholar with Egyptological and biblical training. Together they offer a meticulous examination of historical issues surrounding the narratives in Exodus. They provide one of the best starting points for those interested in this topic.

Homan, M. *To Your Tents, O Israel! The Terminology, Function, Form, and Symbolism of Tents in the Hebrew Bible and the Ancient Near East*. CHANE 12. Leiden: Brill, 2002. This book contains one of the most recent and best analyses of the Israelite tabernacle. It also provides an abundance of information, including pictures and drawings, on similar structures from a variety of time periods.

Levinson, B. M., ed. *Theory and Method in Biblical and Cuneiform Law: Revision, Interpolation and Development*. JSOTSup 181. Sheffield: Sheffield Academic Press, 1994. This set of essays looks specifically at the Covenant Code in Exodus and considers how the code developed and what connections it may have with other ancient Near Eastern legal collections. The authors present differing points of view and thus provide a sense of the ongoing debates in scholarship on biblical law.

Meyers, C. *Exodus*. NCBC. Cambridge: Cambridge Univ. Press, 2005. A medium-length and very readable commentary written by an archaeologist and biblical scholar, this work contains helpful explanations of both ancient Near Eastern evidence and postbiblical Jewish tradition related to Exodus.

Paul, S. M. *Studies in the Book of the Covenant in the Light of Cuneiform and Biblical Law*. VTSup 18. Leiden: Brill, 1970. Although somewhat dated, this book still contains one of the most thorough examinations of the ancient Near Eastern legal material (both law codes and legal documents of practice) relevant for the study of law in Exodus.

Propp, W. H. C. *Exodus 1–18: A New Translation with Introduction and Commentary*. AB 2. New York: Doubleday, 1999; *Exodus 19–40: A New Translation with Introduction and Commentary*. AB 2A. New York: Doubleday, 2006. This is one of the most detailed and scholarly commentaries on Exodus to date. In addition to ancient Near Eastern background material, it includes in-depth analyses of text-critical and interpretive issues. It also contains a rather different English translation of Exodus, designed to give the reader a better feel for what reading the Hebrew text is like.

Sarna, N. M. *Exploring Exodus: The Heritage of Biblical Israel*. New York: Schocken, 1986. Also: *Exodus*. JPS Torah Commentary. Philadelphia: The Jewish Publication Society, 1991. Both of these books contain numerous discussions of ancient Near Eastern history, customs, laws, religion, and social practices. The first takes a detailed look at the major themes in Exodus, while the second proceeds on a verse-by-verse basis through the book.

Walton, J. H. *Covenant: God's Purpose, God's Plan*. Grand Rapids: Zondervan, 1994. Presented from an evangelical perspective, this book provides an insightful overview of the concept of covenant in the Old Testament and other ancient Near Eastern literature, with special attention to the Sinai or Mosaic covenant. A fairly thorough survey of scholarly perspectives and an examination of Christian theological ideas on the topic are important elements in the book.

Weinfeld, M. "The Decalogue: Its Significance, Uniqueness, and Place in Israel's

Tradition." Pages 3–47 in *Religion and Law: Biblical-Judaic and Islamic Perspectives.* Edited by E. B. Firmage, B. G. Weiss, and J. W. Welch. Winona Lake, Ind.: Eisenbrauns, 1990. This extensive essay on the Ten Commandments considers the Decalogue's possible relationship with other ancient law and the role of the commandments both in ancient Israel and in later Jewish tradition.

Westbrook, R. *Studies in Biblical and Cuneiform Law.* CahRB 26. Paris: Gabalda, 1988. This work comes from one of the leading scholars of biblical and ancient Near Eastern law and contains a wealth of insight into the legal systems of ancient Israel and Mesopotamia. While focusing on the topics of abuse of power, systems of punishment, slavery, and theft, the book provides cogent interpretations of a number of difficult texts. It also explains important aspects of the interrelationship of the various law codes.

———, ed. *A History of Ancient Near Eastern Law.* 2 vols. HO 72. Leiden: Brill, 2003. This two-volume set contains the most comprehensive analysis and description of ancient Near Eastern law and practice to date, including that of ancient Israel. It is the result of the collaboration of over twenty scholars and covers more than three thousand years of legal history.

Main Text Notes

1. The term "Israelites" may not actually be appropriate unless it refers to the inhabitants of the independent political entity known as Israel that appears to arise in central Palestine at the end of the second millennium B.C. The most common biblical phrase for designating the group of people under discussion is, literally, "sons of Israel" (often translated "children of Israel"). For the sake of simplicity, however, and because "Israelites" also functions as a legitimate translation of this phrase, this term will be used, even though it may be somewhat anachronistic.

2. A. Mazar, "The Iron Age I," in *The Archaeology of Ancient Israel*, ed. A. Ben-Tor (New Haven, Conn.: Yale Univ. Press, 1992), 285–96.

3. See B. M. Bryan, "The 18th Dynasty before the Amarna Period," in *The Oxford History of Ancient Egypt*, ed. I. Shaw (Oxford: Oxford Univ. Press, 2000), 218–71.

4. See M. Liverani, "The Great Powers' Club," in *Amarna Diplomacy: The Beginnings of International Relations*, ed. R. Cohen and R. Westbrook (Baltimore: Johns Hopkins Univ. Press, 2000), 15–27.

5. On some of the questions surrounding this phenomenon, see Mazar, "Iron Age I," 260–81; B. T. Arnold, *Who Were the Babylonians?* (SBLABS 10; Atlanta: Society of Biblical Literature, 2004), 75–77.

6. D. P. Silverman, *Ancient Egypt* (New York: Oxford Univ. Press, 1997), 10–11.

7. J. K. Hoffmeier, *Israel in Egypt: The Evidence for the Authenticity of the Exodus Tradition* (New York: Oxford Univ. Press, 1996), 52–76.

8. D. B. Redford, *Egypt, Canaan, and Israel in Ancient Times* (Princeton, N.J.: Princeton Univ. Press, 1992), 100.

9. Ibid., 101.

10. B. Halpern, "The Exodus from Egypt: Myth or Reality?" in *The Rise of Ancient Israel*, ed. H. Shanks (Washington, D.C.: Biblical Archaeological Society, 1992), 87–117; Kee, *Cambridge Companion*, 63.

11. Hoffmeier, *Israel in Egypt*, 119–20.

12. Bietak, *Avaris*, 1.

13. The remains at Qantir attest to this; see E. Hornung, *History of Ancient Egypt: An Introduction*, trans. D. Lorton (Ithaca, NY: Cornell Univ. Press, 1999), 109.

14. E. Uphill, *The Temples of Per-Ramesses* (Warminster: Aris and Phillips, 1984), 1.

15. COS, 3.2:11.

16. R. Caminos, *Late-Egyptian Miscellanies* (London: Oxford, 1954), 106. Cf. K. Kitchen, "From the Brickfields of Egypt," *TynBul* 27 (1976): 143–46.

17. W. T. Pitard, "Before Israel: Syria-Palestine in the Bronze Age," in *The Oxford History of the Biblical World*, ed. M. D. Coogan (New York: Oxford Univ. Press, 1998), 65.

18. N. Na'aman, "Habiru and Hebrews: The Transfer of a Social Term to the Literary Sphere," *JNES* 45 (1986): 271–88. For scholarly debate on the topic, cf. A. F. Rainey, "Unruly Elements in Late Bronze Canaanite Society," in *Pomegranates and Golden Bells: Studies in Biblical, Jewish and Near Eastern Ritual, Law, and Literature in Honor of Jacob Milgrom*, ed. D. P. Wright, D. N. Freedman, and A. Hurvitz (Winona Lake, Ind.: Eisenbrauns, 1995), 481–96.

19. COS, 3.11:35–36.

20. Laws of Eshnunna 32; Laws of Hammurabi 194; Malul, "Adoption," 107–8; G. Robins, *Women in Ancient Egypt* (Cambridge, Mass.: Harvard Univ. Press, 1993), 88–90; R. Westbrook, "Old Babylonian Period," *HANEL*, 1:409; K. Slanski, "Middle Babylonian Period," *HANEL*, 1:514.

21. OEAE, 2:438.

22. See the Neo-Babylonian case (Nbk 365) discussed in M. Dandamaev, *Slavery in Babylonia: From Nabopolassar to Alexander the Great (626–331 B.C.)*, trans. V. A. Powell (DeKalb, Ill.: Northern Illinois Press, 1984), 462–63.

23. See R. K. Ritner's discussion and translation of the so-called Harem Conspiracy Case in COS, 3.8:27–30.

24. Redford, *Egypt, Canan, and Israel*, 272. See also R. Giveon, "Toponymes Ouest-Asiatiques à Soleb," *VT* 14 (1964): 244; M. C. Astour, "Yahweh in Egyptian Topographic Lists," in *Festschrift Elmar Edel, 12 Marz 1979*, ed. M. Görg and E. B. Pusch (Ägypten und Altes Testament 1; Bamberg: M. Görg, 1979), 17–34.

25. "Horeb may refer to the wilderness region and Sinai to the mountain itself, or vice versa, or Horeb may be a range and Sinai a particular peak within it" (N. M. Sarna, *Exploring Exodus: The Heritage of Biblical Israel* [New York: Schocken, 1986], 38). The precise relationship between Horeb and Sinai is simply not clear.

26. R. J. Clifford, *The Cosmic Mountain in Canaan and the Old Testament* (Cambridge, Mass.: Harvard Univ. Press, 1972), 9–97. See also M. S. Smith, *The Ugaritic Baal Cycle* (VTSup 55; Leiden: Brill, 1994), 225–34.

27. H. Niehr, "Zaphon," *DDD*[2], 927–28; Smith, *Ugaritic Baal Cycle*, 122.

28. M. S. Smith, "The Baal Cycle," in *Ugaritic Narrative Poetry*, ed. S. B. Parker (SBLWAW 9; Atlanta: Scholars Press, 1997), 110; see COS, 1.86:251. Another example is the Canaanite goddess Anat, who lived on a mountain called ꜣInbubu in Ugaritic texts (see COS, 1.86:243 n. 9).

29. C. Houtman, *Exodus*, trans. J. Rebel and S. Woudstra (Historical Commentary on the Old Testament; Kampen: Kok, 1993), 1:334–35.

30. For other biblical texts, such as Num. 22:22–35, where there appears to be overlap between the identity and activity of God and that of an angel/messenger, see S. A. Meier, "Angel of Yahweh," *DDD*[2], 53–59.

31. COS, 1.109:385. See also the discussion of divine messengers in S. A. Meier, *The Messenger in the Ancient World* (HSM 45; Atlanta: Scholars Press, 1988), 119–28.

32. W. H. Propp, *Exodus 1–18* (AB; New York: Doubleday, 1999), 198–99.

33. Meier, "Angel of Yahweh," 59.

34. U. Cassuto, *A Commentary on the Book of Exodus* (Jerusalem: Magnes, 1985), 33.

35. W. K. Simpson, ed., *The Literature of Ancient Egypt: An Anthology of Stories, Instructions, Stelae, Autobiographies, and Poetry*, 3rd ed. (New Haven, Conn.: Yale Univ. Press, 2003), 58; see COS, 1.38:79.

36. Smith, "Baal Cycle," 158; see COS, 1.86:271.

37. For a summary of scholarly viewpoints, see Houtman, *Exodus*, 1:356–58.

38. P. L. King and L. E. Stager, *Life in Biblical Israel* (Library of Ancient Israel; Louisville: Westminster John Knox, 2001), 113–14.

39. Ibid., 104–6.

40. See the discussion in Propp, *Exodus 1–18*, 223–26.

41. J. Assmann, *The Search for God in Ancient Egypt*, trans. D. Lorton (Ithaca, N.Y.: Cornell Univ. Press, 2001), 83–87.

42. Ibid., 85 (citing the Pyramid Texts, spell 366, §§628–29).

43. Ibid., 87.

44. For what is still one of the more detailed discussions of this point, see E. A. W. Budge, *Egyptian Magic* (New York: Univ. Books, 1899), 157–81; see also E. Hornung, *Conceptions of God in Ancient Egypt: The One and the Many*, trans. J. Baines (Ithaca, N.Y.: Cornell Univ. Press, 1982), 86–91.

45. A. Erman, *Life in Ancient Egypt*, trans. H. M. Tirard (London: MacMillan, 1894), 354.

46. *ANET*[3] 13; see COS, 1.22:34.

47. Ibid.

48. Ibid.

49. A. H. McNeile, *The Book of Exodus*, 3rd ed. (London: Methuen, 1931), 42, quoting A. Macalister.

50. Houtman (*Exodus*, 1:439–47) lists a wide range of other opinions on this point.

51. For a positive view of Moses' action, see T. E. Fretheim, *Exodus* (Interpretation; Louisville: John Knox, 1991), 42–43.

52. For a detailed discussion of this concept, see P. Barmash, *Homicide in the Biblical World* (Cambridge: Cambridge Univ. Press, 2005), 4–115.

53. On the idea in Greece, see ibid., 100–101 n. 22.

54. The text is *ADD*, 321. See T. Kwasman, *Neo-Assyrian Legal Documents in the Kouyunjik Collection of the British Museum* (Studia Pohl Series Maior 14; Rome: Pontificio Istituto Biblico, 1988), 393; Barmash, *Homicide*, 63–64, 106.

55. *CAD*, B 42. The text is ARM 3.18.

56. Barmash argues that even accidental killers would be "guilty in some sense" (*Homicide*, 102) and that the death of the high priest would serve as expiation—that which eliminates the pollution—for the homicide (ibid., 103). In Moses' case, however, the death of an Egyptian ruler would not have the same expiatory effect as that of an Israelite priest.

57. H. W. Attridge and R. A. Oden, Jr., *Philo of Byblos—The Phoenician History: Introduction, Critical Text, Translation, Notes* (CBQMS 9; Washington, D.C.: Catholic Biblical Association of America, 1981), 57.

58. Note, however, that there may have been important differences in the Egyptian and Israelite methods of circumcision; see J. M. Sasson, "Circumcision in the Ancient Near East," *JBL* 85 (1966): 473–76.

59. Houtman, *Exodus*, 1:447.

60. W. H. C. Propp, "That Bloody Bridegroom," *VT* 43 (1993): 495–518.

61. For Mesopotamia, see J. Bottéro, *Religion in Ancient Mesopotamia*, trans. T. L. Fagan (Chicago: Univ. of Chicago Press, 2001), 149–64. For Egypt, see A. J. Spalinger, "Festivals," in *The Ancient Gods Speak: A Guide to Egyptian Religion*, ed. D. B. Redford (Oxford: Oxford Univ. Press, 2002), 125–32.

62. G. Beckman, "How Religion Was Done," in *A Companion to the Ancient Near East*, ed. D. C. Snell (Blackwell Companions to the Ancient World; Oxford: Blackwell, 2005), 346.

63. See, e.g., K. van der Toorn, *Family Religion in Babylonia, Syria and Israel* (Leiden: Brill, 1996), 83.

64. See W. Helck, *Die Beziehungen Ägyptens zu Vorderasien im 3. und 2. Jahrtausend v. Chr.*, 2nd ed. (ÄgAbh 5; Wiesbaden: Harrassowitz, 1971), 446–73.

65. Ibid., 448.

66. C. F. Nims, "Bricks without Straw?" *BA* 13 (1950): 26–27.

67. K. A. Kitchen, *Ramesses II: Royal Inscriptions* (vol. 2 of *Ramesside Inscriptions: Translated & Annotated*; Series A: Translations; Oxford: Blackwell, 1996), 520.

68. K. A. Kitchen, *Ancient Orient and Old Testament* (Downers Grove, Ill.: InterVarsity Press, 1966), 156–57.

69. J. K. Hoffmeier, "The Arm of God versus the Arm of Pharaoh in the Exodus Narratives," *Bib* 67 (1986): 378–87; M. Görg, "'Der Starke Arm Pharaos'—Beobachtungen zum Belegspektrum einer Metapher in Palästin und Ägypten," in *Hommages à François Daumas* (Montpellier: Université Paul Valéry, 1986), 323–30.

70. Kitchen, *Ramesses II: Royal Inscriptions*, 10; see COS, 2.5A:36. The god Montu was a solar deity, who developed into the role of war god, but was subordinate to Amun, whom many ancient Egyptians viewed as the chief creator deity (E. K. Werner, "Montu," in *The Ancient Gods Speak: A Guide to Egyptian Religion*, ed. D. B. Redford [Oxford: Oxford Univ. Press, 2002], 230–31).

71. See, e.g., K. A. Kitchen, *Ramesses I, Sethos I and Contemporaries* (vol. 1 of *Ramesside Inscriptions: Translated & Annotated*; Series A: Translations; Oxford: Blackwell, 1993), 6, 10; and COS, 2.4F:30.

72. EA 147:12, 286:12, 287:27, 288:14. See translations in W. L. Moran, ed., *The Amarna Letters* (Baltimore: Johns Hopkins Univ. Press, 1992).

73. *ANET*³, 448. On divine revelatory statements in Egypt, see S. Morenz, *Egyptian Religion*, trans. Ann E. Keep (Ithaca, N.Y.: Cornell Univ. Press, 1973), 31–33.

74. *ANET*³, 449–50. Cf. M. Greenberg, *Understanding Exodus* (New York: Behrman, 1969), 130–31.

75. Another explanation has to do with the idea that Exodus was put together from earlier sources or versions, which contained many of the stories now found in Genesis and Exodus. These versions differed in the details of some of the narratives. Thus, the revelation of the name Yahweh in Ex. 6 may well be the first time that one of these sources introduces that name. This is why the text can claim that Abraham, Isaac, and Jacob did not know the name Yahweh. For further discussion of both possibilities, see Propp, *Exodus 1–18*, 266–68, 271–72, 283.

76. All of these come from J. Goody, "Adoption in Cross-Cultural Perspective," *Comparative Studies in Society and History* 2 (1969): 55–78.

77. Cf. J. L. R. Melnyk, "When Israel Was a Child: Ancient Near Eastern Adoption Formulas and the Relationship Between God and Israel," in *History and Interpretation: Essays in Honour of John H. Hayes*, ed. M. P. Graham, W. P. Brown, and J. K. Kuan (JSOTSup 173; Sheffield: Sheffield Academic Press, 1993), 245–59.

78. Propp, *Exodus 1–18*, 273.

79. C. Walker and M. Dick, *The Induction of the Cult Image in Ancient Mesopotamia* (SAALT 1; Helsinki: Neo-Assyrian Text Corpus Project, 2001), 10–13.

80. Incantation tablet 3 (probably from the second quarter of the first millennium B.C.) in ibid., 149.

81. Cf. the "opening of the mouth" ritual in Egypt. On this, see Budge, *Egyptian Magic*, 192–203; D. Lorton, "The Theology of Cult Statues in Ancient Egypt," in *Born in Heaven, Made on Earth: The Making of the Cult Image in the Ancient Near East*, ed. M. B. Dick (Winona Lake, Ind.: Eisenbrauns, 1999), 122–210.

82. On this verse, see V. A. Hurowitz, "Isaiah's Impure Lips and Their Purification in Light of Mouth Purification and Mouth Purity in Akkadian Sources," *HUCA* 60 (1989): 39–89.

83. On this practice at Nuzi in northern Mesopotamia, see J. Paradise, "Daughters as 'Sons' at Nuzi," in *Studies on the Civilization and Culture of Nuzi and the Hurrians*, ed. D. I. Owen and M. A. Morrison (Winona Lake, Ind.: Eisenbrauns, 1987), 2:203–13. For Emar, see T. Kämmerer, "Zur sozialen Stellung der Frau in Emar," *UF* 26 (1994): 169–208; R. Westbrook, "Social Justice and Creative Jurisprudence in Late Bronze Age Syria," *JESHO* 44 (2001): 22–43.

84. See, e.g., D. Arnaud, "Mariage et remariage des femmes chez les Syriens du Moyen-Euphrate," *Semitica* 46 (1996): 12–13. See also R. West-

brook, "Emar and Vicinity," *HANEL*, 1:680–81.

85. S. B. Noegel, "Moses and Magic: Notes on the Book of Exodus," *JANESCU* 24 (1996): 49.

86. J. Quaegebeur, "On the Egyptian Equivalent of Biblical ḥarṭummim," in *Pharaonic Egypt: The Bible and Christianity*, ed. S. Israelit-Groll (Jerusalem: Magnes, 1985), 162–72; R. K. Ritner, *The Mechanics of Ancient Egyptian Magical Practice* (SAOC 54; Chicago: Oriental Institute, 1993), 220–22.

87. *CANE*, 3:1747.

88. *CANE*, 3:1780.

89. Assmann, *Search for God*, 3.

90. Simpson, ed., *Literature of Ancient Egypt*, 191–92; see COS, 1.42:94. See also Noegel, "Moses and Magic," 50–51.

91. J. Black, *The Literature of Ancient Sumer* (Oxford: Oxford Univ. Press, 2004), 197–204. The myth is also known as Inanna and the Gardener; see S. N. Kramer, *History Begins at Sumer*, 3rd ed. (Philadelphia: Univ. of Pennsylvania, 1981), 73.

92. W. W. Hallo and J. J. A. van Dijk, *The Exaltation of Inanna* (YNER 3; New Haven, Conn.: Yale Univ. Press, 1968), 21; see COS, 1.160:519–20.

93. Lesko, *Great Goddesses*, 267–68; Wilkinson, *Complete Gods and Goddesses*, 229.

94. Simpson, ed., *Literature of Ancient Egypt*, 21–24.

95. Wilkinson, *Complete Gods and Goddesses*, 229.

96. See Ritner, *Mechanics*, 119–36. See also Noegel, "Moses and Magic," 48–49; Noegel points out the connection between the narrative in Ex. 7 and the aspect of Egyptian magic described by Ritner.

97. Ritner, *Mechanics*, 128 n. 583.

98. H. Hermann, "Das steinharte Herz," *Jahrbuch für Antike und Christentum* 4 (1961): 77–107; J. E. Currid, "Why Did God Harden Pharaoh's Heart?" *BRev* 9 (Dec 1993): 46–51; N. Shupak, "*Hzq, Kbd, Qšh Leb*: The Hardening of Pharaoh's Heart in Exodus 4:1–15:21 — Seen Negatively in the Bible but Favorably in Egyptian Sources," in *Egypt, Israel, and the Ancient Mediterranean World: Studies in Honor of Donald B. Redford*, ed. G. N. Knoppers and A. Hirsch (Probleme der Ägyptologie 20; Leiden: Brill, 2004), 389–403. Cf. R. R. Wilson, "The Hardening of Pharaoh's Heart," *CBQ* 41 (1979): 18–36; G. K. Beale, "An Exegetical and Theological Consideration of the Hardening of Pharaoh's Heart in Exodus 4–14 and Romans 9," *TJ* 5 (1984): 129–54.

99. See Currid, "Why Did God Harden Pharaoh's Heart?"

100. See Shupak, "*Hzq, Kbd, Qsh Leb*: The Hardening of Pharaoh's Heart." Shupak states that the first view — that the biblical terms relate to the weighing of the heart in the afterlife — is utterly wrong" (401).

101. Ibid., 395.

102. Ibid., 396.

103. For "gnats," Childs opts for mosquitoes (*The Book of Exodus: A Critical, Theological Commentary* [OTL; Philadelphia: Westminster, 1974], 156); Propp for lice (*Exodus 1–18*, 350). With respect

to "flies," scholars often tend to use the Hebrew word *ʿārōb*, without translating it.

104. A. S. Yahuda, *The Language of the Pentateuch in Its Relation to Egyptian* (Oxford: Oxford Univ. Press, 1933), 1:66–67.

105. K. A. Kitchen, *Merenptah and the Late Nineteenth Dynasty* (vol. 4 of *Ramesside Inscriptions: Translated & Annotated*; Oxford: Blackwell, 2003), 24.

106. *HALOT*, 1:212.

107. *CAD*, D 134–35.

108. See, e.g., *COS*, 2.4A:24, 2.4C:27, 2.4E:29.

109. *COS*, 2.119A:301.

110. *COS*, 2.119A:302.

111. See also the comments in *COS* 2.113A:263 n. 25; and M. de Odorico, *The Use of Numbers and Quantifications in the Assyrian Royal Inscriptions* (SAAS 3; Helsinki: Neo-Assyrian Text Corpus Project, 1995).

112. Propp, *Exodus 1–18*, 332. Cf. C. M. Doughty, *Travels in Arabia Deserta* (2 vols.; New York: Random House, 1936), 2:511; Hoffmeier, *Israel in Egypt*, 161 n. 131.

113. See, e.g., the treaty (c. 750 B.C.) between Ashurnerari V and Matiʾilu (Matiʾel) and the Esarhaddon vassal treaties (c. 670 B.C.). For translations, see *ANET*³, 533 (col. iv) and 538 (sec. 39), respectively. On the idea of divine disapproval, see further A. M. Kitz, "The Curse behind the Plague of Boils," *Maarav* 11 (2004): 219–32.

114. On this text, see D. Pardee, *Les textes para-mythologiques* (Ras Shamra-Ougarit 4; Paris: Éditions recherche sur les civilisations, 1988), 119–52. Cf. P. Bordreuil and D. Pardee, "Le Combat de *Baʿlu* avec *Yammu* d'après les textes ougaritiques," *MARI* 7 (1993): 63–70.

115. For numerous references, see *CAD*, Š/2 377–78.

116. See J.-M. Durand, "Le mythologème du combat entre le dieu de l'orage et la mer en Mésopotamie," *MARI* 7 (1993): 41–61.

117. *OIP* 2:85, cited in *CAD*, Š/2 377.

118. Propp, *Exodus 1–18*, 228.

119. Hoffmeier, *Israel in Egypt*, 154–55.

120. Propp, *Exodus 1–18*, 335.

121. See O. Borowski, *Agriculture in Iron Age Israel* (Winona Lake, Ind.: Eisenbrauns, 1987), 37.

122. Ibid.

123. *ANET*³, 538 (sec. 47).

124. The letter is preserved on Papyrus Anastasi V and Sallier I. The translation is from Caminos, *Late-Egyptian Miscellanies*, 247.

125. Cf. T. E. Fretheim, "The Plagues as Ecological Signs of Historical Disaster," *JBL* 110 (1991): 385–96.

126. J. Bright, *A History of Israel*, 3rd ed. (Philadelphia: Westminster, 1981), 330.

127. See W. F. Albright, "The Gezer Calendar," *BASOR* 92 (1943): 16–26; S. Talmon, "The Gezer Calendar and the Seasonal Cycle of Ancient Canaan," in *King, Cult and Calendar in Ancient Israel: Collected Studies* (Jerusalem: Magnes, 1986), 89–112. On other ancient Near Eastern evidence related to this issue, cf. R. S.

Hess, "Multiple-Month Ritual Calendars in the West Semitic World: Emar 446 and Leviticus 23," in *The Future of Biblical Archaeology: Reassessing Methods and Assumptions*, ed. J. K. Hoffmeier and A. Millard (Grand Rapids: Eerdmans, 2004), 233–53.

128. Propp, *Exodus 1–18*, 384. Propp cites an example from the Dead Sea Scrolls. Part of a commentary on Habakkuk (1QpHab 11:4–8) refers to the "Wicked Priest" who "attacked the 'Righteous Teacher' on a day that the latter, but not the former considered Yom Kippur" (ibid.).

129. See the beginning of the Mishnah *Rosh Hashanah*; see also Sarna, *Exploring Exodus*, 81–85.

130. E. Reiner, "Plague Amulets and House Blessings," *JNES* 19 (1960): 148–55.

131. D. Bodi, *The Book of Ezekiel and the Poem of Erra* (OBO 104; Freiburg: Universitätsverlag, 1991), 52–68.

132. Ibid., 109. This excerpt is from tablet V of the poem, lines 57–58.

133. *COS*, 3.46:116–17.

134. See M. Liverani, "A Seasonal Pattern for the Amarna Letters," in *Lingering Over Words: Studies in Ancient Near Eastern Literature in Honor of William L. Moran*, ed. T. Abusch, J. Huehnergard, and P. Steinkeller (Atlanta: Scholars Press, 1990), 337–48.

135. Hoffmeier, *Israel in Egypt*, 179–81.

136. On the Wadi Tumilat, see C. Redmount, "On an Egyptian/Asiatic Frontier: An Archaeological History of the Wadi Tumilat" (Ph.D. diss., Univ. of Chicago, 1989).

137. Spalinger, *War in Ancient Egypt*, 147–48.

138. Ibid., 149–50.

139. M. Broshi and R. Gophna, "Middle Bronze Age II Palestine: Its Settlements and Population," *BASOR* 261 (1986): 73–90.

140. M. Broshi and I. Finkelstein, "The Population of Palestine in Iron Age II," *BASOR* 287 (1992): 47–60.

141. See E. L. Greenstein, "Kirta," in *Ugaritic Narrative Poetry*, ed. S. B. Parker (SBLWAW 9; Atlanta: Scholars Press, 1997), 9–48.

142. On this point, see the comments of G. A. Rendsburg, "An Additional Note to Two Recent Articles on the Number of People in the Exodus from Egypt and the Large Numbers in Numbers I and XXVI," *VT* 51 (2001): 392–96.

143. Propp cites a number of ancient sources (Pseudepigrapha, Josephus, even Gal. 3:17) that accept the inclusion of the time in Canaan within the 430 years. Propp, himself, finds the shorter version — the one that omits "in the land of Canaan" — to be original (*Exodus 1–18*, 365).

144. J. H. Breasted, *Ancient Records of Egypt* (Leipzig: Harrassowitz, 1906–1907), 3.226–28 (§§538–542).

145. See Halpern, "Exodus from Egypt," 95–98.

146. See J. Tigay, "On the Meaning of *t(w)tpt*," *JBL* 101 (1982): 321–31.

147. Cf. Lev. 25:47–49. The classic study on this is R. Yaron, "Redemption of Persons in the Ancient Near East," *RIDA* 6 (1959): 155–76; see also R.

Westbrook, "The Development of Law in the Ancient Near East: Slave and Master in Ancient Near Eastern Law," *Chicago-Kent Law Review* 70 (1995): 1651–56.

148. A. H. Gardiner, "The Ancient Military Road between Egypt and Palestine," *JEA* 6 (1920): 99–116.

149. See Hoffmeier, *Israel in Egypt*, 183–87; M. Abd el-Maksoud, *Tell Heboua (1981–1991)* (Paris: Éditions recherche sur les civilisations, 1998).

150. COS, 2.2A:8 (Thutmose III); COS, 2.4A:24 (Seti I); *ANET³*, 255 (Ramesses II). It should be noted that Tjaru is sometimes translated as "Sile," the name of a Roman-period fortress, which actually may or may not be the same as Tjaru (see Hoffmeier, *Israel in Egypt*, 196 n. 112).

151. T. Dothan, "Deir el-Balahʾ," *NEAEHL* 1:343–47; idem, "The Impact of Egypt on Canaan during the 18th and 19th Dynasties in the Light of the Excavations at Deir el-Balahʾ," in *Egypt, Israel, Sinai*, ed. A. F. Rainey (Tel Aviv: Tel Aviv Univ., 1987), 121–35, esp. 128–29.

152. Dothan, "Impact of Egypt," 129.

153. Hoffmeier, *Israel in Egypt*, 199.

154. See the extensive discussion in ibid., 199–222.

155. B. Batto, "The Reed Sea: *Requiscat in Pace*," *JBL* 102 (1983): 27–35.

156. For a summary of these, see Hoffmeier, *Israel in Egypt*, 210–12.

157. J. K. Hoffmeier, *Ancient Israel in Sinai: The Evidence for the Authenticity of the Wilderness Tradition* (Oxford: Oxford Univ. Press, 2005), 85–89.

158. Cross, *Canaanite Myth*, 156–63.

159. Ibid., 149.

160. See, e.g., *ANET³*, 134; COS, 1.86:249; Cross, *Canannite Myth*, 151; M. Weinfeld, "'Rider of the Clouds' and 'Gatherer of the Clouds,'" *JANES* 5 (1973): 421–26.

161. For the ancients, lightning would have been seen as akin to fire (Propp, *Exodus 1–18*, 549).

162. W. F. Albright, "Exploring in Sinai with the University of California African Expedition," *BASOR* 109 (1948): 16.

163. A. Sneh, T. Weissbrod, and I. Perath, "Evidence for an Ancient Egyptian Frontier Canal," *American Scientist* 63 (1975): 542–48. See also Hoffmeier, *Israel in Egypt*, 164–75.

164. Hoffmeier, *Israel in Egypt*, 170.

165. CANE, 1:295.

166. Ibid., 296. See also A. R. Schulman, "The Egyptian Chariotry: A Reexamination," *Journal of the American Research Center in Egypt* 2 (1963): 75–98; idem, "Chariots, Chariotry, and Hyksos," *Journal of the Society for the Study of Egyptian Antiquities* 10 (1979–1980): 105–53.

167. COS, 2.5A:34.

168. See M. Weinfeld, "Divine Intervention in War in Ancient Israel and in the Ancient Near East," in *History, Historiography and Interpretation: Studies in Biblical and Cuneiform Literature*, ed. H. Tadmor and M. Weinfeld (Jerusalem: Magnes, 1986), 121–47.

169. Ibid., 144.

170. Simpson, ed., *Literature of Ancient Egypt*, 17–18.

171. J. Braun, *Music in Ancient Israel/Palestine: Archaeological, Written, and Comparative Sources*, trans. D. W. Stott (The Bible in Its World; Grand Rapids: Eerdmans, 2002), 113–64.

172. C. Meyers, *Exodus* (NCBC; Cambridge: Cambridge Univ. Press, 2005), 117.

173. C. Meyers, "Mother to Muse: An Archaeomusicological Study of Women's Performance in Ancient Israel," in *Recycling Biblical Figures*, ed. A. Brenner and J. W. van Henten (Leiden: Deo, 1999), 66–73.

174. See Noegel, "Moses and Magic," 55–56.

175. See, in general, D. R. Redford, "Execration and Execration Texts," *ABD*, 2:681–82; Ritner, *Mechanics*, 136–42.

176. J. M. Weinstein, "Egyptian Relations with Palestine in the Middle Kingdom," *BASOR* 217 (1975): 11–13.

177. *ANET³*, 329.

178. See The Baʿlu Myth in COS, 1.86:241–74; see also Propp, *Exodus 1–18*, 557–59.

179. Smith, *Baal Cycle*, 115.

180. For further discussion of this point with more extensive consideration of the Ugaritic evidence, though from a slightly different perspective, see B. F. Batto, *Slaying the Dragon: Mythmaking in the Biblical Tradition* (Louisville: Westminster John Knox, 1992), 128–52.

181. For a selection of such texts, see M. Nissinen, *Prophets and Prophecy in the Ancient Near East* (SBLWAW 12; Atlanta: Society of Biblical Literature, 2003), 13–52.

182. M. A. Powell, "Weights and Measures," *ABD*, 6:903.

183. Sarna, *Exploring Exodus*, 117.

184. See the discussion in ibid., 117–18.

185. See Durham, *Exodus*, 230.

186. E. Dombradi, *Die Darstellung des Rechtsaustrags in den altbabylonischen Prozessurkunden* (FAOS 20; Stuttgart: Steiner, 1996), 1:295–302.

187. "The wide agreement of terms used at different times shows how closely pre-judicial and judicial situations resembled each other. In rhetoric the pre-judicial quarrel was carried on much like a quarrel conducted according to the procedures of the official court" (H. J. Boecker, *Law and the Administration of Justice in the Old Testament and Ancient Near East*, trans. J. Moiser [London: SPCK, 1980], 33).

188. See, e.g., *ANET³*, 133; cf. Smith, "Baal Cycle," 95, 116.

189. Cross, *Canaanite Myth*, 26–28.

190. For ancient Israel, see I. M. Young, "Israelite Literacy: Interpreting the Evidence, Part I," *VT* 48 (1998): 239–53; idem, "Israelite Literacy: Interpreting the Evidence, Part II," *VT* 48 (1998): 408–22; idem, "Israelite Literacy and Inscriptions: A Response to Richard Hess," *VT* 55 (2005): 565–68; R. S. Hess, "Literacy in Iron Age Israel," in *Windows into Old Testament History: Evidence, Argument, and the Crisis of "Biblical Israel"* (Grand Rapids: Eerdmans, 2002), 82–102. For Egypt, see J. Baines and C. J. Eyre,

"Four Notes on Literacy," *GM* 61 (1983): 65–96; B. M. Bryan, "Evidence for Female Literacy from Theban Tombs of the New Kingdom," *Bulletin of the Egyptological Seminar* 6 (1985): 17–32; L. H. Lesko, "Some Comments on Ancient Egyptian Literacy and Literati," in *Studies in Egyptology: Presented to Miriam Lichtheim*, ed. S. Israelit-Groll (Jerusalem: Magnes, 1990), 2:656–67. For Mesopotamia, see C. Wilcke, *Wer las und schrieb in Babylonien und Assyrien: Überlegungen zur Literalität im Alten Zweistromland* (SBAW Philosophisch-historische Klasse, Jahrgang 2000, Heft 6; Munich: Bayerische Akademie der Wissenschaften, 2000).

191. P. T. Daniels and W. Bright, eds., *The World's Writing Systems* (Oxford: Oxford Univ. Press, 1996), 33, 73.

192. Ibid., 2, 261. Cf. B. Sass, *The Genesis of the Alphabet and Its Development in the Second Millennium B.C.* (Wiesbaden: Harrassowitz, 1988); idem, *Studie alphabetica: On the Origin and Early History of the Northwest Semitic, South Semitic and Greek Alphabets* (Freiburg: Universitätsverlag, 1991).

193. E. Himelfarb, "First Alphabet Found in Egypt," *Archaeology* 53 (Jan/Feb 2000): 21; S. Feldman, "Not as Simple as A-B-C: Earliest Use of Alphabet Found in Egypt," *BAR* 26 (Jan/Feb 2000): 12.

194. P. K. McCarter Jr., "Hebrew," in *The Cambridge Encyclopedia of the World's Ancient Languages*, ed. R. D. Woodard (Cambridge: Cambridge Univ. Press, 2004), 319.

195. D. Pardee, "Canaanite Dialects," in *The Cambridge Encyclopedia of the World's Ancient Languages*, 386–90.

196. Hess, "Literacy," 95.

197. Young, "Israelite Literacy … Part I," 241–44.

198. For the Egyptian estimate, see Baines and Eyre, "Four Notes," 67. But see the rebuttal in Lesko, "Some Comments."

199. See, e.g., D. Arnaud, "La Syrie du moyen-Euphrate sous le protectorat hittite: contrats de droit privé," *AuOr* 5 (1987): 229–31 text no. 11.

200. See D. Arnaud, *Emar VI: Recherches au pays d'Aštata* (Paris: Éditions recherche sur les civilisations, 1985–87), texts 83 and 217 in volumes 3 and 4.

201. On the Assyrian texts, see S. Parpola and K. Watanabe, *Neo-Assyrian Treaties and Loyalty Oaths* (SAA 2; Helsinki: Helsinki Univ. Press, 1988).

202. This list comes from G. Beckman, *Hittite Diplomatic Texts* (SBLWAW 7; Atlanta: Scholars Press, 1996), 2–3.

203. For possible reasons, see J. H. Walton, *Covenant: God's Purpose, God's Plan* (Grand Rapids: Zondervan, 1994), 13–46.

204. For a helpful overview of issues related to the Ten Commandments, see M. Weinfeld, "The Decalogue: Its Significance, Uniqueness, and Place in Israel's Tradition," in *Religion and Law: Biblical-Judaic and Islamic Perspectives*, ed. E. B. Firmage,

B. G. Weiss, and J. W. Welch (Winona Lake, Ind.: Eisenbrauns, 1990), 3–47.

205. B. Alster, *Wisdom of Ancient Sumer* (Bethesda, Md.: CDL, 2005), 60–69.

206. *COS*, 2.12:60–61.

207. Ibid.

208. This view is articulated well in J. H. Walton, *Ancient Near Eastern Thought and the Old Testament* (Grand Rapids: Baker, forthcoming).

209. See R. Byrne, "Lie Back and Think of Judah: The Reproductive Politics of Pillar Figurines," *NEA* 67 (2004): 137–51.

210. On this point in general, see J. M. Hadley, *The Cult of Asherah in Ancient Israel and Judah: Evidence for a Hebrew Goddess* (Cambridge: Cambridge Univ. Press, 2000); W. G. Dever, *Did God Have a Wife? Archaeology and Folk Religion in Ancient Israel* (Grand Rapids: Eerdmans, 2005).

211. O. Keel and C. Uehlinger, *Gods, Goddesses, and Images of God in Ancient Israel*, trans. T. H. Trapp (Minneapolis: Fortress, 1998), 195–98.

212. T. N. D. Mettinger, "Israelite Aniconism: Developments and Origins," in *The Image and the Book: Iconic Cults, Aniconism, and the Rise of Book Religion in Israel and the Ancient Near East*, ed. K. van der Toorn (Contributions to Biblical Exegesis & Theology 21; Leuven: Peeters, 1997), 176–77.

213. On aniconism, see T. N. D. Mettinger, *No Graven Image? Israelite Aniconism in its Ancient Near Eastern Context* (ConBOT 42; Stockholm, 1995), 13–38; Mettinger distinguishes between what he calls *de facto* aniconism (worship practice that did not involve images) and programmatic aniconism (worship ideology that demanded there be no images).

214. Translation from S. Dalley, *Myths from Mesopotamia* (Oxford: Oxford Univ. Press, 1989), 236.

215. On this point, see the comments of R. S. Hendel, "Aniconism and Anthropomorphism in Ancient Israel," in *The Image and the Book: Iconic Cults, Aniconism, and the Rise of Book Religion in Israel and the Ancient Near East*, ed. K. van der Toorn (Contributions to Biblical Exegesis & Theology 21; Leuven: Peeters, 1997), 205–28.

216. For a list of statues and figurines that may be representations of Yahweh, see ibid., 212–18. For a possible representation of Yahweh as a bull, see A. Mazar, "The 'Bull Site'—An Iron Age I Open Cult Place," *BASOR* 247 (1982): 27–42. For discussion of a possible drawing of Yahweh at the site of Kuntillet ʿAjrud, see B. B. Schmid, "The Aniconic Tradition," in *The Triumph of Elohim: From Yahwisms to Judaisms*, ed. D. V. Edelman (Kampen: Pharos, 1995), 75–105. For other possibilities, see B. Sass, "The Pre-Exilic Hebrew Seals: Iconism vs. Aniconism," in *Studies in the Iconography of Northwest Semitic Inscribed Seals*, ed. B. Sass and C. Uehlinger (Göttingen: Vandenhoeck & Ruprecht, 1993), 194–256, esp. 232–34.

217. See A. Berlejung, "Washing the Mouth: The Consecration of Divine Images in Mesopotamia," in *The Image and the Book: Iconic Cults, Aniconism, and the Rise of Book Religion in Israel and the*

Ancient Near East, ed. K. van der Toorn (Contributions to Biblical Exegesis & Theology 21; Leuven: Peeters, 1997), 45–72.

218. Ibid., 72.

219. For further discussion of this point, see Walton, *Ancient Near Eastern Thought.*

220. Roth, "Age at Marriage."

221. See the explanation of Meyers, *Exodus*, 172–73.

222. See S. Lafont, "La procédure par serment au Proche-Orient ancien," in *Jurer et maudire: Pratiques politiques et usages juridiques du serment dans le Proche-Orient ancien*, ed. S. Lafont (Paris: L'Harmattan, 1997), 185–98.

223. All of these examples are listed by Sarna, *Exploring Exodus*, 147.

224. Meyers, *Exodus*, 132–33.

225. R. Albertz, "Hintergrund und Bedeutung des Elternsgebots im Dekalog," *ZAW* 90 (1978): 348–74; E. Otto, "Biblische Altersversorgung im altorientalischen Rechtsvergleich," *ZABR* 1 (1995): 83–110.

226. M. Stol, "The Care of the Elderly in Mesopotamia in the Old Babylonian Period," in *The Care of the Elderly in the Ancient Near East*, ed. M. Stol and S. P. Vleeming (SHCANE 14; Leiden: Brill, 1998), 62–63; K. R. Veenhof, "Old Assyrian and Ancient Anatolian Evidence for the Care of the Elderly," in *The Care of the Elderly in the Ancient Near East*, 127–36.

227. Ibid., 129–30.

228. Ibid., 71.

229. "It is impossible to determine whether the verse in the Decalogue, Exod 20:13, refers to any slaying or solely to intentional homicide" (Barmash, *Homicide*, 121 n. 15).

230. See the discussion in Barmash, *Homicide*, 20–70.

231. R. Westbrook, "Adultery in Ancient Near Eastern Law," *RB* 97 (1990): 542–80.

232. For discussions related to this point, cf. M. Malul, *Knowledge, Control and Sex: Studies in Biblical Thought, Culture and Worldview* (Tel Aviv: Archaeological Center Publications, 2002), 313–74; J. M. Sprinkle, "Sexuality, Sexual Ethics," in *DOPT*, 741–53.

233. See Malul, *Knowledge, Control and Sex*, 299–310.

234. Translation from Roth, *Law Collections*, 105. The phrase "the wife's master" refers to the wife's husband.

235. Translation from ibid., 158.

236. B. Wells, "Sex, Lies, and Virginal Rape: The Slandered Bride and False Accusation in Deuteronomy," *JBL* 124 (2005): 63–70.

237. B. S. Jackson, "Reflections on Biblical Criminal Law," in *Essays in Jewish and Comparative Legal History* (SJLA 10; Leiden: Brill, 1975), 59–61; S. E. Loewenstamm, "The Laws of Adultery and Murder in Biblical and Mesopotamian Law," in *Comparative Studies in Biblical and Ancient Oriental Literatures* (AOAT 204; Kevelaer: Butzon & Bercker, 1980), 146–53.

238. See B. Wells, *The Law of Testimony in the Pentateuchal Codes* (BZABR 4; Wiesbaden: Harrassowitz, 2004), 112–16.

239. I. L. Seeligmann, "Zur Terminologie für das Gerichtsverfahren im Wortschatz des biblischen Hebräisch," in *Hebräische Wortforschung: Festschrift zum 80. Geburtstag von Walter Baumgartner*, ed. B. Hartmann et al. (VTSup 16; Leiden: Brill, 1967), 262–63.

240. For further discussion of false testimony in Israel and Mesopotamia, see Wells, *Law of Testimony*, 133–57.

241. V. Donbaz, "An Old Assyrian Treaty from Kültepe," *JCS* 57 (2005): 63–68.

242. This translation is adapted from ibid., 65.

243. For a discussion of scholarly problems related to this collection of laws, see R. Westbrook, "What Is the Covenant Code?" in *Theory and Method in Biblical and Cuneiform Law: Revision, Interpolation and Development*, ed. B. M. Levinson (JSOTSup 181; Sheffield: Sheffield Academic Press, 1994), 15–36.

244. See G. C. Chirichigno, *Debt-Slavery in Israel and the Ancient Near East* (JSOTSup 141; Sheffield: Sheffield Academic Press, 1993), 182–84; E. Otto, review of J. Van Seters, *A Law Book for the Diaspora: Revision in the Study of the Covenant Code* (*Review of Biblical Literature* [www.bookreviews.org]). Chirichigno's book has extensive discussions of the ancient Near Eastern laws and practices related to debt-slavery.

245. R. Westbrook, "Slave and Master," 1643–45.

246. The text is Emar 16. See Arnaud, *Emar VI*, text 16 in volumes 3 and 4.

247. R. Westbrook, "The Female Slave," in *Gender and Law in the Hebrew Bible and the Ancient Near East*, ed. Victor H. Matthews, Bernard M. Levinson, and Tikva Frymer-Kensky (JSOTSup 262; Sheffield: Sheffield Academic Press, 1998), 215–20, 235–37.

248. Ibid.

249. Westbrook uses the two categories of revenge (physical penalties) and ransom (financial penalties) to describe the options available to victims (*Studies in Biblical and Cuneiform Law* [CahRB 26; Paris: Gabalda, 1988], 39–88). The latter could choose which type of penalty to inflict on the guilty party. In the case of murder, the victim's family could choose the death penalty as their form of revenge.

250. Translation from Barmash, *Homicide*, 63.

251. For these and other possibilities, see C. Houtman, "Eine schwangere Frau als Opfer eines Handgemenges (Exodus 21,22–25)," in *Studies in the Book of Exodus*, ed. M. Vervenne (Leuven: Peeters, 1996), 381–97; T. Frymer-Kensky, "Israel," *HANEL*, 2:1033.

252. LL d and e (see Roth, *Law Collections*, 26–27 for this enumeration), LH 209–214, HL 17–18, and MAL 50–51.

253. T. Frymer-Kensky, "Tit for Tat: The Principle of Equal Retribution in Near Eastern and Biblical Law," *BA* 43 (1980): 230–34.

254. See Westbrook, *Studies*, 39–88.

255. See J. J. Finkelstein, *The Ox That Gored* (Transactions of the American Philosophical Society 71; Philadelphia: American Philosophical Society, 1981), 17–20.

256. Bottéro, "The 'Code' of Ḥammurabi," 156–84.

257. For the view that Exodus rejects it, see S. M. Paul, *Studies in the Book of the Covenant in the Light of Cuneiform and Biblical Law* (VTSup 18; Leiden: Brill, 1970), 82–83; D. P. Wright, "The Laws of Hammurabi as a Source for the Covenant Collection (Exodus 20:23–23:19)," *Maarav* 10 (2003): 22, 24–25. For the opposite view, see Westbrook, *Studies*, 57–61.

258. R. Westbrook, "A Matter of Life and Death," *JANES* 25 (1997): 61–70.

259. On these provisions, see E. Otto, "Die rechtshistorische Entwicklung des Depositenrechts in altorientalischen und altisraelitischen Rechtskorpora," in *Kontinuum und Proprium: Studien zur Sozial- und Rechtsgeschichte des Alten Orients und des Alten Testaments* (OBC 8; Wiesbaden: Harrassowitz, 1996), 139–63.

260. B. M. Levinson, *Deuteronomy and the Hermeneutics of Legal Innovation* (New York: Oxford Univ. Press, 1997), 112 n. 37.

261. See ibid., 112–3; Wells, *Law of Testimony*, 100.

262. On Israel, see P. K. McCarter Jr., "The River Ordeal in Israelite Literature," *HTR* 66 (1973): 403–12. On Mesopotamia and the rest of the ancient Near East, see T. Frymer-Kensky, "The Judicial Ordeal in the Ancient Near East" (Ph.D. diss., Yale Univ., 1977).

263. See A. G. McDowell, *Jurisdiction in the Workmen's Community of Deir El-Medina* (Egyptologische Uitgaven 5; Leiden: Nederlands Instituut voor het Nabije Oosten, 1990), 107–41; Jasnow, "New Kingdom," *HANEL*, 1:347–49.

264. R. Jas, *Neo-Assyrian Judicial Procedures* (SAAS 5; Helsinki: Neo-Assyrian Text Corpus Project, 1996), 17–19 (no. 7), 21–24 (nos. 10 and 11).

265. Frymer-Kensky, "Tit for Tat."

266. R. Westbrook, "The Deposit Law of Exodus 22,6–12," *ZAW* 106 (1994): 390–403.

267. See, e.g., Dombradi, *Darstellung des Rechtsaustrags*, 1:138–50.

268. See S. A. Nigosian, "Anti-Divinatory Statements in Biblical Codes," *Theological Review* 18 (1997): 21–34.

269. J. A. Scurlock, "Magic (ANE)," *ABD*, 4:465.

270. Roth, *Law Collections*, 172.

271. A. M. Kitz, "The Hebrew Terminology of Lot Casting and Its Ancient Near Eastern Context," *CBQ* 62 (2000): 207–14.

272. Scurlock, "Magic (ANE)," *ABD*, 4:470.

273. Roth, *Law Collections*, 16.

274. Ibid., 133.

275. N. Lohfink, "Poverty in the Laws of the Ancient Near East," *TS* 52 (1991): 34.

276. On this point, see S. Hermann, "Weisheit im Bundesbuch: Eine Miszelle zu Ex 23,1–9," in *Alttestamentlicher Glaube und Biblische Theologie: Festschrift für Horst Dietrich Preuß*, ed. J. Hausmann and H.-J. Zobel (Stuttgart: Kohlhammer, 1992), 56–58.

277. *AEL*, 2:158–59 (all from Chapter 20); see *COS*, 1.47:120.

278. See M. Haran, *Temples and Temple-Service in Ancient Israel: An Inquiry into the Character of Cult Phenomena and the Historical Setting of the Priestly School* (Oxford: Clarendon, 1978), 295–96; M. S. Smith, *The Pilgrimage Pattern in Exodus* (Sheffield: Sheffield Academic Press, 1997), 60–61.

279. See D. E. Fleming, "The Israelite Festival Calendar and Emar's Ritual Archive," *RB* 116 (1999): 8–34.

280. J. Milgrom, "'You Shall Not Boil a Kid in Its Mother's Milk': An Archaeological Myth Destroyed," *BRev* 1 (Fall 1985): 48–55.

281. See, e.g., J. P. Hyatt, *Exodus* (NCBC; Grand Rapids: Eerdmans, 1971), 249–50.

282. Milgrom, "'You Shall Not Boil,'" 50–51. See also R. J. Ratner and B. Zuckerman, "On Rereading the 'Kid in Milk' Inscription," *BRev* 1 (Fall 1985): 56–58.

283. Ibid., 54–55.

284. See D. Charpin et al., *Archives épistolaires de Mari I/2* (ARMT 26/2; Paris: Éditions recherche sur les civilisations, 1988), 32–34; M. Anbar, "Deux cérémonies d'alliance dans Ex 24 à la lumière des Archives royales de Mari," *UF* 30 (1998): 1–4.

285. N. M. Sarna, *Exodus* (JPS Torah Commentary; Philadelphia: Jewish Publication Society, 1991), 157.

286. Ibid.

287. See *CAD*, B 286–89 for numerous ancient Near Eastern examples. For "house of Yahweh," see, e.g., Ex. 23:19; 34:26; Deut. 23:19; Josh. 6:24; Judg. 19:18; 1 Sam. 1:7, 24.

288. E. Matsushima, "Divine Statues in Ancient Mesopotamia: Their Fashioning and Clothing and Their Interaction with the Society," in *Official Cult and Popular Religion in the Ancient Near East*, ed. E. Matsushima (Heidelberg: Universitätsverlag C. Winter, 1993), 209–19.

289. See B. A. Levine, "The Descriptive Tabernacle Texts of the Pentateuch," *JAOS* 85 (1965): 308.

290. On this view and the Near Eastern parallels, see V. A. Hurowitz, *I Have Built You an Exalted House: Temple Building in the Bible in Light of Mesopotamian and Northwest Semitic Writings* (JSOTSup 115; Sheffield: Sheffield Academic Press, 1992), 168–70.

291. C. L. Seow, "The Designation of the Ark in Priestly Theology," *HAR* 8 (1985): 185–98.

292. See R. de Vaux, "Ark of the Covenant and Tent of Reunion," in *The Bible and the Ancient Near East*, trans. D. McHugh (Garden City, N.Y.: Doubleday, 1971), 136–51; C. L. Seow, "Ark of the Covenant," *ABD*, 1:388–89.

293. On these creatures and on ancient Near Eastern representations of other composite creatures, see O. Keel, *The Symbolism of the Biblical World* (New York: Seabury, 1978), 167–71; E. Bloch-Smith, "Solomon's Temple: The Politics of Ritual Space," in *Sacred Time, Sacred Place: Archaeology and the Religion of Israel*, ed. B. M. Gittlen (Winona Lake, Ind.: Eisenbrauns, 2002), 85–86; J. G. Westenholz, *Dragons, Monsters and Fabulous Beasts* (Jerusalem: Bible Lands Museum, 2004).

294. See Milgrom, *Leviticus 1–16*, 2092.

295. See C. L. Meyers, *The Tabernacle Menorah* (ASOR Diss. Series 2; Missoula, Mont.: Scholars Press, 1976), 57–93.

296. Ibid., 79.

297. Ibid., 84.

298. See C. L. Meyers, *The Tabernacle Menorah: A Synthetic Study of a Symbol from the Biblical Cult*, 2nd ed. (Piscataway, N.J.: Gorgias Press, 2003), 95–130.

299. On the temple, see E. Bloch-Smith, "'Who Is the King of Glory?': Solomon's Temple and Its Symbolism," in *Scripture and Other Artifacts: Essays on the Bible and Archaeology in Honor of Philip J. King*, ed. M. D. Coogan, J. C. Exum, and L. E. Stager (Louisville: Westminster John Knox, 1994), 18–31. See also the literature cited in M. S. Smith, "Like Deities, Like Temples (Like People)," in *Temple and Worship in Biblical Israel*, ed. J. Day (Library of Hebrew Bible/Old Testament Studies 422; London: T. & T. Clark, 2005), 7 n. 12.

300. On these and the subsequent parallels, see G. J. Wenham, "Sanctuary Symbolism in the Garden of Eden Story," in *"I Studied Inscriptions from Before the Flood": Ancient Near Eastern, Literary, and Linguistic Approaches to Genesis 1–11*, ed. R. S. Hess and D. T. Tsumura (Sources for Biblical and Theological Study 4; Winona Lake, Ind.: Eisenbrauns, 1994), 399–404.

301. Homan, *To Your Tents*, 155.

302. Cassuto, *Exodus*, 353–54.

303. Sarna, *Exodus*, 157–58; Homan, *To Your Tents*, 155–56.

304. On these texts, see D. E. Fleming, "Mari's Large Public Tent and the Priestly Tent Sanctuary," *VT* 50 (2000): 484–98.

305. See ibid.

306. See, e.g., S. Gitin, "Incense Altars from Ekron, Israel and Judah: Context and Typology," *EI* 20 (1989): 52–67.

307. *OEANE*, 3:95.

308. See R. R. Stieglitz, "Commodity Prices at Ugarit," *JAOS* 99 (1979): 19; C. van Dam, *The Urim and Thummim: A Means of Revelation in Ancient Israel* (Winona Lake, Ind.: Eisenbrauns, 1997), 56–57, 64–67.

309. Ibid., 76–80.

310. See the collection in N. Avigad and B. Sass, *Corpus of West Semitic Stamp Seals* (Jerusalem: Israel Academy of Sciences and Humanities, 1997).

311. Van Dam, *Urim and Thummim*, 71–76.

312. For an overview of interpretations, see ibid., 9–38.

313. Ibid., 221–32; quote from 232.

314. See, e.g., the comments on the faience die at Tel Dan (mentioned below) in King and Stager, *Life in Biblical Israel*, 329–30.

315. A. Biran, *Biblical Dan* (Jerusalem: Israel Exploration Society, 1994), 199.

316. See Kitz, "Hebrew Terminology for Lot Casting"; A. Taggar-Cohen, "The Casting of Lots among the Hittites in Light of Ancient Near Eastern Parallels," *JANES* 29 (2002): 97–103, although Taggar-Cohen doubts that practices specifically referred to as the casting of lots were forms of divination, which is exactly what the Urim and Thummim seem to be. Cf. W. Horowitz and V. A. Hurowitz, "Urim and Thummim in Light of a Psephomancy Ritual from Assur (LKA 137)," *JANES* 24 (1992): 95–115.

317. Hoffmeier, *Ancient Israel in Sinai*, 217; C. N. Reeves, *The Complete Tutankhamun: The King, the Tomb, the Royal Treasure* (London: Thames & Hudson, 1990), 154.

318. V. W. Turner, "Religious Specialists," in *Magic, Witchcraft, and Religion: An Anthropological Study of the Supernatural*, ed. A. C. Lehmann and J. E. Myers (Palo Alto, CA: Mayfield, 1985), 81–88.

319. G. J. Wenham, *The Book of Leviticus* (NICOT; Grand Rapids: Eerdmans, 1979), 18–75.

320. See, e.g., D. E. Fleming, *The Installation of Baal's High Priestess at Emar: A Window on Ancient Syrian Religion* (HSS 42; Atlanta: Scholars Press, 1992); COS, 1.222:427–31.

321. COS, 1.123:433.

322. Cf. the anointing rituals described in D. E. Fleming, "The Biblical Tradition of Anointing Priests," *JBL* 117 (1998): 401–14.

323. Powell, "Weights and Measures," 6:904.

324. See S. Gitin, "The Four-Horned Altar and Sacred Space: An Archaeological Perspective," in *Sacred Time, Sacred Place: Archaeology and the Religion of Israel*, ed. B. M. Gittlen (Winona Lake, Ind.: Eisenbrauns, 2002), 95–123, esp. 96–101.

325. Ibid., 99.

326. A. Ben-David, "The Philistine Talent from Ashdod, the Ugarit Talent from Ras Shamra, the "PYM" and the N-Ṣ-P," *UF* 11 (1979): 29–45; see also Powell, "Weights and Measures," 6:906.

327. Powell, "Weights and Measures," 6:906–7.

328. E. Shany, "A New Unpublished Beqaᶜ Weight in the Collection of the Pontifical Biblical Institute, Jerusalem, Israel," *PEQ* 99 (1967): 54–58. The calculations assume that one ounce is equal to 28.35 grams.

329. See, e.g., I. Cornelius, *The Iconography of the Canaanite Gods Reshef and Ba'al: Late Bronze and Iron Age I Periods (c. 1500–1000 B.C.E.)* (OBO 140; Göttingen: Vandenhoeck & Ruprecht, 1994), 112–24, 226–29, and elsewhere; and Keel and Uehlinger, *Gods, Goddesses, and Images of God*, 191–94.

330. Keel and Uehlinger, *Gods, Goddesses, and Images of God*, 191–94.

331. See, e.g., the use of animals that symbolized attributes of a deity, the use of trees or plants, and the use of astral bodies to represent gods and goddesses, even though the depicted items were not considered to be the deities themselves (ibid., 133–75).

332. G. J. Janzen, "The Character of the Calf and Its Cult in Exodus 32," *CBQ* 52 (1990): 597–607.

333. *HALOT*, 2:1019. The notion of laughing comes mainly in the Qal stem; the other concepts occur mainly in the Piel and can generally be distinguished by their use or non-use of the direct object marker and certain prepositions (see ibid.).

334. See the comments along this line in Janzen, "Character of the Calf."

335. Ibid., 597–99.

336. See, e.g., J. J. Finkelstein, "Some New *Misharum* Material and its Implications," in *Studies in Honour of Benno Landsberger on His Seventy-Fifth Birthday*, ed. H. G. Güterbock and T. Jacobsen (AS 16; Chicago: Univ. of Chicago Press, 1965), 233–51.

337. Smith, "Baal Cycle," 156; see COS, 1.86:270.

338. A different approach comes from D. Frankel, "The Destruction of the Golden Calf: A New Solution," *VT* 44 (1994): 330–39. Frankel argues that the first part of v. 20—about Moses taking the golden calf and burning it—should actually be placed at the end of v. 20. This would mean that the actions of grinding, putting dust in water, and making the Israelites drink all apply not to the golden calf but to the tablets that Moses smashes as he descends the mountain.

339. S. M. Paul, "Heavenly Tablets and the Book of Life," *JANES* 5 (1973): 345–53.

340. Ibid., 346.

341. Ibid., 345.

342. Ibid.

343. For a detailed discussion of this festival, see M. E. Cohen, *The Cultic Calendars of the Ancient Near East* (Bethesda, Md.: CDL, 1993), 400–453. Cf. J. Bidmead, *The Akitu Festival* (Piscataway, N.J.: Gorgias, 2002).

344. Roth, *Law Collections*, 137, 139.

345. Hadley, *Cult of Asherah*. See also S. M. Olyan, *Asherah and the Cult of Yahweh in Israel* (SBLMS 34; Atlanta: Scholars Press, 1988), 1–37.

346. For a concise discussion of this site and the textual finds there, see Z. Meshel, "Kuntillet 'Ajrud," *ABD*, 4:103–9. A similar reference to the goddess Asherah was found in a tomb inscription (late eighth century B.C.) at Khirbet El-Qom in southern Judah. See W. G. Dever, "Iron Age Epigraphic Material from the Area of Khirbet El-Kôm," *HUCA* 40–41 (1970): 139–204; cf. Z. Zevit, *The Religions of Ancient Israel: A Synthesis of Parallactic Approaches* (London: Continuum, 2001), 359–70.

347. On how to distinguish stones with cultic significance from other stones, see E. Bloch-Smith, "*Maṣṣēbôt* in the Israelite Cult: An Argument for Rendering Implicit Cultic Criteria Explicit," in *Temple and Worship in Biblical Israel*, ed. J. Day (Library of Hebrew Bible/Old Testament Studies 422; London: T. & T. Clark, 2005), 28–39.

348. See Zevit, *Religions of Ancient Israel*, 217–18.

349. W. H. C. Propp, "The Skin of Moses' Face: Transfigured or Disfigured?" *CBQ* 49 (1987): 379 n. 18.

350. See, e.g., J. M. Sasson, "Bovine Symbolism and the Exodus Narrative," *VT* 18 (1968): 380–87.

351. See, e.g., the representation of the Mesopotamian king Naram-Sin in his so-called "Victory Stela" (late third millennium B.C.), which portrays him with a horned crown and thus signifies his divinity. Naram-Sin was the first Mesopotamian king and one of only a relatively few from Mesopotamia to take on the status of god. See the discussion of this stela in J. Westenholz, "The King, the Emperor, and the Empire: Continuity and Discontinuity of Royal Representation in Text and Image," in *The Heirs of Assyria* (Melammu Symposia 1; Helsinki: Neo-Assyrian Text Corpus Project, 2000), 99–125, esp. 101–2.

352. Propp, "The Skin of Moses' Face," 375–86.

353. S. L. Sanders, "Old Light on Moses' Shining Face," *VT* 52 (2002): 400–406.

354. Ibid., 403.

355. Cf. the statement describing the god Enlil, "whose horns gleam like the rays of the sun" (*CAD*, Q 139).

356. Cf. M. Haran, "The Shining of Moses' Face: A Case Study in Biblical and Ancient Near Eastern Iconography," in *In the Shelter of Elyon: Essays on Ancient Palestinian Life and Literature*, ed. W. B. Barrick and J. R. Spencer (JSOTSup 31; Sheffield: Sheffield Academic Press, 1984), 159–73. Haran compares the possible shining of Moses' face with the Mesopotamian concept of *melammu*, "the brilliant light that radiates from the gods and seems to be taken as mostly surrounding their heads" (ibid., 168).

357. V. A. Hurowitz, "The Priestly Account of Building the Tabernacle," *JAOS* 105 (1985): 28–29. See the translation of this portion of The Ba'lu Myth in COS, 1.86: 260–61.

358. This is essentially the argument of Hurowitz, "The Priestly Account," 21–30.

359. Ibid., 26.

360. The translation is adapted from that of ibid., 27. See also E. Sollberger, "Samsu-iluna's Bilingual Inscription B, Text of the Akkadian Version," *RA* 61 (1967): 39–44.

361. R. P. Wright, "Technology, Gender, and Class: Worlds of Difference in Ur III Mesopotamia," in *Gender and Archaeology*, ed. R. P. Wright (Philadelphia: Univ. of Pennsylvania Press, 1996), 79–110.

362. This is known mainly from the Old Babylonian period. See R. Harris, "The *nadītu* Woman," in *Studies Presented to A. Leo Oppenheim*, ed. R. Biggs and J. Brinkman (Chicago: Oriental Institute, 1964), 106–35; C. Janssen, "Samsu-iluna and the Hungry *nadītums*," *Northern Akkad Project Reports* 5 (1991): 3–40.

363. The evidence for this comes primarily from Mesopotamia. See P.-A. Beaulieu, "Women in Neo-Babylonian Society," *Bulletin of the Canadian Society for Mesopotamian Studies* 26 (1993): 7–14. This practice would have been different from what is sometimes called sacred or cultic prostitution. The latter refers to sexual acts performed by women, connected to a temple, not for pay but as part of religious ceremonies and rituals, perhaps designed to elicit blessings of fertility from the gods. Recent scholarship has been very skeptical of the idea that sacred prostitution was actually practiced in Mesopotamia. See D. Arnaud, "La prostitution sacrée en Mésopotamie, un mythe historiographic?" *RHR* 183 (1973): 111–16; E. J. Fisher, "Cultic Prostitution in the

Ancient Near East? A Reassessment," *BTB* 6 (1976): 225–36; R. Oden, "Religious Identity and the Sacred Prostitution Accusation," in *The Bible without Theology: The Theological Tradition and Alternatives to It* (San Francisco: Harper & Row, 1987), 131–93; J. Cooper, "Sacred Marriage and Popular Cult in Early Mesopotamia," in *Official Cult and Popular Religion in the Ancient Near East*, ed. E. Matsushima (Heidelberg: Universitätsverlag C. Winter, 1993), 81–96. Some have even argued that the evidence for ordinary prostitution in texts from Mesopotamia is much more scarce than previous scholarship has recognized. See J. Assante, "The *kar.kid/ḥarimtu*, Prostitute or Single Woman? A Reconsideration of the Evidence," *UF* 30 (1998): 5–96.

364. T. Lambdin, "Egyptian Loan Words in the Old Testament," *JAOS* 73 (1953): 153.

365. On the etymology of the word and the nature of the material, see Hoffmeier, *Ancient Israel in Sinai*, 212.

366. A. L. Oppenheim, "Akkadian *pul(u)ḫ(t)u* and *melammu*," *JAOS* 63 (1943): 31–34.

Sidebar and Chart Notes

A-1. See I. Shaw's discussion of Egyptian chronology in *The Oxford History of Ancient Egypt*, ed. I. Shaw (Oxford: Oxford Univ. Press, 2000), 1–16, 479–83. The list of New Kingdom kings is taken from there.

A-2. *ANET*[3], 259; see COS, 3.4:16–17.

A-3. H. C. Kee, et al., *The Cambridge Companion to the Bible* (Cambridge: Cambridge Univ. Press, 1997), 62.

A-4. It is also referred to as Tel ed-Dab'a (see Redford, *Egypt, Canaan, and Israel*, 102, 114).

A-5. M. Bietak, *Avaris, the Capital of the Hyksos: Recent Excavations at Tell el-Dab'a* (London: British Museum Press, 1996), 54.

A-6. Ibid., 55–63. For an older but more technical discussion of the finds at this site, see M. Bietak, *Tell El-Dab'a II: Der Fundort im Rahmen einer archäologisch-geographischen Untersuchung über das Ägyptische Ostdelta* (Vienna: Österreichische Akademie der Wissenschaften, 1975).

A-7. Redford, *Egypt, Canaan, and Israel*, 114–15.

A-8. D. B. Redford, "The Literary Motif of the Exposed Child," *Numen* 14 (1967): 209–28.

A-9. B. Lewis, *The Sargon Legend: A Study of the Akkadian Text and the Tale of the Hero Who Was Exposed at Birth* (Cambridge, Mass.: American Schools of Oriental Research, 1980), 97–101.

A-10. Translation from ibid., 24–25.

A-11. M. Malul, "Adoption of Foundlings in the Bible and Mesopotamian Documents: A Study of Some Legal Metaphors in Ezekiel 16.1–7," *JSOT* 46 (1990): 97–126, esp. 105. The reference to the "dog's mouth" was a common way to refer to abandonment. The other name could imply that because the child was found on the river, it is the river that compensated the adoptive parent for the latter's lack of bio-

logical children. Cf. C. Wunsch, "Findelkinder und Adoption nach neubabylonischen Quellen," *AfO* 50 (2003/2004): 174–244.

A-12. It may actually be more accurate to say that there are only three consonants in the name: *y-h-w*. The final *h* may have been used simply to represent a long vowel sound at the end of the word (D. N. Freedman, "יהוה," *TDOT*, 5:500–521, esp. 501–11).

A-13. Ibid., 501–11. See also, e.g., Clement of Alexandria, *Strom.* 5.6.34. He refers to "the mystical tetragrammaton," which, he says, is pronounced *Iaoue* and is to be translated as "he who is and who will be." For a full translation of the passage, see A. le Boulluec et al., *Les Stromates*, vol. 1 (SC 278; Paris: Cerf, 1981), 81.

A-14. See *DDD*[2], 910–19, on these meanings and others.

A-15. Shortened names were not uncommon in the ancient Near East and are known to scholars as *hypocoristica* (*hypocoristicon* in the singular); see H. B. Huffmon, *Amorite Personal Names in the Mari Texts: A Structural and Lexical Study* (Baltimore: Johns Hopkins Univ. Press, 1965), 130–40.

A-16. F. M. Cross, *Canaanite Myth and Hebrew Epic: Essays in the History of the Religion of Israel* (Cambridge, Mass.: Harvard Univ. Press, 1973), 69–71.

A-17. Huffmon, *Amorite Personal Names*, 131–32.

A-18. There remains some disagreement among scholars, though, regarding how to interpret the name Yahweh Sebaoth. For a summary of the discussion, see *DDD*[2], 920–24.

A-19. For further discussion, see Freedman, "יהוה," 513–16.

A-20. E. V. Hulse, "The Nature of Biblical 'Leprosy' and the Use of Alternative Medical Terms in Modern Translations of the Bible," *PEQ* 107 (1975): 89–90. Some recently cited evidence, however, may indicate the existence of Hansen's disease in Mesopotamia; see J. Scurlock and B. Andersen, *Diagnosis in Assyrian and Babylonian Medicine* (Urbana, Ill.: Univ. of Illinois Press, 2005), 70–73.

A-21. Ibid., 95–97; H. Avalos, *Illness and Health Care in the Ancient Near East: The Role of the Temple in Greece, Mesopotamia, and Israel* (HSM 54; Atlanta: Scholars Press, 1995), 311–16.

A-22. E.g., Num. 12:12. See Hulse, "The Nature of Biblical 'Leprosy,'" 92–93.

A-23. K. E. Slanski, *The Babylonian Entitlement narûs (kudurrus): A Study in Their Form and Function* (Boston: American Schools of Oriental Research, 2003), 73.

A-24. CAD E, 246; citing original text published in *RA* 23 (1926), text number 28, p. 148. For more information on leprosy in Mesopotamia, see *CAD* S, 36–37.

A-25. Translation from Redford, *Egypt, Canaan, and Israel*, 206. See also the translation in Caminos *Late-Egyptian Miscellanies*, 188.

A-26. See, e.g., R. B. Coote, *Early Israel: A New Horizon* (Minneapolis: Fortress, 1990).

A-27. See., e.g., Hoffmeier, *Israel in Egypt*, 226.

A-28. For an attempt to marshal archaeological and other historical evidence in this regard, see ibid. The evidence that Hoffmeier uses, however, only explains how an exodus of Israelites might have been possible. While it can corroborate a few of the details in the biblical text, such as some of the place names in Exodus, there is nothing in the data he discusses that confirms that there were Israelites who left Egypt.

A-29. See Redford, *Egypt, Canaan, and Israel*, 208–9, 221–27; C. Redmount, "Bitter Lives: Israel in and out of Egypt," in *The Oxford History of the Biblical World*, ed. M. D. Coogan (New York: Oxford Univ. Press, 1998), 79–121, esp. 98–103.

A-30. After defeating the city of Megiddo in northern Palestine, Thutmose is said to have brought back over a thousand slaves (see A. J. Spalinger, *War in Ancient Egypt: The New Kingdom* [Ancient World at War; Oxford: Blackwell, 2005], 95).

A-31. Redmount, "Bitter Lives," 85–86.

A-32. *ANET*[3], 247; see COS, 2.3:22.

A-33. M. T. Roth, "Age at Marriage and the Household: A Study of Neo-Babylonian and Neo-Assyrian Forms," in *Comparative Studies in Society and History* 29 (1987): 715–47.

A-34. W. C. Kaiser, Jr. et al., *Hard Sayings of the Bible* (Downers Grove, Ill.: InterVarsity Press, 1996), 140–42. Kaiser argues that Amram and Jochebed are not parents of Moses but came several generations before him.

A-35. Simpson, ed., *Literature of Ancient Egypt*, 13.

A-36. Ibid., 15–16.

A-37. R. H. Wilkinson, *The Complete Gods and Goddesses of Ancient Egypt* (London: Thames & Hudson, 2003), 220–28.

A-38. See D. Meeks, "Demons," in *The Ancient Gods Speak: A Guide to Egyptian Religion*, ed. D. B. Redford (Oxford: Oxford Univ. Press, 2002), 106. See also the texts cited by Budge, *Egyptian Magic*, 79–84.

A-39. As B. S. Lesko notes, "The risen serpent (Egyptian *i'rt*, interpreted by the Greeks as *ouraios* and Latinized as Uraeus) is to be understood as a divine cobra protector of royalty, guardian of the crown" (*The Great Goddesses of Egypt* [Oklahoma City: Univ. of Oklahoma Press, 1999], 72).

A-40. From the Pyramid Texts, spell 221. Translation from R. O. Faulkner, *The Ancient Egyptian Pyramid Texts* (Oxford: Clarendon, 1969), 49.

A-41. COS, 2.5A:37.

A-42. Lesko, *Great Goddesses*, 73.

A-43. G. Hort, "The Plagues of Egypt," *ZAW* 69 (1957): 84–103; *ZAW* 70 (1958): 48–59. A number of scholars (e.g., Hoffmeier, *Israel in Egypt*, 146–49) have followed her lead.

A-44. See, e.g., Z. Zevit, "The Priestly Redaction and Interpretation of the Plagues Narrative in Exodus," *JQR* 66 (1975): 193–211. Zevit argues that the plagues symbolize a reversal of cre-

A-45. J. E. Currid, *Ancient Egypt and the Old Testament* (Grand Rapids: Baker, 1997), 104–20. Currid goes through each plague and identifies possible deities that were targeted.

A-46. Wilkinson, *Complete Gods and Goddesses*, 6.

A-47. This god is to be distinguished from a god by the same name that was one of the sons of the god Horus. On the former, see O. E. Kaper, "Myths," in *The Ancient Gods Speak: A Guide to Egyptian Religion*, ed. D. B. Redford (Oxford: Oxford Univ. Press, 2002), 256. On the latter, the son of Horus, see A. Dodson, "Four Sons of Horus," in *The Ancient Gods Speak*, 132–34.

A-48. Currid, *Ancient Egypt*, 110–11.

A-49. Simpson, ed., *Literature of Ancient Egypt*, 164.

A-50. H. Sanchez-Arroyo, "Largest Swarm," in *University of Florida Book of Insect Records*, ch. 27 (http://ufbir.ifas.ufl.edu/chap27.htm).

A-51. http://www.hindu.com/seta/2004/08/12/stories/2004081200251400.htm.

A-52. *ANET*[3], 366; see COS, 1.25:37–40.

A-53. Lichtheim, *AEL*, 2:96–100; COS, 1.28:44–46; Simpson, ed., *Literature of Ancient Egypt*, 278–83.

A-54. This is similar to the "Lord's Supper" being instituted on the basis of the Passover celebration—a prior festival being given new historical associations.

A-55. The most extensive development of this theory is by L. Rost, "Weidewechsel und altisraelitischen Festkalendar," *ZDPV* 66 (1943): 205–16; for a convenient summary see Childs, *Exodus*, 189; for some variant ideas concerning the liminal period between years (a seasonal rite of passage), see Propp, *Exodus 1–18*, 442–43.

A-56. Ibid, 401, 437.

A-57. S. Loewenstamm, *The Evolution of the Exodus Tradition* (Jerusalem: Magnes, 1972), 197–98; J. Milgrom, *Leviticus 1–16: A New Translation with Introduction and Commentary* (AB; New York: Doubleday, 2001), 1081; this understanding of the verb is also represented in the LXX and Symmachus.

A-58. Milgrom, *Leviticus 1–16*, 1081.

A-59. *ANET*[3], 259.

A-60. See B. M. Bryan, "The 18th Dynasty before the Amarna Period," in *The Oxford History of Ancient Egypt*, ed. I. Shaw (Oxford: Oxford Univ. Press, 2000), 245–48; D. Redford, *The Wars in Syria and Palestine of Thutmose III* (Leiden: Brill, 2003). Spalinger states that with the campaigns of Thutmose III, the "Egyptian supremacy in Palestine was thus cemented, with Beth Shan and Megido serving as the two most important points" (*War in Ancient Egypt*, 116).

A-61. See Halpern, "Exodus from Egypt," 93–94.

A-62. Hoffmeier states: "the appearance of Raamses/Ramesses in the Exodus narrative strongly suggests that the tradition [of Piramesse being associated with the Israelites' enslavement] likely came from the period when the Ramesside capital flourished, between 1270 and 1210 B.C." (*Israel in Egypt*, 119).

A-63. See, e.g., L. E. Stager, "Merneptah, Israel, and the Sea Peoples," *EI* 18 (1985): 56–64.

A-64. Simpson, ed., *Literature of Ancient Egypt*, 360, see COS, 2.6:40–41.

A-65. G. Rendsburg, "The Date of the Exodus and the Conquest/Settlement: The Case for the 1100s," *VT* 42 (1992): 510–27; M. Bietak, "Israelites Found in Egypt: Four-Room House Identified in Medinet Habu," *BAR* 29 (Sep/Oct 2003): 49, 82.

A-66. E.g., Halpern, "Exodus from Egypt," 99. See also S. Israelit-Groll, "Historical Background to the Exodus: Papyrus Anastasi VIII," in *Gold of Praise: Studies on Ancient Egypt in Honor of Edward F. Wente*, ed. E. Teeter and J. Larson (SAOC; Chicago: Oriental Institute, 1999), 159–62.

A-67. See, e.g., J. I. Durham, *Exodus* (WBC 3; Waco, Tex.: Word, 1987), xxvi.

A-68. For a recent detailed and balanced discussion of the major positions on this issue, see J. H. Walton, "Exodus, Date of," in *Dictionary of the Old Testament: Pentateuch*, ed. T. D. Alexander and D. W. Baker (Downers Grove, Ill.: InterVarsity Press, 2003), 258–72.

A-69. A. Mazar, "The Iron Age I," in *The Archaeology of Ancient Israel*, ed. A. Ben-Tor (New Haven, Conn.: Yale Univ. Press, 1992), 265–71.

A-70. *ANET³*, 262–63.

A-71. Cross, *Canaanite Myth*, 121–25.

A-72. S. Lafont, "Considérations sur la pratique judiciaire en Mésopotamie," in *Rendre la justice en Mésopotamie: Archives judiciaires du Proche-Orient ancien (IIIᵉ–Iᵉʳ millénaires avant J.-C.)*, ed. F. Joannès (Saint-Denis: Presses Universitaires de Vincennes, 2000), 16–18.

A-73. See T. M. Willis, *The Elders of the City: A Study of the Elders-Laws in Deuteronomy* (SBLMS 55; Atlanta: Society of Biblical Literature, 2001), 33–88.

A-74. F. R. Magdalene, *On the Scales of Righteousness: Neo-Babylonian Trial Law and the Book of Job* (BJS 348; Providence, R.I.: Brown Judaic Studies, 2007), 65.

A-75. T. G. Pinches, *Cuneiform Texts from the Babylonian Tablets in the British Museum* (CT 2; London: British Museum, 1896), text no. 50.

A-76. C.-F. Jean, *Contrats de Larsa* (TCL 11; Paris: P. Geuthner, 1926), text no. 245.

A-77. H. Klengel, *Altbabylonische Rechts- und Wirtschaftsurkunden* (Vorderasiatische Schriftdenkmäler 18; Berlin: Akadamie-Verlag, 1973), text no. 1. Trans. adapted from R. Westbrook, *Old Babylonian Marriage Law* (AfO 23; Horn, Austria: Berger & Söhne, 1988), 135.

A-78. J. N. Strassmaier, *Inschriften von Cyrus, König von Babylon (538–529 v. Chr.)* (Babylonische Texte 7; Leipzig: Eduard Pfeiffer, 1890), text no. 332.

A-79. H. H. Figulla, "Lawsuit concerning a Sacrilegious Theft at Erech," *Iraq* 13 (1951): 95–102, text copy on p. 96.

A-80. A. Tremayne, *Records from Erech: Time of Cyrus and Cambyses (538–521 B.C.)* (YOS 7; New Haven, Conn.: Yale Univ. Press, 1925), text no. 15.

A-81. A. Kerkeslager, "Mt. Sinai—in Arabia?" *BRev* 16 (2000): 32–39, 52.

A-82. For a recent review of possible locations, see Hoffmeier, *Ancient Israel in Sinai*, 112–48.

A-83. See, e.g., H. Shanks, "Frank Moore Cross, an Interview (Part I: Israelite Origins)," *BRev* 8 (Aug 1992): 23–32, 61–63, esp. 24–25 and 32.

A-84. Kerkeslager, "Mt. Sinai," 35–36.

A-85. Ibid., 36–39.

A-86. Cf. G. I. Davies, "Hagar, El-Hegra and the Location of Mount Sinai," *VT* 22 (1972): 152–63.

A-87. For a different perspective, one that argues against the idea that Mount Sinai is in Midian, see Hoffmeier, *Ancient Israel in Sinai*, 130–40. One of his more important points is that, if one takes the Israelite itineraries in Exodus and Numbers literally, then the distances described in those texts do not fit well with a Midian location for Mount Sinai. Hoffmeier favors placing Mount Sinai in the southern Sinai Peninsula.

A-88. *CANE*, 1:471.

A-89. J. Bottéro, "The 'Code' of Ḥammurabi," in *Mesopotamia: Writing, Reasoning, and the Gods*, trans. Z. Bahrani and M. van de Mieroop (Chicago: Univ. of Chicago Press, 1992), 156–84; M. T. Roth, "The Law Collection of King Hammurabi: Toward an Understanding of Codification and Text," in *La Codification des lois dans l'antiquité: Actes du Colloque de Strasbourg, 27–29 Novembre 1997*, ed. E. Lévy (Travaux du Centre de Recherche sur le Proche-Orient et la Grèce antiques 16; Paris: De Boccard, 2000), 9–31.

A-90. See, e.g., D. Patrick, *Old Testament Law* (Atlanta: John Knox, 1985), 198–200; R. Westbrook, "Cuneiform Law Codes and the Origins of Legislation," *ZA* 79 (1989): 201–22.

A-91. Published as text no. 108 in R. H. Pfeiffer, *Excavations at Nuzi II: The Archives of Shilwateshub, Son of the King* (HSS 9; Cambridge, Mass.: Harvard Univ. Press, 1932).

A-92. The translation is that of the author.

A-93. See T. Frymer-Kensky, "Suprarational Legal Procedures in Elam and Nuzi," in *Studies on the Civilization and Culture of Nuzi and the Hurrians in Honor of Ernest R. Lacheman*, ed. M. A. Morrison and D. I. Owen (Winona Lake, Ind.: Eisenbrauns, 1981), 115–31.

A-94. M. Homan, *To Your Tents, O Israel! The Terminology, Function, Form, and Symbolism of Tents in the Hebrew Bible and the Ancient Near East* (CHANE 12; Leiden: Brill, 2002), 177–80.

A-95. For arguments that make the length of the inner section smaller by about one third, see R. E.

Friedman, "Tabernacle," *ABD*, 6:292–300; Hoffmeier, *Ancient Israel in Sinai*, 198–200.

A-96. King and Stager, *Life in Biblical Israel*, 338. See also M. Aharoni, "Arad: The Israelite Citadels," *NEAEHL*, 1:82–85.

A-97. For the details of this comparison between the tabernacle and Ramesses' camp, see M. Homan, "The Divine Warrior in His Tent: A Military Model for Yahweh's Tabernacle," *BRev* 16 (Dec 2000): 22–32, 55; idem, *To Your Tents*, 111–16.

A-98. See, e.g., R. J. Clifford, "The Tent of El and the Israelite Tent of Meeting," *CBQ* 33 (1971): 221–27.

A-99. For a variety of other parallels, see Homan, *To Your Tents*, 89–128.

A-100. See the comments of Hoffmeier, *Ancient Israel in Sinai*, 201–2.

A-101. *ANET*[3], 207–9.

A-102. On these depictions and their possible relation to the Israelite tabernacle, see Hoffmeier, *Ancient Israel in Sinai*, 213–14.

A-103. Ibid., 213.

LEVITICUS

by Roy E. Gane

Gezer standing
stones
Z. Radovan/
www.BibleLand
Pictures.com
▲

Introduction

For a reader who has not enjoyed much exposure to the riches of ancient Near Eastern discoveries that illuminate biblical backgrounds,
the present commentary will have an over-
whelming impact. Leviticus, the central book
of the Torah (= Pentateuch, consisting of Genesis through Deuteronomy), has to do with the
areas of ritual worship and religious, criminal,
and civil law, which were central to the cultural
life and governance of all ancient Near Eastern societies and generated a vast quantity of
preserved texts and objects. So the scope for
relationships between this biblical book and
parallel materials is practically limitless.

More breathtaking than the sheer volume of parallels is the fact that so many of them are so close. We will find, for example, similar ritual procedures, infrastructure, terminology, and concepts, as well as similar approaches to law in terms of literary context, formulation, reasoning, and content. It is abundantly clear that Leviticus was meant to communicate with and address the needs of real people in the context of their ancient Near Eastern culture, which contained a number of positive elements worthy to be affirmed and continued. At the same time, we will recognize crucial differences that highlight and give depth perspective to the uniqueness of Israel's God and his timeless message through Leviticus, which was countercultural in important respects.[1]

Historical Setting

According to the narrative framework of the Pentateuch, God gave the legislation of Leviticus to Israel through Moses in the Sinai Desert during the first month of the second year after the Israelites exited from slavery in Egypt and before they moved on toward the land of Canaan (cf. Ex. 40:17 and Num. 1:1). Within the framework of biblical chronology, this was during the second half of the second millennium B.C. An accumulating body of textual and archaeological data from the ancient Near East, of which some significant samples are presented in the present commentary, has shown that Leviticus is firmly rooted in its ancient Near Eastern historical setting, especially that of the second millennium B.C., when nations such as the Hittite empire flourished.[2]

Literary Setting

Some major features of Leviticus relate to similar aspects of other ancient Near Eastern texts.

1. Divine speech in a narrative setting. Compare, for example, the Sumerian Cylinder A of Gudea, which extensively quotes the deities Ningirsu and

Er-Raha Plain at the foot of Mount Sinai (Jebel Musa)
Todd Bolen/www.BiblePlaces.com
▶

Nanshe regarding construction of the Eninnu temple in Lagash.[3]
2. Instructions for performance of rituals and festivals. Compare the Ugaritic rites for the vintage.[4]
3. Rules for priests and other persons regarding their treatment of sacred things. Compare the Hittite instructions to priests and temple officials.[5]
4. Laws grouped by topic. Compare the Hittite and Mesopotamian law collections.[6]
5. Blessings and curses after laws (ch. 26). Compare the epilogues to the laws of Lipit-Ishtar and Hammurabi.[7]

Ritual and Ritual Texts in the Ancient Near East

Rituals are activity routines that are believed to do something special through interaction with someone (such as a deity or demon) or something (such as sin or ritual impurity) ordinarily beyond reach of the ordinary mundane world.[8] For ancient Near Eastern peoples, whose worldviews teemed with friendly and unfriendly gods and demons having awesome power over every aspect of human life and death, rituals were essential for survival and well-being. Keeping friendly forces happy by establishing, maintaining (by care and feeding), and remedying relationships with them, and waging "spiritual warfare" against unfriendly ones by enlisting supernatural aid required a wide array of rituals (including magic) and expert personnel to properly perform them.

The monotheistic religion of the Israelites reflected in Leviticus, according to which the real Presence (not a mere idol) of the one all-powerful, divine Creator dwelt at his sanctuary in their midst, liberated them from the complexity and fear (especially of demons) that burdened their polytheistic neighbors.[9] It is true that the Israelites, like other peoples,

had a sanctuary/temple, authorized and trained cultic personnel, sacred times, and regulations to guard the sanctity and purity of holy things and sacred precincts, and they performed a variety of rituals to interact with their divine Lord. Of these kinds of ritual, sacrifices (ritual offerings to deity) were central, just as sacrifice was an important part of worship all over the ancient world. But unlike their neighbors, the Israelites were supposed to offer sacrifices as tokens of relational transactions (including atonement/reconciliation) with a supreme deity who made specific moral demands and required obedience within a covenant context.

Laws of Ur-Nammu
Ji Y. Son, courtesy of the Archaeological Museum, Istanbul, Turkey

Ritual texts have the purpose of preserving knowledge regarding several aspects of ritual procedures: items needed for their performance, instructions on how to carry out their activities, and their goals or meanings.[10] Some ancient Near Eastern ritual texts, which are legal in nature, *prescribe* how rituals ought to be done on any number of occasions. For example, Leviticus 1–7 provides instructions for several basic kinds of sacrifices, and Akkadian tablets from Emar outline elaborate rituals involved in the *Zukru* Festival.[11] Although ritual prescriptions do not specify every detail of performance, they serve as procedural rules for standardizing crucial elements of proper performance so that rituals can achieve their goals.[12]

Other ritual texts, which are narrative in nature, *describe* how ritual performances were actually carried out on specific occasions. For example, Leviticus 8–10 recounts the one-time complex of ceremonies that consecrated and inaugurated the Israelite sanctuary and its priesthood. Similarly, Cylinder B of Gudea tells how the ruler gave offerings when the gods Ningirsu and Baba were inducted into their new Eninnu temple.[13]

Law Collections and Treaties in the Ancient Near East

While there are some narrative portions in Leviticus (1:1; chs. 8–10; 24:10–23), the book is mostly a collection of laws. In terms of content, laws in the latter part of Leviticus (the so-called "Holiness Code"; chs. 17 or 18 to 26 or 27) overlap Mesopotamian and Hittite law collections in the criminal law categories of sexual offenses (18:6–20, 22–23; 19:20–22; 20:10–21); dishonesty and injustice, including lying and stealing (19:11–16, 35–36); murder and assault (24:17–21); and the civil law categories of property ownership, slavery, and debt (25:8–55).[14]

Whereas law collections outside the Bible devote considerable space to procedures and principles governing various facets of commercial and family economic life, such civil matters are a lower priority in the Pentateuch, including Leviticus. Conversely, some topics in Leviticus are not represented in the extrabiblical collections: commands to show respect for parents and the elderly (19:3, 32; 20:9), provisions for care of the poor and resident aliens (19:9–10, 33–34), regulation of inner attitudes (19:17–18), and prohibitions against divination (19:26, 31; 20:6, 27).[15] By far the biggest difference is that Leviticus includes religious law as the most important component (chs. 1–7; 11–17; 21:1–24:9; ch. 27) alongside "secular" law, and in places interspersed with it (ch. 19; even integrated in the same law in 19:20–22!). Only in biblical law collections "are moral exhortations and religious injunctions combined with legal prescriptions; elsewhere … these three distinct spheres are found in separate independent collections."[16]

The facts that Leviticus—unlike ancient Near Eastern law collections outside the Bible—marries religion to social ethics, makes commands regarding attitudes of the heart (such as "love") that only God could enforce, and opposes all forms of divination that compete with reliance on the Lord's knowledge are symptoms of a fundamental distinction. Outside Israel, human behavior was guided by the ideal of an outwardly well-ordered society, with individuals harmoniously fitting into their communities. Israel also possessed a strong sense of communal solidarity and the need for order rather than disorder, but a deeper level of motivation was added: an inner conviction of right versus wrong, which we would call "morality."[17] This morality was based on Israel's relationship with the Lord, to whom his people were accountable for inner attitudes as well as outward actions.

Whereas Mesopotamian and Hittite law collections were promulgated by human beings, especially kings, who were responsible for maintaining social order, the one portrayed as Lawgiver in the Bible was none other than Israel's covenant Lord, who ruled a theocracy. The security of Yahweh's covenant and system of ethical absolutes, conveyed to Israel through a permanently valid revelation, depended on Yahweh's absolute freedom as the sole deity. This kind of assurance was unavailable to polytheists, whose gods were not fully free to consistently keep their promises or reward righteousness because they were constrained by the will and power of other deities.[18]

Biblical law (also in Exodus, Numbers, and Deuteronomy) is presented within a religious framework and is permeated with religious concepts that reflect and showcase the just character of the divine King rather than of a human monarch.[19] Thus the civil provisions of Leviticus 25 regarding property ownership, slavery, and debt are placed within the context of sacred time (Jubilee Year) in the Promised Land. Even in criminal law, where some offenses and penalties are formulated almost identically in Leviticus and extrabiblical collections, we see Israelite religious priorities of primary accountability to God (rather than to society) and paramount interest in life rather than property (see comments on 20:10; 24:17–19).

The laws of Leviticus were stipulations given to Israel by the superior party (God) in a covenant/treaty formulation, as shown by inclusion of covenant blessings and curses near the end of the book. So in this sense the overall literary function of Leviticus is equivalent to that of ancient Near Eastern treaty documents (see comment on 26:3) rather than law collections. However, the Israelite treaty differs from the extrabiblical agreements between human rulers in that it was contracted between a nation and their God, who required not simply loyalty but a loyalty shown by comprehensively living in harmony with his own holy character (11:44–45; 19:2).

The Burnt Offering (1:1–17)

Burnt offering (1:3). This category of sacrifice, in which all edible material was burned, served as a basic and general gift for invoking the deity (cf. Gen. 8:20; Num. 23—by non-Israelites). Burnt offerings were practiced by other ancient Syro-Palestinian peoples, whose rituals were closest to those of the Israelites. They were also performed in Anatolia, but apparently not in Egypt or Mesopotamia. In Ugaritic literature, where words for several kinds of outwardly similar (but by no means identical) sacrifices parallel Hebrew terms, burnt offerings are often coupled with well-being offerings (so-called "peace" or "fellowship" offerings; see comments on Lev. 3), as they are in the Bible (Ex. 20:24, etc.).[20] So we see that Israelite sacrifice was not an isolated phenomenon.

From the herd (1:3). In Leviticus 1, sacrificial victims are logically presented in descending order of size and value. Similarly, a Punic sacrificial tariff (the so-called Marseilles Tariff) lists fees for priestly officiation in descending order, corresponding to the decreasing sizes of animal victims.[21]

Lay his hand on the head (1:4). In Hittite ritual, the same gesture appears to carry the same function of identifying the owner as the one who is giving the sacrifice. For example: "The Old Woman takes one so[ur loaf of thickbread] of one handful, one che[ese] and one jug of wine. She hol[ds] them forth to the offerer(s). They place their hand on. She breaks up the loaf of thickbread and the cheese and she libates the wine." D. P. Wright explains:

> Hand placement attributes the offering and offering act to the offerer. Though

another functionary performs the actual distribution of the offering, the offering is to be ritually attributed to the one who performs the gesture. To put it analogically, hand placement is the signature on a letter delivered to the god by means of a cultic postman. When the god receives the letter, he recognizes that it is from the one who signed the letter (i.e., the one who performed the gesture), not from the postman who delivered it.[22]

To make atonement for him (1:4). Hebrew *kipper* (translated here "make atonement") refers to the removal of evil that disrupts the divine-human relationship, providing ritual impurity or a prerequisite to forgiveness, as part of a process of reconciliation (at-one-ment). In the past, it was common for scholars to connect *kipper* with Arabic *kafara* ("cover") and interpret a ritual accomplishing *kipper* as covering sin

(see Gen. 3:6–7; Zech. 3:3–5). However, in the context of purification offerings (so-called "sin offerings"), *kipper* followed by the preposition *min* ("from") denotes removal (rather than covering) of sin or ritual impurity *from* a person (Lev. 4:26; 12:7) or from the sanctuary (16:16).[23]

The idea of removal is also present in the Akkadian cognate *kuppuru*. In ritual or medical usage, this term usually denotes a physical wiping that is directly applied to persons or things from which evil is removed.[24] Nevertheless, Hebrew *kipper* refers to the goal of a ritual rather than to a specific physical activity. So in Hebrew the emphasis is on the meaning of the removal activity within the context of one's relationship with the Lord.

Shall bring the blood and sprinkle it (1:5). Blood represented life, and ritual application of animal blood to the Israelite altar enacted ransom of human life (17:11).[25] By contrast to the Israelite ritual system, in which blood was intentionally and meaningfully applied in various ways (splashing, sprinkling, daubing, etc.) to objects, areas, and persons, Mesopotamian and Ugaritic cults lacked such ritual use of blood.[26]

In some ancient cultures (Hittite, Greek), blood could be used for libations to *underworld* deities, conveyed to them by means of ritual holes in the ground.[27] Just after such an activity (slaughter of a sheep in a ritual pit), a ritual involved in establishing a new Anatolian temple for the "Goddess of the Night" purifies the new deity and temple by bloodying the golden image, the wall, and all the implements of the deity.[28] The Israelite sacrifices, by contrast, were offered to a *celestial deity*, Yahweh.

A Greek ritual for purification from homicide called for slaughtering a piglet over the head of the person undergoing purification and then rinsing off the blood. In another Greek purification ritual, officials carried a piglet around the city square in Athens, then slaughtered it, sprayed its blood over the seats, and discarded the carcass. These practices somewhat resembled Israelite purification (so-called "sin") offerings, the blood of which was used to purify persons, objects, and places (see comments on 4:3, 26; 16:14).[29] Unlike the Greek purifications, Israelite sacrifices applied blood to part of the sanctuary/temple of their deity, such as an altar. Although Yahweh is a heavenly divinity, he is concerned with life, represented by blood.

An offering made by fire (1:9). This translation assumes that the Hebrew term derives from the word for "fire." Weakening this idea, the original word can refer to food portions that are eaten rather than burned (Deut. 18:1), but it is not used of purification offerings, which are always burned. So scholars have found an alternative in an Ugaritic cognate (same word in another language) that means "gift."[30] This concept fits the biblical contexts well: An offering is *given* to God, whether it is burned or not, and the purification offering is not a gift because it is a mandatory token payment of "debt."[31]

An aroma pleasing to the Lord (1:9). Other ancient Near Eastern peoples also viewed deities as favorably disposed by the smell of incense and offerings.[32] But whereas Israel's deity does not need human food (Ps. 50:12–13), other gods were thought to be dependent on such sustenance. In the Ugaritic myth of the god Baal, when the god ꜣIlu (El) sees the goddess ꜣAtiratu coming to him, he says to her: "Are you really hungry (because) you've been wandering?"[33] In the Babylonian epic Atraḫasis, the gods suffer from hunger and thirst during the great flood because there are no humans to offer them sacrifices. So when Atraḫasis (the "Noah" figure) subsequently offers his sacrifice, the gods smell the offering (cf. Gen. 8:20–21) and crowd around like flies.[34] Unlike Yahweh, they enjoy the smell because it promises an end to their hunger. In a prayer, the Hittite King Mursili II pointedly used the gods' need for food as an argument to plead that they remove a plague from his land lest they suffer because of a lack of humans to serve them.[35]

The Grain Offering (2:1–16)

Grain offering (2:1). Throughout the ancient Near East, people frequently presented sacrifices consisting of grain, which was the staple human diet. While grain offerings could be independent (as in Lev. 2), they were often served with drinks as accompaniments to animal sacrifices (Num. 15), so that the deity received a well-rounded meal (cf. Gen. 18:6–8). Thus, on the fifth day of the Hittite Ninth-Year Festival of Telipinu, this god was to be offered choice meat portions (of 10 bovines and 200 sheep!), plus thick breads and drink offerings (see sidebar on Lev. 24).[36]

Baked in an oven (2:4). Ancient Israelites ate grains, especially barley or wheat, in

---

▶ An Ugaritic Sacrifice

The Ugaritic Kirta (often formerly called Keret) Epic contains a description of a sacrifice, in which several elements relate to Israelite sacrifice: preparatory purification of hands (cf. Ex. 30:19–21), domestic flock animals as victims (Lev. 1:10–13), sacrifice as a gift of food (Num. 28:2), a bird as victim (Lev. 1:14–17), a drink offering of wine (Num. 15:5, 7, 10), honey (excluded from an altar sacrifice in Lev. 2:11), going up to a place of sacrifice (Gen. 22:2, but see Ex. 20:26), raising hands in connection with sacrifice (1 Kings 8:22), and invoking the deity to earthly interaction (Lev. 9:24; 1 Kings 18:38).[A-1]

various states. However, Leviticus 2 limits grain offerings for the Lord's altar to unleavened products of fine-quality wheat flour, that is, semolina. For more on this subject, see sidebar on "Ancient Grain-Processing and Bread-Making."

You are not to burn any yeast or honey (2:11). Apparently the reason for excluding yeast from the altar was that leavening involves a kind of decay through fermentation, which was associated with mortality/impurity and thus had to be separated from intimate contact with God's sphere of holiness and life. Along the same lines, honey (most likely of fruit; cf. 2 Chron. 31:5) was banned from the altar because of its susceptibility to fermentation (cf. Num. 6:3–4).[37]

Non-Israelite peoples, whose deities were not dissociated from death in the same way, frequently offered honey to their gods. Thus in Assyria and Anatolia, honey (along with other liquids, such as oil and wine) could be poured into a ritual hole in the ground as a libation for an underworld deity.[38] The final ritual of the fifth day of the Babylonian New Year Festival of Spring was a burnt offering to celestial gods that included honey, along with ghee and oil.[39]

Salt of the covenant of your God (2:13). In antiquity, parties who shared salt (here the Lord and the Israelites) were united by mutual obligations. Thus, a letter from Neo-Babylonia refers to a tribe's covenantal allies as those who "tasted the salt of the Jakin tribe." Similarly, the Greeks salted their covenant meals, and in Ezra 4:14 those who tasted the salt of the Persian king's palace were bound to loyalty to him (Ezra 4:14).[40]

Since human allies establishing a covenant would commonly share a meal featuring salted meat, it made sense for salt with Israelite sacrifices to serve as a reminder of the covenant between God and Israel. Because salt was employed as a preservative, its use in a covenant context also emphasized the expectation that the covenant would last for a long time, a meaning attached to salt in Babylonian, Persian, Arabic, and Greek covenant contexts. Because salt inhibits the leavening action of yeast, which represented rebellion, salt could additionally stand for that which prevented rebellion. A different reason for the appropriateness of salt in connection with covenant is found in its association with agricultural infertility: "In a Hittite treaty, the testator pronounces a curse: if the treaty is broken may he and his family and his lands, like salt that has no seed, likewise have no progeny."[41]

The Well-Being (So-Called "Fellowship" or "Peace") Offering (3:1–17)

Fellowship offering (3:1). The Hebrew term for this kind of sacrifice is from the same root as the well-known word for "well-being/peace" (šālôm) and is better understood as "well-being offering."[42] A sacrifice designated by a noun from the same Semitic root appears frequently in Ugaritic ritual texts, especially in tandem with burnt offerings (see comment

▶ **Ancient Grain-Processing and Bread-Making**

Archaeological finds have enriched our understanding of ancient grain-processing and bread-making. For example, a jar of semolina has been discovered in early Iron Age Beth Shemesh, a number of grinding stones have been found in various places, and excavators at Gezer found a loaf of bread preserved through a fire (1800–1400 B.C.).[A-2]

Production of breads in Egypt, which could take numerous shapes, is illuminated by pictures on walls of tombs, statuettes, and models of steps in the bread-making process, and by the discovery of actual loaves.[A-3] While the Bible speaks of several varieties of breads, including wafers, biscuits, round loaves, and so on, Mesopotamian vocabularies list about three hundred kinds, which varied in their flours and fillings, shapes and sizes. In Mesopotamia, ground grain was made into porridge, mush, leavened or unleavened bread, or beer.

Ancient Egyptian model of a bakery
Kim Walton, courtesy of the Oriental Institute Museum

◀

on 1:3). The chief difference between the two kinds of sacrifices was that offerers (and others with whom they could share) ate meat from their own well-being offerings as sacred meals shared with their deity, but they were not permitted to partake of a burnt offering.

As food (3:11). Offerings presented to the Lord at the outer altar are called the "food" of God (Lev. 21:8; Num. 28:2, etc.). Non-Israelite peoples also offered food, but they regarded their deities as needing to consume it (see comment on Lev. 1:9). As part of the daily care and feeding of the gods, Egyptians, Hittites, and Babylonians regularly placed various kinds of food and drink on tables or stands before idols in their temples.[43] A. L. Oppenheim describes the way Mesopotamian deities consumed their food:

> Food was placed in front of the image, which was apparently assumed to consume it by merely looking at it, and beverages were poured out before it for the same purpose. A variant of this pattern consisted of presenting the offered food with a solemn ritual gesture, passing it in a swinging motion before the staring eyes of the image.[44]

Food offerings
Frederick J. Mabie

◀

In Hittite cults, consumption of bread offered to a deity could be symbolized by breaking it.[45] In Egypt, care of gods included not only feeding them, but also washing and clothing their idols and even providing them with makeup paint.[46]

To complicate matters, many ancient Near Easterners believed that dead people continued to live on in divine form. This meant that they were required to provide food and drink for these powerful and potentially dangerous spirits, lest they return from the grave hungry, thirsty, and angry.

> Much Mesopotamian religion was animistic in character, and particularly as far as ordinary people were concerned, religion was probably more about placating the spirits and demons rather than the major gods who had temples and images of their own.[47]

By contrast with the highly anthropomorphic rituals of other peoples,[48] the Israelites were to limit similarity between the Lord and his people. While he accepted food to affirm that he dwelt among them, he did not need its nourishment (Ps. 50:12–13). Therefore, the food was burned up so that he only received the smoke.

Horned incense altar from Megiddo

Kim Walton, courtesy of the Oriental Institute Museum

The Purification (So-Called "Sin") Offering (4:1–35)

Sins unintentionally (4:2). In the ancient Near East, deities were believed to possess superhuman powers of perception and to hold human beings accountable for their faulty actions, whether they knew that they had done wrong or not. Therefore a person could suffer evil consequences without knowing why. So an Egyptian prayer asks a god for mercy: "Visit not my many offenses upon me, I am one ignorant of himself. I am a mindless man, who all day follows his mouth, like an ox after grass."[49] This kind of uncertainty was compounded by the difficulty of knowing what deities wanted. A Mesopotamian "righteous sufferer" expressed this problem: "I wish I knew that these things were pleasing to a god! What seems good to one's self could be an offense to a god. What in one's own heart seems abominable could be good to one's god!"[50]

Such uncertainty demanded a solution. Besides knowing which sacrifices, incantations, or magical rituals to perform in order to appease deities or otherwise turn away evil (which could be demonic), priests often practiced divination to sort out the variables, such as why the gods reacted as they did and what would placate them.[51] However, divination was not always successful.[52]

In Israel, divination was unnecessary because several factors greatly simplified reconciliation with the Lord:

1. In monotheism there was no need to determine which deity to approach.
2. Sin that required a ritual remedy was defined as violation of a command that the Lord had communicated to the Israelites.
3. Israelites who committed inadvertent wrongs were liable for offering purification offerings only when they came to know what they had done wrong (Lev. 4:14, 23, 28; but see comment on 5:17).
4. A limited number of ritual types (burnt, purification, and reparation offerings) were prescribed to remedy a wide range of offenses.

As a sin offering (4:3). This sacrifice purified offerers (throughout the year) or parts of the sanctuary (at its consecration and on the Day of Atonement) from moral faults and/or physical ritual impurities, which were not sins in the sense of moral faults (12:6–8; 14:19, etc.). Thus, the name of the sacrifice is better translated "purification offering."[53] The procedure was unique in requiring application of blood to the horns of the outer altar or the incense altar. This ritual has no close parallel outside Israel (cf. comment on 1:5).

Burn it in a wood fire on the ash heap (4:12). There is no indication that remnants of Israelite purification offerings were regarded as having absorbed dangerous demonic impurity. By contrast, a Hittite law warns: "If anyone performs a purification ritual on a person, he shall dispose of the remnants (of the ritual) in the incineration dumps. But if he disposes of them in someone's house, it is sorcery (and) a case for the king."[54] Israelites were not subjected to this kind of fear because the sources of their impurities were human beings and some kinds of animals, not demons.

And he will be forgiven (4:26). The idea of reconciliation with a just deity who mercifully remits sin also appears in the Mesopotamian Poem of the Righteous Sufferer.[55]

The Graduated Purification (So-Called "Sin") Offering (5:1–13)

Public charge to testify (5:1). In the ancient Near East, it was common for heralds to make public proclamations and summons.[56] For example, a law of Hammurabi reads: "If a man should harbor a fugitive slave or slave woman of either the palace or of a commoner in his house and not bring him out at the herald's public proclamation, that householder shall be killed."[57] The procedure was similar in Israel, where compliance of witnesses, whose negligence could easily go undetected by human beings, was enforced by the deity. Following discovery of a crime, the "legal process began with the pronouncement of an ʾalah, a general imprecation that demanded that anyone with knowledge step forward. Divine punishment would follow the person who knows something but keeps quiet."[58]

Serving as a witness against a member of one's community could be uncomfortable or even hazardous. So the early Mesopotamian Shuruppak Composition advised: "Do not loiter about where there is a dispute. Do not appear as a witness in a dispute" (cf. Prov. 26:17).[59] In Leviticus 5 the concession of amnesty through a purification offering for the deliberate sin of failure to respond to a binding summons to testify would encourage reticent witnesses to speak up even though they have delayed.[60]

He will be held responsible (5:1). Literally, "he will bear his culpability." Culpability is viewed as a burden that inevitably leads to punishment, unless or until someone takes it away.[61] To illustrate the concept that a higher authority requires the punishment of the culpable, compare the Turin Judicial Papyrus regarding judgment on conspirators against Pharaoh Ramses III: "And they examined them; they found them guilty; they caused that their punishment overtake them; their crimes seized them."[62] Here the judges are human, but in Leviticus 5 it is God who sees to it that culpability bears its fruit, even if the guilty party is not apprehended by other human beings.

Confess (5:5). Confession is necessary here because the faults in question are not inadvertent but have been hidden deliberately (v. 1) or were the result of forgetfulness (vv. 2–4).[63] Other ancient Near Eastern peoples were also keenly aware that confession is a vital part of restoration.[64] A Sumerian poem of confession and reconciliation shows several important points of contact with biblical teaching regarding the sinful nature of the present human condition, need for recognition of sins, distinctions between sins in terms of whether they are recognized/visible or forgotten, and the value of sincere (rather than artful) confession and supplication in gaining reconciliation with the deity so that joy rather than punishment results (cf. Ps. 51).[65]

The Reparation (So-Called "Guilt") Offering (5:14–6:7)

In regard to any of the LORD's holy things (5:15). Such respect for holy things, such as gifts dedicated to a deity (cf. Num. 18), was basic to all ancient Near Eastern religion. The Hittite document Instructions to Priests and Temple Officials takes pains to specify and prohibit several categories of sacrilege, including temple personnel appropriating sacrificial portions that are not theirs or taking dedicated things from the temple for their families, and farmers cheating gods out of property or delaying presentation of dedicated offerings.[66] At one point the document warns: "You may steal it from a man, but you cannot steal it from a god. It (is) a sin for you."[67]

Guilt offering (5:15). Because the unique element associated with this sacrifice was literal reparation, J. Milgrom prefers to call it the "reparation offering."[68] While problems of impurity, culpability, and sacrilege addressed by purification and reparation offerings were widespread in the ancient Near East and various rituals were devised to remedy them, no close parallels to the mandatory Israelite sacrifices of expiation (removal of evil) have been found in other ritual systems.

Even though he does not know it, he is guilty (5:17). Here the reparation offering addresses the problem of suspected but unidentified sin, which could be sacrilege that would lead to adverse consequences, regardless of intention.[69] A prayer of Assurbanipal expresses similar uncertainty: "[Through a misdeed] which I am or am not aware of, I have become weak!"[70] Notice that circumstances indicate divine disfavor. Similarly, when the Anatolian deity Telipinu became angry, he disappeared and took fertility with him until ritual reconciled him.[71] Unlike other ancient Near Eastern people, when an Israelite could identify no particular sin but was led by circumstances to suspect that he/she was no longer enjoying divine favor, there was only one deity to approach and only one kind of sacrifice to offer (see comment on 4:2).

Unfaithful to the LORD by deceiving his neighbor (6:2). Verses 1–7 deal with cases of sacrilege that involve fraud: misuse of the divine name by swearing falsely to avoid human detection of an act that takes advantage of another person. In the ancient Near East, oaths were used to resolve disputes when other evidence was insufficient. For example, the Mesopotamian Laws of Eshnunna make the provision:

> If the man's house has been burglarized, and the owner of the house incurs a loss along with the goods which the depositor gave to him, the owner of the house shall swear an oath to satisfy him at the gate of (the temple of) the god Tishpak: "My goods have been lost along with your goods; I have not committed a fraud or misdeed"; thus shall he swear an oath to satisfy him and he will have no claim against him.[72]

Like Leviticus 6, the Egyptian Instruction of Amenemope also speaks of false oaths as a way to satisfy greed, but warns of accountability to superhuman power.[73]

Additional Instructions for the Priests (6:8–7:38)

The fire must be kept burning on the altar (6:9). The Hittite Instructions to Priests and Temple Officials also regulate fire at the residence of a deity. However, the concern is the opposite: to put the fire out at night so that it does not burn down the temple.[74] Unlike the Hittite fire, the sacred, eternal flame on the Israelite altar had to be kept burning because it was lit by the deity (9:24).

They belong to the priest who makes atonement with them (7:7). In ancient Near Eastern religious cultures, it was common for priests to eat portions of food that had been dedicated to deities. Thus on the fourth day of the Hittite Ninth Year Festival of Telipinu, the priests eat sacrificial meat that has been presented to the god Telipinu.[75]

The Hittite Instructions to Priests and Temple Officials stipulate that all sacrificial food and drink must first be offered to the god. Then the priests and their family members consume it on the same day if possible, but if necessary, they may have up to three days (cf. Lev. 7:16–17, which gives a two-day limit).[76] So human consumption of the food is secondary, after it is regarded as utilized by the god. Some Hittite food or drink items are permitted only to priests and some must be consumed within the sacred precincts (as in Lev. 6:16, 26; 7:6; 24:9, of food).[77] While such Hittite procedures showed important similarities to Israelite ritual practice, Yahweh did not utilize human food before his priests ate it, so their consumption was not secondary.[78]

Besides edible portions, the hide of an animal was valuable and could serve as payment for an officiating priest both in Israelite (7:8) and Emar (Syria) ritual systems.[79] The Punic Marseilles Tariff not only regulates distribution of dedicated items among priests and offerers; it sets monetary fees for some offerings in proportion to the size of the animals.[80]

Expression of thankfulness (7:12). Gratitude and vows (7:12, 16) could also motivate non-Israelites to make offerings to their deities. For example, the Phoenician king Yeḥawmilk gratefully gave works of art to his goddess.[81] The Aramean king Bir-Hadad set up a stele "for his lord Melqart, to whom he made a vow and who heard his voice."[82] Here fulfillment of a votive obligation is also an expression of gratitude.[83]

That person must be cut off from his people (7:20). This terminal penalty for very serious sin (cf. Num. 15:30–31) is administered by God himself and denies the offender an afterlife, most likely through extirpation of his line of descendants.[84] So it makes sense that a wrongdoer could be put to death and "cut off" as well (Lev. 20:2–3).

Non-Israelites also referred to the punishment of losing posterity. The Hittite Instructions to Priests and Temple Officials warn of consequences if the temple burns down because of neglect to properly extinguish the fire on the hearth: "He who commits this sin will perish along with his descendants. Of those in the temple none will be left living. They will perish together with their descendants."[85]

Consecration of Priests and Sanctuary (8:1–36)

Bring Aaron and his sons (8:2). Preparing the Israelite sanctuary and its priesthood for their sacred function was an elaborate week-long procedure that purified and sanctified them by ritual agents such as water, anointing oil, and sacrificial blood.[86] Non-Israelites also used rituals to consecrate objects and persons. For example, establishing a satellite temple as a new place of worship for the Goddess of the Night in Anatolia was a seven-day process (five days for the old temple and two days for the new temple) that included purification of new sancta with blood on the last day (see comment on 1:5).[87]

All ancient Near Eastern religious systems employed cultic officials of various hierarchical levels to promote positive human interactions with deities by administering and maintaining temples, protecting boundaries of the sacred sphere, performing rituals, seeking to ascertain the divine will through oracles or divination, and leading corporate worship, including performance of festivals. These were weighty responsibilities, so priests at the top of the hierarchy were invested with great power and prestige, and inducting such a person into office could require an elaborate process (see sidebar in "Installing a High Priestess of the Storm God at Emar").

Anointing oil (8:10). To symbolize divine designation for leadership positions that involved special contracts/covenants with Yahweh, Israelites anointed individuals to change their status (verb for "anoint" + preposition "to/as" + a

Replica of a Philistine period oil jar
Copyright
1995–2009 Phoenix
Data Systems

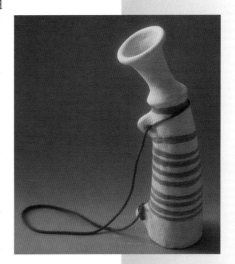

▶ Installing a High Priestess of the Storm God at Emar

Here are some highlights of the Emar procedures, which lasted nine days:

Day 1. The new high priestess is selected by use of sacred lots, oil from the palace and a temple are placed on her head, and sacrifices are offered to the storm god.

Day 2. The high priestess is shaved, a sacrifice of homage is performed for the storm god on behalf of the high priestess, some men feast at the storm god's temple, more oil is poured on the head of the high priestess, and sacrifices are presented to various gods.

Day 3. A sacrifice of homage to the storm god is performed on behalf of the high priestess, she is seated on her throne, gold earrings are put on her ears, the storm god's gold ring is put on her right hand, and her head is wrapped with a red wool headdress.

Days 3–9. During a feast celebrating installation of the high priestess, which lasts seven days,[A-4] sacrifices are offered every day, and the high priestess must give two gold figurines to the storm god and Hebat (his consort).

Day 9. The high priestess leaves the house of her family with her head covered like a bride, she performs sacrifices in several locations, some men feast at the storm god's temple, and the high priestess is settled into her new residence.[A-5]

title) to that of priest or king. Elsewhere in the ancient Near East, symbolic anointing of persons could accompany business contracts, marriage, liberation of slaves, and vassal treaties (to represent obligation and a conditional curse that would take effect if the party that received the oil were to break the treaty).[88] Outside Israel, anointing could also represent protection from supernatural beings and/or elevation of status, including elevation to priesthood. Thus the Reforms of Uru-inim-gina refer to "the anointed priests."[89]

Ram for the ordination (8:22). The word for "ordination" here is derived from the idiom for "ordain," which is literally "fill the hand" (v. 33). The Akkadian cognate expression illuminates the meaning of the idiom: It can refer to authorization for a particular official role, which could be symbolized by filling one's hand with the relevant tool or insignia, such as a scepter for a king.[90]

Inauguration of the Sacrificial System (9:1–10:20).

Aaron lifted his hands toward the people and blessed them (9:22). "The meaning here is that Aaron faced the people. His hands, of course, were raised toward heaven (Ex. 9:29, 33)."[91] This was just after the first high priest had finished officiating the inaugural sacrifices and before the Lord consumed them with fire. In the Ugaritic epic that bears his name, Kirta's hand-raising and sacrifice also functioned together to invoke a celestial deity (see sidebar "A Ugaritic Sacrifice" at 1:9).[92] In the ancient Near East, raising hands before a superior human power (such as a military conqueror) was a gesture of submission.[93] Thus, raising them toward God or heaven could accompany humble petition through prayer (see also 1 Kings 8:22, 54; cf. 1 Tim. 2:8).

The glory of the LORD appeared (9:23). When Aaron and his sons initiated the ritual system by performing their first priestly officiation, Yahweh's glory appeared,[94] and he consumed the sacrifices with fire to complete his acceptance of the sanctuary. Compare the Sumerian Cylinder B of the ruler Gudea, which describes initiation festivities when the god Ningirsu and his consort Baba, as represented by their idols, were settled into their new temple. Their entrance was accompanied by offerings as well as purifica-

Relief from
the tomb of
Horemheb at
Memphis shows
foreigners raising
their hands to
implore a royal
servant.
Erich Lessing/Art
Resource, NY, cour-
tesy of Rijksmuseum
van Oudheden,
Leiden, The Neth-
erlands

◀

tion and divination procedures. Gudea presented "housewarming gifts" to the divine
couple (cf. Num. 7), prepared a banquet for
Ningirsu, and offered animal sacrifices.[95]

Comparison between the Israelite and
Sumerian procedures yields a stunning contrast. The protocol for Ningirsu and Baba
followed the standard ancient Near Eastern
pattern: Installation of deities, represented by
images, was part of a ritual process carried
out by human beings. But Yahweh moved
himself, not his image, into his Israelite tabernacle *before* any consecration or inauguration rituals were performed (Ex. 40:34–35)
to rule out the possibility that anyone could
think that humans had moved him in! By
implication, of course, he could also leave on
his own if he chose to do so (Ezek. 9–11).

They offered unauthorized fire (10:1).
Burning incense as an offering to a deity had
to be done right. Thus in the daily ritual in
the temple of the god Amun-Re at Karnak
(Egypt), the high priest was obliged to follow a detailed protocol: reciting spells for
striking the fire, taking the censer, placing
the incense bowl on the censer arm, putting
incense on the flame, and advancing to the
sacred place.[96] The ritual mistake of Aaron's
two sons was burning incense to Yahweh with
"unauthorized fire," which apparently refers
to live coals from a fire other than that which
God himself had just lit on the altar in the
courtyard (9:24; cf. 16:12; Num. 16:46).

Offering incense
Brian J. McMorrow

▼

Do not let your hair become unkempt, and do not tear your clothes (10:6). Forbidden here (see also 21:10–12) are ancient Near Eastern mourning customs (cf. Gen. 37:34; Job 1:20; see comment on 19:28). In a Mesopotamian myth, when the goddess Ishtar descended to the underworld and fertility ceased, "Papsukkal, vizier of the great gods, hung his head, his face [became gloomy]; He wore mourning clothes, his hair was unkempt."[97]

You and your sons are not to drink (10:9). All over the ancient Near East, wine and beer were regularly served to the gods with their sacrificial meals.[98] The idea that deities could become intoxicated by such beverages is reflected in Ugaritic mythology and in the Babylonian Creation Epic (*Enuma Elish*), where partying gods make a momentous decision to exalt Marduk above other gods while they are "under the influence."[99] There is nothing like this in the Bible with regard to Israel's God.[100] Rather, he makes his tabernacle an alcohol-free zone so that his priests can make clear decisions between crucial categories.

The Hittite Instructions to Priests and Temple Officials recognize that drunken priests could cause disturbance or quarreling or could disrupt a festival. Rather than directly restricting alcohol use, however, these instructions mandate beating as punishment for obnoxious behavior and warn priests that they are accountable for proper performance of festivals, which implies the need for mental clarity.[101]

A Holy Diet (11:1–47)

These are the ones you may eat (11:2). From the rather extensive taxonomy of animals in this chapter (cf. Deut. 14), a modern reader could gain the impression that meat constituted a substantial portion of the ancient diet. However, such was not the case:

> Regardless of the place or period in question, diets in antiquity were predominantly vegetarian. The use of animal products was

in large measure confined to milk curds and cheeses.... Most people could afford to eat meat only on special occasions. Typically accompanying these was a sacrifice of some sort. Indeed, it was not uncommon for a single animal to provide both the sacrifice and the meal. Every use of meat thus became a sacral meal, and every act of animal slaughter a sacrifice.[102]

There were also restrictions on diet in ancient Egypt and Mesopotamia, but these were unrelated to each other or to the biblical ones, and unlike the latter, they did not comprise overall dietary systems. In Egypt restrictions were localized, and generally in each geographic area they dealt with only one species that was prohibited for a religious reason. For example, it was forbidden to eat a cow where the principal god was Hathor, who takes the form of a bovine (cf. the sacred cow in India). Mesopotamians were supposed to avoid particular activities at certain times, which could include eating some kinds of animals on specific days of the month. They were also to avoid violating taboos, which perhaps in some cases could involve eating food reserved for deities.[103]

Leviticus 11 does not provide an explicit rationale for its division of animals into clean/permitted versus unclean/forbidden categories. Interpreters have proposed a wide variety of possible rationales, including effects on human physical health, reflection of societal values (Mary Douglas), analogy to God's holy sacrificial "diet" (Edwin Firmage), the need to teach reverence for the sanctity of life (within the context of the opposition between holiness-life and impurity-death that pervades the ritual system) by limiting animal slaughter (Jacob Milgrom), and the concept that nonpermitted animals depart from the creation ideal of life in that they are associated with death in various ways (Jiri Moskala). The last three of these rationales are the most persuasive because they are based on the reason given in Leviticus 11 for this dietary legislation as a whole: the requirement that God's people should be holy as he is (11:44–45; cf. Deut. 14:21).[104]

And the pig ... is unclean for you (11:7). Of all animals in Israel's environment, only the pig has cloven hooves but does not chew cud. "With this one exception, all unclean animals could have been excluded simply by the requirement that they have cloven hooves."[105] So the rules in Leviticus 11 implicitly single out the pig for exclusion from the holy Israelite diet.

Pigs, along with dogs, were regarded with contempt in the ancient Near East because of their roles as scavengers. For example, the Hittite Instructions to Priests and Temple Officials warn against letting a pig or dog into rooms containing sacred bread.[106] A Mesopotamian saying goes: "The pig is unholy [...] bespattering his backside, Making the streets smell ... polluting the houses."[107] Nevertheless, texts and archaeological remains (especially bones) in Egypt and Mesopotamia, as well as Syria-Palestine and North Africa, confirm that pigs were commonly raised for food by non-Israelites.[108] In some ancient cultures (Hittite, Greek, Roman), unlike Israel, pigs could be offered as sacrifices—especially of purification—to underworld deities. In such a sacrifice, the offerer received none of the meat. Pigs could also be utilized in nonsacrificial rites of purification, including symbolic/magical elimination of impurity or plague.

Wash his clothes, and he will be unclean till evening (11:25). Ablutions with water for ritual purification were also practiced outside Israel. For example, in a Sumerian inscription, Gudea prepares to offer a sacrifice by bathing before dressing.[109] While the concept of evening-ending impurity appears to be unique to Israel, a Ugaritic text views sunset as a boundary for another ritual category: "At the descent of the sun, the day is profane. At the setting of the sun, the king is profane."[110]

Remedy for Physical Ritual Impurity Resulting from Childbirth (12:1–8)

Ceremonially unclean for seven days (12:2). Throughout history, many cultures all over the world have treated genital discharges, including those involved in menstruation and childbirth, as causing ritual impurity (see comments on Lev. 15).[111] For example, a Hittite birth ritual text requires a sacrifice on the seventh day after birth and says that a male infant is pure by the age of three months, but a female is pure at four months.[112] As in Leviticus 12, there is a weeklong initial period of impurity, and purification of a girl takes longer (cf. vv. 4–5).[113] However, whereas the Hittite process has to do with the baby's impurity, Leviticus is concerned with that of the mother. Also, the Hittite sacrifice is offered at the end of the first week, but Israelite sacrifices come after the entire period of purification.

The fact that concepts of impurity connected with human reproduction are so widespread indicates that their origin "must reside in some universal human condition that has evoked the same response all over the globe."[114] For the Israelites, this condition had to do with "the birth–death cycle that comprises mortality."[115] Because the God of Israel is immortal (Deut. 5:26), he required Israelites to keep their physical ritual impurities, which emphasized their mortality, separate from his sacred domain.

Diagnosis of Ritually Impure Scale Disease (13:1–59)

An infectious skin disease (13:2). A more accurate rendering is "a scaly affection" (NJPS).[116] Here the issue regarding scaly (with lesions) skin disease is not infection/contagion in the sense that it makes other people physically sick. Rather, the concern is with protection of the sphere of holiness, centered at the sanctuary, from defilement by ritual impurity, which is a conceptual category associated with mortality (cf. Num. 5:3; 12:10–12).

The maladies lumped in Leviticus 13–14 under the heading of scale disease cannot be simply equated with modern "leprosy" (i.e., Hansen's disease). The Hebrew term applies to a complex of conditions, including some that resemble psoriasis and vitiligo, just as

Hippocrates used Greek *lepra* for several skin diseases.[117] In Leviticus, scale disease is not even restricted to human beings, but could also affect a house (see comment on 14:34). In some instances, white discoloration of skin or hair could be a factor among others that was symptomatic of the impure affliction. For a similar dim view of white discolorations, compare Mesopotamian omens.[118]

The Lord can smite people with scale disease as punishment, especially for sacrilege (Num. 12; 2 Kings 5:20–27; 2 Chron. 26:16–21; cf. Deut. 28:27).[119] The idea that skin disease could be severe divine punishment, signifying rejection by one's deity, has been known elsewhere in the ancient Near East, especially in Mesopotamian curses, but also among the Greeks, Persians, and the Nuer people of Africa.[120]

He must live outside the camp (13:46). Some Mesopotamian curses also speak of ostracizing persons afflicted with scale disease.[121] Compare the rule where Babylonian cultic functionaries who became ritually impure by purging the Ezida cella of the god Nabû on the fifth day of the Babylonian New Year Festival of Spring were required to remain outside the city of Babylon for the duration of the festival.[122]

Caper plant thought to be hyssop
Kim Walton

Remedy for Physical Ritual Impurity Resulting from Skin Disease (14:1–57)

Two live clean birds (14:4). This elimination ritual symbolically transfers ritual impurity from the recovered person to the living bird by means of the blood of the (other) slain bird, in which (along with water) the living bird is dipped. Then the living bird is set free and carries the impurity away.[123] Birds were also used in Anatolian and Mesopotamian elimination rituals. For example, a Hittite ritual to remove evil dispatches a goat (cf. Lev. 16:21–22) and releases an eagle and a hawk.[124]

In a Mesopotamian *namburbi* ritual to get rid of evil portended by a bird (in an omen), a male and female partridge are obtained. The patient raises them with his hands and recites an incantation before Shamash that includes a request that the evil be distanced from the patient. Upon completion of the rite, the male bird is released to the east, before the sun god. Unlike the biblical ritual, the freed bird does not receive a transfer of impurity, but by its physical form represents the evil (cf. Num. 21:6–9).[125]

Fresh water (14:5). It is appropriate that (lit.) "living water," meaning fresh flowing water (Gen. 26:19), should remedy impurity generated by the living death of scale disease and other defilements resulting from mortality (Lev. 15:13; Num. 19:17).[126] Hittites and Babylonians also regarded fresh flowing water, such as rivers, as superior sources of purification. On the fourth day of the Ninth-Year Festival of Telipinu, Hittites take images of Telipinu and other gods, plus a cult pedestal, to a river and wash them.[127] During the Babylonian New Year Festival of Spring, the high priest is to bathe in water from the Tigris and Euphrates rivers (see comment on Lev. 16:4).[128]

A spreading mildew in a house (14:34). J. Milgrom translates "a fungous infection."[129] In Mesopotamia, fungus in the walls of a house could be a good or bad omen. Black fungus portended brisk trade and wealth at that address, but green and red fungi (cf. Lev. 14:37) were ominous: "The master of the house will die, dispersal of the man's house."[130] By contrast, while fungus in an Israelite house could generate the need to replace some of its material and ritually purify it—or (in a worst case scenario) could lead to its condemnation and demolition—the problem was limited to the house and did not indicate other kinds of dangers (caused by demons, etc.) for future inhabitants. So there was inconvenience, but once again, the religion of Israel's God eliminates superstition and the fear that results from it.

An elaborate two-day Anatolian ritual invokes underworld deities to come up, take evil(s) (impurity, perjury, bloodshed, curse, threat, tears, sin, quarrel, and/or gossip) haunting a house, and transport them back down into the nether regions. At the end of the process, safe disposal of the ritual paraphernalia takes place out in the steppe country.[131] In terms of the nature of evils remedied, deities involved, and procedures implemented, the Anatolian ritual differs greatly from Israelite purification of a fungous house. However, there are some strikingly specific points of contact: use of water ("water of purification"—cf. Num. 8:7; 19:9; spring water—cf. Lev. 14:51), the number seven (drawing water and pouring it out; cf. seven days in 14:38–39), red wool (cf. 14:49), contact of a slain animal with water (but libating a lamb before slaughtering it, unlike 14:50), and slaughter of birds (but cooked for sacrifice, unlike 14:50–52). Such similarities reinforce the concept that the Israelite ritual system and the worldview associated with it shared much with common ancient Near Eastern heritage, but important differences made Israelite religion unique in crucial ways.

Physical Ritual Impurity Resulting from Genital Flows (15:1–33)

A bodily discharge (15:2). The male impurity stems from an abnormal urethral discharge that could consist of pus or excessive mucus and which could be caused by gonorrhea.[132]

As an alternative, J. V. Kinnier-Wilson has suggested that it could be caused by infectious urinary bilharzia, an ailment known to have been a problem in antiquity, which was produced by the parasite *schistosoma*, related to snails in water systems that have been detected by archaeologists.[133] The abnormal female condition in Leviticus 15 has to do with a chronic vaginal discharge of blood, which arises from a disorder of the uterus.[134]

Whoever touches any of the things that were under him will be unclean (15:10). A discharge from the genitals directly contaminated objects underneath, such as a bed or chair, which would secondarily contaminate anyone else who touched them. A Mesopotamian incantation also speaks of secondary contamination by sleeping on the bed, sitting in the chair, eating at the table, or drinking from the cup of an accursed person.[135] In this and other Mesopotamian texts, the contagion is demonic: "The common notion in these contexts was that the sinner, or defiled, or diseased individual was liable to demonic attack, and it is the demons themselves who are the contagious agents."[136] For Israelites, such terrible fear was gone and no exorcism was necessary.

When a man has an emission of semen (15:16). A Mesopotamian omen says: "If a man ejaculates in his dream and is spattered with his semen—that man will find riches; he will have financial gain."[137] But in the Israelite religious system, any seminal discharge, including nocturnal emission (Deut. 23:11), generated ritual impurity. Nevertheless, this impurity simply disqualified a person from coming in contact with holy things. There was no acknowledgment of the belief held by some ancient people (such as Hittites) that nocturnal emissions indicated sexual relations with spirits, even with deceased family members.[138]

An Israelite who engaged in sexual relations was barred from entering the sacred precincts of the sanctuary until evening. The situation was similar for Egyptians, but differed in other religious cultures,

▶ The Daily Routine in an Egyptian Temple

In an Egyptian temple, the routine begins with the royal representative entering the chapel. He spreads incense and opens the *naos* to reveal the cult image. Thereafter follow spells of prostration, praise, and offerings, after which the cult statue is removed, salved, clothed, adorned, and provided with unguent and eye paint. In the concluding rites, fresh sand is strewn on the chapel floor, and the god is purified by water and natron and replaced in the *naos*. On exiting, the priest sweeps away his footprints, banishing impurities and demonic forces.[A-6]

Even such daily access was restricted to authorized persons. Ancient Near

Eastern temples were not places of public worship like our churches or synagogues today because they were regarded as possessing or containing sanctity that had to be guarded against profanation or defilement.[A-7]

where ritualized sex flourished. The Hittite "Instructions to Priests and Temple Officials" prohibit cultic functionaries from defiling sancta (on pain of death for a kind of intentional violation; cf. Lev. 22:9) by approaching sacrificial loaves and libation vessels without bathing after sexual intercourse. But that is all. There is no waiting period and no prohibition of sexual activity elsewhere in the temple precincts.[139] So all in all, the Israelite system put greater emphasis on the difference between the holy, immortal deity and mortal human beings, whose creative/reproductive functions only generate more human beings subject to death.

The Day of Atonement (16:1–34)

Into the Most Holy Place (16:2). By contrast to the Israelite high priest, who was permitted to enter the inner apartment of the sanctuary only once per year, other ancient Near Eastern priests were required to enter the inner sanctums of their temples every day in order to care for and "feed" (images of) their gods (see comment on 3:11; see sidebar on "The Daily Routine in an Egyptian Temple").

Behind the curtain (16:2). The Israelite sanctuary had three curtains: a screen (*māsāk*) at the entrance to the court (Ex. 38:18; Num. 3:26), another screen (*māsāk*) at the entrance to the outer sanctum (Ex. 26:36–37; 36:37), and an inner curtain (*pārōket*; Ex. 26:31–35). In Leviticus 16:2 the Hebrew word is *pārōket*, which only denotes the curtain that formed the boundary of the inner sanctum by separating the two apartments of the tabernacle. This special usage agrees with the fact that the Akkadian cognate *parakku* refers to a defined sacred space around the presence of a deity (or divine symbol/image).[140] So the best translation of *pārōket* would be "inner curtain." The Israelite sanctuary was not unique in having such a curtain; a Mesopotamian omen refers to "the linen curtain of a temple (in front of the cult statue)."[141]

He must bathe himself with water (16:4). Non-Israelites also purified themselves with water before engaging in ritual activity. In a Sumerian inscription, the ruler Gudea prepares to offer a sacrifice to his god Ningirsu by bathing before dressing.[142] In Babylon during the New Year Festival of Spring (= Akitu Festival), the high priest was to do the following: "On the 5th day of the month *Nisannu*, during the final four hours of the night, the High Priest arises and bathes in the waters of the Tigris and Euphrates rivers."[143] By washing with water from these special sources, which also provided water for later sprinkling the temple to remove ritual impurity, the high priest attained a degree of ritual purity necessary for subsequent officiation,

which involved entering the presence of the high god Bēl (= Marduk) and his consort (see comment on 22:2).[144]

Making atonement by sending it into the desert (16:10). Azazel's nonsacrificial "tote" goat (NIV translates "scapegoat") served as a ritual "garbage truck" to purge the Israelite community of moral faults through a process of transfer and disposal.[145] Other ancient Near Eastern rituals included transfer and disposal. For example, the Hittite Ambazzi and Huwarlu rituals closely parallel the Israelite ritual "in that they use live animals as bearers of the evil and lack the motif of substitution."[146] The Ritual of Ambazzi to rid people of "evil sickness" and "evil tension" goes as follows:

> She wraps a little tin on the bowstring. She puts it on the right hand (and) feet of the offerers. Then she takes it away and puts it on a mouse (saying): "I have taken

Footprints of deity lead through two chambers to the inner niche at the temple at Ain Dara.
John Monson
▼

away from you evil and I have put it on the mouse. Let this mouse take it to the high mountains, the deep valleys (and) the distant ways." She lets the mouse go (saying): "Alawaimi, drive this (mouse) forth, and I will give to you a goat to eat." [Offerings to Alawaimi and other gods follow.][147]

Unlike the biblical ritual, a deity is entreated (by words and sacrifice) for help in getting rid of the animal bearing the evil.[148]

The Ritual of Huwarlu had the purpose of removing an evil "magical word" from the king and queen and from their palace. A small live dog was waved over the couple and inside the palace in order to transfer the evil to the animal. Then an old woman uttered an incantation expressing the dog's ability to bear the evil, and the animal was taken away to a location regarded as designated by the gods. By contrast, the oral component of the Israelite ritual was confession (by the high priest; Lev. 16:21) rather than an incantation, and the power of the biblical procedure was from the Lord rather than magical in nature.[149] Nevertheless, acting out transfer and disposal provided powerful assurance to the Israelites that their community was freed from the sins they had committed during the past year.

As a scapegoat (16:10). Translating $la^{ca}z\bar{a}^{\flat}z\bar{e}l$ here, we should read instead "to Azazel" (NRSV; NJB).[150] We know that $^{ca}z\bar{a}^{\flat}z\bar{e}l$ should be the proper name of a party capable of ownership because a lot ceremony designated one goat *layhwh*, "belonging to Yahweh," and the other goat as $la^{ca}z\bar{a}^{\flat}z\bar{e}l$, "belonging to Azazel" (16:8). However, we do not know what the name "Azazel" means.[151]

A number of scholars have attempted to answer the question by reconstructing etymologies based on ancient Near Eastern parallels. For example, in accord with the rabbinic tradition that during the Second Temple period Azazel's goat was driven over a cliff to its death (*m. Yoma* 6:6), G. R. Driver took Azazel to mean "jagged rocks/

precipice," derived from the Semitic root *ʿzz*, from which also comes the Arabic word *ʿazâzu(n)*, "rough ground."[152] O. Loretz suggests a linguistic relation between Azazel and the Ugaritic divine name *ʿzbʿl*.[153] Based on their interpretation of the Hurrian term *aza/ušḫi* in light of Akkadian use of the root *ʿzz*, which refers to divine anger, B. Janowski and G. Wilhelm interpret the "Azazel" ritual as expulsion of a goat in order to overcome divine anger.[154]

If Azazel is a proper name, $la^{ca}z\bar{a}^{\flat}z\bar{e}l$ in 16:10 following the words "by sending it into the desert" most naturally indicates the one to whom the live goat is sent: "to Azazel" (cf. 16:26). This rules out the common interpretation of $^{ca}z\bar{a}^{\flat}z\bar{e}l$ as "(e)scapegoat," referring to the goat itself. Obviously the goat would not be sent "to the scapegoat."[155]

The fact that Yahweh, owner of the goat slain as a purification offering (16:9, 15), is supernatural suggests that Azazel, owner of the live goat, is also some kind of supernatural being. Because transporting a load of Israelite toxic waste, consisting of moral faults, to Azazel in the wilderness and abandoning it there by the command of Yahweh (16:10, 22; cf. Zech 5:5–11) is a singularly unfriendly gesture, it appears that Azazel is Yahweh's enemy.[156] Therefore, Azazel is most likely some kind of demon (so Jewish tradition recorded in *1 En.* 10:4–5), who dwells in an uninhabited region (cf. Lev. 17:7; Isa. 13:21; 34:14; Luke 11:24; Rev. 18:2).[157]

The biblical ritual expels moral faults *to* Azazel, who is apparently the ultimate source of their sins (cf. Gen. 3; Rev. 12:9). By contrast, non-Israelite rituals involving demons were concerned with expelling the demons themselves.[158] For example, a ritual for purifying the Ezida shrine of the god Nabû on the fifth day of the Babylonian New Year Festival of Spring began by covering the shrine with a golden canopy. Then the high priest and a group of artisans recited an incantation invoking the gods to exorcise demons who could be lurking there: "Marduk purifies the temple, Kusu designs the plan, and Ningirim

▶ Use of Incense in the Ancient World

Incense was highly valued for sweetening the environment. It was often attributed qualities regarded as associated with or capable of reaching the sphere of deities, who enjoyed its smell. A love poem about the Mesopotamian deities Nabû and Tashmetu includes the words: "Let the pure scent of juniper incense circulate in the sanctuary!"[A-8]

Outside the Bible, incense was used in various ways:

1. In funerary rites to facilitate the passage of dead persons into the afterlife, incense was burned for purification, protection, and divine-human communication, and unburned incense was used for embalming (Egypt, Phoenicia, Mesopotamia).
2. During daily and festival worship, incense was burned for purification, consecration, protection, or appeasement (Egypt, Mesopotamia). Ascending incense smoke could be regarded as carrying prayers up to heaven or enhancing the environment in which an oracle could be received (Mesopotamia).[A-9]
3. Magical rituals used incense to purify persons or places and

protect them from evil spirits and to invoke deities for aid in exorcising demons (Egypt, Mesopotamia). Movements of incense smoke could also be read as omens (Mesopotamia).
4. Throughout the Near East, incense was used as a cosmetic to enhance the attractiveness of persons, their clothes, or rooms, and it was burned at parties to sweeten the atmosphere. Some chewed it to eliminate bad breath.

In the Hebrew Bible, burning incense sweetened the sanctuary both daily (Ex. 30:7–8) and on the annual Day of Atonement, when it protected the high priest from God's Presence (Lev. 16:12–13). Unburned incense was added to some grain offerings (2:1–2, 15–16). On one occasion Aaron burned incense to "atone" (*kipper*) for the Israelites in the sense of turning away God's wrath and thereby stopping a divine plague (Num. 16:46–48 [Heb. 17:11–13]). In secular use, incense could serve as a cosmetic (e.g., Ps. 45:8[9]; Prov. 7:17) and apparently as a kind of medicine (Jer. 8:22; 46:11; 51:8).[A-10]

casts the spell. Whatever evil resides in this temple, get out! Great demon, may Bēl kill you! May you be cut down wherever you are!"[159] The Israelites didn't need to worry about such demons because the Lord's Presence would keep them away. The people's concern was to acknowledge and banish the sins they had committed.

Take some of the bull's blood (16:14). On the Day of Atonement, the high priest purged (*kipper*, usually rendered "atone") the three major consecrated components of the

sanctuary—inner sanctum, outer sanctum, and outer altar—on behalf of the priests and nonpriests by applying the blood of special purification offerings (bull and goat) to parts of them (vv. 14–19, 20, 33).

Non-Israelite peoples also periodically cleansed their sacred precincts and/or sacred objects contained in them, but they generally used substances other than blood.[160] The Sumerian Nanshe Hymn mentions purification of the temple belonging to the goddess Nanshe: "[ ] her house

Relationship to a Man	Leviticus 18	Leviticus 20	Laws of Hammurabi	Hittite Laws
mother	forbidden		forbidden	forbidden
daughter	implicitly forbidden		forbidden	forbidden
son	implicitly forbidden			forbidden
full sister	implicitly forbidden			
father's wife	forbidden[177]	forbidden	forbidden if she was the principal wife who had borne children	forbidden with step-mother only while father is alive
half sister	forbidden	forbidden		
grandchild	forbidden			
stepsister	forbidden			
aunt	forbidden		forbidden	
daughter-in-law	forbidden	forbidden	forbidden	
brother's wife	forbidden	forbidden		forbidden only while brother is alive
woman + her daughter or mother	forbidden	forbidden		forbidden if he is married to one or the other[178]
woman + her granddaughter	forbidden			
sister of wife while wife is alive	forbidden to marry			forbidden

of men to their sisters, daughters, or even mothers were regarded as acts of piety.[175] However, most ancient societies discouraged incest. The Babylonian Laws of Hammurabi and the Hittite Laws viewed some sexual liasons in ways that are paralleled in Leviticus 18 and 20.[176] The accompanying chart basically follows the order in Leviticus 18.

Here are some points of comparison between Leviticus and the Hittite laws:

1. The Hittite laws explicitly label sexual relations between a man and his daughter or son "an unpermitted sexual pairing." These cases are not specified in Leviticus but are covered, along with the case of a full sister, by the general principle that "no one is to approach any close relative to have sexual relations" (18:6).[179]

2. The Hittite laws forbid sexual union of a man with his brother's wife only while his brother is alive and mandate: "If a man has a wife, and the man dies, his brother shall take his widow as wife. (If the brother dies) his father shall take her. When afterwards his father dies, his (i.e., the father's) brother shall take the woman whom he had."[180] This is like levirate (brother-in-law) marriage in Deuteronomy 25:5–10, which is more restricted in that it applies only if the widow has no son and does not provide for the event that her brother-in-law subsequently dies. However, in Genesis 38 Tamar tricks her father-in-law into impregnating her after his son died.

3. In the Hittite laws, a man is not permitted to sexually approach his wife's daughter. If he is married to a daugh-

ter, he may not sexually approach her mother or sister. However, "if a man's wife dies, [he may take her] sister [as his wife.] It is not an offense."[181] This cluster of provisions would include the situation addressed in Leviticus 18:18—"Do not take your wife's sister as a rival wife." Some have argued that "sister" here broadly refers to any other woman, so that this is a blanket prohibition of polygamy.[182] But the immediately preceding context is incest, and in the parallel Hittite legislation "sister" is obviously used narrowly and literally within the immediate family, along with "daughter" and "mother."

4. The Hittite laws introduce a subjective element not present in Leviticus: a man's knowledge of relationships between women. If he "sleeps with free sisters who have the same mother and with their mother—one in one country and the other in another, it is not an offense." But if this occurs in the same place and he knows that the women are related, "it is an unpermitted sexual pairing."[183]

5. Unlike Leviticus 18 and 20, the Hittite laws include permitted liaisons, cover situations in which male relatives sleep with the same woman, and address cases involving slaves or prostitutes, in which incest standards are lowered.

Do not lie with a man as one lies with a woman (18:22). This verse and 20:13 categorically and unambiguously condemn male homosexuality as an abomination to God, punishable in 20:13 by death.[184] There is plenty of evidence for homosexuality and bestiality in the ancient Near East.[185] A Mesopotamian omen (concerned with results rather than morality) prognosticates: "If a man has anal sex with a man of equal status—that man will be foremost among his brothers and colleagues."[186] However, the Middle Assyrian laws have a different attitude, which is closer to that of Leviticus: "If a man sodom-

izes his comrade and they prove the charges against him and find him guilty, they shall sodomize him and they shall turn him into a eunuch."[187] In harmony with this negative assessment, a confession of righteousness in the Egyptian Book of the Dead affirms: "I have not copulated with a boy."[188]

Do not have sexual relations with an animal (18:23). Unlike the Bible, Ugaritic mythology describes bestiality by deities. For example, when Motu threatens Baʿlu (Baal) with death, the latter seeks to guarantee himself a form of afterlife through progeny by repeatedly copulating with a cow, which conceives and bears him a male.[189] This is not so surprising because mixed beings were common in the realm of the gods throughout the ancient Near East.[190]

As with homosexuality, the Bible bans bestiality because it violates the order of sexual pairings (heterosexual within a species) that God established at creation (Gen. 1–2). The Hittite laws condemn a person who engages in bestiality with certain kinds of animals (cow, sheep, pig, dog) to death unless the king grants him mercy, which may also be extended to the animal. Even if the monarch hears his case, the offender may not personally appear before him lest the king be (secondarily) defiled.[191] For the concept that illicit sexual activity defiles, compare Leviticus 18:20; Numbers 5:13, etc. (adultery), and Leviticus 18:23 (bestiality).

Comprehensively Holy Living (19:1–37)

Be holy because I, the LORD your God, am holy (19:2). The Egyptian Instruction of Amenemope presents the divine standard as unattainable for human beings:

> God is ever in his perfection,
> Man is ever in his failure.
> The words men say are one thing,
> The deeds of the god are another...
> There is no perfection before the god,
> But there is failure before him;

Cuneiform cone
with the Reforms
of Uru-inimgina
Mike Beuselinck,
courtesy of the
Louvre
▼

If one strains to seek perfection,
In a moment he has marred it.[192]

By contrast, Yahweh commands his people to emulate him in character by following his standards of right living, which are exemplified in his laws (see also 11:45; 20:26). This implies that his moral standards are attainable, as explicitly stated in Deuteronomy 30:11–14. Compare the Sumerian Nanshe Hymn, according to which temple dependents are judged by their faithfulness (or lack thereof) to the personal cultic and ethical standards of the goddess.[193]

Do not turn to idols (19:4) Ancient Near Eastern peoples regarded their deities as powerful living beings, but they worshiped gods through idols identified with them, which were believed to somehow partake of the divine essence.[194] By contrast, the God of Israel refused to be identified with material representations, which would limit and distort human perceptions regarding him (Deut. 4:15–18).

To "turn to" another power, such as a god represented by an idol, is to switch allegiance to it, as exemplified by a treaty between the Hittite king Muršili and Duppi-Tešub:

Do not turn your eyes towards another (land)!…

But [if] you commit [trea]chery, and while the king of Egypt [is hos]tile to My Majesty you secretly [send] your messenger to him [and you become hosti]le to the king of Hatti, and [you cast] off the hand of the king of Hatti becoming (a subject) of the king of Egypt, [thereby] you, Duppi-Tešub, will break the oath.[195]

So an Israelite who practiced idolatry rejected Yahweh in a most basic way.

Do not pervert justice (19:15). Throughout the ancient Near East, justice was a high priority and rulers prided themselves on carrying out their god-given responsibility to protect weaker members of society from oppression (cf. Ex. 22:22, etc.).[196] The Sumerian king Uru-inimgina of Lagash (c. 2351–2342 B.C.) appears to have pioneered a long tradition of social justice in the ancient Near East by establishing the first known systematic legal reforms. Later laws and hymns echoed the ideals that Uru-inimgina expressed as follows:

A citizen of Lagash living in debt, (or) who had been condemned to its prison for impost, hunger, robbery, (or) murder—their freedom he established. Uru-inimgina made a compact with the divine Nin-Girsu that the powerful man would not oppress the orphan (or) widow.[197]

Human justice and mercy were thought to reflect attributes of divinities, such as the sun-god (Šamaš/Utu), who was the patron of justice.[198] Deities could use their special powers, including perception, to assist socially disadvantaged persons (cf. Ps. 146:9).[199] Therefore it is no surprise that Yahweh, who combined in himself the roles of deity and king of Israel, would express concern for maintaining social justice in harmony with his good character.

Do not go about spreading slander among your people (19:16). Ancient Near Eastern texts similarly discourage slander of various kinds. The Instruction of Amenemope admonishes:

> Guard your tongue from harmful speech,
> Then you will be loved by others...
> Do not shout "crime" against a man,
> When the cause of (his) flight is
>   hidden.[200]

In an Old Aramaic inscription, King Panamuwa boasts that he did away with war and slander (lit., "sword and tongue") from his father's house.[201] At Nuzi, the penalty for slander was payment of one ox.[202] In the Middle Assyrian Laws, a man who goes around spreading baseless rumors or falsely claims in a public quarrel that everyone sodomizes another man is punished with fifty blows, service to the king, a haircut, and a fine of 3,600 shekels of lead.[203]

Love your neighbor as yourself (19:18). Such an attitude is illustrated by the covenanted love between David and Jonathan, who loved him "as he loved his own life"

(1 Sam. 18:3, etc.). Similar loyal love is described in a treaty between the Hittite king Tudḫaliya IV and Kurunta of Tarḫuntašša.[204] Leviticus 19:34 extends the command to love as oneself to the resident alien, who is to be treated like a native citizen. Similarly, a Mesopotamian treaty text from Alalakh provides that "[if people of my land] enter your land to preserve themselves from starvation, you must protect them and you must feed them like (citizens of) your land."[205]

Do not mate different kinds of animals (19:19).
In ancient Near Eastern art and literature, mixed beings are prevalent in the superhuman sphere of gods and demons (cf. Ezek. 1:5–11; see comment on Lev. 18:23). In Mesopotamia, demons, monsters, and minor protective deities were depicted as bulls and lions with human heads, lion-centaurs, snake-dragons, goat-fish, bird-men, scorpion-people, and so on.[206] Similarly, in Israel mixtures belonged to the sacred realm: Fabric of mixed wool and linen was reserved for parts of the tabernacle, high priest's garments, and belts of ordinary priests (Ex. 26:1, 31; 28:6, 15; 39:29). Moreover, the yield resulting from planting two kinds of seed in a vineyard would become holy and therefore forfeited to sacred ownership by the sanctuary (Deut. 22:9).[207]

Yet they are not to be put to death, because she had not been freed (19:20). The violation does not call for the death penalty, as it would if the woman possessed the power of consent belonging to a free woman (Deut. 22:23–24), provided that an inquest confirms her status, along with determining the amount of compensation due to her owner (6:4–5).[208] Compare the Mesopotamian Laws of Ur-Namma and Laws of Eshnunna, according to which a man who deflowers a slave woman must pay her owner.[209]

In Mesopotamia, Shamash was the sun god and was responsible for justice.
Z. Radovan/
www.BibleLand
Pictures.com
◄

Liver model used
for divination
Marie-Lan Nguyen/
Wikimedia Com-
mons, courtesy of the
Louvre

▶

Sketch of diviner
interpreting a
liver in their
workshop
Alva Steffler/Susanna
Vagt

▶

▶ Divination in the Ancient Near East

Divination attempts to predict the future, but magic/sorcery goes further by attempting to alter the future through occult means.[A-11] Forms of divination that sought answers from the Lord, such as legitimate prophecy and the Urim and Thummim worn by the high priest (Ex. 28:30), were permitted for Israel, but divination that failed to trust in God's knowledge and wisdom by resorting to other sources was forbidden (see also Lev. 19:31; 20:6; Deut. 18:10–12). Necromancy (divination by consulting the dead) was especially serious and punishable by death (Lev. 20:27) because it claimed to bring up underworld spirits by what amounted to a kind of sorcery (1 Sam. 28:13–15).[A-12] Sorcery, which purported to draw on superhuman power apart from that of God and thereby denied his exclusive sovereignty, was a capital crime (Ex. 22:18).

Outside Israel, divination was ubiquitous. In fact, cuneiform tablets preserved from ancient Babylonia include more omen texts than any other genre of literature.

Divination manifested itself in many forms and with a wide variety of techniques. Omens could be derived from practically anything, such as oil patterns on water, patterns of incense smoke, flight of birds, positions of heavenly bodies (astrology), casting lots, dreams, and characteristics of organs (especially the liver) in the body of a slaughtered animal.[A-13]

Among Israel's neighbors, divination was regarded as indispensable for ascertaining the thinking of the gods (see comment on 4:2) and to make crucial decisions in time of war (cf. Ezek. 21:21). Some forms of sorcery, such as exorcising demons, countering black magic, and using magic against enemy nations,[A-14] were also viewed as legitimate. On the other hand, black magic to harm others belonging to one's own society was a serious crime in Anatolia and a capital offense in Mesopotamia and Egypt.[A-15]

Do not eat any meat with the blood still in it. Do not practice divination (19:26). J. Milgrom's translation is more accurate: "You shall not eat over the blood."[210] This is not simply a reiteration of the command, based on respect for life, to abstain from eating meat (not including fish) from which the blood is not drained out at the time of slaughter (17:10–14; cf. Gen. 9:4; Acts 15:20, 29). The prohibition in Leviticus 19:26 appears related to the rest of the same verse, which forbids various kinds of divination (not including "sorcery"). Because we know that some ancient peoples poured blood into the ground as libations to underworld deities (see comments on 1:5; 17:7), the prohibition of eating *over* the blood was presumably designed to prevent Israelites from associating with some pagan practice, such as a form of divination that consulted ancestral spirits (cf. 19:27–28; Deut. 14:1–2; Jer. 48:37; Ezek. 33:25).[211] See sidebar on "Divination in the Ancient Near East."

Do not cut your bodies for the dead (19:28). Lacerating oneself in mourning was a heightened expression of sorrow (Jer. 16:6, 41:5). In the Ugaritic Myth of Baal, when the chief god ʾIlu (El) learns that Baʿlu (Baal) is dead, he goes into paroxysms of grief that emphasize the magnitude of the catastrophe:

> He pours dirt of mourning on his head, dust of humiliation on his cranium, for clothing, he is covered with a girded garment. With a stone he scratches incisions on (his) skin, with a razor he cuts cheeks and chin. He harrows his upper arms, plows (his) chest like a garden, harrows (his) back like a (garden in a) valley.[212]

Do not use dishonest standards (19:35). Honesty through use of standard weights and measures was a common topic in ancient Near Eastern literature. For example, in the

Wall painting in the tomb of Panekhmen depicts metal-workers weighing gold on scales.
Werner Forman Archive/E. Strouhal
◀

Book of the Dead, an Egyptian claims innocence: "I have not added to the weight of the balance. I have not tampered with the plummet of the scales."[213] The Laws of Hammurabi require standardization for repayment of debts and for purchases.[214] The "Instruction of Amenemope" provides a reminder of accountability to divine power:

> Do not move the scales nor alter the
>   weights,
> Nor diminish the fractions of the
>   measure…
> Do not make for yourself deficient
>   weights,
>   They are rich in grief through the
>   might of god.[215]

More on Morally Pure Life (20:1–27)

Who gives any of his children to Molech (20:2). This was human sacrifice that involved passing one's child through/in fire as part of Syro-Palestinian worship of the underworld god Molech.[216] In addition to terminally condemning anyone who engages in this hideous

Lev 19:27 forbids cutting the hair at the sides of the head. Relief shows an Asiatic with long side-locks.
Manfred Näder, Gabana Studios, Germany
◀

Penalties for Adultery and Related Sexual Offenses in Israelite Law

Offender(s)	Offense	Penalty	Reference
man & married woman	adultery	death	Lev. 20:10; Deut. 22:22
man & betrothed woman	adultery	death	Deut. 22:23–24
priest's daughter	promiscuity	burned	Lev. 21:9
bride	promiscuity (not virgin)	death	Deut. 22:20–21
man	rape of betrothed woman	death	Deut. 22:25–27
man	rape of unbetrothed woman	50 shekels, forced marriage, no right of divorce	Deut. 22:28–29
man	seduction of unbetrothed woman	bride price, forced marriage at discretion of father	Ex. 22:15–16

practice, Leviticus 20 condemns anyone who tolerates a Molech worshiper. Compare the threat, "But it will go badly for that man," in the Anatolian Telipinu Edict against anyone who fails to deliver a sorcerer to justice.[217]

In the ancient world, the Phoenicians were notable for child sacrifice, and archaeologists have found evidence for the practice at Punic Carthage in North Africa and in Sardinia.[218] Desperate circumstances, such as imminent military defeat (2 Kings 3:27 — King Mesha of Moab), could motivate people to sacrifice their children as supreme gifts to the gods whose aid they sought. But Yahweh categorically rejected such sacrifices (Deut. 18:10).[219]

Both the adulterer and the adulteress must be put to death (20:10). Whereas the laws in Leviticus 18 are apodictic commands that simply state principles ("You shall [not] ..."), chapter 20 is formulated in the more common ancient Near Eastern style of case law ("If/When ..."), which adds punishments. Because adultery was a grave sin against God, an absolute wrong, it was punishable by death to both parties, and even the husband of an adulteress had no right to lessen her punishment or that of her lover.[220] Circumstances could indicate whether or not a sexual encounter was adultery or rape (Deut. 22:23–27), but if it was adultery, circumstances carried no weight in lessening the penalty. The accompanying chart compares penalties for adultery in pentateuchal law with those of other non-incestuous sexual liaisons between men and women that were detected by human beings and punished through the Israelite judicial system.[221]

Mesopotamian law treated premeditated adultery as a crime punishable by death, as in biblical law. However, the Mesopotamians had a more subjective and variable approach to other kinds of cases. There were distinctions between degrees of adultery, depending on degrees of intention, with circumstances affecting the severity of penalties. An adulteress who had not premeditated was under her husband's jurisdiction, and whatever punishment he decided for her was also meted out to her paramour.[222]

As the chart on "Penalties for Adultery and Related Sexual Offenses in Mesopotamian Law" shows, there are common principles for determining penalties in biblical and Mesopotamian laws. The basic factors determining classification of cases are the woman's status (married/betrothed, unbetrothed, or slave) and her intention (consenting, seduced, or forced). For example, married/betrothed woman + consenting = adultery. Circumstances, such as the location and/or reaction of the woman (Deut. 22:23–27; MAL 23; cf. Hittite Laws 197), could help to reveal the woman's intention.

Penalties for Adultery and Related Sexual Offenses in Mesopotamian Law

Key to reference abbreviations: LE = Laws of Eshnunna; LH = Laws of Hammurabi; LU = Laws of Ur-Namma; MAL = Middle Assyrian Laws[223]

Offender(s)	Offense	Penalty	Reference
man & married woman	premeditated adultery and the man knows the woman is married	death	MAL 13
married woman	premeditated adultery	death	LU 4; LE 28; LH 133b
man & married woman	adultery in the act	death or according to husband[224]	MAL 15
married woman	seduces to adultery	according to husband	MAL 16
man & married woman	adultery	according to husband	LH 129; MAL 14, 23a
married woman	adultery as consent to rape	according to husband	MAL 23c
unbetrothed woman	consenting to sex	according to father	MAL 56
man	rape of married woman	death	MAL 12, 23b–c
man	rape of betrothed woman	death	LE 26; LH 130
man	rape or seducing married woman	according to husband	MAL 16
man	rape of unbetrothed woman	price of a virgin, taking rapist's wife, forced marriage at discretion of father, no right of divorce	MAL 55
man	deflowering virgin slave woman	payment to owner	LU 5; LE 31

However, a slave-woman was legally incapable of consent and therefore not accountable for her intention (Lev. 19:20).

A man who violated the right of a husband/fiancé committed a criminal action. But one who wronged the father of an unbetrothed woman or the owner of a slave was required to pay civil compensation. The marital status of men involved in illicit sex was not relevant for classification of cases because ancient Near Eastern society tolerated polygamy. Thus, there was a double standard: A married man could have more than one sexual partner at a time, but this was strictly forbidden for a married woman.[225]

The category of promiscuity/harlotry is unique to biblical law. This is consenting immorality by a woman living in her father's house, which disgraces him. If she is the daughter of a priest, whose reputation for holiness is crucial, she suffers the most severe punishment: burning (Lev. 21:9; see also Gen. 38:24), probably after death by stoning (cf. Josh. 7:25).[226]

Holy Lives of Priests (21:1–24)

A priest must not make himself ceremonially unclean (21:1). Ancient Near Eastern priests were required to be ritually pure—through avoiding impurities or undergoing purification rituals—before approaching their deities. Whereas non-Israelites feared demonic impurities, which could even threaten deities (see comment on 16:10), for Israel the sources of impurity were human beings and some kinds of animals. The holiness of Israelite priests demanded that they avoid defilement from dead persons, who epitomized the impure realm of mortality (cf. comment on 12:2).

In a Mesopotamian myth, impurity linked to the domain of death is similarly restricted: Ereshkigal, divine queen of the underworld, cannot be with the holy gods who dwell above because she is impure.[227] However, just as many ancient Near Eastern people worshiped (impure) underworld deities, they could also worship their dead ancestors.[228]

By contrast to the Israelites, for whom death was a major disruption, the Egyptians believed that life continued after death, and therefore the realm of death was positive and holy. A hymn to the god Osiris, who was king of the dead, contains the words: "Eternal lord who presides in Abydos, Who dwells distant in the graveyard," and, "The son of Isis who championed his father, Holy and splendid is his name."[229] Because death was holy, tombs were temples where priests officiated.

None of your descendants who has a defect may come near to offer (21:17). Respect for the deity required that his priestly servants be free from physical defects, just as animals offered to him were not to be defective (22:17–25).

Hittite ritual rules also excluded persons with physical disabilities from intimate access to deity in sacred precincts.[230]

Proper Treatment of Sacrifices (22:1–33)

Treat with respect the sacred offerings (22:2). The Hittite Instructions to Priests and Temple Officials explain the need for priestly purity and proper decorum by means of an apt analogy (cf. Mal. 1:6):

> When the servant stands before his master, he (is) washed. He has clothed (himself) in clean (clothes). He gives him (his master) either to eat or to drink. Since the master eats and drinks, (in) his spirit he (is) relaxed. He is favorably inclined toward him (the servant). When he (is) solicitous(?), his (master) does not find fault (with him). Is the mind of the god somehow different?[231]

It must be without defect or blemish to be acceptable (22:21). Following the same principle centuries earlier, Gudea sacrificed to his god Ningirsu, "properly arranging perfect ox and perfect he-goat."[232] Cheating the Lord by sacrificing defective animals (except for some defects allowed in freewill offerings; 22:23) was forbidden (cf. Mal. 1:6–14).[233] This ruled out substituting defective animals for acceptable ones previously designated as sacrifices. Like Malachi, the Hittite Instructions warn that the deity holds people accountable for such cheating.[234]

Holy Occasions (23:1–44)

These are the LORD's appointed feasts (23:4). Numbers 28–29 complements the liturgical calendar of Leviticus 23 by specifying communal sacrifices to be performed

Egyptian festival
list from Kom
Ombo
Mark Watson

◀

Egyptian festival
list from Kom
Ombo
Mark Watson

of some extraordinarily elaborate Hittite festivals (AN.TAḪ.ŠUM and *nuntarriyšḫaš*) that lasted for several weeks and apparently involved royal tours/pilgrimages to cultic centers around the empire.[238]

Outside Israel, festivals often commemorated mythic events. For example, the Babylonian New Year Festival included celebration of Marduk's elevation to supremacy over the gods.[239] Fertility was a major festival theme, and some mythic events, such as the death of Baal in the fall and his revival in the spring (Canaanite), were related to renewal of agricultural cycles.

As with Israelite festivals (especially Elevated Sheaf, Weeks, Booths), cyclical holy days and sacrifices of other peoples could punctuate the agricultural calendar at crucial points, such as harvest time. This was because agricultural bounty, which was crucial for survival and well-being, was regarded as dependent on the favor of deities. Thus, there were yearly celebrations of the grape harvest at the temple of Baal in Ugarit.[240] Festivals could also include purification of holy places and objects (see comment on 16:14). But non-Israelite festivals did not explicitly commemorate historical deliverance of a people by their deity as did some Israelite sacred times, such as Passover-Unleavened Bread and Booths.

On the first day of the seventh month ... trumpet blasts (23:24). The first month of the Israelite calendar is Nisan in the spring (Ex. 12:2). However, in postbiblical tradition the first day of the seventh month (Tishri) has become *Rosh Hashanah* ("New Year"). This is not a contradiction. In antiquity, a group of people could have more than one New Year's Day to mark half years that commenced with events such as equinoxes, or to initiate different kinds of full years that overlapped each other (cf. Lev. 25:9 and our fiscal year beginning July 1).[241] Once Jewish tradition came to regard the first day of the seventh month as New Year's Day, it was a short step to view it, along with the Day of Atonement, as a day of judgment (*m. Roš Haš.* 1:2, etc.) in harmony with ancient Near

regularly every day, weekly on the seventh-day Sabbath, monthly at new moons, and yearly at the various annual festivals. Aside from the Sabbath, which was unique to Israel, other peoples had similar ritual cycles. For example, at Ugarit there were regular daily sacrifices, new moon sacrifices, and annual festivals, and Hittite cult inventories specify daily offerings and festivals.[235]

Although the Israelites, Babylonians, and Hittites had different ritual and theological systems, they shared some basic concepts concerning the timetable of obligations toward their deities: "the need to provide twice-daily regular offerings and additional offerings on festival occasions and the need to periodically purify sacred objects and/or precincts pertaining to those deities."[236]

From earliest times, ancient Near Eastern people were very religious. Nowhere is this more evident than in their splendid array of cyclical festivals, which could be lengthy. For example, the *Zukru* festival to all the gods of Emar lasted seven days.[237] Hittite festival texts, the largest attested genre of extant Hittite literature, preserve memory

Eastern traditions that placed judgment in the framework of New Year celebrations (see comment on 16:29).[242]

Holy Light, Bread, and Divine Name (24:1–23)

Bake twelve loaves of bread (24:5). Laying offerings of bread before deities in their temples was common among ancient Near Eastern peoples from early times. The practice appears, for example, in a Sumerian inscription of Uru-inimgina of Lagaš (a little before 2350 B.C.)[243] and is well attested among Egyptians, Hittites, and Babylonians as part of the daily care and feeding of gods, represented by their idols (see also comment on 3:11). In the Israelite sanctuary, twelve loaves served as a reminder that the twelve tribes of Israel constituted the human party to the covenant.[244] However, this offering was not to feed Yahweh. The purpose was exactly the opposite: to acknowledge that he supplied the ongoing needs of the Israelites as their resident Creator-Provider.[245]

Sabbath after Sabbath ... as a lasting covenant (24:8). Compare Exodus 31:16–17, where Sabbath signifies a "lasting covenant" between the Lord and the Israelites, whom he makes holy (31:13), because God created the heavens and earth and rested on the seventh day, a day he made holy (Gen. 1–2).[246] A Syrian amulet bears a Phoenician inscription that expresses some parallel motifs: "Ashur has made an eternal covenant with us. He has made (a covenant) with us, along with all the sons of ʾEl and the leaders of the council of all the Holy Ones, with a covenant of the

Stele of Luny showing offering of loaves of bread in bottom register

Marie-Lan Nguyen/ Wikimedia Commons, courtesy of the Louvre

Heavens and Eternal Earth, with an oath of Baʿl."[247] However, lacking are the concepts that one deity created the heavens and earth, sanctified the Sabbath, and makes his chosen people holy.

Blasphemed the Name with a curse (24:11). In the ancient Near East, deities and their names were regarded as holy. For example, the Egyptian Great Hymn to Osiris praises the god: "Holy and splendid is his name."[248] Speaking evil of a deity or blaspheming his/her name (cf. Ex. 22:28) was a serious offense, as shown by harsh Assyrian punishments on blasphemers, including cutting their tongues.[249] In a Syrian treaty between Ebla and Abarsal, one who committed treason by blaspheming his own king, gods, and country could be put to death.[250]

All those who heard him are to lay their hands on his head (24:14). Compare the Mesopotamian treaty (from Alalakh) between Ir-Addu and Niqmepa, which stipulates that witnesses to theft (committed by a person from the other party's territory) "shall set his guilt on his head" and "he will be a slave."[251]

Stone him (24:14). In the Bible, stoning is a common way for the community to execute someone guilty of a crime against it, without holding any one individual responsible for the death of the offender. Outside the Bible, various modes of execution are attested (such as drowning, impaling, burning), but stoning is rare. The Syrian Hadad Inscription condemns any member of the royal household who plots destruction to being pounded with stones by his/her relatives of the same sex.[252]

If anyone takes the life of a human being, he must be put to death (24:17). Outside Israel, a person who committed homicide could receive capital punishment, as in the Laws of Ur-Namm.[253] Alternatively, he could be forced to give up one or more persons who belonged to him (Hittite Laws).[254] If a death occurred during a brawl, the penalty was a monetary fine (Laws of Eshnunna,

▶ A Babylonian Meal Fit for a God

On the fifth day of the Babylonian New Year Festival of Spring, the regular afternoon presentation offering for the god Bēl/Marduk is an elaborate full meal that includes a component resembling the Israelite "bread of the Presence": twelve regular offerings, likely consisting of loaves of bread, on a golden table:

> [... hours ...] the day, the high priest [enters into the presence of B]ēl, and ... He [performs the ceremony of] the golden table:
> He places roasted meats upon it, he places ... [upon i]t, he places the twelve usual (loaves) upon it, he fills a [gold]en ... with salt and places it upon it,
> he fills a [gold]en ... with honey and places it upon it,
> he places ... upon it, four golden containers...

> ... he places [up]on the table, a golden censer
> ... he places [in] front of the table, aromatic material and an aromatic substance of the juniper tree
> [he mixes on top (of the censer)], he pours out a libation of wine.
> ... he recites the following:
> [Marduk], supreme among the gods,
> [Who dwells in Esag]ila, who is the creator of orderliness,
> ... to the great gods,
> ... I praise your power.
> [May] your heart [be sympathetic] to the one who takes your hands.
> [In Esiz]kur, the temple of prayer,
> [In] ... your place, may he lift up his head.
> After he has recited the [sp]eech, he removes the table.[A-16]

Hadad Inscription: Syrian "Hadad Inscription" condemns any member of the royal household who plots destruction to being pounded with stones by his/her relatives of the same sex.
K. Lawson Younger, courtesy of the Vorderasiatische Museum, Berlin

▼

Laws of Hammurabi).[255] According to the Hittite king Telipinu, it was up to the heir of a murdered person to decide whether the murderer would die or pay.[256]

By contrast with this subjective approach, murder, like adultery, is an absolute crime in the Bible. Because of the supreme value of the life of a human being, made in God's image, a person who takes the life of another forfeits his own right to live and there is no alternative to capital punishment (Gen. 9:6; Num. 35:31).[257]

Anyone who takes the life of someone's animal must make restitution (24:18). Law collections outside the Bible present similar remedies. For death of an animal or such serious injury to an ox that it is unusable, the Laws of Hammurabi stipulate replacement with an animal of comparable value. For other permanent injuries, money payments suffice.[258] The Hittite Laws mandate

money payments for death or permanent injuries to animals.[259]

Whatever he has done must be done to him (24:19). Outside Israel, retaliatory punishments are first attested in the eighteenth-century B.C. Laws of Hammurabi from Babylonia (LH 116, 196–197, 200, 210, 229–30),[260] which are earlier than the biblical laws. Such penalties also appear later in the Middle Assyrian Laws (MAL A 20, 50, 52, 55). In their time, retaliatory punishments administered by civil courts were a major advance for the cause of justice by curbing unlimited retribution (cf. Gen. 4:23) and ensuring that rich and poor were treated in a way that affected them equally.[261] Biblical law authorized by Yahweh accepted the principle of talion, which was pioneered by

Hammurabi, but Yahweh tailored its applications to suit the Israelite judicial system.

Holy Land (25:1–55)

Proclaim liberty (25:10). The Hebrew word for "liberty" here is $d^e r\hat{o}r$ (see also Isa. 61:1; Jer. 34:8, etc.). It is related to the Akkadian word *andurāru*, which refers to various kinds of release, including remission of commercial debts and manumission of private slaves.[262] Especially near the beginnings of their reigns, several Mesopotamian kings proclaimed releases similar to the biblical Jubilee in that they provided relief for debtors and return of "land and persons pledged, sold, or enslaved in direct consequence of debt."[263] The purpose of such legislation was to restore some economic and social equilibrium.[264]

The main unique feature of the Israelite Jubilee release was its regular recurrence, which gave it predictability and independence from the arbitrary will of an absolute human ruler.[265] Also, whereas exceptions to releases in Mesopotamia could be specified by royal edicts or by contracts,[266] the Israelite Jubilee was designed to benefit all Israelites (but not non-Israelites; Lev. 25:44–46).

To his family property ... to his own clan (25:10). Basic to the Israelite economic system was the concept that God was the ultimate owner of all land and granted to each family an inalienable right to use (but not permanently sell) a piece of agricultural real estate. Some Ugaritic real estate documents show similar concern for permanence of land grants.[267] In Egypt, the pharaoh, who was regarded as divine, was the overall owner of land and assigned it to his subjects. Whatever the situation for commoners may have been in actual practice, an Egyptian treatise on kingship recognizes the ideal of free people with use of their own land: Such people are more likely to be contented, unified, and loyal than if their situation is otherwise.[268] Unlike Israel and Egypt, Mesopotamia lacked a unified system of land ownership.[269]

If an Israelite farmer fell on hard times and had to sell (really lease) temporary use of his land, he would have no way to support himself and could be forced into slavery, along with his family members, whether by selling himself (and them) or by being seized as collateral for a debt in default.[270] Other ancient Near Easterners could fall into slavery for similar reasons,[271] and also through defeat in warfare (Deut. 20:10–11; 2 Sam. 12:31).

In Babylonia, debt slaves were theoretically "to be kept in bondage until the debt had been worked off. In practice, however, unless they were redeemed, they remained in the possession of the creditor as long as they lived."[272] The Laws of Hammurabi remedied this grim scenario by limiting the service of a wife and children to three years.[273] Exodus 21 and Deuteronomy 15 went further, extending amnesty to the debtor himself and limiting service to six years, regardless of the size of the debt. Leviticus 25 adds crucial elements: An insolvent Israelite forced to sell his land is to be treated as a hired worker, and release of such servants is coordinated with release of their land, which is essential for their independent survival.[274]

His nearest relative is to come and redeem (25:25). The Laws of Eshnunna contain the provision: "If a man becomes impoverished and then sells his house, whenever the buyer offers it for sale, the owner of the house shall have the right to redeem it."[275] Leviticus 25 provides a higher level of protection for the original owner: An Israelite can redeem his ancestral property anytime, not just when the other party decides to put it up for sale, and even if he is unable to redeem it, his kinsman should step in to keep the property in the extended family (cf. Ruth 4:1–12; Jer. 32:6–15). A kinsman can also redeem an Israelite who has fallen into servitude (Lev. 25:48). Redemption of persons was also practiced in Mesopotamia. In a Sumerian text from Umma, the person who redeems slaves is their mother.[276]

Do not take interest of any kind from him (25:36). Agreements to pay interest were common in the ancient Near East,[277] but the need for avoiding exploitation was well recognized. The Laws of Hammurabi limit the amount of interest that can be charged and cancel interest payments for a year in which a farmer's crop is devastated by an "act of god" (storm, flood, drought).[278] So, as in Israelite law, a creditor was to show mercy to (rather than receiving profit from) an individual beset by unfortunate circumstances.

Covenant Blessings and Curses (26:1–46)

Do not … set up … a sacred stone (26:1). At Bethel, Jacob set up a stone as a pillar to mark the place of his dream and dedicated it to God by pouring oil on it (Gen. 28:18). From very early times, other ancient Near Eastern people also set up religious standing stones, called *maṣṣēbôt* in Hebrew. For example, in the Negev and Sinai Deserts, archaeologist Uzi Avner has identified and documented many prehistoric sites that contain such stone pillars. Avner has demonstrated that some of these *maṣṣebôt* represented groups of deities, just as groups of gods were depicted in sculpture throughout the ancient Near East.[279]

While *maṣṣebôt* and idols differed in that the former represented deities abstractly without attempting to portray physical like-ness, standing stones "were objects of veneration and worship, conventionalized aniconic representations of a deity."[280] So it is no wonder that Israelite law prohibited their use. However, while Jacob earlier set up his stone as a sacred *maṣṣēbâ* to mark the spot where the Lord had appeared to him (Gen. 28:16–22; 31:13), there is no hint that he regarded the stone as an object of worship.

Do not place a carved stone in your land to bow down before it (26:1). Because this kind of idolatrous practice appears only here in the Bible, its nature has been obscure. However, comparison with an Assyrian text has led V. Hurowitz to propose that the "carved stone" is a stone slab placed in the ground, possibly in a doorway, decorated with engraved divine symbols and bowed down upon, enabling the supplicant to kiss the ground with the purpose of having his or her wish granted. We may translate it as "decorated wishing stone."[281]

If you follow my decrees (26:3). These blessings and curses conclude the treaty between God (as the superior party) and Israel recorded in Exodus–Leviticus (cf. Deut. 27–28). In the ancient Near East, blessings and curses (or curses and blessings) could be appended to a law collection in order to encourage obedience.[282] They were also among the components of treaty formulations, such as those given by Hittite emperors of the second millennium B.C. (fourteenth and thirteenth centuries) to other rulers subordinate to them.[283] Following are the most prominent components, not all of which were present in every treaty:

Introduction of the speaker
Historical prologue
Stipulations
Statement concerning the document
Divine witnesses
Curses and blessings[284]

Blessings and curses, usually with an emphasis on curses of increasing severity, combined to form a powerful tool of persuasion that encouraged faithfulness and discouraged disloyal noncompliance with treaty stipulations by placing positive versus negative results in vivid contrast.[285] An Egyptian hymn of praise to the god Amun-Re encapsulates this dynamic: "Who extends His arms to the one He loves, While His enemies fall to the flame."[286]

You will pursue your enemies (26:7). In the ancient world, as in modern times, military protection and victory was a crucial benefit commonly sought from deities. For example, in the Inscription of Zakkur, king of Hamath, the god Ba'lshamayn ("Lord of Heaven") encourages the ruler: "Do not be afraid! Since I have made [you king, I will stand] beside you. I will save you from all [these kings who] have besieged you."[287] In the Inscription of Mesha, this king of Moab claims that his god Kemosh has provided military guidance, deliverance, and victory for the Moabites (against Israel).[288] Divine protection that is explicitly conditional on obedience to treaty stipulations, as in Leviticus 26, also appears in the Hittite treaty between Muršili and Duppi-Tešub.[289]

I will set my face against you (26:17). The negative impact of divine displeasure was keenly felt throughout the ancient Near East. Thus king Mesha viewed the anger of Kemosh against his land of Moab as the cause of her earlier subjugation to Israel.[290] An Egyptian complaint links violation of divine plans to resultant chaos and suffering.[291] Conditional curses in the Aramaic inscription of Hadad-Yith'i on an

Clay tablet from Ugarit with imprint of the stamp seal of King Muršili II
Erich Lessing/Art Resource, NY, courtesy of the National Museum, Damascus, Syria

image are devastating because they call for basic divine rejection, which can negatively impact every aspect of life:

> Whoever removes my name from the furnishings of the house of Hadad, my lord, may my lord Hadad not accept his food and water from his hand, may my lady Sûl not accept food and water from his hand. When he sows, may he not reap.[292]

The sky above you like iron and the ground beneath you like bronze (26:19). The idea of this conditional curse is that heaven will bar any rain from getting through to earth; consequently, the land will dry up and become hard like metal. Deuteronomy 28:23 reverses the metals. Likewise, curses in the Succession Treaty of the Assyrian king Esarhaddon call on the gods to "make your ground like iron (so that) nothing can sprout from it. Just as rain does not fall from a brazen heaven, so may rain and dew not come upon your fields and meadows."[293]

I will send a plague among you (26:25). Compare a prayer of Muršili II, in which the king assumes that a lethal plague on his Hittite people is vengeance from the gods because his father killed a man.[294] In the epilogue to the Laws of Hammurabi, a curse on any who disrespect the royal pronouncements calls on the goddess Ninkarrak to "cause a grievous malady to break out upon his limbs, an evil demonic disease."[295]

Ten women will be able to bake your bread in one oven (26:26). K. L. Younger places this curse formula alongside close parallels in the Te Fakhariyah Inscription (c. 850–825 B.C.), the Sefire Treaty (c. 760–740 B.C.) and the Bukān Inscription (c. 725–700 B.C.), all of which emphasize lack of grain by speaking of multiple women baking bread in one oven. However, whereas the extrabiblical texts describe failure to fill the oven, Leviticus focuses on not having enough to eat. Younger concludes that "there were some stock West Semitic curse formulae that could be drawn from in the composition of curse passages and that these could be adapted to the particular needs of the ancient writers."[296]

You will eat the flesh of your sons and the flesh of your daughters (26:29). Ancient Near Easterners turned to cannibalism only as a desperate last resort to prevent imminent starvation (2 Kings 6:24–30). Frightful curses of cannibalism also show up in Deuteronomy 28:53–57 and in Assyrian treaties of Esarhaddon.[297]

And I will remember the land (26:42). Some historical passages outside the Bible, such as the Moabite inscription of King Mesha and the Mesopotamian "Sun Disk" Tablet of Nabû-Apla-Iddina, also mention cessation of divine anger.[298] Unlike Leviticus 26 and Deuteronomy 30:1–10, these do not explicitly identify repentance as the pivotal factor in restoration of the divine-human relationship.

Dedications to the Sphere of Holiness (27:1–34)

If anyone makes a special vow (27:2). An Israelite could give such a votive offering to the Lord either (1) in hope of a future divine blessing or (2) in fulfillment of a promise to present the offering after a divine favor had been bestowed. Both kinds of voluntary agreements with deities—before or after divine blessings—have parallels elsewhere in the ancient Near East. As an example of type (1), a royal votive inscription of the Mesopotamian king Ibbi-Sin was originally carved on an animal sculpture (leopard?) that he dedicated to the deity Nanna "for the sake of his (Ibbi-Sin's) (long) life."[299] A Hittite conditional promise to give a votive offering of type (2) is as follows:

[The queen] made the following vow [on behalf of] the royal prince, the king of Išuwa: "If the prince recovers from this illness, I will [.........] and I will give to the deity on behalf of the prince, the king of Išuwa, a sword, a dagger(?), and one silver ZI-ornament of unspecified weight."[300]

To dedicate persons to the LORD (27:2). In the ancient Near East, votive objects were various kinds of valuable items that worshipers of deities transferred to their sacred realm. They were often sculptures or replicas of items used in daily life and were often inscribed with prayers.[301] Here in Leviticus 27, the votive object is the monetary work valuation of a person who would otherwise be literally pledged to service at the sanctuary, as Samuel was (1 Sam. 1:11, 25–28; 2:11).

Related to the vow of (the work valuation of) a human being is a situation in which a wealthy person vows to present a deity with a multiple of another person's weight in precious metal. In an Ugaritic epic, King Kirta vows to give the goddess ʾAṯiratu double the weight of princess Hurraya in silver and triple her weight in gold if he succeeds in taking her as his wife.[302] Compare *m. Arak.* 5:1, which tells how a mother vowed her daughter's weight in gold and paid it at Jerusalem.

Set the value of a male between the ages of twenty and sixty at fifty shekels of silver

Sumerian statues from Tel Asmar placed in temple in connection with a vow
Courtesy of the Oriental Institute Museum

(27:3). This expensive valuation of a man in the prime of life (2 Kings 15:20; cf. annual wage in Judg. 17:10) would have been reasonable as the price of a male adult slave in Mesopotamia.[303] However, unlike slave prices, the fixed scale in Leviticus 27 does not fluctuate over time according to market conditions and treats individuals equally by not taking variable factors into account, such as a particular person's strength or speed, which would affect actual productivity.

He must not exchange it (27:10). The Hittite Instructions to Priests and Temple Officials forbid cheating the deity by exchanging high quality animals for inferior ones.[304] The present verse goes further by categorically ruling out any substitution, including even an exchange that could be regarded as upgrading the value: "a good one for a bad one, or a bad one for a good one." So there can be no justification based on rationalizing relative values.

Bibliography

Beckwith, R., and M. Selman, eds. *Sacrifice in the Bible*. Grand Rapids: Baker, 1995. Essays by different authors trace the theme of sacrifice through the Bible and relate Israelite practices to sacrificial rituals elsewhere in the ancient Near East.

Cohen, M. *The Cultic Calendars of the Ancient Near East*. Bethesda, Md.: CDL, 1993. This comprehensive survey of ancient cultic calendars traces cyclical holy times through history in various regions of Mesopotamia.

Gane, R. *Cult and Character: Purification Offerings, Day of Atonement, and Theodicy*. Winona Lake, Ind.: Eisenbrauns, 2005. Close reading and syntactic study of ritual texts (mainly in Leviticus) dealing with purification offerings reveal the underlying theme of divine justice, which relates in fascinating ways to some Sumerian and Babylonian festivals.

_____. *Leviticus, Numbers*. NIVAC. Grand Rapids: Zondervan, 2004. This recent commentary makes the timeless messages of Leviticus and Numbers accessible to modern readers by taking them from the original meaning of each passage through bridging contexts to contemporary application.

_____. *Ritual Dynamic Structure*. Gorgias Dissertations 14, Religion 2. Piscataway, N.J.: Gorgias, 2004. Developing and then applying a methodology for analyzing rituals as human activity systems, this work investigates and compares ancient Israelite, Babylonian, and Hittite festival days of sancta purification. An appendix contains the first published English translation of the Hittite texts pertaining to the Ninth-Year Festival of the god Telipinu.

Haran, M. *Temples and Temple-Service in Ancient Israel*. Winona Lake, Ind.: Eisenbrauns, 1985. This important study explains various aspects of the Israelite sanctuary/temple institution and its priesthood, including the physical structure of the tabernacle and rituals performed there.

Hartley, J. *Leviticus*. WBC 4. Dallas: Word, 1992. For each section of Leviticus, this major commentary includes a bibliography, translation, text (including text-critical) notes, discussion of the form/structure/setting, comment on the content, and further explanation that includes connections with other parts of the Bible.

Klingbeil, G. *A Comparative Study of the Ritual of Ordination as Found in Leviticus 8 and Emar 369*. Lewiston, N.Y.: Mellen, 1998. Klingbeil offers a detailed comparison of an important Emar text and the biblical description of priestly consecration, specifying elaborate procedures for installation of the storm god's high priestess.

Levine, B. *Leviticus*. JPS Torah Commentary. Philadelphia: Jewish Publication Society, 1989. Utilizing his impressive grasp of ancient Near Eastern cultures and linguistics as well as rabbinic literature, Levine has produced a concise and insightful commentary.

Milgrom, J. *Leviticus 1–16, Leviticus 17–22, Leviticus 23–27*. AB 3, 3A, 3B. New York: Doubleday, 1991, 2000, 2001. These three volumes comprise the largest and most comprehensive commentary on Leviticus ever produced. For his exhaustive investigation, Milgrom draws on a wide variety of resources and approaches, which include ancient Near Eastern and rabbinic texts, archaeological data, and anthropology, in addition to close reading, lexical and grammatical study, linguistics, and analysis of literary structure.

Patrick, D. *Old Testament Law*. Atlanta: John Knox, 1985. Here is a clearly understandable introduction to the legal genre in biblical writings, including the structure, scope, formulation, and content of the various collections and series of laws, and relationships between them.

Ross, A. P. *Holiness to the Lord: A Guide to the Exposition of the Book of Leviticus*. Grand Rapids: Baker, 2002. This clear exposition opens up the theological themes of Leviticus and brings them to the modern reader.

Roth, M. T. *Law Collections from Mesopotamia and Asia Minor*. SBLWAW 6. Atlanta: Scholars Press, 1995. Here are up-to-date translations of the Sumerian, Babylonian, Assyrian, and Hittite law collections all together in one handy volume.

Toorn, K. van der. *Sin and Sanction in Israel and Mesopotamia*. SSN 22. Assen: Van Gorcum, 1985. The author compares the civilizations of Israel and Mesopotamia in terms of their respective approaches to maintenance of moral order, a theme central to Leviticus.

Walton, J. H. *Ancient Israelite Literature in its Cultural Context*. LBI. Grand Rapids: Zondervan, 1989. This useful resource introduces the reader to comparison between biblical texts and pieces of ancient Near Eastern literature belonging to the same literary genres. It provides descriptions of ancient works, comparisons between them, discussion of interpretive issues, and bibliographic resources for further study.

Weinfeld, M. *Social Justice in Ancient Israel and in the Ancient Near East*. Jerusalem/Minneapolis: Magnes/Fortress, 1995. Weinfeld explores the biblical theme of maintaining social justice, which is prominent in Leviticus, within the larger context of the ancient Near East.

Westbrook, R., ed. *A History of Ancient Near Eastern Law*. 2 vols. Handbook of Oriental Studies/Handbuch der Orientalistik 72. Leiden: Brill, 2003. This current, comprehensive, and clearly organized survey of ancient Near Eastern (including Israelite) law, covering all major periods and geographical areas, is a major achievement by top scholars and serves as an indispensable reference tool.

Wright, D. P. *The Disposal of Impurity: Elimination Rites in the Bible and in Hittite and Mesopotamian Literature*. SBLDS 101. Atlanta: Scholars Press, 1987. Wright investigates Israelite ritual impurities and their elimination, and compares them with somewhat analogous concepts and procedures in Hittite and Mesopotamian ritual texts.

Zevit, Z. *The Religions of Ancient Israel: A Synthesis of Parallactic Approaches*. London: Continuum, 2001. This major examination of ancient Israelite religious experience thoroughly integrates study of texts with analysis of a wealth of archaeological data.

Main Text Notes

1. On the message of Leviticus, see further R. Gane, *Leviticus, Numbers* (NIVAC; Grand Rapids: Zondervan, 2004).

2. See, e.g., J. Milgrom, *Leviticus 1–16* (AB; New York: Doubleday, 1991), 3–13, esp. 10–12; K. Kitchen, "The Tabernacle—A Bronze Age Artifact," *Bible and Spade* 8 (1995): 33–46; R. Gane, "Schedules for Deities: Macrostructure of Israelite, Babylonian, and Hittite Sancta Purification Days," *AUSS* 36 (1998): 231–44, esp. 244.

3. *COS*, 2.155:419–21, 423–24.

4. Ibid., 1.95:299–301.

5. Ibid., 1.83:217–21.

6. Ibid., 2.19:106–19; 2.130–33:332–61; 2.153–54:408–14.

7. Ibid., 2.131:351–53; 2.154:413–14.

8. R. Gane, *Ritual Dynamic Structure* (Gorgias Dissertations 14, Religion 2; Piscataway, N.J., 2004), 58–61.

9. Speaking of complexity, "the polytheistic cults of Mesopotamia generated ever more deities and temples, 5580 of the former by one count and 1439 of the latter by another" (W. W. Hallo, "Sumer and the Bible: A Matter of Proportion," in ibid., 3:liii).

10. Compare Gary A. Anderson, "Sacrifice and Sacrificial Offerings (OT)," *ABD*, 5:883; D. Baker, "Leviticus 1–7 and the Punic Tariffs: A Form Critical Comparison," *ZAW* 99 (1987): 192–93.

11. *COS*, 1.123:431–36.

12. R. Knierim, *Text and Concept in Leviticus 1:1–9: A Case in Exegetical Method* (FAT; Tübingen: Mohr, 1992), 31, 65, 94–97, 98–106.

13. *COS*, 2.155:432. On the distinction between prescriptive and descriptive ritual texts in the Bible and elsewhere in the ancient Near East, see B. Levine, "The Descriptive Tabernacle Texts of the Pentateuch," *JAOS* 85 (1965): 307–18; B. Levine and W. W. Hallo, "Offerings to the Temple Gates at Ur," *HUCA* 38 (1967): 17–58; *COS*, 3.124:275; A. Rainey, "The Order of Sacrifices in Old Testament Ritual Texts," *Bib* 51 (1970): 495.

14. Compare other major biblical law collections in Ex. 20–23 and Deut. 12–26. For the Mesopotamian and Hittite collections, see *COS*, 2.153–54:408–14 (Sumerian); 2.130–133:332–61 (Akkadian); 2.19:106–19 (Hittite).

15. See J. H. Walton, *Ancient Israelite Literature in its Cultural Context* (LBI; Grand Rapids: Zondervan, 1989), 78.

16. S. Paul, *Studies in the Book of the Covenant in the Light of Cuneiform and Biblical Law* (VTSup 18; Leiden: Brill, 1970), 43.

17. W. G. Lambert describes the difference between the Mesopotamian and Israelite worldviews: "The contrast was not, as among the Hebrews, between morally right and wrong, but between order and disorder. Civilization was the ideal: the well ordered society" ("Destiny and Divine Intervention in Babylon and Israel," *Oudtestamentische Studiën* 17 (1972): 67; cf. K. van der Toorn, *Family Religion in Babylonia, Syria and Israel: Continuity and Change in the Forms of Religious Life* (Leiden: Brill, 1996), 94–95; T. Abusch, "Ghost and God: Some Observations on a Babylonian Understanding of Human Nature," in *Self, Soul and Body in Religious Experience*, ed. A. Baumgarten, J. Assmann, and G. Stroumsa (Studies in the History of Religions; Leiden: Brill, 1998), 381. On the related social-ethical implications of the Egyptian concept of *maʾat*, see J. Assmann, "A Dialogue Between Self and Soul: Papyrus Berlin 3024," in *Self, Soul and Body*, 395–96, 401–3.

18. J. J. Finkelstein, "Bible and Babel: A Comparative Study of the Hebrew and Babylonian Religious Spirit," in *Essential Papers on Israel and the Ancient Near East*, ed. F. Greenspahn (New York: New York Univ. Press, 1991), 368–73.

19. On the need for Mesopotamian law collections to express royal ideals of justice and deal with changes in society, versus the lack of such collections in Egypt because the pharaohs and gods existed by an order of rightness in nature and society (*maʾat*) that was built into the universe at creation, see Walton, *Ancient Israelite Literature*, 86–87, 91–92.

20. For an overview of the kinds of sacrifices practiced in various parts of the ancient Near East, including Ugarit, see M. J. Selman, "Sacrifice in the Ancient Near East," in *Sacrifice in the Bible*, ed. R. Beckwith and M. Selman (Grand Rapids: Baker, 1995), 88–104. For examples of Ugaritic sacrificial procedures, including burnt and well-being offerings, see *COS*, 1.95:299–301. For some parallel kinds of Punic sacrifices, see ibid., 1.98:306–7. On Greek sacrifices, see Dennis E. Smith, "Meal Customs (Greco-Roman)," *ABD*, 4:653–55.

21. *COS*, 1.98:306–8.

22. D. P. Wright, "The Gesture of Hand Placement in the Hebrew Bible and in Hittite Literature," *JAOS* 106 (1986): 443.

23. R. Gane, *Cult and Character: Purification Offerings, Day of Atonement, and Theodicy* (Winona Lake, Ind.: Eisenbrauns, 2005), ch. 6.

24. B. Levine, *In the Presence of the Lord: A Study of Cult and Some Cultic Terms in Ancient Israel* (SJLA; Leiden: Brill, 1974), 123; D. P. Wright, *The Disposal of Impurity: Elimination Rites in the Bible and in Hittite and Mesopotamian Literature* (SBLDS 101; Atlanta: Scholars, 1987), 291–99; Milgrom, *Leviticus 1–16*, 1080–82; *CAD*, 8:179.

25. For the connection between blood and life, compare the fact that in the Babylonian epic Atraḫasis, human beings are created from the flesh and blood of a slain god (W. G. Lambert and A. R. Millard, *Atra-Ḥasis: The Babylonian Story of the Flood* [Winona Lake, Ind.: Eisenbrauns, repr.

1999; orig. 1969], 59). Regarding an animal ransoming a human life, compare Hittite Laws 166—"a man who sows seed over another man's seed is torn apart by oxen, which are also killed"—with 167 (reformed law): "But now they shall substitute one sheep for the man and two sheep for the oxen. He shall give 30 loaves of bread and 3 jugs of ... beer, and reconsecrate (the land?)" (M. T. Roth, *Law Collections from Mesopotamia and Asia Minor* [SBLWAW 6; Atlanta: Scholars, 1995], 233–34).

26. T. Abusch, "Blood in Israel and Mesopotamia," in *Emanuel: Studies in Hebrew Bible, Septuagint, and Dead Sea Scrolls in Honor of Emanuel Tov*, ed. S. Paul et al. (VTSup; Leiden: Brill, 2003), 675–84; G. del Olmo Lete, *Canaanite Religion according to the Liturgical Texts of Ugarit* (trans. W. Watson; Bethesda, Md.: CDL, 1999), 41.

27. H. Hoffner, "Second Millennium Antecedents to the Hebrew *ʾob*," *JBL* 86 (1967): 390–92, 395–96, 399; see also M. Cohen, *The Cultic Calendars of the Ancient Near East* (Bethesda, Md.: CDL, 1993), 459; cf. 325.

28. COS, 1.70:176.

29. See Edwin Firmage, "Zoology (Fauna)," *ABD*, 6:1132.

30. G. R. Driver, "Ugaritic and Hebrew Words," *Ugaritica* 6 (1969): 181–84.

31. Milgrom, *Leviticus 1–16*, 161–62, 253.

32. See, e.g., COS, 1.143:474. However, W. G. Lambert points out that in ancient Babylonia (unlike Israel), there was no custom of burning slaughtered animal victims to ashes. Incense was the only Babylonian offering material completely consumed by fire ("Donations of Food and Drink to the Gods in Ancient Mesopotamia," in *Ritual and Sacrifice in the Ancient Near East*, ed. J. Quaegebeur [Orientalia Lovaniensia Analecta; Leuven: Peeters, 1993], 194).

33. COS, 1.86:259.

34. Lambert and Millard, *Atra-Ḥasis*, 98–99.

35. H. Hoffner, *Alimenta Hethaeorum: Food Production in Hittite Asia Minor* (AOS 55; New Haven, Conn.: American Oriental Society, 1974), 216; COS, 1.60:159.

36. Gane, *Ritual Dynamic Structure*, 256, 361; cf. COS, 1.83:220.

37. Milgrom, *Leviticus 1–16*, 188–90.

38. Hoffner, "Second Millennium Antecedents," 389, 391–92, 394–95; Cohen, *Cultic Calendars*, 459; cf. COS, 1.68:170 and 1.125:440–41. See comment on 1:5 regarding similar libations of blood.

39. Gane, *Ritual Dynamic Structure*, 210–13; cf. Cohen, *Cultic Calendars*, 447.

40. Milgrom, *Leviticus 1–16*, 191.

41. *IVPBCCOT*, 122.

42. Ibid., 220–21.

43. See, e.g., A. Blackman, "The Sequence of the Episodes in the Egyptian Daily Temple Liturgy," *Journal of the Manchester Egyptian and Oriental Society* (1918–1919): 27–53; Hoffner, *Alimenta Hethaeorum*, 216; G. Barton, "A Comparison of Some Features of Hebrew and Babylonian Ritual," *JBL* 46 (1927): 85–86; E. Kingsbury, "A Seven

Day Ritual in the Old Babylonian Cult at Larsa," *HUCA* 34 (1963): 26–27; *ANET*, 343–45.

44. A. L. Oppenheim, *Ancient Mesopotamia* (Chicago: Univ. of Chicago Press, 1964), 191–92; cf. Selman, "Sacrifice," 90–92.

45. Hoffner, *Alimenta Hethaeorum*, 217.

46. COS, 1.34:55; see comment on Lev. 16:2.

47. Selman, "Sacrifice," 91; see also 92.

48. Lambert reminds us that in Sumerian and Babylonian literature, "the human race was created solely to serve the gods by providing their food and drink. The whole matter is conceived anthropomorphically. 'Sacrifice' is a misnomer applied to this conceptual world" ("Donations of Food and Drink," 198).

49. COS, 1.29:47; cf. 1.114:416–17.

50. Ibid., 1.153:488; K. van der Toorn, *Sin and Sanction in Israel and Mesopotamia* (SSN 22; Assen: Van Gorcum, 1985), 94–97. On the problem of unwitting sin in the ancient Near East, see also Milgrom, *Leviticus 1–16*, 361–63.

51. COS, 1.78:205; cf. 204.

52. Ibid., 1.60:160; cf. 157.

53. The Hebrew term was derived from the same root as the verb for "purify" in Ex. 29:36 and Lev. 8:15; Milgrom, *Leviticus 1–16*, 253–54.

54. COS, 2.19:110.

55. Ibid., 1.153:490; cf. 487.

56. See, e.g., ibid., 3.138:307—announcement that a slave is freed.

57. Ibid., 2.131:338.

58. T. Frymer-Kenski, "Israel," in *A History of Ancient Near Eastern Law*, ed. R. Westbrook (HO 72; Leiden: Brill, 2003), 2:994.

59. COS, 1.176:569.

60. A. Phillips, "The Undetectable Offender and the Priestly Legislators," *JTS* 36 (1985): 150.

61. See B. Schwartz, "The Bearing of Sin in the Priestly Literature," in *Pomegranates and Golden Bells: Studies in Biblical, Jewish, and Near Eastern Ritual, Law, and Literature in Honor of Jacob Milgrom*, ed. D. Wright, D. N. Freedman, and A. Hurvitz (Winona Lake, Ind.: Eisenbrauns, 1995), 8–15.

62. COS, 3.8:27; see also 28–30; cf. K. Koch, "Is There a Doctrine of Retribution in the Old Testament?" in *Theodicy in the Old Testament*, ed. J. Crenshaw; trans. T. Trapp (IRT; Philadelphia/London: Fortress/SPCK, 1983), 60–82; Gane, *Cult and Character*, ch. 16.

63. Milgrom, *Leviticus 1–16*, 298–302.

64. A Mesopotamian text contains passionate confession of a wide range of faults (W. G. Lambert, "*dingir.šà dib.ba* Incantations," *JNES* 33 [1974]: 275, 281, 283, 285, 287).

65. COS, 1.179:574–75.

66. Ibid., 1.83:218–21.

67. Ibid., 220.

68. Milgrom, *Leviticus 1–16*, 339–45.

69. Ibid., 333–35, 343–44.

70. COS, 1.144:475; cf. 1.151:485.

71. Ibid., 1.57:151–53.

72. Roth, *Law Collections*, 65; cf. COS, 2.130:334; 3.10:32; 3.65:160.

73. COS, 1.47:117; cf. 118, 120.

74. Ibid., 1.83:220.
75. Gane, *Ritual Dynamic Structure*, 248, 252–53, 359; cf. COS, 1.124:437 regarding animal portions belonging to the supervising "diviner."
76. COS, 1.83:218.
77. Ibid.
78. R. Gane, "'Bread of the Presence' and Creator-in-Residence," *VT* 42 (1992): 194–98.
79. COS, 1.124:438–39.
80. Ibid., 1.98:305–9.
81. Ibid., 2.32:151.
82. Ibid., 2.33:152–53.
83. Regarding vows, see comments on 27:2.
84. D. Wold, "The Meaning of the Biblical Penalty *Kareth*" (Ph.D. dissertation, Univ. of California at Berkeley, 1978), 251–55; Milgrom, *Leviticus 1–16*, 457–60; Schwartz, "Bearing of Sin," 13.
85. COS, 1.83:220; cf., 1.148:480.
86. On use of oil in ancient Near Eastern dedication ceremonies, see V. Hurowitz, *I Have Built You an Exalted House: Temple Building in the Bible in Light of Mesopotamian and Northwest Semitic Writings* (JSOTSup; Sheffield: Sheffield Academic Press, 1992), 278–79. For oil and blood together (Lev. 8:30; 14:14–18, 25–29), cf. part of the *Zukru* festival at Emar: "Total: four calves and forty sheep for the consecration. After eating and drinking they rub all the stones with oil and blood" (COS, 1.123:433; see also 435).
87. COS, 1.70:176.
88. On anointing of Israelite kings and the ancient Near Eastern background of this practice, see T. Mettinger, *King and Messiah: The Civil and Sacral Legitimation of the Israelite Kings* (ConBOT; Lund: Gleerup, 1976), 185–232.
89. COS, 2.152:407.
90. See *CAD*, 10/1:187.
91. Milgrom, *Leviticus 1–16*, 587.
92. COS, 1.102:335; cf. 1.95:301.
93. *ANEP*, 89 and 91, showing submission to superior Egyptian forces.
94. Cf. *CAD*, 10/2:9–10, on the Akkadian word *melammu*, which refers to "radiance, supernatural awe-inspiring sheen (inherent in things divine and royal)."
95. COS, 2.155:431–32; cf. 2.123A:312 regarding celebration that attended restoration of the Ehulhul temple in Haran by the Neo-Babylonian King Nabonidus. See also Baal's inaugural banquet upon completion of his palace (ibid., 1.86:261–62, The Baʾlu Myth).
96. Ibid., 1.34:55.
97. Ibid., 1.108:382.
98. See, e.g., *ANET*, 338–41, 343 (in Mesopotamia).
99. COS, 1.97:303–4; 1.111:396–97; *ANET*, 66.
100. On *šēkār* (so-called "strong/fermented drink") offered in the Israelite tabernacle, see Gane, *Leviticus, Numbers*, 750–51.
101. COS, 1.83:220.
102. See Firmage, "Zoology," 1120.
103. Ibid., 1125–26.
104. Gane, *Leviticus, Numbers*, 206–8, referring to M. Douglas, *Purity and Danger: An Analysis of Concepts of Pollution and Taboo* (London: Routledge & Kegan Paul, 1966), 41–57; E. Firmage, "The Biblical Dietary Laws and the Concept of Holiness," in J. A. Emerton, ed., *Studies in the Pentateuch* (Leiden: Brill, 1990), 177–208; Milgrom, *Leviticus 1–16*, 735; J. Moskala, *The Laws of Clean and Unclean Animals of Leviticus 11: Their Nature, Theology, and Rationale (an Intertextual Study)* (ATSDS 4; Berrien Springs, Mich.: Adventist Theological Society Publications, 2000).
105. Firmage, "Zoology," 1125.
106. COS, 1.83:217, 220.
107. W. G. Lambert, *Babylonian Wisdom Literature* (Oxford: Clarendon, 1960), 215.
108. Firmage, "Zoology," 1131–35.
109. COS, 2.155:427.
110. Ibid., 1.95:300; cf. 301.
111. Milgrom, *Leviticus 1–16*, 763–65; G. Beckman, *Hittite Birth Rituals*, 2nd ed. (SANE 29; Wiesbaden: Harrassowitz, 1983), esp. 251; M. F. Small, "A Woman's Curse? From Taboo to Time Bomb: Rethinking Menstruation," *The Sciences* (January/February 1999), 24–29.
112. Beckman, *Hittite Birth Rituals*, 135, 137, 143, 219.
113. Since slight vaginal bleeding can occur in a newborn girl, perhaps the doubled time of the mother's purification could be based on the actual and potential genital discharge of both females (J. Magonet, "'But If It Is a Girl She Is Unclean for Twice Seven Days …': The Riddle of Leviticus 12.5," in *Reading Leviticus: A Conversation with Mary Douglas*, ed. J. Sawyer [JSOTSup 227; Sheffield: Sheffield Academic Press, 1996], 152).
114. Milgrom, *Leviticus 1–16*, 765.
115. H. Maccoby, *Ritual and Morality: The Ritual Purity System and its Place in Judaism* (Cambridge: Cambridge Univ. Press, 1999), 49; see also 31–32, 48, 50, 207–8; cf. Milgrom, *Leviticus 1–16*, 767–68, 1002–3; idem, "The Rationale for Biblical Impurity," *JANES* 22 (1993): 107–11.
116. See also J. Milgrom, *Leviticus 23–27* (AB; New York: Doubleday, 2001), 1913, but in v. 3, where the disease is pronounced impure, he renders "scale disease."
117. E. V. Hulse, "The Nature of Biblical 'Leprosy' and the Use of Alternative Medical Terms in Modern Translations of the Bible," *PEQ* 107 (1975): 88–89; Milgrom, *Leviticus 1–16*, 817. Greek *lepra*, from which our word "leprosy" is derived, was used for scale disease in the LXX and the New Testament (Matt. 8:3; Mark 1:42; Luke 5:12–13). R. K. Harrison makes a detailed medical argument that biblical scale disease could have at least included an ancient form of what we now call "leprosy" ("Leper; Leprosy," *ISBE*, 3:103–6; idem, *Leviticus: An Introduction and Commentary* [TOTC; Leicester: Inter-Varsity Press, 1980], 136–45, 241–46).
118. COS, 1.120:426.
119. On Gehazi's offense as sacrilege in the sense that he robbed God of credit for healing Naaman, cf. van der Toorn, *Sin and Sanction*, 74.
120. Milgrom, *Leviticus 1–16*, 820–21; see also van der Toorn, *Sin and Sanction*, 73.

121. Milgrom, *Leviticus 1–16*, 820; van der Toorn, *Sin and Sanction*, 30–31, 73–75.
122. *ANET*, 333; Cohen, *Cultic Calendars*, 445–46.
123. On Israelite, Mesopotamian, and Hittite ritual use of birds to carry away evils, see Wright, *Disposal of Impurity*, 75–86. For use of cedar in Mesopotamian rituals, compare *ANET*, 335–36; *CAD*, 4:277–78.
124. Wright, *Disposal of Impurity*, 83.
125. Ibid., 81, 84.
126. Cf. the "water of life" motif in Mesopotamia (COS, 1.164:534 and 1.170:549–50).
127. Gane, *Ritual Dynamic Structure*, 261–62, 265–66, 273, 358–59.
128. *ANET*, 332; Cohen, *Cultic Calendars*, 444.
129. Milgrom, *Leviticus 23–27*, 1917.
130. COS, 1.120:424.
131. Ibid., 1.68:168–71.
132. *Blennorrhea urethrae* or *Gonorrhoea benigna*, not to be confused with the venereal *Gonorrhoea virulenta*, which has appeared more recently. See M. M. Kalisch, *A Historical and Critical Commentary on the Old Testament, with a New Translation: Leviticus* (London: Longman, Green, Reader, and Dyer, 1872), 2:155.
133. J. V. Kinnier-Wilson, "Medicine in the Land and Times of the Old Testament," in *Studies in the Period of David and Solomon*, ed. T. Ishida (Winona Lake, Ind.: Eisenbrauns, 1982), 358.
134. B. Levine, *Numbers 1–20* (AB; New York: Doubleday, 1993), 185.
135. Erica Reiner, *Šurpu: A Collection of Sumerian and Akkadian Incantations* (AfOB 11; Graz, Austria, 1958), 16.
136. M. J. Geller, "The Šurpu Incantations and Lev. V.1–5," *JSS* 25 (1980): 188.
137. COS, 1.120: 425.
138. H. Hoffner, "Some Contributions of Hittitology to Old Testament Study," *TynBul* 20 (1969): 42; Milgrom, *Leviticus 1–16*, 927; cf. COS 2.19:118 (Hitttite Laws 190).
139. COS, 1.83:220; Walton, Matthews, and Chavalas, *IVP Bible Background Commentary*, 130.
140. *AHw*, 2:827–28; R. Gane and J. Milgrom, *"pārō-ket," TDOT*, 12:95; see also 96.
141. COS, 1.120:424.
142. Ibid., 2.155:427.
143. Cohen, *Cultic Calendars*, 444; cf. *ANET*, 332.
144. Cohen, *Cultic Calendars*, 445; *ANET*, 333; cf. Gane, *Ritual Dynamic Structure*, 221–22.
145. See further in Gane, *Cult and Character*, ch. 11; Gane, *Leviticus, Numbers*, 273–74, 288–91.
146. David P. Wright, "Day of Atonement," *ABD*, 2:74.
147. Wright, *Disposal of Impurity*, 57. For analysis of the Israelite "scapegoat" ritual in relation to a number of Hittite and Mesopotamian parallels, see 15–74. For an apparent Ugaritic parallel, in which an elimination ritual involves driving a goat away to a far place, see K. Aartun, "Eine weitere Parallele aus Ugarit zur kultischen Praxis in Israels Religion," *BO* 33 (1976): 288; O. Loretz, *Leberschau, Sündenbock, Asasel in Ugarit*

und Israel (UBL; Altenberge: CIS–Verlag, 1985), 35–49.
148. Wright, *Disposal of Impurity*, 58.
149. Ibid., 58–60; cf. H. Hoffner, "Hittite-Israelite Cultural Parallels," in COS, 3:xxxii; see also Walton, Matthews, and Chavalas on the "scapegoat" concept in the ancient Near East, *The IVP Bible Background Commentary*, 131.
150. See also Milgrom, *Leviticus 23–27*, 1921; cf. NJPS: "for Azazel."
151. For surveys of suggested explanations, see B. Levine, *Leviticus* (JPS Torah Commentary; Philadelphia: Jewish Publication Society, 1989), 250–53; Wright, *Disposal of Impurity*, 21–22; Milgrom, *Leviticus 1–16*, 1020–21; A. Treiyer, *The Day of Atonement and the Heavenly Judgment from the Pentateuch to Revelation* (Siloam Springs, Ark.: Creation Enterprises International, 1992), 231–58.
152. G. R. Driver, "Three Technical Terms in the Pentateuch," *JSS* 1 (1956): 98.
153. Loretz, *Leberschau*, 56–57.
154. B. Janowski and G. Wilhelm, "Der Bock, der die Sünden hinausträgt: Zur Religionsgeschichte des Azazel–Ritus Lev 16,10.21f," in *Religionsgeschichtliche Beziehungen zwischen Kleinasien, Nordsyrien und dem Alten Testament*, ed. B. Janowski, K. Koch, and G. Wilhelm (OBO 129; Freiburg/Göttingen: Universitätsverlag/Vandenhoeck & Ruprecht, 1993), 134–62.
155. C. D. Ginsburg, *Leviticus* (The Handy Commentary; Grand Rapids: Zondervan, 1961), 151; cf. S. R. Driver and H. A. White, *The Book of Leviticus* (SBONT; New York: Dodd, Mead, 1898), 81.
156. R. Gane, *Altar Call* (Berrien Springs, Mich.: Diadem, 1999), 248–50; Gane, *Cult and Character*, ch. 11.
157. A. Noordtzij, *Leviticus*, trans. R. Togtman (BSC; Grand Rapids: Zondervan, 1982), 162–63; B. Levine, "Leviticus, Book of," *ABD*, 4:315. For Babylonian belief in *alu*-demons who lived in deserted wastelands, see *CAD*, 1:376. On the Azazel episode in *1 Enoch*, see P. D. Hanson, "Rebellion in Heaven, Azazel, and Euhemeristic Heroes in 1 Enoch 6–11," *JBL* 96 (1977): 220–27.
158. Y. Kaufmann, *The Religion of Israel*, trans. and abridged M. Greenberg (Chicago: Univ. of Chicago Press, 1960), 114.
159. Cohen, *Cultic Calendars*, 446; see also *ANET*, 334.
160. However, blood was used for purifying a new Anatolian temple: COS, 1.70:176.
161. Ibid., 1.162:530; cf. T. Jacobsen, *The Harps That Once …: Sumerian Poetry in Translation* (New Haven, Conn.: Yale Univ. Press, 1987), 138.
162. Gane, *Ritual Dynamic Structure*, 261–62, 264–66, 273, 358–59.
163. Ibid., ch. 5; see also *ANET*, 333–34; Cohen, *Cultic Calendars*, 445–46. On the ritual events of this festival and their function, see further in J. Bidmead, *The Akitu Festival: Religious Continuity*

and Royal Legitimation in Mesopotamia (Piscataway, N.J.: Gorgias, 2002).

164. Kaufmann, *Religion of Israel*, 103–5; Milgrom, *Leviticus 1–16*, 1068–69.

165. For further explanation, see Gane, *Leviticus, Numbers*, 169, 276–77; Gane, *Cult and Character*, ch. 8; cf. J. Milgrom, "Confusing the Sacred and the Impure: A Rejoinder," *VT* 44 (1994): 557–58.

166. *ANET*, 333; Cohen, *Cultic Calendars*, 445–46.

167. See also the behavior of Jews at Elephantine (Egypt) in a time of disaster: COS, 3.51:127–28.

168. See Gane, *Cult and Character*, ch. 14.

169. Ibid., 1.147:478.

170. Ibid., 1.162:528. For further analysis of this text and comparison with Leviticus, see Gane, *Cult and Character*, ch. 17. For other Mesopotamian texts in which New Year days are days of inspection, see COS, 1.173:557–58; W. Heimpel, "The Nanshe Hymn," *JCS* 33 (1981): 110; K. van der Toorn, "Form and Function of the New Year Festival in Babylonia and Israel," in *Congress Volume: Leuven, 1989*, ed. J. A. Emerton (VTSup 43; Leiden: Brill, 1991), 5.

171. J. Milgrom, *Leviticus 17–22* (AB; New York: Doubleday, 2000), 1462.

172. Compare Milgrom, *Leviticus 1–16*, 1021, 1072. H. Tawil, "ʿAzazel The Prince of the Steppe: A Comparative Study," *ZAW* 92 (1980): 48–52.

173. Milgrom, *Leviticus 1–16*, 1072.

174. Hoffner, "Second Millennium Antecedents," 395.

175. M. Schwartz, "The Old Eastern Iranian World View According to the Avesta," in *The Cambridge History of Iran*, ed. I. Gershevitch (Cambridge: Cambridge Univ. Press, 1985), 2:656. Regarding incest among Elamite kings, see F. Vallat, "Susa and Susiana in Second-Millennium Iran," in *CANE*, 2:1029.

176. COS, 2.131:345; 2.19:118. Interestingly, a negative confession in the Egyptian Book of the Dead refers to a kind of sexual activity that is not mentioned in the Bible: "I have not masturbated" (ibid., 2.12:61).

177. See also Deut. 22:30; 27:20; 1 Cor. 5:1.

178. However, "If anyone sleeps with an *arnuwala*-woman, and also sleeps with her mother, it is not an offense" (Roth, *Law Collections*, 237).

179. S. Rattray, "Marriage Rules, Kinship Terms and Family Structure in the Bible," *SBLSP* 26 (1998): 542. A Hittite treaty condemns sex with one's sister, cousin, or sister-in-law (G. Beckman, *Hittite Diplomatic Texts*, 2nd ed. [SBLWAW; Atlanta: Scholars, 1999], 31–32).

180. Roth, *Law Collections*, 236. Cf. COS, 1.120:425 (a Mesopotamian omen).

181. Roth, *Law Collections*, 236.

182. A. Tosato, "The Law of Leviticus 18:18: A Reexamination," *CBQ* 46 (1984): 202–8; cf. *Temple Scroll* 57:17–18, trans. Y. Yadin, in *The Temple Scroll* (Jerusalem: Israel Exploration Society, 1983), 2:407; *Damascus Document* 4:21, trans. G. Vermes, *The Complete Dead Sea Scrolls in Eng-lish* (New York: Allen Lane/Penguin, 1997), 130.

183. Roth, *Law Collections*, 236.

184. Regarding how this legislation applies today, see Gane, *Leviticus, Numbers*, 325–30.

185. H. Hoffner, "Incest, Sodomy and Bestiality in the Ancient Near East," in *Orient and Occident*, ed. H. Hoffner (AOAT 22; Kevelaer/Neukirchen-Vluyn: Butzon and Bercker/Neukirchener, 1973), 81–90.

186. COS, 1.120:425.

187. Roth, *Law Collections*, 160.

188. COS, 2.12:60 n. 8.

189. Ibid., 1.86:261–62.

190. See, e.g., *Dragons, Monsters and Fabulous Beasts*, ed. J. G. Westenholz (Jerusalem: Bible Lands Museum, 2004).

191. COS, 2.19:118. Although copulating with a horse or mule is a sin and prevents a man from approaching the king or ever becoming a priest, it is not a punishable offense (ibid., 118–19).

192. Ibid., 1.47:120.

193. Ibid., 1.162:526–31; Heimpel, "Nanshe Hymn," 65–139; Jacobsen, *Harps That Once . . .*, 125–42; cf. comment on Lev. 16:29.

194. See, e.g., COS, 1.35:65; A. Berlejung, "Washing the Mouth: The Consecration of Divine Images in Mesopotamia," in *The Image and the Book: Iconic Cults, Aniconism, and the Rise of Book Religion in Israel and the Ancient Near East*, ed. K. van der Toorn (Leuven: Peeters, 1997), 45–72; E. M. Curtis, "Images in Mesopotamia and the Bible: A Comparative Study," in *The Bible in the Light of Cuneiform Literature—Scripture in Context III*, ed. W. W. Hallo, B. W. Jones, and G. L. Mattingly (Ancient Near Eastern Texts and Studies; Lewiston, N.Y.: Mellen, 1990), 31–56; M. B. Dick, ed., *Born in Heaven, Made on Earth: The Making of the Cult Image in the Ancient Near East* (Winona Lake, Ind.: Eisenbrauns, 1999); W. W. Hallo, "Cult Statue and Divine Image: A Preliminary Study," in *Scripture in Context II: More Essays on the Comparative Method*, ed. W. W. Hallo, J. C. Moyer, and L. G. Perdue (Winona Lake, Ind.: Eisenbrauns, 1983), 1–17; V. Hurowitz, "Picturing Imageless Deities: Iconography in the Ancient Near East," *BAR* 23/3 (1997): 46–48, 51, 68; J. J. M. Roberts, "Divine Freedom and Cultic Manipulation in Israel and Mesopotamia," in *Unity and Diversity: Essays in the History, Literature, and Religion of the Ancient Near East*, ed. H. Goedicke and J. J. M. Roberts (Baltimore: Johns Hopkins Univ. Press, 1975), 181–90; J. M. Sasson, "On the Use of Images in Israel and the Ancient Near East: A Response to Karel van der Toorn," in *Sacred Time, Sacred Place: Archaeology and the Religion of Israel*, ed. B. M. Gittlen (Winona Lake, Ind.: Eisenbrauns, 2002), 63–70.

195. COS, 2.17B:96; cf. 2.17C:99.

196. See the eloquent Egyptian Instruction of Amenemope, which exhibits a number of similarities to biblical law and wisdom teachings (ibid., 1.47: 116, 118, 119, 120, 121; cf. 1.35:62, 65).

NUMBERS

by R. Dennis Cole

Kadesh Barnea
region
Z. Radovan/
www.BibleLand
Pictures.com

Introduction

Title

The title "Numbers" derives from the Septuagint name *Arithmoi*, based especially on
the census materials in chapters 1–4 and 26.
The Hebrew title (*b*^e*midbar*; "In the Wilderness") describes the geographical setting of
much of the book—from the Wilderness of

Sinai to the arid Plains of Moab, across the
Jordan River from Jericho.

Geographical Setting

Numbers contains three geographical settings, providing a thematic and theological program for the book. The first and the

The question of where Moses and Israel encountered God has intrigued biblical scholars at least since the Byzantine period. Eusebius[1] cites the preference for the traditional Mount Sinai at Jebel Musa in the rugged south central mountains, which towers up to 7,505 feet, while others proposed Jebel Serbal (6,791 feet) in the western ridge of the Sinai peninsula. The Christian preference for Jebel Musa led to the construction of the famous St. Catherine's Monastery in the sixth century A.D., further strengthening that tradition.

No less than twenty different suggestions have been tendered through the centuries for other locations for Mount Sinai, such as Jebel Sin Bisher in the west-central Sinai peninsula (2,755 feet), Jebel Helal and Har Karkom in northeast Sinai, and even Jebel al-Lawz in northwest Saudia Arabia.[2] The strongest support historically and geographically is for Jebel Musa, though the Jebel Sin Bisher location meets as many of the criteria (see esp. comments on 33:16). Locating Israelite campsites between Mount Sinai and Kadesh Barnea is dependent on the location of Mount Sinai (see charts in ch. 33).

Historical Setting

Archaeologists and historians date the Israelite wilderness sojourn to the middle or latter part of the Late Bronze Age (1550–1200 B.C.) in the ancient Near East. The world of Egypt, the eastern Mediterranean, and Mesopotamia experienced dramatic political and territorial transitions during this era. Egypt conquered the lands of Canaan and beyond under Eighteenth Dynasty kings Thutmose I and Thutmose III, only to see it diminish during the reign of Akhenaton. During the fifteenth century B.C. Egypt exacted extensive political and economic control over the region.

Yet in the fourteenth century as the Amarna letters reflect, the Egyptians experienced a significant loss of power among loyal Canaanite puppet-kings because of invasions from the Hapiru, Shasu, and other marauding bands. Then the Nineteenth Dynasty

last are specific locales. The *Wilderness of Sinai* (1:1–10:10) is where the Israelites spent almost a year encamped at the base of Mount Sinai, the mountain of God. There Moses and the Israelites encountered God, received the gift of the law, and constructed the tabernacle and its holy furnishings. The final location was the *Plains of Moab* (22:1–36:13), where the second generation of Israelites prepared for the conquest of their promised inheritance.

Between these two locales is the *journey* through several rugged wilderness regions from the central Sinai peninsula to the Paran Wilderness (10:11–12:16), to the central Negev region of Kadesh Barnea and the Zin Wilderness (13:1–20:22), then into the arid southern Jordan regions of the Wadi Zered (20:22–21:9), then northward through the territories of the Moabites and Amorites, where God gave victory over Sihon and Og. These travels should have taken several months but lasted nearly forty years.

kings Seti I and Ramesses II restored the Egyptian hegemony over much of Canaan, having established a boundary with the Hittites at Qadesh on the Orontes River. Early Hebrew chronologists place the Exodus about 1442 B.C., under either Thutmose III or Amenhotep II, placing the forty-year wilderness sojourn during the reigns of Amenhotep II and Thutmose IV. Late Hebrew chronologists place both the Exodus and the wilderness period under Ramesses II.[3]

Whichever chronological scheme is taken, the *terminus ad quem* for Israel's existence in Canaan is the mention of "Israel" in the Merneptah Stele (ca. 1209 B.C.). By that time Israel had established itself as a significant enough entity in the central hill country to be mentioned as one of the peoples defeated in the land of Canaan by the pharaoh Merneptah.[4] By the end of the Late Bronze Age, because of massive migrations of peoples such as the Sea Peoples (including the Philistines, Sherdan, and Danoi) and international warfare, empires such as the Egyptians and Hittites and city-states such as Ugarit experienced dramatic collapse and even destruction.

Most important is that under either chronological scheme, God delivered the Israelites from Egypt during the reign of a powerful pharaoh who oversaw a vast empire that stretched through much of Canaan. The wilderness sojourn as described in Numbers came when the Egyptians focused on maintaining the lucrative trade routes through northern Sinai and into Canaan. The southern two-thirds of the Sinai region was less in focus during this era. Thus the Israelites' experiences with God were less likely to be impacted by the imperial pursuits of her former taskmasters.

The First Census of Israel's Military (1:1–54)

Tent of Meeting (1:1). Israel's worship center is known from Egyptian sources dating to as early as the Old Kingdom period (2700–2200 B.C.). Kitchen demonstrates parallels of several Egyptian "dismountable

Eighteenth and Nineteenth Dynasty Egyptian Pharaohs	
Eighteenth Dynasty	
Pharaoh	Regnal Dates
Thutmose I	1524–1518 B.C.
Thutmose II	1518–1504 B.C.
Thutmose III	1479–1425 B.C. ** (25 YEAR GAP)
Hatshepsut	1479–1457 B.C.
Amenhotep II	1453–1419 B.C.
Thutmose IV	1419–1386 B.C.
Amenhotep III	1402–1364 B.C.
Akhenaton	1352–1336 B.C.
Smenkhare	1336–1334 B.C.
Tutankamun	1337–1333 B.C.
Ay	1334–1325 B.C.
Horemhab	1323–1295 B.C.
Nineteenth Dynasty	
Ramesses I	1295–1294 B.C.
Seti I	1294–1279 B.C.
Ramesses II	1279–1213 B.C.
Merneptah	1213–1203 B.C.

tabernacles" of the third through second millennia B.C.[5] Mobile tent shrines with wooden pillars are depicted in ritual purification scenes on tomb murals.[6] These structures used vertical and horizontal poles, metal fittings of copper, gold, or silver, and draped fabrics.

The war tent of Ramesses II presents a similar style of mobile sanctuary. Also the "secular tabernacle" of Queen Hetepheres, mother of Khufu (ca. 2600 B.C.), consisted of wooden poles and horizontal frames, assembled with tendon and socket joints. Gold decorations adorned the poles.[7] Other mobile sanctuaries are known from Mari (eighteenth century B.C.) and Ugarit (thirteenth century B.C.), the latter contemporary with Moses.[8] The Ugaritic Keret Texts use the same term *mšknt.hm* ("their tents") as the Hebrew *hammiškān* ("the tent," 3:7) for the mobile sanctuary. From the Mari texts of the Middle Bronze Age (2000–1550

B.C.), tents are described as being supported by wooden frames, called *qeršu* in Akkadian (cognate to the Heb. *qᵉrāšîm*, "frames").[9] The Ugaritic term *qeršu* describes the tent of El in the Baal Epic.[10]

Desert of Sinai (1:1). On the location of Mount Sinai and route taken by the Israel-ites, see the introduction.

First day of the second month of the second year (1:1). This chronological state-ment places the military conscription census on a "New Moon" festival, a year and two weeks after the Exodus, which took place on the 14th of Abib (=Nisan), the first month. This notation also occurs after the events described in chapters 7–9. The presentation of gifts by the twelve tribes for the service of the tabernacle (7:1–89) took place at the conclusion of the construction of the mobile shrine, which Exodus 40:17 places on Abib 1, almost a year after the Exodus. Then came the second Passover, celebrated on Abib 14 (Num. 9:1–5). The Israelite departure from Sinai took place on the twentieth day of the second month, less than three weeks after the census. See chart on "Chronology of Events in Exodus, Leviticus, and Numbers" at 7:1.

Take a census (1:2). A census for mili-tary conscription purposes was common in the Bible and texts of the ancient Near East (cf. Num. 25; 2 Sam. 24:1–17; 1 Chron. 21:1–17). In numerous other cases, a simple total of the military conscripted for battle is given.[11] The census involved a head count—the idiomatic Hebrew terminology reads literally "lift up the head" and "every male by their skulls"—of capable military men age twenty years and up.

A troop census before going to battle was common in the warfare plans of ancient Sumer, Akkad, and Assyria. Sargon of Akkad (ca. 2350 B.C.) had an army of 5,400 who dined at his table after victories in Amurru.[12] His son and heir to the throne fought with armies of 10,000 or more. In terms of the sizes of armies conquered, Shalmaneser I (ca. 1275–1245 B.C.) claims to have slaughtered 14,400 Hittites and Ahlamu troops.[13]

Twenty years old or more (1:3). Twenty years of age was the accepted age of full maturity in the Bible for military conscription (cf. 26:2; 2 Chron. 25:5), even though marriage often took place in the late teens. This age requirement is confirmed in the Dead Sea Scrolls.[14] No upper age limit is given, though military capability is delineated. Levitical service began at age thirty, with an upper limit of fifty (Num. 4:3, 23, 30). Milgrom notes that twenty was the military age requirement in Sparta, though eighteen was the minimum at Athens.[15]

Total number (1:46). The large numbers in Exodus and Numbers have long posed problems for interpreters. With an able militia of over 600,000 and an additional population of 22,273 Levites, the total population of Israel coming out of Egypt would have easily exceeded two million (cf. also Ex. 12:37; 30:12–16; 38:26; Num. 11:21). Internal evidence from the Bible and external data cause considerable difficulty in accepting these figures at face value. See sidebar on "Large Numbers in the Book of Numbers."

Levi (1:47–51). The three clans of the Levites are not counted in the military conscription census because of their noncombatant role. Priests in ancient Near Eastern societies were similarly not required to carry arms in battle, but served to carry symbols of the national deity(s) into battle and do

other nonfighting functions. Though the Levites are not technically priests—that position is restricted to those in the direct line of Aaron—they perform duties similar to those in the priestly circles of ancient Ugarit, Mari, Emar, Assyria, and Babylon.[16]

Standard (1:52). Comparison of the Hebrew *degel* with the usage of Akkadian terms *dagalu* and *diglu* in the second millennium B.C. suggests that this is something that is seen (e.g., a banner or flag), which served as an identity feature for the given tribal troop unit.[17] In later Hebrew and Aramaic this term refers to a military troop unit of a thousand men who lived together with their families and functioned as a legal and economic entity.[18] Milgrom notes: "This situation corresponds closely to the makeup and function of the Israelite tribes in the wilderness."[19]

Arrangement of the Tribal Camps (2:1–34)

Around the Tent of Meeting (2:2). See comment on 1:1.

Each man under his standard (2:2). Each tribal leader is to camp according to the standard that signifies his ancestral house, around and away from the tabernacle.[20] The terms *degel* ("standard") and *'ōtôt* ("signs") refer to some kind of banner or flag (see comment on 1:52). In the War Scroll from the Qumran caves, distinguishable standards were to be carried by each division within the ancestral tribe.[21]

Priests carrying standards
Guillaume Blanchard/Wikimedia Commons, courtesy of the Louvre

▶ Large Numbers in the Book of Numbers

The numbering of the Levites at 22,000 for the redemption of the firstborn of Israel's males (well over 603,550, if firstborn males under age twenty are included) would mean that the average Israelite woman bore more than twenty-seven males, plus females. In the Old Testament the largest number of males born to a single male (Jacob) is twelve, and they were through multiple wives and concubines (Gen. 29:31–30:22; 35:18, 22–36). Deuteronomy 7:1 describes "seven nations greater and stronger than you [Israel]" in the Promised Land, whom the Lord would drive out from before the Israelites. If Israel were two million, this figure would yield an aggregate population of Canaan of fifteen to twenty million, far more than the modern population of the region. The optimum estimates of the total population of the region in the Late Bronze Age and Iron I period that have come as

a result of archaeological surveys and demographic distribution studies come to less than one million.

Thus, evangelical scholars have suggested several possible solutions. (1) The figures represent hyperbole to show the fulfillment of God's promise to make a nation through Abraham that would be as numerous as the stars in the heavens (Gen. 13:16; 15:5). (2) Fouts has compared this military census with those of Assyrian and Babylonian military conscription texts, suggesting such figures were used to demonstrate the power of ancient kings in their conquest annals.[A-1] (3) The Hebrew term translated "thousand" (ʾelep) has been taken to mean "military unit" (vocalized ʾallup, from the same Semitic root); hence the total would be 598 units yielding a total militia of 5,550 combat-ready soldiers in this chapter and 5,730 men in 596 units in the second census of chapter 26.[A-2]

The Tribal Encampments of Israel around the Tabernacle
▼

The tribal encampments and the order of their marching through the wilderness had a definite structure. See "The Tribal Encampments of Israel around the Tabernacle."

Sacred Responsibilities of the Levites (3:1–4:49)

Family of Aaron and Moses (3:1). The genealogical record (Heb. tôlēdôt) of the family of Aaron and Moses stands firmly within the biblical and ancient Near Eastern tradition of recounting one's ancestry in societal ritual. Genealogical records served several purposes: (1) to provide historical connection in the present in relationship to a pivotal point in the past, (2) to preserve familial community and organization within the larger societal structure, (3) to justify one's present position by providing an historical precedent from one's family line, or (4) to provide future generations with a source of pride and presence.[22]

Typically in the Bible genealogies link the present generation with the past and then describe the role of the present generation in the life of the religious community. In the Atraḫasis Epic (a version of the Babylonian flood account), the concluding statement of each of the three tablets functions like a modern title page with information about date of composition, authorship, and title. Like the genealogical statements of Genesis (e.g., Gen. 2:4; 5:1; 6:9; 10:1), Harrison suggests that Moses used his records of the census to "validate his authority and that of his brother, Aaron."[23]

Nadab the firstborn (3:2). Normative in ancient Near Eastern law during the Bronze Ages and later were the rights of primogeniture, by which the eldest son received a double portion of the family inheritance. But he had certain responsibilities, such as care for the aged parents and their eventual proper burial, and maintaining ancestral worship.[24] This pattern also ensured the orderly disposition of property from one generation to the next. If the firstborn died, as in the case of Nadab (and then Abihu), the responsibility went to the next living kin (Eleazar and then Ithamar).

Sometimes the rights of primogeniture were displaced by divine preference (e.g., the choice of David as king, 1 Sam.

16:1 – 13) or by negotiation (e.g., Jacob and Esau, Gen. 26:24 – 34). According to the Laws of Hammurabi, a father could choose the son of preference, as Jacob did in conferring the status on Judah instead of Reuben after the latter slept with Bilhah, his father's concubine.[25] Daughters could also sometimes inherit property, as in New Kingdom Egypt. Texts from Emar provide some of the closest examples to Israelite law on these issues.[26]

Put to death (3:10). The Levites served as guardians of the sanctuary, functioning as a lightning rod for the fiery wrath of God against potential encroachment on the sanctuary. Elsewhere human and divine guardians were positioned to prevent violation of the temples and cities. For example, gargoyles and various creatures in Egypt and Mesopotamia (symbols of divine entities) were positioned at the entrances to temples.[27] Priests at Mari on the Euphrates and at the Hittite capital of Hattusas performed night-time guard duty, for which improper performance of duty was punishable by death.[28]

Levites are mine (3:12 – 13). Rather than having individual clan rights of primogeniture for maintaining the sanctuary and ancestral worship, Israel has an entire tribe dedicated to proper worship of God. In the exodus event, the Lord commanded that every firstborn male of humans and animals be dedicated or sacrificed to the Lord as a sign of faithfulness (Ex. 13:1 – 16). The Levites became the substitute for the firstborn males of Israel.

Ancestral worship practices were common in ancient Near Eastern cultures. In Egypt the Book of the Dead emphasized the proper care and provision for the deceased. At Ugarit, mortuary ritual attended to deceased royal ancestors so that they might bring blessing to the

Gigantic Lamassu figures guarded the entryway to temples and palaces, threatening harm to trespassers.
Marie-Lan Nguyen/ Wikimedia Commons, courtesy of the Louvre

▶ Redemption Money in the Ancient Near East

The concept of redemption finds a parallel in Babylonian literature, where the term *padû* denotes a form of monetary payment equivalent to the market value of an object or person, remitted in order to transfer property from one party to another. Often this redemption fee was the payment of an original debt, whereby a debt-slave could gain his freedom through monetary or property transfer, performance of a determined period of servitude, or a general cancellation of the debt.[A-3] Property yielded in payment of debt could be redeemed at an agreed price. Slaves or indentured servants could obtain their freedom by paying the redemption price.

Most of the Israelite firstborn were redeemed via the substitution of the Levites, with the excess number of males to be redeemed by the price of five shekels of silver (2.1 ounces according to the twenty-gerah sanctuary shekel). The redemption price for each Israelite delivered from bondage in Egypt was one-half shekel (Ex. 30:11–16), provided to support the service of the Tent of Meeting. Five shekels was the standard price of a slave in Late Bronze Egypt and Mesopotamia and amounted to six months' wages for the average day laborer.[A-4] In early Israel the redemption rate of five shekels was the value set on a small male child; an adult male was valued at fifty shekels (Lev. 27:1–8).

current king.[29] In Mesopotamian ritual the cult of the dead included practices whereby a "caretaker" made funerary offerings and poured out water libations while invoking the name of the deceased.[30] Such practices became common in Israelite popular religion, but were condemned by the law and the prophets (Deut. 14:1–2; 18:10–11; 26:12–15; Isa. 19:3; Jer. 16:5–9).

The money for the redemption (3:48). On the issue of redemption money, see sidebar on "Redemption Money in the Ancient Near East."

Hides of sea cows (4:6). This translation of *taḥaš* is unlikely since sea cows, porpoises, or dolphins are unclean animals (aquatic life with fins but not having scales and thus prohibited from consumption or other usage; see Lev. 11:9–12). According to Milgrom, *taḥaš* should be rendered "yellow-orange."[31]

Cloth of solid blue (4:6). The "blue cloth" covering mentioned in verses 6–14 was actually bluish purple (*tᵉkēlet*), and the "purple" (*ʾargāmān*; NIV "purple cloth") refers to a reddish-purple dye (4:13). These dyes were produced from the various murex

shells, with the *Murex trunculus* used in producing the bluish-purple dye, and the *Murex brandaris* and *Thais haemastoma* shells yielding the reddish-purple extract.[32] The use of these shells along the shorelines of the Mediterranean basin is attested in archaeological surveys and excavations of sites dating to the early second millennium B.C., from Greece to Asia Minor in the north, and from Ugarit to Tyre in the east.[33]

Purification Laws for the Sacred Community (5:1–31)

Send away from the camp (5:1–4). The sacred camp of Israel has been numbered and organized with its concentric circles of holiness, with the priests and Levites constituting the first level of human presence in proximity to the sanctuary, the Tent of Meeting. The twelve tribes encamp symmetrically around the central sanctuary and its attendants, constituting the second level of human presence in the camp. Now the next level of the encampment is described in terms of relative cultic isolation on the perimeter of the camp of those with various impurities.

Mary Douglas posits that humans developed social distinctions of conformity and disunity based on their observations of natural forces. She defines "dirt" or "uncleanness" as that which is "out of place" in society, and "holiness" as that which is in harmony with nature, having "wholeness and completeness."[34] With regard to biblical purity she highlights the human understanding of Levitical legislation as denoting an ideal for humanity.

But the Hebrew Bible provides further distinction between the common and the unclean, as well as between the holy and the pure. Douglas sees in Leviticus and Numbers a "paradox insofar as they legislate against impurity without designating any social category as inherently impure or liable to contaminate others."[35] But the Torah in fact legislates against any kind of class system, even to the point of giving resident aliens status in worship and purification under the same matrix of law as the Israelite. Ethical and moral distinctions, not class systems, play a significant role in the understanding of these distinctions. Hence Douglas observes, "the Judaism of Leviticus and the book of Numbers is not among the exclusive religions, nor do its commands weigh heavily upon its congregation. Purification is easy, and open to all who wish for it."[36]

Skin disease (5:2). Scholars have debated extensively the meaning of ṣāraʿat, translated "leprosy" in earlier versions. Some have questioned whether leprosy (known today as Hansen's disease) even existed in the ancient world.[37] Harrison and Wenham argue for the inclusion of this disease among ancient infectious skin diseases.[38] The extensive description of the disease, its effects and treatment, and the purification process after having had the disease, as well as the adjudication by the priest at the conclusion of the purification rituals, all evidence a disease with some symptoms similar to Hansen's and some dissimilar.

Other serious skin infections, such as psoriasis or eczema, may be intended by this ritual exclusion. In each case the form of skin disease was considered by the ancients to be at discord with the harmony of nature, indicating to an adjudicating priest that "the world is no longer in balance, and that its fundamental categories have been violated."[39]

Full restitution (5:7). The sanctity of the community applies to economic relationships, whereby monetary compensation for fraud or extortion between individuals provides stability and justice in society. By comparison, the Law Code of Hammurabi called for restitution penalties ranging from a one-sixth to 100 percent addition to the principal amount of the damage incurred for defrauding another person under oath. For example, if a person deposited gold or silver with another person in the presence of witnesses, and later denied the transaction, the witnesses would be called to testify on behalf of the depositor, and the repayment was double the original amount (see comment on Lev. 6:1–7).[40]

If a man's wife goes astray (5:12). This particular case concerns a woman suspected by her husband of having an adulterous affair.[41] In Mesopotamian as well as biblical law, if a man or a woman was caught having intercourse with another's spouse, they were both executed. In Law 129 of the Code of Hammurabi, the man and woman were to be bound together and thrown into the river.[42] A trial by ordeal places punishment in the hands of God for a case of unapprehended adultery.[43] Westbrook argues that the ancient Near Eastern societies shared a set of legal traditions, among them marriage and divorce codes.[44] See sidebar on "Suspected but Unobserved Adultery."

Grain offering (5:15). The Šurpu purification ritual from Assur of the Middle Babylonian period (ca. 1350–1050 B.C.) used flour in relation to a variety of misdemeanors, including a case where a man had intercourse with a neighbor's wife. A "magic

▶ Suspected but Unobserved Adultery

Two laws from the Code of Hammurabi relate to cases of suspected but unobserved adultery. Law 132 contains a trial by ordeal, in which the woman is thrown to the divine realm of the river gods: "If a citizen charges a woman with adultery,[A-5] but has no evidence, then she is to be tried by ordeal in the river to restore the honor of her husband. If she survives she must pay a fine." Law 131 focuses on false accusation by a husband, whereby the woman must simply swear an oath of innocence: "If a citizen falsely accuses his wife of adultery, and she swears an oath of innocence before the divine patron of her household, then she may return home."[A-6] In both cases ultimate adjudication is rendered into the hands of the divine.

Unlike the Babylonian parallels, the biblical text only addresses cases in which the husband brings the accusation. Milgrom notes that even "if the rumor originated in the community it was still only the husband who could press charges (v. 15)."[A-7] In a practical consideration of the case, Brichto notes that the focus of the trial by ordeal should be placed on "assessing the degree of probability of the eventuation of the punishment.... A jealous husband, possessing not a scintilla of evidence against his wife, is asked to subject her to a test in which all the cards are stacked in her favor."[A-8]

circle of flour" was placed around a brazier, then wiped over the offender in an atonement (*ukappar*) ritual. This act was accompanied by several sympathetic magic rituals involving onions, dates, matting, and wool, which were then thrown into the brazier's fire with some of the flour.[45]

Loosen her hair (5:18). The unbinding of one's hair was a sign of mourning or disgrace (Lev. 10:6, 13:45; 21:10). In ancient Greek literature, the loosening of the hair was a sign of one's unmarried state or a potential sign of freedom, including sexual immorality and eroticism,[46] but similar customs are not evident in the ancient Near East.

Drink the bitter water (5:24). From the archives of Mari comes a case in which a water potion made with dirt from the gate of the city is consumed by the accused and then is followed by an oath before the gods.[47] Water mixed with dust may not be bitter to the physical taste, which would normally be alkaline, but bitter in terms of the potential distress and bitterness of the life situation being tried.[48]

Nazirites (6:1–21)

Vow (6:2). Vows among ancient Near Eastern cultures from Mesopotamia, Anatolia, and the Levant reflect the following pattern: (1) The vow grows out of a situation of need or distress; (2) it is made by a human to the gods; (3) it is generally conditional in nature; (4) a responsive votive offering is offered publicly at a cultic place at the conclusion of the vow conditions.[49]

Abstain from wine and other fermented drink (6:3). Restrictions for the Nazirite are more stringent than those for the priest here, because the priest need only refrain from fermented beverage during his period of service in the sanctuary (Lev. 10:9). A Nazirite must abstain from all vineyard products at all times, defined in detail down to the grape hulls, pits, and even the vines.

The intoxicant beverages are listed as "wine" (*yayin*) and "other fermented drink" (*šēkār*). Wine was the most common form of grape beverage, produced in the late summer and early fall in ancient Israel in winepress

Relief from the tomb of Petosiris, High Priest of the god Thoth, shows the grape harvest, and people pressing grapes. Erich Lessing/Art Resource, NY

◄

installations and then stored in subterranean bell-shaped caves for fermentation. Numerous examples of these installations from the Bronze and Iron Ages have been excavated in Israel, such as those at Gibeon, Beth Shemesh, Samaria, and el-Burj.[50]

The "other fermented drink" has historically been translated as "beer," a common Mesopotamian and Egyptian beverage known from inscriptions and carved or painted murals, or as "strong drink." L. E. Stager suggests that *šēkār* may refer to a grape distillate such as grappa or brandy, a term that gave rise to the verb *šākar* ("to be drunk"). Such a product had an alcohol content of 20 to 60 percent by comparison to wine's 12 to 14 percent.[51] The emphasis here is total abstinence from anything associated with the vineyard, lending support to the interpretation of *šēkār* as an intoxicating beverage produced from vineyard produce.[52]

No razor may be used on his head (6:5). The visible distinctiveness of allowing the hair to grow long and remain uncut for the duration of the vow set the Nazirite apart from societal norms. In Mesopotamian and Mediterranean law codes, hair played a significant role in ritual and legal practices. In Hammurabi's law code, cutting one's hair was a form of punishment and humiliation for bringing a false accusation against another man's wife in matters of property.[53] In a ninth-century B.C. Cypriot bowl inscription, a person's hair was presented to Astarte as a memorial offer-ing.[54] In a Hellenistic era temple repair and rededication ritual, the king's hair was cut and presented as an offering to the local deity in a special votive vessel.[55]

In contrast to Canaanite priestly practices, levitical regulations prohibited Israelite priests from allowing their heads to be shaved bald or trimming the edges of the beard, as well as cutting themselves (Lev. 19:26–28; 21:5–7). Olyan notes that shaving rites mark a ritual transition, altering the status of the one shaved. By shaving the head one entered into the realm of social control, whereas long hair symbolized separation from social control.[56] From Emar, a ritual for the installation of the high priestess (NIN.DINGIR) of the storm god involved

Model of Egyptian beer makers Anthony M. Warnack, courtesy of the Rosicrucian Egyptian Museum

▼

a "Shaving Day," which was concluded by anointing the head with oil.[57]

He must not go near a dead body (6:6). Touching or even coming into close proximity with a corpse was a common means of ritual contamination. To maintain the sanctity of a vow, a Nazirite could not participate in the standard ritual mourning for the dead, even a member of one's own family. Verses 9–12 provide for accidental contamination, whereby the Nazirite removes the outward symbol of identification by shaving the hair and offering it to Yahweh at the conclusion of the period of uncleanness. Restriction also included the levitically prohibited participation in ritual associated with the cult of the dead. This practice stood in contrast to pagan ritual related to the cult of the dead[58] (see comment on 3:12–13).

Drinking wine to the point of drunkenness was also part of the pagan cult of the dead ritual, as described in the *Ilu's Marzihu* account from Ugarit (cf. Heb. *marzēaḥ*, "funeral meal").[59] The story of Samson implies that the restriction also applied to animal corpses since he withheld from his parents the knowledge that the honey he presented them was gathered from the carcass of a lion he had killed with his bare hands (Judg. 14:5–9).

Boiled shoulder of the ram (6:19). Normally the breast and the upper portion of the right hind leg were reserved for priestly consumption (Lev. 7:30–35). A similar practice seems apparent in Egyptian, Mesopotamian, and Hittite texts and murals in which the right thigh was the choice portion for presentation to various deities.[60] The boiling of sacrifices is known from pre-Israelite Lachish[61] and pre-monarchical Shiloh (1 Sam. 2:13–14).

Wave offering (6:20). To wave or elevate an offering before Yahweh is a ritual act signifying the transfer of the offering from the property of the offerer to Yahweh (see comment on 18:11).

Priestly Blessing over the Sacred Community (6:22–27)

Bless the Israelites (6:23). That this blessing was important to the ancient Israelites is attested in the copy found in the excavations of Ketef Hinnom on the southwest of Mount Zion and the Old City in Jerusalem, where archaeologist G. Barkai unearthed a late seventh- to sixth-century B.C. burial complex. Among the remains was a phylactery containing two silver scrolls the size of a small cigarette, on which were written two versions of the priestly blessing.[62] Both inscriptions contain additional appellations to YHWH as "the restorer and rock" and as "the warrior and the rebuker of evil."[63]

These texts had been used as amulets either while these individuals were alive or as burial pendants. The text on the larger one is nearly identical to this passage; an abbreviated version of the second and third blessings was written on the smaller. Containing the oldest attestation to the tetragrammaton (YHWH = Yahweh) in Jerusalem, these texts indicate the authenticity and antiquity of this "priestly benediction." Its text became a standardized liturgical form no later than the end of the preexilic period. Ancient Near Eastern texts from the second millennium B.C. contain parallels to the themes of divine countenance, the lifting up of the face, and the blessing of well-being (*šālôm*).[64]

Thigh offering
Rama/Wikimedia
Commons, courtesy
of the Louvre

The LORD make his face shine upon you (6:25). The metaphor portraying God's face as light shining on his people occurs in numerous biblical and extrabiblical texts (Ps. 80:3; 44:3). This imagery occurs in several Mesopotamian and Ugaritic contexts, in which the gods bestow gifts and extend mercy to individuals or nations.[65] An Egyptian text from the First Intermediate period (ca. 2134–2040 B.C.) has a letter to the dead inscribed on a tubular jar stand: "You live for (me), The Great One shall praise you, and the face of the Great God will be gracious over you; he will give you pure bread with his two hands."[66] While this text parallels the priestly blessing in form and content, its broader context is significantly different insofar as it focuses on petitioning the deceased father for assistance in producing a male heir.

They will put my name on the Israelites (6:27). Placing the name of a deity on a place or a people asserted the claim of deity and established his presence. In Akkadian usage, the phrase *šuma šakānu* is used in the same way.[67]

Offerings at the Dedication of the Tabernacle (7:1–89)

When Moses finished setting up the tabernacle (7:1). For chronology, see sidebar and comment on 1:1.

Offerings for its dedication (7:12–83). The pattern of enumeration here reflects an administrative record following the traditional pattern of temple records of the ancient Near East. Levine suggests that the original text was a tabular list,

> intended to be read both horizontally and vertically.... The system of numeration employed in Num 7:12–88 is perhaps the most revealing feature of all, because it directly links biblical records to known methods of ancient Near Eastern accounting. In Num 7:12–88 the sequence of numeration is (a) item, (b) numerical quantity.[68]

Wenham proposes that the repetitive nature of the material is primarily theological, to emphasize that every tribe has an equal stake in the worship of God and that each is fully committed to the support of the tabernacle and its priesthood.[69]

Sanctuary shekel (7:13). The craftsmen of the three types of utensils use the sanctuary shekel, a cultic measurement for weighing gifts and sacrifices or determining their monetary value. The term "shekel" was used throughout the Levant and Mesopotamia as a standard weight measure, generally ranging from ten to thirteen grams. Milgrom and Wenham compute the resultant weights of the objects as approximately three pounds for the large silver plate, two pounds for the silver basin, and four ounces for the small gold ladle for the incense.[70]

Menorah and Levites (8:1–26)

Lampstand (8:1–4). This tree of light recalls the tree of life of Genesis 2:10; 3:22–24, a common life motif in Mesopotamian texts and iconography; it is crafted with seven tiers, symbolic of God's perfect presence and life illumination.[71] Mesopotamia and Egypt offer no evidence of lampstands in cultic contexts,[72] but the motif of vase altars with trees on them in worship scenes is

Ketef Hinnom silver scrolls
Z. Radovan/www.BibleLand
Pictures.com

▶

Chronology of Events in Exodus, Leviticus, and Numbers		
Date (Month/Day/Year)	Scripture	Event
1/14/1	Ex. 14:6, 31–32	Exodus from Egypt
3/14/1	Ex. 19:1	Israelites arrive at Sinai
1/1/2*	Ex. 40:2, 17	Tabernacle erected with Tent of Meeting
	Lev. 8:1–36	Priestly sanctification begins
	Lev. 1:1–7:38	Altar offerings commence
	Num. 7:1, 3	Tribal offerings begin
	Num. 9:15	Cloud covers tabernacle
1/8/2	Lev. 9:1	Priestly sanctification concluded
1/12/2*	Num. 7:78–83	Tribal offerings completed
1/14/2	Num. 9:1	Second Passover
2/1/2	Num. 1:1–2	First census commences
2/14/2	Num. 9:11	Second Passover for the unclean
2/20/2	Num. 10:11	Cloud moves—Israel departs Sinai

Artist's version of the lampstand from the model of the tabernacle at Timna
Todd Bolen/www. BiblePlaces.com
▶

extant in the iconography from the earliest periods.[73] In later periods palm branches are replaced with conical fires, at times with seven flames.[74]

Shave their whole bodies (8:7). Egyptian priests shaved their bodies every three days as a means of purification.[75] The purification ritual sequence of shaving, bathing, and washing (clothes) was also practiced among Mesopotamian cultures.[76] For instance, the high priestess at Emar was shaved in preparation for her installation.[77]

The cleansing process ensured ritual purification, so that a level of holiness could be maintained for those in service for the Lord. A slightly higher level of holiness was maintained for the priests who received new clothes when they were consecrated for

service (Lev. 8:12–13). Recent study suggests that shaving was one way to designate a temporary change in status.[78]

Lay their hands (8:10, 12). See comment on Lev. 1:4.

Levites in place of all the firstborn (8:18). The firstborn of people, animals, and plants belonged to Yahweh.[79] In Mesopotamia it was common to give the choicest products to the gods, whether "firstfruit" or firstborn animals,[80] but there is no indication of firstborn sons being regularly consecrated.

Second Passover: New Delineations (9:1–14)

Passover (9:2). One year after the first Passover that precipitated the Exodus from Egypt, the Israelites prepare to celebrate the feast according to the requirements set forth in Exodus (see sidebar on "The Passover" at Ex. 12). Originally called Abib, the first month was later called by the Babylonian name Nisan. At Emar, the first month was called AbT and marked a lunar cycle of numerous offerings on days 1–8, 14, 16, 17, 19, 20, 25–27, and the day of the concluding/beginning new moon.[81]

Yahweh in the Cloud (9:15–23)

The cloud covered it (9:15). The imagery of clouds for deity is ubiquitous in the ancient Near East. In Akkadian texts the term *melammu* describes the cloud aura that surrounded the gods and their sanctuaries. The term *puluḫtu* denoted the attendant garment of fire in the temple precinct. In Egyptian murals, deity is often depicted as a winged sun disc surrounded by storm clouds. In the Creation Epic from Ugarit, Baal is often referred to as the "Cloud-Rider," who brought forth the fertility of the soil through beneficent rains.[82] Yet the psalmist declared that Yahweh, God of Israel, was the one who truly "rides on the clouds," who dwells in his holy sanctuary and champions the cause of widows and orphans (Ps. 68:4–6). His power over the natural elements was exemplified in withholding rain in the days of Ahab.

Israelites set out (9:17). The rhythmic pattern here echoes ancient epic poetry of the second millennium B.C., such as the Ugaritic Epic of Keret. Harrison notes that "the repetitions in the text, a feature of both Hebrew and Ugaritic literature, give coherence both to the narratives themselves and to the spiritual attitude of the Hebrews that the sources reflected."[83] The rhythmic presentation of the journey motif is resumed in Numbers 33 (see comments).

Silver Trumpets (10:1–10)

Trumpets of hammered silver (10:2). The silver trumpets are to be distinguished from the ram's horn in function as well as appearance. The ram's horn (*šôpār*) announced the Day of Atonement throughout the land (Lev. 25:9) and was used in the marching around Jericho (Josh. 6:2–21). The bright pitch of the silver trumpet called the people to march through the wilderness and was blown by Phinehas in the battle against Midian (Num. 31:6).

These trumpets were likely styled after those known from Egypt during the Late Bronze Age, examples of which were found in King Tutankhamun's tomb.[84] These instruments were about two feet long with narrow tubes;[85] when blown in certain patterns they emitted a bright and piercing sound that communicated clearly to the people the desired intent. In Egypt they were used both in cultic and military contexts.[86]

Trumpet blast (10:5). The trumpets were blown with varying tones and lengths of blast. The two trumpets were likely of slightly different size, producing varying tones so that both could be distinguished. In terms of length of blast, the short blast alerted the camps to break camp and begin a journey (vv. 5–6); the long blast called the assemblies together (vv. 3–4, 7).[87]

Priests are to blow the trumpets (10:8). Blowing the silver trumpets was limited to the Aaronic priests. In the Qumran War Scroll, a major role of the Levites and priests in the great eschatological battle was to sound the trumpets, which were inscribed with such phrases as "God's mighty deeds to scatter the enemy, and to put to flight all opponents of justice, and disgraceful retribution to the opponents of God."[88] This section

Trumpet from the tomb of Pharaoh Tutankhamen, Eighteenth Dynasty
Scala/Art Resource, NY, courtesy of the Egyptian Museum, Cairo

Winged sun disk from Medinet Habu
Neil Madden

looks ahead to the time when the people will be battling their enemies for occupation and control of the territory God granted them and celebrating the bounty of God's blessing and his salvation activities in their festivals.

Whole burnt offerings for consecrative atonement and peace offerings for community celebration were accompanied by the long blast of the silver trumpets during the pilgrimage festivals of Passover, Pentecost, and Tabernacles, and during the monthly New Moon rites.

Leaving Sinai (10:11–36)

Desert of Sinai … Desert of Paran (10:12). The geographical parameters of this initial movement are the Sinai and Paran Deserts. According to 33:16–18, the Israelites camped at Taberah (11:3), Kibroth Hattavah (11:34–35), and Hazeroth (12:16) on their way to the Paran Desert, the parameters of which are difficult to outline. No cartographic mapping remains from this period identifying these regions. From the biblical data Paran was west of Midian and east of Egypt, extending from some point north or northeast of Mount Sinai—north toward Kadesh Barnea and east to the Arabah.[89]

Kadesh is associated with both the Paran and Zin Deserts. Paran seems to encompass a broader geographical area, which included in its northeast quadrant, the Desert of Zin, more narrowly defined by the Nahal Zin and its water drainage basin. Hence, the text shifts from the general Paran Desert region (10:17; 13:26) to a context in which greater specificity is needed, as in the listing of the itinerary of the spies (13:21) and later the rebellion of Moses (20:1–13; 27:14). Paran's relationship to Midian is confirmed later in history when the Edomite king Hadad fled from Solomon to Egypt via Midian and Paran (1 Kings 11:18). Most of the forty years of wilderness sojourn were spent in the Paran-Zin Desert region.

Hobab (10:29). Some suggest the dual names Reuel (Ex. 2:18) and Jethro (father of

Paran Wilderness in Sinai near Hazeroth
Todd Bolen/www. BiblePlaces.com

Zipporah, 3:1) may refer to variant patriarchal clan leaders of this tier of the Midianites, with the patriarchal clan founder named "Reuel" and the actual father-in-law of Moses named "Jethro." Others suggest Jethro and Reuel are the same person, since dual names are common in Bronze Age texts from Mesopotamia and the Levant.[90] The Hebrew *ḥōtēn* can mean "brother-in-law" (preferred here) or "father-in-law" (Ex. 3:1).

Traveled for three days (10:33). The Battle Song of the Ark is preceded by a dual chronological marker about the first stage in the movement of Yahweh's cloud, the distance of a three-day journey (i.e., about thirty-five to forty-five miles). This journey is reminiscent of Moses' request to Pharaoh to allow the Israelites to journey three days into the wilderness to worship their God (Ex. 8:27).

First Rebellion: Murmuring at Taberah (11:1–3)

Taberah (11:3). Taberah ("burning"), referring to the form of fiery judgment, often comes by means of lightning, though the mode of igniting the fire is not specified. This form of judgment parallels that meted out against Nadab and Abihu (Lev. 10:1–3), though that fire came out from the tabernacle. Natural disasters such as those caused by lightning were considered acts of divine judgment by people of the ancient Near East, even cases of fire caused by lightning in sacred precincts such as the Esagila in Babylon or the Assur Temple in Assyria. Fire was considered a divine quality that gave light to the people and fire for cooking sacred meals. The fiery judgment of the gods could be summoned by a diviner to bring down destruction upon one's enemies.[91]

Second Rebellion: Complaint about Food (11:4–35)

Meat (11:4). Meat was available in Israel's livestock and herds, but those were reserved for festive occasions and their supply of milk products. Goshen in the eastern Nile Delta was the breadbasket of Egypt, lush with vegetation and abounding with natural and man-made canals, whose waters teemed with fish and were replete with nutrients for abundant crop production. The foods listed are among the most commonly grown in the region: "cucumbers, melons, leeks, onions and garlic."[92] Several of these are represented in Egyptian tomb murals. All require ample amounts of water for irrigation.

Manna (11:7). The description of manna demonstrates that the Israelites' claims are spurious. This botanical and culinary description of the manna refutes each point of the people's complaint. See sidebar on "Manna."

Prophesied (11:25). Ecstatic prophets are known from the texts at Mari and Babylon, where they were called *maḫḫu* (or *muḫḫum*; female *muḫḫutum*) and functioned as one category of divination personnel. The *maḫḫu* would go into a frenzied trance and speak utterances believed to be derived from gods or goddesses like Ishtar, Nergal, or Adad.[93] These "prophets" (or better "diviners") were sometimes considered madmen because of their abnormal behavior (see also comments on Deut. 13:1).

Quail (11:31). An east wind and a south wind descend on the camp with provision of meat. Writers through history have described the movement of quail (genus *coturnix coturnix* or *coturnix vulgaris*) across the Sinai, generally northward in the spring (as here) and southward in the fall. Fowling using low-slung nets is known from several Egyptian tomb murals, including

Wall painting from the tomb of Userhet shows the gift of loaves, figs, a pomegranate, a cucumber (?), grapes, and a honeycomb.
Werner Forman Archive

▼

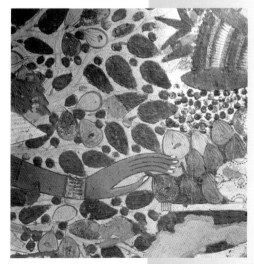

▶ **Manna**

Precise identification of "manna" with known agricultural products of ancient or modern times is somewhat tentative. The association with coriander seed is likely an indicator of its taste, since that seed is used for flavoring (similar to sesame or poppy seeds),[A-9] in which case "manna" may refer to a variety of small seeds produced by desert plants.

Physical description seems intended in the comparison to bdellium, a loan word in English from the Semitic root *budulchu* (Akk.) via the Greek *bdellion*, generally associated with a pale yellow or white aromatic resin.[A-10] Generally manna has been associated with a by-product of the tamarisk tree found in northern Arabia. B. Childs notes:

> There forms from the sap of the tamarisk tree a species of yellowish-white flake or ball, which results from the activity of a type of plant lice (*Trabutina mannipara* and *Najococcus serpentinus*) or aphids. The insect punctures the fruit of the tree and excretes a substance from this juice. During the warmth of the day it (the substance) melts, but it congeals when cold. It has a sweet taste. These pellets or cakes are gathered by the natives in the early morning and, when cooked, provide a sort of bread. The food decays quickly and attracts ants. The annual crop in the Sinai Peninsula is exceedingly small and some years fails completely.[A-11]

The hardened resinous manna could be ground on millstones or in a mortar, typically made from basalt or hard limestone, and then boiled and formed into cakes. The taste is compared to the rich creamy olive oil that comes from the upper layer of the first pressing of the olives. In Exodus 16:31, the taste of manna cakes is compared to honey. The manna appeared in the early morning, blown in from the heavens during the night so that enough could be gathered for the daily consumption after the morning dew had evaporated.

Fowling using low-slung nets
Z. Radovan/
www.BibleLand
Pictures.com

those of Kagemni at Saqqarah dating to the Sixth Dynasty.[94] Israelite fowling with nets is mentioned in Hosea 7:12.

The fourteenth-century A.D. Arab writer Al-Qazwini described the fowling activity of the people El-ʿArish in the north coastal Sinai. This area is known to have between one and two million quail in the autumn migration of these small birds.[95] The extraordinary quantity of quail here is swept in "from the sea" (probably from the Gulf of Aqaba if the wind is from the east), and then downward toward the encampment of Israel.

The magnitude of the quail is measured in three ways. (1) Breadth: a day's journey in each direction (about twelve to fifteen miles, hence an area of more than four hundred square miles). (2) Height: three feet (two cubits) above the ground, referring either to the height of the birds' flight or the depth of the piles of quail. (3) Quantity: each person gathering at least ten homers over a two-day period, a volume estimated at between thirty-eight and sixty-five bushels.[96] Some of the birds are eaten right away, while most of them are spread out around the camp, presumably for drying the meat in the hot sun after cleaning and salting them.[97]

Plague (11:33). In their greed the people probably consume unprocessed meat and are struck down with food poisoning, since the name of the site, Kibroth Hattaavah ("Graves of Craving"), evidences a form of talionic justice for those who protest against Yahweh.

Kibroth Hattaavah ... to Hazeroth (11:35). The location of these sites is conjecture and dependent on the location of Mount Sinai. If Mount Sinai is Jebel Musa, then Hazeroth may be associated with the Wadi Hudeirat region, forty miles northeast of Jebel Musa. If Mount Sinai is located at Jebel Sin Bisher, then Kibroth Hattaavah and Hazeroth may be situated along the route eastward across the central Sinai region toward Elath and Mount Seir.

Third Rebellion: Challenge to Moses' Authority (12:1–16)

Cushite wife (12:1). The geographical setting is Hazeroth (see comment on 11:35). 'Cush' has a few possible identifications:[98] (1) On the basis of Genesis 2:13; 10:6; Psalm 68:31; Isaiah 18:1, Cush, the first son of Ham, is identified with Nubia in modern Sudan, bordering ancient Egypt on the south. If this connection is assumed, Moses' Cushite wife would be a woman other than Zipporah, his Midianite wife from the clan of Jethro and Reuel. Some have suggested

that Zipporah died and the Cushite wife is of a recent marriage.[99] (2) The synonymous parallel cola in Habakkuk 3:7 suggest an association of Cushan with the Midianites, giving credence to the identity of the Cushite woman with Zipporah. (3) The term Cushite may refer to a distinguishable physiological trait, such as that of the deeply tanned Midianites from northwest Arabia.

Ethnic purity was an important issue in ancient Israel; note the commands to drive out and/or annihilate the Canaanites from the Promised Land (33:51–56). The Pentateuch, however, contains explicit instructions that there was to be one code of law for the native Israelite and the sojourning foreigners in their midst. In 9:14, aliens living among the Israelites could even celebrate the Passover if they did so according to the statutes related to its commemoration, including circumcision as an indicator of that individual's coming under the covenant relationship with the God of Israel (Ex. 12:48–49; cf. also Lev. 24:22; Num. 15:14–16, 29). It would seem, then, that Miriam's complaint against Moses on the basis of ethnicity is not the real reason for her objections.

Leprous like snow (12:10). On the Hebrew word ṣāraʿat ("skin disease, leprosy"), see comments on 5:2. Harrison suggests that "ṣāraʿat is a generic term for a group of pathological conditions and serves the same sort of function as the term *cancer*, which covers a wide range of degenerative tissue states."[100] Miriam probably does not suffer from Hansen's disease, as skin deformity in leprosy is seldom "white as snow." This description is the same as that with which God afflicted Moses at his point of unbelief at the burning bush (Ex. 4:6).

"Leprosy" in the ancient Near East and in the Bible was often seen as punishment for offenses against God (or the gods).[101] The reference to Miriam's degenerating

Statue of Nubian woman
Mulhu, courtesy of the Museum of Fine Arts, Boston

to the appearance of "a stillborn infant," whose scaly flesh sometimes peels off with the amniotic fluids when handled after birth, may indicate a severe form of eczema.

Desert of Paran (12:16). The Paran Desert is in the southeast Negev or northeast Sinai region.[102] The Desert of Paran was the goal of the first phase of the journey (10:11), and from that area the spies are sent to explore the Promised Land (13:3).

Fourth Rebellion: Rejection of the Land (13:1–14:45)

Grapes (13:20). This is the time of the first harvest of the vineyards, hence late summer or early fall, several months after the departure from Mount Sinai in early spring.[103]

Desert of Zin as far as Rehob, toward Lebo Hamath (13:21). The twelve Israelite men launched their exploration of the land from the Paran Desert. The Desert of Zin was the region of the drainage basin around the Nahal Zin, an expanse westward on a line from just south of the Dead Sea that includes

the wilderness, as well as Kadesh Barnea to the west (v. 26). They reached as far north as Rehob of Lebo Hamath in southeast Lebanon. The exact location of this Rehob is unknown, though the region of Lebo Hamath suggests a site in southern Lebanon, such as Beth Rehob near Tel Dan on the southern flank of Mount Hermon.[104]

Lebo Hamath has been identified with modern Lebweh on the Orontes River, on the southern border of the ancient kingdom of Hamath and about fourteen miles north-northeast of Baalbek. Lebo is recounted as a city on the northern border of the Promised Land (Num. 34:7–8) and later of the Israelite kingdom of David and Solomon (1 Kings 8:65).

Negev (13:22). The scouts headed north through the hill country regions later known as Judah, Samaria, and Galilee, starting in the Negev ("southland"). In the Old Testament, the Negev region stretched south from Hebron (Qiryath ʿArba) into the Desert of Zin (e.g., Gen. 12:9; 13:3, 14; 20:1; 24:62; Num. 21:1; 33:40); in modern geography the term denotes the region from the

Desert of Zin
Jack Hazut
▸

Hebron (Tel
Rumeida)
Z. Radovan/
www.BibleLand
Pictures.com

Arad and Beersheba region south to Elat on the Gulf of Aqaba.

Hebron ... Zoan in Egypt (13:22). Hebron, formerly known as Qiryath ʿArba, is located about twenty miles south of Jerusalem in the central hill country. It must have been a prominent city at this time because of its comparison with the Egyptian stronghold of Zoan. The ancestry of the Hebronites is highlighted by the mention of three clans of the Anakites, namely Ahiman, Sheshai, and Talmai. These names are Semitic in origin, reflecting the fact that the inhabitants of the land spoke a Semitic dialect.

The name "Anak" is associated with a people feared for their great size and military prowess; it may also be associated with the ethnic phrase Iy-ʿanaq found among the Egyptian Execration Texts of the early second millennium B.C.[105] The LXX of verse 33 translates the term as "giants," and they were associated with the Rephaim in Deut. 2:11 (cf. also 9:2). Remnants of these giants survived into the time of the Judges and the beginning of the Israelite monarchy.

Hebron was said to have been fortified seven years before Zoan, which was in the eastern Nile Delta. This name is the equivalent of the Egyptian Djaʿnet, which was vocalized by the Greeks as Tanis, long identified with the modern site of San el-Hagar. Early excavators thought this was the site of the city of Ramesses mentioned in Exodus 1, but it is now known that Pi-Ramesses is located at Tel ed-Dabʿa (= Avaris/Qantir), twelve miles south of Zoan/Tanis.[106] Earliest indicators suggest that Zoan was founded in the twelfth century B.C. For more information concerning the confusion of these two sites, see comment on Genesis 47:11.

Forty days (13:25). The scouts' forty-day exploration of the land accords with the approximate time such a journey would have taken on foot. The number forty is often used in the Bible for an indefinite period in excess of a month. Having trekked from the Desert of Zin all the way to Lebo Hamath and back again means they would have covered from 350 to 500 miles while reconnoitering the hill country and valleys. According to the annals of the campaigns of Thutmose III and Ramesses II, a day's journey was approximately twelve to fifteen miles.

Kadesh in the Desert of Paran (13:26). Kadesh (Barnea) is usually identified with ʿAin el-Qudeirat in the upper reaches of the Desert

Fruit-bearers on
Assyrian relief
Z. Radovan/
www.BibleLand
Pictures.com

of Zin, about fifty miles southwest of Beer-sheba. The springs produce a volume of about forty cubic meters of water per hour (there are no fortifications from the Late Bronze Age or Iron I periods there). Pottery remains suggest this spring area was often the stopping point for nomadic groups since the late Neolithic period through the Bronze Ages.[107] An Israelite fortress was constructed there in the tenth century B.C. and destroyed by the Babylonians in 586 B.C. The spies' report concludes with a listing of the various Semitic and non-Semitic tribes living throughout the country.

Milk and honey (13:27). This classic description of the abundance of natural flora and fauna of Canaan (e.g., Ex. 3:8, 17; 13:5; 33:3; Lev. 20:24; Deut. 6:3; 11:9) is echoed in the Egyptian travel account The Story of Sinuhe, where the princely emissary describes the land of Yaa (see comment on Ex. 3:8).

Amalekites (13:29). The Amalekites were a seminomadic tribe whose origins were in the region of Edom and who ranged throughout the southern Levant, from northern Sinai to the hill country of Samaria. Hormah (Tel Masos in the Negeb) may have been one of their cities (Num. 14:45;

cf. Gen. 36:16; Judg. 12:15; 1 Sam. 15:7).[108] No reference is found to the Amalekites in ancient Near Eastern documents.

Hittites (13:29). Among the numerous ethnic inhabitants of the central highlands were clans of the Hittites, such as are known from the patriarchal period (Gen. 23:3–20). Their origins in eastern Anatolia dating to the third millennium B.C. are well known from historical and archaeological records.[109] The Hittite empire flourished in the Late Bronze Age (1550–1200 B.C.), centered in Hattušas, and extended from central Anatolia to the upper Euphrates and to the northern Levant. For discussion of the relationship between the Hittites in Canaan and in Anatolia, see comment on Gen. 23:3.

Jebusites (13:29). The Jebusites were a non-Semitic clan who lived in Jerusalem during the Middle Bronze through Iron I periods (2000–1000 B.C.); they controlled the city through most of the early history of Israel until the time of David (see Josh. 15:8, 63; 18:16; Judg. 1:8, 21; 2 Sam. 5:6–9). They are unknown outside the Bible, and scholars have suggested they may have been a subclan of the Perizzites or related to the Hurrians.[110]

Faience tiles por-
traying various
people groups
from the Levant
Z. Radovan/
www.BibleLand
Pictures.com
◀

The Table of Nations lists the Jebusites as descendants of Canaan (Gen. 10:16).

Amorites (13:29). The term "Amorite" can refer in general to a number of the inhabitants of the Levant, including areas known today as Syria, Lebanon, Jordan, Israel, and Palestine. It may also refer more specifically to an ethnic descendant of Canaan as delineated in Genesis 10:16.[111] Referred to as the *Amurru* ("Amorites" or "westerners") in Akkadian records at Mari and the *Martu* in Sumerian texts of the third and second millennia B.C., some of this people group established city-states in Syria while others were more nomadic, migrating southeast into southern Sumer and southwest into the Levant. Egyptian records describe their territory as extending from the Negev to the heights of Lebanon.

Canaanites (13:29). During much of the Late Bronze Age, the land of Canaan was controlled by Egypt under the Eighteenth and Nineteenth Dynasties (see introduction), as reflected in the temple texts of Thutmose I, Thutmose III, Amenhotep II, the Amarna Letters of the fourteenth century B.C., and the texts of Ramesses II.[112]

The region extended along the Mediterranean Sea from the Wadi el-ʿArish to Lebo Hamath in Lebanon, and inland to the Jordan Valley region. The inhabitants of Canaan included numerous ethnic subgroups. The designation of "Canaan" may derive from the Akkadian *kinannu* ("red purple"), based on the production of red-to-purple dyes produced along coastal regions of Lebanon from the abundant murex shells found there. Other scholars point to the Semitic root *k-n-ʿ* meaning "to bend, be subdued." The earliest reference to "Canaan" comes from the eighteenth century B.C. in Mari.[113]

Nephilim (13:33). Referring to the descendants of Anak as Nephilim was designed to instill fear in the hearts of the Israelites in the face of their enemies, to make them feel like grasshoppers. Grasshoppers were the smallest of edible creatures permitted for Israelite consumption (Lev. 11:22). The Nephilim ("fallen ones"; "giants" in the LXX) are noted in Genesis 6:4 (see comments) as the product of the "sons of God" ("angelic beings" or "divine warriors") and the "daughters of men."

Tore their clothes (14:6). Tearing one's clothes was a form of self-debasing lament in the Old Testament; it was widely practiced in the ancient Near East in mourning for the dead, in expressing sorrow over disease or plague, or in prefacing a prophetic lament of judgment against an individual or nation.[114] In the Tale of Aqhat from Ugarit, Paghat (daughter of Daniʾilu) laments the coming drought that has been foretold:

> Paghat weeps in her heart, cries in her
>   inward parts
> She rends the garment of Daniʾilu the
>   man of Rapaʾu
> The cloak of the valiant man of
>   Harnam....[115]

Route to the Red Sea (14:25). The "Way of the Red Sea Wilderness" was the trade route connecting to Ezion Geber on the Gulf of Aqaba/Elath from Kadesh Barnea through the Desert of Zin and the southern Arabah. A second leg of the route then extended westward across the central Sinai peninsula toward Egypt.

Hormah (14:45). Hormah has been identified tentatively with Tel Masos in the Beersheba Valley region, though other sites have also been suggested.[116] Hormah is mentioned in the Middle Bronze Age Egyptian sources, including the Execration Texts and an inscription in a Sinai mine dated to the reign of Amenemhet III (1831–1786 B.C.).[117]

Offerings from the Land and Other Laws (15:1–41)

For special vows or freewill offerings or festival offerings (15:3). Vows involved a verbal act of commitment to a task or to consecration of oneself or one's property to the Lord; sacrificial offerings (votive) were part of the obligation or, in the case of the Nazirite, oaths of abstinence.[118] The peace, vow, and freewill offerings were of the communion type, in which certain portions of the animals were offered to God as a savory aroma,[119] and the remainder were consumed by the priests and the offerer in the communal setting of the tabernacle or temple. Hence, the totality of the Israelite community engaged in a corporate meal that celebrated the unity of the community of faith.

Unlike the descriptions noted in Mesopotamian ritual texts, which depict the gods as consuming the sacrifices as necessary to their survival,[120] God's pleasure in the Israelite sacrifices is described in anthropomorphic terms of a pleasing aroma that ascends in the smoke into the invisible realm of the heavenly abode.

The first of your ground meal (15:20). During the spring harvest of barley and wheat (the season of Passover, Unleavened Bread, and Pentecost), the grain firstfruit offering was presented to God. Even the mundane daily practice of kneading dough for making bread was a time of worship and celebration of God's benevolence and faithfulness. The first or choicest dough made from the first coarsely ground flour of the season was set aside for honoring God.

Bread was the essential food staple, and hence a sacred sacrifice was rendered back to God as the giver of life and the provider of grain from which the bread was made. Similarly, wine and grapes from the vineyard, olive oil and olives from the orchard, and fruit juices from the fall fruit harvest were offered unto God. According to 18:11–16, all firstfruits and products brought to Yahweh were supplied to the priests.

Sins defiantly (15:30). The raised right hand with the outstretched arm was a common symbol of strength and power in ancient Near Eastern literature and iconography.[121] The sinner with a high hand feels no guilt; thus, the offense is not sacrificially expiable. Such a defiant person must suffer the ultimate of judgment, the "cutting off" (*karet*) reserved for the most heinous or sacrilegious offenses.[122] Milgrom delineates five categories of infractions in which the *karet* was meted out: (1) violation of sacred time, as in the neglect of certain holy days, (2) violation of sacred substance, such as in the consumption of blood, (3) neglect of purification ritual, such as circumcision, (4) illicit worship, such as idolatry or sorcery, and (5) illicit sexual activity, such as incest or bestiality.[123]

Tassels (15:38). In the ancient Near East, special garments were made for priests and royalty that identified them within their communities and to the outside world. Several examples of garments with corded fringes come from the statue of Puzur-Ishtar, governor of Mari in the Ur III period (ca. 2060–1955 B.C.), from Asiatics depicted in the Beni Hasan tomb of the Egyptian Khnum-hotep II in the nineteenth century B.C., and from later Neo-Assyrian murals.[124]

Rebellion of Korah and Reubenites (16:1–17:13)

Korah … became insolent (16:1). In tribal and clan-structured societies of the ancient Near East, the position of leadership often fell on the eldest son of the family patriarch. The men of Reuben, Jacob's firstborn, sought to claim what they perceived as their rightful positions in Israel, thereby usurping the role of Moses, with Korah supplanting Aaron. Korah's lineage is traced back fully through three major figures in the levitical line. As a Kohathite, Korah was among the favored clan of the Levites whose responsibility was to transport the sacred furnishings of the tabernacle after being packed by the Aaronic priests (4:1–20).[125]

Take censers … and put fire and incense in them (16:6–7). The censers for incense were pans or shallow bowls at the end of long handles (Lev. 10:1). These pans carried hot coals on which incense could be sprinkled, creating a savory aroma. Such censers are believed to have originated in Egypt, where they were used in the performance of apotropaic magic for driving away evil deities or

Egyptian relief showing tassels on Asiatic garment
Manfred Näder Gabana Studios Germany
▲

Incense censer
Loic Evanno/Wikimedia Commons, courtesy of the Louvre
▼

▶ Incense

Incense was often burned on small incense altars or cultic stands made of bronze, stone, or ceramics. In ancient Near Eastern cultic contexts, incense was often offered to pacify or appease the wrath of gods and goddesses and to soothe their spirits. Incense enhanced the sweet-smelling aroma of burning sacrifices that ascended into the heavens, symbolically entering into the nostrils of God (or the gods) (cf., e.g., Lev. 1:9, 13, 17; 2:2, 9, 11; 3:5, 16).

Incense was produced from the sap, bark, roots, and fruits of a variety of trees and shrubs, especially from East Africa and Arabia. In the Gilgamesh Epic the gods savored the sweet smell of the burning cedar and reeds offered up by Utnapishtim in "seven and seven" cultic bowls following the great flood.[A-12]

In Egypt (where incense is called "the eye of the Horus"), incense was used in funerary rites, including the embalming process and ensuing ceremonies, for warding off evil spirits[A-13] and for appeasing the divine. Egyptian reliefs portray the pharaoh (a divine figure) looming over the city as the princes and priests offer incense in an attempt to allay the slaughter of their people.[A-14]

demonic forces by waving them in a ritual manner.[126]

Alive into the grave (16:33). The grave (Sheol) at this point in Israel's history was perceived to be a shadowy, unknown realm of the dead—the netherworld of both good and evil where one was gathered to one's fathers at death.[127] Normally, one places a dead person in a cave or man-made tomb, where the body slowly deteriorated. Later the bones of the deceased were added or gathered to those of one's ancestors in the ancestral burial site. But in this incident the bodies of the rebels (and perhaps their families as well as their possessions) plummeted into a gaping abyss, which soon closed over them with collapsed dirt and rock of the desert terrain. The second census informs us that Korah's fate was the same as of Dathan and Abiram (26:10).

Sheol is described as opening it mouth to receive the dead (Prov. 1:12; Isa. 5:14; Hab. 2:5) in a manner parallel to the Canaanite god Mot. In the Baal Cycle, the champion deity admonishes his emissaries to Mot to beware "lest he put you in his mouth like a lamb, and crush you like a kid in his jaws." Later Baal himself is mortally wounded and descends into the belly of Mot, who "stretched out his tongue to the stars, Baal entered his innards, he descended into his mouth."[128] Here the realm of Sheol and the dead is under the sovereign power of Israel's God; since Moses pronounces the curse prior to the event, no one can mistake the judgment as circumstantial.

Fire came out from the LORD (16:35). A fiery storm of divine judgment from the god Enlil is depicted in the Lament over the Destruction of Sumer and Ur, in which the city, its crops, and its inhabitants are destroyed.[129] Phenomena that today are considered "natural" disasters were not thought of as natural in the ancient world.[130] Lightning was considered fire from heaven. The god Enlil is said to make stones and fire rain upon his foes.[131] The Assyrian king Ashurbanipal reports on one occasion that fire fell from heaven and consumed his enemies.[132]

Write the name of each man on his staff (17:2). The staff was the official symbol of the tribal chieftain, which in Babylonia and Egypt often were designed so as to signify its owner.[133] The word *matteh* means both "tribe" and "staff/scepter" and hence carried some representation of the tribe's identity. In this context the names were inscribed for unmistakable identification.

The use of wood articles to discern the will of the gods is well documented in the ancient Near East, wherein the wooden symbols of Asherah, Astarte, or Ishtar are used in fertility rites. Even in Egypt Asherah was combined with Hathor during the Nineteenth Dynasty and represented as a nude figure standing on a lion and holding snakes and flowers.[134] In the Ugaritic Incantation against Sorcery, Baal drives off a man's accuser with his staff into the underworld.[135] Such cultic practices were forbidden and condemned elsewhere in the Old Testament.[136]

The Priests and Levites: Additional Responsibilities and Provisions (18:1–32)

Offenses against the sanctuary (18:1). The priests and Levites provided a layer of security for the nation as a holy and undefiled people and defined its prophetic destiny as God's people in the midst of a defiled world. Encroachment by any outside or unauthorized person on the holy objects was punishable by death. Priests were also culpable of violating the sanctity of the Holy Place if they allowed an unauthorized person within its defined sacred space. The priests themselves were prohibited from going beyond the veil and entering the Most Holy Place; only the high priest was permitted to enter that sanctum on the Day of Atonement.

Levine defined the phrase "offenses against the sanctuary" and its proper adjudication as "infractions against the purity of the sanctuary.... Impurity was viewed as an external force which entered the person or attached itself to him. The primary purpose of expiation was, therefore, to rid one's self of this foreign force."[137] A Hittite work entitled Instructions to Priests and Temple Officials warns the priests against taking for themselves or their families food or precious objects that belonged to the temple.[138] It also indicates the need for diligence in guarding access to sacred space at all times.[139]

They must not go near (18:3). The full sanctuary of ancient Israel consisted of concentric zones of holiness: (1) The inner tier was the ark of Yahweh in the Most Holy Place, (2) extending outward to the priestly court within the curtains of the Holy Place, (3) then to the realm of the priests and three clans of Levites, (4) moving to the four triads of the tribes of Israel, and then (5) outside the camp of the holy where unclean persons were designated during their term of impurity.[140] In the ancient world the temple complex was likewise a sacred zone,

Sesostris here holds the kherep scepter. There were numerous scepters in Egypt that designated different powers. The kherep pictured here was an insignia of office that could also be used by others besides the king.

Werner Forman Archive

▶ The Firstborn Male

The firstborn were the first male issue from the womb of its mother,[A-16] whether human or animal. Animals defined by the law as clean, such as cattle, sheep, and goats, were offered as sacrifices. Since humans could not be sacrificed physically, nor could unclean animals, a redemption price was set by which a substitutionary value was rendered to the priesthood.

Milgrom states that human firstborn redemption was mandatory, whereas animal firstborn redemption was optional (he reads the imperfect as permissive rather than imperative).[A-17] According to Exodus 34:19 the unclean donkey could be redeemed with a lamb, otherwise its neck was to be broken. Other unclean animals are not discussed, probably since they were of little use to the priesthood or the average Israelite. The process of human and animal redemption had a didactic purpose of reminding the Israelites of their redemption from Egypt, an object lesson of history rehearsed in every generation so the people would not forget the Lord's benevolence and the heavy price paid for their deliverance to freedom and blessing. No practices comparable to these have yet been found in the ancient Near East.

in the seasoning of the elements, but it also contributed to the quality of the covenant relationship between humanity and God (Lev. 2:13).[146]

In Ezra 4:14 the Sanballatid leaders in Samaria pledged their loyalty to the Persian government with the expression, "We have salted the salt of the palace."[147] With these concepts in mind, the covenant of salt between Yahweh and the Aaronic priesthood emphasized the quality and permanence of the relationship. That relationship was evidenced outwardly through the perpetual statute of the Israelite supplying of tribute to Yahweh, which then provided the means of sustenance for the priests and their families (see also comments on Lev. 2:13).

Tithes (18:21). The concept of tithing is known from ancient Near Eastern sources in the Levant and Mesopotamia. Not only were agricultural goods tithed, but also various commodities such as metals and goods produced by craftsmen. The usage of the Ugaritic $m^c\acute{s}rt$[148] evidences a royal temple structure in which contributions to the given sanctuary could be used by the royalty. A kind of royal priesthood is evidenced in the account of Melchizedek in Genesis 14:18–24.

In Babylon of the sixth century B.C., cattle contributed as tithes were branded for the temple treasuries, and other goods were earmarked on storage jars and other receptacles.[149] In the Iron II Israelite kingdom period, goods collected for the royal provision were inscribed with the term *lmlk* ("for the king"). Whether some of these may

Deir al-Bah(a)ri model of livestock count
Gerard Ducher/Wikimedia Commons, courtesy of the Cairo Museum
▼

have been dedicated for the temple stores is unknown, but there is little doubt that some means of identifying the tithed goods was employed during the First Temple period (see also comment on Gen. 14:20).

Grain ... juice (18:27). These were two key agricultural products to be set aside by the Levites for their tithe: the best grain from the threshing floor and the finest juice from the wine vat. From the painted wall murals of Egypt to the hewn murals of the Hittites in central and eastern Anatolia and the Assyrians of Mesopotamia, the activities and products of grain processing and wine production were esteemed as sacred aspects of human endeavor in utilizing these gifts from the gods. Rites associated with bread and wine held significant places in ancient cultic activities, as they did in ancient Israel. Cultic activities were associated with threshing floors and winepresses, as well as olive presses. In Numbers particular attention is given to the bread, oil, and wine accompaniments to a number of animal sacrifices.[150]

Red Heifer Purification Ritual (19:1–22)

Red heifer (19:2). The process begins with the selection of a quality red cow (a roan or reddish-brown color)[151] that is unblemished and has never been harnessed with a yoke.[152] In that the cow has never been yoked for any physical task, it is probably young and strong. Elsewhere a bull was sacrificed as a sin offering for the high priest and his family (Lev. 4:3–12; 16:6, 11) or for the community as a whole (4:13–21), and so the female is specified here. The cow offers the maximum potential yield of purification ashes so the ritual need not be repeated often.[153]

The redness of the cow reflects on the color of blood, as do the other sacrificial elements burned with the cow: red cedar wood, crimson wool, and hyssop.[154] The plant species translated "hyssop" is probably not the Greek *hyssopos* (from which the English was derived) since it is not native to this region.

Perhaps it is marjoram, sage, or thyme, the leaves of which are very absorbent.[155]

The use of reddish materials along with other colored elements in ritual sanctification is echoed in texts from the Assyrian holy city of Ashur, known as The Ritual Followed by the Kalū-Priest When Covering the Temple Kettle-Drum. The assembly and sanctification of the bronze kettle-drum was accompanied by "cypress, one-half pound of sweet-smelling reed ... of roses, ten shekels of aromatic *annuba* ... two *qa*-measures of wine ... one-half *qa*-measure of cedar sap ... white ... cloth, one red ... cloth ... pounds of wool ... seven pounds of blue wool," as well as other materials.[156]

Wash his clothes and bathe himself with water (19:7). The priest (Eleazar) who carries out the slaughtering and sprinkling, the assistant[157] who burns the cow (v. 8), and the one who gathers and stores the ashes (v. 10) are each rendered unclean by touching this purification (sin) offering. But this was a lesser state of uncleanness than one who touches a dead body. After taking the prescribed ritual bath, they are permitted to reenter the camp and remain unclean only until evening.[158] Hittite and Ugaritic ritual texts prescribe the wearing of clean clothes and taking ritual baths for both kings and priests, especially to prepare for ceremonial and festival days.[159]

Aliens living among them (19:10). In future generations this purification offering and ritual becomes one of the more commonly applied purification offerings because of the continual potentiality of becoming unclean through the death of someone in the family, of a neighbor, or of a sojourner in the land. The ritual guidelines apply to both the native Israelite and to resident aliens. The openness of Israelite ritual law to resident aliens who desire to identify with the community of faith stands in contrast to some other religious practices in the ancient Near East. Hittite temple ritual prohibited foreigners from bringing anything to the gods or even approaching them.[160]

Whoever touches the dead body of anyone (19:11). The time period of the impurity is the common maximum length for persons who have become unclean. Yet with some forms of impurity, such as contact with the red cow during the preparation process, one is rendered impure only until sundown. The attention to death impurity stands in contrast to the prevalent cults of the dead in the ancient Near East, where ritual practice shows no concept of contracting contamination or impurity from a corpse.[161]

The cult of the dead consisted of elaborate rituals on behalf of dead family members in order to assure life in the hereafter and placate the gods of death and the underworld. This process began with funerary rites of the deceased family member and continued well after the initial event. Mesopotamian texts from Mari (eighteenth century B.C.) prescribe offerings for the dead four times a year, in which the name of the dead person was invoked, food presented, and a water libation rendered.[162]

Defiles the LORD's tabernacle (19:13). The severity of death impurity is evidenced in the ritual ablution on the third and seventh days, the potential of defiling the sanctuary from a distance if left unpurified, and the potential penalty of *karet* (being cut off from the community for failure to comply with the ordinance).[163] In the Hittite text Instructions for Priests and Temple Officials, priestly sins against the sanctuary in the matter of a profane fire carried a similar penalty toward the offender and his family: "He who commits this sin will perish along with his descendants. Of those in the temple none will be left living. They will perish together with their descendants. Be extremely careful concerning the matter of fire."[164]

Unclean for seven days (19:11, 14, 16). Impurity specifically because of corpse contamination is not attested in the ancient Near East (see comment on 19:13), but a notable Babylonian text evidences a seven-day period of isolation for one who comes

in contact with the "dust from a place of mourning." The ritual includes reciting a *namburbi* incantation to protect from evil, offering libations to the god Shamash, taking a ritual bath, and changing clothes, after which the offender remains secluded in his house for seven days.[165]

From the Desert of Zin to the Plains of Moab: The Last Rebellions (20:1–21:35)

First month (20:1). Chapter 20 begins with Miriam's death and concludes with Aaron's death.[166] The first month, Abib (=Nisan), in the spring of the fortieth year, commences the conclusion of Israel's punishment in the wilderness. This was the month of the deliverance from Egypt, in which they should have been celebrating the Passover and Festival of Unleavened Bread in the Promised Land. Instead, they find themselves back at Kadesh after some forty years of wilderness nomadic shepherding, and again they grumble about their water supply, just as the first generation had done soon after they crossed the Red Sea (Ex. 15:23–26; 17:1–7). On Kadesh and the Desert of Zin, see comment on Num. 13:26.

Staff (20:8). The staff was taken from the Lord's presence, implying this is the staff of Aaron that budded, blossomed, and produced almonds in the divine confirmation of his priestly authority after the Korah rebellion.[167] It was kept before the ark of the testimony as a sign to any future grumbling rebels so that their murmuring might be summarily dismissed (17:10).

The actions of Moses have been examined against the backdrop of Egyptian and Mesopotamian magicians and diviners as well as in the context of the nature of God as seen in the Pentateuch. Magical acts in the ancient world were usually performed after appropriate sacrifices were made, ritual actions performed, and incantations recited. In these ways, Moses' behavior here would not have looked or sounded like that of the

Egyptian lector priests (the magicians that he faced during the plagues, see comments on Gen. 41:8; Ex. 7:11). Nevertheless, Moses' actions were tantamount to that of an idolatrous pagan magician, in which the prophet ascribes miraculous, almost god-like, powers to himself and Aaron. Israel must be freed of its pagan background.[168]

Water gushed out (20:11). No parallel accounts exist in the ancient Near East of deities providing water in this way. But geographers and biblical interpreters have written of the extensive aquifers that exist beneath the surface of the sedimentary rock strata of the Sinai peninsula. Oases such as those at Serabit al-Khadem, Ain Hawarah, and Ain el-Qudeirat (Kadesh Barnea) provide examples of such abundant water supply.[169] Still, aquifers would not normally provide nearly enough water to care for the needs of a group the size of the Israelites.

King of Edom (20:14). The classical Edomite territory extended from the Wadi Zered (Wadi el-Hasa) on the north to the Gulf of Aqaba (Elath) on the south and to the Arabian Desert on the east. Topographically it is characterized by reddish-purple mountains on the east side of the southern Arabah Valley, and then by intermittent sections of arable land in the northern half, extending from near Petra and the Wadi Musa to Bozrah and the Wadi Zered. Deep valleys such as the Wadi Rum provided east-west passage across the region.

The Israelites may have been seeking passage from the south along the King's Highway from its origin on the Gulf of Aqaba and then moving north. More likely, however, their intentions were to enter the region from the Arabah near Tamar into the Edomite highlands through one of the wadis (such as the Wadi Feifa), and then past Bozrah, the Edomite capital city during the Iron Age.[170]

That Edom should possess a king at this time has caused concern for interpreters since the publication of Nelson Glueck's definitive works on the settlement of Transjordan during the Bronze and Iron Ages.[171] As a result of his surface surveys in southern Jordan between 1934 and 1940, he observed that there was a gap in the material remains during the Middle Bronze to Iron IA periods.

Wadi Zered from east
Todd Bolen/www.
BiblePlaces.com

identity of Jebel Nebi Harun ("Mount of the Prophet Aaron") near Petra,[179] Jebel Medra about six miles east northeast of Kadesh, or Jebel Madurah about fifteen miles northeast of Kadesh Barnea. Jebel Madurah is generally on the way from Kadesh Barnea to the Arabah along the route of the Atharim, and the surrounding terrain fits the general picture where the Israelites could observe the initial events from afar.

Aaron will be gathered to his people (20:26). This phrase conveys the idea of being reunited with one's ancestral families in Sheol, the place of the dead. Being left unburied or "ungathered" was viewed as an ignominious end of life (cf. Jer. 8:2; see comments on Num. 16:33; Deut. 21:23).[180] But both Aaron and Moses were buried on separate mountains in a land that did not belong to their ancestors, for they had rebelled against God's word (see comment on Gen. 25:8).

King of Arad (21:1). After Aaron's death the Israelites set out from Mount Hor to circumnavigate Edom along "the road to Atharim." Arad here cannot be Tel Arad in the eastern Negev, which was a substantial urban center during the Early Bronze Age,

was destroyed about 2650 B.C., and remained unoccupied until the early Israelite monarchy.[181] Several alternative suggestions have been suggested. (1) The reference to the "king of Arad" may be a regional designation (like "king of Edom" in 20:14), who may have ruled from the city of Hormah (21:3) or even in the vicinity of Yeroham.[182] Hormah has been identified with Tel Malhata (Tel el-Milh),[183] a city of the Middle Bronze and Iron Ages about eight miles southwest of Tel Arad.[184] (2) Others place Arad at Tel Malhata at this point in history, in keeping with the occasional transference of a city name to another location,[185] and then locate Hormah at Tel Masos, three miles west of Tel Malhata.[186] The occupational history of these two sites is similar.[187]

Note that Hormah (meaning "destruction") is a name given to the site after the defeat of the Canaanites in this part of the Negev. Multiple cities are said to have been completely or utterly destroyed by the Israelite armies, and the use of the toponym Hormah in verse 3 may designate a single key city of this campaign or the region of the defeated towns.[188]

Tel-Malhatah
Z. Radovan/
www.BibleLand
Pictures.com
▶

Road to Atharim (21:1). This road is described by Aharoni as "leading from Kadesh-barnea to Arad," along which the fortresses of Bir Hafir, Oboda, and Aroer were built during the Israelite monarchy.[189] Budd suggests it may refer to the road leading to Tamar, or Ein Tamar, located about ten miles south of the Dead Sea.[190] Modern Israeli mapping designates a mountain along this route as Hor Hahar (Mount Hor, 20:22; 21:4), about eighteen miles southwest of Ein Tamar. Thus the Canaanites of the Arad region may have perceived the Israelites as encroaching on their territory and attacked them as they did a generation before (14:35).

Along the route to the Red Sea (21:4). According to Aharoni, this trade route extended from Elath on the eastern finger of the Red Sea in the Gulf of Aqaba northward through the Arabah to the Dead Sea. Hence this desert route has them approaching the northern end of the Arabah from the west-southwest, then crossing the Arabah between Tamar and Zalmonah.[191]

Venomous snakes (21:6). "Venomous" (*ś^{e}rāpîm*, "burning") may refer to the burning pain from the lethal injection of venom through the serpents' fangs or to a species of snake whose bite caused a burning sensation.[192] Lawrence described his encounters with horned vipers, puff-adders, cobras, and black snakes in eastern Jordan.[193] The carpet viper (*Echis carinatus* or *Echis coleratus*) is a highly poisonous viper known from Africa and the Middle East—thus a likely candidate.[194] Other suggestions include the puff-adder and sand viper, neither of which is as lethal as the carpet viper.

Make a snake and put it up on a pole (21:8). The antidote for the snakes' venom is a copper image of the snake mounted on a signal pole. The function of the image resembles a form of homeopathic and apo-

tropaic ritual, whereby a votive form of the source of the disease (homeopathic element) is used in a ritual to ward off evil (apotropaism)—here, death from snake bite.[195]

The use of a copper or bronze serpent in a worship context was found in the excavated remains of a temple to Hathor at Timna, a copper mining site of Egyptian origin (Bronze Age) and later Midianite (Iron I, Judges period) occupation located on the west side of the Arabah about fifteen miles north of Elath. Excavations and surveys by the Rothenberg expedition from 1959–1969[196] uncovered mining shafts, smelting facilities, wall carvings, and a small cultic center dedicated to Hathor, the patron deity of Egyptian artisans. Temple remains unearthed in 1969 from the later Midianite occupation included a five-inch long copper snake with a gilded head, representative of some deity in the local cult and of a typology of cultic activity well attested in Egyptian literature and iconography.[197] A coiled copper snake form about eight inches long was excavated at Tel Mevorakh in the northern Sharon Plain, dating to the Late Bronze Age.[198] Joines noted that miniature models of serpents were worn as amulets by the Egyptians in order to prevent snake bites.[199]

In 1850 Layard's excavations at Nimrud[200] unearthed a large cache of bronze bowls brought there as tribute from somewhere in the Levant, probably by Sargon or Sennacherib. This hoard includes about seventy decorated bowls. One of these bowls depicts a winged serpent on a pole. Since the serpent Moses set

Snake standard from Hazor
Z. Radovan/
www.BibleLand
Pictures.com

Five-inch copper snake with a gilded head from the later Midianite occupation of the Hathor Temple at Timna
Z. Radovan/
www.BibleLand
Pictures.com

up had survived until the eighth century and was worshiped as Nehushtan until Hezekiah destroyed it (2 Kings 18:4), one theory is that this bowl carried its image. The argument has been bolstered because sixteen of the bowls have West Semitic names etched on them, apparently to indicate their owner. Unfortunately, with the exception of one name (Aḥiyo = Aḥiyahu), none are demonstrably Hebrew. Furthermore, the winged serpent on a pole is an image connected to Eshmun, the Phoenician god of healing.[201]

Waheb in Suphah ... ravines (21:14).[202] "Waheb" is an unknown site in the vicinity of the Arnon River. "Ravines" probably refers to the entire drainage basin of the eastern Arnon system with its numerous tributaries. The upper reaches of the Wadi al-Wala, a northern tributary of the Arnon, can also be included.[203] The deep gorge and precipitous ravines formed a formidable boundary for the northern part of Moab, though later the Moabites expanded into the tablelands, hills, and valleys in the area of Heshbon. Additionally some of the ravines led to "Ar"—probably Ar of Moab, a city, district, or region (Num. 21:28; Deut. 2:9, 18, 29).[204]

Israel sang this song (21:17). The epic narrative poem continues the journey motif from the well of Beer to the sites of Mattanah ("gift"), Nahaliel ("river of God"), Bamoth ("high place, cultic center"), the valley that is in the Moabite countryside, and the top of the Pisgah mountains, which overlooks the "wasteland" (Jeshimon) (21:19–20). Translators and commentators alike have faced the problem of whether these are place names or descriptive terms. Translating several of the toponyms yields the following versification:

> The well dug by princes; its excavation
>   the nobles of the people,
> with scepter and with staves;
>   from the wilderness a gift (Mattanah),
>   from a gift (Mattanah), the river of God
>   (Nahaliel),
>   and from the river of God (Nahaliel),
>   high places (Bamoth);

> from the high place (Bamoth), which is in
>   the valley of Moab,
> the top of the Pisgah [range], which
>   is overlooking the face of the
>   wasteland.[205]

Poised on the top of Mount Nebo in the Pisgah mountains, Moses was later granted a glimpse of the Promised Land (Deut. 34:1–4).

Mattanah has not been identified, though Khirbet el-Medeiyineh (Madaynah) has been suggested.[206] Y. Aharoni identified Kh. el-Medeiyineh with Iye Abarim (Iyyim).[207] The mound is located about eleven miles northeast of Dibon and contains pottery from the end of the Late Bronze Age and in Early Iron I. Nahaliel has not been located, though this may refer to the Wadi Zerqa-maʿin, which flows from the central highlands to the Dead Sea.

Nor has Bamoth ("high places, cultic centers") been identified, though it could have been preserved in the longer form "Bamoth Baal" (22:41) or "Beth-bamoth" of the Mesha inscription.[208] Bamoth was a common toponym that is combined with names or titles of deities in the naming of important worship centers among Canaanites and Amorites. This Bamoth seems to have been located somewhere near Mount Nebo in the Pisgah range. The Pisgah peak provided an excellent vantage point over the wilderness areas on the northern side of the Dead Sea. On a clear winter day from the traditional Mount Nebo, one can see where the Jordan River flows into the Dead Sea, the northern end of the Judean wilderness and the Jericho oasis, as well as the regions to the north on both sides of the Jordan.

The valley in verse 20 may be the Wadi ʿAyûn Mûsâ, about two miles northeast of the corner of the Dead Sea. Finally, Aharoni identified the "wasteland" as a place name with Beth Jeshimoth, part of the realm of Sihon of the Amorites conquered by Israel (Josh. 12:3).

Messengers ... to Sihon king of the Amorites (21:21–22). Diplomatic envoys were sent to negotiate passage northward along the King's Highway in the Transjordan highlands and then westward down the hillsides to the shores of the Jordan River (see comment on 20:17). The Amorites were a large ethnic group that formed in Upper Mesopotamia near the end of the Early Bronze Age and extended westward to the Mediterranean coastlands (see comment on 13:29). Sometimes "Amorite" is used generically in the Bible as a reference to the population of Canaan.

But Sihon would not let Israel pass through (21:23). Biblical and extrabiblical evidence locates Jahaz somewhere between Dibon and Madaba.[209] The Amorite kingdom of Sihon is said to have spread from the Arnon to the Jabbok Rivers, a length of about fifty miles, flanked by the fortified towns of the Ammonites on the eastern and northern sides. The early Ammonite kingdom is evidenced by the discovery and excavation of a Middle to Late Bronze Age temple near the Amman airport[210] as well as other sites in the region, such as Tel el-Umeiri,[211] Hesban,[212] Jalul, and Tell el-Jawa.

Heshbon was said to have been the key city of Sihon at the time of the Israelite conflicts, though remnants are meager from the Middle or Late Bronze ages at Tel Heshban, located about eleven miles southwest of Amman. Few Late Bronze potsherds and no architectural remains were uncovered at the site during the 1968–76 Andrews University excavations. The archaeological record at Tel Hesban parallels that of Arad, Ai, Hebron, and other sites of the Israelite campaigns. Horn suggested that the Heshbon of Sihon may have been located at Jalul[213] or other nearby sites, which do have occupational remains. Younker notes the complexity of the social and political structures of early Moab and cautions against ascribing aspects of formal statehood to these early tribally oriented groups.[214]

Chemosh (21:29). Chemosh first appears among the deities at Ebla about 2600–2250 B.C. and is associated with mud brick production.[215] He is mentioned twelve times in the Mesha Stele, including

Plain north of Amman
Todd Bolen/www.BiblePlaces.com

in the appellation Ashtar-Chemosh, as the god who enabled Mesha to break the yoke of Israel's domination and recapture and rebuild a number of his cities, including Jahaz (l. 19; cf. Num. 21:23), Dibon (l. 21; also Dibon Gad in 33:45–46), Beth Dibla-then (l. 30; cf. 33:46–47), and Madaba (l. 30; cf. 21:30).[216] Heshbon is not preserved in the Mesha Inscription, though it remained a vital city of this period in Moab's history.

Jazer (21:32). Jazer may not have been an Amorite town originally, but may have come under Amorite dominion in the expansion of Sihon or Og into the Ammonite region. Jazer was both the name of a region (32:1) and its principal city (32:3), located in the valley of the Wadi Kefrein.[217] The city was identified by Simons with Khirbet-Gazzir (Jazer), about ten miles west-northwest of Amman.[218] The battle ensued at Edrei (21:33), generally associated with modern Derʿâ on the Syrian-Jordanian border and thirty miles east of the Sea of Galilee.[219]

Og king of Bashan (21:33). The capital of the kingdom of Og of Bashan was located at Ashtaroth, situated on a northern tributary of the Yarmuk River (Deut. 1:4). Later Edrei was included in the tribal territorial allocation

of the eastern half of the tribe of Manasseh (Josh. 13:31). Though no other battles in this campaign are recounted in Numbers, sixty cities from the kingdom of Og were subjected to the stipulations of holy war (Deut. 3:4–6).

The Book of Balaam (22:1–24:25)

Plains of Moab (22:1). This area is the broad plain between the Transjordanian highlands and the Jordan River, extending about ten miles from just north of the Dead Sea. From this locale the campaign into the promised land of Canaan will be launched.

Balak ... king of Moab (22:2, 4). Unknown outside the Bible, Balak is called a "king of Moab," meaning he was the titular head of an emerging tribal confederation (as were other groups in Transjordan, such as the Edomites and Ammonites). Territorial borders of these clans were not well defined until the Iron Ages, when classical Moab extended from the Wadi Zered border on the south with the Edomites to the Arnon River gorge on the north, and from the Dead Sea on the west to the desert on the east. At various times Moabite domain reached north to Heshbon and the surrounding plains.

Elders of Midian (22:4). The Midianites have their origins in northern Arabia and southern Transjordan; they were descendants of Abraham and Keturah (Gen. 25:1–6). Their loose-knit, seminomadic culture carried them from Arabia to Sinai and Egypt (Ex. 2:15–22; Num. 10:29); occasionally they made forays into Canaan as traders (Gen. 37:25–36) and as invaders (Judg. 6:1–6). In this narrative a group of Midianite elders (note, no king is cited) joins the emissaries from Balak in enlisting the services of Balaam to curse Israel. Later the alliance with Moab is reflected in the idolatrous incident at Baal Peor (Num. 25). For these two affairs they are condemned and suffer the consequences in the Midianite reprisal campaign (Num. 31).

Pethor, near the River (22:5). Pethor is likely Pitru, situated thirteen miles south of

Upper Euphrates
Region
▼

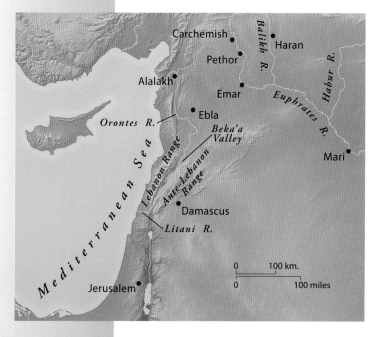

Carchemish on the Sajur River tributary west of the Euphrates. Pitru is cited in the annals of Shalmaneser III (859–824 B.C.), and earlier a Pedru is mentioned in the annals of Thutmose III (ca. 1467 B.C.).[220] The phrase translated in the NIV "in his native land" is probably better rendered "in the land of Amaw," a region west of the Euphrates possibly mentioned in Egyptian and Mari inscriptions.[221] The distance from Pethor to Moab exceeded four hundred miles, making each leg of the journey by the emissaries and Balaam a twenty- to twenty-five-day trek.

Curse (22:6). Ancient Near Eastern texts recount the power of diviners, magicians, and sorcerers to discern, intervene, and even manipulate the will of the gods through augury, special sacrificial rituals such as extispicy (ritual dissection of a liver or entrails), and incantations aimed at blessing or cursing an individual or group, forecasting the future, and advising kings and other leaders.[222]

The reading of omens through observing various aspects of nature was considered a skilled science. Glossaries of omens and detailed lists of animals and objects and their potential use in divination are found among the texts of the Hittites, Babylonian, Assyrian, Egyptian, and other cultures. Knowledge of the ways, workings, and occasional whims of the divine and the skill of cajoling these deities into bringing beneficial or detrimental results was a highly prized craft. A parallel to the Hebrew concept of curse ($^c\bar{a}rar$) is found in the following Akkadian text:

> May the great gods of heaven and the
> nether world curse him (*li-ru-ru*),
> his descendants, his land, his soldiers, his
> people, and his army with a
> baneful curse; may Enlil with his
> unalterable utterance curse him
> with these curses so that they speedily
> affect him.[223]

Fee for divination (22:7). This phrase describes the men "carrying divination in their hands" (*ûqsāmim b^eyādām*), which

various scholars have translated as a divination fee, divination equipment, or an idiom describing the emissaries of Balak as men "versed in divination."[224] Hurowitz, developing the lead of J.-M. Durand, delineates several parallel contexts from Mari in which objects used in the process of divination were presented, dispatched, and used in the negotiation with the recipient of the divination. These included such items as clay models of intestinal entrails, livers, or other parts used in the practice of extispicy, the art of ritual dissection. Hurowitz concludes: "If Balaam was, among his various magico-religious talents, a *bārū*, and if extispicy was practiced in Moab as it was at Canaanite Hazor and Megiddo and Ugarit, then the q^esāmîm referred to may well have been baked clay models of the entrails predicting Moab's downfall and Israel's ascendancy."[225] Fear of the Israelites may have so alarmed Balak's own trained diviners that they sought a person of great renown as Balaam, who might exercise his expertise in allaying Moab's potential destruction by cursing Israel.

Opened the donkey's mouth (22:28). Three times Balaam's female donkey observes the angel of the Lord in a manner more perceptive than that of the renowned seer of the gods. The vineyard scene indicates that the theophany took place in the arable highlands of Transjordan, probably between Damascus and Rabbath Ammon. Piles of stones gathered from the area for planting were used to create boundaries between neighboring vineyards.

Tales of talking animals in the ancient world often contain warning, irony, or satire. In the Egyptian Story of Two Brothers, a cow advises one of the brothers to flee because his brother was seeking to kill him with a lance.[226] From the Aramaic Words of Ahiqar (seventh century B.C.) comes a conversation between a lion, a leopard, a bear, and a goat, each representing a human characteristic in facing the struggles of life before the gods.[227]

Interpretation of this donkey event has given rise to two general options: (1) God

gave the female the power of speech similar to how he empowered Ezekiel to speak after a prolonged period of silence (Ezek. 3:27; 33:22); (2) the donkey's normal braying was heightened such that it was perceived and interpreted by Balaam in a human manner.[228] The scene is replete with irony in that the female donkey is more perceptive of God and is able to speak God's word in a manner superior to the internationally renowned expert. Balaam is reminded he will only be allowed to speak what Yahweh, God of Israel, permits him to speak.

Kiriath Huzoth (22:39). The "city of plazas" (as the name translates) may have been a central market area for Moab. Biran, the excavator of Tel Dan in northern Israel, has noted a series of official buildings in the market plaza outside the gate of the Iron Age city that seem to have served as offices for oversight of commercial activity.[229]

Bamoth Baal (22:41). See comment on 21:18. Balak apparently thinks that Yahweh, God of Israel, might be more apt to be manipulated from a cultic center dedicated to a primary deity of the region (Baal, the champion of creation in the mythology of Ugarit). Bamoth (see comment on 21:17) is found in several compound names in the Old Testament, but does not occur as a topographical name anywhere but in Moab.[230]

Seven altars (23:1). Multiple altars are not attested elsewhere in the Old Testament, though the number seven denotes completeness or fulfillment. The importance of the number seven is reflected in the days of creation, the sanctity of the Sabbath, the sprinkling of the blood of the sin offerings on Yom Kippur, and the series of sevens in Revelation. A parallel use of seven is found in a Babylonian text in which a worshiper is instructed to "erect seven altars before Ea, Shamash, and Marduk, to set up seven censers of cypress, and then pour out [as a libation offering] the blood of seven sheep."[231]

A bull and a ram (23:2). In ancient Near Eastern culture, the bull and ram were the most prized of animals and the obligatory

Dan Iron Age gate complex where remains of a market plaza were excavated
Todd Bolen/www. BiblePlaces.com

sacrifices for persons from the upper echelon of society. The bull was the required offering of the high priest (Lev. 4:3–8) and the ram for a guilt offering (5:14–6:6). These animals are also a regular part of special offerings in the Canaanite-type culture at Ugarit in the mid-second millennium.[232] For a divination context, this is a large offering reflecting the importance of the situation—a king acting on behalf of his people in an international crisis. Usually a sacrifice performed in connection with divination was just one animal whose entrails were then examined for an answer.[233] Here Balaam offers the sacrifices in order to try to induce Yahweh to deliver prophecy through him.

Stay here beside your offering (23:3). Here the king himself acts on behalf of the Moabite people, performing a priestly role not uncommon among Northwest Semitic people.

Field of Zophim on the top of Pisgah (23:14). The field of Zophim ("field of the watchmen") was probably named so because of its strategic observation location. Several scholars interpret this location as a known place for observing heavenly omens and making astrological observations.[234] The Phoenicians referred to an astrologer as a *tsope šamem* ("watcher of the skies"). Balaam may have sought to observe the omen of bird movements at Zophim according to the common practice of augury known in Mesopotamia and in the Deir ʿAlla texts (ll. 7–9). Pisgah (cf. 21:18–20) is one of the prominent mountain peaks in the Abarim Range just northeast of the Dead Sea. There Moses will commission Joshua (Num. 27:12–23), and later God provides Moses an overview of the Promised Land (Deut. 34:1–12).

Change his mind (23:19). Unlike the gods of Mesopotamia, who were often whimsical and malleable, Israel's God was unchangeable and therefore of incomparable integrity. Note the incantation from the Namburbi Texts of Mesopotamia: "The evil

of the lizard which fell upon me, the portent of the evil that I saw—Ea, Shamash, and Marduk turn it into a portent of good, an oracle of good for me."[235] This incantation shows that the gods were believed capable of exploiting the ambiguity of omens to their pleasure. Ishtar, a principal Mesopotamian goddess, is known for possessing paradoxical, and at times mutually exclusive, traits.[236]

In this text "changes" denotes making idle or deceptive promises or failing to follow through on one's words. In other words, it concerns integrity. Though the gods of the ancient world sometimes changed their posture on certain issues and even evidenced a change in character, they could normally be taken at their word (though sometimes their words were intentionally ambiguous and thus could mislead).[237]

Wild ox (23:22). Israel's strength was totally in her God; by his power she is compared to a ravaging wild ox. Hammurabi of Babylon declared himself to be like "the fiery wild ox who gores the foe."[238] Ancient Near Eastern deities were often depicted as horned bulls or as humans with the head and/or horns of the bull.[239] Baal is depicted as wearing the horns of a bull or wild ox in a bas relief from Ugarit.[240]

No sorcery against Jacob (23:23). Israel did not need augurs, sorcerers, diviners, or magicians; in fact these were condemned. Augury included reading cloud patterns, bird movements, and other activities in the skies (see comment on 22:6). No such

Obverse of the Narmer Palette portraying wild ox
Werner Forman Archive/The Egyptian Museum, Cairo

Pharaoh striking
with scepter
Frederick J. Mabie

▶

activity was the source of Israel's defense, nor could such powers be effectively used against her. God would use a pagan diviner to communicate divine revelation for the purpose of blessing those whom Balaam had been expected to condemn.

Top of Peor (23:28). Peor is another of the peaks in the Abarim Range near Pisgah (see comment on 23:14), near the cultic site of Baal Peor, where some Israelites entered into idolatrous activity at the instigation of Balak and Balaam (25:1–19; 31:16). The site afforded a view to the north-northwest of the area of Jeshimon ("wasteland"—cf. Beth Jeshimoth in 33:49) on the southern end of the Plains of Moab near the Dead Sea.

Agag (24:7). King Agag ruled the Amalekites at the time of King Saul (1 Sam. 15:8). The Amalekites were Israel's greatest enemy in the time of Moses, routed by Israel soon after the Exodus (Ex. 17:8–16); they defeated Israel after she rejected the gift of the land (Num. 14:43–45). Agag seems to have been a dynastic name among the Amalekites, and this oracle depicts a future victory in the exaltation of Israel.

Balak ... struck his hands together (24:10). Fierce clapping of the hands was a sign of derision or defiance when used with this particular verb (Job 27:23; 34:37; Lam. 2:15).[241] The same meaning is evident in Esarhaddon's Prism Inscription, where the gesture accompanies mourning in response to what he calls the wicked behavior of his father.[242]

Star ... scepter (24:17). It is difficult to document the star used as a symbol or metaphor for kingship in ancient Near Eastern literature. In later literature, this passage served as a basis for the star used on the coinage of Alexander Janneus (103–76 B.C.) to elevate the status of his kingship.[243] Rabbi Akiba in the second century A.D. proclaimed Simon bar Kosiba to be Bar

Kochba ("son of the star"), thereby claiming fulfillment of this messianic passage. The "scepter" symbolized royal power in both heavenly and earthly realms, as seen in royal monuments of the ancient Near East in iconographic and epigraphic forms. Thutmose III subdues his captives with his scepter in a relief from the temple of Amon at Karnak.[244]

Kenites (24:21–22). The Kenites were a nomadic clan living in the eastern Sinai region, whose roots are traced biblically to the descendants of Cain and are associated with metallurgical craftsmanship (Gen. 4:17–24). In Judges 1:16 the association is made between the Kenites and Moses' in-laws (the Midianites Jethro, Reuel, and Hobab), the descendants of whom settled in the Negev near Arad. Later Kenites are found living as far north as the territory of Naphtali (cf. Ex. 2:11–3:1; 18:1–5; Num. 10:29–32; Judg. 4:17; 5:24–27). The present text notes a group of Kenites who, like some Midianites, become enemies of Israel and are eventually subdued.[245]

Asshur (24:24). This probably refers not to the later Assyrian empire of the ninth to seventh centuries B.C., or even the Middle Assyrian peoples of the Late Bronze Age, who seldom ventured west of the Euphrates. Rather, this citation denotes the relatively unknown Asshurites, a nomadic group of the Negev region mentioned in Genesis 25:3, 18 and Psalm 83:8. They were descendants of Abraham and his concubine Keturah.

Kittim (24:24). Kittim is one of the ancient terms for Cyprus (Gen. 10:4), derived from its major city Kition (thus Kitionites). In several Old Testament passages the term is used generically for the islands of the Mediterranean and their inhabitants (Jer. 2:10; Dan. 11:30). The Kittiyim mentioned in the Arad inscriptions are probably Greek and Cypriot mercenaries serving in the Judean army in border fortresses.[246] During the Hellenistic age Kittim became a byword for the archenemies of God, a prominent motif in the Qumran scrolls in reference to the Greeks and then the Romans.

Eber (24:24). Eber occurs in the genealogy of Shem, from whom the Hebrews descended (cf. Gen. 10:21; 11:14–17); this offers no solution here since God will then be fighting against his own people. Eber perhaps can be associated with the Mesopotamian king Ibrim known from the Ebla Tablets of northern Syria of the third millennium B.C., but this reference antedates our context by more than a thousand years.

Idolatry at Baal Peor (25:1–18)

Shittim (25:1). The geographical link to previous and later material is derived from the references to Shittim (Num. 33:49, i.e., "Abel Shittim"; Josh. 2:1; 3:1), Baal (Num. 22:41, "Bamoth Baal"), and Peor (Deut. 3:29). "Shittim" is an example of a floral toponym, derived from the word for "acacia tree," which is prominent in these arid regions. Glueck identified Abel Shittim with Tell el-Khefrein, though Tell el-Hamman, a site located at the mouth of the Wadi Kefrein, has also been suggested.[247] Josephus identified the site with Abila of his day, a site about three miles east of the Jordan and five miles north of the Dead Sea.[248] This general area "on the plains of Moab by the Jordan across from Jericho" (Num. 26:63; 31:12; 33:48, 50; 36:13) is the geographical setting for the rest of Israel's sojourn prior to entering the Promised Land.

Baal of Peor (25:3). This is the first occurrence of the god Baal in the Hebrew Bible, who becomes the primary antagonist to Yahweh for the hearts of the Israelites. In the latter half of the Late Bronze Age, Baal was emerging as one of the major operative deities in Canaan. From Ugaritic texts Baal was the agent of the creative order, who with his consort Anath defeated the forces of evil, namely, Yammu (Sea), Mot (Death), and Lotan (Leviathan, "Sea Monster").

Baal was a lesser-known deity in Mesopotamia during the Early Bronze Age and in the beginning of the Middle Bronze (patriarchal) period. Milgrom simply states that "the patriarchs did not know him."[249] His

Wadi es-Sir is roughly the area where Abel Shittim is to be found.
Todd Bolen/www.BiblePlaces.com

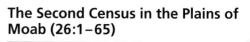

The storm-god Adad stands on a bull, brandishing a flash of lightning. Basalt bas-relief on a stele is from Arslan-Tash, eighth century B.C.
Rama/Wikimedia Commons, courtesy of the Louvre
▶

first appearance as a prominent deity in Canaan surfaces in Hyksos period texts from Egypt in the latter half of the Middle Bronze Age (ca. 1720–1570 B.C.). The Egyptians bemoaned the fact that the "foreign rulers" from the land of the Hurru and Retenu were not worshipers of Amon-Re, but of a god called Baal-hazor, which they associated with their god Seth.[250] With the emergence of the classical Canaanites in the southern Levant, apparently a mix of Northwest Semitic peoples and some non-Semitic elements such as the Hurrians and Hittites, came the emergence of Baal as a primary deity in the cults of the land.[251]

Kill them (25:4). The instructions given to Moses are severe but necessary to accomplish the purging of the sins of the

people. Moses is charged literally to "take all the leaders of the people and impale them to Yahweh before the sun." That is, Moses must round up all the tribal leaders, those representatives of the people who presumably should have either prevented the idolatrous activities or carried out the punishment of the guilty members of their tribes, and execute them by impaling them on poles so that their bodies hang out in broad daylight.[252] The term "impale" is a rare Hebrew verb that has been variously translated as "kill, execute, impale, dismember."[253]

Exposure to the elements usually followed this form of execution, as with Saul's sons (2 Sam. 21:8–13). Such public exposure was reserved for only the most heinous of crimes in ancient Israel and Mesopotamia. Later Assyrian bas relief murals depict rebellious vassals impaled on poles and left for public viewing, presumably to deter further insurrection.[254] That the guilty parties were to be executed as "unto Yahweh" means that they were rendered unto Yahweh in order to expiate the divine wrath as evidenced in the plague.

The Second Census in the Plains of Moab (26:1–65)

Israelites who came out of Egypt (26:4). The second census of Israel's military provides genealogical information not listed in the first census (see ch. 1; on the purpose of genealogies, see comment on 3:1). Lists of successive kings of Sumer, Assyria, and Babylon were common among the cuneiform

Stone relief from the palace of Sennacherib depicts the assault on the gate tower of Lachish and impalement of captives.
Werner Forman Archive/The British Museum
▶

texts excavated at Nineveh and Babylon.[255] The genealogical census lists in Numbers connect the second generation of Israelites with the first generation, whom God delivered from Egypt. The familial relationships also form the basis for the land distribution by lot noted in 26:52–56; 33:53–54 (see comments on 1:20–46).

The total number of the men of Israel was 601,730 (26:51). See the sidebar on "Large Numbers in the Book of Numbers" at 1:46. If one takes the interpretation of *'elep* ("thousand") as "troop, clan," the second census total is 596 troops, totaling 5,730 men (a growth of 180 men).

Distributed by lot (26:55). The antiquity of these texts is echoed in the practice of census taking in the ancient Near East of the second millennium B.C. Census taking for military and land distribution purposes is known from the royal archives of Mari dating to the nineteenth century B.C.[256] Milgrom also notes the clan register is reflective of the "premonarchical period, when Israelite society was based solely on clan structure."[257] The principle of proportion is described in explicit terms—greater territory for larger tribes, smaller portions for the less populated. Clan apportionment is assumed under the aegis of their ancestral tribe.

The proportional distribution takes into consideration the percentage of arable land available or accessible by clearing or irrigation. Joshua will later challenge tribes to harvest forested areas for ample farming acreage (Josh. 17:17–18). The second principle governing land allocation is that of providential probability. The Lord oversees the tossing of the lots and thereby brings his decision to pass. Distribution of land for tribal inheritance follows this method; that inheritance is to remain within the tribal family for posterity.[258]

Zelophehad's Daughters (27:1–11)

Daughters of Zelophehad (27:1). In the two census tallies only male descendants are registered. If a man dies without a male heir, a male relative will redeem the land so that the territory remains within the clan. The levirate land responsibilities are outlined in Leviticus 25:23–28 for cases in which land is sold to pay one's debts, and in the Year of Jubilee land debts are fully restored (25:8–17).

The present account provides an example of the development of casuistic legislation early in Israelite history. (1) The specific case is presented at the entrance to the Tent of Meeting (vv. 1–4); (2) appeal is made to divine legislative authority (v. 5); and (3) precedent-setting decision is issued, accompanied by derived principles (vv. 6–11). Zelophehad perished ("he died for his own sin") without a rightful male heir through which his family would receive its share in the allotment of the land. The concern shared by his daughters was that their family would be passed over in the apportionment and thus their name be forgotten in posterity.

The potential disappearance of one's family name is a matter of grave concern, often associated with divine judgment leading to societal abandonment. The entreaty within the clan allotment derives from the principles set forth in 26:52–56. Thus the daughters of Zelophehad desire status and inheritance rights within the Makirite clan of Manasseh. Later the Makirites receive an inheritance in the Gilead region of Transjordan (32:39–42).

Parallels to female inheritance in the Pentateuch occur in ancient Near Eastern texts from several countries. Ancient Sumerian law from Nippur and the decrees of Gudea of Lagash (ca. 2150 B.C) allowed a woman to inherit property when there were no sons.[259] Z. Ben-Barak cites numerous other cases from Babylon, Nuzi, and elsewhere, including one from sixth-century B.C. Athens, which stipulated that the woman marry within the family.[260] Egyptian laws seem to develop progressively from the Middle to New Kingdom periods, moving from a case in which a woman's husband

Akhnaten and
Nefertiti offer
votive images
Erich Lessing/Art
Resource, NY, cour-
tesy of the Egyptian
Museum, Cairo
▲

The fifteenth day of the seventh month (29:12). This was the Feast of Tabernacles (Sukkoth). The *sukkâ* was a hut or tent constructed during the wilderness period to protect from the elements of the desert. First called the Feast of Ingathering, the celebration commemorated God's provision in the fall harvest of the vegetable crops, vineyards, and olive orchards.

Such a celebration was common among ancient Near Eastern cultures, such as the Emar *zukru* ("remembrance") rituals on the eighth and fifteenth days of the seventh month of Zarati.[274] When the Israelites settled the Promised Land, they were to imitate their ancestors by building a *sukkâ* adjacent to their homes and live in it during the seven days of the festival (Lev. 23:39–43), to remind them of God's protection and provision during the forty-year sojourn. The association of Sukkoth with the Exodus from Egypt provided a continuation of the salvation-redemption-providence-preservation motifs of Passover, Unleavened Bread, and Pentecost.

Women's Vows (30:1–16)

When a man makes a vow (30:2). Vows are binding on all community members, with special exceptions for women. Making vows was voluntary, but anyone who did so or swore an oath in an obligatory relationship had to fulfill that commitment. Vows involve a verbal act of commitment to a task or to consecration of oneself or one's property to the Lord; sacrificial offerings are part of the obligation, and in the case of the Nazirite also an oath of abstinence. Cartledge distinguishes between vows and obligations; the former is "a conditional promise, made in the context of petitionary prayer," the latter "an oath of abnegation."[275] Biblical vows are made only to deity, intensifying the solemnity of the pledge. To break a vow in which God's name has been evoked is to profane that name (see Lev. 27).

Vows to the gods for favors were common in the ancient Near East in requests for victory in battle, healing, deliverance, childlessness, or the love of a woman. The recitation of a vow was often inscribed on a stele. Examples include those made by kings and other worshipers in Mesopotamia,[276] Ugarit,[277] and Aram.[278] Conditional vows were rare in Old Kingdom Egypt, the few taking the form of a declaration of promise. In the New Kingdom, several prayers of the poor reflect vows to praise the god Ptah in response to his beneficent acts.[279]

Woman still living in her father's house (30:3). Concerning the binding nature of vows or pledges made by a woman while still living under the patriarchal headship of her father, Cartledge notes: "Male dominance becomes the controlling rule: any dependent woman may make vows, but such vows are subject to cancellation on first hearing by the male authority figure on whom the woman is dependent, whether father or husband."[280] The young female lived under her father's care and authority until she married (usually in the late teenage years), at which time her husband assumed that responsibility. A father may confirm such a vow or permit it to remain in effect by choosing no course of action.

Widow or divorced woman (30:9). A woman no longer under the patriarchal authority of her father or her husband, whether by his death or by divorce, possessed the same status and responsibility of a man with regard to vows and obligations. Independent women were afforded a significant position in Israelite society, being permitted to buy and sell property, negotiate contracts, operate businesses, and make vows and pledges (cf. Prov. 31:10–31).

A woman living with her husband (30:10). Vows that might be detrimental to the woman, her husband, or the husband-wife relationship could be annulled by the husband. Special considerations were given to the circumstances and time sequence of when the wife took a vow or oath, when the husband was apprised of the commitment, and when and how he responded to the information. Childlessness was a common concern in the Bible and the ancient Near East (e.g., Hannah, 1 Sam. 1:11; the mother of Samson, Judg. 13:1–23). In Mesopotamia severe childhood disease or mortality is deemed the result of unpaid vows.[281]

The Midianite Campaign (31:1–54)

Midianites (31:2). The Midianites are an enigmatic people in biblical, historical, and

archaeological research (for more on this people group, see comments on 10:29; 12:1; 22:4). Moses fled to the region of Midian from Egypt, labored in the Midianite household of Jethro (Reuel), married one of his seven daughters (Zipporah), and first encountered the Lord in the theophany at the burning bush (Ex. 2:15–3:4). Egyptian records seem to subsume groups such as the Midianites under the heading of the *shasu*, a group of pastoralists and village raiders. Recent excavations in northwest Arabia and at Timna in the southern Arabah have yielded a stylistic pottery from the thirteenth to the twelfth centuries B.C. that may be Midianite.[282]

Vengeance (31:3). Here are the demands of all-out holy war: (1) driving out human populations (33:50–53), and in some cases the total annihilation of human life in a given area for purging of idolatry and its temptations (Deut. 20:16–19); (2) subjugating women who are not killed (21:10–14); and (3) banning certain objects and materials from the public usage (7:5, 24–26; Josh. 6:18–19). These requirements were intended for Israel during the period of the late second to early first millennia B.C.; regarding the moral and ethical concerns of holy war, God often provided a prior option that would alleviate destruction (i.e., conversion).

The Mesha Stele from Moab (ca. 830 B.C.) describes a similar holy war strategy when King Mesha celebrated the rebellion and victory against Israel: "So I went by night and fought against it from the break of dawn till noon, taking it and slaying all, seven thousand men, boys, women, girls, and maidservants, for I had devoted them to destruction for (the god) Ashtar-Chemosh."[283]

Articles from the sanctuary (31:6). Scholars have debated which holy implements may have been taken from the sanctuary into battle. Some have suggested the ark of the covenant, but others disagree.[284] It seems, however, that if the ark of the covenant were intended by this phrase, it would have been mentioned as when the Israelites tried to

Timna
Bible Scene Multimedia/Maurice Thompson
◀

use it against the Philistines in the battle of Aphek-Ebenezer (1 Sam. 4:3–11). Noordtzij and Milgrom suggest these vessels were the Urim and Thummim, but Ashley notes that this is unlikely since they were kept by the high priest.[285] Harrison suggests these are the signal trumpets, which were kept in the sanctuary for their regular cultic usage and for waging battle (see comment on 10:9).

Evi, Rekem, Zur, Hur and Reba (31:8). The names of the five kings are recounted again in the same order in the battle summary of Joshua 13:21, where they are called princes of Sihon. The precise political relationships among the Amorites, Moabites, and Midianites remain somewhat nebulous. These Midianites chieftains may have been subject to Sihon prior to the defeat of the Amorites and then gained their independence through the earlier Israelite victory.

Zur was the father of Cozbi, the Midianite woman killed by Phinehas along with her Israelite paramour, Zimri ben Salu (Num. 25:14–18). Zur and Zimri are both regarded as patriarchal clan leaders.[286] On the title "king" (*melek*), see comment on 20:14.

Purify yourselves (31:19). The purpose of holy war was the eradication of all impure elements from the geographical region or ethnic territory placed under the ban. Coming on the heels of an idolatrous and adulterous affair at Baal Peor involving Israelite and non-Israelite participants, a cleansing of the camp was needed for the sanctity and purity of the community. The violence of war brings death and a state of ritual impurity through contact with the dead.

Gold, silver ... put through the fire (31:22–23). This new ordinance has to do with the purification of metallic products by means of fire because they can withstand the high temperatures. Perishable goods such as glass beads, clothing, wood, leather, animals, and other organic commodities are to be purified with water, probably through washing, and then put through the waters of purification made from fresh water and the ashes of the red cow.

Divide the spoils (31:27). This instruction for distributing the spoils of war among the community members sets the standard for the coming campaigns in the Promised Land. In many other marauding cultures of the ancient Near East, the warriors retained whatever goods or persons they captured during and after battle, with certain portions being allocated to the king and his court and other portions rewarded to the priesthoods of the patron deity of that people.

Tribute (31:28). The term for tribute (*mekes*) occurs three times in this chapter but nowhere else in the Hebrew Bible. This term is attested in Ugaritic (*mekes*) and Akkadian (*miksu*) and occurs often in later rabbinic sources.[287] The tradition in Abraham's day was a tithe of ten percent presented to the temple priesthood, as he did with the spoils of war confiscated from the battle against the four kings of Mesopotamia (Gen. 14:1–24).

Plunder remaining (31:32). These totals are much higher than those confiscated in the campaign of Thutmose III of Egypt (ca. 1460 B.C.) during his campaign against Megiddo and other northern Canaanite cities. The Karnak temple account lists booty of 1,929 cattle, 2,000 goats, 20,500 sheep, and 2,503 slaves (men, women, and children), along with a variety of physical objects such as gold bowls and ebony statues.[288] Wenham

Booty: flocks captured from Arabs
Todd Bolen/www. BiblePlaces.com

suggests an adjustment should be made to the numbers by analogy with the two census summaries of 1:1–46 and 26:1–51. Humphreys' analysis and assessment of the number of people in the Exodus from Egypt are in order here to clarify the interpretation.[289]

Gold articles (31:50). The amount of the gold offered by Israel's commanders on behalf of their troops exceeds the minimal requirement of one-half shekel per person, a ransom of some 6,000 shekels, or about 2,500 ounces = 158 pounds of gold. Instead, they present nearly three times the minimal amount, with a combined weight of the armlets, bracelets, signet rings, earrings, and necklaces totaling 16,750 shekels = 7,000 ounces = 440 pounds of gold.

This much gold seems phenomenal considering the seminomadic nature of the Midianites. Yet they traveled the caravan routes into Arabia and beyond by which such wealth could have come, and adornment in gold is still prized today among Bedouins.

Samples of such wealth occasionally find their way into burials. Note the excavation of Tel Beth Shean, in which material goods from a child burial from the Middle Bronze II (Hyksos) period (ca. 1700 B.C.) include an ornate white alabaster vase, four gold earrings, and a gold ring with an etched amethyst mounted on it with gold thread.

Settlement of the Transjordan Tribes (32:1–42)

Lands of Jazer and Gilead (32:1). Having journeyed through the more arid regions south of the Arnon (such as Edom and Moab), the Gadites and Reubenites observe how the more northern region of Gilead is more fertile with highland grassy regions for grazing, and with valleys and hillsides suitable for grain and fruit orchards. Gilead extended through the Transjordan highlands from the Bashan and Golan regions in the north to the Jabbok River in the south, rising to more than 4,000 feet in elevation. Rivers

Region of Gilead
Peter White

Tell Hesban from
north
Todd Bolen/www.
BiblePlaces.com

▶

such as the Yarmuk, Jabesh, Jabbok, and their tributaries, as well as the numerous springs in the region, provide ample water supply for humans and animals alike.

Gilead is perhaps *gl'd* mentioned in the texts from Ugarit,[290] and *ga-al'a[a]-(za)* of Akkadian texts of Tiglath-pileser III, a possible reference to Ramoth Gilead bordered on the north by the Aramaeans.[291] The land of Jazer is an arable region northwest of Amman, generally associated with the area around Khirbet Jazzir, located about ten miles west-northwest of Amman and twelve miles south of the Jabbok.

Ataroth, Dibon, Jazer, Nimrah, Heshbon, Elealeh, Sebam, Nebo and Beon (32:3). These cities are located in the arable highland plains of Transjordan on the east side of the Dead Sea, advantageous for farming, grazing, and animal husbandry.

Ataroth is identified with Khirbet 'Attarus, located between Machaerus and Libb, just over ten miles northwest of Dibon. Ataroth and Dibon are cited in the Mesha Stele (ca. 830 B.C.) as a land and a town formerly occupied by Gad (l. 11–12).[292]

Dibon (modern Dhiban) was the Moabite capital, located about 3.3 miles north of the Arnon River gorge and twelve miles east of the Dead Sea.[293] Jazer is cited above.

Nimrah is identified with Tel Beleibel just north northeast of Tel Nimrin, a Roman-Byzantine site that retains the ancient name. Note Beth Nimrah in verse 36 and the "waters of Nimrim" in Isaiah 15:6 and Jeremiah 48:34.

Heshbon is associated with Tel Hesban, about twelve miles southwest of Amman, Jordan (see comment on 21:23).

Elealeh is identified with Tel el-'Al, about two miles northeast of Heshbon.

Sebam is generally identified with Khirbet Carn el-Kibsh, between Heshbon and Mount Nebo.

Nebo (Kh. El-Mukhayyit) is located just south of its mountain namesake in the Abarim range of Moab; the Mesha Stele suggests a cultic center was dedicated to Yahweh there (l. 14–19).

Beon is identified with Ma'in, four miles southwest of Madaba; it seems to be the conflation of Baal Meon in verse 38.[294]

If we have found favor (32:5). After the list of the cities conquered from the Amorites and an acclamation that Yahweh their God was responsible for granting them the victory, the Israelites make a request of Moses and Israel's other leaders. A similar entreaty for a land grant in proper protocol format is found in diplomatic correspondence of the ancient Near East, including the basic letter-writing language found in the Lachish, Arad, and Samaritan ostraca.[295]

Pens (32:16) The "pens" (*gidrōt ṣōʾn*—"stone pens for sheep" or simply "sheepfolds") are perhaps the V-shaped stone enclosures found in Transjordan and the Arabah for protecting sheep, goats, and cattle during times of danger.[296]

If you will do this (32:20). The compromise proposed by the Gadites and Reubenites is structured as a covenant with stipulations in the formula of blessing and curse: "If you do X, then you will have Y blessing; but if you do *not* do X, then Z curse will come to you." The covenant between the Gad and Reuben tribes and the other ten tribes has Moses as the mediator and Yahweh as the witness and guarantor of the commitment made by the two tribes.[297]

Gadites (32:33). The Gadites are allocated land grants in the southern part of the former kingdom of Sihon of the Amorites, most of which are cited in verse 3. Gad shares its northern border with the half-tribe of Manasseh. The cities listed for Gad in the Old Testament suggest a narrow strip of land in the Jordan River plain extending from the Jabbok River to the Sea of Galilee. Aroer (mod. ʿAraʿir) was located on the King's Highway, just north of the Arnon. The Gadite cities are detailed in Joshua 13:24–28.[298]

Reubenites (32:33). These people receive the area and cities generally allocated south of those belonging to Gad. Among the cities are Heshbon, the former capital of Sihon's Amorite kingdom, Elealeh, Kiriathaim ("twin cit-ies"?), Nebo, and Baal Meon (see also Josh. 13:15–23).[299] Simons identifies Kiriathaim with Khirbet el-Qureiyat, six miles northwest of Dibon, though Aharoni's suggestion of Khirbet el-Mekhaiyet, northwest of Madaba, seems more likely.[300]

The half-tribe of Manasseh (32:33). The allocation to the half-tribe of Manasseh is generally north of Gad, extending from the region of Gilead into Bashan and the Golan. Only the cities of Havoth Jair and Kenath Nobah are mentioned here (but see Josh. 13:29–32).[301]

Triumphal March from Egypt to the Promised Land (33:1–56)

Stages of the journey (33:1–49). The toponymic list of the stages of Israel's departures

Israelite Itinerary in the Wilderness
▼

Cycle 1—From Ramesses to the Red Sea

Numbers 33	Bible: Ex. 12–17; Num. 1–21; Deut. 1–4, 10	Variant readings: additional sites, location/identification
Ramesses (3, 5)	Ramesses (Ex. 12:37)	Pi-Ramesses: Heb. *R-ʿ-m-s-s* = Egyptian *R-ʿ-m-s-s*, identified as Khataana-Qantir (not = Tanis; Avaris loc. at Tel Daba).[A-23] Built by and named after Ramesses II, est. size 4 x 2 miles.[A-24] Israelites lived in District of Ramesses (Gen. 47:11).
Sukkoth (5–6)	Sukkoth (Ex. 12:37; 13:20)	W. of Sea of Reeds and SE of Ramesses, Heb. *Sukkoth* ("Booths"), Egyptian *Tjeku*, recently identified with Tell el-Maskhutah in Wadi Tumilat, 40 miles SE of Pi-Ramesses[A-25]
Desert of Etham (6–7)	Etham (Ex. 13:20)	Part of or near to the Shur Wilderness (Heb ??r = "wall" but not = an Egyptian *khetem* = "wall, fortress"). Perhaps *ʾi(w)-(l)tm* or similar word meaning "isle/mound of Atum"
Pi-Hahiroth (7–8)	Pi-Hahiroth (Ex. 14:2); between Migdol and Sea, opp. Baal Zephon, Yam Suph crossing (Ex. 14:21–31); Shur Wilderness (Ex. 15:22)	MT—*miphney-hahiroth*—"from facing the gorge"—SP, Syriac, Vulgate, Sebourin = *Pi-Hahiroth* ~ "Mouth of the canals," which empty into Sea of Reeds, near location of Sea crossing[A-26] -Probably in Bitter Lakes or Lake Timsah area.
Marah (8–9)	Marah (Ex. 15:23), bitter waters made sweet	Traditionally located at ʿAin Hawara (Bir el-Muwarah), just inland 8 miles E from city of Suez; alt. perhaps ʿUyun Musa.
Elim (9–10); 12 springs and 70 palms	Elim (Exod. 15:27); 12 springs, 70 palms, water	Trad. JM[A-27]—Oasis in Wadi Gharandel, 75 miles SSE of Bitter Lakes. JSB—area of ʿUyun Musa or Wadi Riyanah[A-28]
Yam Suph (10–11)	Yam Suph—Sea crossing site name (Ex. 14:21–31), but not same location. Here camp by Yam Suph shoreline, S of crossing.	Sea of Reeds / Red Sea (see comment on Num. 21:4).[A-29] JSB or JM—Somewhere along the E shoreline of Suez Gulf, SE of sea crossing (v. 7) but N of the Wadi Feiran.

Thutmose III on Seventh Pylon with a list of enemies defeated
Frederick J. Mabie

and encampments from Ramesses in Egypt to the plains of Moab stands in the tradition of itineraries of ancient Near Eastern kings in their travels and conquests. Coats has demonstrated that the list in Numbers 33 is a genuine ancient Near Eastern itinerary.[302]

This compares with the Late Bronze Age itineraries of Thutmose III from Karnak, which were both military and economic expeditions that included topographical, geographical, and toponymic information.[303] Later in the ninth and eighth centuries B.C., Assyrian kings such as Shalmaneser III and Tiglath-Pileser III listed cities and geographical features in their conquest annals.[304]

Sinai (33:16). One of the key issues for locating sites in the second through fifth cycles is the location of Mount Sinai (see comments in introduction; also at 11:35). If the request of Moses before Pharaoh to journey three days into the desert to celebrate a festival to the Lord

Cycle II—The Deserts of Sinai: Sin, Sinai, and Paran

Numbers 33	Bible: Ex. 12–17; Num. 1–21; Deut. 1–4, 10	Variant readings: additional sites, location, identification
Sin Wilderness (11–12)	Sin Wilderness (Ex. 16:1–15)—between Elim and Sinai on 15th day of 2nd month. Complaint of food, God gives manna and quail.	Probably coastal area of NW Sinai along Gulf of Suez[A-30] since quail generally do not migrate into the mountains. JM—Dibbet el-Rammleh JSB—SE of Bitter Lakes, E of city of Suez
Dophkah (12–13)		LXX—Raphaka. Trad. Serabit el-Khadim and Wadi el-'E?? uncertain[A-31]—remains unknown.
Alush (13–14)		SP—Alish—Unknown location—in desert region between Suez Gulf and central mountain wadis.
Rephidim (14–15); no water for people to drink	Rephidim (Ex. 17:1)—No water; people quarrel; Massah and Meribah; Amalekite attack, Israel's victory	Trad. Wadi Refayid (30 miles NNW of S tip JSM—Prob. Wadi es-Sudr if Israel moved south; or Refidim if E, 35 miles E of Bitter Lakes (neg—in Shur Wilderness) (to JSB = 55 miles)
Sinai Wilderness (15–16)	Sinai Wilderness (Ex. 19:1–2—Moses w/ God, Mount Sinai)	Trad. following Wadi Feiran to Jebel Musa and Central S. Sinai region, mt. 2,285m elev. JSB—Jebel Sin Bisher (618m elev.) vicinity and Wadi es-Sudr; other locations?[A-32]
Kibroth Hattaavah (16–17)	Paran Desert (Num. 10:12); Kibroth Hattaavah (Num. 11:34)	JM—between Jebel Musa and Ein Hudrah JSB—Suggest upper Wadi es-Sudr or upper Wadi Gheidara
Hazeroth (17–18)	Hazeroth (Num. 11:35) Paran Desert (Num. 12:16)	JM—Wadi Hudeirat region and Ein Hudrah, 35 miles NE of Jebel Musa JSB—Region of Wadi Gheidara

(Ex. 8:3) is to be applied to the quest for the mountain's locale, then the sacred summit must be closer to the Egyptian border fortresses than most of the suggested mountains except Jebel Sin Bisher. The most explicit passage bearing on this question is the statement in Deuteronomy 1:2 that the distance from Horeb (= Sinai) to Kadesh Barnea via Ezion Geber is a distance of eleven days or about 140 to 150 miles.[305]

Rithmah (33:19). The sites recorded in cycles III and IV of the desert itinerary largely belong to the wilderness wandering period. Most of the sites are

Cycle III—Spies Sent from Paran Desert (13:3), Return to Kadesh in Paran Desert (13:26)

Numbers 33	Bible: Ex. 12–17; Num. 1–21; Deut. 1–4, 10	Variant readings: additional sites, location, identification
Rithmah (18–19)		Location unknown.
Rimmon-Perez (19–20)		Location unknown.
Libnah (20–21)		SP (Gk)—Lebonah; Location unknown.
Rissah (21–22)		Location unknown.
Kehelathah (22–23)		LXX—Makellath (w/ v. 25), thus some scholars suggest that Kehelathah may be an alt form of Macheloth. Location unknown.
Mount Shepher (23–24)		Location unknown.
Haradah (24–25)		Location unknown.

Initially referred to as the Baal Hadad Stele, this is now considered by many to represent the moon god.

Cycle IV—Kadesh to the Arabah

Numbers 33	Bible: Ex. 12–17; Num. 1–21; Deut. 1–4, 10	Variant readings: additional sites, location, identification
Makheloth (25–26)	Kadesh in Zin Wilderness (Meribah?)	Location unknown.
Tahath (26–27)		LXX—Kataath. Location unknown.
Terah (27–28)		Location unknown.
Mithkah (28–29)		SP—M^etikah. Location unknown.
Hashmonah (29–30)		LXX—Selmona. Location unknown.
Moseroth (30–31)	Moserah in Deut. 10:6	Location unknown.
Bene Jaakan (31–32)	Deut. 10:6	Deut. 10:6 has order as Bene Jaakan, Moserah, Gudgodah, Jotbathah. Location unknown.

unknown to the rest of Scripture, later history, and modern historical geographers.

Carved images (33:52). Those images of deity carved from wood (e.g., Asherim)[306] or sculpted from stone or ivory (e.g., the stylistic stele of Baal Hadad found at Bethsaida) are included.[307] This kind of iconography represents a form of mimesis whereby a representation of the given deity functions as a record of the perception of reality conceived by the worshiper in relationship to the deity.[308]

Cast idols (33:52). Molten cast images (*massēkôt*) of deities are those in which clay or molten metal, such as copper or bronze, was poured into a pottery mold forming the shape of the deity.[309] Numerous deity forms and their molds have been uncovered in excavations throughout Israel/Palestine.[310]

Cycle V—Desert Journeys to Edom and the Death of Aaron

Numbers 33	Bible: Ex. 12–17; Num. 1–21; Deut. 1–4, 10	Variant readings: additional sites, location, identification
Hor Haggidgad (32–33)	Gudgodah in Deut. 10:7	Few MSS, LXX, Vulg—*Har*-Haggidgad SP—Haggidgadah
Jotbathah (33–34)	Deut. 10:7	JM—ʿAin Tabah and et-Tabah, 6 miles S of Elat (etymologically weak) Modern Yotvata in southern Arabah?
Abronah (34–35)	Lacking	Suggestion: ʿAin Defiyeh?
Ezion Geber (35–36)	Lacking, but "Way of Red Sea" mentioned in Num. 21:4	Probably Jezirat Faroun island in northern Gulf of Aqaba, S of Elat[A-33] vs. trad. Tell el-Kheleifeh, just NE of modern Elat, probably not Ezion Geber.[A-34]
Kadesh (36–37) in Zin Wilderness	Kadesh (Num. 20:1)—Miriam dies; Waters of Meribah	Trad. ʿAin Qudeirat
Mount Hor (37–41)	Mount Hor (Num. 20:22) near border of Edom; Aaron dies at age 123, 40 yrs. after Exodus	Others: Hormah (and Arad) Deut. 10:6—Aaron dies at Moserah. On the border of Edom. Trad.—J. Madeirah, S of Petra, too far East. Possible mountain in north-central Nahal Zin region such as Hor Hahar
Zalmonah (41,42)	Lacking	Unknown elsewhere in OT. Perhaps in region of Wadi Salmana, E of ʿEin Hatzevah

Cycle VI—Punon to the Plains of Moab

Numbers 33	Bible: Ex. 12–17; Num. 1–21; Deut. 1–4, 10	Variant readings: additional sites, location, identification
Punon (42–43)	Lacking	Trad. Feinan, 31 miles S of Dead Sea on E side of Arabah (ancient copper mining center).[A-35] Roman—Phaenon
Oboth (43–44)	Oboth (Num. 21:10)	Suggestions: ʿAin el-Weibeh (Simons) on W edge of the Arabah, 18 miles W of Feinan. Alt. site N of Kh. Feinan toward Kh. Ay[A-36]
Ijeabarim (44) Iyim (45)	Iye Abarim—E of Moab, then to Zered, Mattanah, Nahaliel, Bamoth, Pisgah (Num. 21:11)	Add'l sites: Wadi Zered, Mattanah, Nahaliel, Bamoth, Pisgah cited in Num. 21:13–20. Iye Abarim = "ruins of Abarim (Mts.)" Thutmose III cites "Iyyin"—Possibly Muhai, 11 miles SE of Mazar nr. E edge of Moab; or Medeiyineh on N edge of W. Zered canyon.[A-37]
Dibon Gad (45–46)	Dibon in Num. 21:30 proverb	Add'l sites: Jahaz, Heshbon, Jazer, Edrei (Num. 21:23–35). Egyptian t-b-n-i; modern Dhiban—3 miles N of Arnon River gorge.[A-38] Ramesses II—"Qarho (Dibon)."
Almon Diblathaim (46–47)		= Beth-diblathaim? (Jer. 48:22 w/ Dibon and Nebo), Mesha Stele, line 30.[A-39] Near Baal-meon and Madaba. Deleilat el-Gharbiyeh.[A-40]
Mounts Abarim (47–48) before Nebo	cf. Iye Abarim above (Num 21:11); Mount Nebo in Abarim Mts. in Deut. 32:49	Abarim = ridge of mountains separating Transjordan plateau from Jordan Valley, W of Madaba and Heshbon. Mount Nebo traditionally identified w/ mountain of 802 meters elev., 5 miles NW of Madaba.
Plains of Moab (48–49) by Jordan from Beth Jeshimoth up to Abel Shittim	Plains of Moab (22:1); Balaam encounters	Beth Jeshimoth = Tel ʿAzeimah, 12 miles SE of Jericho near Dead Sea.[A-41] Abel-shittim = Tell Kefrein, 5 miles E of Jordan and 7 miles N of Dead Sea (Josephus)[A-42]—or Tel Hammam Thutmoses III, Ramesses II—"Abel"

High places (33:52). The phrase "high places" translates the Hebrew *bāmôt*, which may or may not refer to an elevated site or structure. With the variety of usage in the Old Testament, a generic phrase such as "sacred site" or "cultic installation" may better render this kind of worship center.[311] Such a site may include (1) an altar on which animal, grain, vegetable, incense, or other product is rendered unto the deity; (2) cultic symbols and/or figurines, (3) standing stones (*maṣṣēbôt*), or (4) other cultic instruments.[312]

Boundaries of the Promised Land (34:1–15)

Canaan (34:2). Canaan was a definable geographical entity in Egyptian onomastica as early as the fifteenth century B.C., since Egypt controlled much of Canaan (Retenu) during the Eighteenth and Nineteenth Dynasties.[313] Though the detailed borders are not as explicitly demarcated in the Egyptian records of the Late Bronze and Early Iron Ages, the cities and towns listed in both sets of documents encompass substantially the same region.

Southern side (34:3). The southern boundary begins with the Desert of Zin, from which the original scouts were sent (ch. 13), and extends first east northeast to the southern end of the Dead Sea (Salt Sea), avoiding Edomite territory (on the west side of the Arabah). The boundary then moves westward from the Desert of Zin, gradually turning more northwest toward the Great Sea, the Mediterranean.

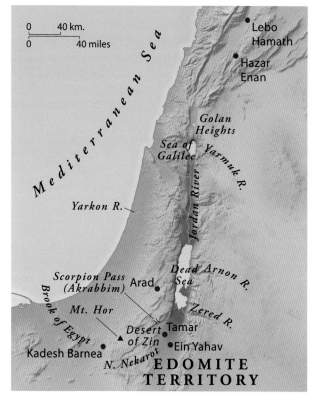

The Edomites
occupied the hilly region south of the Nahal
Zin, southwest and west of Ein Khatseva
and Ein Yahav, and in the basin of the Nahal
Nekarot. In fact, the Edomites are now
known to have moved even further northwest into the area just south of Arad in the
Israelite kingdom period.[314]

**Scorpion Pass ... Kadesh Barnea
(34:4).** The southern border passes just
south of the famous "Scorpion Pass,"[315]
a winding road from the Nahal Zin basin
into the Negev south of Mampsis.[316] On
Kadesh Barnea, see comments on 13:26.
The border continues on to Hazar Addar
and Azmon (cf. Josh. 15:3, the southern
border of Judah); the locations of these two
towns are unknown, though they probably
lie along a natural geographical and topographical line between Kadesh Barnea and

the Brook of Egypt (Wadi el-
ʿArish). Aharoni identifies Hazar
Addar with Ain Qedeis, Azmon
with Ain Muweilih, and Karka of
Joshua 15:3 with Qetseimeh.[317]
These three sites lie along the
watershed between the Wadi el-
ʿArish and the smaller Nahal Zin
basin.

Western boundary (34:6).
The natural western boundary is
the Great Sea (i.e., the Mediterranean). A stormy body of water
in the fall, winter, and early parts
of spring, and often unpredictable
even in the summer, all ancient
peoples respected it. In Ugaritic
mythology the sea was believed to
be the abode of an often malevo-
lent deity Yammu and his associate, the great sea serpent Lotan
(Leviathan of the Old Testament).
The western border extends along
the shoreline from the Brook
of Egypt in the south to a point
west of Mount Hor and Lebo Hamath. These
coastal plain regions were occupied by the
Philistines (south of the Yarkon River) and
various Sea Peoples and Phoenicians during the Iron I and Iron II periods; they were
under Israelite control only briefly during the
reigns of David and Solomon.[318]

Northern boundary (34:7). The northern
boundary extends on a line from the Great
Sea toward Mount Hor, which is likely one
of the Lebanon mountain peaks just north of
Byblos (perhaps Jebel Akkar).[319] The northern border town of Hethlon (Ezek. 47:15) is
identified with modern Heitela on the lower
slope of Jebel Akkar.

Lebo Hamath ("the entrance to
Hamath"), perhaps so named because of its
geographical location as a southern access
route to the city state of Hamath, is generally identified with modern Lebweh near
one of the sources of the Orontes River. It
was the northern border of Israel during the
monarchy of David and Solomon (1 Kings

Though many confine the Edomites to
the east side of the Arabah, the geographical
patterns here and in 20:14 – 21:12 (see comments) suggest otherwise.

8:65). Joshua 13:4 contains the additional site of Aphek, identified with modern Afqa, about fifteen miles east of Byblos.

Zedad is associated with the modern town of Tsada (Tsadad), about thirty-five miles northeast of Lebweh; Ziphron remains unknown. Milgrom suggests that Ziphron and Hazar Enan be identified with two oases east of Zedad, namely Hawwarin[320] and Qaryatein. Ezekiel 47:17 places Hazar Enan on the northwest border of the territory of Damascus.

Eastern boundary (34:10). The eastern border of the Israelite inheritance begins at Hazar Enan, where the northern boundary leaves off (v. 9). The border continues toward Shepham, south toward Riblah, around the east side of Ain, and on to the eastern edge of the Sea of Galilee ("Sea of Chinnereth"). Shepham is unknown; Riblah here is not the Riblah on the Orontes mentioned in 2 Kings 25:6. The LXX has "Arbela," a mountain and town of that name on the prominent escarpment on the west side of the Sea of Galilee. Ain ("spring") could be one of the springs that serve as the sources of the Jordan (i.e., the springs at Iyyon [Ijon][321] near Tel ed-Dibbin, at the base of Tel Dan, or at Banias [Caesarea Philippi in the New Testament]).

The border then follows the eastern side of the Upper Jordan Valley, descending toward the Sea of Galilee, including the strip of land on the eastern side up to the slopes of the ridge that extends from Caesarea Philippi southward along the western edge of the Golan Heights to the Yarmuk River. The sea was originally named Chinnereth, presumably because the lake looked like a harp from distant vistas such as Mount Arbel. From that sea the eastern border then follows the Jordan down to the Dead Sea, about sixty miles, though the river itself meanders back and forth for about eighty-five miles.

All these borders reflect the ideal territorial limits for the land of Israel, but they were not fully realized until the time David and Solomon (2 Sam. 8:1–18; 10:1–19; 2 Chron. 18:1–20:3).

Levitical Cities and the Cities of Refuge (35:1–34)

Give the Levites towns to live in (35:2). Circumscribed portions of land on the perimeter of forty-eight cities are prescribed for Levite utilization in pasturage and farming, including the six cities of refuge. Parallel to the encampment of the priests and Levites around the tabernacle during the wilderness journey (ch. 2), the Levites provide a constant visible presence among the twelve tribes to remind them of the need for holiness and righteousness as God's people. This distribution parallels the Eighteenth Dynasty of Egyptian administration of Canaan in which royal land grants were made, administered by the priesthood.[322] These fortified cities

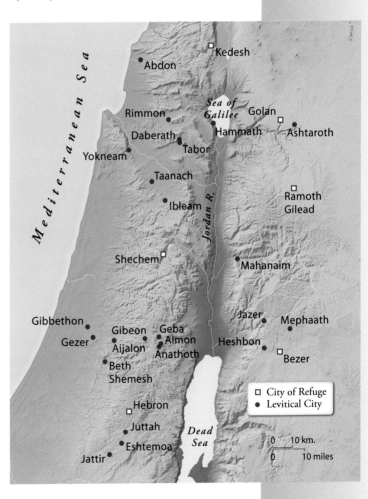

Levitical Cities and the Cities of Refuge

□ City of Refuge
● Levitical City

0   10 km.
0   10 miles

collected tribute from the region, providing wealth to the priesthood in Egypt.

Instead of being granted a designated portion of the land, the Levites' inheritance is Yahweh himself (18:20). The Levitical pasturelands around the grant cities are to extend outward 1,000 cubits (about 1,500 feet) from the wall of the city, and the territory is described as 2,000 cubits (about 3,000 feet) on each of the sides. Levite presence facilitates the rendering of the tithes by the Israelites (18:21–24, 30–32) to the Lord. The Levite land grants are primarily for pasturage of animals, not for crop production (Josh. 21:11–12). On the specific areas where the Kohathites, Gershonites, and Merarites lived, see Joshua 21.[323]

Cities of refuge (35:11). Six cities are to be set aside to provide refuge for a person who causes an accidental death of someone else (cf. Deut. 4:41–43). The manslayer must flee to the appointed city immediately after committing the act to be afforded the opportunity for refuge from a potential kinsman avenger. For the names and placement of these six cities, three on each side of the Jordan and all somewhat equidistant from each other, see Joshua 20:7–8.

Avenger (35:12). The "avenger" (Heb. gōʾēl; cf. vv. 19–27) is the same term used of the "kinsman-redeemer" in Ruth 2:20 and 4:4, 6; he is someone who "redeems" property or persons from another. In Leviticus 25:33 gʾl denotes the redemption of property of the Levites that has been sold, and in 25:47–54 it relates to the redemption by a kinsman of persons sold into slavery.

The "avenger of blood" is a kinsman who redeems the lost life of a relative by exacting the life of the murderer.[324] The responsibility to carry out this judgment falls to the nearest surviving relative (father, then eldest brother, and on down the line). The city of refuge provides a safe haven for the manslayer until the community has opportunity to ascertain the nature of the crime and determine whether murder or manslaughter has been committed.

Murderer (35:16). Case laws governing murder and manslaughter are stated in a formula of option,[325] with the first set of laws governing murder and the avenging adjudication by the blood kinsman (vv. 16–21), and second set governing manslaughter and the responsibilities of the community in such cases (vv. 22–29).[326]

If without hostility (35:22). According to Joshua 20:4, one seeking asylum must appear at the entrance to the city gate, where the city's elders and judges hear and settle a variety of judicial cases. If the case is determined accidental, the Levitical city will offer asylum and sanctuary. The sending of a person convicted of manslaughter "back to the city" (Num. 35:25) suggests that the trial takes place just outside the city walls, whereby also a person convicted of murder can be rendered readily to the blood kinsman for execution. One convicted of manslaughter must remain in the city of refuge until the death of the high priest, which marks the end of an era in Israelite cultic history, similar to the ancient practice of a king or governor granting amnesty or pardon to convicted felons. In effect the death of the individual or the high priest ransoms the death of the victim.

Testimony of witnesses (35:30). No one can be executed on the basis of a single witness to a crime; a minimum of two witnesses is necessary for conviction of a capital crime. This is consistent with cases delineated in Deuteronomy as well as ancient Near Eastern law codes, such as that of Hammurabi.[327] Bribery, ransom, or other forms of compensation for the death of a human being are strictly prohibited, whether the death is murder or manslaughter.

Zelophehad's Daughters Revisited (36:1–12)

Ancestral inheritance (36:3). The particular concern of the larger Gileadite clan is the possible loss of land to another Israelite tribe should the daughters of Zelophehad marry outside the tribe of Manasseh. Under the Lord's direction, Zelophehad's daughters are granted territorial inheritance rights, thereby setting a legal precedent that the land should remain within the family or tribe. The Gileadite leaders bring to the judicial proceedings the other legal precedent of the Lord's direction for the distribution of tribal territory by lot, and territorial sovereignty of each tribe is to be maintained.

With these two precedents on the judicial table, the Gileadites present their case in two parts before Moses and the Israelite leadership for a legal decision. First is the question of one of the daughters of Zelophehad marrying outside the Manassite tribe, in which case the property would accrue to the husband's tribe, thereby violating tribal territorial sovereignty. Tribal sovereignty is maintained by requiring Zelophehad's daughters to marry within the tribal clan. This decision settles a potential conflict within property laws related to the year of Jubilee, during which property reverted to its original tribal or clan owner and indentured slaves were emancipated (Lev. 25:13–55). Since the Jubilee statutes applied only to purchased property and not to inherited property, this case sets a precedent for future potential litigation.

Bibliography

Boling, Robert. *The Levitical Cities: Archaeology and Texts*. Winona Lake, Ind.: Eisenbrauns, 1985. Boling examines the setting, form, and function of the Levitical cities from a historical and archaeological standpoint. These studies provide unique insights into the role of the Levites within the larger Israelite society.

Cartledge, T. W. *Vows in the Hebrew Bible and the Ancient Near East*. JSOTSup 147. Sheffield: Sheffield Academic Press, 1992. The context and content of oaths and vows in ancient Near Eastern cultures are examined to shed light on practices described in Old Testament narratives and legal texts. Contrasts are also made with Near Eastern oaths and vows before various deities, which involved potions, sorcery, or forms of divination.

Cole, R. Dennis. *Numbers*. NAC. Nashville: Broadman & Holman, 2000. This commentary provides a theological and literary analysis of Numbers as a unified composition in its presentation of the wilderness tradition of ancient Israel. Historical, geographical, and archaeological data complement the literary analysis of this pivotal Pentateuchal book.

Fleming, Daniel E. *Time at Emar: The Cultic Calendar and the Rituals from the Diviner's Archive*. Mesopotamian Civilizations 11. Winona Lake, Ind.: Eisenbrauns, 2000. For comparative analysis of the Israelite holy day calendar, Fleming presents parallels from the agricultural festival calendar from Emar in Upper Mesopotamia. Since the biblical patriarchs come from this general region, this presentation provides helpful insights into the world of sacrificial systems and festival calendars in order to study the unique historical elements of the Israelite celebrations.

Fouts, David. *The Use of Large Numbers in the Old Testament*. Ann Arbor: Univ. Microfilms, 1991). Idem, "A Defense of the Hyperbolic Interpretation of Large Numbers in the Old Testament," *JETS* 40 (1997): 377–87. In his dissertation and several derived articles, Fouts analyzes the military census passages in Numbers in light of the comparative literature of military census taking in Egyptian, Babylonian, and Assyrian records.

Hoffmeier, James K. *Israel in Egypt: The Evidence for the Authenticity of the Exodus Tradition*. New York: Oxford, 1996. Idem, *Ancient Israel in Sinai: Evidence for the Authenticity of the Wilderness Tradition*. New York: Oxford, 2005. In these two books Hoffmeier examines the recent historical, geographical, and archaeological data bearing on Israel's sojourn in the Nile Delta region of Egypt and their movement into the Sinai desert region. The location of Mount Sinai and various sites on the Israelite journey are analyzed.

Milgrom, Jacob. *Numbers*. JPS Torah Commentary. Philadelphia: Jewish Publication Society, 1990. Milgrom's expertise in Israelite cult, history, and law is fleshed out in this thoroughgoing commentary on Numbers. This work is a must for any serious student of this book. Milgrom also provides an insightful new translation of the Hebrew text. The extensive excurses provide in-depth analysis of key themes and literary structures.

Walsh, C. E. *The Fruit of the Vine: Viticulture in Ancient Israel*. HSM 60. Winona Lake, Ind.: Eisenbrauns, 2000. Walsh presents a thoroughgoing analysis of vineyard agriculture and wine production in the context of ancient Israel. Included is the utilization of wine in the various aspects of the sacrificial system delineated in the Old Testament, with some corollary elements from viticulture in Egypt and Mesopotamia.

Main Text Notes

1. Eusebius, *Onomasticon* 14.5.9.
2. For a detailed analysis of the location of Mount Sinai, see G. I. Davies, *The Way of the Wilderness: A Geographical Study of the Wilderness Itineraries in the Old Testament* (Cambridge: Cambridge Univ. Press, 1979); idem, "Sinai, Mount," *ABD*, 6:48; G. Kelm, *Escape to Conflict: A Biblical and Archaeological Approach to the Hebrew Exodus and Settlement in Canaan* (Fort Worth: IAR Publications, 1991), 80–92; M. Harel, "Sinai," *Encyclopaedia Miqraith*, 5:1021–22; idem, "The Route of the Exodus of the Israelites from Egypt" (Ph.D. diss.; New York Univ., 1964); G. E. Wright, "Sinai," *IDB*, 4:376–78; Y. Aharoni, *The Land of the Bible*, rev. ed. (Philadelphia: Westminster, 1979), 197–99. Survey results in northern Sinai are found in E. I. Oren, "Sinai," *OEANE*, 5:41–47.
3. For extensive discussion of the early date for the Exodus, see B. Waltke, "Palestinian Artifactual Evidence for the Early Date of the Exodus," *BibSac* 129 (1972): 33–47; J. Walton, "Exodus, Date of," *DOTP*, 258–72.
4. J. K. Hoffmeier, *Israel in Egypt: The Evidence for the Authenticity of the Exodus Tradition* (New York: Oxford, 1996), 126. See 107–34 for additional data on the literary and chronological evidence for Israel in Egypt.
5. K. A. Kitchen, "The Tabernacle—A Bronze Age Artifact," *ErIsr* 24 (1993): 121–29; idem, *On the Reliability of the Old Testament* (Grand Rapids: Eerdmans, 2003), 275–83.
6. K. A. Kitchen, "Some Egyptian Background to the Old Testament," *TynBul* 5–6 (1960): 7–13; *Reliability*, 276–83; A. M. Blackman, *The Rock Tombs of Meir V* (Oxford: Oxford Univ. Press, 1977), pl. 42, 43; G. A. Reisner and W. S. Smith, *A History of the Giza Necropolis II: The Tomb of Hetep-heres* (Cambridge, Mass.: Harvard Univ. Press, 1955).
7. Reisner and Smith, *A History of the Giza Necropolis*.
8. For Mari texts see D. E. Fleming, "Mari's Large Public Tent and the Priestly Tent Sanctuary," *VT* 50 (2000): 484–98. Fleming notes that the earlier precedents for the tent sanctuary argue against a late priestly tradition for the tabernacle, that some critics argue was based on the extant temple in Jerusalem. For Ugarit see Keret A and B texts, *ANET*, 142–47 (146 iii.18).
9. Fleming, "Mari's Large Public Tent," 484–98.
10. Translation in *ANET*, 133.
11. E.g., Num. 31:3–6; Josh. 7:3–4; 8:3; 1 Sam. 11:8; 13:1–5; 30:9; 2 Sam. 10:6; 1 Kings 20:15.
12. S. N. Kramer, *The Sumerians* (Chicago: Univ. of Chicago Press, 1963), 324.
13. A. K. Grayson et al., eds., *Royal Inscriptions of Mesopotamia* (Toronto: Univ. of Toronto Press, 1987), 1:184. See also D. Fouts, *The Use of Large Numbers in the Old Testament* (Ann Arbor: Univ. Microfilms, 1991); idem, "A Defense of the Hyperbolic Interpretation of Large Numbers in the Old Testament," *JETS* 40 (1997): 377–87.
14. See 1QSa 1.9–11; L. Schiffman, *Sectarian Law in the Dead Sea Scrolls: Courts, Testimony, and the Penal Code* (Chico, Calif.: Scholars Press, 1983), 55–65.
15. J. Milgrom, *Numbers* (JPS Torah Commentary; Philadelphia: Jewish Publication Society, 1990), 5.
16. A. M. Blackman, *God, Priests, and Men: Studies in the Religion of Pharaonic Egypt* (New York: Columbia Univ. Press, 1998); M. Haran, ed., *Temples and Temple Service in Ancient Israel: An Inquiry into Biblical Cult Phenomena and the Historical Setting of the Priestly School* (Winona Lake, Ind.: Eisenbrauns, 1985); W. R. Millar, *Priesthood in Ancient Israel* (St. Louis: Chalice, 2001); E. Matsushima, *Official Cult and Popular Religion in the Ancient Near East* (Heidelberg: Carl Winter, 1993); K. Watanabe, ed., *Priests and Officials in the Ancient Near East* (Heidelberg: Carl Winter, 1997).
17. For a depiction of this type of standard, see Y. Yadin, *The Art of Warfare in Biblical Lands* (New York: McGraw-Hill, 1963), 122, 139. Note the extensive discussion of *degel* in B. A. Levine, *Numbers 1–20: A New Translation with Introduction and Commentary* (AB; New York: Doubleday, 1993), 146–48.
18. Note the usage of *degel* in the Arad ostraca (#12), in which it refers to the military garrison at Arad, and the Elephantine papyri of the fifth century B.C. See also A. Temerev, "Social Organizations in Egyptian Military Settlements of the Sixth-Fourth Centuries B.C.E.: *Dgl* and *Mtʾ*," in *The Word of the Lord Shall Go Forth: Essays in Honor of D. N. Freedman*, ed. C. L. Meyers and M. O'Connor (Winona Lake, Ind.: Eisenbrauns, 1983), 523–25.
19. Milgrom, *Numbers*, 10; also 300, n 2.
20. Lit., "Each man according to his standard with the signs of the house of their fathers, the children of Israel shall camp; outwardly surrounding the Tent of Meeting they shall camp." See Milgrom, *Numbers*, 12.
21. 1QM 3.27–43.
22. Ancient Near Eastern literature abounds in genealogical formulae, parallel to the *tôlᵉdôt* records in the Old Testament. Van der Toorn notes that "genealogical lists are a family history in telegraphic style," and that "the ancestor cult is the setting in which such genealogist functioned and—presumably—originated; the cult also fostered a sense of connection with the past" (*Family Religion in Babylonia, Syria, and Israel: Continuity and Change in the Forms of Religious Life* [Leiden: Brill, 1996], 54). See also chs. 3 and 8.
23. R. K. Harrison, *Numbers* (Grand Rapids: Baker, 1992), 13–14, 61–63. For Atraḫasis Epic see *COS*, 1.130.
24. For detailed discussion of rights and responsibilities of primogeniture, see R. Westbrook, *History*

of Ancient Near Eastern Law (Leiden: Brill, 2003), 57–58, 118–19, 278, 678. In one Old Kingdom Egyptian case a man designated himself as the "eldest son" and "heir" because he buried his mother and acted as her mortuary priest (125). For additional information see F. E. Greenspahn, "Primogeniture in Ancient Israel," in *Go To the Land I Will Show You*, ed. J. Coleson and V. Matthews (Winona Lake, Ind.: Eisenbrauns, 1996), 69–80; B. J. Beitzel, "The Right of the Firstborn in the Old Testament (Deut. 21:15–17)," in *A Tribute to Gleason Archer*, ed. W. C. Kaiser Jr. and R. F. Youngblood (Chicago: Moody, 1986), 179–90. See also the comment on Gen. 25:31.

25. *ANET*, 173–75, laws 168–71. See also "Primogeniture" in P. J. King and L. E. Stager, *Life in Biblical Israel* (Louisville: Westminster John Knox, 2001), 47–48; I. Mendelsohn, "On the Preferential Status of the Eldest Son," *BASOR* 156 (1959): 38–40. See also van der Toorn, *Family Religion*, 222–23.

26. Westbrook, *History of Ancient Near Eastern Law*, 278. Cf. van der Toorn, *Family Religion*, 222–23.

27. Note the discussion of the protective powers of winged deities in O. Keel and C. Uehlinger, *Gods, Goddesses, and Images of God in Ancient Israel*, trans. T. H. Trapp (Minneapolis: Fortress, 1998), 248–62. See also the discussion of "Labor-Gods" in L. K. Handy, *Among the Host of Heaven: The Syro-Palestinian Pantheon as Bureaucracy* (Winona Lake, Ind.: Eisenbrauns, 1994), 154.

28. For Mari, see *ARM* 10.50.16–17; for Hittite temple laws see "Instructions for Temple Officials," *ANET*, 209.10–11. See also Milgrom, *Numbers*, 341–42 (excursus 4, "The Levites: Guards of the Tabernacle").

29. T. J. Lewis, *Cults of the Dead in Ancient Israel and Ugarit* (HSM 39; Atlanta: Scholars Press, 1989), 56–59; scholars debate whether the deceased royalty were in fact deified or simply granted a place with the divine in death. In the excavations of the necropolis at Ras Shamra, pipelines were uncovered that functioned to supply water for the dead; see C. F. A. Schaeffer, "Les fouilles de Ras Shamra-Ugarit," *Syr* 19 (1938): 193–255.

30. M. Bayliss, "The Cult of the Dead Kin in Assyria and Babylonia," *Iraq* 35 (1973): 115–25; also van der Toorn, *Family Religion*, 222–23.

31. Milgrom, *Numbers*, 25–27.

32. Ibid. (Excursus 38: "The Tassels: *Ṣiṣit*," 411).

33. For a discussion of the purple dye industry see L. B. Jensen, "Royal Purple of Tyre," *JNES* 22 (1963): 104–18; J. Doumet, *A Study in Ancient Purple Color*, trans. R. Cook (Beirut: Imprimerie catholique, 1980); I. Zederman, "First Identification of Authentic *Tekelet*," *BASOR* 265 (1987): 25–36; F. W. Danker, "Purple," *ABD*, 5:557–60; King and Stager, *Life in Biblical Israel*, 159–62.

34. M. Douglas, *Purity and Danger* (London: Routledge & Kegan Paul, 1966), 1–55.

35. M. Douglas, *In the Wilderness: The Doctrine of Defilement in the Book of Numbers* (JSOTSup 158; Sheffield: Sheffield Academic Press, 1993), 158.

36. Note also E. Jan Wilson, *"Holiness" and "Purity" in Mesopotamia* (AOAT 237; Neukirchen-Vluyn: Neukirchener Verlag, 1994); J. Sklar, *Sin, Impurity, Sacrifice, Atonement: The Priestly Conceptions* (Hebrew Bible Monographs 2; Sheffield: Phoenix Press, 2005); K. van der Toorn, *Sin and Sanction in Israel and Mesopotamia* (Assen: Van Gorcum, 1985), 30–31, 72–75.

37. See J. F. A. Sawyer, "A Note on the Etymology of *ṣāraʿat*," *VT* 26 (1976): 137–38; Levine, *Numbers 1–20*, 184–86. Cf. also S. G. Browne, "Leprosy in the Bible," in *Medicine and the Bible*, ed. B. Palmer (Exeter: Paternoster, 1986), 101–26; J. V. Kinnier Wilson, "Medicine in the Land and Times of the Old Testament," in *The Period of David and Solomon*, ed. T. Ishida (Winona Lake, Ind.: Eisenbrauns, 1982), 354–58.

38. Harrison, *Numbers*, 100–101; G. Wenham, *Numbers* (TOTC; Downers Grove, Ill.: InterVarsity Press, 1981), 76–77; idem, *Leviticus* (NICOT; Grand Rapids: Eerdmans, 1979), 120. J. Scurlock and B. Andersen, *Diagnoses in Assyrian and Babylonian Medicine* (Urbana, Ill.: Univ. of Illinois Press, 2005), 70–73, have now demonstrated that the symptoms of Hansen's disease are attested in Mesopotamia.

39. F. H. Cryer, *Divination in Ancient Israel and Its Near Eastern Environment: A Socio-Historical Investigation* (JSOTSup 142; Sheffield: Sheffield Academic Press, 1994), 318.

40. *ANET*, 168–71. Note the example in law 124. See also Westbrook, *History of Ancient Near Eastern Law*, 555–56, 936–62; P. Galpaz-Feller, "Private Lives and Public Censure—Adultery in Ancient Egypt and Biblical Israel," *NEA* 67 (2004): 152–61.

41. M. Fishbane, "Accusations of Adultery: A Study of Law and Scribal Practice in Numbers 5:11–31," *HUCA* 45 (1974): 25–45.

42. *ANET*, 171, 181; V. H. Matthews and D. C. Benjamin, *Old Testament Parallels: Laws and Stories from the Ancient Near East*, 2nd ed. (New York: Paulist, 1997), 115–16.

43. Milgrom, *Numbers*, 37; idem, "A Husband's Pride, A Mob's Prejudice," *BR* 13 (1996): 21. See also T. Frymer-Kensky, "The Strange Case of the Suspected Sotah," *VT* 34 (1984): 11–26; B. Wells, "Sex, Lies and Virginal Rape: The Slandered Bride and False Accusation in Deuteronomy," *JBL* 124 (2005): 25–40; H. C. Brichto, "The Case of the *Sota* and a Reconsideration of Biblical 'Law,'" *HUCA* 46 (1975): 55–70. See also R. Westbrook, "Adultery in Ancient Near Eastern Law," *RB* 97 (1990): 575–76.

44. R. Westbrook, "Biblical and Cuneiform Law Codes," *RB* 92 (1985): 247–64; idem, *Studies in Biblical and Cuneiform Law* (Paris: Gabalda, 1988); and idem, "What is the Covenant Code," in *Theory and Method in Biblical and Cuneiform Law: Revision, Interpolation, and Development*, ed. B. Levinson (JSOTSup 181; Sheffield: Sheffield Academic Press, 1994), 15–36.

45. M. J. Geller, "The ÒURPU Incantations and Lev. V.1–5," *JSS* 25 (1980): 181–92.

46. C. H. Cosgrove, "A Woman's Unbound Hair in the Greco-Roman World, with Special Reference to the Story of the 'Sinful Woman' in Luke 7:36–50," *JBL* 124/4 (2005): 675–92.

47. *ARM*, 10.9. The context of the text is different, in that the gods and goddesses consuming the potion promise to not sin against the city and its protective deity. See also discussion in J. J. M. Roberts, *The Bible and the Ancient Near East: Collected Essays* (Winona Lake, Ind.: Eisenbrauns, 2002), 125.

48. T. R. Ashley, *The Book of Numbers* (NICOT; Grand Rapids: Eerdmans, 1993), 129–31; B. Lafont, "The Ordeal," in *Everyday Life in Ancient Mesopotamia*, ed. J. Bottéro, trans. A. Nevill (Baltimore, Md.: Johns Hopkins Univ. Press, 2001), 199–209.

49. T. Cartledge, *Vows in the Hebrew Bible and in the Ancient Near East* (JSOTSup 147; Sheffield: Sheffield Academic Press, 1992), 114.

50. C. E. Walsh, *The Fruit of the Vine: Viticulture in Ancient Israel* (HSM 60; Winona Lake, Ind.: Eisenbrauns, 2000), 142–65. See also R. Frankel, *Wine and Oil Production in Antiquity in Israel and Other Mediterranean Countries* (JSOT/ASOR Monographs 10; Sheffield: Sheffield Academic Press, 1999); J. Pritchard, *Winery, Defenses, and Soundings at Gibeon* (Philadelphia: Univ. of Pennsylvania Museum, 1964), 10–26; idem, "Gibeon," *NEAEHL*, 2:511–14. For an extensive analysis of wine as a divine fluid in ancient Near Eastern and Mediterranean cultures, see E. R. Goodenough, *Jewish Symbols in the Greco-Roman Period* (New York: Pantheon, 1957), 5:99–142; 6:126.

51. L. E. Stager, "The Fury of Babylon: Ashkelon and the Archaeology of Destruction," *BAR* 22 (1996): 66; King and Stager, *Life in Biblical Israel*, 101–3.

52. See also O. Borowski, "Eat, Drink, and Be Merry: The Mediterranean Diet," *NEA* 67 (2004): 96–107; M. Homan, "Beer and Its Drinkers: An Ancient Near Eastern Love Story," *NEA* 67 (2004): 84–95.

53. *ANET*, 171 §127.

54. Milgrom, *Numbers*, 356.

55. *ANET*, 339–40.

56. S. Olyan, "What Do Shaving Rites Accomplish and What Do They Signal in Biblical Ritual Contexts?" *JBL* 117 (1998): 611–22, esp. 622. Cf. Deut. 21:12–13.

57. D. Fleming, "The Biblical Tradition of Anointing Priests," *JBL* 117 (1998): 401–14.

58. S. M. Olyan, "Cult," *OEANE*, 2:84, esp. Ancestor Cults; C. Kennedy, "Dead, Cult of the," *ABD*, 2:105–8.

59. D. Pardee, *Ritual and Cult at Ugarit* (SBLWAW 10; Atlanta: SBL Press, 2002), 167–70.

60. For examples of the right thigh usage in the ancient Near East, see Epic of Gilgamesh, 6.160–67; *ANET*, 85, 348 (L49–50).

61. O. Tufnell et al., *Lachish 2* (London: Oxford Univ. Press, 1940), 93–94. Tufnell notes a collection of right thigh bones found near the Late Bronze fosse temple and interprets them as remnants of special portions provided for the cultic personnel.

62. G. Barkai, "Excavations on the Hinnom Slope in Jerusalem," *Qadmoniot* 17 (1984): 94–108 (Heb); also "The Divine Name Found in Jerusalem," *BAR* 9/2 (1983): 14–19. For a general treatment of the excavations and inscriptions see J. P. Dessel, "Ketef Hinnom," *OEANE*, 3:285–86.

63. G. Barkai et al., "The Challenges of Ketef Hinnom: Using Advanced Technologies to Reclaim the Earliest Biblical Texts," *NEA* 66 (2003): 162–71.

64. C. Cohen on the theme of the "shining divine countenance and of the lifting of the divine countenance" as having late second millennium B.C. parallels in Middle Babylonian and Late Bronze Ugaritic texts in "The Biblical Priestly Blessing (Num 6:24–26) in the Light of Akkadian Parallels," *Tel Aviv* 20 (1993): 228–38. On the Akkadian and Ugaritic background of the gods providing protection and peace (well-being), A. Rainey states: "It is probable that expressions of blessing drawn from social and official contexts, originally having no bearing on the cult, provided the discrete components of the fixed liturgical benedictions" ("The Scribe at Ugarit, His Position and Influence," *Israel Academy of Sciences and Humanities* 3 [1968]: 126–46). See also Levine, *Numbers 1–20*, 236–37.

65. E. Dhorme has collected numerous examples of Akkadian parallels in "L'emploi métaphorique des noms de parties du corps en hébreu et en akkadien," *RevBib* 30 (1921): 383–412. From the 6th-century B.C. context of the reign of Nabunaid comes a blessing by the goddess Gula, who "turned her countenance toward me (the king), with a shining face she faithfully looked at me and actually caused (him, i.e., Marduk) to show mercy" (H. Lewy, "The Babylonian Background of the Kay Kâûs Legend," *AnOr* 17 [1949]: 51–63).

66. S. R. Keller, "An Egyptian Analogue to the Priestly Blessing," in *Boundaries of the Ancient Near Eastern World*, ed. M. Lubetski, C. Gottleib and S. Keller (Sheffield: Sheffield Academic Press, 1998), 338–45, esp. 339.

67. S. Richter, *The Deuteronomic History and the Name Theology* (BZAW 318; Berlin: de Gruyter, 2002); see *CAD* Š/3, 290, d); 293, c); and *CAD* Š/1, 143–44.

68. B. Levine, *Numbers 1–20*, 246–60, notes that "in biblical texts quantities are usually registered differently as … (a) numeral (quantity), (b) item," yet numerous examples suggest otherwise (e.g., 2 Kings 18:19). In 2 Chron. 30:24 both systems are used for delineating the quantities of bulls, sheep, and goats sacrificed during a Passover held in Hezekiah's reign.

69. Wenham, *Numbers*, 93.

70. Milgrom, *Numbers*, 55; Wenham, *Numbers*, 92–93. Estimates for these articles range from 2.86–3.43 lbs. for the silver plate, 1.54–2.00 lbs. for the silver basin, and 3.5–5.0 oz. for the gold ladle.

71. C. L. Meyers, *The Tabernacle Menorah* (Winona Lake, Ind.: Eisenbrauns, 1976). Summarized by Milgrom, *Numbers*, 60; cf. also excursus 17: "The Menorah," 367.

72. Meyers, *The Tabernacle Menorah*, 59.

73. Ibid., 60; figs. on 206–7.

74. Ibid., 65.

75. Herodotus, *History* 11.37.

76. R. I. Caplice, *The Akkadian Namburbi Texts: An Introduction* (Malibu: Undena, 1974). See also Milgrom, *Numbers*, 62.

77. D. Fleming, *The Installation of Baal's High Priestess at Emar* (HSS 42; Atlanta: Scholars Press, 1992), 181–82. For more examples, mostly from Neo-Assyrian and Neo-Babylonian, see *CAD* G, "*gullubu*," 129–31.

78. Olyan, "What Do Shaving Rites Accomplish?" 611–22.

79. Extensive treatment of biblical materials regarding the firstborn, from consecration to inheritance, may be found in G. Brin, *Studies in Biblical Law* (JSOTSup 176; Sheffield: Sheffield Academic Press, 1994), 166–281. But he has little to offer regarding any practice of firstborn consecration in the ancient Near East.

80. Cf. *rēštu CAD* R, 272–77; for Ugarit see Pardee, *Ritual and Cult at Ugarit*, 53 (RS 24.266:31).

81. D. E. Fleming, *Time at Emar: The Cultic Calendar and the Rituals from the Diviner's House* (Winona Lake, Ind: Eisenbrauns, 2000), 175–89.

82. COS, 1.86; *CTA*, 2.iv.8, 29; 3.iii.1; 3.iv.53. Also see COS, 1.103, i.43–45.

83. Harrison, *Numbers*, 164.

84. J. Braun, *Music in Ancient Israel/Palestine* (Grand Rapids: Eerdmans, 2002), 92–93. Other archaeological evidence is found in the example excavated from Beth Shean and a fourteenth-century painted pottery sherd picturing a man playing one.

85. The precise dimensions were 22 7/8 in. long, 1/2 in. wide tubes, with the bell flanging to 3 1/4 in. See also H. Hickmann, *La Trompette dans l'Egypte ancienne* (Cairo: Institut francaise d'archaeologie orientale, 1946), 46; F. W. Galpin, *Music of the Sumerians and Their Immediate Successors the Babylonians and Assyrians* (Freeport, N.Y.: Books for Libraries, 1936), 21 and plate XI, 25; C. C. J. Polin, *Music of the Ancient Near East* (New York: Vantage, 1954), 40–42. Silver metallurgy dates to the Early Bronze Age in Mesopotamia (3300–2300 B.C.). After a piece of processed silver was hammered into a thin sheet, it could then be hammered and molded around a trumpet form, and then heated again to temper the metal.

86. H. te Velde, "Music," *OEAE*, 2:450. They are less frequently attested in Mesopotamian contexts.

87. The later rabbis defined the long blast *taqaʿ* as three times the length of the short blast (*m. Roš. Haš.*). Cf. Wenham, *Numbers*, 102; Milgrom, *Numbers*, 74–75, excursus 21: "Trumpet and Shophar, 372–73.

88. F. G. Martinez, ed., *The Dead Sea Scrolls Translated* (Leiden: Brill, 1994), 57. In peaceful times they used other trumpets, inscribed with phrases like "The peace of God and his holy ones."

89. Cf. Gen. 14:6; 21:21; Num. 10:12; 12:16; 13:3, 26; Deut. 1:1; 33:2; 1 Kings 11:18; Hab. 3:3. Additionally, the LXX reads "Paran" instead of "Maon" in 1 Sam. 25:1. If Mount Sinai is to be located in the south-central Sinai peninsula (Jebel Musa), then the Paran Desert would include the northeast quadrant of the peninsula. If Mount Sinai is identified with Jebel Sin Bisher, Paran would be more to the east-northeast and associated with the present-day location of the Wilderness of Paran.

90. C. H. Gordon, *Before the Bible* (London: Collins, 1962), 236–38. Cf. W. F. Albright, "Jethro, Hobab, and Reuel in Early Hebrew Tradition," *CBQ* 25 (1963): 1–11.

91. *CAD* I/J, 228–29.

92. Note O. Borowski, *Agriculture in Iron Age Israel* (Winona Lake, Ind.: Eisenbrauns, 1987), 137–38.

93. *CAD*, "M: Part I," 90. Cf. also A. Malamat, *Mari and the Early Israelite Experience* (Schweich Lectures, 1984; Oxford: Oxford Univ. Press, 1989), 85–86.

94. D. Brewer, "Hunting, Animal Husbandry and Diet in Ancient Egypt," in *History of the Animal World in the Ancient Near East*, ed. B. J. Collins (Leiden: Brill, 2002), picture, 455.

95. For a discussion of quail, see O. Borowski, *Every Living Thing: Daily Use of Animals in Ancient Israel* (Walnut Creek, Calif.: AltaMira, 1998), 151–55. Cf. J. Gray, "The Desert Sojourn of the Hebrews and the Sinai-Horeb Tradition," *VT* 4 (1954): 148–54; also Aristotle, *The History of Animals* in *The Complete Works of Aristotle: The Revised Oxford Translation*, ed. J. Barnes (Bollingen Series 71/2; Princeton, N.J.: Princeton Univ. Press, 1984), 1:934.

96. Estimates for the volume of the homer range from 3.8–6.5 bushels. Cf. M. A. Powell, "Weights and Measures," *ABD*, 6:903; O. R. Sellers, "Weights and Measures," *IDB*, 4:834–35. Cf. Wenham, 500 gallons = 2,200 liters, *Numbers*, 109; Harrison, 60 bushels, *Numbers*, 191; Gray, 100 bushels, *An Exegetical and Critical Commentary on Numbers* (ICC; Edinburgh: T. & T. Clark, 1986), 119.

97. For further background on the phrase "spread them out around the camp" (for drying), cf. Ezek. 26:5 and possibly Jer. 8:12. Herodotus (*History* 2.77) describes this as an Egyptian practice.

98. See discussion in E. Yamauchi, *Africa and the Bible* (Grand Rapids: Baker, 2004), 35–75 (only the first few pages deal with this specific issue; the rest is a study of Nubia in Old Testament times).

99. R. B. Allen, "Numbers," *EBC*, 2:797–98.

100. Harrison, *Numbers*, 197. See also his article, "Leper, Leprosy," *ISBE*, 3:103–6.

101. J. Milgrom, *Cult and Conscience* (Leiden: Brill, 1976), 80–82.

102. The Wilderness of Paran seems to have denoted a large arid region in the northeast Sinai, extending north to Kadesh Barnea and the Nahal Zin

drainage basin (Num. 13:3,26; 20:1; Deut. 1:1) and east to the Arabah and the regions of Mount Seir (Edom) and the Midianites (Gen. 14:6; 1 Kings 11:18).

103. The Qumran sectarians described the celebration of a firstfruits festival on Ab 3, seven weeks after Shavuoth, which likewise suggests a date in the last week of July or the first two weeks of August (11QTemple 19.11–20.10); see G. Vermes, *Dead Sea Scrolls in English*, 4th ed. (New York: Pelican), 156–57.

104. Cf. J. Simons, *Geographical and Topographical Texts of the Old Testament* (Leiden: Brill, 1959), 7; G. W. van Beek, *IDB*, 1:396.

105. *COS*, 1.32.

106. Cf. Hoffmeier, *Israel in Egypt*, 117–19; K. A. Kitchen, *New International Dictionary of Biblical Archaeology* (Grand Rapids: Zondervan, 1983), 384; Harrison, *Numbers*, 204–6.

107. See M. Dothan, "The Fortress at Kadesh-barnea," *IEJ* 15 (1965): 134–51; idem, "Kadesh-barnea," *EAEHL*, 3:697–98 (1977). See also I. Gilead and R. Cohen, "Kadesh-barnea," *NEAEHL*, 3:841–47.

108. See Z. Herzog, "Enclosed Settlements in the Negeb and the Wilderness of Beersheba," *BASOR* 250 (1983): 41–49; B. Rothenberg, *Negev: Archaeology in the Negev and the Arabah* (Jerusalem: Massada, 1967), 92–97 (Hebrew). G. Mattingly, "Amalek," *ABD*, 1:169–71.

109. See T. Bryce, *The Kingdom of the Hittites* (Oxford: Clarendon, 1998).

110. S. Reed, "Jebus," *ABD*, 3:652–53.

111. The later annals of Sennacherib list the kings of Phoenicia, Edom, Moab, Ammon, and Philistia among the Amorites whom he conquered in his campaign of 701 B.C. (*ANET*, 287).

112. Note numerous references to the "land of Retenu," in *ANET*, 238–57.

113. J. A. Hackett, "Canaan" and "Canaanites," *OEANE*, 1:408–14.

114. Gen. 37:29; 2 Sam. 1:11; 3:31; 13:19; 1 Kings 21:27; Ezra 9:3–5; Isa. 36:22; 37:1; Jer. 36:24.

115. *ANET*, 153, "AQHT C," L35–49; D. Pardee, "The Aqhatu Legend," in *COS*, 1.103, i.19–ii.93.

116. Y. Aharoni, "Nothing Early and Nothing Late," *BA* 39 (1976): 55–76; see "Masos, Tel," *NEAEHL*, 3:986–89; "Ira, Tel," *NEAEHL*, 2:642–46; "Malhata, Tel," *NEAEHL* 3:934–39.

117. *ANET*, 328.

118. See Cartledge, *Vows in the Hebrew Bible*.

119. For example, the fat and the blood were always presented to the Lord at or upon the altar (Lev. 7:22–27). In the case of the fellowship/peace offering, the breast was presented as a wave or elevation offering before the Lord and then given to the Aaronic priests along with the right thigh portion.

120. Note the starved deities taking the form of flies in order to consume the sacrifices of Utnapishtim in the Babylonian account of *Enuma Elish*.

121. See "Poems of Baal and Anath," *ANET*, 130–35, IIIAB/B., lines 38–40; also IIAB.vii.38–41. Common in the iconography of Baal is the standing form with the raised right hand wielding a sword, lightning bolt, or club.

122. For an expanded treatment of this means of punishment, see J. Milgrom, *Numbers*, excursus 36: "The Penalty of 'Karet,'" 405–8; also D. J. Wold, *The Biblical Penalty of Kareth* (Ann Arbor: Univ. Microfilms, 1978).

123. J. Milgrom, *Numbers*, 406.

124. Cf. also S. Bertman, "Tasseled Garments in the Ancient East Mediterranean," *BA* 24 (1961): 119–28; F. J. Stephens, "The Ancient Significance of Sitsith," *JBL* 50 (1931): 59–70. For an expanded treatment of these garment fringes, see Milgrom, *Numbers*, Excursus 38: "The Tassels: Ṣiṣit," 410–14; "Of Hems and Tassels," *BAR* 9/3 (1983): 61–65.

125. Cf. Ex. 6:16–25, where the early lineage of the Levites is found, including the name of Korah.

126. K. Nielsen, *Incense in Ancient Israel* (VTSup 38; Leiden: Brill, 1986); "Incense," *OEANE*, 3:147–49; King and Stager, *Life in Biblical Israel*, 344–48; C. Meyers, "Censers," *ABD*, 1:882.

127. For a thorough treatment see P. Johnston, *Shades of Sheol* (Downers Grove, Ill.: InterVarsity Press, 2002). For discussion of the netherworld in early Mesopotamian thinking see D. Katz, *The Image of the Netherworld in Sumerian Sources* (Bethesda, Md.: CDL, 2003).

128. See *CTA*, 4.8.17–20; 5.5.2–40. Note also the Mesopotamian parallels in the Descent of Ishtar to the Nether World and A Vision of the Nether World (*ANET*, 106–110) to the gates and gatekeepers of the underworld described in the Bible in Job 38:17; Ps. 9:13; 107:18; Isa. 38:10. See T. J. Lewis, "Dead, Abode of the," *ABD*, 2:101–105.

129. *COS*, 1.166, esp. L258–60, 338–418.

130. F. Wiggermann, "Mythological Foundations of Nature," in *Natural Phenomena: Their Meaning, Depiction and Description in the Ancient Near East*, ed. D. J. W. Meijer (Amsterdam: Royal Netherlands Academy of Arts and Sciences, 1992), 279–306.

131. *CAD* I/J, "išatu," 228.

132. Ibid.

133. *ANEP*, 14 (fig 43), 156 (454), 134 (382), 154 (457), 174 (511), 188 (563), etc.

134. *ANEP*, 162–64 (figs. 470–74).

135. *COS*, 1.96.

136. Lev. 19:26–31; Deut. 18:9–14; Isa. 8:19; 57:3; Hos. 4:12–14; etc.

137. B. Levine, *In the Presence of the Lord: A Study of Cult and Some Cultic Terms in Ancient Israel* (SJLA 5; Leiden: Brill, 1974), 76–77.

138. *COS*, 1.83, §§7–8.

139. Ibid., §10.

140. See P. Jenson, *Graded Holiness* (JSOTSup 106; Sheffield: Sheffield Academic Press, 1992), 89–114; cf. Haran, *Temples and Temple Service in Ancient Israel*.

141. Cf. discussion of Egyptian temples by J. Baines, "Palaces and Temples of Ancient Egypt," *CANE*, 1:303–17.

142. *ANEP*, 192, 197–99, figs. 576, 601–6.

143. Note the description in A. P. Ross, *Holiness to the Lord: A Guide to the Exposition of the Book of Leviticus* (Grand Rapids: Baker, 2002), 192.

144. For an expanded discussion of these, see Milgrom, *Numbers*, excursus 43: "First Fruits," 427–28. The first processed foodstuffs included also fruit syrup, leavening, and kneaded dough (Num. 15:20–21). From the sheep came the first sheared wool. Cf. also Ex. 23:16–19; Lev. 2:14; 23:17–18; Deut. 18:4; 26:1–11.

145. Cf. those things devoted to destruction in Lev. 27:29; Deut. 7:28; 13:18.

146. Note the connection between the expressions in Lev. 2:13, "every offering of your grain you shall season with salt; you shall not allow the salt of the covenant of your God to be lacking from your grain offering"(NRSV). Cf. also Ezek. 43:24.

147. The Aramaic expression "that the salt of the palace we have salted" was used in the context of demonstrating their loyalty to the king and suggesting that the Jews of Jerusalem might rebel and not submit their required tribute. As a result the royal household would thus suffer damage (v. 13) both financially and politically. Implied, of course, is that the Samaritans had demonstrated their loyalty by paying the required tribute.

148. Perhaps vocalized as *ma'sratu*, similar to the Hebrew *ma'ăśēr*; see C. Gordon, *UT*, 462.

149. For an extensive discussion of the tithe in Israel and the ancient Near East, see Milgrom, *Numbers*, excursus 46: "The Tithe (18:21–32)," 432–36.

150. See 15:1–21; 18:8–12; 28:1–29:40. However, Nazirites were restricted from touching or using any products of the vineyard as part of their vow (Num. 6:2–4), until after the completion of their period of avowal. At that point sacrifices of bread and wine were offered by the Nazirite in addition to the animals of the purification (sin) and peace offerings (6:14–17, 21).

151. For further explanation of this color, see A. Brenner, *Colour Terms in the Old Testament* (JSOTSup 21; Sheffield: Sheffield Academic Press, 1982), 62–65.

152. The rabbinical interpretation extends the red and perfect characteristics to mean the cow is entirely red: "Two hairs of another colour on its body were sufficient to disqualify it" (J. H. Hertz, ed., *The Pentateuch and Haftorahs*, 2nd ed. [London: Soncino, 1978], 652).

153. So remarks Milgrom, *Numbers*, excursus 48: "The Paradox of the Red Cow," 440 (cf. Ashley, *Numbers*, 364).

154. Crimson red dye was derived from the crimson worm (*Kermes bilicus*), and was also used in the production of priestly garments and curtains for the Tent of Meeting (Ex. 36:8, 35, 37; 39:1–2).

155. *Fauna and Flora of the Bible*, 129–30. The species *origanum maru or origanum marjorana* grows in Syria and Palestine to a height of about 1 meter from the ground or rock crevices. Its leaves and branches are hairy and its flowers white. Its aromatic leaves when dried are used as a condiment. When collected in bunches it can be used for sprinkling, as its hairy leaves hold liquid for application, whether sprinkling or painting.

156. *ANET*, 336, text A:L3–20.

157. Whether this person (or the one who gathered the ashes) was a priest, Levite, or layperson is unspecified in the text. He simply had to be ritually clean to handle the purification elements.

158. Though not explicitly stated, I agree with Milgrom, *Numbers*, 162, that bodily cleansing for the person who collects the ashes is understood, as well as explicitly stated for the other two individuals. This brief period of impurity compares to the seven days of uncleanness for a person rendered impure by a dead individual (v. 11).

159. G. McMahon, "Instructions to Priests and Temple Officials," COS, 1.83, 2,14; D. Pardee, "Ugaritic Prayer for a City Under Siege," COS, 1.88.

160. "Instructions for Temple Officials," ii.9–11, *ANET*, 208.

161. Lewis, *Cults of the Dead*, 164; D. Wright, *The Disposal of Impurity* (Atlanta: Scholars Press, 1987). In Nergal and Ereshkigal, Ereshkigal, divine queen of the underworld, claims that she cannot be with the holy gods who dwell above because she is impure (COS, 1.109:388), but it is not clear that this has to do with her constant contact with the dead.

162. C. A. Kennedy, "Dead, Cult of," *ABD*, 2:105–8.

163. Milgrom, *Numbers*, excursus 36: "The Penalty of 'Karet,'" 405–8. The *karet* penalty carried both human and divine consequences—human execution and divine extirpation of the line and loss of the hereafter.

164. COS, 1.83, 13.

165. Caplice, *The Akkadian Namburbi Texts*, 19, text 10; E. Ebeling, "Beitrage zur Kenntnis der Beschwörungsserie Namburbi," *RA* 48 (1954): 178–81.

166. According to the detailed itinerary of the victory march from Egypt to the Plains of Moab in Num. 33, Aaron died on Mount Hor on the first day of the fifth month of the fortieth year after the Exodus (33:38–39).

167. Those commentators identifying the rod as Aaron's include: Harrison, *Numbers*, 264; Gray, *Numbers*, 262; Wenham, *Numbers*, 149; A. Noordtzij, *Numbers* (SBC; Grand Rapids: Zondervan, 1983), 176. Contra is Milgrom (*in loc.*), who has suggested "it was more likely the rod of Moses as was used in the performance of God's miracles in the wilderness," especially in the case of Moses' striking of the rock to produce water in Exod. 17:5–6.

168. Milgrom, *Numbers*, excursus 50: "Magic, Monotheism, and the Sin of Moses," 452. Note also the context of God's blessing at Meribah within the psalmist's calling of Israel to repentance because of her idolatrous activities (Ps. 81:6–10).

169. Note discussions in N. Glueck, *Rivers in the Desert* (New York: Norton, 1968), 22; C. S. Jarvis, *Yesterday and Today in Sinai* (Edinburgh: Blackwood, 1931), 174–75.

170. For an analysis of the travel itineraries through Edom found in Num. 20:14, 22–23; 21:1–4, 10–13 as compared with 33:36–45, see Aharoni, *The Land of the Bible*, 200–209; T. Brisco, *Holman Bible Atlas* (Nashville: Broadman & Holman, 1998), 71–73.

171. N. Glueck, *Explorations in Eastern Palestine*, II & III (AASOR 15, 18–19; New Haven, Conn.: ASOR 1935, 1938–39); his other earlier publications included "The Boundaries of Edom," *HUCA* 11 (1936): 141–57; "The Civilization of the Edomites," *BA* 10 (1947): 74–83; *Rivers in the Desert* (New York: Norton, 1968); *The Other Side of the Jordan* (New Haven, Conn.: ASOR, 1940).

172. Cf. J. R. Bartlett, *Edom and the Edomites* (Sheffield: Sheffield Academic Press, 1989), 55–82; "The Land of Seir and the Brotherhood of Edom," *JTS* 20 (1969): 1–20; "The Rise and Fall of the Edomite Kingdom," *PEQ* 104 (1972): 26–37; J. A. Dearman, *Studies in the Mesha Inscription and Moab* (Atlanta: Scholars Press, 1989); P. Bienkowski, ed., *Early Edom and Moab: The Beginnings of the Iron Age in Southern Jordan* (Sheffield Archaeological Monographs 7; Sheffield: Collis, 1992); B. Macdonald, *Ammon, Moab, and Edom* (Amman, Jordan: Al-Kurba, 1994); D. V. Edelman, ed., *You Shall Not Abhor an Edomite for He Is Your Brother* (Atlanta: Scholars Press, 1995).

173. Note the "chieftains of Edom" (Ex. 15:15).

174. Note also that an abbreviated form of this correspondence form is found in 21:21–22. More lengthy correspondence is found in Aramaic in Ezra 4:9–16, 17–22; 5:6–17. The Samaritan Pentateuch expands upon v. 14 with details from Deut. 2:2–6.

175. Levine, *Numbers 1–20*, 492; M. Noth, *Numbers* (OTL; Philadelphia: Westminster, 1968), 151; Bartlett, *Edom and the Edomites*, 90–93; Gray, *Numbers*, 266.

176. Ashley, *Numbers*, 391. Ashley cites 34:3–5 and Josh. 15:1–12 as corroborating evidence that the statements imply general proximity, since the border of Judah was said to be touching the border of Edom.

177. Note remarks by C. R. Krahmalkov, "Exodus Itinerary Confirmed by Egyptian Evidence," *BAR* 20/4 (1994): 54–62, 79. Note also contra Krahmalkov, D. Redford, "A Bronze Age Itinerary in Transjordan (Nos. 89–101 of Thutmoses III's List of Asiatic Toponyms)," *Journal of the Society of Egyptian Archaeology* 12 (1982): 55–74.

178. According to Deut. 10:6 Aaron died after the journey from Bene Jaakan to Moserah, which R. K. Harrison suggested was an etiological toponym based on the events there; *Numbers*, 272.

179. An identification at least to the 1st century A.D., cited by Josephus, *Ant.* 4.4.7.

180. Cf. Levine, *Numbers 1–20*, 494.

181. R. Amiran, O. Ilan, and M. Aharoni, "Arad" *NEAEHL*, 1:75–87. Cf. Y. Aharoni, "Arad: Its Inscriptions and Temple," *BA* 31 (1968): 31–32; R. Amiran, O. Ilan, and A. Herzog, "Arad," *OEANE*, 1:169–76.

182. An Arad *yrchm* is known from the tenth-century B.C. annals of Shishak, and an example of two cities having the same toponymic preface. Arad *yrchm* is often identified with Jerahmeel of 1 Sam. 27:10; 30:27, but perhaps could be a site near the modern Israeli town of Yerocham, eighteen miles south-southeast of Beersheba, twenty-four miles south-southwest of Tel Arad, and seventeen miles south-southwest of Tels Masos and Malhata.

183. M. Kochavi, "Tel Malhata," *NEAEHL*, 3:934–37.

184. This would be compatible with the early date of the exodus and conquest according to the revised chronology of J. Bimson, *Redating the Exodus and Conquest* (JSOTSup 5; Sheffield: Sheffield Academic Press, 1978), 203–5.

185. E.g., a second Arad is known from the annals of Shishak, called Arad *yrchm*, or perhaps Yerucham.

186. Aharoni, *Land of the Bible*, 201.

187. A. Kempinski, "Tel Masos," *NEAEHL*, 3:986–89. V. Fritz, "Tel Masos," *OEANE*, 3:437–39.

188. In the conquest Arad and Hormah are separate towns with individual kings (Josh. 10:40; 12:14), probably included among those defeated in the Negev.

189. Aharoni, *Land of the Bible*, 58.

190. P. Budd, *Numbers* (WBC; Waco, Tex.: Word, 1984), 230.

191. See Brisco, *Holman Bible Atlas*, 72, map 32.

192. Ashley, *Numbers*, 404–5. D. J. Wiseman translated it as "venomous" in "Flying Serpents," *TynBul* 23 (1972): 108–10. The former view of this term referring to a species seems more likely in the broader context.

193. T. E. Lawrence (of Arabia), *Revolt in the Desert* (New York: Doran, 1927), 93.

194. See discussion in Harrison, *Numbers*, 276.

195. A biblical parallel to this ritual is the Philistine votive gold offerings in the form of the disease (perhaps boils formed on the body from bubonic plague) and the determined instrument of the disease (mice), offered to the Lord by placing them in the ark of the covenant and returning it to the Israelites at Beth Shemesh (1 Sam. 5:6–6:18).

196. B. Rothenberg, *Timna: Valley of the Biblical Copper Mines* (London: Thames & Hudson, 1972), esp. 125–207, fig. 41and color plates XIX-XX; idem, *The Egyptian Mining Temple of Timna* (London: Thames & Hudson, 1988). See also B. Rothenberg and J. Glass, "The Midianite Pottery," in *Midian, Moab, and Edom*, ed. J. F. A. Sawyer and D. J. A. Clines (JSOTSup 24; Sheffield: Sheffield Academic Press, 1983), 65–124.

197. For an analysis of the role of serpent iconography in the history of the cults of Israel and Egypt, see K. R. Joines, "The Bronze Serpent in the Israelite Cult," *JBL* 87 (1968): 245–56; idem, *Serpent Symbolism in the Old Testament* (Haddonfield, N.J.: Haddonfield House, 1974), 85–96; Wiseman, "Flying Serpents," 108–10.

198. E. Stern, "A Late Bronze Age Temple at Tell Mevorakh," *BA* 40 (1977): 89–91.

199. Joines, "Bronze Serpent," 251.

200. Ancient Kalḫu; Layard at the time believed he was digging at Nineveh and published the bowls in *Monuments of Nineveh II* (1953), plates 56–68.

201. For much of this information, including a record of the find and a list of all the names, see R. D.

Barnett, "Layard's Nimrud Bronzes and Their Inscriptions," *ErIsr* 8 (1967): 1*–7*.

202. Perhaps meaning "Waheb in a Storm-wind/whirlwind."

203. For further analysis of the northern border of Moab during the Iron Age, see P. M. M. Daviau, "Moab's Northern Border: Khirbet al-Mudayna on the Wadi ath-Thamad," *BA* 60/4 (1997): 222–28.

204. In Isa. 15:1 Ar is paralleled with Kir of Moab, a title for the capital of the Moabites. The destruction of Ar and/or Kir represents the destruction of the entire country.

205. My translation, taking vv. 19–20 as a continuation of the song, since neither of the verbs of journey ("they departed" or "they encamped") occurs here.

206. Cf. Simons, *Geographical and Topographical Texts*, 62; Harrison, *Numbers*, 282.

207. Aharoni, *Land of the Bible*, 436.

208. *ANET*, 320, line 27. Beth-baal-meon of line 30 could be another possibility since it is mentioned with Madaba and Beth-diblathen, which are also in this general vicinity.

209. The Mesha Stele (lines 18–20) mentions a Jahaz close to Dibon, which belonged to the Moabites during their expansion northward in the late tenth to early ninth century B.C. (cf. Josh. 13:18; Judg. 11:20; and the oracles against Moab in Isa. 15:4; Jer. 48:34). Aharoni located it at Kh. el-Medeiyineh (also Iye Abarim), eleven miles northeast of Dibon and the same distance southeast of Madaba. There are other suggestions; cf. also Simons, *Geographical and Topographical Texts*, 262.

210. L. Herr, "The Amman Airport Structure and the Geopolitics of Ancient Transjordan," *BA* 46 (1983): 223–29. Herr also edited *The Amman Airport Excavations, 1976* (ASOR Annual 48; Winona Lake, Ind.: ASOR/Eisenbrauns, 1983).

211. See L. Geraty, "'Umeiri, Tell el-," *OEANE*, 5:273–74; L. Geraty et al., *The Madaba Plains Project: The 1984 Season at Tell el-Umeiri and Vicinity and Subsequent Studies* (Berrien Springs, Mich.: Andrew Univ. Press, 1989), as well as subsequent volumes.

212. L. Geraty, "Hesban," *OEANE*, 3:20–22; idem "Heshbon," *ABD*, 3:181–84; R. Boraas et al., *Heshbon, 1968–76*, vols. 1–10 (Andrews Univ. Monographs; Berrien Springs, Mich.: Andrews Univ. Press, 1969–78).

213. S. Horn, "Heshbon," *EAEHL*, 510–14; J. A. Dearman, "Roads and Settlements in Moab," *BA* 60/4 (1997): 205–13.

214. R. W. Younker, "Moabite Social Structure," *BA* 60/4 (1997): 237–48. Cf. also G. Mattingly, "The Culture-Historical Approach and Moabite Origins," in *Early Edom and Moab: The Beginnings of the Iron Age in Southern Jordan*, ed. P. Bienkowski (Sheffield Archaeological Monographs 7; Sheffield: Collis, 1992), 55–64. Surveys and excavations continue in the Madaba Plains Project.

215. G. Mattingly, "Moabite Religion," in *Studies in the Mesha Inscription and Moab*, ed. P. J. King (Atlanta: Scholars Press, 1989), 216–27; idem, "Chemosh," *ABD*, 1:895–97; H.-P. Müller, "Chemosh," *DDD²*, 186–89.

216. Cf. translation of W. F. Albright, "The Moabite Stone," in *ANET*, 320–21.

217. Noth, *Numbers*, 236–37.

218. Simons, *Geographical and Topographical Texts*, 119, 300.

219. Ibid., 124, 302; G. Mattingly, "Edrei," *ABD*, 2:301. This site, located sixty miles south of Damascus on an eastern tributary of the Yarmuk River, contains remnants of a Late Bronze occupation.

220. *ANET*, 278.

221. W. F. Albright, "Some Important Recent Discoveries: Alphabetic Origins and the Idrimi Statue," *BASOR* 118 (1950): 15–16. Idrimi, the fifteenth-to fourteenth-century B.C. king of Alalakh, is said to have ruled over the regions of Mukishkhe, Ni, and Amau. See also A. Millard, "The Hazael Booty Inscriptions," in *COS*, 2.40; also 2.113. ii.35b–40a, 81b–86a.

222. M. Weinfeld, "Ancient Near Eastern Patterns in Prophetic Literature," in *The Place is Too Small for Us: The Israelite Prophets in Recent Scholarship*, ed. R. Gordon (Winona Lake, Ind: Eisenbrauns, 1995), 32–49. For additional resources on prophecy in the ancient Near East, see also T. Abusch, *Babylonian Witchcraft Literature* (BJS 132; Atlanta: Scholars Press, 1987); T. Abusch and K. van der Toorn, *Mesopotamian Magic* (Groningen: Styx, 1999); Cryer, *Divination in Ancient Israel*; U. Jeyes, *Old Babylonian Extispicy* (Istanbul: Nederlands Historisch-Archaeologisch Instituut, 1989); M. Nissinen, *References to Prophecy in Neo-Assyrian Sources* (SAA 7; Helsinki: Helsinki Univ. Press, 1998); idem, *Prophecy in its Near Eastern Context* (Atlanta: Scholars Press, 2000); idem, *Prophets and Prophecy in the Ancient Near East* (SBLWAW 12; Atlanta: Scholars Press, 2003); S. Parpola, *Letters from Assyrian and Babylonian Scholars* (SAA 10; Helsinki: Helsinki Univ. Press, 1993); idem, *Assyrian Prophecies* (SAA 9; Helsinki: Helsinki Univ. Press, 1997); T. Abusch, *Mesopotamian Witchcraft: Toward a History and Understanding of Babylonian Witchcraft Beliefs and Literature* (Ancient Magic and Divination 5; Leiden: Brill-Styx, 2002); L. Ciraolo and J. Seidel, *Magic and Divination in the Ancient World* (Leiden: Brill-Styx, 2002).

223. *CAD* I, "A" Part II, 235; cf. R. Harper, "Code of Hammurabi," xliv, L83, 89; *ANET*, "The Code of Hammurabi: The Epilogue," 178–79 (L19–97).

224. Cf. M. Ginsburger, *Pseudo-Jonathan (Thargum Jonathan ben Usiel zum Pentateuch)* (Berlin: S. Calvary, 1903); Milgrom, *Numbers*, 187; A. B. Ehrlich, *Randglossen zur Hebräischen Bibel: Textkritisches, sprachliches, und sachliches* (Leipzig: Hinrichs, 1909), 193.

225. V. Hurowitz, "The Expression *ûqsāmîm bᵉyādān* (Numbers 22:7) in Light of Divinatory Practices from Mari," *HS* 33 (1992): 5–15, esp. 12–13.

226. *ANET*, 24.

227. *ANET*, 428–29.

228. Harrison notes that "as the donkey brayed, she conveyed a message of anger and resentment that the seer understood in his mind in a verbal form" (*Numbers*, 300); cf. Milgrom, *Numbers*, 191; Cole, *Numbers*, 392–93.

229. A. Biran, "The *husot* of Dan," *ErIsr* 26 (1999): 25–29; idem, "Sacred Spaces: Of Standing Stones, High Places and Cult Objects at Tel Dan," *BAR* 24/5 (1998): 39–45, 70–2; see picture and caption on 44.

230. Bamoth alone in the Mesha Stele, L3 as well as Isa. 15:2; 16:12; Jer. 48:35; Beth Bamoth in Mesha L27; and Bamoth Baal here and in Josh. 13:17.

231. R. Largement, "Les oracles de Bileam et la mantique suméro-akkadienne," in *Memorial du cinquatenaire 1914–1964* (Paris: Travaux de l'Institut de Paris, 1964), 46. Also in Virgil's *Aeneid* seven head of cattle and seven sheep are offered as sacrifices, 6.38–39.

232. Cf. in the Baal Cycle in the dedication of Baal's house (*CAT*, 1.4 VI:40–43) and in the mourning when Baal has died (*KTU*, 1.6, I:18–29); for translations see Smith, *Ugaritic Narrative Poetry*, 134, 152. For tabulation of animals in ritual texts from Ugarit, see Pardee, *Ritual and Cult at Ugarit*, 224–25.

233. For larger discussion of animal sacrifices, see J. Scurlock, "Animal Sacrifice in Ancient Mesopotamia," in *History of the Animal World in the Ancient Near East*, ed. B. J. Collins (Leiden: Brill, 2002), 389–404.

234. Milgrom, *Numbers*, excursus 19: "Balaam: Diviner or Sorcerer?" 471–73; cf. Noordtzij, *Numbers*, 219.

235. R. I. Caplice, "The Namburbi Texts in the British Museum," *Or* 54 (1965): 116; idem, *The Akkadian Namburbi Texts: An Introduction*, 199.

236. R. Harris, "Inanna-Ishtar as Paradox and a Coincidence of Opposites," in *Gender and Aging in Mesopotamia* (Norman, Okla.: Univ. of Oklahoma Press, 2000), 158–71.

237. A couple of examples include Ea's misleading advice to Adapa regarding the food and drink that Anu would offer him (*COS*, 1.129), and the same god's advice to Atraḫasis on how to mislead the people of Shuruppak when the flood was approaching (*COS*, 1.130, 452 lines 29–49).

238. *ANET*, 165.

239. *ANEP*, 168, 170. Note the Apis bull of Egypt, *ANEP*, 190–91.

240. B. Mazar et al., *Views of the Biblical World* (Chicago: Jordan, 1959), 1:228.

241. N. S. Fox, "Clapping Hands as a Gesture of Anguish and Anger in Mesopotamia and Israel," *JANES* 23 (1995): 49–60, esp. 54.

242. Ibid., 50; Akk. *ritti rapasu*, see *CAD* R, 151, 386.

243. C. Roth, "Star and Anchor: Coin Symbolism and the Early Days," *ErIsr* 6 (1960): 13–16.

244. *ANEP*, 312–13.

245. B. Halpern, "Kenites," *ABD*, 4:17–22.

246. Y. Aharoni, *Arad Inscriptions* (Jerusalem: Israel Exploration Society, 1981), 12–13.

247. N. Glueck, *Explorations in Eastern Palestine*, AASOR 25–28 (New Haven, Conn: ASOR, 1945–48): 221, 371–82.

248. Josephus, *Ant.* 4.8.1; 5.1.1. Cf. Ashley, *Numbers*, 516; Harrison, *Numbers*, 335; Milgrom, *Numbers*, 212; Wenham, *Numbers*, 184.

249. Milgrom, *Numbers*, 213.

250. *ANET*, 179.

251. A. Green, *The Storm God in the Ancient Near East* (Winona Lake, Ind.: Eisenbrauns, 2003); D. Fleming, "The Storm God of Canaan in Emar," *UF* 26 (1995): 127–30; N. Wyatt, "The Titles of the Ugaritic Storm-God," *UF* 24 (1993): 403–24; I. Cornelius, *The Iconography of the Canaanite Gods Reshef and Ba'al: Late Bronze and Iron Age I (1500–1000 B.C.)* (OBO 140; Gottingen: Vandenhoeck & Ruprecht, 1994).

252. Cf. the use of the phrase in 2 Sam. 12:12.

253. R. Polzin has suggested the meaning of "dismember" in "'HWQY' and Covenantal Institutions in Early Israel," *HTR* 62 (1969): 227–40. The Qal form of the verb means "dislocate, sprain" as happened to Jacob's hip when he wrestled with the angel at Penuel (Gen. 32:26). Cf. also the Code of Hammurabi, 153.

254. Cf. Joshua and the Israelites' treatment of the five kings of the coalition of southern Canaanite cities who attacked the city of Gibeon, which incident precipitated the southern campaign of the conquest (Josh. 10:11–27).

255. *ANET*, 265, 271–74.

256. *ARM*, 1.42 contains a military census; *ARM*, 1.7.31–45 contains a land census.

257. Milgrom, *Numbers*, 219.

258. A. M. Kitz, "Undivided Inheritance and Lot Casting in the Book of Joshua," *JBL* 119 (2000): 601–18; M. Hudson and B. Levine, *Urbanization and Land Ownership in the Ancient Near East* (Cambridge, Mass.: Harvard Univ. Press, 1999); K. E. Slanski, *The Babylonian Entitlement* Narûs (Kudurrus) (Boston: ASOR, 2003).

259. M. Civil, "New Sumerian Law Fragments," *Assyriological Studies* 16 (1965): 4–6; Gudea Statute B, VII.44–48.

260. Z. Ben-Barak, "Inheritance by Daughters in the Ancient Near East," *JSS* 25 (1980): 22–34. See also G. R. Driver and J. C. Miles, *The Babylonian Laws I* (Clarendon Press: Oxford, 1956), 335–41.

261. J. Vercoutter, "La femme en Igypte ancienne," in *Histoire mondiale de la femme*, ed. P. Grimal (Paris: Nouvelle libraire de France, 1956), 143–46.

262. H. J. Marsman, *Women in Ugarit and Israel* (Leiden: Brill, 2003), 389–400.

263. Cf. also 8:10–13. For laying on the hands in substitutionary identification in the Israelite sacrificial system, see Lev. 1:4; 3:2; 4:22; 8:6–22; 16:21; et al.

264. J. Walton, et al., eds., *The IVP Bible Background Commentary: Old Testament* (Downers Grove, Ill.: InterVarsity Press, 2000), 164. The tombs were published in six volumes by N. de Garis Davies, *The Rock Tombs of El Amarna*, between 1903 and 1908. They were republished by the Egyptian Exploration Society in 2004–2005.

265. C. van Dam, *The Urim and Thummim: A Means of Revelation in Ancient Israel* (Winona Lake, Ind.:

Eisenbrauns, 1997); Harrison, *Numbers*, 359. See also the view of the use of the Urim and Thummim as "lot-oracle" set forth by A. Goetze, *Kulturgeschichte Kleinasiens* (Munich: C. H. Beck, 1957), 148–50.

    See also W. Horowitz, and V. Hurowitz, "Urim and Thummim in Light of a Psephomancy Ritual from Assur (LKA 137)," *JANES* 24 (1992): 95–115.

266. M. E. Cohen, *Cultic Calendars of the Ancient Near East* (Bethesda, Md.: CDL, 1993).

267. J. C. de Moor, *Anthology of Religious Texts from Ugarit* (Leiden: Brill, 1987), 158; idem, *New Year with the Canaanites and Israelites*, 2 vols. (Kampen: Kok, 1972), 1:6; 2:13; M. S. Smith, *Untold Stories: The Bible and Ugaritic Studies in the 20th Century* (Peabody, Mass.: Hendrickson, 2001), 90–92; idem, *Ugaritic Baal Cycle* (Leiden: Brill, 1994), 1:90–106.

268. COS, 1.83, '15.

269. Fleming, *Time at Emar*, 143–89, esp. 175–79.

270. King and Stager, *Life in Biblical Israel*, 87–88.

271. S. A. Scham, "Eating and Drinking in the Ancient Near East," *NEA* 67 (2004): 64–117.

272. Fleming, *Time at Emar*, 193.

273. G. Vermes, *Dead Sea Scrolls in English*, 44, 79–80, 152.

274. Fleming, *Time at Emar*, 133–40, 148.

275. Cartledge, *Vows in the Hebrew Bible*, 25.

276. Ibid., 74–91.

277. KRT A.iv.198–210, ANET, 144–45. See also S. B. Parker, "The Vow in Ugaritic and Israelite Narrative Literature," *UF* 11 (1979): 693–700; C. Virolleaud, "Les nouvelles tablettes de Ras Shamra (1948–1949)," *Syria* 28 (1951): 27–28. Cf. also CTA, I.50 (=UT, 117).

278. W. F. Albright, "A Votive Stele Erected by Ben-Hadad I of Damascus to the God Melcarth," *BASOR* 87 (1942): 23–29; F. M. Cross, "The Stele Dedicated to Melcarth by Ben-Hadad of Damascus," *BASOR* 205 (1972): 36–42; J. C. L. Gibson, *Textbook of Syrian Semitic Inscriptions II* (Oxford: Clarendon, 1971), 1.

279. A. Barucq, *Hymnes et prières de l'Egypte ancienne* (Paris: Cerf, 1980), 36. Cf. *Near Eastern Religious Texts Relating to the Old Testament*, ed. W. Beyerlin, trans. J. Bowden (Philadelphia: Westminster, 1978), 34.

280. Cartledge, *Vows in the Hebrew Bible*, 34.

281. R. Labat, *Traite akkadien de diagnostics et pronostics médicaux* (Paris: Académie internationale, 1951), 37.

282. P. J. Parr, "Midian," *OEANE* 4:25; J. Sawyer and D. Clines, eds., *Midian, Moab, and Edom*, esp. the articles by E. J. Payne ("The Midianite Arc"), E. A. Knauf ("Midianites and Ishmaelites"), and B. Rothenberg and J. Glass ("The Midianite Pottery").

283. ANET, 320.

284. Those favoring the use of the ark include N. Snaith, *Leviticus-Numbers*, 194–95; Ashley, *Numbers*, 592; those against its use in this kind of an operation include Budd, *Numbers*, 330, who suggests that "these objects appear to take the place of the ark." Noth, *Numbers*, 229, states that the ark would have been taken automatically and thus would not be categorized among these items.

285. Noordtzij, *Numbers*, 271; also Targum Pseudo-Jonathan; Milgrom, *Numbers*, 257; contra Ashley, *Numbers*, 592; Harrison, *Numbers*, 383.

286. Note the use of the phrase "house of a father," as in 1:4; 25:14, 15, et al. Similar phrases are used for Zur the Midianite, who was called a "chief (head) of people of a patriarchal house in Midian" (25:15), compared to Zimri the Israelite, who was called a "prince of a patriarchal house of the Simeonites" (25:14).

287. Akkadian *miksu* (CAD 10:63–64) denoted the share paid to the royal palace as owner of the fields, and a *bēt miksi* was a storehouse for taxes collected. For rabbinical sources, see M. Sokoloff, *A Dictionary of Jewish Palestinian Aramaic of the Byzantine Period* (Ramat-Gan, Israel: Bar Ilan Univ. Press, 1992), 308.

288. ANET, 237.

289. C. Humphreys, "The Number of People in the Exodus from Egypt: Decoding Mathematically the Very Large Numbers in Numbers I and XXVI," *VT* 48 (1998): 196–213.

290. C. H. Gordon, *Ugaritic Textbook*, texts 170 and 301; cf. M. Ottosson, "Gilead," *ABD*, 2:1020.

291. H. Tadmor prefers the reading ᵘʳᵘ ga-al-ʿa-[a] (?)-[di] and finds it in Summary Inscriptions 9:r.3 and 4:6, *The Inscriptions of Tiglath-Pileser III King of Assyria* (Jerusalem: Israel Academy of Sciences and Humanities, 1994), 186–87.

292. ANET, 320.

293. "Dibon," *OEANE*, 2:175–77.

294. Baal Meon is also called Beth Baal Meon in Josh. 13:17 and the Mesha Stele (l. 31), and Beth Meon by Jeremiah in his oracle against Moab (48:23).

295. See ANET, 322; Gibson, *Textbook of Syrian Semitic Inscriptions I*, 49–54; cf. Ezra 5:7–17; Dan. 2:4.

296. Milgrom, *Numbers*, 270. Cf. G. L. Harding, "The Cairn of Hani," *Annual of the Dept. of Antiquities of Jordan* 2 (1953): 8–56.

297. Noordztij, *Numbers*, 281.

298. Note also the discussion of the Gadite territory and cities in Simons, *Geographical and Topographical Texts*, 119–23; Aharoni, *Land of the Bible*, 207. See also D. Howard, *Joshua* (NAC; Nashville: Broadman & Holman, 1998), 313–14.

299. Note also the discussion of the territory of Reuben and its cities in Simons, *Geographical and Topographical Texts*, 115–19; Aharoni, *Land of the Bible*, 207–8.

300. Simons, *Geographical and Topographical Texts*, 118; Aharoni, *Land of the Bible*, 142, 337, 438.

301. Simons, *Geographical and Topographical Texts*, 123–25; Aharoni, *Land of the Bible*, 314. Cf. Howard, *Joshua*, 314–15.

302. G. W. Coats, "The Wilderness Itinerary," *CBQ* 34 (1972): 135–52; G. I. Davies, *The Way of the Wilderness: A Geographical Analysis of the Wilderness Itineraries in the Old Testament* (SOTSMS 5; Cambridge: Cambridge Univ. Press, 1979); idem, "The Wilderness Itineraries: A Comparative Approach," *TynBul* 25 (1974): 46–81; idem, "The

Wilderness Itineraries and the Composition of the Pentateuch," *VT* 33 (1983): 1–13.

303. Cf. D. Redford, "A Bronze Age Itinerary in Transjordan (Nos. 89–101 of Thutmose III's List of Asiatic Toponyms)," *JSSEA* 9 (1982): 55–74; Hoffmeier, *Israel in Egypt*, 176–98.

304. *ANET*, 276–87.

305. A standard "day's journey" was twelve to fourteen miles in Late Bronze Egypt, and the statement in Deut. 1:2 is a distance statement rather than a chronological statement concerning how many days the Israelites journeyed.

306. See J. Day, "Asherah," *ABD*, 1:483–87;

307. For a detailed discussion of the stone-working industry see P. R. S. Moorey, *Ancient Mesopotamian Materials and Industries: The Archaeological Evidence* (Winona Lake, Ind.: Eisenbrauns, 1994), 21–110.

308. For a discussion of iconography in its conception and function see Z. Bahrani, *The Graven Image: Representation in Babylonia and Assyria* (Philadelphia: Univ. of Pennsylvania Press, 2003), 73–88.

309. For a detailed discussion of the metallurgical industry, see Moorey, *Materials and Industries*, 216–301, esp. 224–25, 255–73.

310. For examples and discussion see King and Stager, *Life in Biblical Israel*, 348–53; O. Keel, "Iconography and the Bible," *ABD*, 3:358–74; D. I. Block, *The Gods of the Nations: Studies in Ancient Near Eastern National Theology* (Grand Rapids: Baker, 1988, 2000), 68–71.

311. See discussion in Z. Zevit, *Religions of Ancient Israel* (New York: Continuum, 2001), 262–3; J. T. Whitney, "Bamoth in the Old Testament," *TynBul* 30 (1979): 125–47; M. D. Fowler, "The Israelite *bāmâ*: A Question of Interpretation," *ZAW* 94 (1982): 203–13; J. M. Grintz, "Some Observations on the 'High Place' in the History of Israel," *VT* 27 (1977): 111–13; E. C. LaRocca-Pitts, *Of Wood and Stone* (HSM 61; Winona Lake, Ind.: Eisenbrauns, 2001), 127–59; J. E. Catron, "Temple and *Bamah*: Some Considerations," in *The Pitcher is Broken: Memorial Essays for Gösta W. Ahlström*, ed. S. W. Holloway and L. K. Handy (JSOTSup 190; Sheffield: JSOT, 1995), 150–65; A. Biran, "Sacred Spaces: Of Standing Stones, High Places and Cult Objects at Tel Dan," *BAR* 24 (1998): 38–45, 70; B. Alpert Nakhai, *Archaeology and the Religions of Canaan and Israel* (Boston: ASOR, 2001), 161–200; idem, "What's a Bamah? How Sacred Space Functioned in Ancient Israel," *BAR* 20/3 (1994): 18–29, 77–78.

312. Compare finds from the open-air bull site found in a survey of the Dothan region of Samaria (A. Mazar, "The Bull Site: An Iron Age I Cult Place," *BASOR* 247 [1982]: 27–42); a worship center at Kuntillet ʾAjrud about thirty miles south of Kadesh Barnea (Z. Meshel, "Kuntillet ʾAjrud," *ABD*, 4:103–9); or the high place at the entry to Bethsaida (R. Arav, "Bethsaida Rediscovered," *BAR* 26/1 [2000]: 48–49).

313. *ANET*, 234–55.

314. I. Beit-Arieh, "Edomites Advance into Judah: Israelite Defensive Fortresses Inadequate," *BAR* 22/6 (1996): 28–36. Fortresses built by the Israelites throughout the southern Negev region during the ninth and eighth centuries B.C., and possibly even earlier, may have been constructed with this potential threat in mind from Edomites.

315. Better translated as "from the south of the Ascent of the Scorpions."

316. Portions of the Roman Maʾale Aqrabbim can be seen today just west of the modern road.

317. Aharoni, *Land of the Bible*, 72.

318. Cf. Josh. 13:2–6; Judg. 1:19, 27, 29, 31; 3:3 for the unconquered lands of the early Israelite emergence in Canaan. See also 2 Sam. 5:17–25; 8:1–14; 2 Chron. 2:1–16 for the Israelite relations with Hiram, king of Tyre of the Phoenicians.

319. Cf. Milgrom, *Numbers*, 286; Aharoni, *Land of the Bible*, 72–73.

320. So also Aharoni, *Land of the Bible*, 73.

321. See Gray, *Numbers*, 461.

322. *ANET*, 247, 483–90. See also R. Boling, *The Levitical Cities: Archaeology and Texts* (Winona Lake, Ind.: Eisenbrauns, 1985); A. Taggar-Cohen, "Law and Family in the Book of Numbers: The Levites and the *Tidennutu* Documents from Nuzi," *VT* 48 (1998): 74–94.

323. For extensive discussion of the form and function of Levitical cities, see Milgrom, *Numbers*, excursus 74: "The Levitical Town—An Exercise in Realistic Planning," 502–4.

324. R. L. Hubbard Jr., "The *Goʾel* in Ancient Israel: Theological Reflections on an Israelite Institution," *BBR* 1 (1991): 3–19.

325. Brin, *Studies in Biblical Law*, 90–101.

326. For expanded discussion of the concept and function of the cities of refuge, see M. Greenberg, "The Biblical Conception of Asylum," *JBL* 78 (1959): 125–32; Milgrom, *Numbers*, excursus 75: "Asylum Altars and Asylum Cities," 504–9.

327. *ANET*, 166, L9–11, 13. Cf. Deut. 17:6; 19:15; Matt. 18:16; John 8:17; 2 Cor. 13:1; Heb. 10:28.

Sidebar and Chart Notes

A-1. Fouts, "Use of Large Numbers," 27–38; idem, "Defense of the Large Numbers," 377–87.

A-2. The basic Semitic root ʾlp vocalized as ʾelep is attested as "thousands" in Aramaic, Arabic, Sabean, and others. The alternative vocalization ʾallup is generally translated "chief" as in Ex. 15:15 or "clan" in Gen. 36:15; Zech. 12:5, 6. The interpretation is supported by the LB Mari usage of ʾlp as "clan" (ARM, 1.23.42; 6.33.65); see A. Malamat, "A Recently Discovered Word for 'Clan' in Mari and Its Hebrew Cognate," in *Solving Riddles and Untying Knots: Biblical and Epigraphic and Semitic Studies in Honor of Jonas C. Greenfield*, ed. Z. Zevit, S. Gitin, and M. Sokoloff (Winona Lake, Ind.: Eisenbrauns, 1995), 177–79.

A-3. Westbrook, *HANEL*, 43, 666–68; G. Beckman, "Family Values on the Middle Euphrates," in *New Horizons in the Study of Ancient Syria*, ed. M. Chavalas and J. Hayes (Bibliotheca Mesopotamia 25; Malibu: Undena, 1992), 68–71.

A-4. G. J. Wenham, "Leviticus 27:2–8 and the Price of Slaves," *ZAW* 90 (1978): 254–65. Cf. also Harrison, *Numbers*, 75–78.

A-5. Literally, "points a finger," *ANET*, 171 §132.

A-6. Matthews and Benjamin, *Old Testament Parallels*, 105. Note also the Middle Assyrian code of Tiglath-pileser I (1115–1007 B.C.), which cites the case of a suspected adulterous woman who is tried by ordeal in the river (ibid., 116 art. 17).

A-7. Milgrom, *Numbers* (excursus 8: "The Judicial Ordeal," 347).

A-8. Brichto, "The Case of the *Sota*," 66.

A-9. W. E. Shewell-Copper, "Coriander," *ZPEB*, 1:960; Borowski, *Agriculture in Iron Age Israel*, 98; *Fauna and Flora of the Bible* (New York: United Bible Societies, 1980), 110–11. Also cf. J. M. Renfrew, *Palaeoethnobotany: The Prehistoric Food Plants of the Near East* (New York: Columbia Univ. Press, 1973), 171, who notes that though coriander has not yet been found in excavations of Syro-Palestine, samples have been unearthed in the tomb of Tutankhamun in the Valley of the Kings and in the Neo-Assyrian fortress of Nimrud.

A-10. See Milgrom, *Numbers*, 84, 308; D. Bowes, "Bdellium," *ZPEB*, 1:494; *Fauna and Flora of the Bible*, 96.

A-11. B. S. Childs, *The Book of Exodus* (Philadelphia: Westminster, 1974), 282. See also F. S. Bodenheimer, "The Manna of Sinai," *BA* 10 (1947): 2–6 (reprinted in *BARead*, 1:76–80).

A-12. COS, 1.132.

A-13. *ANET*, 328.

A-14. *ANEP*, 106–8, 117–18.

A-15. COS, 1.83 §19.

A-16. This phraseology is found elsewhere only in Ex. 13:2, 12–15; 34:19; Num. 3:12; 8:16; Ezek. 20:26. Male firstlings are specified in Ex. 34:19–20.

A-17. Milgrom, *Numbers*, 152; also excursus 45: "The First-Born," 431–32.

A-18. On the use of the Urim and Thummim and the *goral*-lot, see Cryer, *Divination in Ancient Israel*, 273–77.

A-19. Cf. an eighth-century date suggested by J. Naveh, "The Date of the Deir ʿAlla Inscriptions in Aramaic Script," *IEJ* 17 (1967): 256–58; a seventh-century date by F. M. Cross, "Notes on the Ammonite Inscription from Tell Sôrân," *BASOR* 212 (1973): 12–15; in contrast to the original dating by the excavator to the Persian sixth century, see H. J. Franken, "Texts from the Persian Period from Tell Deir ʿAlla," *VT* 17 (1967): 480–81.

A-20. See the paleographic discussions in J. Hackett, *The Balaam Text from Deir ʿAlla* (HSM 31; Chico, Calif.: Scholars Press, 1984), 1–19. Note also Milgrom, *Numbers*, excursus 60: "Balaam and the Deir ʿAlla Inscription," 473–74. See also B. A. Levine, "The Deir ʿAlla Plaster Inscriptions," in COS, 2.27.

A-21. Milgrom, *Numbers*, 476.

A-22. Translation that of the author based on the combinations of J. Hackett.

A-23. M. Bietak, *Tell ed-Daba*, 2 (Untersuchungen der Zweigstelle Kairo des Osterreichischen Archäologischen Instituts, Band I; Wien: Osterreichischen Akademie der Wissenschaften, 1975), 179–221. See also idem, *Avaris and Piramesse: Archaeological Exploration in the Eastern Nile Delta* (Proceedings of the British Academy 65; London: Oxford Univ. Press, 1986); Hoffmeier, *Israel in Egypt*, 63–65.

A-24. See Kitchen, *Reliability*, 254–56; J. Dorner, *Ägypten und Levante* 9 (1999): 121–33.

A-25. Hoffmeier, *Israel in Egypt*, 120; Kitchen, *Reliability*, 257–59.

A-26. Hoffmeier, *Israel in Egypt*, 169–71; 188–89.

A-27. For Cycles I–IV sites are suggested relative to locating Mount Sinai at either Jebel Sin Bisher (JSB) or Jebel Musa (JM). SP = Samaritan Pentateuch, LXX = Septuagint.

A-28. Kitchen, *Reliability*, 271.

A-29. Hoffmeier, *Israel in Egypt*, 182–83; 199–222. Yam Suph in the Bible is the name applied to what is today the Red Sea and its upper fingers the Gulf of Suez (W) and the Gulf of Aqaba (E). Recent geological surveys suggest that the Gulf of Suez extended into the Bitter Lakes region during the Late Bronze Age.

A-30. The southern route would have bypassed most of the Egyptian presence in the region except for the copper/turquoise mines of Serabit el-Khadim, which were worked during the fall and winter months, but not in the spring and summer because of extremely high temperatures. See Kitchen, *Reliability*, 268, 558 n.60.

A-31. Davies, *Way of the Wilderness*, 84.

A-32. For a detailed analysis of the location of Mount Sinai, see Davies, *The Way of the Wilderness*; idem, "Sinai, Mount," *ABD*, 6:48:1; Harel, "Sinai," 5:1021–22; idem, "The Route of the Exodus"; G. E. Wright, "Sinai," *IDB*, 4:376–78; Aharoni, *The Land of the Bible*, 197–99. Survey results in northern Sinai are found in E. I. Oren, "Sinai," *OEANE*, 5:41–47; Hoffmeier, *Israel in Egypt*, 126; see 107–34 for additional data regarding the literary and chronological evidence for Israel in Egypt.

A-33. B. Rothenberg, "Tell el-Kheleifeh: Ezion Geber: Elath," *PEQ* 94 (1962): 44–56; G. Pratico, "A Reappraisal of the Site Archaeologist Nelson Glueck Identified as King Solomon's Sea Port," *BAR* 12/5 (1986): 24–35; M. Lubetski, "Ezion-Geber," *ABD*, 2:723–26.

A-34. Identified as such by N. Glueck, "Ezion-geber," *BA* 28 (1965): 70–87; idem, "The Third Season of Excavation at Tel el-Kheleifeh," *BASOR* 79 (1940): 2–18.

A-35. Simons, *Geographical and Topographical Texts*, 439; E. A. Knauf, "Punon," *ABD*, 5:556–57. Knauf suggests Punon is the name of the district rather than simply a village site. Note also P. J. Parr, "Aspects of the Archaeology of North-West Arabia in the First Millennium B.C.," in *L'Arabie préislamique et son envione-*

ment historique et culturel, ed. T. Fahd (Leiden: Brill, 1988), 39–66.

A-36. Davies, *Way of the Wilderness*, 90.

A-37. G. Mattingly, "Iye-Abarim," *ABD*, 3:588.

A-38. See W. H. Morton, "Summary of the 1955, 1956, and 1965 Excavations at Dhiban," in *Studies in Mesha Inscription and Moab*, ed. A. Dearman (Atlanta: Scholars Press, 1989), 239–46; A. D. Tushingham, "Dibon," *ABD*, 2194–96; *OEANE*, 2:156–58.

A-39. *ANET*, 320.

A-40. Simons, *Geographical and Topographical Texts*, 440, suggests the existence of twin cities of Almon Diblathaim and Beth Diblathaim to be identified with the mounds of Keleilat el-Gharbiyeh and Deleilat esh-Sherqiyeh respectively, due north of Dhiban.

A-41. Near the Dead Sea, ten miles south of Jericho according to Eusebius, *Onomasticon.*

A-42. Following Milgrom, *Numbers*, 282, and Rabba bar Hana, estimates are that the Israelite encampment would have covered about 4,020 yards square = 2.28 x 2.28 miles = 5.2 square miles (3 x 3 Persian parsangs; 1 parsang = 1,219 meters).

DEUTERONOMY

by Eugene E. Carpenter

Introduction

Historical Setting

In three powerful speeches, Moses expounds the law (*tôrâ*, 1:5) forty years after the Lord has delivered Israel from Egypt. The people have "wandered" forty years in the wilderness of the Sinai Peninsula, including spending a year at Mount Sinai, where God made a covenant with his people (Ex. 19–24). At this time Egypt is weakening, but still ruled the ancient Near East. The pharaohs have stopped major expeditions into the land of Canaan, which now allows Israel a providential opportunity to gain a foothold in the land.

Plowing with donkey and ox.
Jim Monson, Bible Backgrounds

The larger historical-cultural milieu for Israel's experiences with Egypt was the New Kingdom Empire (ca. 1550–1069 B.C., Dynasties 18–20). After a decline in the New Kingdom after Ramesses II (1279–13 B.C.), a brief revival occurred under Ramesses III (1185–1154); but thereafter the Egyptian influence declined into the late periods of the nation (Dynasties 21–30).[1]

The date of the Exodus fixes the date of these three speeches of Moses. Two approximate dates vie for recognition currently: an early date (ca. 1446 B.C.) and a late date (ca. 1269 B.C.). Allowing forty years for the wilderness wanderings places Moses in the Plains of Moab at about 1406 or 1229. Thutmose III (1479–25 B.C.) and Amenophis II (1427–1396) would have been in power during an Eighteenth Dynasty exodus, while Seti I (Sethos, 1294–79 B.C.) and Ramesses II (1279–13) would likely have been in power during a Nineteenth Dynasty exodus event.[2] The next pharaoh, Merneptah (1213–1203 B.C.), erected a stele in western Thebes that records many of his victories. In a small section, he mentions Israel, as a people, already in Canaan in 1209 B.C. While he claims to have wiped out the seed of Israel, ironically his stele is the earliest extrabiblical witness to their presence in the land of Palestine.[3]

Moses' exposition of the Sinai covenant occurs in the plains of Moab, which is just north-northeast of the northern tip of the Dead Sea and on the eastern side of the Jordan River. Moses views the future extent of Israel's promised inheritance from Mount Nebo.[4]

Literary Setting

Deuteronomy shares many affinities with literature from the ancient Near East. The most evident is its relationship to the various law collections or "codes" that have been recovered.[5] These collections have come from as early as 2000 B.C. and before—e.g., Sumerian Laws of Ur Nammu (2064–46), Lipit-Ishtar (1875–64), Old Babylonian Laws from Eshnunna (ca. 1850), and Hammurabi king of Babylon (1792–50). The Old Testament contains both comparison and contrast with these collections in subcategories of types of laws, such as case law, apodictic law, laws involving curses, motive clauses, and so on.[6]

Deuteronomy displays a form and structure that reflects a close relationship with suzerain-vassal treaties.[7] The parallels extend to the variety and flexibility of these ancient documents and the covenants and treaties in the Old Testament. The set structures of these treaties are reflected in Deuteronomy and the basic elements are clearly evident (see commentary). Kitchen and McCarthy both make the important point that these treaties were hybrids as well, adapting their form and structure as needed to accommodate differing situations. The basic structure of a suzerain-vassal treaty is best placed within the years 1400–1200 B.C.[8]

There are many other types of parallels in Deuteronomy, which set it squarely within it ancient Near Eastern cultural context. Oaths were a feature of ancient Near Eastern covenantal documents. The poetry of chapters 32–33 reflects poetic features, style, and theological content found in the literature of Ugarit (Ras Shamra) near the Mediterranean coast. The curses and blessings of Deuteronomy reflect relationships with ancient Near Eastern traditions of such literature reaching

---

New Kingdom Kings (1550–1069)

Early Exodus: Eighteenth Dynasty (1550–1295)

Thutmose III	1479–1425
Amenhotep II	1427–1400
Thutmose IV	1400–1390

Late Exodus: Nineteenth Dynasty (1295–1186)

Seti I (Sethos)	1294–1279
Ramesses II	1279–1213
Merneptah	1213–1203
Wilderness Wanderings	c. 1446–1406 or 1269–1229
Merneptah Stele	1209
Moses' Exposition of Law	1406 or 1229

to the third millennium B.C. The centrality of love for the suzerain and among the great kings of the Near East, expressed in religious ritual and covenantal and literary documents, reflects the supreme commandment of love in Deuteronomy for the Lord and for one's fellow human being.[9]

Religious Setting

Deuteronomy celebrates covenant renewal, specifically the renewal of the covenant at Sinai (see Exodus and Leviticus). If Israel are to claim and retain the land promised to them, they must maintain this covenant. The covenant is renewed again in Joshua 24. In each case, the call to worship and to commitment is paramount; in each case the form and content of the covenantal renewals reflect ancient Near Eastern suzerain-vassal treaty/covenant patterns with necessary changes made to fit special circumstances.

Preamble (1:1–5)

These are the words Moses spoke (1:1). The traditions of the Israelites contained in the Hebrew Bible witness to Moses, the extraordinary leader of ancient Israel. Many ancient leaders are known only through written or oral traditions that have been left behind. Historians of the ancient Near East are finding real history lying behind these stored memories.[10] Scholars have noted that if Moses had not lived, he would have to be invented. He stands between God and the people to deliver the Lord's words. He delivers a covenant that reflects, but also adapts and goes beyond other ancient Near Eastern treaties and covenants. Mediators were common in ancient Near Eastern treaty processes, but they always stood outside of the covenant itself. Moses is the chosen mediator, but also a member of the covenant community.

Tafileh
Todd Bolen/www. BiblePlaces.com

The true sovereign in Israel is the Lord God himself, the suzerain.[11] The scenario that Israel experiences during this historical era could have called forth just such a leader as Moses.[12]

Desert east of the Jordan (1:1). This area is in the Arabah, the Jordan Rift Valley, usually limited to the valley from the south end of the Dead Sea to the Gulf of Aqaba (though the Arabah also refers to the Jordan Rift Valley from the Gulf of Aqaba to the southern end of the Sea of Galilee). The locations mentioned in verse 1 are situated in various places along Israel's travels from Egypt to the plains of Moab.

The location of Suph is not known. Paran seems to be located south of Israel, west of Edom, and north of Sinai, but exactly where is not known. Tophel has possibly been correctly identified with et-Tafileh (twenty miles southeast of the Dead Sea). Laban has not been located for certain, but the village may have been the sixth encampment of Israel after leaving Egypt (Num. 33:20–21). Hazeroth probably lay about forty miles north of traditional Sinai, Jebel Musa (Mountain of Moses), at the 'Ain el-Khadra. The location of Dizahab is not certain, but Dhahab may be Dizahab, located on the southwest side of the Gulf of Aqaba.[13]

The author's list of geographical locations here seems to reflect an itinerary (see Num. 33 for a schematized itiner-ary), including locations where the words of Moses were delivered before, during, and after Sinai—words that are now to be expounded on the plains of Moab.

From Horeb to Kadesh (1:2). It took eleven days,[14] traveling about fifteen miles per day, to journey from the traditional site of Horeb[15] at Jebel Musa, in southern Sinai, to Kadesh (ca. 170 miles). Kadesh is called Kadesh Barnea and Kadesh in the Old Testament.[16] See sidebar on "Kadesh."

Mount Seir road (1:2). This ancient travel and trade route ran from the Gulf of Aqaba north through the area of Seir (Edom), a mountainous region east of the Arabah. The route intersected the trade route coming east from Kadesh Barnea and continued north across the Brook Zered and into Moab (see 1:44).

In the fortieth year (1:3). Ancient chronology had no fixed points for dating purposes. Events were related to various key events (e.g., see Amos 1:1 and the dating formula, "before the earthquake").[17] The Exodus birthed the people of Israel as a nation and the proclamation of the Torah; these words in Deuteronomy took place in the fortieth year after Israel came out of Egypt, whether in the fifteenth century or thirteenth century B.C.[18] Solomon laid the foundation of the temple 480 years after the exodus (1 Kings 6:1). The "eleventh month" in Israel's calendar is Tebet, which overlaps with our modern December–January.

This was after he had defeated Sihon ... Og (1:4). These battles refer to Israel's defeat of relatively petty kingdoms located in the Transjordanian territory.[19] The chief city of the Amorites, Heshbon, was located northeast of the northern tip of the Dead Sea. Only Heshbon has been excavated.

The "Amorites" (Sumerian, *Martu*, Akkadian, *Amurru*) migrated from Syria into Canaan as far back as about 2500 B.C.[20] Other scholars place them in Canaan by the Middle Bronze Age II (1800–1650 B.C.) They featured a tribal structure that reached beyond the city-state system, for a "coun-

Ashtaroth being captured by Tiglath-pileser III
Z. Radovan/
www.BibleLand
Pictures.com

▶ **Kadesh**

Kadesh means "holy place." It lay on the southern boundary of Canaan and later served as a southern boundary marker of Judah. It was about fifty miles southwest of Beersheba in the Wilderness of Zin. Its modern archaeological designation places it near Ein el-Qudierat,[A-1] where a large spring supplied (and still does) an abundance of water that encouraged the growth of vegetation.[A-2]

Archaeologists have uncovered three levels of fortresses at Kadesh dating from about the tenth century B.C. to the seventh or sixth century B.C. Only six miles away, ʿAin Qadis has also been proposed. Perhaps this general area is what the biblical writer has in mind.[A-3] At least two significant trade routes ran through this area.

The Israelites did not encamp en masse at this spot for forty years. They had been barred from the land of Canaan and sentenced to wander some years in this desert area.[A-4] The archaeological evidence indicates that they would need to move about in this area to obtain sufficient sustenance to live. Probably they often returned to Kadesh, using it as a base camp.[A-5] Israel's use of tents[A-6] left no definitive evidence of their wanderings in the vicinity.[A-7]

Kadesh Barnea region
Z. Radovan/
www.BibleLand
Pictures.com
◀

cil of the Amorites" is noted in a letter.[21] A text from Mari on the Euphrates mentions Canaan/Canaanites and refers to an ethnic or geographical group/area.[22] The name is in Amarna texts, texts from Ugarit,[23] and Egyptian texts in about 1430–1400 B.C.[24] It is present in the Merneptah Stele (1209 B.C.).[25]

Bashan was situated east-northeast of the Sea of Galilee and north of the Yarmuk River. The modern Golan area in Israel covers some of this territory, but in ancient times Bashan extended to Mount Hermon in the north and to the Yarmuk River in the south, and was bounded on the west by the Jordan Valley and on the east by the great eastern desert. It was lush and fertile and noted for its rich grazing lands. The city of Edrei was located in south central Bashan and is identified with modern Darʿa. Ashtaroth, Og's capital, was due east of Galilee on one of the tributaries of the Yarmuk River. It was mentioned in Egyptian, Assyrian, and possibly Ugaritic texts[26] and is designated as Tell ʿAshtarah today. Bashan was plundered later in history by Shalmaneser III of Assyria (858–34 B.C.).[27] See 1:7; 2:24; 3:1.

Historical Prologue (1:6–3:29)[28]

Long enough at this mountain (1:6). Israel camped at Sinai ("this mountain") for about eleven months. They arrived at Sinai three months after exiting Egypt (Ex. 19:1) and

▶ Canaan

Canaan encompassed the Mediterranean coast from the Brook of Egypt to Mount Hor just north of Byblos with a southern border running from this brook along Kadesh and Tammar to Zoar on the Dead Sea. Its eastern border was the Jordan and then east to just south of Salecah. It turned north then to Hazarenan and west to Zedad and Lebo-Hamath and on to Mount Hor on the coast.[A-8] Later Egyptian references seem to refer more to southern Palestine.

The Canaanites were the original inhabitants of Canaan, with ethnic groups assimilated among these natives. Texts from ancient Ugarit (Ras Shamra), 130 miles north of Canaan, suggest much about these peoples with their pantheon, rituals, festivals, practices, and worldviews. L. L. Grabbe has, however, rightly cautioned about explaining the references in the Old Testament to Canaanite religious issues by appealing to the Ugaritic texts indiscriminately as if they were Canaanite texts.[A-9] Texts from Ras Ibn Hani also describe more about the culture of this people, as do Ebla materials (Tell Mardikh).[A-10] There are texts from Egypt and later inscriptions from Carthage and Phoenicia as well. Archaeological

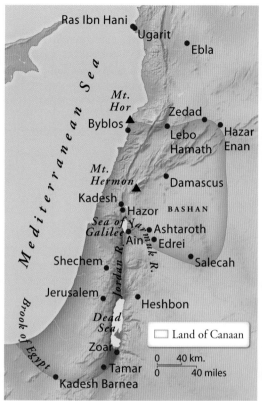

artifacts, such as temples, images, cultic sites, altars, and other cultural remains have been uncovered in Canaan. Many of these discoveries help to some extent to differentiate Israelites and Canaanites from each other.[A-11] The name was used sometimes to describe all the inhabitants of Canaan. Canaanite/Amorite appears

departed from Sinai one year and two months after leaving Egypt (Num. 10:11).

Advance into the hill country of the Amorites (1:7). This description of Canaan recalls the description of the land given in Genesis 15:18–21. Palestine divides into four longitudinal regions running north-south: a coastal plain that stretches from beyond the northern city of Tyre south along the Mediterranean Sea to the El-Arish (River of Egypt); a central mountain range that runs north from the Negev beyond Upper Galilee into Lebanon and is crossed only by the Jezreel Valley near Megiddo; a Jordan Rift Valley (Arabah) that runs from the southern end of the Sea of Galilee south to the Gulf of Aqaba; a Transjordanian mountain range that rises parallel to and east of the Jordan Rift Valley (see 1:25).[29]

At the time the Israelites entered Palestine, the Amorites occupied much of the

to be interchangeable in some cases.[A-12]

But although Ugarit is located just north of Canaanite boundaries, their beliefs probably reflect much of the life and times of the Canaanites.[A-13] Based on hundreds of cuneiform documents found at ancient Ugarit near the Syrian coast, we catch at least some glimpses about these people.

The Canaanite worldview(s) included a cult of the dead, the worship of many gods, especially El (the high god) and Baal. Female goddesses abounded (Anat, Asherah). Many high places, sacred prostitutes, and possibly Molek cults (human sacrifice?) are evidenced. The Canaanites or West Semitic peoples developed the alphabet much earlier than previously thought[A-14] and greatly influenced Israel's cult and several other areas as well.

Proto-Canaanite inscription
The Schøyen Collection MS 5180, Oslo and London

◄

Topographical Zones of Canaan

▼

Transjordanian mountain area just north of the Arnon River. Historically they had lived on both sides of the Jordan in the hill country (Num. 13:29).[30] Thus, the entire land of Palestine may be in mind here or only the Transjordanian hill country.[31]

The "Arabah" refers to the eastern edge of the Dead Sea and the Jordan Rift Valley running up to the Sea of Galilee. The "mountains" evidently refer to the central hill country running along the western side of the Jordan Rift Valley and up to the southern end of the Sea of Galilee and into Upper Galilee. The "western foothills" (Shephelah) are the low-lying areas of the central mountain range that extend down to the Mediterranean coastal plain.

The "Negev" served as the southern border of Judah; it was essentially desert and extended east from Beersheba to the southern end of the Dead Sea and west to Gaza near the coast. Its southern extensions merged with the highlands of the Sinai Peninsula and reached to the Gulf of Aqaba. Its eastern border was the Arabah running from the Dead Sea to the Gulf of Aqaba.

"The land of the Canaanites" stretched at various times from the River of Egypt (Wadi

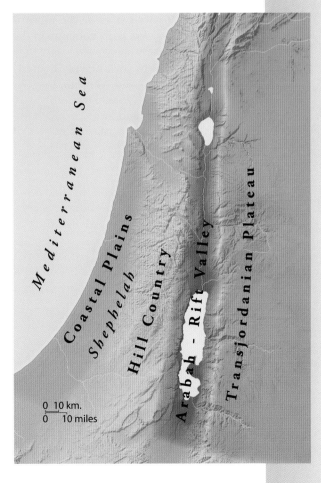

El-Arish) to Lebo Hamath north of Damascus. Strong textual evidence indicates that there were both a geographical area called Canaan and a people there who were called Canaanites, earlier possessors of Palestine.[32] In this context its northern territory is in mind and probably the coastal area there.[33] "Lebanon," which ran parallel to the Phoenician coast, indicates a northeast boundary of the land. The northwestern branch of the Euphrates River served as the northeastern border of the area. Similar clichés for boundary markers were common in the ancient Near East, e.g., "from the Euphrates to the great sea where the sun sets."[34]

I charged your judges at that time (1:9). The recollection of the establishment of Israel's judicial structures begins here (1:9–18; but cf. also Ex. 18:13–27; Deut. 16:18–29; 17:6–2).[35] Israel's judicial system, though not always the laws per se or the motivations for the laws, was fairly common in the ancient Near East.[36]

Three spheres of government "housed" the constitutional and administrative law: the divine (gods, king, and dynasty), state, and local authorities.[37] Outside of Israel the king was at the top of the pyramid in constitutional and administrative law and judicial procedures. Kingship originated from heaven (the gods) and was passed on to the king, who could claim to be ruler of the world and as such could promulgate laws.[38] He was ultimately the head of any legislative group and acted as supreme judge, who especially championed the cause of the widow, the orphan, the poor, and the oppressed.

There was typically some kind of central

administration as well as provincial or city-state administrative structures. The courts recognized the king as supreme judge along with supportive royal judges under him, and there were evidently local judges as well.[39] A "commissioner" (*mashkim*) functioned, who researched legal or economic matters. He came from among the common people, for he could be a scribe, barber, or the manager of an estate.[40]

In Mesopotamia levels of the judicial system are evident. A town assembly of elders was established. Then additional local, temple, or royal officials could get involved, often serving as witnesses. The parties involved in a case represented themselves, for there were no lawyers or professionals involved.[41]

In Egypt the king and his royal staff administered justice and ruled the land. An "eloquent peasant" could appeal to Pharaoh himself, if necessary, to seek justice.[42] The king derived his authority from the gods. D. Lorton asserts that there was no group of legal professionals in Egypt before 700 B.C. or legal theory per se that has yet been uncovered.[43] Egyptian law codes have not been uncovered, but royal decrees or edicts have been.[44] But references in ancient writings imply that such laws did exist, at least to some extent.[45] There were "judges" and supporting court personnel.[46] There was a scribal class who functioned as "quasi-lawyers," and court and legal procedure functioned in rudimentary form.[47] *Maʾat* represented a natural abstract concept of universal order and harmony. Justice was available to the poor as well as the rich. Some persons (judges) were charged to see that "law" (*maʾat*) was used to the good of all humanity.[48]

We have records of Hittite instructions to officers in the thirteenth century (Tudhalias IV). Officers are classified as commanders of thousands, designated as majors, and so on. Officers in the military served as judges. The king, however, was the one who gave out the commands and instructions. Extremely difficult cases for the various judges could be refused; justice was to be passed in all cases to those involved, with no partiality shown for the rich or the poor. In Egypt similar actions are recorded in a fourteenth-century Stele of Horemheb, where we read that he sought out men of integrity and excellent character to serve as judges. Thutmose III gave similar instructions to the new vizier, Rekhmire, who was to "regard him whom you know like him whom you do not know."[49]

Among the Hittites the king served in the highest court, the royal court, which was also a court of appeals. He was the steward of the land of Hatti under the creator storm-god,[50] who owned the land, just as Yahweh owned the land in Israel. The king also served as the chief priest of the gods.[51]

Israel's tribal organization is possibly reflected in Egyptian texts and designated *shasu* (*sh sw*) (nomads, wanderers; cf. Arameans, people of Seir, Edom).[52] At Mari documents refer to a pastoral population of West Semitic elements featuring tribal aspects that parallel Israel's earliest tribal features.[53] In early Israel the tribal system served as a foundation and source for the development of a justice system (1:23; 29:18).[54]

The Valley of Eshcol (1:24). This valley was probably a fertile wadi, housing a vineyard, located just north of Hebron (Num. 13:22–25), a city renowned for its viticulture and olive production. Perhaps its ancient name is still evident in the Wadi Burj Haskeh, situated two miles north of Hebron, where grapes, grapevines, and related products were and are cultivated and harvested.[55] Viticulture was vital to Israel's national prosperity. To create and nurture a prosperous viticulture took many years and a stable community.[56] Cultivation of the vine

and its products flourished as early as the third millennium on the Levant.[57] Hillside terraces had to be planted, but were grown from plant cuttings and shoots. The vines were manicured and manipulated in many ways (cf. Isa. 5:1–7).

The viticulturist harvested early grapes in June/July and harvested the best grapes in August/September. Grapes were cut in clusters from the vine with sharp knives. Winepresses were used to tread on the grapes with bare feet (beam presses were used later). The wine was received into a lower receptacle, collected, and stored in a cool place. Grapes were dried in the sun to make raisins and "dibs," a honey produced from fruit.

It is a good land that the LORD our God is giving us (1:25). The land in general was well endowed with agricultural potential,[58] but it was not rich in natural resources, although the Dead Sea provided some salt and bitumen and small amounts of iron have been found. Some turquoise is present in the Negev.[59] Large desert areas were neither fruitful nor fertile. Certain regions were suited to produce wine, grain, and olive oils in abundance (Gen. 27:28; Deut. 7:13); some regions were capable of sustaining cattle, flocks, and herds in great numbers, such as Gilead.[60] The Mediterranean coastal area, the Sea of Galilee, and the Jordan River provided an abundance of fish. Other features of the land offered many challenges to its inhabitants. See sidebar on "Climate and Agriculture."

The Anakites (1:28). Egyptian Execration Texts (from about 1860, 1830, 1780 B.C.) may refer to the Anakites (also termed Anakim).[61] Kitchen believes it is probable that the city of Yaʾanaq, mentioned in all three main series of these texts, is to be tied to the Anakim of the Old Testament (esp. Josh. 11:21–22). Yaʾanaq has three rulers mentioned. In Joshua two groups of three cities (Hebron, Debir, Anab; Gaza, Gath, Ashdon) are mentioned where Anakites dwelt. Perhaps the biblical "triplets" suggest an ancient tradition.[62] In a thirteenth-century Egyptian papyrus (Anastasi I), Bedouin in Canaan are cited as nearly nine feet tall.[63]

▶ Climate and Agriculture

Climate varied from north to south and from east to west. In general the rainfall decreased as one moved from the north to the south and from the west to the east. It increased with higher elevations and was greater on the western sides of the central and Transjordanian mountains than on the eastern side. Some areas experienced abundant rainfall; others received only enough rain for subsistence living, and some areas were scorching, unproductive desert.[A-15]

The annual rainfall varied considerably, from forty inches in Upper Galilee to two inches in the desert areas, such as the Negev and the Judean Desert. A year featured two main seasons, a wet season (October–March/April) during which early autumnal rains from October–December fell, and late, spring rains, in January–April.

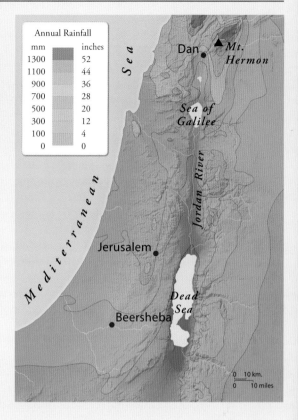

Annual Rainfall	
mm	inches
1300	52
1100	44
900	36
700	28
500	20
300	12
100	4
0	0

Mediterranean Sea

Dan • ▲ Mt. Hermon

Sea of Galilee

Jordan River

Jerusalem •

Dead Sea

Beersheba •

0 10 km.
0   10 miles

Epic of Tukulti-
Ninurta I
The British Museum;
© Dr. James C.
Martin
▼

In fire by night and in a cloud by day (1:33). This flame or fire was probably covered by a cloud in the day, but was visible at night.[64] Niehaus concludes that the pillar of cloud and pillar of fire represented both a messenger of God and God himself.[65] Speculations that this biblical phenomenon was the result of local volcanic activity or that it is to be tied to the smoke and fire signals that "led" caravans are far off the mark.[66]

Mann observes the "remarkable similarities" between the

▶ Moab

The kingdom of Moab, featuring tribalism rather than "statehood" per se, had a significant population and presence during the Late Bronze Age (1550–1200 B.C.). This was not always the case. Some sites not mentioned in the biblical text indicate a Late Bronze Age occupation, while some sites in the biblical text do not (see 2:24, for Heshbon). Moab is mentioned in Egyptian texts from the time of Ramesses II (ca. 1270 B.C.), and a Moabite king may be represented in a stele from the Late Bronze Age.[A-20] Dibon, one of Moab's capital cities, based on irrefutable evidence,[A-21] existed in 1270 B.C. References from Ebla (southwest of Aleppo; twenty-fifth century B.C.) and from southern Moab (tenth to ninth century B.C.) mention the chief Moabite god Chemosh. The name is also in the ritual texts at Ugarit (fourteenth century) and is present in theophoric names at Ebla, such as the city name Carchemish (Kar-Kamish).[A-22] Mesha, a Moabite king, is identified on the Moabite Stone (ca. 830 B.C.) found at Dibon (cf. 2 Kings 3). Babylon crippled Moab in 582–581 B.C.,[A-23] but it seems to have limped into Hellenistic times. By the time of Rome, Ammon, Moab, and Edom were gone.[A-24]

Several cities, areas, and peoples are mentioned in this text (2:9–33). The designation Ar may refer to a city, area, or to all of Moab.[A-25] Here and in verse 29 below, the word refers to a region or to the entire land of Moab.[A-26] The location of Ar is placed at competing locations in Moab, Khirbet el-Balu being the most probable.[A-27]

Arnon Gorge
Bible Scene
Multimedia/Maurice
Thompson
◀

The word applies to ancient warrior heroes who served the god Baal.[110]

The OT refers to the spirits of "the dead" as $r^e p\bar{a}^\flat im$ (Ps. 88:11–12; Isa. 14:9; 26:14, 19;[111] see also Prov. 2:18; 9:18; 21:16). The Rephaites as spirits of the elite dead is also found in Phoenician and Punic-Latin texts/inscriptions.[112] The sarcophagus inscriptions of Tabnit use the term to describe the "shades/spirits" of the common person.[113] It is fair to say that the Rephaites in both categories are still puzzling. O. Loretz argues with some effectiveness that Israel historicized this latter view of the Rephaites.[114]

For Anakites see comments on 1:28. Verse 11 here indicates that the Anakites were also considered Rephaites, as were the Emites. The fear felt by the Israelites had some basis in fact, based on what the names of these peoples suggest.

The Ammonites also dispossessed the Rephaites, whom they named the Zamzummites. Hence, the basic stock of giants in these areas were called Emites by the Moabites, but Zamzummites by the Ammonites and were all huge like the Anakites.

Horites (2:12). Horites inhabited the territory of Seir. Some scholars have closely tied them to the Hurrians, a non-Semitic people. These people located in various places, such as Mitanni, Syria, Anatolia, and Palestine. They were found in Syria and Palestine, and they had spread there from territory east of the Tigris River in Mesopotamia.[115] This identification is still held by some,[116] but other scholars recently strongly disavow the identity of the Horites and the Hurrians, asserting that the resemblance of names is

only incidental.[117] The name "Horites" may be derived from Hebrew *hor* ("cave") and, hence, refers to mountainous cave dwellers in the regions of Seir, which both the geology and geography of the region would support.[118] See comments on Hivites at 7:1.

Zered Valley (2:13). The Brook (Heb. *naḥal*) Zered (cf. Num. 21:12) flowed through and gave its name to this valley. The valley extends from its southeastern origin westward for about thirty-six miles to the southeast corner of the Dead Sea, where its small stream enters the Dead Sea.[119] Today it is identified as the Wadi-el-Hesa. The valley averages about three and one-half miles in width at its widest. It provided a natural boundary between Moab to the north and Edom to the south. The Zered Brook and tributaries drained the northern area of the Jebel esh-Shera as it descended 3,900 feet to sea level. Israel crossed it and ceased wandering (Num. 21:12), entering a new territory and a new era for her.

The LORD's hand was against them (2:15). The "hand of the LORD" or "his hand" is a biblical and ancient Near Eastern expression.

Wadi Zered
Todd Bolen/www.
BiblePlaces.com

In Akkadian literature it often refers to the punishing, destructive, or threatening hand of a particular god. The poor sufferer of I Will Praise the Lord of Wisdom can complain of his god that "heavy was his hand [upon me], I could not bear it."[120] In biblical texts it stood for the power/might of Israel's God (Ex. 3:20; 9:15; Deut. 3:24; 7:8). In Egyptian documents (annals, historical texts, oracles, and prophecies) the expressions "hand of Pharaoh" or the "strong arm of Pharaoh" were metaphors for the power/might of Egypt (Ex. 3:8; 18:9). The equivalent expression "outstretched arm" (Ex. 6:6; Deut. 4:34; 11:2) was often used in and even combined with the "mighty hand of the LORD" (4:34; 5:15; 7:19; 9:29; 11:2; 26:8).

These terms are found ubiquitously in Egyptian literature since Pharaoh was known as "lord of the strong arm" (*Neb Khopesh*).[121] Ramesses II affirmed that his god Seth had made Ramesses' arm "mighty to the height of heaven and my strength to the width of the earth!"[122] In Egypt "man in the hand of the God," an equivalent expression, occurs.[123]

The phrase is found in literature at Mari as well.[124] The Hittite king Mursili conquered the enemy "with [his strong] arm."[125] These idioms were also used in Canaan as evidenced by the Amarna letters.[126] It is considered an "Egyptianism" in Hebrew.[127]

Ammonites (2:19). The Ammonites were related to the Israelites through Lot (Gen. 19:38) and so the Lord gave them territory in Transjordan, from the Arnon River to the Jabbok River, covering a north-south distance of about thirty-nine miles. Archaeology shows the Ammonites as a people before the Neo-Assyrians arose. Early Bronze (3100–2650 B.C.), Middle Bronze (1800–1650 B.C.), and Late Bronze (1500–1200 B.C.) materials testify to this. The national god Molech is mentioned in texts at Ebla (twenty-fifth century B.C.) and also at Ugarit, where he is equated to the god Rpu (Rapiʾu). Ugaritic texts and Egyptian texts mention the city of ʿAshtarot, an earlier cultic location for the worship of Molech/Rapiʾu.[128] The capital city was Rabbah (modern Amman). There is sufficient evidence at Transjordanian sites (e.g., Tell Safut) to suggest that the Iron Age Ammonites continued the Late Bronze Age people.[129]

In the reign of Tiglath-Pileser, the Neo-Assyrian annals refer to the Land of Benammanu (KUR.Benammana) and the House of Ammon (Bit-Ammon).[130] Ammonite kings are known from Assyrian records kept by kings, including Shalmaneser III (853 B.C., Qarqar), Sennacherib (704–681 B.C.), and Esarhaddon (680–669 B.C.). The Ammonites, as a mini-power, ceased to exist in around 582–581 B.C., when the Babylonians defeated them. They continued to play minor but troublesome roles in Israel's history down to the second century.[131]

Zamzummites (2:20). The Zamzummites are the same as the Zuzites in Genesis 14:5. "Rephaites" (shades, ghosts), "Emim" (frightful ones),

Pharaoh with arm raised to strike enemy
Olga Sorokoletova
◄

and this word all indicate dread or discomfort surrounding their appearance (see comments on 2:10).[132] The LXX renders "Zamzummites" as "mighty ones," an even closer fit to the other two words. Ullendorf and Christensen identify this as the use of a foreign word in Hebrew.[133] The personal name Zammabu is found in an Old Babylonian king list.

Avvites (2:23). The Avvites lived south of the key Philistine city, Gaza, both before and after the conquest of Palestine (Josh. 13:3). The LXX renders this word as "Hivites." Perhaps they were a part of the displaced Sea Peoples who landed in or migrated to this area. Some scholars tie the Avvites to the Hyksos settlements that were followed later by the Aegean Sea peoples.[134] Their dwellings (ḥaṣērîm; NIV "villages") are understood to have been small unwalled villages or even seminomadic tent encampments.[135]

Caphtorites (2:23). The Caphtorites may have been a part of the Philistines at an early stage (Jer. 47:4; Amos 9:7). They stemmed from Crete rather than Cyprus, as some have argued.[136] Caphtor (Heb. *kaptôr*) is ancient Kaptara (Crete), and Mari texts from the second millennium mention a king of Hagor who sent gifts to Kaptara. Egyptian texts mention *kefl(i)u*, a variant of Kaptara.[137]

Arnon Gorge ... Sihon the Amorite, king of Heshbon (2:24). The Arnon Gorge, identified as Wadi el-Mujib today, is a perennial stream that opens into the east side of the Dead Sea almost opposite Ein-Gedi. It is about thirty miles long, with breathtaking canyon views. It served once as a heavily fortified border area[138] of Ammon (Ammonites) and of Moab (Deut. 3:12, 16; Judg. 11:18–19). It functioned as the southern border of the tribe of Reuben. It is mentioned in the Mesha Stone (Moabite Stone) dating from about 830 B.C. Mesha (ca. 849 B.C.), mentioned in 2 Kings 3:4, claims to have retaken Moabite territory formerly conquered by Israel, including the Arnon Gorge, and claims that he made a road for travel in the Arnon.[139]

Sihon, the king of Heshbon, was also king of the Amorites (Num. 21:21–31). A poetic piece (Num. 21:27) celebrates the takeover of Heshbon from Sihon and Israel's subsequent rebuilding of it. Sihon's petty kingdom centered around Heshbon, but Amorites over a larger area were affected (Deut. 3:6–8). The origin of Heshbon goes back to the thirteenth century B.C.[140] The modern site of Heshbon is possibly Tell Hesban and excavations show that it was inhabited from at least the twelfth century. Heshbon may, however, prove to be a Bronze Age city represented by Tell el-Jalul or Tell el-Umeiri.[141]

Terror and fear of you (2:25). The peoples and kings of the nations will be terrified of Israel, a special people. In Egyptian literature the terror of Amun, god of Egypt, overwhelmed the enemy. Hittite, Assyrian, and Babylonian texts feature divine warriors and armies who struck fear into the enemy. The king led the army in the Old Babylonian era, but he was amply supported by the gods, whose will was discerned through diviners. In the Middle Babylonian eras and throughout the Assyrian epochs, the divine hosts helped to overwhelm the enemy. These gods accompanied and supported their troops.[142] A similar situation functioned in Hittite military activity.[143]

Desert of Kedemoth (2:26). There was a Transjordanian city of Kedemoth north of the Arnon and a wilderness area around it to the southeast and southwest, here translated as "Desert of Kedemoth."[144] The city was allotted to the tribe of Reuben (Josh. 13:18). Its identification is not certain, but it is usually considered to be ʿAleiyan, es-Saliyeh, or er-Remeil. The second of these suggestions may be the best option since it lies on the edge of the desert.[145]

The act of sending messengers reflects common ancient Near Eastern practice,[146] for they were employed by Sumerians, Babylonians, Akkadians, Hittites, Ugaritians, and Egyptians, among whom Israel had lived. They were part of the fabric of ancient Near Eastern military protocol. Messengers were especially important in order to spot the military presence of a people, especially in Sumer and Egypt.[147]

When Sihon ... came out to meet us in battle at Jahaz (2:32). The Israelites defeated Sihon and the Amorites at Jahaz in Transjordan (cf. Num. 21:21–31; Deut. 2:30–35; 3:5; Judg. 11:20).[148] The Moabite Stone describes it (ca. 830 B.C.) as a city taken back from the Israelite king who had rebuilt or fortified it.[149] It was given to Reuben and became a Levitical city (Josh. 21:36; 1 Chron. 6:78). Prophetic oracles mention it (Jer. 48:34), and it is possibly to be identified with Khirbet el-Medeiniyeh.

Completely destroyed them (2:34). This agrees with the practice of devoting things to destruction (herem) in the Old Testament, especially during times of war. To violate this instruction was a serious offense, punishable by death.[150] The practice of herem was practiced elsewhere in the ancient Near East. King Mesha of Moab took the city of Nebo from Israel and devoted all in it to destruction to his god Ashtar-Chemosh.[151] The ban as already noted functioned at

Mari,[152] where a nearly equivalent phrase was "eating the taboo" (asakkan akālum). The "taboo" belonged to a god or king and to "eat it" violated its holy/cursed or special nature. The asakkum concept functioned at Mari as in Israel for the Israelite soldiers. Soldiers could not take any spoils of war to themselves, for these items were the asakku of the gods Adad and Shamash.[153]

Aroer on the rim of the Arnon Gorge (2:36). Aroer was located on the northern rim of the Arnon Gorge (Wadi el-Mujib; see also 4:48). It was a fortified city (Num. 32:34) and served as a natural border checkpoint with Moab (Deut. 4:48; Josh. 2:2). It is located by modern ʿarahir, about three miles southeast of biblical Dibon. The Syrian king Hazael controlled it in the ninth century. It is mentioned in the Moabite Stone by King Mesha (ca. 830 B.C.) as a city that Mesha fortified or "built."[154]

Gilead (2:36). This area of central Transjordan has yielded an abundance of archaeological data from the Late Bronze Age and Iron Age.[155] The name appears in extrabiblical texts at Ugarit and in Assyria at Nimrud both as a name of a place and of a person.[156] The area flourished in the Late Bronze Age (1550–1200 B.C.), with a fortress attributed to Mesha.[157] Temples and inscriptions were discovered at Ammon and Deir ʿAlla.[158] Gilead marked the boundary of the Ammonites to the north and the Moabites to the south. It included the area of Transjordan north of Sihon's kingdom and northwest of the Ammonites and extended to Bashan, spanning the Jabbok River. Sihon's central authority was exercised from the Arnon River to the Jabbok River (Num. 21:24).[159]

Course of the Jabbok (2:37). The Jabbok, located about twenty-five miles north of the Dead Sea, becomes a swift-flowing stream by the time it enters the Jordan River. Its modern name is Wadi Zerqa. It begins near Rabbah of the biblical Ammonites, flows east and north, and then descends westward into the Jordan.

Og king of Bashan (3:1). This king is not attested outside of the Bible. A note in 3:11 refers to a tradition that he was a Rephaite (cf. 2:10) and that his bedstead or "sarcophagus of basalt" (*ʿereś barzel*) was on display at Rabbah, the Ammonite capital. Many sarcophagi have been recovered in Bashan and may (1) favor this translation of the phrase and (2) support a historical basis for this tradition.[160] Millard has presented a cogent argument for considering the bed as a piece of furniture, a decorated, gilded bed with iron, based on its purported Late Bronze Age origin, a time when iron was scarce and therefore highly valued.[161]

Argob (3:4). This refers to a confederation of cities within the larger Bashan area or to a region to the east of the Jordan. In 3:13 it is described as bounded by the Maacathites and Geshurites to the northeast and east respectively. A small Geshurite kingdom lay due east of the Sea of Kinnereth (see 3:12–17). Later Argob is included in the sixth Solomonic administrative district (1 Kings 4:19) and comprised the fertile land north of the Yarmuk River.[162]

All these cities were fortified (3:5). Fortified cities were a feature of the culture of Mesopotamia, Aram/Syria, Palestine, and Egypt across the centuries and millennia in the ancient Near East. See sidebar on "Ancient Fortified Cities."

Arnon Gorge as far as Mount Hermon (3:8). Mount Hermon (Jebal ash-Shaykh), the highest peak (9,200 ft.) on the Anti-Lebanon Range, sat at the northern extent of Israel's conquests. The discovery of numerous temples around and on it reveals its sacred character for the inhabitants of the area.[163] The sources of the Jordan originate in its western slopes. The Sidonian name Sorion was used by the scribes of Ugarit[164] and is found in Egyptian texts[165] of the eighteenth century. Shalmaneser II (858–24 B.C.) called Mount Hermon "Senir" when he encountered Hazael of Damascus in battle.[166] Mursilis II, a Hittite king, refers to it as *Sariyana*,[167] and it is mentioned in Old Babylonian fragments of the Gilgamesh Epic.[168]

It is still in Rabah (3:11). Huge objects such as this bedstead (sarcophagus) and the giant sword of Goliath were kept as a memorial that recalled these ancient giants (1 Sam. 21:9), along with the victory the Lord gave Israel over them.

The land that we took over at that time (3:12). A number of cities are noted here (cf. Num. 32; Josh 12:1–6; 13:8–32). Relatively recent archaeological surveys have increased our knowledge of these areas. In general Late Bronze II–Iron IA levels of occupation are present.[169] See previous references for most of these sites and features of Transjordanian territory allotted to Reuben, Gad, and half of the tribe of Manasseh.

Geshurites inhabited a tiny kingdom of Aramaeans north-northeast of the Sea of Kinnereth (Galilee). Mazar cites probable references to Geshur in the Amarna letters.[170] Gilead was at their southern border; Bashan was on their eastern boundary, and Mount Hermon was to the north of

▸ Ancient Fortified Cities

Troy, in Anatolia, still witnesses to the massive fortifications produced there.[A-28] The multiplication of cities in ancient Mesopotamia created competition between them, and they became heavily fortified for protection and security purposes as early as 2800 B.C. Palaces housed the political and military machinery of the cities. Here too walls, gates, and moats encircled the cities.[A-29] Arsenals were located near city walls. Siege and warfare were part of life in ancient Mesopotamia.

In the Levant military fortifications developed rapidly (Megiddo, Jericho, Taanach, Arad, Ai) and walls, buttresses, bastions, glacis, gates, and towers proliferated. The same is true for Egypt, although archaeological remains are fewer. In the early and middle second millennium, powerful fortified cities appeared in Syria and Palestine. Moats were often a part of Middle Bronze Age fortifications (ca. 1800–1550 B.C.).[A-30] They appear in pictures and are mentioned in texts of the Late Bronze Age/Iron Age II.[A-31]

Ramparts were constructed on one or both sides of massive walls (or no wall!) to hinder an attacking enemy, although scholars interpret the function of ramparts differently.[A-32] City gates were constructed to serve as a vital part of these fortified cities.[A-33]

In the Late Bronze Age fortified cities continued, but a dramatic reduction of them occurred because of Egypt's oppressive policies at the end of the Middle Bronze Age.[A-34] Egyptian records mention these fortified sites encountered in Palestine. In the Iron Age (1200–800 B.C.) the Philistine cities of Ekron, Ashkelon, and even Ashdod featured huge city gates and massive walls.[A-35] These urban features of Palestine, much abated, continued into the Iron Age.[A-36] The presence of these cities and towns struck fear into the Israelites. As noted above, recent archaeological and demographic/social studies have indicted that there was a decided depletion of fortified cities, centers of concentrated power, in the Late Bronze Age that controlled large rural areas as well.[A-37] Walls were only one possible component used to fortify a city (e.g., Jericho); powerful cities without walls existed. Thus, Israel faced other threats of fortified cities as they entered the land in the Late Bronze Age.[A-38]

Iron Age fort at Arad showing intimidating walls
Kim Walton

them (Josh. 13:11). Their relationship to Israel was ambivalent. Some of their cities were taken by Manasseh, but later recovered (1 Chron. 2:22–33). David took a Geshurite wife, Maacah, from whom Absalom was born.[171] The Maacathites were a small Aramaean kingdom south of Mount Hermon whose land went to the half-tribe of Manasseh (Josh. 12:5; 13:11). They lived north of the Geshurites, northeast of the Sea of Kinnereth, west of the Jordan Rift Valley. Mount Hermon was far to the north.

Both of these peoples and territories lay within the high plateau area of Bashan. Tadmor now rejects a possible mention of Abel Beth-Maacah in the annals of Tiglath-pileser III as unsustainable. Abel-shittim is suggested instead.[172] Egyptian execration texts refer to Maacah.[173] Israel did not conquer it. They had a checkered relationship with King David, but eventually became his vassals (2 Sam. 10:6; 1 Chron. 19:7).

Its western border was the Jordan in the Arabah (3:17). The Kinnereth and the Sea of the Arabah refer to the Sea of Galilee and the Dead Sea (Salt Sea) respectively. Kin-

nereth indicates the shape of a lyre, a musical instrument; the lake resembles the instrument. It is located in the Jordan Rift Valley. Today it is thirteen miles long by seven miles wide. It lies about 700 feet below sea level and is 160 feet deep on average; it is rich in various kinds of fish and other products. It was a northern boundary for Israelite territory in its early stages of settlement. The ancient Jewish writer Josephus gives a description of the lake and refers to it by several different names.[174]

The LORD your God has given you this land to take possession of it (3:18). This phrase refers to God's giving of the land to Israel, but it also describes his parceling out of land to the Edomites, Moabites, and Ammonites. In the ancient Near East a nation's god/gods were the ones who gave the land to its inhabitants. From the Moabite point of view Chemosh, god of Moab, gave the land of Moab back to the Moabites after Israel, under Yahweh, had captured it.[175]

Pisgah (3:27). Pisgah is a peak in a mountain in a range (Abarim) of several mountains formed out of the high tableland of Trans-jordan that also included Mount Nebo. If Pisgah, in fact, refers to a peak named Ras es-Siaghah today, it is located slightly northwest of Mount Nebo.[176] Both peaks are located on Jebel/Shayhan.[177] But its identity is not certain. Other scholars consider Pisgah to be the summit of Mount Nebo or even the same mountain.[178] Pisgah always occurs in the Hebrew text with the definite article, indicating that it was well known. Balaam tried to offer sacrifices and curse Israel from this peak (Num. 23:14). Pisgah, if correctly located, is 2,329 feet high; Nebo is over four hundred feet higher at 2,740 feet.[179]

Beth Peor (3:29). Beth Peor (meaning "house of Peor") was located almost due east of the northern tip of the Dead Sea, in or next to the plains of Moab, southwest of Heshbon in Transjordan.[180] Modern Khirbet (city) el-Meḥatta is its probable site, although some prefer Khirbet ʿAyunmusa,[181] located about a mile north of Mount Nebo. Decades ago Vernes presented a case for the recognition of Beth Peor as a Moabite sanctuary, a position that is still firm.[182] The name "Peor" was the name of a mountain in northwest Moab and served as a short name of the god Baal Peor.

Introduction to the Stipulations (4:1–49)

Hear now, O Israel, the decrees and laws I am about to teach you (4:1). This call to Israel introduces the stipulations of the Sinai covenant as renewed in Deuteronomy.[183] Features of ancient Near Eastern treaties are clearly discernible in this chapter.[184] Israel's laws shared in both the literary tradition of the laws, treaties, and covenants in the ancient Near East and, to a lesser but important extent, in its content and legal presentations.[185] Westbrook notes, however, that the biblical law differs chiefly from cuneiform law in its firm presentation of a "voice of dissent." It is not a mere rubber stamp of the establishment.[186]

Pisgah is a peak in the Abarim range to the northwest of Nebo. As this picture looks northwest from Nebo, Pisgah, about 400 feet lower in elevation, is near the center left.
Todd Bolen/www.BiblePlaces.com

Nine law "codes" have been discovered, some intact and some only in part. In the ancient Near East seven are now identifiable: Ur-Nammu (CU), Lipit Ishtar (CL), Eshnunna (CE), Hammurabi (CH), Assyrian Laws (AL), Hittite Laws (HL), and Neo-Babylonian Laws (NBL). Two "codes" are found in the Bible: Exodus (21:1–22:16) and Deuteronomy (chs. 12–26). Deuteronomy 4 serves as the introduction to the covenantal stipulations (ch. 5=basic; chs. 6–11, 12–26=specific), following the pattern of Hittite treaties from 1400–1200 B.C.[187]

The decrees and laws I am about to teach you (4:1). The basic stipulations in the Sinai Covenant, as it forms the framework for Deuteronomy, are found in chapter 4 and fit into the ancient Near Eastern pattern of treaties between 1400–1200 B.C. This chapter introduces basic stipulations and accompanying exhortations.[188] While the form of the covenant between Israel and their God has many ancient Near Eastern analogues, the enactment of a covenant between a god and that god's people featuring divinely imparted laws in even subsequent promulgations and revisions has not, so far, been evidenced in detail. The extent and depth to which covenant, history, and law are combined is not matched in the ancient Near Eastern materials.[189]

Take possession of the land that the LORD, the God of your fathers, is giving to you (4:1). "The God of your fathers" is a key Old Testament concept within Israel's worldview (cf. Ex. 3:13–16; Deut. 1:11, 21). Such terminology has turned up in the Mari documents.[190] Kings of the cities of Aleppo and Qatna use the phrase. On the familial level this kind of god was inherited/passed on from father to sons, sons to grandsons, and, interestingly, the god named on a family seal served to identify the family rather than an individual person. The father's seal passed on in the family bore the name of the father's god. "The god mentioned in the father's seal was also his son's, not because the son had decided it that way, but by virtue of his membership (and now leadership) of the family."[191]

Family gods tended to stay in the family (e.g., Adad). This practice is traceable back to 2500 B.C.[192] The family god was not exclusive to the particular family, for "family god" does not occur in the terminology. These gods were effective beyond the boundaries of the family, as was Israel's God, the God of the fathers.[193]

Do not add … do not subtract (4:2). This "canonical formula" (cf. 13:1–3) is common to ancient Near Eastern treaty literature. It is found essentially in Egyptian scribal guidelines and in Assyria (Esarhaddon) as warnings against changing any part of a covenant/treaty.[194] Hammurabi included this charge in his epilogue[195] and called down curses on anyone who would change his laws. The same language obtains in the prologue/epilogue of the Lipit-Ishtar law code.[196]

Baal Peor (4:3). Baal Peor was, in addition to a geographical location, a major deity of Moab, Ammon, and Midian.[197] Israel played the (religious) harlot at Baal Peor (Num. 25:1–5) while camped at Shittim. "Baal" as used here refers to a local manifestation of the Canaanite god or gods, Baal, a fertility/weather god.[198]

I have taught you decrees and laws … so that you may follow them (4:5). The creation and collection of law(s) in the ancient Near East was, as here, considered proof of wisdom in those law codes and clearly stated as such. Hammurabi asserted that his laws would be an object of splendor to the wise man, and he threatened those who did not heed them with curses and with dispersion.[199] The various laws of the different nations reflected their character and culture in some basic national worldviews (e.g., polytheism vs. monotheism).[200] Underlying axioms to some extent were imbedded and emphasized in the laws.[201]

You stood before the LORD your God at Horeb (4:10). Horeb refers to Sinai once in Deuteronomy (1:6), but elsewhere it refers to a desert region called Horeb.[202] In

33:2 only Sinai is used.²⁰³ Horeb/Sinai is most likely located in southern Sinai. Some argue for other locations, such as Midian, Mount Bisher, northwest Saudi Arabia, and Edom.²⁰⁴ Most scholars prefer a southern location for Sinai at Jebel Musa, Jebel Serbal, or Ras Safsafah.²⁰⁵

He declared to you his covenant ... and then wrote them on two tablets (4:13). Israel's distinctiveness was their God and the acts and words he established with only them. He assigned other beings to guide the other nations (see 4:19–20; 32:8–9). While the external form of the Lord's covenant with Israel reflects ancient Near Eastern covenant/treaty traditions, there is a flavor, a spirit, a monotheistic view, and a unique God involved. How God and his people patterned and emphasized the ideas of God/people, covenant/law/history, is the key to Israel's unique covenant and worldview with its two foundational tablets of ten laws (words).²⁰⁶

No form (4:15). The Hebrew word translated "form" (*tᵉmûnâ*) is found in a Phoenician text describing Astarte, a female goddess,²⁰⁷ represented by an image resembling a man/woman, a practice forbidden in Israel. The Egyptian pantheon was symbolically filled with animal representations for all the key gods. The dung-beetle, cow (Hathor), baboon, falcon, and more were used to represent Egypt's gods.²⁰⁸

Beyond the world of Israel, I. Cornelius has noted the many faces of the gods, the varied representations of the divinity.²⁰⁹ Egypt, Amarna, Mesopotamia, Anatolia, and Syria-Palestine each had their way of depicting the gods. The puzzling and shocking presentation of Egyptian gods is informative as well as surreal. Hornung asserts—probably correctly—that the presentation of a god(s) with various human and/or animal features at one time gives "allusions to essential parts of the nature and function of deities."²¹⁰ Hence, the goddess Hathor may be depicted with human and bovine features, for she possessed the tenderness of motherly care and the essence of a human person. As partially snake, she was sly, wise, and mysterious; bearing horns she reflected strength; and as a lion she portrayed power. It seems that while

Jebel Musa, traditional Mount Sinai
Z. Radovan/
www.BibleLand
Pictures.com

▶ Ancient Near Eastern Treaties and Covenants

Covenantal thinking and documents constituted a vital component of ancient Near Eastern culture and functioned in manifold ways. The Bronze Age (3500–1200 B.C.) produced many treaties. The treaty between Hattusilis/Ramesses II (ca. 1280 B.C.) displays a treaty form and model that fits the treaty form at Sinai (Ex. 19–24) and its various renewals in Deuteronomy (chs. 1–28) and Joshua (chs. 24). Covenants with similar treaty components stem from even earlier times, such as Early Bronze (3500–2300 B.C.) at Byblos. Late Bronze Age (1550–1200 B.C.) examples are abundant. The key features of these treaties were:

1. Title
2. Historical prologue
3. Stipulations
4. Provision for the deposition and public reading of the treaty text
5. List of witnesses to the treaty
6. Listing of blessings and curses.[A-39]

Feature 2 is notably missing in the late Neo-Assyrian treaties of the seventh century B.C., as well as the blessings of feature 6.

The Iron Age (1200–ca. 539 B.C.) documents display a covenantal structure and content different from those of the Late Bronze Age. Iron Age loyalty oaths/treaties varied in style and content. Usually they included:

1. Preamble
2. Identification of the Assyrian ruler(s)
3. Invocation of deities
4. Definition of responsibilities of a vassal (which, if not observed, brought curses)
5. Curses brought on an unfaithful vassal[A-40]

It is evident that the cultural, historical, and literary connections of the covenant at Sinai, as reiterated in Deuteronomy, are closely connected with the Late Bronze covenants. Those from the Iron Age and later lack either a preamble or blessings, as well as some technical vocabulary found in earlier documents. The covenant concept in Israel was evidently early.[A-41] Covenantal ideas were already hundreds of years old and common in the ancient Near East when Israel's God established his covenant.[A-42]

K. A. Kitchen has cogently demonstrated the connection between Israel's Sinai covenant and Hittite treaties/covenants.[A-43] The Hittite body of treaties and the Sinai covenant are probably to be placed within the years 1400–1200 B.C. and nowhere else, according to Kitchen. At the very least this parallel establishes

these mixed features were suggestive of the deity, still the true form of the deity remained hidden.[211]

Out of the fire (4:15). Yahweh speaks to Israel "out of the fire" eight times in Deuteronomy.[212] In the ancient Near East, at Ugarit, the messengers for the god

the fact that the covenantal idea and actual covenants similar in form to the Sinai covenant were in the ancient Near East by the time of Moses.[A-44] Within the broader issue of historiography, it is clear that this covenant form allowed and encouraged a story-type of historiography (preamble, etc.) in Hittite documents[A-45] as it also did when used on a much more expanded and developed way by the author-editor of Deuteronomy.

Treaty between Ramesses II and the Hittites from the battle of Qadesh engraved on temple wall at Karnak
Todd Bolen/www.BiblePlaces.com

Yam (sea) were pictured as two flames of fire like burnished swords.[213] In the Babylonian Creation Epic, the god Ea takes the halo or bright *melammu* ("divine fire") of the god Apsu and encloses himself with it. At Ugarit *pd* was Baal's garment, signifying divine brilliance, and was essential to his royalty and kingship. Yam sought to remove it in order to dethrone Baal.[214] The gods gave protective rays of light (*melammu*) to Humbaba, enemy of Gilgamesh.[215] Both Marduk and Humbaba were divested at some point of their rays or mantles and became weak.[216] The *melammu* was not separate from the gods but emanated from them as a part of their awesome presence.

The sun, the moon and the stars (4:19). These heavenly bodies were considered gods all across the ancient Near East. See sidebar on "Astrology in the Ancient Near East."

prophets. Saggs summarizes the essential truth of this assertion in Babylonian religion.[235] The "divine" image itself was cut and carved from a piece of wood, decorated with precious stones, or made from metals. At the time of a ceremony called Opening the Mouth,[236] the divinity actually began to dwell in the statue. The ceremony took two days and was performed alongside a river bank. The human workers asserted that not they, but the craft-god had made the idol. The wood became a special bright wood, which was connected to both the underworld and the heavens. Later Esarhaddon, a Neo-Assyrian king, believed that the craftsmen who made the images were themselves divinely chosen. Diviners were employed to choose the lucky workers.

Gods could abandon their idols or be humbled by injuries sustained by the statues. The idols could become famished without food. Supposedly these idols in certain ceremonies or festivals could dine on beer, honey, fruit, and meat served up on golden platters. Neither Moses nor the later prophets would have any of this foolishness (Isa. 44:10–20).[237]

For the LORD your God is a merciful God (4:31). From hoary antiquity the concept of a compassionate/merciful god was present in the ancient Near East. This assertion is made about the god El, "the gracious, the merciful," at Ugarit.[238] Even within the brutal Assyrian kingdom favor and grace were not unknown. The great king Assurbanipal, representing his great Assyrian god Assur, claimed to have extended grace and favor toward some of his rebellious vassals at Qedar and at other locations.[239] In these texts the attitude of the king is a reflection of the god as well. In this case the Assyrian god would be the great god Assur, Mullissu, and Nabu, to whom Assurbanipal prayed passionately for mercy.[240]

Has anything so great as this ever happened, or has anything like it ever been heard of? (4:32). Ancient Near Eastern gods intervened in history, in the lives and affairs of their subjects over whom they ruled.[241] Egypt touted the antiquity of her nation, her ancient past, and her famous heroes.[242] "From the day it was founded" is probably an Egyptianism, as Couroyer has argued.[243]

However, in at least several ways, the Lord's actions toward Israel seem unparalleled in the ancient Near East. (1) Yahweh took his people out *from another nation* (v. 34); (2) the *means* he used to accomplish this was unparalleled in variety, quality, intensity, and purpose; (3) the rescue/taking of a people was only one component in a long-term plan stretching over centuries, even millennia.[244] The "migrations" of the Sea Peoples, while acts of God, did not bring about the results of the exodus of Israel.[245] The purpose of God's actions was made clear by his word/act in the past, present, and future. History was covenantally driven (teleology) in Israel, and the ultimate goal was Yahweh enthroned among his own people.

Then Moses set aside three cities east of the Jordan (4:41). "Bezer" may refer to modern el-ʾAmad, northeast of Medeba; the name is found in the Mesha Stele (ca. 830 B.C.) as a city of Mesha, king of Moab,[246] who rebuilt it. This may refer to Bezer in the mountains of Bashan or to Bezer (Tell Jabul) east of Medeba.[247] "Ramoth" is modern Tell Ramith between the upper Yarmuk and Jabbok rivers. Others suggest a Ramoth in the Argob region in Bashan. "Golan" is modern Sahm el-Jolan; it is east of Galilee by about seventeen miles.[248]

Basic Stipulations (5:1–33)

Hear, O Israel, the decrees and laws I declare in your hearing today (5:1). No concentrated collection of laws from the ancient Near East matches this crystallization of "ten words," the Decalogue.[249] Yet these words and commands are at home in their broader ancient Near Eastern setting,[250] which illuminates their structure and even content.[251] These commands are apodictic in form and state unequivocal prescriptions and proscriptions, but they do not define the penalties for breaking them.[252] Ancient Near Eastern law collections do not feature this type of law, but rather use, like most biblical law, case law (casuistic law).

Covenantal and treaty stipulations featured apodictic law, indicating that these "ten words" of instructions were to function as part of a covenant (see sidebar on "Ancient Near Eastern Treaties and Covenants" at 4:13). Apodictic formulation is also found in the wisdom literature of the ancient Near East, and in Israel divinely given wisdom often centers around the instructions of the Ten Commandments and the larger Torah. Apodictic instruction is used in the Instructions of Shuruppak (2600–1100 B.C.): "Do not steal something; do not kill yourself";[253] in the Instructions of Ur-Ninurta: The godfearing man "keeps ... swearing away from his house";[254] in the Counsels of Wisdom: "May you pay attention to the words of your mother as to the words of your god";[255] and in Egyptian literature: "Do not set your heart on wealth."[256]

The LORD our God made a covenant with us at Horeb (5:2). The basic stipulations of Israel's ancient Sinai Covenant reflect significant aspects of ancient Near Eastern covenants. The eternal validity and ongoing application of its apodictic law is hinted at in other ancient Near Eastern treaties/covenants, though Israel's covenant was uniquely monotheistic and powerfully futuristically oriented.[257] Esarhaddon's Assyrian treaty (ca. 680–69 B.C.) included persons who would live in the future: "your sons who will live after this treaty."[258] Assur, the great Assyrian god, transacted a covenant with some West Semitic peoples, an eternal covenant with them, including the divine sons of El and all of the divine council and with the heavens and earth.[259]

The LORD spoke to you face to face out of the fire (5:4). The ancient Near Eastern king was the immediate source and author of their laws. Hammurabi, commissioned by the god of justice, Shamash, put forth his laws as expressions of his own words. Shamash met "face to face" with Hammurabi on the eight-feet-high stele on which a prologue, 282 laws, and an epilogue were inscribed. The laws of Lipit-Ishtar were his own.[260] The laws express cosmic order that lies in a matrix behind or beyond the gods, but the king, at the top of the social pyramid,[261] promulgates laws to prosper the people, establish justice, and stabilize his government.[262] But in Israel the Lord is the origin and author of the laws, their transcendent source.

I am the LORD your God ... out of the land of slavery (5:6). This assertion identifies Yahweh as the liberator of Israel, the

Hammurabi's collection of legal sayings
Z. Radovan/
www.BibleLand
Pictures.com

Great King and Creator, of this covenant. It parallels the preambles found in many ancient Near Eastern covenants and treaties, especially those involving the Hittites and their vassals (ca. 1400–1200 B.C.). The Great King Sumilumiuma says in his preamble that he has "taken you, Aziru, as my subject" (cf. v. 9).[263]

You shall have no other gods before me (5:7). The central requirement of the covenant is total allegiance, unfeigned covenant love, to Yahweh alone. The exclusivity of Yahweh is vaguely paralleled in other ancient Near Eastern treaty texts, but in the form of an allegiance of the human vassal to his human suzerain and his many gods. Yahweh alone is God; he does not function in or with a community of gods, as the gods of the other nations did.[264] Idols were hardly separate from their gods in the ancient Near East,[265] and idols in Israel became a problem because a "god" was somehow tied to his idol (see comment on 4:28).

You shall not make for yourself (5:8–10). It follows that no images are to be used to represent or mediate the Lord.[266] The power of art forms to carry religious messages and to communicate ideology, class status, and so on was utilized abundantly in the ancient Near East.[267] But Yahweh's form was never revealed to Israel. An Egyptian papyrus at

Thebes from the close of the reign of Ramesses II asserts that Amun's real appearance was unknown even to the other gods, for Amun (meaning "hidden") hid himself from them.[268] Yet the sun was an emanation of Amun, and its worship flourished in Egypt.[269]

Sins of the fathers to the third and fourth generations (5:9). The third and fourth generations of a family covers the generations in a family that a person normally sees during their lifetime. It was also recognized in the ancient Near East (cf. Job 42:16). In a seventh-century inscription from Nerab, a priest of Sahr in Nerab had inscribed on his sepulcher that he had lived long enough to see "children of the fourth generation."[270] The mother of Babylonian king Nabonidus, in a sixth-century text, relates that she either lived for 104 years or saw her descendants to the fourth generation.[271] The anger of kings and gods to effect family punishment toward those who sin and threaten national and familial solidarity is well illustrated by Hittite literature. These ancient Near Eastern texts indicate that the biblical writer is stressing the duration of God's anger here.

During the reign of the Hittite king Mursilis II (1339–1306 B.C.) a devastating plague ravaged his land.[272] The king believed that his father Suppiluliumas had "sinned" against the word of a storm god, breaking covenant and angering the storm god. The plague rendered divine retribution for that fault. Mursilis II admits *his own* guilt as a result of his father's failures, praying that the pestilence will cease: "It is only too true, however, that the father's sin falls upon the son. So my father's sin has fallen upon me." In

▶ Aniconism in the Ancient Near East

Deuteronomy 5:8–10 is central to biblical theology.[A-56] From the beginning aniconism (which means "without idols"; the worship of gods is done via symbols rather than through icons") was a feature of Israel's religion at Sinai, a position that resonates with recent studies that argue that standing stones (maṣṣēbôt) with aniconic functions originated in the Negev and deserts of Sinai.[A-57] This was a move toward monotheism and God as Spirit.

In a similar vein this concept is found in certain eras and in certain ways in other nations. In Egypt an experiment with monotheism, a "strict practical monotheism," was recognized by some persons under Akhenaten (ca. 1380 B.C.) with respect to the deity Aten, and a relative aniconism with respect to Amun.[A-58] Some scholars hold that this universalistic flavor and trend toward monotheism was in the air before Akhenaten and the Amarna Revolution in Egypt.[A-59]

Aniconic elements may also be found in the Kassite era of Mesopotamia and perhaps in the cult of Assur in Assyria. In Syria (Bronze Age) and Anatolia aniconic features of religious cults are found. But standing stones (maṣṣēbôt) that represented deities are featured in this era, thought these standing stones are probably de facto aniconic themselves.[A-60]

No programmatic, theologically reasoned literary source repudiating iconism or affirming aniconism in a systematic way has been found or deciphered. This law sets off Israel firmly from her ancient Near Eastern neighbors.[A-61] The self-presentation of the Lord (v. 9) as found here is common to royal inscriptions in the ancient Near East: "I am Yawmelk, king of Byblos," or "I am Kulamuwa, son of Ḥayya."[A-62] So also, Mesha king of Moab introduces himself: "I am (ʿnk) Mesha the son of … the king of Moab."

Horned crown regularly used to represent the god Anu
Rama/Wikimedia Commons, courtesy of the Louvre

Seal depicts a bearheaded priest before divine symbols of the goddess Ishtar (star) and the god Sin (moon crescent) set on altars.
Werner Forman Archive/The British Museum

is most often prescribed (e.g., Laws 6–7, 9–10, 22, 25).[309] This could be avoided in some cases (Law 6) if the thief had the means to do so. In other cases a fine was permitted (Laws 25–26, 265).[310]

The Middle Assyrian Laws (ca. 1100–400 B.C.) on theft (e.g., Laws 3–6) call for a variety of punishments depending on the parties involved. Punishments included death, waiver of punishment, or horrible disfigurements.[311] Hittite laws treat a variety of thefts of animals and related actions.[312] Ordinary theft called for restitution as did most other types of theft (fraudulently keeping something, finder's keeper deception).[313] Key laws on theft and stealing are discussed in the Lipit-Ishtar Code (Law 9) and the Laws of Eshnunna (Laws 12–13).[314]

You shall not give false testimony (5:20). Bearing false witness was a serious breach of covenant faith in Israel. It was a basic fault in the rest of the ancient Near East as well. In a Sumerian proverb failing to keep a promise makes a person a liar,[315] and a person who speaks in a case but knows nothing about it is an abomination.[316]

In Mesopotamian laws if false testimony or witness was born and discovered, it was nullified, as in the Lipit-Ishtar Code (Law 17).[317] In Hammurabi's Code (Laws 1–4, 11), out of five laws, four condemn the guilty person to death. Only in a case dealing with grain or money was the guilty person able to pay a penalty instead.[318]

You shall not covet your neighbor's wife (5:21). This commandment prohibits an internal motivation or condition that desires (*ḥmd*, stimulated by vision) what a person is prohibited from having—the wife of another man. A different word is used (*ʿwh*, inner need) to prohibit taking of things. The verb *ḥmd* in this context has the connotation of "to appropriate" as well. The phrase "covet this city" occurs in a Phoenician text.[319] The commandment lies behind previous commands that destroy relationships.

The phrase "his land [field]" is coupled with "house" and is used in legal documents in the ancient Near East, especially at Ugarit.[320] In an Egyptian document recording the negative confessions of a deceased person, the deceased denies that he had been covetous. The fabled wise Egyptian Ptah-Hotep inveighed against covetousness as a deadly vice. In the Ramesside era the covetous person was considered a fool and covetousness a sin. Wealth, a poor man's possessions, a nobleman's wealth—none of these were to be coveted.[321]

The now famous Eloquent Peasant of Egypt expected a leader to be free from covetousness, and a covetous person would not enjoy success. One's own house should fill all of one's needs.[322] The inwardness of these admonitions is paramount, for the heart was regarded as "the god who dwells in man."[323] This central concept seems to be absent from Mesopotamian law; there is an emphasis on the act of appropriation, which was condemned.[324] In ancient wisdom literature, "coveting murders" and is an abomination to the gods Ninurta and Enlil.[325]

Two stone tablets (5:22). See comments on 4:13.

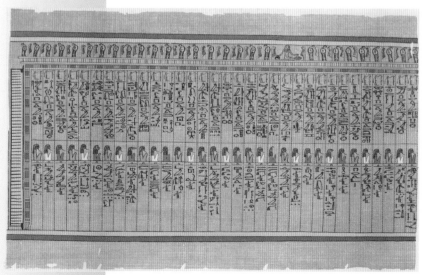

▶ Truth in Egyptian Society

The Egyptian goddess/god Maat represented truth, which was also a deified concept: order. This order was to be sought and maintained by the pharaoh in the divine and human/social realms. Maat nourished even Re, the sun god. In the human realm the goal was harmonious social cohesion; in the divine realm, since the king was divine, social stability and solidarity of the pharaonic state was the goal. The pharaoh was responsible for the temples and communicated with the gods and goddesses, always seeking harmony—ma'at.[A-63]

The triumph of the god Horus was a time when *maat* would prevail on earth, a time of peace and well-being.[A-64] In this sense *maat* was an ultimate goal, a present condition to be realized, not an abstract concept or goal toward which all things were moving. The gods had established truth and justice, and every pharaoh was to maintain or, if necessary, restore *maat*. Hence, a false witness disabled justice.[A-65] Faithfulness and trust was necessary among persons; therefore, false testimony was not an option among a covenant people.[A-66]

Horus and Maat
Werner Forman
Archive/The Egyptian Museum, Cairo

We have heard his voice from the fire (5:24). See comments on 1:33.

Then tell us whatever the LORD our God tells you (5:27). On the one hand, Moses plays a typical ancient Near Eastern role as a covenant mediator,[326] chosen by a god and/or a people. On the other hand, his role and the Lord's role are uniquely adapted to the Lord's covenant with his people.[327] It was customary to seek out the proper sacred officials of the temple or other sacred precincts in the ancient Near East so that a relevant answer could be given to a concerned inquirer.[328] The will of the deity was revealed in this way. Pharaoh Akhenaten was a mediator of his god's will in a unique sense, one that approaches Moses' position.[329]

Be careful to do what the LORD our God has commanded you (5:32). The people involved in the covenant/treaty processes and ceremonies are to pledge and respond at the conclusion of the covenant or treaty ceremony. Responses are to be from the whole heart in words expressing a treaty commitment and conclusion. In an eighth-century Aramaic treaty made between Bar-gahayah, king of KTK, and Matiḥel of Arpad, the words "you do swear" appear; they also appear in vassal treaties of Esarhaddon.[330] One of his treaties with a vassal includes a loyalty oath involving words, lips, and heart.[331] The same

Proto-Canaanite inscription shows a form of writing from this period
Z. Radovan/
www.BibleLand
Pictures.com

can be said of a Hittite text that contains ratification responses concerning Hatti and Hurrians represented by their king Kurtiwaza.[332] Those pledging were to assert in essence, as the Israelites did at Sinai, "we will listen and obey" (5:27).

Detailed Stipulations (6:1–11:32)

Flowing with milk and honey (6:3). This phrase occurs often (e.g., 11:9; 26:9, 15; 27:13; 31:20; cf. Ex. 3:8; Lev. 20:24; Num. 13:27). It is closely paralleled in Ugaritic poetry. "The heavens fat did rain, The wadies flow with honey!"[333] Milk and fat are mentioned as a blessed feature of the world ordered by Enki, who determined Sumer's destiny.[334] This hyperbolic metaphorical phrase stresses both the richness of Canaan and the special favor God has bestowed on it as the dwelling place for his people.

The LORD is one (6:4). This uniqueness of Yahweh is diametrically opposed to the multiplicity of gods in Canaan. Even the one god Ptah in Egypt could be referred to as "the one god in nineness."[335] Yahweh is the one and only God, not one god among many.[336]

His special character is safeguarded in this assertion.[337] Ancient Near Eastern scholars have suggested reading this as "Yahweh is our God, Yahweh is 'One'" or perhaps, "Yahweh our God is the Unique."[338] But there is only one unique God by definition. In the ancient Near East there were many gods, which created all kinds of confusion for they often opposed one another. Not Israel's One, Unique God![339] In a Sumerian

inscription, Enlil was declared to be king alone (his oneness);[340] likewise, Baal or the god Mot asserted "I am one," but also ruled over other "gods."[341] It appears that one god was supreme and ruled over other divine beings, "gods."

Several scholars in different fields of expertise have recently demonstrated that monotheism in a recognizable form, practical and conceptual, was around at least as early as the fifteenth to fourteenth centuries B.C.[342] In Egypt a hymn to Amun (ca. 1500/1400 B.C.), well before Akhenaten's religious revolution in Egyptian religion (1350–1340), sets forth Amun as "creator" of the other gods.[343] Akhenaten attempted to establish the sun-god Aten as the god, demoting all other gods to nongods.

Baines recognizes the monotheism of Akhenaten in Egypt as perhaps the only case of real monotheism.[344] Propp cogently but cautiously argues a monotheistic presence in the second millennium. He rejects arguments that Israelite monotheism was a product of the postexilic era after 586 B.C.[345] Egyptian religion in general rejected Akhenaten's attempt to deny the reality of a multiplicity of deities and accepted what Assmann calls the Ramesside approach, in which the multiplicity of deities reflects, in fact, various forms and manifestations of the one single transcendent god.[346] Amun was the "apogee of religious thought in ancient Egypt. He was the fashioner of himself who formed his own body, the first creator who was never born, without parallel and who oversees all."[347]

Love the LORD your God with all your heart (6:5). God's command to love him demands a single-minded love, a heart focused and centered on him alone as God

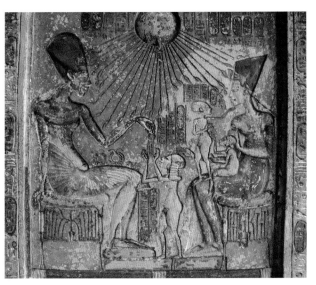

Aten pictured
as sun disk with
hands reaching
Akhenaton and
his family
Gerard Ducher/
Wikimedia Com-
mons, courtesy of the
Cairo Museum

The concept of the heart is central to the theological anthropology of the ancient Near East. In a hymn to Aten, the pharaoh says, "Thou art in *my heart* and there is no other that knows thee."[348] In Egypt the heart was nothing less than "the god who dwells in man." The heart itself dwelt in its shrine.[349] A righteous Egyptian worshiper was said "to hold Amun in his heart."[350]

The Great King, the suzerain, in a suzerain-vassal treaty in the ancient Near East expected his vassal to love him, not merely in a legal way but with fervor and emotional commitment. Correspondence between the great kings of that era is replete with expressions of love toward one another. Kings of Egypt, Babylon, Assyria, Hatti, Mitanni, and doubtless others—the "club" of royal brothers—exude mutual brotherhood, loyalty, and love to one another.[351] In Hittite parlance the vassal and his lord were to love each other as they loved themselves. Love unto death, the greatest love, was expected toward the suzerain from the vassal.[352] And love was expected of those surrounding the king (e.g., Esarhaddon, Assurbanipal), as they loved their own lives.[353] The vassal was to hate the enemy of his lord and the lord was to hate the enemy of his vassal. The subjects of the king, his people, were to love him.[354]

Upon your hearts (6:6). Heart in the sense of reason and cognitive functions is by far the most important bodily organ mentioned in the Old Testament.[355] In Ugaritic literature the heart is often paired with the liver as the internal organs of joy and laughter.[356] Its use in Gibson's translation portrays the heart as the seat of emotions and feeling.[357] In the Memphite Theology of Egypt the heart of the god Ptah functions both as a center of conceptual thinking and feeling through the senses. The heart is paired with the tongue and the control of all limbs. The tongue repeats what the heart formulates, while the heart gathers information from all of the senses.[358]

Putting words on one's heart and soul is expressed in loyalty oaths of the ancient Near East, as in Hittite treaties of Mursilis II and oaths of allegiance to Assyrian king Esarhaddon.[359] In an intimate didactic wisdom text (ca. 900–500 B.C.), a father, Ka-nakht, instructs his son to give ear to his words, "to put them in their heart."[360] The heart of the pharaoh was the key to his thinking and behavior and is mentioned hundreds of times in ancient Egypt literature.[361]

Impress them on your children (6:7). The inculcation of moral principles and wisdom in youth was practiced widely in the ancient Near East. See sidebar on "Education of Youth."

Tie them as symbols on your hands and bind them on your foreheads (6:8). "Your forehead" is literally "between your eyes" (cf. 11:18). This picturesque phrase is found in Ugaritic texts referring to the forehead of Judge River (Nahar)—that is, between the eyes of Nahar.[362] It was an obvious vital and vulnerable spot where an accurately placed blow could kill a person or disable a god. The forehead was considered a prominent location where some balm, the hairs of a dog, might be placed to help someone recover from drunkenness,[363] and it is mentioned as a place where a birth deformity might appear in omen texts.[364]

In the Aqhat Legend at Ugarit the appearance of Dan(i)el's forehead revealed worry and stress.[365] The Egyptian pharaoh wore a Ureaus, a protective serpent, on his forehead, a symbol also worn by the gods.[366] In Egypt during the New Kingdom, children wore cylindrical amulets containing strips of papyrus. Inscriptions on the tiny papyrus strips protected them from various dangers. No ambiance of magic surrounded an Israelite's display of God's law; this symbol reminded them to follow the covenant stipulations.[367]

Write them on the doorframes of your house, and on your gates (6:9). Doorposts or doorframes seem to be related to Akkadian *manzazu* ("stand, position, door, socket").[368] Silver plaques written in ancient Hebrew script have been unearthed (eighth or seventh century B.C.).[369] All types of

Modern Jew wearing phylacteries
Jack Hazut

materials and writing surfaces were used to display important written materials, including silver amulets in Egypt,[370] with textual material on them. They were fastened to a person's arm, hand, or neck and bore important messages.

Plastered walls and doorways, more germane to this biblical text, were used at Kuntillet ʿAjrud (eighth century B.C.). Gates of cities also provided exposure for important notices. Papyrus, stone, copper, bronze, arrowheads, seals (clay), waxed wood boards, and leather—all of these were employed in writing.[371] These materials and the inscriptions on them provided an opportunity to tie a person to a god who protected them and whom they wanted to constantly revere, as well as to serve as a memorial sign in the presence of the deity.[372]

A land with large flourishing cities (6:10–11). In many cases these "cities" were taken over, not built for the first time. This was common in the ancient Near East where whole peoples and nations could be uprooted and their land and cities taken over by intruders[373] or conquerors.

Stager describes what we know about the ancient Canaanite "houses" that Israel took over,[374] including the building materials used to construct them. A typical rectilinear house may have featured: (1) two, three, or four rooms, (2) three rooms formed by rows of longitudinal pillars that created a central large room, and (3) a back room or broad room for storage. Small windows were left in the walls. Ceramic lamps, flax wicks, and olive oil for fuel created artificial light in the houses. The door pivoted in sockets. The lintel over the doorframe was supported by two doorposts. The threshold was usually a single block of stone. Wooden bolts and tumble locks were used in the doors of palaces, temples, granaries, storage facilities, and domestic houses. Houses supported by pillars always had roofs. In some cases stairs led up to the roof. The "typical" four-room pillared Israelite house has been found outside of Israel and may have been simply a

► Education of Youth

In Egypt teaching and instruction were used from at least 2500 B.C. up until the time of the Ptolemies (ca. 300 B.C.).[A-67] Rules of conduct and learning were prepared for sons. From moral issues to royal protocol children were trained in the home or in the king's palace. Order, truth, and justice (all together equaled Egyptian *maat*) were important.

Proverbs 1–9 present a wisdom that resembles Egyptian *maat*. An especially close relationship exists between Proverbs 22–23 and the teaching of Amenemope.[A-68] In Mesopotamia likewise, Sumerian literature includes the advice of a father to his son.[A-69] Several famous works of a didactic nature come from Mesopotamia.[A-70] The Words of Ahiqar, although extant in texts from ca. 500 B.C., was certainly composed far earlier than the time of Esarhaddon

(680–669).[A-71] Repetition by mouth and copying texts and strict discipline (the rod!) were the two main pedagogical means of "impressing" a desired curriculum on a student or child. This was done both in the home and in any place of learning available.[A-72]

Covenantal conditions and stipulations were passed on so that following generations would know and pursue them diligently—and, of course, for political purposes. Esarhaddon declared a curse on anyone who would not pass on the traditions and conditions of his vassal treaties: "If you … do not transmit it to your sons who will live after this treaty.…" He continues, "May your sons and grandsons because of this fear, in the future, your god Assur and your lord, the crown prince designate Assurbanipal."[A-73]

common Canaanite house, not an innovation by Israel.

"Wells" (*bôrôt*) were used from ancient times, as far back as the sixth millennium. Wells at Lachish, Tell Sheva, existed in biblical times. Water shafts were connected to springs at Hazor, Megiddo, Gibeon, and Jerusalem. Over one hundred wells were located at the Philistine city of Ashkelon. Pools were constructed around wells for watering animals. Some translate this word as "cisterns"—that is, artificial reservoirs of water. These were normally hewn out of bedrock.[375]

Take your oaths in his name (6:13). Oaths were common in ancient Near Eastern treaties. This fact appears in the essentials of its literary form, namely, the promulgation of terms of the treaty or covenant and some adumbration of an oath in the list of gods invoked as witnesses or in the curses or blessings. The enactment of the curses or blessings was dependent on the fidelity or infidelity of the covenantal parties to the oath.[376]

Oaths were a part of treaties and covenants from the earliest times in Sumer and Elam (third millennium B.C.), Mesopotamia, Ebla, Mari, and especially

Typical four-room house
Alva Steffler/Susanna Vagt

◄

among the Hittites (parity or vassal treaties), Syria (seventeenth century), and Assyria. Oaths were sworn in Akkadian to the life of the king or to the life of a god,[377] also in Egypt,[378] and in the Canaanite-Phoenician milieu.[379] A ruler in Arpad or Damascus set up a stele to Melquart, patron deity of the city of Tyre in Phoenicia, and made a vow to him.[380] Soldiers took solemn oaths to serve the king, the nation, and its gods. To break this oath could lead to death, abject humility, and shaming.[381]

Do not follow ... the gods of the peoples around you (6:14). All the nations around Israel had multiple gods. See sidebar on "Gods in the Ancient Near East."

Massah (6:16). Massah was located near Horeb (Sinai) and Rephidim (cf. Ex. 17:1) but cannot be pinpointed on a biblical map. Since the name is given to the events there, not the location, it is possible that Massah is Rephidim and the occasional name is not a separate location (cf. also Ps. 95:8).[382]

Drives out before you many nations (7:1). This list features seven nations Israel was to drive out of Canaan. Egypt designated her traditional enemies as the "Nine Bows."[383] This idiom designated the peoples that she conquered and kept in subjection. It is even found in the names of the pharaohs.[384]

Hittites (7:1). The New Kingdom of Hatti, a people who inhabited and ruled

in the area of Anatolia and Syria, began under Tudhaliya I (ca. 1430–1410 B.C.) and expanded until Hattushili III (ca. 1239). They concluded a treaty with Egypt in the twenty-first year of Ramesses II. The Hittite empire lasted from about 1239–1180 B.C.[385] The Hittites vied with Egypt for rule over Canaan and southern Syria, especially the area around Kedesh on the Orontes. They immigrated into upper Syro-Palestine and spread south into upper Canaan. They adapted to Canaanite life and culture. Significant cultural and literary parallels between the texts of the Old Testament and Hittite literature have been addressed.[386]

There is only circumstantial evidence for Hittites in Canaan in the Late Bronze Age (ca. 1600–1200). They were in Emar in Syria.[387] Kitchen argues for Hittites in Israelite territory in the eighteenth century.[388] The migration of the Sea Peoples undoubtedly swept many people along with it or before it into Canaan in about 1220–1200 B.C. or earlier, including Hittites.[389]

Girgashites (7:1). The Girgashites were a subgroup of Canaanites. They descended from Ham (Gen. 10:15–16). At Ugarit the name Girgash and the phrase "son of *Grgs*" are present, suggesting that the name was at least known in early Israel.[390] Some suggest they came from Asia Minor.[391]

Amorites, Canaanites (7:1). See comments on 1:7.

Perizzites (7:1). In the Old Testament the Perizzites are located in the hill country of northern Canaan (Josh. 11:3). Additional references suggest other areas farther south and certain regions of Carmel. Archaeologists and philologists are divided over whether they

▶ Gods in the Ancient Near East

A profile of Canaanite religion in the ancient Near East is taking shape for us in texts coming from Ugarit, a coastal city not far from Canaanite territory to the south.[A-74] Religion there was largely mythological and assumed that the forces of nature manifested the gods and were controlled by the gods. In the cult priestly personnel and their subordinates made appeal to these divine beings through rituals. El was the purported head of the Canaanite pantheon, and he had a consort, Asherah (Athirat). As father of the pantheon, he was rather distant from the common worshiper and even the priests in Ugarit.

The god Baal was in touch with the people and the one through whom the forces of nature and divinity worked. He was recognized under other names, such as Hadad and Dagan, and he manifested himself in various locations, taking to himself the name of that location (e.g., Baal Peor, Baal Berith, Baal Zebul). Hadad was son of Dagan, according to sources from upper Mesopotamia. Possibly Hadad, the storm god from Mari, became Baal elsewhere in Canaan.

Baal achieved hegemony among the other gods in Canaan, such as El, Yam (Sea), Nahar (River), Mot (Death), and Anat (Baal's sister). For Baal, rain was thought to be his semen, impregnating the earth; Asherah, his wife, was goddess of fertility. Asherim (poles, green trees, divine symbols) and sacred stones (*maṣṣēbôt*) marked sacred places and even gods. Israel's "great sin" was that she whored after the gods of Canaan (Judg. 2:17).[A-75]

The neighbors of Israel delighted in their multiplicity of gods: Ammonites (Milcom, chief god, plus nine others), Moabites (Chemosh [Kemosh], Ashtar-Chemosh, both mentioned in the Moabite Stone); Edom (Qaws, chief god; Baal, Hadad, and an unnamed goddess); Byblos (Baal Shemayin, chief deity; Baal Dor, Baal, Baʾalat gbl, "lady of Byblos"); Sidon (Eshmun, Astarte, Resheph, Rehaim), Tyre (Melkart). The list goes on for Serepta and Ugarit (at least three goddesses). A divine council of gods functioned in most areas.[A-76] Chthonic deities (earth/underworld gods) were also common at Ebla, Ugarit, and some Transjordanian areas.

Resheph
Z. Radovan/
www.BibleLand
Pictures.com
◀

Edomite deity,
perhaps Qaws
Z. Radovan/
www.BibleLand
Pictures.com
◀

were possibly Hurrians or a subgroup of Amorites.[392] The personal name Perissi or Perizzi (Hurrian) describes an envoy from Mitanni in both cuneiform and Egyptian texts.[393]

Hivites (7:1). The Hivites "originated" in the areas bordering Egypt and the Hittite empire (ca. twelfth century B.C.). However, some scholars connect them to the Luwians from the area of Cilicia; others identify the Hivites with the Horites/Hurrians (cf. Deut. 2:12, 20).[394] They are found as far south as Edom/Seir.

Figure from the City of David that could be a Jebusite. Jebusites are also perhaps mentioned in a Mari text.
Z. Radovan/ www.BibleLand Pictures.com
▲

Jebusites (7:1). The Jebusites were located in the hill country of Canaan and, at least later, inhabited Jerusalem in the twelfth to eleventh centuries. Their origin is obscure except for circumstantial biblical evidence, which suggests (weakly) that they were from the land of the Hittites. Some scholars continue to tie them to the Hurrians and note the similarities between worship in Jerusalem and the rituals of the Hittites/Hurrians.[395] The Amarna Tablets contain the name of a king of Jerusalem, Abdu-Heba, who would reasonably have been a Jebusite.[396] Only under David were these people finally conquered and the Israelites took over the city.

Destroy them totally (7:2). See comments on 2:34.

Smash their sacred stones, cut down their Asherah poles (7:5). Sacred stones, images, and idols (7:25–26) were found in Hazor from the Late Bronze Age at the time Israel was there.[397] Standing stones,[398] altars,[399] and symbols (poles, trees, figures) of Asherah were part of the furnishings of the cults and rituals in Canaan from 1200–930 B.C.,[400] as were idols/images. The Asherahs (sacred symbols) represented the female aspect of deity.[401]

At Ugarit Athirat depicts the wife of El, head of the pantheon. In Mesopotamia (ca. 1830–1531 B.C.) the female deity Ašratum is equivalent to Athirat at Ugarit. The name of the goddess Asherah appears in kings' names at Amurru, such as in Abdi-Ashirta. This king's name appears in the Amarna letters several times.[402] This word also denoted a symbolic tree or pole.[403] In Egypt the goddess Qdš parallels Asherah/Athirat/Ašratum, especially since this name for Asherah is found at Ugarit.[404] Ašertu, a Hittite

goddess, certainly represents Asherah[405] of the Bible as well. From about 750 B.C. and 800 B.C. respectively we have references to "Asherah of YHWH" from Kuntillet ʿAjrud (ca. forty miles south of Kadesh Barnea) and from Khirbet el-Qom, nine miles west of Hebron.[406] This plethora of cultic female imagery and goddesses, along with potentially sexually charged sacred stones, drove the need for the biblical authors and Israel to contend against seductive and tempting religious objects.

Treasured possession (7:6). Israel's depiction as God's "special possession" translates *segullâ* (used eight times in the Old Testament). This term occurs in the ancient Near East from the first part of the second millennium. In Old Babylonian Akkadian the word *sikiltu* is found in Hammurabi's laws as well as at Alalakh, reflecting eighteenth-century usage. It is found in fifteenth-century Nuzi. At Ugarit the cognate word *sglt* is present, but thereafter, its use was minimal in the ancient Near Eastern documents that we have.[407] The use of these words points to someone who is a special personal possession of his own god. Its meaning shades over into "beloved" and thus singles out[408] Israel before Yahweh. In Hittite texts the word refers to a special position of status for the king at Ugarit based upon a covenant relationship with Hatti.

But it was because the LORD loved you and kept the oath (7:8). The theme of the Lord's love for Israel justifies her special place before Yahweh. This concept has some partial analogues in the ancient Near Eastern literature. In this material apologies or justifications are given for certain individuals, especially rulers, who took power under unusual circumstances.[409] Whole cities such as Babylon fall within this purview, for the Babylonian creation account justifies and proclaims Babylon as the favored of Marduk.[410] Individuals who enjoyed a chosen status, among others, included Hattusilus III of Hatti and Nabonidus of Babylon.[411]

Grain, new wine and oil (7:13). These three products of an agricultural land are often found together in the Old Testament and are present in other ancient Near Eastern literature as well, such as materials from Ugarit.[412] Likewise the increase of herds and flocks as stereotyped expressions (28:4, 18) occurs in Ugaritic literature.[413] These crops and produce were clearly a common feature of the territory.

Disease (7:15). The sicknesses and medicines of Egypt were a part of Israel's historical memory (cf. Ex. 15:26). These diseases are described amply in many ancient Near Eastern texts.[414] The etiology of disease in Egypt traced many illnesses to internal decay; hence, the use of purgatives and enemas was common. Defecation was a process and product that was watched carefully. Hygienic processes were prescribed and followed to thwart possible diseases. Diseases that were certainly present included dental problems (attrition and cavities), broken bones, bone cancer, arthritis, obesity, baldness, and less certain, smallpox, polio, and malaria. Epidemics occurred because of poor sanitation. From a study of Egyptian art, dwarfs, hunchbacks, clubfeet, hernias, and emaciation were the result of poor health conditions in the ancient world. Persons rarely lived beyond forty or fifty years. "Drugs" from vegetables, animals, and minerals constituted an Egyptian pharmacopoeia.[415]

Hornet (7:20). "Hornet" may be a metaphor standing for panic or depression.[416] Or the phrase could be shorthand for invading peoples or armies, as is "flies" or "bees" (Isa. 7:18–19). Rendsburg notes in the latter case that it is interesting

Twelfth-century bronze model from Susa with stylized trees in worship setting
Rama/Wikimedia Commons, courtesy of the Louvre

Stele of Qadesh, a Syrian goddess accompanied by Resheph and Amon-Ra, Nineteenth–Twentieth Dynasty
Rama/Wikimedia Commons, courtesy of the Louvre

that the Egyptian hieroglyphic signs used to designate the pharaoh could be a hornet (*ṣirʿâ*) and may imply the centuries-long military and political involvement of the Egyptians in Canaan. The city-states of the Middle Bronze and Late Bronze Ages were weakened, providentially, by Yahweh during Egypt's hegemony, so that Israel could enter the land successfully.[417] However, a literal meaning is possible, for insects were used as agents of war in the ancient Near East.[418]

Deliver them over to you (7:23–24). The statement that Yahweh is giving Israel's enemies into her power (hand), often so that Israel can "wipe them out" (*ʾābad*), occurs many times in Deuteronomy. This divine activity on behalf of Israel parallels other ancient Near Eastern literature.[419] In the Amarna letters a king of Mitanni tells Amenophis III (ca. 1403–1364 B.C.) that Teshub (a god of Mitanni) has given his enemies into his hand so that he may destroy them.[420] Nebuchadnezzar asserts that Marduk has given many peoples into his hand and he has subdued them. The same divine activity in history is attributed to the sun goddess of Arinna on behalf of a Hittite king, Mursulis I (1330–1295 B.C.).[421]

Israel is to annihilate the Canaanites (Ex. 17:14–16), for Yahweh has given them into her hand. She too had been the object of planned genocide, both in Egypt and in Canaan at the hands of Merneptah (1209 B.C.). He thought that he had decimated the *seed* of the people Israel.[422]

Feeding you with manna (8:3). The Hebrew word *hammān* ("manna"), meaning "What is it?" conveys the inability of

Relief from causeway of Unas at Saqqara shows victims of famine.
Werner Forman Archive/The Louvre

Israel to explain what this phenomenon was. "Tamarisk manna," secreted by an insect and gathered in large amounts in northern Iraq by Kurds for food in May-June, may parallel this at a natural level. It could have been produced in Sinai in the mid-thirteenth century in amounts sufficient to feed a large number of people.[423] But such naturalistic explanations are inadequate at this point in the light of the biblical text. Israel's King-God fed them; God's people had access to the King's table and stood in his grace. The manna-food, though small in amount, was eminently sufficient. Israel would live off of God's "words" primarily, not material provisions.

Eating at the king's table and tasting "the food of the gods" was part of the culture of the ancient Near East. In the last Babylonian era of 900–705 B.C., an already-old tradition is recorded concerning Adad-Nirari III, which permitted the kings to eat "remnants" of divine meals offered to the gods.[424] Perhaps the analogue here is one of a royal, priestly nation, each and every person receiving food from the table of the Great King.

Your clothes did not wear out (8:4). In the Babylonian Epic of Gilgamesh (11:244–46), Utnapishtim, the "Babylonian Noah," puts forth a prayer and hope for Gilgamesh. The hero was encouraged when told that until he finishes his journey to acquire his goal of finding a life-giving plant, his cloak will not have moldy cast but will remain wholly new.[425] In Deuteronomy this is clearly an idiom for expressing God's watchful care over his people Israel, until they reach their goal, the Promised Land, where life will be abundant.[426]

A land with wheat and barley ... bread (8:8). Certain political ancient Near Eastern covenants contained a land grant description with features as are found here,[427] but it is also found in treaties.[428] The essential difference between political treaties and land grant treaties was that in the latter the master obligated himself freely to the vassal or grantee. In the former the vassal was obligated to his master. The land grant is held in perpetuity even if the vassal broke faith and the stipulations of the grant. His descendants would retain the land/property granted.[429] The historical prologues of political treaties could contain land grant features that included careful descriptions of the land in question.[430]

A failure of barley and wheat was a major disaster in time of drought to an agricultural community. When this crop flourished, the god of the nation was given credit.[431] In a good year wheat and barley were produced in abundance by the latter spring rains.[432] A school boy's writing exercise, the Gezer Calendar, contains a record of the months of barley and wheat planting.[433] The land is described similarly in the Egyptian story of Sinuhe (ca. 1960 B.C.), a fugitive from Egypt residing in the land of Canaan. He describes the land as "a good land" producing figs, grapes, abundance of wine, honey, olives, fruit trees, barley, and emmer, and it was full of cattle. The land flowed with an abundance of milk.[434]

A land where the rocks are iron ... dig copper out of the hills (8:9). Copper and iron were found in the Arabah, especially from the Dead Sea to the Gulf of Aqaba and possibly in Transjordan.[435] This expression reveals the author's view of the extent of the Promised Land.[436] Copper was the first metal used in the ancient world and was mined deep in the ground in the Beersheba Valley as far back as the fourth millennium.

Copper metallurgy was practiced in Arad, but most of the metal objects found there came from the Early Bronze II Age.

Copper ores were also used at Timna' on the eastern border of the Arabah.[437] Tin (10 percent) and copper (80 percent) were combined to produce bronze. The ancient sources of tin are uncertain. Iron was, however, scarce in Palestine. Small amounts of surface iron ore deposits are north of the Jabbok River. Significant deposits of iron were found at several other places, such as the Ajlun Hills and ironsmith shops located in Tell Deir ʿAllah and Tell Qasile. Because of the high temperature need, it was not possible to produce cast iron in antiquity.[438]

Inscribed by the finger of God (9:10). This bold anthropomorphism is an example of synecdoche, letting a part stand for the whole. God was the author of the ten words (cf. Ex. 31:18). In Egyptian mythology the finger of the Egyptian God Seth had been used to damage the "Eye of Horus." Until it was removed, Horus's eye would not heal. The phrase "finger(s) of the god(s)" is also found in Mesopotamian texts. In two Babylonian texts Döller notes the outstretched finger of the ritualist while sealing an oath as a sign in that context of danger or threat from the god.[439] This metaphor suggests

Gezer calendar
Z. Radovan/
www.BibleLand
Pictures.com
▲

Timna' copper mine
Christine Thompson
▼

that divine presence and power wrote the Ten Words. Most likely each tablet contained a full copy of the Ten Words.[440]

Taberah, Massah and Kibroth Hattaavah (9:22). Taberah ("burning"; Num. 11:13) and then Kibroth Hattaavah were the first camping sites after Sinai (Num. 11:34; 33:16). Their locations are not certain. At Taberah quail brought on a plague. Both places lay between Hazeroth (Num. 11:35) and Sinai. Kitchen suggests a location around Wadi Saɔl on to Wadi Marra.[441]

Ark out of acacia wood (10:3). The ark of the covenant was a wooden chest carried by poles inserted into rings attached to the corners of the chest. Similar construction patterns have been uncovered in Egypt from the tomb of Tutankhamon (1336–27 B.C.).[442] Kitchen describes the tabernacle in which the ark was housed as a Bronze Age production and presents an example of a portable tabernacle.[443]

Acacia was a primary wood in Egypt for various kinds of carpentry. It grew in the Sinai area and was fairly common in the thirteenth century B.C. It was relatively light but strong and hard, making it ideal for furniture.[444] Sources of acacia today are only a fraction of what was available in antiquity. Hoffmeier has shown convincingly that the use of acacia wood for the ark fits the date of events at Sinai.[443] All of the features of the ark (portable shrine, carrying poles, priestly care for it, winged creatures, gilded wood)

were present in Egypt (1479–1069).[446] The compound wooden bow made of this material was in use then and was bound together by smaller pieces of wood and glue.[447] The strong gates at Lachish were made of acacia wood.[448]

Jaakanites ... Moserah ... Gudgodah ... Jotbathah (10:6–7). The location of the Jaakanites is not certain, but the name possibly relates them to the family of Akan (Gen. 36:27). The location of Moserah is still uncertain; it is near to or the same as Mount Hor.[449] Gudgodah is possibly Bir Taba located on the west side of the Arabah, south of the Dead Sea.[450] Jotbathah was then in the same area, but east of Gudgodah. Both places were probably watering locations. The locations may have been respectively at Ain el-Gattar and Ain el-Weibah, on the east side of the Arabah about twenty miles south of the Dead Sea.[451]

Itineraries similar to this one are known from Mesopotamia (e.g., the annals of Tukulti-Ninurta II, 890–84 B.C.).[452] In fact, such itineraries and geography are found throughout antiquity in the ancient Near East:[453] Old Babylonian itineraries of the eighteenth century,[454] Mari itineraries, and Egyptian itineraries constituting the military directions for New Kingdom pharaohs (sixteenth–fifteenth centuries),[455] with some toponymn lists coming from the Late Bronze Age.[456] This passage and other itineraries in the Old Testament were part and parcel of the ancient Near Eastern world.[457]

Circumcise your hearts ... do not be stiff-necked (10:16). The metaphorical concept of the heart was and is central to biblical anthropology, spirituality, and theology (see comments on 6:5–6). The heart was the focus of moral fortitude and character development and was considered as a gift of the gods; hence, it was metaphorically referred to as a "god."[458] A circumcised heart responded, panting after the law of the Lord and his covenant. It trusted in the moral, ethical, religious, and spiritual guid-

Itinerary from the Annals of Tukulti-Ninurta II
Marie-Lan Nguyen/ Wikimedia Commons, courtesy of the Louvre

ance of the covenant and the Torah. It communed within its chamber with the "law of the LORD" and his presence "day and night" (cf. Ps. 1:2).

Circumcision was practiced in the ancient Near East by many peoples. The Egyptians practiced circumcision as early as the third millennium.[459] West Semitic peoples, such as Israelites, Ammonites, Moabites, and Edomites performed circumcision. Eastern Semitic peoples did not (e.g., Assyrians, Babylonians, Akkadians). Nor did the Philistines, an Aegean or Greek people.[460] However, while the Hebrews amputated the prepuce of the penis, the Egyptians merely incised the foreskin and so exposed the glans penis.[461] To circumcise one's heart in order to become a part of the Lord's covenant people was the internal equivalent of covenantal commitment to the Lord, observable by God, not a human

being. A circumcised Israel loved God from the inside out, and God sustained their trust in him.

The great God, mighty and awesome (10:17). This powerful language recalls the God of the exodus and urges the reader to make the connection (cf. 10:20). Titles were popular in the ancient Near East, especially royal titles. The title "lord of kings" is in a Philistine letter to Pharaoh and also found as a title in Phoenician. The exact title "lord of lords" is present in Assyrian texts, usually occurring before the late kings of Assyria. The "mighty and awesome" god is an epithet also at Ugarit (*mlk rb*).[462]

He defends the cause of the fatherless and the widow (10:18). This language is a mainstay in the laws and the prologues/epilogues in the ancient Near East (e.g., Hammurabi's Law Code; also those found at Ugarit in the Aqhat Epic). Lipit-Ishtar's prologue and epilogue (1934–24 B.C.) imply this act of justice. The concern is expressed among the Hittite kings as well, as kings and gods gave special attention and protection to these groups of people.[463]

Seventy (10:22). The number "seventy" has a rich use in the Bible and in the ancient Near East, primarily in the northwest Semitic and Egyptian areas.[464] The multiplication from seventy persons (literal) who migrated to Egypt into an unlimited host (metaphorical) describes Israel's amazing multiplication into an innumerable number.

Seventy expresses totality. Panamuwa slew seventy of his brothers (all of them) to become king.[465] It indicates potential (cf. Ex. 1:1–7). ʿAnatu slew an innumerable number of sacrificial animals for the god Baal in the Baal Myth at Ugarit—seventy at

a time.[466] The seventy sons (divine) of Athirat are mentioned in texts at Ugarit.[467] In Egyptian literature the phrase "seventy kings in seventy days" may refer to the seventy "creative forces" in Heliopolitan cosmology.[468] The Lord was Israel's sole creative force at creation and in procreation.

Horses and chariots (11:4). Chariots in the ancient Near East for millennia trumped cavalry. Until the Eighteenth or Nineteenth Dynasty, Egypt did not use cavalry except to serve the chariots in battle. In the time of Shalmaneser III (858–824 B.C.) and Tiglath-Pileser III (744–727 B.C.) cavalry began to play a greatly expanded role in warfare.[469]

Irrigated it by foot (11:10). In Egypt agriculture depended on irrigation systems of some kind. By contrast, the land of Palestine soaked up the rain and produced crops over a large area and in many settings.[470] Small channels dug by one's foot watered the small ribbon of irrigated land in Egypt.[471] Land not covered by the annual Nile flood had to be irrigated manually. Watering a plot of land was a constant chore in Egypt and so depicted in the Egyptian Satire on the Trades, for the gardener had to water the vegetables daily or they would fail: "In the morning he waters vegetables, the evening he spends with the herbs."[472] In the fertile land of Canaan, rain sent by the Lord watered the

land, a condition depicted by the Egyptian fugitive Sinuhe.[473]

Some scholars detect a bit of mockery in the phrase "irrigated it by foot" by taking the Hebrew phrase as a euphemistic idiom referring to urination, "waters of the feet." In Egypt land plots were relatively small so that one owner could have watered it by urination.[474] In any case, the potential multiple resources for water in Canaan exceeded those in Egypt.

So if you fully obey ... be careful or you will be enticed to turn away (11:13–16). In ancient Near Eastern treaties the gods rewarded fealty to a treaty or covenant; failure to keep such incurred the wrath of the gods who had been entreated to judge the participants of the document according to the oaths they had taken. Rain was absolutely necessary to the land of Palestine. The Lord would send both early and latter rain to prosper Israel's crops, if she carefully kept the covenant stipulations.[475]

But in Israel, spiritual/moral beliefs merged to a degree not evident in other ancient Near Eastern laws or worldviews.[476] The visitation of pestilence and drought were signs of the displeasure of the god(s), as in the time of a devastating drought in the reign of the Hittite King Mursilis in Hatti (ca. 1330–1295 B.C.) and in Israel in the days of Elijah (ca. 870 B.C.). In Canaan Baal could be the source of devastations. The Egyptian god Seth could create drought conditions in Hatti. The anger of Pharaoh Ramesses II could keep rain from the Hittites.[477] Threats to shut down rain were among the curses in Hittite treaties.[478]

From the desert to Lebanon, and from the Euphrates River to the western sea (11:24). Hittite and Assyrian treaties have similar descriptive approaches for their territories as are depicted in verses 23–25. The Assyrian king Adad-Nirari boasted that his conquered territory stretched "as far as the Great Sea of the Rising Sun (and) from the banks of the Euphrates."[479] The Euphrates River and Mount Lebanon were favorite ancient Near Eastern territorial markers. The "Euphrates my rear line and Mount Lebanon my border"[480] is found in Hittite documents.

I am setting before you a blessing and a curse (11:26). Threats of blessings or curses were tied to covenant fealty in a prophetic utterance found at Mari.[481] A theology of the heart was imbedded within its formal ancient Near Eastern covenant/treaty form. Likewise, Israel's faithfulness to her covenant God determined whether she received a curse or a blessing.

Mount Gerizim ... Mount Ebal (11:29). Mount Ebal, just north of Shechem, stands 3,080 feet high; Mount Gerizim, just south of Shechem, towers 2,849 feet. These mountains, situated on the main north-south road, and the valley between them form an east-west entrance into Canaan. The curses and blessings of the covenant could be recited antiphonally by the participants, positioned in the narrowest part of the valley, opposite each other (cf. 27:13–26).

At Mount Ebal (Jebel Islamiyeh today), two archaeological strata are present, one dating (II) from ca. 1240–1200 B.C. and the other (I) from about 1200–1130 B.C. Excavator A. Zertal is convinced that a cult center is present.[482] Finds from Stratum II possibly include many bones of sacrificial animals. Two Egyptian scarabs dating to the last part of the reign of Ramesses II are present, as is a stone seal dating from the same era. A large altar for burnt offerings (beginning of Stratum 1B, 1200 B.C.) suggests a connection with Israelites and Mesopotamia. Enclosures, evidently imported, suggest a multi-tribal society.[483] It has non-Canaanite elements.

Other interpreters disagree strongly. Kempinski maintains that it is an Iron Age I watchtower, while Dever suggests that it may be a farmhouse.[484] Perhaps it is the precursor to Shiloh.[485] A. Mazar tentatively accepts the cultic character of the site, maintaining that the old traditions in the biblical text go back to the Israelite settlement era.[486]

Mount Gerizim (Jebel et-Tur today) was excavated in 1968 on its lower north slope. A structure built in the Middle Bronze Age (ca. 1650–1540 B.C.) and serving as a temple, was unearthed, an indication of the religious significance of the mountain for Israel.[487]

Detailed Stipulations: Purity and Unity (12:1–26:19)

Laws you must be careful to follow (12:1). Westbrook argues that the biblical laws do not follow entirely the categories of other ancient Near Eastern law collections. He finds Israel's laws reflecting a riddle pattern of arrangement (cf. Prov. 30:18–19, 21–23).[488] Others disagree. At any rate, the laws given in chapters 12–26 find many apparent parallels in other ancient Near Eastern legal materials. See sidebar on "Israel's Law and Other Ancient Near Eastern Laws."

Places on the high mountains and on the hills and under every spreading tree (12:2). In a Sumerian Disputation between Ewe and Wheat, a primordial sacred location is depicted, the Hill of Heaven and Earth. There the "godlings" were generated by An and there they lived and worked. Ewe and Wheat came down to emerge from the Holy

Structure on Mount Ebal considered an altar by many
Z. Radovan/ www.BibleLand Pictures.com

▶ Israel's Law and Other Ancient Near Eastern Laws

Millard notes that the laws of Moses compare favorably with the Code of Hammurabi, so that the common legal traditions of the ancient Near East become evident, though there are also important Israelite "distinctions." One striking differences between Hammurabi's Code and the Mosaic corpus is that in Israelite law persons are clearly more valuable than property or possessions. Crimes against persons or property receive similar punishment in Hammurabi's Code. In biblical law crimes against persons carry physical penalties, while offenses concerning possessions carry monetary or material penalties.[A-77] But in both situations, these so-called codes provide general principles that can be applied in specific cases.

Rendsburg brings attention to the clear relationship between Israel's laws and the Mesopotamian collection in both content and form.[A-78] In addition to what has been said above, he insists that Israel's laws were generated as a reaction against the legal practices of her Canaanite neighbors. Some of these specific issues are noted in the various laws discussed below (e.g., 17:6; 23:16–17; 23:18).[A-79]

Westbrook asserts that the real difference between biblical law and ancient cuneiform law is that biblical law allows for and fosters dissent rather than acquiescence to establishment practice and theory. Israelite kings were condemned for not establishing justice, while ancient Near Eastern kings praised themselves for doing so.[A-80] Many scholars consider the tie between divine covenant and divine law from a *divine* Lawgiver to be unique to Israel.[A-81]

Cultic platform at Tel Dan
Todd Bolen/www.BiblePlaces.com

Hill. From such ancient Near Eastern texts the mountains and hills were recognized as prime spots for worship and ritual.[489]

The phrase "hilltop" is linked with sites featuring leafy green trees and sometimes simply means "everywhere."[490] Trees and mountains were often endowed with a sacred aura in the ancient Near East, both in Israel (Gen. 2:9; 3:22, 14; Prov. 3:18) and in other nations. Mount Hermon was a sacred mountain to many of the nations and their gods. A mountain located near ancient Ugarit was the site of a shrine to Baal,[491] and Ziusudra, the Sumerian Noah, was placed on a Mount Dilmun, far in the east, over the mountains, a faraway and somewhat mythical place.[492] The names of foreign/pagan deities at all these locations were to be erased by destroying all of these objects and removing the names of the deities.

In Hatti the gods assembled under a hawthorne tree.[493] A tree or trees could represent fertility goddesses. The "tree of life for the sunfolk" is men-

tioned in the Great Cairo Hymn of Praise to Amun-Re.[494] The goddess Asherah was connected to a sacred tree or pole, a symbol of fertility and a "place of worship."[495] Being in the presence of a deity was awe-inspiring (cf. Ex. 3:5; 24:9–11) and religious objects at these locations threatened Israel (see Deut. 7:5). Israel was not to worship like the prior inhabitants of the land at the high hills and green trees.[496]

Worship ... in their way (12:4). We now know a fair amount about how the nations of Canaan worshiped, including their mythology and cultic practices.[497] Without exception they were polytheistic with royal pantheons. See sidebar on "Ancient Near Eastern Worship."

Put his Name there (12:5). The names of pagan gods were attached to the places where they appeared or were connected to a given location, especially a cultic location or shrine.[498] As a result of this practice, God instructs Israel that he will put his name at those places where he chooses to be recognized and worshiped. The name of a deity in the ancient Near East defined in an essential way the character and nature and function of a deity. Hence, when a god's name was "placed" somewhere (e.g., Baal Peor), the god was there. S. L. Richter shows that the language source for the term "to place his name there" (*lāśûm et šᵉmô šām*) was the equivalent Akkadian idiom *šuma šakānu*. The Lord claimed the Promised Land by placing his name there as the previous kings of Mesopotamia and Canaan had. The conquered kings, whose names were then "removed," are gone.[499]

But you must not eat the blood (12:16). Proper worship involved the character and attitude of the worshiper, not the sacrifice per se. However, certain things were to be observed, and eating blood was prohibited. Certain words in ancient Near Eastern literature are found in pairs, as they are in the Hebrew Bible. Blood and life are two such words, and they are found in Israelite, Ugaritic, and Akkadian inscriptions or literature;[500] hence, drinking or eating blood was equivalent to consuming life. The blood was properly drained from a slain animal before it could be eaten (cf. 12:21; 14:21). Wine was the "blood" (life) of the grape (32:14).[501]

Enemy soldiers facing a terrifying defeat at the hands of the Assyrian king Assurbanipal slit the stomachs of their camels and drank the blood.[502] Perhaps there was some kind of parallel between the "water of life," special drink or food, and the interplay of life/blood in the Old Testament.[503] The Babylonian creation epic describes human beings as made from the shed blood of the god Qingu (Kingu), who had stirred up war. Abusch argues that this accounts for the concept of blood as "life," the blood of a god.[504] In the Atraḫasis Epic a god is slain and humans made by mixing his "flesh" and blood with clay.[505] These insights may be helpful, but at a deeper level there is as yet no parallel to Israel's view and use/nonuse of blood.[506]

They ... burn their sons and daughters in the fire as sacrifices to their gods (12:30–31). In a study of human sacrifice in the ancient Near East, A. Green concludes that the ritual took various expressions. In Mesopotamia there was ritual killing of attendants to important people, as well as building foundation sacrifices and adult substitute sacrifices for kings. In Syria-Palestine expiatory sacrifices in times of crises took place and also propitiatory sacrifices on special occasions.[507] More recently Heider has reviewed the evidence for child sacrifice carefully and concludes that there is good reason to believe that religious child sacrifice was practiced in Mesopotamia, but absolute proof is lacking.[508] However, human sacrifice in late texts at Carthage (Punic) is certain.[509]

F. M. Cross has argued that a text from Idalion mentions child sacrifice (ca.

Atraḫasis Epic
The Schøyen Collection MS 5108, Oslo and London
▲

▶ Ancient Near Eastern Worship

Ancient Near Eastern people were much concerned with the care and feeding of the gods.[A-82] At Ugarit (thirteenth century), on the northern edge of Canaan, there were temples, one for Baal and one for Dagan. The Baal temple is typical of the Middle Bronze Age in Syria and has typical features for that era.[A-83] Most of the cultic furniture has been unearthed as well. The palace chapel was the most conspicuous part of the royal cult. It was a raised construction to which the many gods "go up"[A-84] and was dedicated to Dagan and Baal.[A-85] Altars of crafted masonry were found with steps leading up to them, a violation of Israel's practice (Ex. 20:26).

There was a temple at Shechem as well (twelfth century B.C.). The high god El in Canaan was connected with the bull symbol and was considered the creator of the earth and human race, as well as the progenitor of the gods, while Athirat was the progenitress.[A-86] But Baal, who came to rival Yahweh in Israel, was the most active and popular god. He manifested himself in various places and his name appeared in various locations, thus binding him to that location. He controlled rain, lightning, and thunder.[A-87]

The people at Ugarit worshiped Anat, goddess and consort of Baal.[A-88] A yearly schedule of sacrifices was scheduled at the various temples, including "holocausts" (whole burnt offerings), peace/well-being offerings, and libation offerings. Often the king had a part in the ceremonies.[A-89] Gods visited these temples during worship. A full temple staff functioned in Ugarit, offering sacrifices for various types of sin(s). Confession of sins occurred at both Ugarit and among Hittite kings. The collective guilt of a people or community could be expressed.[A-90] A Ugaritic "Day of Atone-ment" is described, and a day of purification for the king.[A-91] Most Hebrew offerings are analogous to those in the cult at Ugarit and/or Egypt.[A-92]

In temples at larger cities like Emar, Ebla, and Hazor (thirteenth to twelfth centuries) seven-year cycles were observed. High priestesses were part of the temple personnel, and a nine-day ritual from Emar recounts the installation of the high priestess of the storm god and the removal of a previous high priestess. A seven-day feast is celebrated during this time.[A-93]

Official cultic prostitution is considered by some to have been a part of worship at Ugarit, but the evidence for it is not definitive.[A-94] Most recent studies conclude that there probably was no cultic prostitution at Ugarit. The term *qdšt* (consecrated female holy person) does not occur at Ugarit, but *qdš* (consecrated male holy person) does, as does *qdšm* (masculine plural).[A-95]

Divination at Ugarit employed models of livers, as it did in many parts of Canaan. Omens were read when unusual births, deformed births, and the unusual behavior of animals took place.[A-96] This latter practice recalls similar practices in the Babylonian text *Shuma izbu*[A-97] and many other Mesopotamian divination texts.[A-98] Prayer for national safety and well-being went up at Ugarit, a common theme in all royal divination systems.[A-99]

Farther south in Canaan no written rituals are extant, but remains of more and better-preserved temples have been unearthed. At Lachish, a mud-brick altar is located near a thirteenth-century temple, which was rebuilt twice by 1230 B.C. Divine images were housed in niches in a rear wall, where gifts also could be deposited.[A-100] Entire assemblages of the remains of offerings and ritual texts have been unearthed. Among the

Temple of Baal at Ugarit
Copyright 1995–2009 Phoenix Data Systems
◀

Baal Epic, *CTA* 6, the account of Baal's death and his victory over Mot
Rama/Wikimedia Commons, courtesy of the Louvre
◀

remains are various animal bones, bird bones, and complex processes. Incense was used in rituals.[A-101] High places, however, are more scarcely attested.[A-102]

Archaeology suggests that child sacrifice was practiced, but it cannot prove that it did occur in Mesopotamia, Syria, or Palestine. But the Old Testament witnesses to child sacrifice and high places among the Canaanites.[A-103] Later classical authors mentioned child sacrifice among the Phoenicians. Divination, sacred prostitution, a cult of the dead,[A-104] prayer, and a kingly role in the cult are all witnessed to, in part at least, by extant texts and archaeological indicators. The shades of the dead (*reₚāʾîm*) were deified and even worshiped at Ugarit. Some scholars now believe that all uses of the term *reₚāʾîm* refer to the deified dead, often kings.[A-105] While much of this ritual and cult helps us see the commonly shared aspects of Israel and her world, polytheism, mythology, nature worship, divination, divine kingship, omens, necromancy, ancestor worship, and idolatry all stand in sharp contrast to the way Israel was to worship before her God.[A-106]

350–300 B.C.), and so may the Mit Rahineh urn.[510] In current scholarship the opinion that the practice took place in Syria-Palestine is high.[511] However, the evidence for cremation and strong involvement in rituals for the dead has been proven in both Syria-Palestine and Mesopotamia, and this may be what is being condemned here.[512]

A prophet, or one who foretells by dreams (13:1). This section treats the problem of disloyalty to Yahweh. Dreams were a means of obtaining knowledge/wisdom from the gods across the ancient Near East and were also recognized channels of revelation in Israel.[513] No dream could supersede the covenantal laws given by the Lord at Sinai. Immorality and unfaithfulness to divine moral precepts were condemned by all wisemen outside or inside Israel. Instructions to Merikare in Egypt (ca. 1450–1400 B.C.) assert, "More acceptable is the character [or, loaf] of the upright than the ox of the wrongdoer" (cf. 1 Sam. 15:22).[514] While the prophets of Assyria might condone a violation of morality, a righteous people or

city was extolled, such as the city of Nippur or Borsippa in Babylon.[515] It is clear that "basic forms as well as basic motifs of classical prophecy are rooted in ancient Near Eastern literature."[516] See sidebar on "Ancient Near Eastern Prophecy."

Stone him to death (13:10). Execution by stoning is prescribed in the Hadad Inscription to deal with a possible assassin or murderer, whether male or female.[517] Hittite, Aramaic, and Assyrian treaties deal openly and gravely with sedition and rebellion.[518] Levinson has argued convincingly for both a text-critical and cuneiform ancient Near Eastern background for this harsh verse, dealing primarily with rebellion, apostasy, and disloyalty to Israel's God. Stoning a person clearly means to execute the guilty party.[519]

Esarhaddon's succession treaty deals with the possibility of disloyalty to himself or his son Assurbanipal. Disloyalty is treated severely by immediate and summary execution of a disloyal subject or anyone in the royal house when the king's life is endangered by such an act. In this case even the relatives of a rebel were to be executed. This conclusion is further supported by the stipulations in the Zakatu Treaty.[520] Hence, execution of a false prophet who foments disloyalty toward the Lord falls into place in its ancient Near Eastern setting.

Gather all the plunder of the town into the middle of the public square and completely burn the town (13:15 – 16). This constitutes a typical ancient Near Eastern covenantal curse/threat.[521] A city was burned so that it would not be rebuilt from the same materials. Ruin reflects the Hebrew word *tel* (Arab. *tell*), meaning a heap, ruin. This ultimate curse could befall a city—to become a ruin instead of a place of joyful habitation.[522] The ancient city of Ur (ca. 2000 B.C.) was laid waste and became a ruin because of the anger of the gods toward it.[523] The Sefire treaty inscription (ca. 750 B.C.) between Bargaḥah and Matiḥel records curses against Matiḥel, king of Arpad, if he breaks the covenant, including: "And may Arpad become a mound [ruin] to [house the desert animal].... May [this] city not be mentioned."[524]

These ruins through time became hills or huge mounds of successive layers of debris from the destruction of cities and villages across the centuries and millennia. In this case the city was to remain so permanently. The threat of a flood could likewise turn a city and its land into an uninhabitable ruin.[525] The treaty of Ushshur-Nerari II with the Hittite king records a threat against the Hittites if they are disloyal: "Then may Assur, father of the gods, who grants kingship, turn your land into a battlefield, your people to devastation, your cities into mounds, and your houses into ruins."[526] In the Ugaritic Baal Myth two ruin-mounds (mountains) seem to set off the land of the dead from the land of the living, thus making a plausible parallel between those mythological constructs and historical cities that lay dead in ruins.[527]

Do not cut yourselves or shave the front of your heads for the dead (14:1). For a discussion of this passage, see the sidebar on "Ancient Funerary Rites."

Beersheba with large, open courtyard just inside gate
Kim Walton

▶ Ancient Near Eastern Prophecy

Prophecy in the ancient Near Eastern style was well developed by the time Israel appeared on the scene, but Israel's monotheism and covenantal constitution transformed and modified the key aspects, character, function, and content of prophecy at its core. Contrasts between ancient Near Eastern prophetic parallels with biblical prophecy are as important as likenesses. Biblical prophecy can be helpfully contrasted with ancient Near Eastern omens and other means of divination that also served to guide the behavior of its hearers.[A-107] This is clearer now that the evidence for an extrabiblical presence of prophecy has become clear. Even cognate analogues of the Hebrew terms for prophets/prophecy have come to light.[A-108]

In the Old Babylonian era and the late second millennium at Emar, Egypt, and Byblos, prophetic activity included predictive assertions by "the ancients."[A-109] So it goes for Syria, Palestine, Hamath,[A-110] and Jordan in the first part of the first millennium. From the Neo-Assyrian era of Esarhaddon and Assurbanipal (seventh century B.C.) oracles/prophecies are extant. Some touch on Esarhaddon's rise to power or Assurbanipal's rise to kingship as well as his wars. Bel declares to Esarhaddon, "I will deliver all the countries into your hands."[A-111]

"False prophecy" meant what did not agree with, or spoke against, the official ideology of the king or state. A prophet at Mari dared to speak on his own;[A-112] this occurred rarely in Assyrian circles.[A-113] Prophetic assertions were often written down not only for preservation,[A-114] but to test the fulfillment of prophecies.[A-115] While much remains to be examined from divination texts, ritual texts, and sociological settings of the prophets,[A-116] by the time of Israel's prophets there was a common prophetic tradition in the ancient Near East. This tradition from the past gave Israel's prophetic activity a historical integrity within and outside of Israel.[A-117]

Although the materials have not yet been published (2003), at Ebla, Syria, the word *nabi'tum* (cognate to Heb. *nābi'*, "prophet") is found. Fleming holds that newer texts at Mari and Emar indicate that there a prophet was one who actively invoked or called forth the gods, not "one who was called or invoked (passive)" by the gods.[A-118] Huehnergard has responded that, among other things, the Hebrew active form (Qatēl) never indicates active agent nouns.[A-119]

In the Old Babylonian era at Eshnunna, King Ibalpiel II received prophetic words from Kititum, the local "Ishtar," who probably spoke through prophets in the local temple.[A-120] Prophets were active at Mari (Tell el-Hariri, nineteenth to eighteenth centuries B.C.) on the Euphrates. Lemaire notes significant geographical parallels, linguistic features, and ethno-sociological features between the Old Testament and the materials at Mari.[A-121] At Mari prophetic messages could be delivered by an ordinary person, man or woman. Aspects of prophecy there included intercession for other persons, especially for a king; acting as a spokesperson (male/female) for another person, and the like. The spokesperson spoke "as moved" or in response to others. The respondents were termed *apilu*.

Prophets spoke of victory, healing/death, and wise counsel, and they gave consultation. Kings could be warned, though rarely, about their actions or words. Prophets sometimes warned kings of Assyria, Mari, and Egypt concerning their sins (cf. Dan. 4:24). This confused mix of divination, omens, and various devices served to check the truth of a given prophecy.

This scenario holds in the Egyptian and the Hittite empires. Both true and false prophets operated in Egypt (e.g., the prophecy of Neferti). In the Egyptian documents Instruction for Merikare (ca. 2000 B.C.) and Admonitions of Ipuwer (1900–1800 B.C.), "predictive" prophecy is present. The speaker presents his messages based on their faithfulness to the central religious ideology of the state and/or the words of a god imparted to him. An Aramaic text (seventh century B.C.) in Deir ʿAlla in Jordan reflects a tradition tied to Balaam, a biblical pagan prophet.[A-122] In the end, Israel's prophets had only the Lord's revealed national and royal "ideology" as their absolute reference point to pursue and promulgate. They could not create their own ideology with its messages, nor could they deviate from Israel's religious worldview as housed in their divine covenant and laws.

Pig (14:8). Why Israel was not to eat pigs is unclear.[528] Some level of Egyptian society considered pigs unclean. The god Seth injured Horus's eye, transformed himself into a black pig/boar, and injured it further. The god Re healed the eye and then pronounced the pig an abomination (*bwt*) for Horus's sake. This spell explained why, according to the gods, the pig was an abomination to Horus. The concept became a part of Egyptian culture, though pork was eaten in Egypt by at least the lower classes of the land,[529] and it was a staple of the working class at Amarna in the Egyptian New Kingdom. In certain dream oracles if a person copulated with a pig it was a bad sign, indicating that the person would lose their property.[530] Pigs do not endure arid conditions and so Israel would certainly not have herded pigs through the Sinai Desert.[531]

In the ancient Near East the pig was cheap, contemptible, and not, evidently, eaten in rituals.[532] They were a part of Hittite rituals that were tied to chthonic deities,[533] especially the Sun Goddess of the Earth,[534] connected to the dead in some way,[535] and they were considered unclean. A pig could be sacrificed to settle a domestic quarrel.[536] Mesopotamian religion rarely used pigs as food or as sacrifices. In general it was unclean and "not fit for a temple … an offense to all the gods."[537]

The pig and wild boar were probably used in Canaanite and/or Syrian rituals, and perhaps the Israelites did not use them partly because of a connection with these nearby pagan nations.[538] There is no definite evidence in Canaan for a cultic use of pigs in the Bronze Age (3500–1200 B.C.). In the Middle Bronze Age (ca. 2000–1550) in Syria and Palestine pig remains decrease near cities, especially large cities, but remains are found in rural areas. Philistines living on or near the coastal areas herded pigs, but the herding and eating of pigs were basically taboo in the highlands of Canaan where Israel settled.[539] The herding and production of pigs actually competed with more productive and profitable agricultural activities. Perhaps this also helps to explain the biblical prohibition.[540]

Do not cook a young goat in its mother's milk (14:21). This prohibition (cf. Ex. 23:19; 34:26) still puzzles exegetes; even after the discovery of the Ugaritic texts that were thought to contain a significant parallel, Moses Maimonides may have the last

Pig remains excavated at Tell es-Safi
Joshua Walton, courtesy of the Tell es-Safi excavations

▶ **Ancient Funerary Rites**

Not surprisingly ancient Near Eastern parallels to the rites mentioned in 14:1 are found at Ugarit, since there was a cult of the dead there.[A-123] Ugaritic kings were divinized after their death and became $rp^{\circ}m$ ($r^e p\bar{a}^{\circ}\hat{\imath}m$).[A-124] Interaction with spirits of the dead was often tied to the use of a pit (Heb. $b\hat{o}r$) in both ancient Near Eastern and Greek settings.[A-125] But also the family at Ugarit was obliged to care for their deceased in order to stabilize the family.[A-126]

In a mourning rite El lacerates himself with a stone, cutting off his locks and making furrows in his cheeks and skin with a knife.[A-127] Lewis understands the text describing El's mourning over Baal's death as an illustration of the fact that "the parallels from Ugarit clearly show that the mourning ritual involving self-laceration was a Canaanite practice and, hence, outlawed by normative Yahwism."[A-128] In the Aqhat Legend professional mourners cut or possibly bruised their skin.[A-129] An Akkadian text from Ugarit describes persons who lacerate themselves on behalf of a dying righteous person.[A-130]

In Mesopotamian texts a cult of the dead is evident,[A-131] and abundant funerary offerings are required to sustain the dead.[A-132] Monthly sacrifices were presented to the dead at Mari,[A-133] as many types of texts support offerings to various classes of deceased people, even the common person.[A-134] West Semitic texts describe offerings and the care of dead kings.[A-135] In Egypt a cult of the dead, involving ancestor worship, functioned; in the Old Kingdom only the king and nobles could take part in it. It featured elaborate rituals and sacrifices.[A-136] In Canaanite culture these rituals could obtain blessings and favors from the dead—and placate the dead as well.[A-137] Because of her separation to Yahweh, Israel was not to foster any such rituals.[A-138]

say when he noted correctly that something is prohibited that was practiced among the heathen nations.[541] The Ugaritic text that supposedly throws some light upon this text is highly suspect.[542] J. Milgrom argues that the writer is forbidding the practice of a foreign cult, probably from Ugarit.[543]

The use of milk for cooking in Canaan is described in the Tale of Sinuhe (ca. 1960 B.C.).[544] Schäfers long ago noted the common use of milk in ancient Canaan,[545] but Gibson notes that the claimed parallels with 14:21 are not likely based on syntax, context, and diction of the two texts. The verbs "slaughter" (Ugar.)/"boil" (Heb.) do not match.[546] Perhaps this prohibition was to protect the immigrating Israelites from this (for some reason) practice of the Ugaritians and surrounding peoples, including Canaanites farther south.[547]

At the end of every seven years you must cancel debts (15:1). A cycle of seven years occurs in the Ugaritic calendar, but it may reflect mere literary convention. It was tied to the agricultural year and agricultural prosperity, not to debt release.[548] Some debt-release regulation is practically ubiquitous in the ancient Near East. Westbrook notes that "the broadest and most complex form of legislation was debt-release decrees, which cancelled not only taxes and debts owed to the crown but also debts arising out of private transactions, as well as persons pledged, sold, or enslaved in direct consequence of debt."[549] Decrees releasing debts were promulgated by kings in many locations: Aleppo, Alalakh, Emar, Babylon, and Assyria.[550]

In the Old Babylonian period, for example (which had Sumerian antecedents), *mešarum* edicts were issued by the kings, the guardians of social justice, to cancel debts;[551] they canceled debts, released some hostages or slaves, and helped the oppressed and impoverished persons in Babylonian society. Land reverted to its original owners. The most outstanding example is the one issued by Ammisaduqa, the tenth king in the dynasty of Hammurabi (ca. 1646–1626 B.C.).[552] Assurbanipal claims to have been created by the gods with these features, *kittum u mišarum*.[553] The close Hebrew cognate is *mêšārîm*.

These *mešarum* were issued at "fairly regular" intervals at the word of a particular king.[554] They were general royal decrees, while *anduraru* was a particular state or occurrence of release.[555] Some scholars argue that Israelites adapted this policy as the Sabbatical Year (Lev. 25; Deut 15:1–4) for the covenantal community of Yahweh.[556] However, there is more contrast between the relevant texts than comparison with Israel's weekly Sabbath, Sabbatical Year, and Jubilee (see comment on 15:7). Hallo sums up two key contrasts: sabbatical cycles versus lunar calendars; divine instruction versus royal whim.[557]

If there is a poor man among your brothers (15:7). The homeless, powerless, or disadvantaged in the ancient Near East were ideally defended and supported in various ways by righteous kings.[558] In Sumerian hymns the goddess Nanshe is lifted up as a goddess who cares for and "knows" the widow, the poor, the orphan (a mother of the orphan), the oppressed debtor, and the weak.[559]

Justice and righteousness for these persons was the special "task of the king."[560] Concern for the poor, along with the alien and the widow, is emphasized in the prologues and/or epilogues of the law codes from Mesopotamia (e.g., Hammurabi, Ur-Nammu, Lipit-Ishtar of Isin). Hammurabi cared for the poor, as did Babylonian kings Urukagina and Ur-Nammu in the third millennium B.C.[561] Sinuhe, an Egyptian returned home, exalts the pharaoh with, "You deliver the poor from harm."[562] Canaanite documents from Ugarit and Egyptian tomb inscriptions prescribe special care and concern for these persons.[563]

But only Israel actually constructs legislation directly on behalf of the poor and other groups in her laws, as opposed to grandiose assertions in prologues/epilogues. Ideally, in Israel God, the divine King, is in charge. His will prevails and the poor are to be taken care of without fail. Ancient Near Eastern kings usually issued these decrees at the beginning of their reigns, but only sporadically thereafter.

If a fellow Hebrew, a man or a woman, sells himself to you and serves you six years (15:12). Servitude was a permanent and endemic part of ancient Near Eastern society, providing a social safety for some persons. Over the centuries laws were crafted to deal with the situation. The Laws of Hammurabi (ca. 1728–1686 B.C.) established three years of servitude as the maximum time a slave was to serve. During these years a noble/free man was able to work off a debt or other obligation. The same time limit applied to a wife, son, or daughter, if they should fall into servitude.[564] Enslavement often occurred because of indebtedness.[565]

The term "servant for life" (perpetual slave) is found in Ugaritic literature and carries a positive connotation.[566] While Middle Assyrian laws allowed a husband to send forth a divorced wife "empty-handed," the same phrase describes how a slave is not to be handled in this situation.[567] Ancient Near Eastern kings put forth decrees sporadically to remove debts, which had possibly caused persons to be enslaved. Israel's

Edict of
Ammisaduqa
© The Trustees of the
British Museum
▲

jurisprudence system attempted to make freeing of slaves a central and regular part of legal social justice.[568]

Take an awl and push it through his ear lobe into the door (15:17). Hurowitz finds a suggestive parallel in Akkadian texts that indicates that piercing the ear of a slave in Israel may have indicated a declaration of ownership of the slave in a public and permanent manner. The Akkadian ritual called for a "parallel" activity in which a peg was driven into the mouth of a small statue of the slave.[569] This act symbolized the slave's becoming the property of his new owner.[570]

In Hammurabi's Law Code (Laws 280, 282) only the slave who disavowed his master is mentioned. The slave had been brave enough to declare that "you are not my master." The master could bring charges and proofs against such a "rebellious" slave to prove that he was his slave. If the master successfully established his claim over the slave, he could cut off the slave's ear and the person became an *unwilling* slave for the rest of his life.[571] In Israel the slave who desired to pledge perpetual love/obedience to his master, because he loved his master, is highlighted. The master happily "adopts" him forever. The mark on the Israelite's ear was a sign of mutually desired ownership, a relationship between slave/master forever. The Great Hittite King Hattusili I (Old Kingdom, ca. 1650–1620 B.C.) urged his subject nobles to be of a single liver (emotions), lungs (life), and single ear (obedience, intelligence, knowledge).[572]

Hired hand (15:18). This law concerns native Israelites and recognizes their inherently superior value, contrasting the service received with that of a mere hired hand. The Code

of Hammurabi treats native slaves, male or female, with respect to their native owners of the slaves, more than for the slaves themselves and their well-being. A slave purchased in a foreign land by someone could be redeemed without cost to their former master(s), if the masters were both natives of the same country.[573] The biblical text rather says a word on behalf of the native Israelite slave.

Month of Abib (16:1). The Old Testament contains certain names of the months that the Israelites shared with or borrowed from their Canaanite neighbors. Four are so used: Abib, the first month; Ziv, the second month; Ethanim, the seventh month; Bul the eighth month. Abib and Ziv have been found in Canaanite or Phoenician sources. In later centuries Israel borrowed Babylonian calendar names: Nisan (1), Sivan (3), Elul (6), Chislev (9), Tebet (10), Shebat (11), Adar (12).[574] The Babylonian Nisanu is equivalent to Hebrew Nisan, which was equal to the older Canaanite Abib, for the first month.[575]

Do not pervert justice or show partiality (16:19). In Mesopotamia an important concept of justice grew up across the centuries. A major part of the king's mission was to establish justice and to liberate the oppressed—a high calling. Nevertheless, justice was elusive and almost inaccessible to the lower classes. The ideal of the king remained.[576]

Social reforms were put into place in Mesopotamia and Egypt to see that justice was rendered, especially with respect to the weak in society.[577] In Mesopotamia various "law codes" (Ur-Nammu, 2064–2046 B.C.; Lipit-Ishtar 1875–1864; Eshnunna, 19th century) were promulgated to "establish justice (*nig-si-sa*)" in the lands.[578] Akkadian anthologies of jurisprudence were compiled by Hammurabi and Eshnunna. Even in societies with three-tiered structures of persons (*awilum* [patrician]; *mukenum* [plebian]; *wardum* [slave]) these efforts tended to protect the less powerful and help the poor and others who were less fortunate.[579]

This socio-theological activity was to enable the kings' servants to serve the gods properly.[580] The kings could issue special proclamations of mercy as needed.[581] In Egypt the king or pharaoh likewise maintained *maat*, order and justice. The vizier, second in command, and his secretary were to see that uprightness was carried out.[582] This theme is carried through into the New Kingdom and beyond (1570–1070 B.C.).[583] Even in the chaotic intermediate periods the attempt to preserve justice was important. Pharaoh Khety says, "[I did] what people love and gods praise: I gave bread to the hungry, clothes to the naked; I listened to the plea of the widow, I gave a home to the orphan."[584] Nordoni finds these same emphases in Egyptian "popular religion."[585] In Canaan the righteous Dan(i)el of Ugarit pursued justice for all.[586]

Defect or flaw (17:1). Neither the Proto-Sinaitic inscriptions nor sacrificial instructions at Ugarit describe conditions of a sacrificial animal.[587] Certain texts may imply a strong concern for a high quality of sacrificial animals, unblemished, in the rituals of the cult.[588] Gudea, a king of ancient Lagash (ca. 2094–47 B.C.), while praising his god Ningirsu, was careful to present only a perfect ox and a perfect he-goat.[589] Scurlock reports a Mesopotamian text in which Anu of Uruk offers "fine, fattened, ritually pure sheep that had eaten barley for two years."[590] The cultic purity of animals is praised in an imagined world by an Akkadian diviner.[591]

City gate (17:5). Disputes and legal trials were handled by the elders of a village or city (cf. 21:19).

The righteous Dan(i)el at Ugarit processed justice and carried out judgment at the city gate.[592] The problems and issues of the town were discussed and justice meted out at the city gate(s), where the elders congregated.[593] Cuneiform documents from Babylonia indicate that these classes of society dealt with the administration of justice: the elders, the priests, and the king, and his officials.[594]

The central public gate was a place of assembly, business, and legal transactions (cf. Amos 5:15). Impressive flagstone pavement was used to garnish the gate at Tell Dan.[595] Offerings during festivals were sometimes presented at city gates to honor the gods at the Zukru festival at Emar. In this case the name of the gate was the Gate of the Upright Stones (for the storm god and Hebat, his consort).[596] The gate area constituted special space in the ancient Near East that separated the city from tilled ground; hence, it was the center of many religions and social activities.[597] At Megiddo over four hundred people could gather just outside its central gate.[598]

On the testimony of two or three witnesses a man shall be put to death (17:6). Certain Middle Assyrian laws possibly

Iron Age gate at Bethsaida
Todd Bolen/www.
BiblePlaces.com

Antediluvian king
list

The Schøyen Collection MS 2855, Oslo
and London

▲

Pharaoh crowned
by gods

Frederick J. Mabie

▼

required a minimum of two witnesses (secs. A 12, 17, 40), although this is not certain. The law has a plural form for witnesses and does not limit them explicitly to two, and this seems to suggest what we have in this Mosaic text. In Middle Assyrian Law 41 the number of witnesses needed was five or six,[599] in order to establish the validity of a woman's claim to be a man's principal wife.

Take them to the place the LORD your God will choose (17:8). In the second millennium there were locations where cases were examined and judgments rendered, as well as specific places where judgments were enacted. See sidebar on "Ancient Court Systems."

Let us set a king over us like all the nations (17:14). Israel does ask for this king in 1 Samuel 8:4–5. Samuel sets before the people the political, military, and economic reality they are asking for. The real cost of a king like the kings of the nations is enormous. The state machinery of a monarchy demands crops and personal property, to say nothing of "state enslavement" for cheap labor. Mari, Ugarit, Alalakh, and later cities and mini-kingdoms should have made Israel

aware of the cost of kingship.[600] In times of war oppression intensified beyond imagination.[601] The model put forth here tries to control major abuses beforehand and to set Israel's kingship within a Yahwistic covenantal framework that circumscribes its practice and ideology over against the current Realpolitik and its abuses.[602]

Models of kingship abound in the literature of the ancient world. In Egypt the god-king-priest was central and was to imitate, control, guarantee, and communicate the order of the cosmos and society, as well as regulate religious, moral, political, and military issues. In Mesopotamia, Assyrian and Babylonian kings ate the food of the gods and were to provide a paragon of rulership and virtue.[603] Prior to human kings, gods had purportedly ruled,[604] but then they had subsequently lowered kingship down to humans at Ur[605] for finite periods of rulership.[606]

The king the LORD your God chooses (17:15). In the ancient Near East the king was invariably chosen by the chief god(s) of a nation, picked to lead the people and honor the god(s) who had chosen him. For a king to be successful a legitimate chain of approval, including connections with the chief god and the people, was necessary.[607] If no immediate link or legitimacy existed for the new king, it had to be created. The gods put the right king on the throne—which had to be the case.[608]

Hattusilis III (1275–45 B.C.) was chosen by the goddess Shaushga to be the Great King of the Hittites. Sargon, king of Agade (2296–2240 B.C.), was anointed and given kingship by Enlil and Anu (sky god). Hammurabi was chosen by the sun god Shamash and Marduk, Babylon's patron god.[609] Likewise, Assyrian kings (e.g., Tiglath-pileser, 1114–1076 B.C.) were chosen by the gods and Neo-Babylonian and Persian kings were chosen by their gods.[610]

Do not place a foreigner over you (17:15). Neither Israel nor Judah ever had a "foreign ruler." Given the way

▶ Ancient Court Systems

Egypt had persons entitled "overseer of the law courts" that continued from the Old Kingdom. They served evidently at the "six great houses." They could cite the laws issued by Pharaoh or his close attendant(s). A group called "the thirty" acted as "judges." Judgment was pronounced at the gates or entrances of temples or palaces.[A-139] The New Kingdom featured great courts where high-ranking members served and lesser courts functioned under them. The vizier oversaw both town and temple courts. Justice also was meted out at temple gates, palaces, porticos, or forecourts.[A-140]

In the Old Babylonian period a mayor and elders governed a city and served as court functionaries. Wards were established in the city. The king was the highest court and the authority of final appeal. The palace functioned somewhat as a supreme court building.[A-141] Similar structures and personnel operated in the Middle Babylonian, Middle Assyrian, and Nuzi eras.[A-142] The Hittites, as well as cities such as Emar, Alalakh, and Ugarit, and much of Syria-Palestine had many of these same features.[A-143]

In Canaanite city-states kings acted as judges, as did also priests. At Sidon (ca. 500 B.C.) the king was also called "priest of Astarte." The elders in Israel and at Ugarit pronounced judgments and took oaths.[A-144] The elders were especially important in Israel, but also at Alalakh, Ugarit, and in texts from El-Amarna. At Alalakh the elders were involved in international cases as well as local affairs.[A-145] In an El-Amarna text a city elder appeals to the pharaoh of Egypt.[A-146] In Mesopotamia some elders engaged in areas of specialization and rendered decisions.[A-147] In Israel as in Mesopotamia, the temple and tabernacle were places where oaths were taken by various persons, including accusers, accused, elders, priests, and others.[A-148]

foreign rulers tended to oppress the native populations in the ancient Near East, it was to Israel's advantage, during the monarchy or during the twin kingdoms, not to have had one. Egypt suffered under the foreign rule of the Hyksos (shepherd-kings or possibly "rulers of foreign lands," ca. 1649–1540 B.C.). Their rule was oppressive in certain areas. The ancient historian of Egypt, Manetho, described this period: "A blast of god smote us."[611] The Egyptians finally cast off this foreign element under Ahmose (ca. 1552–1527 B.C.).

A foreign ruler would most likely be an enemy of the god of the conquered land, as when the Elamites conquered Babylon, carried the god Enlil to Elam, and installed a ruler who was not of Babylonian descent.[612] Because of Israel's theocracy it was imperative that her king be of Davidic descent. A foreign king was simply theologically and biologically impossible in Israel.

In Mesopotamia, Babylonian kings gave way to the Kassites, a people from the Zagros Mountains area, east of the Tigris.[613] They held power for about four hundred years (ca. 1530–1155 B.C.). Although they were relatively successful rulers, the Babylonians removed them and seized their own destiny. Both the Kassites and the Hyksos became acculturated to some extent in the countries they conquered. But they remained a foreign element, separate

Kamose Stele from Karnak describes Hyksos being driven out
Todd Bolen/www. BiblePlaces.com

from the peoples they had subjugated. They powerfully influenced the culture and religion of those over whom they ruled. While they adopted the gods of the nations they controlled, they also changed and added to their pantheons. Such an action was strictly forbidden in Israel.

Assyrians ruled Babylon several times by placing an Assyrian on the throne, thus creating practically a dual monarchy.[614] This empire greatly influenced the Babylonians since the position of king included the charge to represent the people and the gods over whom he ruled.

Horses (17:16). The animal of consummate prestige was the horse, and its appearance fostered the development of the chariot and chariotry warfare. It appeared in Egypt in the Second Intermediate era (ca. 1674–1553 B.C.).[615] The privileged elite of the military classes valued the horse. The god Shamash is depicted riding a horse. Shamash, the Assyrian god Assur, and the Babylonian god Marduk cultivated their own herds of horses to pull their chariots or to ride. Assur preferred white horses; Marduk chose his own horses

as royal divine horses and they were cared for accordingly.[616] Israel was to trust in her God for victory, not horsemen, war horses, or chariots (Ps. 20:7).

In time mounted cavalry made up a part of ancient warfare (ca. 900 B.C.).[617] Instruction manuals about horses, their care and handling, including discussions of horse diseases, have been found in Hittite, Ugaritic, and partial Akkadian inscriptions.[618] A hippiatric text at Ugarit highlights the care and cure of horses.[619] Hittites purified horse chariots in a special ceremony.[620] Kassite, Mitannian, and Cappadocian records refer to horses.

The Hyksos rulers of Egypt (18th–16th centuries B.C.) produced the first references to horses in the eastern Mediterranean world,[621] and Egyptians bred horses during the second millennium. Ramesses II sent horses to the Hittite king, as did the king of Babylon. Pharaoh Osorkon IV sent horses to Sargon II of Assyria (ca. 622 B.C.).[622] Israel did not rely greatly on horses until Solomon's reign, when kingship and horses became central.[623]

Wives (17:17). Creation theology presents the familial state as a united male and

So-called stables at Hazor
Dr. Tim Bulkeley,
www.eBibleTools.com

female, one man one woman. In the present verse the prohibition was political and intended to keep Israel from striking covenants with foreign nations. This injunction forbids marriages for political purposes for they might bring devastating religious consequences and were a means of filling the king's harem. The history of the ancient Near East is replete with these arrangements between nations and royal dynasties.

A few sample illustrations can be offered, but the point could be multiplied many times over. Each foreign wife represented a connection to a foreign god as well as to a pagan political entity. The king's wives, in effect, made up a royal harem that had its own living quarters in or near the royal palace. Amenophis III of Egypt (1403–1364 B.C.) offered to marry the daughter of Arzawa in a shrewd political move against the Hittites.[624] He would recognize the gods of King Tarhumdaradu of Arzawa and that king would reciprocate, thus sealing a religious-political-military coup by a treaty cemented through marriage. Amenophis also married the daughter of Tushratta, Taduhepa of Mitanni.

Similarly, the Great King of Hatti strengthened his relationship with his subjects by giving the subject rulers a female relation of the Great King as wife.[625] A Mitannian princess married Thutmose IV to demonstrate both friendship and agreement between the two kings.[626] Babylon and Assyria sealed their rapprochement by way of the daughter of Assur-uballit given to the son of Burnaburiash II.[627] Elam and Babylon, Assyria and smaller states, secured their treaties and friendships with dynastic marriages.[628]

Silver and gold (17:17). The accummulation of large amounts of silver and gold threatened to turn a king's heart from the Lord to the glitter of his wealth. All Solomon's wealth certainly did not foster his trust in the Lord. The kings of the Near East prided themselves in the accumulation of wealth. Solomon's cache was actually mod-

est compared to the wealth of other kings in Egypt or the Midas of legendary fame. Solomon's twenty tons of gold (666 talents, 1 Kings 10:14) was pocket change compared to the wealth of Pharaoh Osorkon I, who presented 383 tons of gold as offerings to the gods and temples of Egypt. Persian wealth of over one thousand tons of gold was taken by Alexander the Great out of one capital alone: Susa.[629]

Write for himself on a scroll (17:18). Some kings in the ancient Near East could write, and writing was highly developed in Alalakh, Emar, and Ugarit. Much further back, Shulgi (2094–47 B.C.), king during the Third Dynasty of Ur, claimed to be a superb writer of tablets and boasted that he had attended the "tablet-house" for training.[630] Ancient Ebla witnesses to the activity of writing in northern Syria as early as 2300 B.C. Administrative texts, legal texts, letters, and literature attest to this well-established fact.[631]

Kings received praise in ancient Near Eastern texts for their skill in writing, in royal hymns, and in other settings.[632] Trevor Bryce has studied the letters the great kings of the ancient Near East passed among themselves.[633] Texts from Amarna are mostly from the strongly populated areas in the Late Bronze Age in Canaan. Amarna letters of Jerusalem display a sophisticated style addressed to the pharaoh.[634] Hess demonstrates the presence of writing in Jerusalem well before David, as well as during the

Donation stele of Osorkon I
Keith Schengili-Roberts/Wikimedia Commons, courtesy of the Metropolitan museum
▲

entire Iron Age.[635] A strong tribal tradition was likely in Jerusalem, capital of David's empire.

Material from Transjordan features a list of curses (cf. 28:15–68).[636] The Hittite king Mursilis II (ca. 1300 B.C.) expressed himself in such a personal way; many believe that he did write, although he may have dictated to scribes.[637] This injunction (cf. 27:2) reflects epigraphic practice and convention reaching far back into antiquity. However, the hubris and divine claims of these kings stand in stark contrast to the humility expected of Israel's king (17:18–20).

Read it all the days of his life (17:18–19). In the ancient Near East instructions for future kings or leaders were recorded in various works of wisdom literature. In Egypt, Ptahhotep instructed his son about how to be a successful vizier over Egypt.[638] Instructions by Amenemope with an emphasis on inwardness[639] come from the time of the Ramesside kings. Pharaoh Amenemhet I (ca. 1960 B.C.), the first pharaoh of the Twelfth Dynasty, left written instructions for his son and successor to read and study.[640] More words of instruction for a successor come from a pharaoh of the Twenty-Second Dynasty. Among other things he enjoins the future king to "advance the great men, so that they may carry out thy laws," and further to "copy thy fathers and thy ancestors."[641]

According to ancient Sumerian wisdom, the king who implemented justice in his land and faithfully observed the worship of his gods would enjoy long life.[642]

The priests, who are Levites (18:1). Priests were the ones who were allowed to approach the gods and perform rituals; some performed priestly menial tasks.[643]

In Egypt the pharaoh was king and high priest, "lord of priests." Under him were those set apart to serve the gods—special state officials who, among other things, cared for the divine images.[644] They observed purity in all aspects of their duties, such as washing several times daily. The pharaoh appointed the priests,[645] of which there were two main levels: (1) servants of god (prophets) and (2) pure ones. The ḥm nṯr priest cared for the cult image in the holy place, and other pure priests (wᶜb) were below him.[646]

In Mesopotamia all temple workers were priests, but the Sanga was the foremost official. The en priest served a city god as his or her spouse.[647] Certain priests were allowed to open the mouths of the gods.[648] Then came singers and musicians.[649]

Various kinds of priests functioned among the Hittites.[650] The king and queen were high priests; the Great King, a ritual expert, was also high priest and was obliged to seek purity at all times. There was also a mother-of-god priestess. "Men of the temple" followed an instruction manual, and a large support staff aided this basic structure. The use of "priestly guards" at Hittite sanctuaries paralleled the function of priests and Levites in Israel who oversaw religious sanctuaries.[651]

Priestly activity was supported by offerings set apart for this purpose.[652] In the West Semitic areas of Ugarit and Phoenicia there were analogous personnel: priests, chief priests (rb khnm), and "consecrated ones" (qdshm; lit., "holy ones"). A lower group was known as "servants of the gods."[653] At Emar there were lists of priestly personnel including a baru, a diviner, and a female "wife or concubine of the god." Priestesses were also part of the personnel.

If what a prophet proclaims in the name of the LORD does not take place (18:22). If God, who hates deception, was the source of prophecy, it had to be true and sound. In Mari, this principle was recognized; prophecies were "tested" to evaluate their validity by getting another opinion. Royal written records were kept about prophecies in order to check their fulfillment or nonfulfillment.[654] This practice was followed in Nineveh as well.[655] In this way prophecies could be tested over a long period of time if necessary.

False prophecy often confirmed a shrewd political maneuver. In Egypt, Amenemhet (1990–1960 B.C.), founder of the Egyptian

Twelfth Dynasty, was supported by a *vaticana ex eventu* ("prophecy after the event"), the prophecy of Neferti.[656] This prophecy was set forth originally in the time of Snefru, Fourth Dynasty (2600 B.C.); it predicted Amenenhet I as a redeemer figure for the current era. Similarly, false prophecy is found in Tales of the Magicians.[657] In the story of The Shipwrecked Sailor a prognostication concerning the weather is featured.[658]

The avenger of blood might pursue him in a rage (19:6). Because of the kin-based social structure of Israel, the relative (*gōʾēl haddām*) of a slain person was authorized to avenge/reclaim the blood of his relative. To control this volatile situation Israel set up a unique institution in the ancient Near East, cities of refuge. These cities, not paralleled in the ancient Near East, provided protection for the person who had slain another person. Cities of refuge were not paralleled in Babylon or Assyria at the familial level because of different social, political, religious, and economic factors.[659] See sidebar on "Dealing with Homicide."

If a man hates his neighbor and lies in wait for him, assaults and kills him (19:11). Killing a person with prior intent defined murder and is reflected in the Mesopotamian laws of Ur-Nammu and in some Hittite laws.[660] In the Hittite Laws (e.g., 1–2) there is an assumption of intent to kill a person even though it is during a "quarrel."[661] As Haase indicates, there is a clear concern for intent here.[662] In the Old Babylonian period premeditated killing was punished by death.[663] In the case of premeditation the guilty person could not find asylum by fleeing to a city of refuge like the person who had committed manslaughter, a crime committed without prior intent.[664]

Do not move your neighbor's boundary stone (19:14). Stones (*kuddurus*) often marked boundaries and they were not to be moved under threat of heavy penalties. Inscriptions on them appealed to divine sanction and divine protection for the owner's rights. The first such stones are found after the time of Hammurabi (ca. 1600 B.C.). They appear in the eleventh and tenth centuries in Babylon. Some features of these stones reflect Israel's covenantal forms/content.[665]

Some Hittite laws of the Old Kingdom (1650–1500 B.C.) concern boundaries and property rights (e.g., Law 168). They assert that the one who takes even a furrow of another's field will, as a penalty, pay a fine and lose a section of his own field to the owner of the field he has violated. In Law 169 a violator confesses his guilt and presents an offering to the sun god or storm god.[666]

A Babylonian inscription (ca. 893 B.C.), similar to a *kudurru* stone, engraved on a

Babylonian boundary stone
Todd Bolen/www.
BiblePlaces.com

▼

▶ Dealing with Homicide

The Treaty of Sefire (3.9–14) calls for the assassination of a ruler or any relative to be avenged by a treaty partner. The ruler would avenge a slain fellow ruler, a grandson would avenge a slain grandson of the ruler, and so on. Surprisingly, the "slayer" or guilty party to be slain could be a city as well as an individual.

The Babylonian king Burnaburiash (fourteenth century) demanded that the Egyptian pharaoh Amenophis IV apprehend and slay certain murderers who had killed Babylonians in Egypt on business.[A-149] Outside of Israel, a "lord of blood" (*bēl damê*), referring to both the slayer and the representative from the family of the slain person, seems to have operated among the royal families. In a proclamation the Hittite king Telipinu, in order to ensure proper dynastic succession, declares that the "lord of the blood" would determine whether any guilty person would live or die, except

that a person who had slain a king would die without recourse.[A-150]

In the laws of Mesopotamia the formal jurisdiction of the state dealt with homicide and blood feuds and the families of both the slain and the slayer were involved. Thus, cities of refuge were not needed.[A-151] In this milieu biblical and Mesopotamian law (and the rest of the ancient Near East) differed greatly. In Mesopotamia there were no "blood avengers," for state institutions, including the king or other judges, remedied certain homicide cases. Assyria permitted a role for the family of the slayer and the victim.[A-152]

An axhead that flies off the handle and kills someone is used as an example of accidental homicide. This axhead is from Iron Age II A.
Kim Walton, courtesy of the Oriental Institute Museum

▶

hard black stone, records a royal grant of land and income to a priest.[667] The movement of a boundary marker was worthy of a curse (27:17). The wisdom saying in chapter 6 of the Egyptian Work of Amenemope, who determined the boundaries of the land,[668] forbade carrying off landmarks of arable land or encroachment.

Malicious witness (19:16–19). In this type of case, according to the Code of Hammurabi, the person committing perjury "shall be put to death."[669] The Laws of Lipit-Ishtar (ca. 1934–1924) state that an accuser of another person who is not knowledgeable about the malicious accusation he is making and cannot establish the accusation must endure the penalty the person he has wrongly charged would have had to suffer, had that person been culpable.[670] On the other hand,

the Code of Ur-Nammu instructs that a person guilty of perjury merely be fined fifteen shekels of silver.[671]

Eye for eye (19:21). This law should be read in the light of the principle set out in 19:16–19: the malicious accuser will suffer the penalty he wished upon his potential victim. This tit-for-tat principle was applied in the Code of Hammurabi, but only when the two persons were of the same socioeconomic standing. If a seignior injured someone in the aristocratic class, he would receive poetic justice (e.g., eye for eye, Law 196; bone for bone, Law 192; tooth for tooth, Law 200). But a seignior would receive a lesser penalty if the victim was a commoner (a commoner's eye put out: penalty to seignior, one mina of silver; eye of a slave put out: penalty, one-half slave's value).[672]

Shared cultural class and experience explains many parallels in these laws in the ancient Near East. Some prefer to see them as examples used in common in a "scholastic tradition."[673] The eye, tooth, foot, bone, finger, hand, nose, and collarbone are mentioned in the various law codes.[674] In the Hittite Laws an eye for an eye or a tooth for a tooth was not followed, but compensation of twenty or forty shekels of silver was paid and the injured person was cared for.[675] The Laws of Ur-Nammu (2112–2095 B.C.) record more humane treatments; for example, ten shekels is the penalty "if a man cuts off the foot of another man."[676]

When you go to war against your enemies (20:1). In the ancient Near East war at the command of a god was common. Priests (*barum*) sought the signs that indicated whether a nation should go to war, using various methods (e.g., divination, omens, oracles, dreams, and magic). A frequently sought formulaic answer was "god X delivers the enemy into the hand of X."[677] The king in the ancient Near East performed as leader of the army and often as priest. Scribes were in the vanguard of ancient Near Eastern armies to render encouragement to the troops, to record battles, and to serve as experts on the technicalities of military procedure.[678]

The god was the divine warrior (cf. Ex. 15:3), and war was part of the divine plan, especially according to Egyptian thinking. A pharaoh engaged in war by divine commission only. Divine warriors in Mesopotamia and Hatti included the gods Ninurta or Teshub respectively. Among Hittites and Mesopotamians war could be a lawsuit with the god serving as judge-warrior. The gods in the ancient Near Eastern worldview were invoked to participate in warfare and even the battle itself in Egypt and Mesopotamia from the earliest ages (ca. 2500 B.C.). The Hittite king won battles only with the aid of his divine warrior god.

The conquered enemy became the property of the god, the divine warrior. Among the Hittites they were subject to *ḥerem* ("total destruction").[679] Victory was always attributed to the divine warrior gods, never to the king alone, and the enemies engaged were ultimately the enemies of the gods. Divine wars and victories were then remembered in cult rituals and were recorded in the annals of the state. Moreover, the playback in the "ritual battle is beyond the actual historicity of the battle, even though the battle was rooted in a historical event."[680]

The officer shall say to the army (20:5). Military officers also announced acceptable conditions under which some soldiers could refrain from going to battle. Gilgamesh, the great Sumerian hero, finds fifty men to help him accomplish his journey to the distant land of the living. He allows only single males to accompany him; those who have a house or a mother can go to their house or mother.[681] He requests that only soldiers stout of heart accompany him against Kish.[682]

As many as seven ranks of officers were used in the Hittite army, and the highest level of officers was even allowed to function in place of the king to direct military operations.[683] Officers also kept rituals that bolstered the morale of the Hittite army when needed.[684]

Siege (20:12). Siege warfare was a terrifying experience. A city was literally starved, humiliated, and battered into submission. Ugaritic literature contains a prayer for a city under siege.[685] The siege usually was planned to begin just before the city could harvest its ripened grains, thus cutting them off from their lifeline of food supply.

Stele of Naram-Sin
Erich Lessing/Art Resource, NY, courtesy of the Louvre

In Hittite siege warfare, when an offer of surrender was refused, the exits of the city were blocked, cutting off supplies and reinforcements. No communications from the city were permitted. The gates of the city were watched closely and eventually seized. Night attacks were especially effective. Any wood in the walls or gates of a city were set on fire, and battering rams were constructed and used to loosen and weaken walls and gates. Sappers tunneled under walls, loosening bricks and weakening the foundations of the walls. Siege towers threatened the walls, while great ramps of earth were built to reach the tops of the walls or to cross over moats.

Psychological warfare created a "fifth column" within the ranks of the enemy. Starvation of the city set in, and the atrocious conditions of plague, pestilence, internal dissension, and incessant violence and death began.[686]

You may take these as plunder for yourselves (20:14). Warfare was endemic in the ancient Near East. Hittite military procedures illustrate this devastating horror. In general a conquered city was looted and torched. The leaders may have been spared, but usually they were executed and the common people were perhaps spared. Sometimes the Hittites respected the deities of a conquered city so that they were moved to spare it. Normally various valuables, herds, and people were collected and used to augment the wealth and strength of the conquering nations. Some of these persons ended up as slaves, some as new faithful subjects of their conquerors. Others ended up serving on the estates of the pagan deities of the Hittites.

The site of the destroyed city might be sown with fennel weeds to erase its previous existence. Certain conquered cities could be offered treaties that would be confirmed by oracles. Tribute was imposed on defeated peoples and their cities.[687] This basic scenario played out repeatedly in Egypt, Syria-Palestine, and Mesopotamia.[688] This picture of doom and gloom can be lightened only slightly by reports of certain humane actions towards conquered enemies.[689]

Do not destroy its trees by putting an ax to them (20:19). The flora in the land of Canaan was vital to the survival of its inhabitants. Over fifteen species of trees are mentioned in Scripture. Nearly every part of a date palm tree (34:3) was used in daily life. Pomegranates, fig trees, grape vines, sycamore trees, almond trees, and pistachio trees were crucial to life.[690]

The Lord did not instruct Israel to follow a scorched-earth policy. Egypt's warrior king, Thutmose III (1490–36 B.C.), often pursued just such a policy, cutting down all kinds of trees in his Asiatic campaigns. In the Barkal Stele he records that he cut down all the fruitful groves: "I took away the *very sources of life*, for I cut down their grain and felled all their groves and their pleasant trees."[691] He used the wood to construct siege equipment.[692] Hasel argues that this lone reference fits the second millennium milieu.[693]

In the first millennium B.C. it is clear that the Assyrians cut down fruit trees. Hasel argues that it happened only after a city had been destroyed, but never for the purpose of building siege works from the wood. The Assyrian Shalmaneser attacked Hazael of Damascus and in his annals records, "I cut down his orchards."[694]

If a man is found slain (21:1). In Old Kingdom Hittite laws, if a dead person is found in a field in the open country, desig-

Egyptians cutting
down the trees of
a defeated enemy
in the upper left
hand corner of
the relief.
Lenka Peacock

nated persons (village elders, councils, civil officials, priests, local judges, etc.) measured out a radius of three miles in every direction. The village(s) that fell within that radius were forced to present payments to the heir of the dead person. If no village lay within that area the heir forfeited his claim.[695] In the case of robbery, the city and governors in whose territory the robbery took place made up the lost property or paid one mina to the relative(s) of a person who was killed.[696] Blood spilled on the ground at Ugarit threatened the fertility of the ground.[697] In the Aqhat Legend, Dan(i)el locates the place where his son was murdered and curses the unknown murderer and the cities near the crime.[698] At Nuzi likewise the nearest town was held responsible for any unsolved crime.[699]

Shall take a heifer (21:3). The purpose of killing the heifer was to atone for the death of the victim beside a flowing stream and at an area of land not cultivated. This served to eliminate the bloodguilt created by the crime from the community, while killing a cow reenacted the murder as well. Both Hittite and Mesopotamian texts seem to suggest likewise. These rites "remove pollution from the community or inhabited area to an area uninhabited or separate from the community's concerns."[700]

Wright cites Hittite rituals that dispose of impurity in seas, rivers, enemy lands, mountains, and open country (e.g., the Ambazzi ritual and the Tunnavi ritual). A female ritualistic priestess would throw combs used to cull evil from a patient into a river nearby.[701] In Mesopotamia the Akitu festival and the Shurpu rituals contained rites that removed evil from a person by taking it into open country. A priest decapitated a ram and eventually threw its carcass in the river. The same was done with the ram's head. Before this slaughter the room was wiped with the carcass of the dead ram and incantations of exorcism were carried out.[702]

Our hands did not shed this blood (21:7). An exculpatory oath is also found in Ugarit where it concerns a woman whose husband was murdered in the city of Arzigana. The local leaders must declare, "We did not kill the husband of the woman, brother of x, in the city. We do not know who killed him."[703]

Rights of the firstborn (21:16). In Israel the firstborn son received a double portion of the inheritance.[704] See sidebar on "Inheritance Practices in the Ancient Near East."

A stubborn and rebellious son (21:18). In a West Semitic Hadad inscription from near Zenjirli death by stoning was administered to persons, male or female, who had committed an assassination, an understandable penalty for such a crime.[705] Rebellion against established authority was the major issue, whether against the royal house of king Panamuwa I of Samʾal or the parental line of authority set up by God in Israel. The Code of Hammurabi discusses a son who commits a grave offense against his parents and sets forth the penalty as disinheritance.[706] Penalties elsewhere involved enslavement, mutilation, or disinheritance.[707]

The parallel law in Exodus 21:15 requires the death penalty for a son who strikes his parents, an act that is probably included in the rebelliousness in mind in this passage.[708] In Israel rebellion against one's parents was equivalent to rebellion against the Lord. In the ancient Near East it was basically a societal issue, but still was a grave offense.

▶ **Inheritance Practices in the Ancient Near East**

Primogeniture functioned in the ancient Near East, but not everywhere, nor was it, if present, always observed.[A-153] In Hammurabi's Code (Law 165) other divisions of property are allowed.[A-154] In Lipit-Ishtar's Laws the inheritance goes equally to the children of two wives; in Hammurabi's Code the first wife's firstborn receives a preferential share.[A-155] Thus the ancient provenance and some shared features of Israel's law are evident.

At Mari a legal decision granted a double portion to the natural firstborn son; at Nuzi (fifteenth century) the same provision was followed.[A-156] At Alalakh on the Orontes a father was aware of but did not have to recognize the law of primogeniture in his will. He could designate a first son for inheritance purposes.[A-157] Primogeniture was recognized at Emar where the son received an "extra share." Each son first claimed a bride price from the inheritance.[A-158] A daughter could rarely be an equal heir with the sons in Mesopotamia.[A-159]

In Egypt by the Middle Kingdom the law of primogeniture could be disregarded by the dying person; property could be willed to a brother.[A-160] In the New Kingdom era the oldest son was the expected heir, but the entire family or an appointed trustee could become the heir.[A-161] In the Tale of Sinuhe, a fugitive Egyptian in Canaan, upon departing from Egypt, turned over all of his possessions to his family, both men and property to be given to his firstborn son.[A-162]

In Neo-Babylonian laws the sons of a first wife received two-thirds of the inheritance while the sons of the second wife received one-third.[A-163] Sons who were different in status might fare differently, since sons of the first and main wife could receive the major inheritance. Among sons, in a Middle Assyrian law the oldest son inherited the largest portion; the rest of the inheritance was divided according to set instructions.[A-164] In some cases the kind of property to be divided up determined how it could be distributed.[A-165]

You must not leave his body on the tree overnight (21:23). The burial of the dead was important for several reasons in the ancient Near East, and improper burial was a catastrophe as far back as ancient Sumer. Improper burial could lead to baneful consequences involving ghosts, demons, and other evils.[709] The Assyrians used the practice of hanging a person on a tree in a time of war instead of burying them so that birds would eat the corpse. The dead bodies of the enemy were also mutilated, fed to animals, and finally removed.[710] The threat of not being buried continued into the Persian era and even later.[711]

In Babylonian anthropological thinking the physical body provided the habitation for the dead person's ghost (*etemmu*) to be received by the community of the dead. The body was to be buried. Burial of the body maintained the identity of the deceased. Rites that would feed and renew the memory of them then provided for the dead. Destroying a person's corpse deprived the person of a future identity among the dead. Burning, mutilation, or the consumption of a body by animals also destroyed the person's identity and future life. Those whose bodies were not buried had a gruesome chaotic existence to face.[712]

At the city of Emar the dead were referred to as divine beings or "gods." According to certain Sumerian texts the dead should be buried within "the shade of one's house," so that they would enjoy their new lives among the dead in this vicinity.[713]

Within this religious and cognitive kind of thinking it is easy to see why in Israel a dead body desecrated the Lord's land, both literally and symbolically.[714]

If you see your brother's ox or sheep straying (22:1). Rather than envy the property of their neighbors, the Lord instructs the Israelites to be their brother's helper and keeper (vv. 1–4). Israelite houses had a stable area on the ground floor where animals were kept and cared for. A lost animal was to be treated as one's own.[715] The Hittite Laws of the Old Kingdom (ca. 1650–1500 B.C.) instructed a person who found a stray animal (ox, horse, mule) to take it to the gate of the king or to the elders of the nearest town. The finder could use the animal until the owner happened to locate it with the finder. The finder would be considered a thief if he were not to turn the animal over to the owner.[716] The Code of Hammurabi has near parallels, but they are in a different context and the issue is more clearly theft by the finder.[717]

A woman must not wear men's clothing (22:5). Transvestism was prohibited in the ancient Near East, except as punishment. In the Epic of Aqhat at Ugarit, after Aqhat's murder, his sister Pughat seeks revenge against his murderer Anat, goddess of love and war. She dresses as a male, using cosmetics, clothing, and other male paraphernalia. She covers all of this by putting on a woman's clothing.[718] It is not clear whether this is transvestism, and the reaction to it in the Ugaritic texts is not clear. Is it heroic or perverted action? It is a weak rendition of the power goddess Ishtar, "who was androgynous, marginal, ambiguous" — androgynous both psychologically and physiologically.[719] She shatters the boundaries of male/female, war/love, divine/human, and more.[720] Known also as Inannu-Ishtar, she breaks all gender and socioeconomic distinctions.

Israel would have none of this. Therefore, some scholars suggest that Israel's reaction to this type of description/perversion was to prohibit its occurrence in Israel. Mentioning the woman first with respect to this issue in Israel's law may be simply a reflection of the Ugaritic text, for elsewhere in Israel's laws the male is addressed first.

Hittite texts illuminate the larger issue of gender confusion as abnormal and depict it as a shaming technique in certain circumstances.[721] In Ritual and Prayer to Ishtar of Nineveh, males captured by the Hittites have their manhood shamefully insulted and removed by dressing them like women. A scarf worn by women is placed on them and they are forced to do women's work with a distaff and spindle in their hand.[722] This act is equivalent to making males/male soldiers into women.[723] Turning them into women punished soldiers who broke an oath of allegiance to the king.[724] The "scarf" noted above may be pictured in the famous Beni Hasan painting in Egypt.[725] Lambert records some wisdom texts that refer to homosexual or tranvestism practices apparently by Amorites.[726]

Make a parapet around your roof (22:8). An Israelite is to fulfill his responsibilities

Impaled captive from Khazazu on the Balawat Gates of Shalmaneser III
Werner Forman Archive/The British Museum

Caring for cow
Frederick J. Mabie

Ashurbanipal's lion hunt relief shows hunters returning with a dead lion, but also pictured is one hunter carrying a nest of baby birds in one hand and grasping the mother bird in the other hand. This brings to mind the exhortation in Deut 22:6.

Erich Lessing/Art Resource, NY

▲

toward the safety of others when they are on his property. Law 58 of Eshnunna indicates that when a wall collapses and causes the death of a freeman, it is a capital offense and must be brought before the highest legal authority in the land, the king.[727] Westbrook notes that a specific punishment is not set here in Deuteronomy, but he suggests that "the guilt of bloodshed" may refer to polluting the building or making it unclean, or to actually bringing bloodguilt on the household. The penalty for the latter could be execution.[728] In Hittite Law 6, a general case refers to a fine of a portion (cubit?) of the owner's property.[729]

Do not plant two kinds of seed in your vineyard (22:9). The rationale for the prohibitions in verses 9–11 is not clear. Certain mixtures of foodstuffs were not acceptable legally (Lev. 19:19; Ezek. 4:9); the same idea may be in effect here.[730] The principle may go back to creation and to attempts to keep "creation distinctions" clear and functioning, "holy" and separated unto Yahweh and his created order.[731] Old Kingdom Hittite laws forbade, on pain of death, one man to sow his seed on another man's seed; the penalty was later mitigated.[732]

Do not plow with an ox and a donkey yoked together (22:10). Ancient Sumerian laws (prior to 2500–2342 B.C.) were reformed by Uruinimgina (2351–2342), but the laws had formerly permitted the *šanga*-priests to yoke together goring oxen and donkeys as teams.[733]

Do not wear clothes of wool and linen (22:11). At a Midianite tent shrine at Timnah colored cloth of mixed wool and linen was found, but this was permissible for priests in the sphere of the holy.[734] Persons at Kuntillet ʿAjrud wove forbidden fabrics by

mixing woolen threads and linen threads,[735] but this probably involved a sacerdotal activity, not a common everyday usage (where it was prohibited).[736]

Make tassels on the four corners of the cloak you wear (22:12). Tassels were attached to the "outer garment" (*keꜱût*; cf. Num. 15:37–41) used by Israelite men. Both men and women wore an outer cloak and wrapped it around their bodies or draped it over the shoulder. A belt secured it to protect a person from inclement weather. It functioned as a cover during the night and was considered valuable enough to secure a debt (Exod. 22:26–27; Deut. 24:10–13). The Black Obelisk (ca. 820 B.C.) contains a picture of King Jehu of Israel with a fringed outer garment laid over his left shoulder.[737]

If a man takes a wife and, after lying with her, dislikes her (22:13). A man could take a wife and subsequently divorce her, but not without being challenged in many instances. He could not slander or impugn her. A Babylonian dossier from the reign of Samsu-iluna (ca. 1749–1712 B.C.) touches on a provision in the Code of Hammurabi involving a charge of the Ama-sukkal against his bride of not being a virgin when he married her. His charge was not sustained.[738] Charges against a virgin in the laws of Lipit-Ishtar also failed.[739] It was of great value to a woman, her father, and her family for her to be a virgin at marriage.[740] Cases at Mari and Nippur indicate that a betrothed woman who was penetrated before marriage had broken her vow and could be divorced.[741]

There the men of her town shall stone her to death (22:21). This penalty is not paralleled in the ancient Near East, if the sexual activity is understood to have taken place before a betrothal. This legal equality between a married woman and a betrothed woman is mirrored in various laws of the ancient Near East. In the Laws of Eshnunna (Law 26) a man who rapes a betrothed daughter is executed.[742] The woman's death

Parallels between Hammurabi's Code and the Bible

Hammurabi's Code	Topic	Mosaic Law
# 1	False witness	Deut. 19:16–21
# 14	Kidnapping	Deut. 24:7
# 15	Fugitive slaves	Deut. 23:16–17
# 117	Servitude	Deut. 15:12–18
# 129	Adultery	Deut. 22:22
# 130	Rape of virgin	Deut. 22:23–27
# 141	Marital discord/violence	Deut. 22:13–19
## 154–58	Incestual relationships	Deut. 27:20–23

by stoning demonstrated that this was not a "sacrificial" act.[743]

If a man is found sleeping with another man's wife (22:22). The laws in verses 22–29 treat in three scenarios sexual sins that can dissolve a marriage or betrothal covenant or pledge. Adultery was termed the "great sin" in various documents in Egypt and Ugarit and in the ancient Near East in general.[744] Code of Hammurabi Law 129 parallels verse 22 and assigns the penalty for both of the persons involved; they were to be bound and drowned. The husband could show mercy to his wife; if so, then the guilty man could be set free also.[745]

Hittite laws and Middle Assyrian laws[746] recognize these same conditions. In Hittite laws the manner of execution is not given.[747] In Egypt adultery was prominent in legal cases, but there was evidently no officially enforced death penalty. Adulterers were rebuked or possibly beaten, sometimes in public. A betrayed husband was urged to get a new wife. In a famous list of sins confessed by deceased persons, they asserted that they did not commit adultery.[748]

Extramarital activities by the husband were not punishable offenses in ancient Mesopotamia, but an adulterous wife was put to death.[749]

Drowning and impalement were vicious punishments, but forgiveness from the husband was possible, and both the offending wife and her paramour could go free. In the case of adultery by the wife, the sins and accusations set forth in the case invariably involved more that adultery: sorcery, deceit, and slander were included in the charges. In Israel it appears that adultery was considered a religious crime against the Lord.[750] There is little from Ugarit on adultery.[751]

If a man happens to meet in a town a virgin pledged to be married (22:23). The circumstances of rape/adultery helped determine blame and penalty in each case in Israel and in the ancient Near East. This text discusses a betrothed virgin (fiancée). Similar conditions for a married woman are noted in Hittite laws, where the woman is culpable if the rape is in a populated area and she does not cry out.[752] Law 150 in the Code of Hammurabi describes a situation in which a man clearly overpowers and holds

Tassels on clothing
Kim Walton, courtesy of the Oriental Institute Museum

▶ Eunuchs

In certain cases of adultery or sodomy in the Middle Assyrian era, the guilty parties were turned into eunuchs by having their testicles crushed.[A-166] Hittite texts attest to the presence of eunuchs in the "house of the king,"[A-167] indicating that eunuchs played a major role in the royal structure of the ancient Near East and in Hittite administration,[A-168] but they did not serve in the military. Anuwanze, a eunuch, served as supervisor over the scribes who wrote/copied a Hittite New Kingdom text concerning the founding of a new temple.[A-169] Their presence at Mari is well attested mostly as elite military troops.[A-170]

In Assyria eunuchs were disqualified from serving as priests, but they served in lower capacities. They could serve as a treasurer of the temple or (rarely) as a temple administrator. The Chief Eunuch[A-171] was a high-ranking military leader, and eunuchs held other high military positions.[A-172] Eunuchs were normally made, not born. At an early age a child was castrated or their testicles were crushed. Captives from war or persons given in tribute were the main source for eunuchs.[A-173] The mother goddess Ninmah created some from birth, according to ancient Sumerian tradition.[A-174] In Israel emasculation disqualified a priest from serving and from offering animals for sacrifice (Lev. 21:20; 22:24). Sacrificial animals should be without defect, with a few exceptions in Israel as listed.

Hittite documents record the attempt of scribes and priests and other temple officials in an unusual situation to discover the reason for the anger of the gods and the occurrence of unfavorable omens. Several possible solutions to this dilemma included the fact that two "deficient and mutilated people" had entered the temple. This required the performance of a rite by an old Hittite woman with respect to the god involved. Among other possible reasons for the unfavorable situation was the fact that a dog had approached the table, once knocking the sacrificial bread off of its table and at another time eating portions of sacrificial bread.[A-175]

was frowned upon.[784] Israel condemned taking interest from a fellow Israelite because of covenantal compassion.[785]

Loans at high rates of interest were extended throughout the ancient Near East, and temples were often the most used creditors.[786] In some cases interest could be forfeited, such as if a catastrophe struck the debtor.[787] Since the purpose of a loan was to help the poor or someone in a crisis situation, it was unjust to exact interest from the debtor.[788] The excessive rates charged reached 25 percent or more a year, with additional demands tacked on. Certain Assyrian Aramaic inscriptions (ca. 650 B.C.) had this provision.[789]

Especially in a time of need or crisis among the people of Israel interest was not to be placed on fellow Israelites, but Israelites could charge interest to foreigners. In Ugarit class-conscientious free men did not charge each other interest.[790] Persons could stand in pledge and serve as laborers in place of interest.[791] Surety for debt was firmly exacted.[792]

Vows (23:21). Vows in Israel could involve sacrifice before a certain event occurred or afterward. Both situations are covered in this instruction. Old Babylonian vows are recorded in royal inscriptions and in literary texts. One involves offering the image of a dog to the goddess Narina for a future blessing. The other vow offering, a sculpture of a dog to Nintinuga, goddess of healing, expects healing by dogs (licking wounds). Dogs were sacred to Nintinuga.[793]

Cartledge recognizes the function of vow offerings in many sources across the ancient Near East: Sumerian, Akkadian, Egyptian, Hittite, Ugaritic, Old Aramaic, Punic, and Neo-Punic. The function of these offerings reflects uniformly similar usage and purposes as are present in Israel.[794] He observes that vows from the ancient Near East were everywhere (including Egypt) made to a god and conditioned. Fulfillment of vows was public, and prompt performance of vows was often necessary, motivated by personal and/or possibly national distress.[795]

If a man marries a woman who becomes displeasing to him (24:1). In the ancient Near East divorce was taken seriously. See sidebar on "Divorce."

Recently married (24:5). The joy of a new marriage is respected and adulated. The possibility of producing a child and heir in the family is highest during the first year in the cultural milieu and age spans of the ancient Near East.[796] Note that a military exemption could be suspended in unusual circumstances.[797] This custom was observed at Ugarit, but it was waived in the case of war undertaken on behalf of King Keret in the Ugaritic epic texts.[798]

Millstones (24:6). Millstones were necessary for a household to produce groats, meal, or flour for cooking and food preparation, usually operated by women, slaves, or servants (cf. Ex. 11:5; Isa. 47:2). Two stones were used, so that to take one as a pledge or guarantee removed a family's means of sustenance and livelihood. This insensitive seizing of property was an exception to what the creditor could normally do with property of a debtor.[799]

Millstones were used in homes, and the officials of the state in milling houses used large millstones. The millhouse existed as a part of Mesopotamian culture. Two stone slabs were used, one concave lower stone and an upper stone shaped like a loaf. Grain was placed on the lower stone to be ground. The upper stone was moved up and down by hand on the lower stone to grind the grain between them. Sixteen grindstones have been found in place at Ebla.[800]

Upper and lower millstone for grinding grain
Z. Radovan/
www.BibleLand
Pictures.com

Kidnapping (24:7). Kidnapping was a form of theft and murder because by removing a person from the community, it cut off a fellow Israelite from the community of God's people and from the promised covenant land itself.[801] Kidnapping dealt with persons as if they were merchandise. Code of Hammurabi Law 14 says that the person who kidnapped a young man must be executed. In the Old Babylonian period kidnapping slaves and free persons for enslavement was common.[802]

In Hittite laws, kidnapping did not carry a death penalty. Depending on who the abductor was and who was abducted, the abductor was subject to various penalties: the abductor's house could be taken, six persons in place of the

The goddess of healing, Gula, was often portrayed as a dog.
Marie-Lan Nguyen/
Wikimedia Commons, courtesy of the
Louvre

but they probably worked fewer hours. The hired man depended on his daily wage to survive and to care for his family.[816] The Bible strongly condemns any failure to pay the wages of a day laborer.[817]

Fathers shall not be put to death for their children (24:16). In Middle Assyrian law a husband and children could not suffer a penalty for a wife who had blasphemed.[818] This seems to refer to the disallowance of vicarious liability for the act of a wife/woman only, for a woman was responsible for any debts, crimes, or offenses of her husband.[819]

In the Code of Hammurabi several laws (e.g., Laws 230–32) stipulate a talion (eye for eye) mentality in the punishments. If faulty construction of a house resulted in the death of the owner's son or slave, the builder's son or slave was to be put to death. If the house caused the destruction of property or goods, they must be replaced. Greenberg maintains that Israel's laws differed from other ancient Near Eastern laws that allowed vicarious punishment and maintains that a principle of individual responsibility was both early in Israel and governed all biblical law.[820]

Alien (24:17). This powerful injunction of social justice is widespread and found in documents at Ugarit, in Akkadian texts, and in texts from Nuzi.[821] A common social and legal concern for this class of persons was part of the ancient Near Eastern culture, but nowhere as it was in Israel.[822] Four classes of persons outside the normal safety nets of these ancient societies are highlighted: widow, orphan, alien (*gēr*),[823] and poor.[824] The alien is not mentioned along with the other three in the law collections outside Israel.[825]

The Moabite Stone records the death of *grn* and *grt*, male and female sojourners, among those whom Mesha, the king of Moab, killed in his war against Israel.[826] All four groups were vulnerable and subject to abuse. Israel had experienced firsthand what it was to be an alien in a strange land and culture, and thus the alien was specifically written into her laws. Showing hospital-

ity to the stranger was far from providing for them in the laws of a nation.[827] These aliens were resident in various countries but did not enjoy citizenship; hence, they were denied significant legal rights. Israel's God heard their cry.

Widow (24:17). The widow throughout the ancient Near East was often cared for by special legislation.[828] See sidebar on "Widows, Orphans, and the Poor."

Flogged in his presence … not give him more than forty lashes (25:2–3). This law seeks to protect a guilty party from being destroyed emotionally and spiritually by excessive humiliation. The Code of Hammurabi (Law 202) limits the number of lashes to sixty for insubordination. Note also the New Testament, where thirty-nine lashes were prescribed to ensure that the law not be broken (2 Cor. 11:24).[829] The "lashes" were likely administered with something like a rod (cf. Ex. 21:20). In the Hammurabi Code an oxtail whip was used in public to administer punishment. In the Middle Assyrian Laws flogging normally entailed from thirty to a hundred lashes.[830] Fifty lashes was the most often prescribed penalty, though the total range was from five to a hundred.

Tablet A (57) instructs the punishment to be done "in the presence of the judges."[831] This provision guaranteed that the penalty was administered and was delivered as prescribed. According to the status of the guilty person and what the offense had been, an appropriate penalty was framed. A harlot who was spotted in the street wearing a veil to disguise herself was flogged fifty times with staves or rods, and hot pitch was poured on her head.[832]

Do not muzzle an ox while it is treading out the grain (25:4). In Israel work animals were to be treated with compassion (cf. 5:14, 19).[833] The ox was an immensely important piece of property and an invaluable work animal throughout the ancient Near East (cf. Ex. 21:28–32, 35–36).[834] It was the primary work animal in agriculture. Oxen pulled sledges that had been outfit-

▶ Widows, Orphans, and the Poor

Assyrian laws required sons to care for their mothers.[A-187] A creditor could not seize a widow's cloak.[A-188] In the ancient Near East kings were supposed to be guarantors of social righteousness, and a righteous king did not deliver up a widow or orphan to abuse. The ancient reform laws of Uruinimgina (ca. 2400 B.C.), Hammurabi (1728–1686), and Ur-Nammu all contained a provision similar to this. Judicial reforms and special acts of concern by the king were also embedded in the matrix of society to protect these classes of persons when necessary. The king's own royal subordinates were to follow his example.[A-189]

As in Israel, a king's reign or his own life could be extended if he protected this group.[A-190] Such righteous action pleased the gods. The gods themselves (e.g., Shamash, Ningirsu, Amon, Re, Ptah) were expected to care for these classes of individuals. The wisdom literature of the ancient Near East expressed its concern about the welfare of these persons.

In Mesopotamian wisdom literature (e.g., Babylonian Theodicy, ca. 1000 B.C.), concern and care for the weak is stressed. In Egyptian literature the poor, the widow, and the orphan were the objects of special care of kings and monarchs from at least the time of the twelfth dynasty (ca. 1991–1000). In such works as the Eloquent Peasant,[A-191] Instructions of Merikare, Instructions of Amenemhet, and Instructions of Amenemope, concern is evident. Ramesses III boasts to the god Ptah of caring for widows and orphans.[A-192]

At Ugarit the famous righteous man Dan(i)el set himself to judge diligently the cause of the widow and orphan.[A-193] In Israel one Lord, not multiple gods, exercised justice and was the source of righteous laws protecting the widow, orphan, poor, or alien. To abuse the rights of any of these persons led to a curse from the Lord. The Supreme Judge set forth the way and all others were to follow that lead.[A-194]

Emaciated man holding a bowl
Werner Forman Archive/The Egyptian Museum, Berlin
◀

ted with studs of flint or basalt embedded into wooden boards. They pulled these across the grain to loosen the grain from the stalks. In Sumerian laws, later reformed by Uruinimgina (ca. 2351–2342 B.C.), the "oxen of the gods" plowed the onion garden of the king. These were oxen dedicated to temple service and its holy precincts.[835]

Oxen were watched carefully, controlled, and properly contained according to Hittite law (prior to ca. 1650 B.C.; cf. Ex. 21:26–36) and according to the Laws of Eshnunna.[836] Specific laws governed the rental of an ox for hire.[837] The seemingly ubiquitous case of a goring ox is now also known at Nuzi,[838]

Ox treading grain in Egyptian wall painting
Manfred Näder, Gabana Studios, Germany
◀

but is not yet paralleled in Egyptian texts. However, an Egyptian relief pictures an ox that has stopped to eat grain and it has no muzzle on it.[839]

Duty of a brother-in-law (25:5). Hebrew *yābām* refers to "brother-in-law," while Latin *levir* means "husband's brother." See sidebar on "Issues in Levirate Marriage."

The Family of the Unsandaled (25:10). Sandals of various types were worn in Canaan, Syria, and Mesopotamia from the most ancient times. They could be used in a symbolic way at Nuzi, perhaps as token payments.[840] At Nuzi the seller removed his foot from a piece of land he was selling and placed the buyer's foot in its place. Then shoes were transferred. A pair of shoes and garments is presented as a fictitious payment to "accommodate" some unusual transactions.[841] The brother-in-law (25:10) who refused to honor his dead brother by preserving his seed and inheritance brought shame on himself and his house. Honor, shame, and covenant relations were central concerns in the ancient Near East.[842]

If two men are fighting (25:11). The harshness of the penalty in this law is surprising.[843] In the Middle Assyrian Laws, if in a fight between two men, a woman intervenes and crushes a testicle of one of them, one of her fingers is cut off. If the man suffers the damage or loss of the other testicle because of complications, then the woman's eyes were torn out (or, possibly, both nipples were ripped off).[844] In the second case, in both Deuteronomy and the Middle Assyrian Laws, the penalty approaches lex talionis and the offender suffers punishment according to her deed.

Differing weights (25:13). Israel's God loved honesty and hated deception. In the ancient Near East the king was especially responsible to see that the weights used in business or personal transactions were fair and that everyone used the same set of weights. Unfortunately a uniform universal system of weights was not adopted in ancient times, but whatever system was used to begin a transaction had to be used to complete it. A lender could potentially sell using one set of weights, but receive payment using another set.[845] In the Laws of Ur-Nammu (2112–2095 B.C.) a faltering attempt was made to standardize weights and measures.[846]

In the Egyptian Instruction of Amenemope, the falsification of weights was prohibited, as well as "leaning" on them. Measuring devices were not to be tampered with, and the god Thoth had his sacred ape (or baboon) that watched constantly over the system of scales in use.[847] In the document relating the "negative confession of sins," the confessor asserts that he has not "added to ... the balance" or "tampered with ... plummet of the scales."[848] The Elegant Peasant in Egypt mentions the evil practice of "tipping the scales" in one's favor.[849]

In Mesopotamia a specific provision in a contract could stipulate that a certain standard be employed, such as the mina of Shamash (i.e., the system of balances employed in transactions in the temple of Shamash).[850] A cheating merchant, if caught, could forfeit everything due to him.[851] In a hymn to the god Shamash, it is asserted that Shamash was especially wary of a misuse of honest weights and measures.[852]

Amalek (25:19). The Amalekites were nomadic/seminomadic people and were descendants of Esau. It was not only Israel who blotted out memories of whole peoples at the command of her God, such as Amalek (Ex. 17:14–16), who had, in fact, first tried to destroy Israel at her birth at the exodus. Pharaoh Merneptah (1209 B.C.) laid down his claim that he had stamped out the seed of Israel—"its seed is not."[853] The irony of the claim is that it is, in fact, presently our major ancient Near Eastern unequivocal

Fighting men
Manfred Näder,
Gabana Studios,
Germany

▶ Issues in Levirate Marriage

The practice described here (still followed among some Arabs today) was well known in the ancient Near East. The family was perpetuated and the inheritance was kept in the family.[A-195] Levirate marriage was practiced at Ugarit, at least at the royal level of society (ca. 1345–1336 B.C.), with reference to the childless Arhalba and his brother Niqmepa.[A-196] Hittite laws and possibly laws at Nuzi recognized this marriage practice.[A-197] In Hittite law a widowed wife may, if necessary, marry her brother-in-law, her father-in-law, or the son of her brother-in-law.[A-198]

In some Hittite and Assyrian laws the issue is not whether the deceased had sons, but rather the need to support the widow in whom the father had a large investment through the bride price.[A-199] More recent textual finds from Emar emphasize the desire of legislation like this to keep property within the family.[A-200] Concern for the preservation of seed and inheritance is found[A-201] late into the time of Ptolemy II Philadelphus (273/272 B.C.).

In the more ancient Middle Assyrian laws the wife of a son who died could be given by the son's father to another of his sons, even if he were betrothed to someone else but not yet married. But if the father of that betrothed daughter does not agree to this, the father of the deceased son may proceed as planned and give the betrothed bride to his son. Or he may withdraw from the entire process. If a betrothed daughter dies before the marriage, her father may give his prospective son-in-law another daughter, or the betrothed groom may withdraw.

If a wife's husband dies while they are living in her father's house, if she has borne no children, her father-in-law may marry her to the son of his choice, or she could be given in marriage by her father to her father-in-law. This option was not permitted in Israel (cf. Gen. 38:26). If her husband and father-in-law both died, she became a widow and was free to do as she pleased. If the wife had borne children, she was free to live in a house for her and her son in her father's household.[A-202]

witness to the existence of Israel's "seed" in the land of Canaan at this early date!

Wandering Aramean (26:5). The Arameans are attested as early as the fourteenth century (Amenophis III, 1380; Merneptah, 1200 B.C.) on the west bend of the Euphrates River. They then appear in Syria, to the west and south.[854] The Israelites clearly recognized a biological and geographical connection between themselves and the Arameans. Nahor, Bethuel, and Laban had remained in Aram as Arameans. Wives of Isaac and Jacob came from this Aramaic branch of the family (Gen. 24:28). Hence, Deuteronomy 26:5 seems justified, as an assertion of origin for Israel, as a particular branch of the much larger classification

1/3 mina

5 shekels

10 shekels

1/2 mina

4 shekels

3 shekels

2 shekels

1 shekel

3/4 shekel

2/3 shekel

1/2 shekel

1/3 shekel

1/4 shekel

1/6 shekel

1/7 shekel

1/8 shekel

1/16 shekel

Complete set for weighing precious metals in the palace
The Schøyen Collection MS 5088/1-55, Oslo and London

of people known as Arameans (cf. Gen. 10:22–23). Some scholars prefer to see "Aramean" as primarily a geographical term rather than an ethnic term.[855]

It is not possible to write a comprehensive history of the Arameans, but Lemaire thinks this verse probably indicates a genuine connection of Israel with those Arameans who appear in the Mari texts (ca. 1100–960 B.C.). Assyrian royal inscriptions mention them, and the oldest Aramaic inscriptions are located in the second half of the ninth century. Fleming suggests that "Israelites who settled the north-central hill country during the Iron I period carried with them the tradition of Syrian origins."[856] He suggests that these Aramean connections could have been imbedded in persistent social or political institutions across time.[857]

Tenth of all your produce in the third year (26:12). God's people were to care for each other. By giving a tithe ("tenth") of their produce for the needy they demonstrated their compassion for their neighbor. Social concern and charity have been evidenced by archaeological finds at Arad in the Negev. There "mixing bowls" were found in which food had been placed for a poor man.[858] Israel was enjoined to care for the widow, orphan, and poor. The Levite, a central player in Israel's

cultic and ritual activities, lived off of the cult and produce from the levitical cities. "Holy" bowls dedicated to the priests have been found and were used by priests with respect to their portion of sacrificial foods (cf. Lev. 22:14–16).

Then say to the LORD your God (26:13–14). After a positive affirmation of obedience to protocol, a negative confession in verse 14 disavows any sacrifice to the dead, a ritual prescribed by even the wise Ahikar: "My son, pour out the wine upon the graves of the righteous and do not drink it with iniquitous men."[859] In this instruction it is possible to see a reference to giving a part of one's tithe to Baal, the "Dead One," who, however, was purportedly resurrected again and again in the spring according to the fertility rites recorded in the Baal Epic at Ugarit.[860] This is also, of course, a reference to the fact that a funerary cult was to be avoided that involved feeding, nourishing, and communicating with the dead of a family.

Such tasks were passed on within the family at Nuzi, Emar, and perhaps at Ugarit.

Mari and Ebla seem to lack these practices.[861] This negative confession formula was also spoken in Egypt, and the confessor specifically disavowed ever having been guilty of any sins with respect to the temple, gods, or other holy things, including foods.[862]

You have declared this day.... And the Lord has declared this day ... (26:16–19). Assyrian kings and their vassals exchanged oaths.[863] Various ancient Near Eastern treaties/covenants reflect this clearly. Later Assyrian treaties include the assertions by the vassal that the vassal "does swear" to the terms of the treaty; later vassal treaties include actions by word and ceremony that were to effect the treaty.

Earlier Hittite treaties/covenants featured this as well. Extensive ratification rites are included in the Hittite treaty between Kurtiwaza and Suppiluliumas. In this case "Hatti proclaims the form and content of the oath [r. 11–34] and Kurtiwaza [vassal] himself ['I'] then actually pronounces the oath for himself and his Hurrian subjects ... then the Hurrians themselves get into the act."[864] In the expanded covenant/treaty of Deuteronomy these verses connect the material in chapter 26 to chapter 28.[865] Even the gods exchanged oaths in marriage, as when Dumuzi and Inanna were married.[866]

Ceremonies (27:1–10)

Set up some large stones and coat them with plaster (27:2). Some Syrian-Palestinian treaty/covenant sections provided engraved blessings and cursings.[867] These stones were whitewashed with an application of lime plaster, and then laws were written on them (cf. Dan. 5:5).[868] Several such inscriptions are known at Succoth and Kuntillet ʿAjrud. Many other stone inscriptions are well known from the ancient Near East.[869]

This method and type of writing and this peculiar preparation reflects Egyptian influence (cf. Josh. 24:27). In Egypt black ink was used, especially for decorative flourishes or headings. Red ocher or red oxide was substituted for the carbon. In Egypt and Syria-Palestine stone was used for permanence and for public display. Plaster was used to improve the writing quality of the stone.[870]

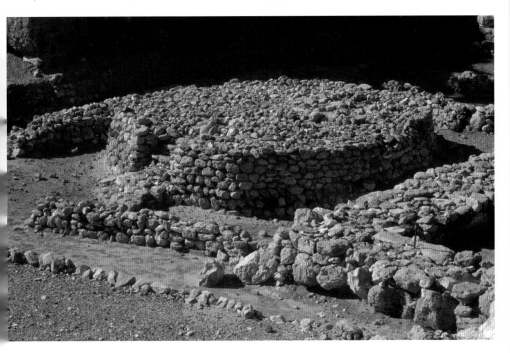

Stone altar from Megiddo
Z. Radovan/
www.BibleLand
Pictures.com

A. Zertal argues that a stone ruin he uncovered on Mount Ebal on the upper part of the northeast part of the mountain should be tied to Deuteronomy 27:1–26 and Joshua 8:30–35.[871] Yet no part of the inscribed stones has been recovered to date, so no final verdict on Zertal's claim is yet possible. Zertal considers the location, type of site, and the probable period of the site as highly suggestive in a positive sense to tie it to this passage.[872] Kempinski challenged Zertal's interpretation of his finds on Mount Ebal, claiming that Zertal has found an Iron Age I watchtower.[873]

Blessings and Curses (27:11–28:68)

These tribes shall stand on Mount Gerizim (27:12). The ceremonial ritual that celebrates Israel's entrance into the land and seals the covenant includes an actual ceremony and recitation of curses and a full inscription of the blessings (28:1–14) and curses (28:15–68). Kitchen lists the oaths (29:12–15) and ceremonies (ch. 27) as additional features of the adapted covenant form employed in Deuteronomy.[874]

Mount Gerizim (2849 ft.) and Mount Ebal (1405 ft.) are twin mountains situated in the central Samarian hills. Mount Ebal is slightly north of Gerizim, and the city of Shechem (modern Nablus) lies slightly east at the base of these mountains. East-west access into the hill country of Samaria/Ephraim is through these mountains. Today a Samaritan community has a synagogue in Nablus and celebrates Passover, Pentecost, and Tabernacles every year on Gerazim.[875]

To bless the people ... to pronounce curses (27:12–13). These introductory verses and the ceremony reciting key curses constitute a ritual that Israel was to carry out when she entered the land. The list of curses and blessings of the renewal of the Sinai covenant is contained in Deuteronomy 28. The presence of blessings *and* curses argues strongly for a Late Bronze Age (ca. 1550–1200 B.C.) origin for the treaty form of Deuteronomy itself.

Kitchen has shown that there are (1) ancient Near Eastern parallels for nearly every curse in Deuteronomy 28, and (2) most parallels (ca. thirty treaties examined

dated before 1200 B.C.) link up to the second millennium much better than with the seventh century. But, significantly, there are "links" with both. Kitchen's claims and results are based on his summary of eighty to ninety documents available for study. He demonstrates parallels to the curses in texts and inscriptions from Zimri-Lim, Eshnunna, Hammurabi, Hittite documents (various kings and vassals), Arameans, Mari, Neo-Assyrian, and Kudurrus (so-called boundary stones from Babylonia). He finds parallels of varying significance to all verses in Deuteronomy 28:16–63. Verses 64–68 repeat and expand on earlier verses.[876] The curses in 27:15–26 are sometimes unique to Israel; sometimes they reflect a common ancient Near Eastern body of laws and curses.

The Levites are to recite and the people are to respond. A text recounting the birth of a "double deity" at Ugarit contains a ceremonial type of rubric. It seems to reflect a cultic-ceremonial usage: "Seven times they are to pronounce (these verses) next to the ʿO-room and those who enter respond."[877]

Leads the blind astray (27:18). The blind were to be treated with care and compassion.

Blindness was relatively common in the ancient Near East (see 10:18; 24:17 and comments). The Egyptian Teaching of Amenemope (ca. 1300 B.C.) prohibits laughing at a blind person or a dwarf or doing injury to a lame person. Blindness could, however, be visited on a mortal who has offended a god in some way.[878] In the myth of Enki, god of wisdom, and Ninmah, the mother goddess, various kinds of handicapped persons are created. Enki gave them appropriate roles. The one born blind was placed before the king in a place of honor as the chief musician. Each disabled person is placed appropriately.[879]

Sleeps with father's wife (27:20). The accursed sexual behaviors mentioned in verses 20–23 are condemned in several ancient law codes. A plethora of punishments were meted out to the persons involved, such as banishment, drowning, monetary restitution, loss of dowry and potential daughter-in-law, burning, or disinheritance.[880] Hittite laws considered sexual relations with one's mother, daughter, or son to be a capital crime, but the king could spare the offender's life.[881] Having sexual relations with a living brother's wife was a capital crime.[882] Bestiality was permitted with certain animals, especially in the Hittite laws. The penalty for lying carnally with cattle, a pig, dog, or sheep was death, but, strangely, not so with a horse or mule (no punishment). But the king could spare the guilty person's life.

Kills his neighbor (27:24). Murder of whatever kind was usually punishable by blood revenge or compensation. In Assyria both options were available in all the periods for which we have texts.[883] Interestingly, among the Hittites only compensatory penalties were in place except for a royal murder, which was still able to be settled by compensation or blood revenge. Hoffner believes that the relatives of a murdered person could demand the death penalty for the murderer if they so desired.[884] In Babylonia, evidence

suggests that the death penalty was an option, at least for wives and their accomplices who were involved in murdering husbands.[885]

Bribe (27:25). The one who took a bribe was usually a judge or official of some kind (cf. 16:18–20), so it is probable that a judge is in mind here.[886] Tigay perceives a reference here to a corrupt death penalty rendered by the judge. In the Code of Hammurabi if a judge who has officially decided a case and rendered a sealed judgment changes his decision, that judge is condemned and ejected from the assembly and place of judgment permanently. Bribery may have blinded him to act perversely.

A text found in Assurbanipal's library (668–663 B.C.), but which undoubtedly has a much earlier origin, praises the universal sun god, Shamash. Shamash punished a person who accepted bribes, because he was perverting justice. This text notes that a person who rejects bribes would likewise intercede for the weak, who could be innocent victims.[887]

Carefully follow all his commands (28:1). Verses 1–3 state the conditions under which the following blessings will be received, a feature common to other ancient Near Eastern lists of blessing. But it is the king whose honor is primary, not the honor of the particular god involved, as it is in Israel. The king implores that those who observe his laws and respect his inscriptions may receive the pleasure and blessing of a god or gods. For example, Lipit-Ishtar, king of the First Dynasty of Isin (1934–1924 B.C.), offers these blessings for the one who respects his laws, promotes his stele, and does not place his name over the kings (pseudepigraphy was strongly condemned centuries before the intertestamental era): "May he be granted life and breadth of long days; may he raise his neck to heaven in the Ekur temple; may the god Enlil's brilliant countenance be turned upon him from above."[888]

Hammurabi implores that those who follow his laws may have their reign lengthened and may shepherd their people with justice by the help of Shamash, god of justice. The kings of Egypt and Hatti wished goodwill on those who kept their treaty/covenant. Hundreds are called upon to bless any Egyptian or Hittite who keeps the Hittite treaty.[889]

All these blessings will come upon you ... if you obey the LORD your God (28:2). The blessings of the covenantal document are all paralleled to some extent in other ancient Near Eastern documents, but no document presents them in their entirety in one place or in the order presented in the biblical text.[890] Blessings are found in ancient, archaic treaties of the third millennium (ca. 2500–2300 B.C.), such as in the Naram-Sin materials; in early law "codes" that were sometimes part of a treaty/covenant from the third millennium into the early second millennium (ca. 2100–1700), such as Ur-Nammu, Lipit-Ishtar, Hammurabi; in treaties/covenants of the late second millennium (ca. 1400–1200), such as Hittite treaties. In Aramaic or Assyrian treaties from about 900–650 blessings are not featured. The Sinai covenant and its renewals with blessings (short) and curses (long) best fit the era 1400–1200 B.C.[891]

Blessed when you come in and blessed when you go out (28:6). The far-ranging blessings of 28:3–6 are covered in a summary way in a treaty hoping for peace, health, happiness, and success on persons and their country in Hittite and Egyptian/Hittite treaties.[892] The higher echelons of society and government receive special emphasis. Suppiluliuma (1370–1330 B.C.) implores that Kutiwaza may return to its high place among the nations that it had before, and that it may prosper and expand.

However, mixed with the blessings for Israel from her God is a clear recognition and realization that she is his holy people, if they keep his covenantal laws. This overarching theological concept is not paralleled in the blessings of the other ancient Near Eastern treaties. To breach or break a covenant or treaty, which was, in fact, an act of unfaithfulness by a covenant partner, brought down terrible curses on an offending party. The Hittite king Mursilis II (ca. 1330–1295 B.C.) attributed a terrible plague upon his people during his reign to the people's failure and the failure of Suppiluliuma I (ca. 1370–1330) to keep a treaty with the Egyptians even though it had been enacted under a previous king.[893]

Whatever one makes of the dating of Deuteronomy and other critical issues involved, it is clear that Israel at some levels functioned as any other ancient Near Eastern nation, but at the significant level of a theological worldview, ethics, and life she was wholly other, a people holy unto their own exclusive God. Exile was the ultimate covenant threat (28:36, 41, 48, 63, 64–68). She would, in fact, in shame and humility retrace her history and birth (v. 68). There is no essential parallel to this overall phenomenon.

The sky over your head will be bronze (28:23). The depiction of a drought featuring a bronze sky and iron ground is matched in a canonical West Semitic inscription that may go back to the seventh century B.C.: "The earth was bronze, the heavens, of iron, the sod, in a bad/arid state."[894] Esarhaddon's vassal treaty curses mention the soil being turned to iron and the sky to copper.[895]

Boils ... tumors (28:25–29). Verses 25–29 encompass curses that result in Israel's complete defeat and humiliation at the hands of her enemies, in addition to a terrifying buffeting by plagues from the Lord because she has broken the covenant (cf. Ex. 15:22–24).[896] Parallels exist in Aramaic and Akkadian with curses listed in the vassal treaties of Esarhaddon, but only partially and not in the same order. This is the situation with most of the curses found in this chapter. Ugaritic, Aramaic, and Akkadian texts speak of blindness as a curse because of murder.[897] The epilogue in the Code of Hammurabi contains relatively close parallels concerning dispersion and exile, defeat by enemies (v. 25), boils, tumors, itch (v. 27), blindness, and mental confusion (vv. 28–29).[898]

Eat the fruit of the womb (28:53). Ugaritic texts describe prayers offered on behalf of a city under siege.[899] Sumerian texts record deaths from famine at the time of the destruction of Ur and Sumer.[900] The horrors of siege warfare often resulted in unbelievable acts of human cannibalism. The ancient story of Atraḫasis contains a description of cannibalism in a city oppressed with hunger.[901]

These conditions were also set forth in the vassal treaties of Esarhaddon (ca. 690 B.C.): "Mother shall [bar the door to] her daughter, may you eat in your hunger the flesh of your children ... let dogs and pigs eat your flesh, and may your spirit have no one to take care of and pour libations to him."[902] A similar description of a kind and gentle person, as given here, depicts the king of Babylon.[903]

Covenant Renewal, Oaths, Restoration, Charges to the Nation (29:1–30:20)

Terms of the covenant (29:1).[904] This chapter, as previous chapters, indicates that Israel was to seal this covenant with an oath. The source of this covenant is the Lord God, not Moses, its human mediator. In Syria the god Assur made a covenant with this people, as recorded on an amulet found at ancient Hadattu, Syria, dating to the seventh century B.C. and written in a local Canaanite dialect using Aramaic script. The text, of course, invokes other gods, such as sons of El, leaders of a group of Holy Ones, Baʾal, and even the heavens and eternal earth.[905] This text involves incantations against demons and other potentially harmful beings, including a demon (the Wolf) that carried off children in the night. On the basis of this eternal covenant with Assur, the person appeals to Assur and his covenant for protection and security. The covenant/incantation ritual is sealed with an oath.

But to this day the LORD has not given you a mind that understands (29:4). God created human beings with the ability to see and hear (Ex. 4:11–12), but spiritual, moral, and intellectual perception is in mind here. All these functions work together in the Egyptian Ennead of gods: "eyes see, the ears' hearing ... to the heart [which] causes every conclusion to emerge."[906] Ears and eyes that function properly inform the heart (*lēb*), which produces knowledge, speech, and action that is also morally and ethically discerning. This is expressed in the action of the Egyptian god Ptah, creator of the world. The sight of the eyes, the hearing of the ears, and the sense of smell are connected to Ptah's heart, understanding, and intelligence.[907]

For Israel to truly "hear" with their whole being they needed to keep the covenant, but they had not done so. Only faithful obedience to the Lord and his covenant could open an epistemological channel leading to God's giving them an understanding mind (*lēb*; cf. 6:4).

I will be safe, **even though I persist in going my own way (29:19).** The vassal treaty of Esarhaddon (690–669 B.C.), with the god Assur as witness, puts forth similar conditions: "If you, as you stand on the soil where this oath (is sworn), swear the oath with *words and lips (only)*, do not swear with your entire heart, do not transmit it to your sons ... if you take this curse upon yourselves but do not plan to keep the treaty of Esarhaddon."[908] Duplicity and deceit were

not acceptable to Assur or to Esarhaddon. How much more so to the Lord of Israel, the God and true King of Israel, who alone was the source of his covenants and knew human hearts.

Salt and sulfur (29:23). Burning, salting, and weeds (?) are mentioned in inscriptions from Sefire in a treaty context as curses on those who break the treaty or covenant.[909] Salt and sulfur wither and dry up vegetation. The cities of Jericho and Shechem experienced this kind of devastation.[910]

It is because this people abandoned the covenant of the LORD (29:25). Assurbanipal records that all of the kings he set up in his provinces rebelled and broke their covenant and oaths. Therefore, he proceeded to punish them with the curses contained in the treaties.[911] Covenant rebels were given their due—the curses of their respective treaties or covenants. The gods involved were the covenant prosecutors and executioners through the legal and military machinery of the suzerain whom the vassals had betrayed.

In the case of Assurbanipal (668–633 B.C.) the treaty language, as in Deuteronomy, anticipates the questions of an astonished rebel vassal who asks, "On account of what have these calamities befallen Arabia?" He himself responds, "Because we did not keep the solemn oaths (sworn by) Assur, because we offended the friendliness of Assurbanipal, the king, beloved of Enlil."[912] The guilty vassals could not claim lack of knowledge, for the terms of the covenant or treaty and the will of the gods and suzerain stood in the publicly accessible document that had been sworn by all the parties involved (cf. 29:29).

What I am commanding you today is not too difficult for you or beyond your reach (30:11). The ancient hero Gilgamesh sought to discover the secret to life by seeking out Utnapishtim (Babylonian Noah). Gilgamesh asserts, "I traversed difficult mountains, and I rowed all the seas,"[913] in

order to gain the secret of life from Utnap-ishtim.[914] He further declares that "man, the tallest, cannot stretch to heaven."[916] The origin of this magnificent epic lies far back into hoary antiquity (ca. 2000 B.C. or earlier). It has Sumerian analogues and predecessors.

Ancient Near Eastern wisdom literature found it impossible to discover the way to life. Hidden was the reasoning and the intentions of the gods, as the Righteous Sufferer declares.[916] In the Babylonian Theodicy the friend of a sufferer indicates that people cannot grasp the divine purpose.[917] The pessimist of Babylonian wisdom asked, "Who is tall enough to ascend to heaven?"[918] The Babylonians believed that mortals who dwell on earth could not attain the wisdom of the gods, who dwell in heaven.[919] Not so for the Israelites, whose God had clearly and publicly set forth what was right in his eyes for his people to follow.

See, I set before you today life and prosperity (30:15). To live was to receive the blessings; to die was to encounter the divine displeasure through the curses. Thus, two ways are set before Israel—life or death. The Babylonian Noah, Utnapishtim, was encouraged to seek life by following the words of the gods, with the result that prosperity and health would follow.[920] Pharaoh Akenaten, who alone knew the Aten (sun disk/god), believed that to follow him was to experience life.[921] The king's heart was to stay focused on his god.[922]

The victory stele of Piye (ca. 734 B.C.), king of Egypt, reports that as he approached a town he sent messengers saying, "Look, two ways are before you; choose as you wish. Open, you live; close, you die." Those who follow the word of his lord prolong their life, but shorten it if they rebel.[923] Moral behavior was a key to a good and long life in Egyptian thinking.[924]

I call heaven and earth as witnesses (30:19). Calling out witnesses and writing down a list of divine witnesses to a covenant or treaty in the Late Bronze Age Hittite documents was tedious but necessary in order to

activate the covenant. In the treaty between the Hittite king Mursilus and Duppi-Teshub the list of deities and witnesses begins, "Let the thousand gods stand by for this oath! Let them observe and listen!"[925] The list runs for forty lines and concludes with "mountains, rivers, springs, great sea, heaven and earth, winds, clouds. Let these be witnesses to the treaty and to the oath!"[926] For the king and country, but also for the king's agents who were faithful, a blessing of long life was extended.[927] In addition to life, health, multitudes of years, and length of days were rewards for the faithful covenant keeper.

Succession, Deposition, and Recitation of Text (31:1–29)

I am now a hundred and twenty years old (31:2). Old age was a blessing from the gods in the thinking of the ancient Near East.[928] The kings before the flood in the Sumerian King List were attributed heroic lives of thousands of years.[929] The age of one hundred and ten represented a fulfilled life in Egypt.[930] Ramesses II lived to be about ninety. Moses reaches the biblical ideal of one hundred and twenty years (Gen. 6:3; cf. 50:26).

Ptah-Hotep, one of Egypt's ancient viziers and wise men, instructed his son concerning how to live and think in order to enjoy a successful and long life. He himself attained to one hundred and ten years through the favor of the king and the god Horus.[931] In more recent texts found at Emar the ideal age of one hundred and twenty years has surfaced and was already known in Enlil and Namzitara.[932] The average lifespan in the ancient Near East was, in fact, only about forty-five years.[933] Moses, Joshua, Job, and a high priest named Jehoida were the only persons, those persons in the patriarchal era, who lived to one hundred years or more.

Various phrases used to describe old age, such as "length of days," have been found outside the Old Testament at Kuntillet 'Ajrud (ninth to eighth century B.C.).

Ancient Near Eastern parallels in West Semitic and Akkadian occur.[934] Nabonidus, a king of the Neo-Babylonian era, had a mother who was made famous for her old age by the god Sin, who extended her life and, more importantly, maintained her full mental capacity and reasoning powers.[935] Nabonidus himself prayed to Sin for a "present life of long days."[936]

At the end of every seven years ... you shall read this law (31:10–11). As elsewhere in the ancient Near East, the Lord required a regular reading of the covenant. See sidebar on "Reading the Covenant Document."

Present yourselves at the Tent of Meeting (31:14). This Tent of Meeting (*ʾōhel môʿēd*; cf. 1:2) refers to the portable sanctuary that the Lord instructed Israel to build and where he met with them to communicate through Moses and the appointed priests (Ex. 25–31; 35–40). In keeping with the small size of portable Near Eastern sanctuaries, Friedman has argued that it was quite small, only 10.5 meters long and 6–8 meters wide.[937] Other scholars have demurred.[938] Tents were ubiquitous in the ancient Near East, and at Ugarit a tent served as the dwelling place of the high god El.[939] The word "assembly" in Akkadian (*puʿuru*) is combined with the Akkadian Hebrew cognate (*môʿidi*) to express "the gathering of the (divine) assembly."[940]

The camp of Ramesses II in the mid-thirteenth century is currently the closest analogue to the tabernacle and its setting in Exodus 25–31; 35–40. It appears on a temple wall at the Abu Simbel temple.[941] Key terminology used of the wilderness tabernacle is present at Mari five hundred years earlier.[942]

Rest with your fathers (31:16). Archaeological evidence in Egypt at the Dothan ancestral tomb suggests that the ancient Near Eastern world thought of the deceased as being reunited with their ancestors upon burial in the family tomb(s). This tomb held levels[943] of interment from 1400–1100 B.C. Pottery, various vessels, furnishings, and personal possessions accompanied a burial and were placed around the body. Everyday needs were provided. The tomb was a temporary "way station" for the deceased on their journey to the netherworld. Burial objects were not added or disturbed until the body had totally decomposed. Then the bones were moved and the process repeated for the next corpse.

This activity and function of the family grave may add some light to the biblical phrase "rest with your fathers."[944] In Mesopotamia families were to care for their dead through a daily cult. A pious son presented regular daily offerings (*kispu ginû*) to his father and other ancestors after their death.[945] Elaborate monthly ceremonies were also observed,[946] along with a yearly "All Souls' Day." This cult preserved the names and identity of ancestors, tying the living to the past—an important function of Israel's traditions.

Sumerian O. B. Texts and texts at Emar indicate that in some shadowy sense the dead were "divine," living among the gods.[947] Although much later, archaeological evidence indicates that family burial in the ancestral graves in Israel was integral to maintaining the family inheritance. Post-mortem care for the dead was important and procured benefits for the living,[948] but this was condemned by official Israelite belief.

Now write down for yourselves this song (31:19). Foster provides a study of Egyptian hymns, prayers, and songs directed to kings, gods, the dead, life, love, and the living.[949] The flexibility of the ancient treaty/covenant forms permitted additional sections to be added. Here the biblical author places witnesses following the blessings and curses, a feature found in Hittite treaties, especially between Tudkhalia IV and Kurunta. There the required deposition of the treaty documents is located between stipulations, and other stipulations are added after the curses and blessings as well as a list of sanctions.[950] The Hittites, Syrians, and Assyrians adjusted treaties depending on whether they were dealing with individuals, "peoples," or king-

▶ **Reading the Covenant Document**

Hittite treaties provided for the deposition of treaty/covenant documents (of whatever material: iron, bronze, clay, stone, silver, etc.). It was desirable to have a copy of these documents on file, but also to make future public periodic reading possible. The document was deposited "before the god" and was read in the presence of the king and the "sons of the Hatti country." Curses were declared against anyone who would be so bold as to remove, damage, destroy, or deface the treaty or covenant document. Curses were set forth for the person who would change the document.[A-203]

At Emar in Syria a *zukru* festival[A-204] reflects a number of significant parallels between it and certain features of the covenant in Deuteronomy. A covenant renewal ceremony was held every seven years, which parallels the seven-year cycle of covenant reading and covenant renewal laid out in 31:10–11 at the Feast of Booths. The ritual calendar of this religious festival began on the first full moon of the year.[A-205] This *zukru* festival included all those who functioned as the essential parties in the festival. The king was there, though he was not the key participant, as was the practice in Israel (v. 12). The seventh year was also special in Ugarit.[A-206]

Seven-year cycles with a preparatory period in the sixth year are also found.[A-207] In the sixth year preparations were made for the seventh year.[A-208] The *zukru* festival was directed to the gods, a total of seventy, and involved a treaty or covenant bond between Emar and its god Dagan (grain god).[A-209]

---

doms. Terminology, structure, and tone could vary with the purpose of the treaty.[951]

Moses wrote down this song that day and taught it to the Israelites (31:22, 30). The interplay between writing and literacy is well illustrated here. Ancient Israel was not a modern literate nation, but she was acquainted with writing. She used it to help disseminate knowledge and wisdom by repeating or teaching it to the people first of all orally, not by the production of a thousand copies of the Song of Moses or the Book of the Law or the Blessings of Moses.

What is clear in these two verses is the oral-literate interplay that was featured. The written words are to be repeated and spoken. The oral world elaborates and gives them a "living" context.[952] Other literature, archives, and libraries in the ancient Near East seem to foster a vibrant interaction between "oral and written mentalities."[953] Ancient Near Eastern materials, such as some letters of Arad, a Deir ʿAlla inscription, the Gezer Calendar, an Izbet Sartah inscription, inscriptions at Kuntillet ʿAjrud, Lachish letters, the Mesha Inscription, and so forth, all reflect the interesting interaction of orality and the written word.[954] Kitchen sets forth a plausible explanation of how the ancient materials of Deuteronomy could have been updated, as was done with other ancient Near Eastern documents from as early as ca. 2500 B.C. to the Greco-Roman culture.[955]

In a covenant between the Hittites and King Kurtiwaza in Mitanni, the covenantal documents were deposited before the gods or goddesses for periodic reading. An inscribed public monument could serve the same function.[956] A copy was placed before the goddess Arina in Hatti and one was placed before Teshub in Mitanni mainly for safe keeping by both parties. But the ancients also considered the words of the text and their reading to aid in keeping the agreement in force. Moses considers the written document to be a divine instrument that has power in its very reading, since it was a word from Israel's living God.[957]

Song of Moses (31:30–32:47)

O heavens … O earth (32:1). Moses sets forth a powerful picture of the future of Israel. Israel's Lord alone, as revealed in the Old Testament, is the sole source for insights like this. Her future, however, hinges on her moral-ethical response of faith or lack thereof toward the Lord and his covenant. In the ancient Near East the future of human beings and nations was decreed by the gods and recorded in the Tablet of Destinies. See sidebar on "The Tablet of Destinies."

Is he not your Father, your Creator? (32:6). The fatherhood of the gods was a common theological feature of the peoples of the ancient Near East and contributed to the idea, for example, that Enlil (Sumer) "was a friendly, fatherly deity who watches over the safety and well-being of all humans, *particularly* the inhabitants of Sumer."[958] However, the overall concept is somewhat jumbled because of the seemingly contradictory way the material is presented and the strangeness of the worldview being propounded.

There were many "father gods." In Sumer (e.g., An, Enlil, Utu), Egypt (Atum, Ptah, Re, Geb), and Ugarit (El, Baal), father gods were involved in the production and creation of the cosmos as well as other gods.[959] As an example, in the Ugaritic myths (ca. 1350 B.C.), Baal, the Bull, is described as the creator of even the gods.[960] In Egypt Amun was the ultimate source and cause of the gods and the cosmos.[961] This language is echoed in the designation of even a subordinate ruler such as Azatiwata, "mother and father" of the Danua people.[962] In the Emar *zukru* festival Dagan (god of grain; storm god) is referred to as the "lord of creation."[963]

Which god fathered what and whom and how this all is to be tied together systematically are practically hopeless until more complete materials are available. In Israel, however, there is no confusion, for the one and only God, Yahweh, was God and Father of everything that exists in heaven and on earth.

When the Most High gave the nations their inheritance, when he divided all mankind (32:8–9). The Hebrew text followed by the NIV reads "according to the sons of Israel." Many scholars prefer the reading of the LXX and some Dead Sea Scrolls, which read "according to the sons of God."[964] This text is closely connected to Genesis 10, where seventy nations are listed, but Israel is not included among them. It is possible that, according to the LXX, God divided (*prd*, in both Gen. 10 and here) the disobedient nations among seventy subordinate, created, divine beings as punishment for their rebellion against the Lord (Gen. 11).[965]

At any rate, some scholars perceive a Ugaritic background to this text that refers to the "seventy sons of Athirat," sired by El,[966] and his council of divine beings.[967] Seventy gods are mentioned at Emar.[968] A divine council of gods was common in the ancient Near East.[969] A Phoenician (also Hittite) inscription refers to the whole "group of the children of the gods" (El). In general in other Babylonian literature we read of the gods distributing the cosmos among themselves, but not the nations.[970] Gods in the ancient Near East could give gifts of cities, as at Ugarit or in Sumer.[971]

This is part of the broader context, but these verses are intended to contrast the fact that the Lord has set Israel *apart unto himself* from among all the nations, and Israel is not numbered with them. The nations have their own "gods," who are mortal, but they do not have Yahweh, who alone does not die and is omnipotent, omniscient, and omnipresent.[972] The great Egyptian god Re grows old with millions of years, suffering from divine age.[973] Marduk chooses Babylon as his chief city where the gods will live with him.[974] Kronos, a chief Greek god, although much later in history, assigns the rulership of Attica to Athena, Byblos to Baaltis, Berytus to Poseidon, and all of Egypt to Tauthos.[975]

Like an eagle (32:11). The Epic of Lugalbanda has relevant imagery.[976] The story of

▶ The Tablet of Destinies

The Tablet of Destinies appears in numerous texts.[A-210] Some scholars believe that *shimtu* (fate) in Mesopotamia was partially expressed through this tablet, and fate was always tied to the gods. It never functioned as an independent force.[A-211] The Tablet of Destinies as mentioned in the Babylonian Creation Epic (ca. 1500 B.C.) was presented to the god Anu by the great god Marduk, who had taken possession of it.[A-212] When Marduk grew weak and old, Erra, a young god, obtained and exercised power through the Tablet of Destinies and would not give it to anyone else.[A-213]

In a Sumerian-Babylonian dialogue "the bowl of Marduk" contained a list of men's deeds.[A-214] Enlil exercised his Enlil-ship—that is, his royal cosmic authority as shown in the Myth of Zu—by possessing the Tablet of Destinies, until Anzu stole it.[A-215] Through the Tablet of Destinies the successes or failures of peoples and kings were set forth as in vassal treaties of Esarhaddon.[A-216]

A royal Assyrian text describes the Assyrian god Assur as the possessor of the Tablet of Destinies, by which he decrees the course of Sennacherib's reign. The tablet hung over Assur's heart, bearing his seal and signifing

Anzu
Marie-Lan Nguyen/
Wikimedia Commons, courtesy of the Louvre
◀

his power, to grant a successful reign to Sennacherib. The tablet functioned as a bond (*markas*) or means (*riksu*) by which the power and relationship between heaven and earth were recognized.[A-217]

In the Sumerian Hymn to Inlil, Enlil, and Ninlil, Enlil decreed the fates. No god could challenge Enlil's proclaimed destinies. In a hymn to Ninurta, god of wrath, the god's judgment was fixed; not even a god could question it.[A-218] Less often noted is the Egyptian text Instruction of Amenemope, where the "plans of the gods" as given in written oracles is no less than "Fate and Destiny" decreed by the gods.[A-219] Israel knew the essential plans of her God and what he desired in order to please him, for it was near her, in her mouth and in her heart (30:14).

Cylinder seal of the twenty-third century B.C. shows Etana ascending on an eagle's back.
Z. Radovan/
www.BibleLand
Pictures.com
▼

Etana, a quasi-historical king of Kish mentioned in the Sumerian King List, rode upon an eagle that cared for him as it carried Etana on his back.[977] Etana ascends on an eagle's back on a cylinder seal of the twenty-third century B.C. This is probably the literary source behind the imagery here, although the actual bird in mind is often considered to be the griffon vulture.[978]

The storyline in the Etana Myth is helpful. It depicts an eagle as the instrument

Demon Pazazu
Z. Radovan/
www.BibleLand
Pictures.com

▶

Image is a statue
of King Che-
phren. The god
Horus in the
shape of a falcon
is sitting on
the back of the
throne protect-
ing the king with
his outstretched
wings.
Werner Forman
Archive/The Egyp-
tian Museum, Cairo

▼

through whom Etana success-fully gets a son. The eagle imagery here and in Exodus 19:4 is tied to the Lord's rescue of his son Israel on eagles' wings. Etana beseeches the eagle to "change my destiny"; the eagle obliges,[979] but only after giving Etana a magnificent but dangerous ride toward heaven and back down to earth. The eagle drops but retrieves Etana at three miles, two miles, one mile, and one meter above the ground.[980]

The parallel with the biblical text is not dependent on naturalists observing certain behavior patterns of eagles with their young, but on the storyline of the Etana text. It took an eagles' wings for Etana's goal to be met: his acquisition of a son. God brought Israel to the mountain of God, Sinai, and birthed/nurtured his only son (cf. 32:8). Some believe that the eagles' wings protective imagery originated in Egypt and moved throughout the ancient Near East. Winged figures with Egyptian features appear in art work found in the Levant as well.[981]

Sacrificed to demons (32:17). Demon possession goes back to a Babylonian worldview and world order.[982] The Sumerian *udug* demon was evil, the Akkadian *šedu* could act as either a demon or a protective spirit. A *rābisu* being was a spy for good or evil. *Dimme* (Sumerian) was a demon who murdered children according to Babylonian and Assyrian thinking. In Babylonian religion demons were sent against a person who sinned. The *āšipu/mašmašu* priest

often sent incantations against these demons.[983]

The Hebrew word for demons in this verse is *šēdim*, a plural (sing. *šēd*). Israel had rebelled by sacrificing to a god(s) *šdym*, "demons" (cf. 32:17; Ps. 106:37; cf. Akk. *šedū*). It appears that the *šdyn*, the Aramaic equivalent to the Hebrew word, were gods worshiped in Transjordan and Canaan and are the same gods referred to in the biblical texts.[984] Whatever they were, they were not worthy of worship. These beings were "no gods."

A uniformly sinister history accompanies these beings. The cognate Akkadian word *šedu* describes only minor deities, if deities at all (cf. Ps. 106:36–38),[985] and the word in Akkadian is connected to spirits of the dead.[986] This word for gods has turned up in Aramaic texts at Deir ʿAlla, and they use the Aramaic word for these gods, *šdyn*.[987] The synonym *šgr* is also used. In these texts these "gods" sit in the divine assembly with other gods and decree a catastrophe on the earth, but these gods inform Balaam of this by a dream or vision (cf. Num. 22:8–9, 12, 19). Hence, as noted, Chavalas and Adamthwaite conclude that these gods were worshiped in Transjordan and possibly Canaan,[988] and they are the gods whom Israel wrongly served (32:17; Ps. 106:37). Their evil intent in these texts tends to support this.

I will hide my face from them (32:20). When God "goes away" or hides his face, he is displeased with his people and catastrophe strikes them. In a famous Egyptian theological treatise a deceased person expresses despair that he can no longer see the face of Atum: "It is too much for me, my Lord, not to see your face."[989] In rituals involving the deity Amun at Karkak, the official's face had to be protected from the god.[990]

When the great god Erra (Nirgal) was enthroned, the other gods "began to look at his face."[991] Telipinu, a weather or storm god of sorts at Hatti, turned his face away and left his people because of their insolence toward him. When he left, he took with him all kinds of blessings, especially fertility. People could not conceive nor could they, if pregnant, give birth. The hills dried up, trees withered, and the grass died. Hunger set in. An incantation finally resulted in the god's return, and subsequent blessings at his return ensued because he was again with his people. The royal house prospered.[992]

The abandonment of a people by its god occurred several times during Babylon's history. In the Tukulti-Ninurta Epic the gods abandon the Kassite Babylonian king because he had broken his covenant with Assyria.[993] The third-century B.C. priest-historian Manetho reported that the Hyksos invasion of Egypt (seventeenth century B.C.) was a result of "God's displeasure upon us."[994] Cyrus the Great (538 B.C.) proclaimed that Marduk, Babylon's chief god, gave Babylon into his power because the last king, Nabonidus, forsook the cult of Marduk and worshiped other gods.[995]

I will heap calamities upon them (32:23). Curses are found in various texts in the ancient Near East. At Ugarit the god Resheph, a storm god, was a god of war[996] and a god of pestilence.[997] These threats became realities in warfare. The support of a national god was crucial for a king, such as Hadad of northern Syria. In this case Panamuwa, son of the king of *y'dy*, Qarli, claimed support from many gods: Hadad, for whom a statue was erected, but also El, Rashap,

Rakib-El, and Shamash.[998] Fulfilled curses include vivid descriptions of a besieged city, such as Sumer and Ur.[999] In several ancient treaties a specific stipulation was followed by a specific curse administered by a particular god.[1000]

Instructions Concerning Moses' Death (32:48–52)

Abarim Range to Mount Nebo (32:49). The Abarim mountain range sits northeast of the Dead Sea. Mount Nebo (ca. 1,435 ft.) is a part of this range (cf. Num. 27:12; 33:47–48).[1001] It is located near the city Nebo (32:3), and the area forms a northwestern rim of the tableland of Moab.[1002] Mount Nebo (cf. Deut. 34:1) is closely connected to Mount Pisgah, which is tied to descriptions of southern Gilead. The Spring of Moses on the north and the Wadi Afirt help frame the mountain.

The view from Nebo is panoramic, including the Dead Sea, Jordan Valley, and Jordan Desert from Tekoa to Jerusalem. Even the mountains of Samaria are visible from it. In the Mesha Stele of Moab (ca.

Mount Nebo and Abarim Range
Todd Bolen/www. BiblePlaces.com

▼

830 B.C.) Nebo is considered an Israelite city conquered by the Moabites.[1003]

Mount Hor (32:50). The location of this mountain, mentioned twelve times in the Old Testament (cf. Num. 20:22; 33:38–9), is not certain. Bible maps suggest a location northeast of Kadesh Barnea. It may have been located at modern Jebel Madurah.[1004] The Hebrew definite article is always used with this name, indicating that the mountain area or ridge is well known. The reference to Aaron's death at Moserah (Deut. 10:6) refers to the punishment rendered by God's judgment there, not to a geographical location.[1005]

Meribah Kadesh in the Desert of Zin (32:51). The geographical location of this event of "strife" is not certain, since it describes an episode, not a physical location. Evidently it was located at or very near Kadesh Barnea (ʾEin Qudeiret). The Desert of Zin is located in the Negev on the border of southern Canaan. It is referred to as the Desert of Kadesh in Psalm 29:8 and was part of "that vast and dreadful desert." It demarcated the boundaries of parts of Judah (cf. Num. 34:3–4). The eastern border extended to Edom and its western extent reached to Kadesh and beyond. An east-west line touching the southern tip of the Dead Sea points out its northern border. Its southern edge merged with the Desert of Paran.[1006]

Blessings of Moses on Israel (33:1–29)

The blessing that Moses the man of God pronounced (33:1). For this chapter compare the blessings of Isaac (Gen. 27) and the blessings of Jacob (Gen. 48–49). Outside of the Old Testament there are similar final blessings recorded in the second millennium, especially in texts at Nuzi. Green finds many features of Yahweh presented in this chapter paralleled by descriptions of the great storm god in the ancient Near East, especially under his name Baal.[1007] In general the Canaanite setting of several

tribes is depicted just before Moses' death. There are close connections with Canaanite mythology, as evidenced in the literary style, language, and vocabulary of the poem. Language reminiscent of the storm gods of the ancient Near East depicts the Lord's kingship and his theophany (see esp. vv. 2–3, 13–16, 26–29).[1008]

Mount Paran (33:2–3). This is clearly a Hebrew poetic parallel with Sinai and Seir (Edom area). Sinai is the primary referent, which is near or possibly in the Desert of Paran.[1009]

The entire theophany here of God's awesome appearance shares features with, among others, texts from Ugarit (Baal) and Mesopotamia (e.g., Assur).[1010] El "shines forth" in a text in Hebrew (Phoenician script) from Kuntillet ʿAjrud.[1011] In Ugaritic texts Baal marches forth.[1012] The divine allies of Baal and ancient Near Eastern storm gods parallel Yahweh's "myriads." A divine assembly to perform the bidding of the chief god is present in Canaanite and similar mythological texts[1013] in Assyrian, Assyrian-Babylonian, and Hittite texts.

Thummim and Urim (33:8). The Urim and Thummim were an ancient means of drawing lots in Israel; the results were determined by the Lord.[1014] The terms probably mean "lights" and "perfections" respectively.[1015] C. van Dam finds no essential parallels to this practice in Mesopotamia, Hatti, Ugarit, or Egypt.[1016] See also sidebar on "The Assyrian Incantation Ritual of Two Stones."

Guarded your covenant (33:9). This phrase has ancient parallels from documents of the second millennium and beyond in Akkadian (*mamitu/ade* or *riksa nas(c)aru*, "to guard the oath or treaty"). Both Kitchen and Weinfeld show the antiquity of this concept.[1017]

Offers incense (33:10). Incense altars from Lachish (ca. 586–538 B.C.) suggest the importance of these cultic objects.[1018] Egyptian kings could offer incense and carry out important functions as shown in the First Beth Shan Stele (ca. 1294 B.C.).[1019]

▶ The Assyrian Incantation Ritual of Two Stones

The closest parallel to Urim and Thummim comes from an incantation ritual text from Assur. The Assyrian ritual process is clearly one of divination by using a black stone (hematite) and a white stone (alabaster). The process is called psephomancy, divination by pebbles. The will of seven gods is sought by lifting up one of these stones.[A-220]

In order to perceive that will,[A-221] Shamash, the god of oracles, is addressed, offerings are made, and two stones are put into the hem of the ritualist's garment to be retrieved at the right time. The ritualist writes the names of seven gods on the ground and then lifts up a stone; a judgment is rendered and a revelation given, if the god so desires (yes). If no revelation or judgment is received, a stone of no desire (no) is given. It is not certain what the "jumping up of a stone" implies. Perhaps it merely refers to the process of picking up the stone by the ritualist. Nor is it stated explicitly which stone stands for desirable/not desirable, but based on other ancient Near Eastern divination texts, white is probably the yes stone, black the no stone.[A-222]

Evidently the ritualist repeats the process three times to confirm the answer given, as was somewhat common in rituals.[A-223] The process involved, the stones involved (light, truth), the binary options available, the technical terms used, the option of no answer, the drawing of stones from a garment, and the types of questions addressed all suggest that the Urim and Thummim, and this process may be related.[A-224]

About Joseph he said (33:13–17). In essence Yahweh fulfills the functions performed by the chief fertility god, Baal, in Canaan.[1020] The "deep waters" are tied to the "abyss" in both Ugaritic liturgy texts and mythological texts.[1021] The bull imagery used in verse 17 has similarities with Ugaritic materials in which Mot and Baal "gore like wild oxen" and El is called "the bull."[1022] A Hittite document describes the strength of the bull that moved a mountain.[1023] Even Horus in Egypt, however, is pictured as a young, strong bull.[1024]

Who rides on the heavens ... clouds (33:26). This language closely resembles language used to depict Baal.[1025] He is presented as a warrior god who prepares to smash his enemies and to take his everlasting kingdom and dominion (cf. Ps. 68:5).[1026] However, Baal was also the bringer of rain.[1027] A bit less striking, but still helpful, is the depiction in a Sumerian myth of the weather god, Ishkur, Enki and the Ordering of the World.[1028] In this case Ishkur is put in charge of the entire weather system. In the case of Yahweh, Israel's God shows that he is in control of all of this to destroy Israel's enemy.

Trample down their high places (33:29). Exactly what high places were is still debated. This discussion accepts the translation of *bāmôtêmô* as "high place."[1029] Several high places (*bāmôt*) have recently been uncovered. These were possibly places where local shrines were situated and pagan religious rites were practiced.[1030] Zevit understands a high place to be a place where *maṣṣēbôt* (standing stones) were located; it was available to the public.[1031] Grintz argues that *bāmôt* originated in Moab.[1032] To Israel's detriment, these places fostered syncretism and enticed Israel to become involved in forbidden worship. Asherim (sacred poles or trees), *maṣṣēbôt*, and altars were featured. These high places often had *liška*, a room for sacred meals, connected to them.[1033]

Death of Moses; Commissioning of Joshua (34:1–12)

Moses climbed Mount Nebo (34:1). From Mount Nebo one enjoys an impressive view of Jericho, a city of great antiquity (before 6000 B.C.). It was important and powerful in the Middle Bronze Age (ca. 2300–1550) and even into the Late Bronze Age (ca. 1550–1200). The "City of Palms" (v. 3) refers to the date palm trees that grow there even today in the Jordan Valley, the Arabah region, and in some areas of the coast. The city is located just west of the Jordan about ten miles north of the northern tip of the Dead Sea. The large fresh water spring ꜥAin es-Sultan was active in antiquity and watered the area even as it does today. Later Jericho served as a border town between Ephraim and Benjamin. This impressive city would fall to Israel to begin her long conquest of the Promised Land.[1034]

Moses' view of the Promised Land scans the horizon and mentions only key points of focus. The view given here surveys the scene by looking straight ahead (north) and then to the left (west). Zoar was probably located at the southern tip of the Dead Sea (cf. Gen. 13:10). This description was possibly written later to present what Moses saw according to the later distribution of the land. Thus the author describes a view of the land that assumes tribal territories yet to be assigned. The city and tribe of Dan was located just south of Mount Hermon, about one hundred miles distant.

And Moses the servant of the LORD died (34:5). The description of Moses as "the servant of the LORD" has connotations of intimacy and of obedience. The legendary King

Area of Jericho viewed from the top of Mount Nebo

Todd Bolen/www. BiblePlaces.com

Keret in the Ugaritic literature is depicted as "the beloved, Lad of El," "the Servant of El [3x]," with the context of each occurrence implying the care and concern of El for his chosen servant.[1035]

A hundred and twenty years old (34:7). Moses' eyesight and vigor are still not gone at 120 years of age. No wonder! In the ancient Near East "the face of a god radiated light and life to those fortunate enough to gaze upon it."[1036] Only kings could, however, claim this blessing. Moses had lived in the presence of God forty days and nights and then conversed with the Lord without his veil for an indefinite period of time. In some ancient Near Eastern traditions the radiant faces of the gods (e. g., Enlil, Assur, Ninlil) strengthened the kings they looked upon. The faces of the gods were both radiant and life-giving, a belief recorded in a Samsiluna inscription (ca. 1749–1712 B.C.), grandson of Hammu-rabi.[1037] The word referring to "strength" or virility (*lḥh*) is found in Ugaritic texts, where it likely means "sexual power."[1038]

Because Moses had laid his hands on him (34:9) This action probably points out Joshua as the object of God's Spirit, who imparted wisdom (cf. Ex. 35:31). The laying on of hands is employed in a Hittite ritual text discussed by D. P. Wright.[1039] The parallel is only suggestive. Hands are placed upon a sacrifice, but how this act illuminates the present text is doubtful; it may suggest that Joshua should be understood as the subject of the process. As a result he receives of Moses' spirit—that is, his wisdom, imparted to Moses by God.[1040]

Face to face (34:10). Moses' excellence was dependent on his being in the presence of God, face to face. The Assyrian king Assurbanipal (668–27 B.C.) enjoyed the gaze of Assur and Ninlil and returned it to his benefit.[1041]

Hittite Law	Topic	Law in Deuteronomy
1–2, 4–5	Murder/killing	5:17; 19:11–13; 27:25
3	Mansluaghter	19:5–6
6	Unsolved murder	21:1–2
7	Eye for eye mitigated	19:21
19–21	Kidnapping	24:7
22–23	Fugitive slaves	23:15
26, 31	Divorce	24:1–4
44B, 111	Sorcery	18:10–14
45, 71	Stealing	5:21
71	Lost animals	27:1
151–152	Hire of animals	19:11–13
166	Two kinds of seed	22:9
168–169	Boundary stones	19:14; 27:17
173A	Judges, officials	16:18
187, 188, 199, 200	Bestiality	27:21
189–191, 194	Incest	22:20
193	Levirate marriage	25:5–10
197	Rape	22:25–26
197–198	Adultery	22:23–24
Telipinu Edict (49)	Murder	5:17; 19:11–13
Sources: *COS*, 2:106–19; *ANET*, 188–97; *CANE*, 555–60		

Bibliography

Ahituv, Shmuel, and Eliezer D. Oren. *The Origin of Early Israel—Current Debate.* Vol. 12. Jerusalem: Bialik Institute, 1998. Contains up-to-date discussions on the issues surrounding the earliest birth and history of Israel.

Albrektson, Bertil. *History and the Gods.* Lund, Sweden: W. K. Gleerup, 1967. An excellent book to challenge some standard views taken on the historiographical concepts of the ancient Near East.

Baker, David W., and Bill T. Arnold, eds. *The Face of Old Testament Studies.* Grand Rapids: Baker, 1999. Helpful chapters that give the current status of issues in Old Testament studies. Useful background discussions.

Bryce, Trevor. *Letters of the Great Kings of the Ancient Near East.* London: Routledge, 2003. An informative and readable presentation of the ideas and relationships that existed among the Great Kings of the ancient Near East.

Christensen, Duane L. *Deuteronomy 1:1–21:9.* WBC 6A. 2nd ed. Nashville: Nelson, 2001. Buried within various discussions are some excellent insights and source materials for Bible background issues.

_____. *Deuteronomy 21:10–34:12.* WBC 6B. Nashville: Nelson, 2002. See above comment.

Craigie, Peter C. *The Book of Deuteronomy.* Grand Rapids: Eerdmans, 1976. This is still an excellent source book for background discussions of the book of Deuteronomy and the ancient Near East, especially with respect to Ugaritica.

Currid, John D. *Ancient Egypt and the Old Testament.* Grand Rapids: Baker, 1997. An interesting and enlightening discussion of Egyptian culture and the Old Testament.

Hoerth, Alfred J., Gerald L. Mattingly, and Edwin M. Yamauchi, eds. *Peoples of the Old Testament World.* Grand Rapids: Baker, 1994. A basic study of the key peoples that Israel encountered in the ancient world.

Hoffmeier, James K. *Israel in Egypt.* New York: Oxford Univ. Press, 1996. A basic and well-informed argument for the historical reality of the Exodus event.

_____. *Israel in Sinai.* New York: Oxford Univ. Press, 2005.

Hoffmeier, James K., and Alan Millard, eds. *The Future of Biblical Archaeology.* Grand Rapids: Eerdmans, 2004. Dynamic and challenging essays that paint the way that responsible archaeology should strive to relate properly to the Old Testament and its history and culture.

King, Philip J., and Lawrence E. Stager. *Life in Biblical Israel.* Louisville: Westminster John Knox, 2001. A basic source book for the cultural world of the Old Testament. It is filled with pictures that bring the Old Testament world to life.

Kitchen, K. A. *On the Reliability of the Old Testament.* Grand Rapids: Eerdmans, 2003. A monumental work that sets forth the ancient Near Eastern world in an informative, lively, and engaging way. The footnotes section is superb, and various topics can be researched further based on the information in them.

Kline, Meredith. *Treaty of the Great King.* Grand Rapids: Eerdmans, 1963. A classic study in which the features of the ancient Near Eastern Hittite vassal treaty are applied to the book of Deuteronomy.

McCarthy, Dennis J. *Treaty and Covenant.* Rome: Biblical Institute Press, 1981. Still a classic study of the texts of treaties and documents of the Old Testament.

Niehaus, Jeffrey J. *God at Sinai.* Grand Rapids: Zondervan, 1995. A classic study of theophanies in the ancient Near East with material relevant to Deuteronomy and other Old Testament books.

Tigay, Jeffrey H. *Deuteronomy.* JPS Torah Commentary. Philadelphia: Jewish Publication Society, 1996. A helpful commentary that from time to time places the biblical text into its ancient context and helps illuminate the text.

Weinfeld, Moshe. *Deuteronomy 1–11.* AB. New York: Doubleday, 1991. A helpful standard background commentary on Deuteronomy. Sometimes the parallels are overstated or not sufficiently nuanced.

Main Text Notes

1. K. A. Kitchen, *Pharaoh Triumphant* (Mississauga, Ont.: Benben, 1982), 238–39.
2. For a discussion of the issues involved concerning the exodus event, see M. W. Chavalas and M. R. Adamthwaite, "Archaeological Light on the Old Testament," in *The Face of Old Testament Studies*, ed. D. W. Baker and B. T. Arnold (Grand Rapids: Baker, 1999), 78–90; J. K. Hoffmeier, *Israel in Egypt* (New York: Oxford Univ. Press, 1996), 122–26; K. A. Kitchen, *On the Reliability of the Old Testament* (Grand Rapids: Eerdmans, 2003), 307–10.
3. *COS*, 2.6.
4. A. R. Rainey and Z. Safrai, *The Macmillan Bible Atlas*, 3rd ed. (New York: Macmillan, 1993), 49, #53.
5. J. Walton, *Ancient Israelite Literature in Its Cultural Context* (Grand Rapids: Zondervan, 1989).
6. See esp. W. Von Soden, *The Ancient Orient*, trans. D. G. Schley (Grand Rapids: Eerdmans, 1994), 131–44; J. H. Walton, *Ancient Israelite Literature*, 69–94; A. Hill and J. H. Walton, *Survey of the Old Testament* (Grand Rapids: Zondervan, 2000), 52–53; H. J. Boecker, *Law and the Administration of Justice in the Old Testament and the Ancient Near East*, trans. J. Moiser (Minneapolis: Augsburg, 1980), 66–176; Kitchen, *Reliability*, 283–306.
7. Kitchen, *Reliability*, esp. 289; D. J. McCarthy, *Treaty and Covenant* (AnBib 21a; Rome: Biblical Institute, 1981), 122–53.
8. Kitchen, *Reliability*, 287–88.
9. See esp. T. Bryce, *Letters of the Great Kings of the Ancient Near East* (New York: Routledge, 2003), 76–94, esp. 76–78; W. L. Moran, "The Ancient Near Eastern Background of the Love of God in Deuteronomy," in *Essential Papers on Israel and the Ancient Near East*, ed. F. E. Greenspahn (New York: New York Univ. Press, 1991), 103–15.
10. A. Millard, *Treasures from Bible Times* (London: Lion, 1985), 80; Kitchen, *Reliability*, 295–99. See these and the items listed below for strong historical/archaeological/cultural suggestive evidence for the probable rise of a leader like Moses, most likely during the time of the New Kingdom in Egypt; cf. D. M. Beegle, "Moses," *ABD*, 4:909–18; J. Hoffmeier, "Moses," *ISBE*, 3:415–25; K. A. Kitchen, "Egyptians and Hebrews, from Raʾmeses to Jericho," in *The Origin of Early Israel—Current Debate*, ed. S. Ahituv and E. D. Oren, (Ben Gurion Univ.: Negev Press, 1998), 88–91; F. Yurco, "Merenptah's Canaanite Campaign and Israel's Origins," in *Exodus: The Egyptian Evidence* (Winona Lake, Ind.: Eisenbrauns, 1997), 27–55. Yurco claims to present visual, pictorial evidence of the Israelites in Egypt. Note also A. Rainey's negative response in the same article (40).
11. McCarthy, *Treaty and Covenant*, 261, 264–65, 273–75; esp. 294.
12. See J. Hoffmeier, *Israel in Egypt*, esp. 52–163; now see idem, *Israel in Sinai* (Oxford: Oxford Univ. Press, 2005), passim, esp. 177–78.
13. See *ABD* for a brief discussion and bibliography of all these place names; see also C. G. Rasmussen, *Zondervan NIV Atlas of the Bible* (Grand Rapids: Zondervan, 1989), for a clear and easy-to-read atlas with narrative; Kitchen, *Reliability*, 268–73, 627–31. This is a masterful resource for the Old Testament and its ancient Near Eastern contexts. See for Dizahab = Dhahab, Kitchen, *Reliability*, 559, n. 64; 680, fig. 30.
14. G. Davies, "The Significance of Deuteronomy 1:2 for the Location of Mount Horeb," *PEQ* 111 (1979): 87–101; B. Beitzel, "Travel and Communication (OT World)," *ABD*, 6:646; discussion in Hoffmeier, *Sinai*, 118–20.
15. For a full discussion of the location of Sinai see Kitchen, *Reliability*, 265–72.
16. D. N. Manor, "Kadesh-Barnea," *ABD*, 2:1–3; Kitchen, *Reliability*, 272–73, 627.
17. J. H. Walton, V. H. Matthews, and M. W. Chavalas, *The Intervarsity Bible Background Commentary: Old Testament* (Downers Grove, Ill.: InterVarsity Press, 2000), 170–71.
18. For a thorough review of the current dating of the exodus, see I. Provan, V. P. Long, and T. Longman III, *A Biblical History of Israel* (Louisville: Westminster John Knox, 2003), 129–32; Kitchen, *Reliability*, 307–12; cf. J. K. Hoffmeier, "NSAP Excavations at Tell el-Borg," in *The Future of Biblical Archaeology*, ed. J. K. Hoffmeier and A. Millard (Grand Rapids: Eerdmans, 2004), 57; Walton, "Exodus, Date of," in *Intervarsity Dictionary of the Old Testament: Pentateuch*, ed. T. D. Alexander and D. W. Baker (Downers Grove, Ill.: InterVarsity Press, 2003), 269.
19. The strategy and wisdom of attacking Sihon is clear. See C. Herzog and M. Gichon, *Battles of the Bible*, (Mechanicsburg, Pa.: Stackpole, 1997), 43; Provan, Long, and Longman, *Biblical History of Israel*, 136.
20. G. E. Mendenhall, "Amorites," *ABD*, 1:199–202.
21. J. J. M. Roberts, "The Ancient Near Eastern Environment," in *The Bible and The Ancient Near East* (Winona Lake, Ind.: Eisenbrauns, 2002), 11.
22. A. Malamat, "The Proto-History of Israel: A Study in Method," in *The Word of the Lord Shall Go Forth: Essays in Honor of D. N. Freedman*, ed. C. L. Meyers and M. O'Connor (Winona Lake, Ind.: Eisenbrauns, 1983), 309; P. C. Schmitz, "Canaan," *ABD*, 1:829–37.
23. For Canaanite religion, see G. del Olmo Lete, *Canaanite Religion*, trans. W. G. E. Watson (Bethesda, Md.: CDL, 1999). For a complete treatment of religious texts in Ugarit, see A. F. Rainey and R. S. Notley, *The Sacred Bridge: Carta's Atlas of the Biblical World* (Jerusalem: Carta, 2006), 100 (excursus 8.1).
24. *ANET*, 246.
25. *ANET*, 378.

26. J. Day, "Ashtaroth," *ABD*, 1:491.

27. M. Weinfeld, *Deuteronomy 1–11* (AB; New York: Doubleday, 1991), 180; *ARAB*, 1:243.

28. For all the treaties see G. Beckman, *Hittite Diplomatic Texts*, 2d ed. (SBLWAW 7; Atlanta: Scholars Press, 1999), 11–114; for a convenient chart of passages that feature a covenant/covenant renewal format see most recently Kitchen, *Reliability*, 284–85.

29. Rasmussen, *NIV Atlas*, 17.

30. Schoville, "Canaanites and Amorites," 166.

31. A. R. Millard, "Amorite," *NBD*, 31–32; M. Weinfeld, *Deuteronomy 1–11*, 132.

32. L. Younger, "Early Israel," in *The Face of Old Testament Studies*, ed. D. W. Baker and B. T. Arnold (Grand Rapids: Baker, 1999), 187–88, esp. n. 58.

33. Weinfeld, *Deuteronomy 1–11*, 133.

34. From an inscription of Assyrian king Adad-Nirari, about 800 B.C., *ANET*, 281; for more examples see Weinfeld, *Deuteronomy 1–11*, 133–34.

35. Weinfeld, *Deuteronomy 1–11*, 140–41, with bibliography listed there; for detail see idem, "Judge and Officer in Ancient Israel and in the Ancient Near East," *IOS* 7 (1977): 65–88; S. Alp, "Military Instructions of the Hittite King Tuthaliya," *Belleten* 11 (1947): 403–14; R. O. Faulkner, "The Installation of the Vizier," *JEA* 41 (1955): 18–29.

36. Walton, *Israelite Literature in Its Cultural Context*, 69–93.

37. R. Westbrook, "The Character of Ancient Near Eastern Law," *HANEL*, 25.

38. Clause Wilcke, *Early Ancient Near Eastern Law: A History of its Beginning: Early Dynastic and Sargonic Periods* (BAW 2; München: Beck, 2003), 29–30; Westbrook, *HANEL*, 26.

39. Westbrook, *HANEL*, 30.

40. Wilcke, *Early Ancient Near Eastern Law*, 31–40; to see how this all works out see W. Hallo, "A Model Court Case Concerning Inheritance," in *Riches Hidden in Secret Places*, ed. T. Abusch (Winona Lake, Ind.: Eisenbrauns, 2000), 141–54.

41. *CANE*, 473.

42. *ANET*, 407–10; *COS*, 1.43, B1 31–51, B2 91–115.

43. *CANE*, 354–55.

44. R. Jasnow, "New Kingdom," *HANEL*, 289.

45. See R. Versteeg, *Law in Ancient Egypt* (Durham, N.C.: Carolina Academic Press, 2002), 9, plus nn. 37–9; 17; Jasnow, "New Kingdom," 289–90.

46. Versteeg, *Law*, 56–62.

47. Ibid., 94.

48. Ibid., 36.

49. As quoted in Weinfeld, *Deuteronomy 1–11*, 141.

50. See A. R. W. Green, *The Storm-God in the Ancient Near East* (BJS 8; Winona Lake, Ind.: Eisenbrauns, 2003), for a full study.

51. G. Beckman, "Royal Ideology and State of Administration in Hittite Anatolia," *CANE*, 529–30.

52. Rainey and Notley, *Sacred Bridge*, excursus 8.3.

53. Shmuel Ahituv, "The Origins of Ancient Israel—The Documentary Evidence," in *The Origin of Early Israel*, 136–37.

54. A. Lemaire, "Mari, the Bible, and the Northwest Semitic World," *BA* 47 (1984): 103.

55. King and Stager, *Life in Biblical Israel*, 98–101.

56. Ibid., 98.

57. M. A. Powell, "Wine and the Vine in Ancient Mesopotamia: The Cuniform Evidence," in *The Origins and Ancient History of Wine*, ed. P. E. McGovern, S. J. Fleming, and S. H. Katz (Amsterdam: Overseas Publishers, 1995), 97–122, esp. 121; C. E. Walsh, *The Fruit of the Vine: Viticulture in Ancient Israel* (HSM 60; Winona Lake, Ind.: Eisenbrauns, 2000); for terracing see L. E. Stager, "The Archaeology of the Family in Ancient Israel," *BASOR* 260 (Fall/November 1985): 5–9 with pictures.

58. *ANET*, 19. Sinuhe describes the land as "a good land, named Yaa. Figs were in it, and grapes. It had more wine than water." He adds honey, olives, fruit, trees, barley, emmer, and cattle to his catalogue of praise for the land of Palestine.

59. G. W. Ahlstrom, *The History of Ancient Palestine* (Sheffield: Sheffield Academic Press, 1994), 70–71.

60. For a pictorial presentation of the produce see further, J. Rogerson, *Atlas of the Bible* (New York: Facts on File, Inc., 1985), 63, or Aharoni and Avi-Yonah, *Macmillan Bible Atlas*, 19.

61. *ANET*, 328–29; for details see Kitchen, *Reliability*, 333–34, 572, n. 64.

62. Kitchen, *Reliability*, 334.

63. R. S. Hess, "Nephilim," *ABD*, 4:1072–73; idem, *Joshua* (TOTC; Downers Grove, Ill.: InterVarsity Press, 1996), 218, n. 5; for text see E. Wente, *Letters from Ancient Egypt* (SBLWAW; Atlanta: Scholars Press, 1990), 107–8; for discussion see Provan, Long, and Longman, *Biblical History of Israel*, 339, n. 95; M. W. Chavalas and M. R. Adamthwaite, "Archaeological Light on the Old Testament," 81.

64. Walton, Matthews, and Chavalas, *IVPBBC-OT*, 89–90.

65. J. Niehaus, *God at Sinai* (Grand Rapids: Zondervan, 1995), 195.

66. See esp. G. A. Lee, "Pillar of Cloud and Pillar of Fire," *ISBE*, 3:871.

67. T. W. Mann, *Divine Presence and Guidance in Israelite Traditions: The Typology of Exaltation* (Baltimore: John Hopkins Univ. Press, 1977), 130–31.

68. *COS*, 1.113, I.10–12, 90–99.

69. Mann, *Divine Presence*, 104, 132–33; G. Mendenhall, *The Tenth Generation* (Baltimore: Johns Hopkins Univ. Press, 1973), 55; Cyrus Gordon, *Ugaritic Textbook* (Rome: Pontifical Biblical Institute, 1965), 458, #1885.

70. Mann, *Divine Presence*, 104, 132–33.

71. M. Weinfeld, "Divine Intervention in War," in *History and Interpretation*, ed. H. Tadmor and M. Weinfeld (Jerusalem: Magnes, 1983), 125, 133–34.

72. *COS*, 1.86, *CTA*, 4.vi.28.

73. Weinfeld, "Divine Intervention," 134.

74. Ibid., 139.

75. *ANET*, 235b, 236a, n. 25; Weinfeld, "Divine Intervention," 124–26, 131–33.

76. *ANET*, 476.

77. Hoffmeier, *Sinai*, 75–109; J. R. Huddleston, "Red Sea," *ABD*, 5:633, 635–42; Kitchen, *Reliability*, 261–63.

78. Kitchen, *Reliability*, 262.

79. Ibid., 272, 630, fig. 30; esp. now Hoffmeier, *Sinai*, fig. 1.

80. Ibid., 404–5.

81. Paul W. Ferris Jr., *The Genre of Communal Lament in the Bible and the Ancient Near East* (SBLDS 127; Atlanta: Scholars Press, 1992), 17–61.

82. W. W. Hallo, "Lamentations and Prayers in Sumer and Akkad," *CANE*, 1872–79, 1881.

83. COS, 1.60; *ANET*, 394–96; see Kitchen, *Reliability*, 405, 586, n. 64, for discussion and additional bibliography.

84. As quoted by Kitchen, *Reliability*, 404–5, 587, n. 63; *KTU*, 1.40.

85. COS, 1.166; 1.164, 165; 1.119

86. Ferris, *Communal Lament in the Bible and the ANE*, 21–25, 48–52; see also Xuan Huong Thi Pham, *Mourning in the Ancient Near East and the Hebrew Bible* (JSOTSup 202; Sheffield: Sheffield Academic Press, 1999), 16–17.

87. Several other sites are possible. See Rainey and Notley, *Sacred Bridge*, 122; J. M. Hamilton, "Hormah," *ABD*, 3:288–89.

88. *ANET*, 488.

89. J. R. Bartlett, *Edom and the Edomites* (JSOTSup 77; Sheffield: JSOT Press, 1989), 41–42.

90. Ibid., 43–44; cf. also Josh. 11:17; 12:7.

91. Rasmussen, *NIV Atlas*, 92, 250.

92. B. MacDonald, *East of the Jordan* (ASOR 6; Boston: ASOR, 2000), 83–84.

93. Kitchen, *Reliability*, 193–94, nn. 93–96; esp. B. MacDonald, *East of the Jordan*, 82–83; D. Baly, *Geography of the Bible*, 2nd ed. (Guildford & London: Lutterworth, 1974), 235–36; cf., however, Rasmussen, *NIV Atlas*, 92.

94. See Dever, *What Did the Biblical Writers Know and When?* 221–28 for discussion, esp. 228; J. W. Betlyon, "Coinage," *ABD*, 1:1076–84.

95. Coinage per se was used in 650 B.C at Sardis, Lydia.

96. King and Stager, *Life in Biblical Israel*, 194–95, 199.

97. O. S. Bianca and R. Younker, "The Kingdoms of Ammon, Moab and Edom," in *The Archaeology of Society in the Holy Land*, ed. Thomas Levy (New York: Facts on File, 1995), 399–415, 407–8; B. MacDonald, "Early Edom: The Relation between the Literary and Archaeological Evidence," in *Scripture and Other Artifacts*, ed. M. Coogan, J. Exum, and L. Stager (Louisville: John Knox, 1994), 230–33, 242–43.

98. Ibid.

99. K. A. Kitchen, "Egyptians and Hebrews, from Raamses to Jericho," in *The Origins of Early Israel—Current Debate* (Beer-sheva: Negev [Ben Gurion Univ.], 1998), 74.

100. S. Ahituv, "The Origins of Ancient Israel—The Documentary Evidence," in *The Origins of Early Israel—Current Debate* (Beer-sheva: Negev [Ben Gurion Univ.], 1998), 136.

101. K. G. Hoglund, "Edomites," *POTW*, 335–47, for excellent resource notes.

102. M. Lubetski, "Ezion Geber," *ABD*, 2:723–26; see Ian Wilson, *The Bible Is History* (London: Weiden-

feld & Nicolson, 1999), 132–33 for a photograph of the island.

103. Weinfeld, *Deuteronomy 1–11*, 160–61.

104. Ø. S. LaBianca and R. Younker, "The Kingdoms of Amon, Moab and Edom: The Archaeology of Society in Late Bronze/Iron Age Transjordan," in *The Archaeology of Society in the Holy Land*, ed. T. E. Levy (New York: Facts on File, 1995), 399.

105. G. L. Mattingly, "Emim," *ABD*, 2:497; R. Hess, "Nephilim," *ABD*, 4:1072–73.

106. COS, 1.103, 19:iv 179; *ANET*, 149d and n. 2.

107. C. E. L'Hereux, *Rank Among the Canaanite Gods El, Baal, and the Repha'im* (HSM 21; Missoula, Mont.: Scholars Press, 1979), 126–27.

108. See Rainey and Notley, *Sacred Bridge*, Excursus 8.1 on Kingdom of Ugarit.

109. S. B. Parker, *Ugaritic Narrative Poetry* (SBLWAW 9; Atlanta: Scholars Press, 1997), 196–205; RSP 34:126; COS, 1.86, CTA, 5.vi 42–44.

110. Parker, *Ugaritic Poetry*, 201; CTA, 22B, ll. 7–9.

111. *ANET*, 182, translates as "shades."

112. M. S. Smith, "Rephaim," *ABD*, 6:674–76; Weinfeld, *Deuteronomy 1–11*, 161–62.

113. COS, 2.56, 8.

114. O. Loretz, "Das Paradigma des Mythos von der *rpum*—Rephaim," in *Ugarit and Bible* (UBL; Münster: Ugarit Verlag, 1994), 191–93.

115. Weinfeld, *Deuteronomy 1–11*, 162–63; M. A. Morrison, "Hurrians," *ABD*, 3:335–6; F. W. Bush, "Horites," *ISBE*, 2:756–57.

116. Cf. Rainey and Notley, *Sacred Bridge*, 27, 61, 114; Kitchen, *Reliability*, 175.

117. Rainey and Notley, *Sacred Bridge*, 114; E. A. Knauf, "Horites," 3:288.

118. D. L. Christensen, *Deuteronomy 1:1–21:9* (WBC 6A; Nashville: Nelson, 2002), 43, bibl. 35–36.

119. Weinfeld, *Deuteronomy 1–11*, 163; G. A. Herion, "Zered," *ABD*, 6:1082; Rasmussen, *NIV Atlas*, 17–18; Rainey and Notley, *Sacred Bridge*, 38, 41; Christensen, *Deuteronomy 1:1–21:9*, 42.

120. *ANET*, 436.

121. Kitchen, *Reliability*, 253–54. For a full discussion of this ancient Near Eastern idiom see further chap. 6, n. 15 of Kitchen; esp. J. D. Hoffmeier, "The Arm of God versus the Arm of Pharaoh in the Exodus Narrative," *Bib* 67 (1986): 378–87. The phrase is in other ancient Near Eastern literature: Ugaritic texts (*UT*, 54:13), and Akkadian texts (EA 35:37). In Amarna letters see 286:12; 287:27.

122. *ANET*, 257; cf. 443.

123. J. J. M. Roberts, "The Hand of Yahweh," in *The Bible and the Ancient Near East* (Winona Lake, Ind.: Eisenbrauns, 2002), 99.

124. *ANET*, 623.

125. Kuhrt, *The Ancient Near East ca. 3000–330 B. C.* (New York: Routledge, 1995), 2:245.

126. Weinfeld, *Deuteronomy 1–11*, 212, and references there; e.g., EA 286:12.

127. J. Currid, *Ancient Egypt and the Old Testament* (Grand Rapids: Baker, 1997), 154–55; Hoffmeier, "The Arm of God," 378–87; Roberts, "Hand of Yahweh," 95.

128. Gordon and Rendsburg, *Eblaitica*, 86.

129. Randall Younker, "Ammonites," *POTW*, 293, 303–4.
130. *ANET*, 282a, 287b, 294a; J.-M. de Tarrogon, "Ammon," *ABD*, 1:194–6; Weinfeld, *Deuteronomy 1–11*, 164.
131. J. A. Thompson, "Ammonites," *ISBE*, 1:111–12.
132. Weinfeld, *Deuteronomy 1–11*, 164.
133. Christensen, *Deuteronomy 1:1–21:9*, 1:44; E. Ullendorf, "The Knowledge of Languages in the Old Testament," *BJRL* 44 (1962): 455–65.
134. S. E. McGarry, "Avvites," *ABD*, 1:531–32;
135. Weinfeld, *Deuteronomy 1–11*, 164.
136. R. S. Hess, "Caphtorites," *ABD*, 1:869–90; Craigie, *Deuteronomy*, 113; Christensen, *Deuteronomy 1:1–21:9*, 43; Weinfeld, *Deuteronomy 1–11*, 165.
137. A. B. Knapp, "Alashiya, Captor/Kefliu, and Eastern Mediterranean Trade: Recent Studies in Cypriote Archaeology and History," *JEA* 12 (1985): 231–50; Kitchen, *Reliability*, 340, nn. 94, 95; *ANET*, 241b, 248, 374b.
138. E. D. Graham, "Arnon," *IDB*, 1:230; *NBD*, "Arnon," 85.
139. *COS*, 2.23, ll 26–7; *ANET*, 320; *DOTT*, 195–98.
140. R. F. Johnson, "Sihon," *IDB*, 4:351.
141. Kitchen, *Reliability*, 195–6, esp. 546, n. 100; J. C. Slayton, "Sihon," *ABD*, 6:22; M. Chavalas and M. Adamthwaite, "Archaeological Light on the O.T.," in *The Face of Old Testament Studies* (Grand Rapids: Baker, 1999), 82–3; G. Mattingly, "Moabites," *POTW*, 322–3.
142. S. Dalley, "Ancient Mesopotamian Military Organization," *CANE*, 415, 417, 421–22.
143. R. H. Beal, "Hittite Military Organization," *CANE*, 546–48, 550, 1552.
144. B. MacDonald, *East of the Jordan*, 93–94; Kitchen, *Reliability*, 194, 546, n. 97; Rasmussen, *NIV Atlas*, 92; J. L. Peterson, "Kedemoth," *ABD*, 4:10–11.
145. Rainey and Notley, *Sacred Bridge*, 123.
146. J. Greene, *The Role of the Messenger and Message in the Ancient Near East* (BJS 169; Atlanta: Scholars Press, 2001), 7–43, 45–76, 88, 165, 232.
147. Ibid., 41; G. H. Oller, "Messengers and Ambassadors in Ancient Western Asia," *CANE*, 1465.
148. Rasmussen, *NIV Atlas*, 92, 94, 101; J. A. Dearmon, "Jahaz," *ABD*, 3:612; Weinfeld, *Deuteronomy 1–11*, 172.
149. *ANET*, 320.
150. P. D. Stern, *The Biblical Herem* (Atlanta: Scholars Press, 1991).
151. *COS*, 2.23, ll 14–18a; *ANET*, 320; M. Chavalas, E. Hostater, "Epigraphic Light on the O.T.," in *Face of Old Testament Studies*, 50.
152. A. Malamat, "The Ban in Mari and the Bible," *Biblical Essays* (Stellenbosch: Univ. of South Africa Press, 1966), 40–49; idem, *Mari and the Early Israelite Experience* (Oxford: Oxford Univ. Press, 1989), 70–79.
153. Lemaire, "Mari," 103; cf. SA-Moon Kang, *Divine War in the Old Testament and in the Ancient Near East* (New York: de Gruyter, 1989), 80–83.
154. *COS*, 2.23, l 26; *ANET*, 320, l. 25; J. M. Miller, "Moab," *ABD*, 4:891.
155. J. F. A. Sawyer and D. J. A. Clines, eds., *Midian, Moab, and Edom: The History of Archaeology of Late Bronze and Iron Age Jordan and North-West Arabia* (JSOTSup 24; Sheffield: Sheffield Academic Press, 1982).
156. M. Ottosson, "Gilead," *ABD*, 2:1020; for description see Rainey and Notley, *Sacred Bridge*, 41.
157. S. Cohen, "Gilead," *IDB*, 2:398–99; Weinfeld, *Deuteronomy 1–11*, 161, 173.
158. Ottosson, "Gilead," 2:1020.
159. Weinfeld, *Deuteronomy 1–11*, 173; J. C. Slayton, "Sihon," *ABD*, 6:22.
160. D. Stuart, "Og," *ISBE*, 3:584; P. W. McMillion, "Og," *ABD*, 5:9; Christensen, *Deuteronomy 1:1–21:9*, 55.
161. A. Millard, "King Og's Bed and Other Ancient Ironmongery," in *Ascribe to the Lord*, ed. L. Eslinger and G. Taylor (Sheffield: Sheffield Academic Press, 1988), 485, 487, 489.
162. H. O. Thompson, "Argob," *ABD*, 1:376; B. Mazar, "Geshur and Maacah," *JBL* 80 (1961): 16–28; Rainey and Notley, *Sacred Bridge*, 176; Rasmussen, *NIV Atlas*, 29.
163. Ami Arav, "Hermon," *ABD*, 3:159; discussion in Hoffmeier, *Sinai*, 111–13.
164. *CML*, 4.VI.18–20; *COS*, 1.86, 4, vi, 18–20; Craigie, *Deuteronomy*, 120, n. 6; *ANET*, 134.
165. R. Arav, "Hermon," *ABD*, 3:158.
166. *ANET*, 280, B, 97–99.
167. *ANET*, 205.
168. *ANET*, 504b.
169. Kitchen, *Reliability*, 198–99, 547, nn. 115–16; but Chavalas and Adamthwaithe, "Archaeological Light on the O.T.," argue that these cities should be placed in the Middle Bronze Age (2100–1550 B.C.), and that the Late Bronze era should be ruled out as a time for the Exodus-Conquest; cf. also Craigie, *Deuteronomy*, 119, n. 2.
170. B. Mazar, "Geshur and Maacah," *JBL* 80 (1961): 16–28; M. Kochavi, "The Land of Geshur Regional Project: Attempting a New Approach in Biblical Archaeology," in *Biblical Archaeology Today* (Jerusalem: Israel Exploration Society, 1993), 725–37.
171. B. Mazar, "Geshur and Maacah," 16–28; G. J. Pelter, "Geshurites," *ABD*, 2:996–97; Rasmussen, *NIV Atlas*, 29.
172. *KAT*, 265; but now see *COS*, 2.117C, ll iii. A. 34–6, and n 5; H. Tadmor, *The Inscriptions of Tiglath-Pileser* (Jerusalem: Israel Academy of Sciences and Humanities, 1994), 139, n to l 6; N. Naʾaman, "Rezin of Damascus and the Land of Gilead," *ZDPV* 111 (1995): 105–6.
173. Mazar, *Archaeology of the Land of the Bible*, 186; Rainey and Notley, *Sacred Bridge*, 52.
174. *JW* 2.573; *JW* 3.57; *Life* 96, 153.
175. *COS*, 2.23, where the idea is expressed repeatedly; *ANET*, 320, esp. ll. 15–20, 30.
176. W. S. LaSor, "Pisgah," *ISBE*, 3:873.
177. G. L. Mattingly, "Pisgah," *ABD*, 5:374.
178. Weinfeld, *Deuteronomy 1–11*, 191; cf. LaSor, "Pisgah," 3:873.
179. Mattingly, "Pisgah," 5:373–74.
180. Rasmussen, *NIV Atlas*, 101.

181. G. L. Mattingly, "Beth Peor," *ABD*, 1:691; cf. Weinfeld, *Deuteronomy 1–11*, 192.

182. V. Vernes, "Le Sanctuare moabite de Beth-Péor: Moise et la promulgation de la loi du Deutéronomie," *RHR* 38 (1917): 240–61.

183. Kitchen, *Reliability*, 284; M. G. Kline, *Treaty of the Great King* (Grand Rapids: Eerdmans, 1963), 7, 8, 31.

184. P. M. Michéle Daviau, J. W. Wevers, and M. Weigl, *The World of the Arameans III* (JSOTSup 326; Sheffield: Sheffield Academic Press, 2001), 97; M. Weinfeld, *Deuteronomy and the Deuteronomic School* (Oxford: Clarendon, 1972), 65–68; J. A. Thompson, *Deuteronomy* (Downers Grove, Ill.: InterVarsity Press, 1974), 17–21, 106.

185. R. Westbrook, "Biblical and Cuneiform Law Codes," *RB* 92 (1985): 246, 249, 255; for a full discussion and sources of the key features and nature of ancient Near Eastern law and Israelite law, see Westbrook, *HANEL*, 1:1–90; for Israel see idem, *HANEL*, 2:975–1046.

186. Westbrook, *Biblical and Cuneiform Law*, 134–35.

187. Kitchen, *Reliability*, 288–89.

188. Ibid., 284–89; Hill and Walton, *Survey*, 132–34.

189. Roberts, "Bible and the Literature of the Ancient Near East," 46. See the comments below, however, concerning finds at Emar and assertions concerning Assur, chief god of Assyria; S. Parpolo and K. Watanabe, *Neo-Assyrian Treaties and Loyalty Oaths* (SAAS 2; Helsinki: Univ. Press, 1988), esp. XXII, XVIII, XXIV (Loyalty Pacts).

190. Lemaire, "Mari," 104; see Mari texts *ARM*, v.20.16; x.113.21; x.156.10–11.

191. K. van der Toorn, *Family Religion in Babylonia, Syria and Israel: Continuity and Change in the Forms of Religious Life* (Leiden: Brill, 1996), 72, 450–52.

192. Ibid., 74.

193. Ibid., 77–78.

194. Craigie, *Deuteronomy*, 130; S. Morenz, *Egyptian Religion*, trans. R. E. Keep (Ithaca, N.Y.: Cornell Univ. Press, 1973), 223; M. Fishbane, "Varia Deuteronomica," *ZAW* 84 (1972): 349–52; H. G. Güterbock, "Mursili's Accounts of Suppiluliuma's Dealings with Egypt," *RHA* 18 (1960): 59–60; Weinfeld, *Deuteronomy 1–11*, 200.

195. *ANET*, 178.

196. *ANET*, 159, 161; *COS*, 2.154, Epilogue.

197. M. S. Smith, "Worship in Canaan and Ancient Israel," *CANE*, 2034.

198. *COS*, 1.86, 4.v. 64–73; Craigie, *Deuteronomy*, 130; see esp. J. G. Jung, "Baal," *ISBE*, 1:378; J. C. Slayton, "Baal and Peor," *ABD*, 1:553.

199. *ANET*, 165, iv, 50–70; 178; xxiv, ll. 60–100; xxv 60–100; cf. M. T. Roth, *Law Collections from Mesopotamia and Asia Minor* (SBLWAW 6; Atlanta: Society of Biblical Literature, 1995), xlix 18–li 91.

200. Thompson, *Deuteronomy*, 35; Weinfeld, *Deuteronomy & Deuteronomy School*, 226, n. 2.

201. P. Machinist, "The Question of Distinctiveness in Ancient Israel," in *Essential Papers on Israel and the Ancient Near East*, ed. F. E. Greenspahn (New York: New York Univ. Press, 1991), 420–42, 424, 429, 431. He observes that the distinctiveness passages focus on God or on the people of Israel (437, n. 22).

202. L. Koehler and W. Baumgartner, *Lexicon in Veteris Testamenti Libros* (Leiden: Brill, 1985), 350, where its Akk. cognate *ḫuribtu* (desert, dry land) is discussed.

203. For a recent discussion see Hoffmeier, *Sinai*, 114–15.

204. R. D. Cole, "The Challenge of Faith's Final Step," in *Giving The Sense*, ed. D. M. Howard Jr. and M. A. Grisanti (Grand Rapids: Kregel, 2003), 340–59, 350–52.

205. G. E. Davies, "Mount Sinai," *ABD*, 6:47–49; more recently, Hoffmeier, *Sinai*, 115–48.

206. Machinist, "Distinctiveness," 424, 429–30.

207. Craigie, *Deuteronomy*, 135, esp. n. 9 for primary texts.

208. Christensen, *Deuteronomy 1:1–21:9*, 86; E. M. Curtis, "Idol, Idolatry," *ABD*, 3:376–80.

209. I. Cornelius, "The Many Faces of God: Divine Images and Symbols in Ancient Near Eastern Religions," in *The Image and the Book*, ed. K. van der Toorn (Leuven: Peeters, 1997), 21–43, with good illustrations.

210. E. Hornung, *Conceptions of God in Ancient Egypt*, (Ithaca, N.Y.: Cornell Univ. Press, 1982), 113–14.

211. Ibid., 124.

212. Ian Wilson, *Out of the Midst of the Fire* (SBLDS; Atlanta: Scholars Press, 1995), 17. This is a helpful study, but does not discuss the ancient Near Eastern background of this concept.

213. *CML*, 2.1:30–33.

214. *CTA*, 2, 1:13–15; Weinfeld, "Divine Intervention," 132 n. 51, 133–34, n. 55; similar terminology found in the *Iliad*, 205–8; cf. Weinfeld, 133, n. 57.

215. Ibid. 134 n. 134; *ANET*, 79, 1v. 38–9.

216. *COS*, 1.113, II.1–10, n 26.

217. P. R. S. Moorey, *Ancient Mesopotamian Materials and Industries* (Winona Lake, Ind.: Eisenbrauns, 1999), 278–91 (iron), 243, 333 (furnaces); Weinfeld, *Deuteronomy 1–11*, 207; T. C. Mitchell, "Furnaces," *NBD*, 199; W. A. Shell, "Furnace," *ISBE*, 2:371.

218. King and Stager, *Life in Biblical Israel*, 138–39, 164–76.

219. *COS*, 2.30, n. 10.

220. Niehaus, *God at Sinai*, 125–36; for divine intervention in general see Kitchen, *Reliability*, 47–50, 174–75.

221. Weinfeld, "Divine Intervention," 136.

222. Ibid., 125.

223. Weinfeld, *Deuteronomy 1–11*, 295–96.

224. J. Hoffmeier, "Moses," *ISBE*, 3:419a.

225. McCarthy, *Treaty and Covenant*, 297; H. A. Bongers, "Der Eifer des Herrn Zebaoth," *VT* 13 (1963): 269–84.

226. Hoffmeier, "Moses," 3:419a; W. Johnstone, "The Ten Commandments: Some Recent Interpretations," *ET* 100 (1989): 456.

227. P. Koschaker, "Zur Interprepation des art. 59 des Codex, Bilalama," *JCS* 5 (1951): 106–9; R. Yaron, "Matrimonial Mishaps at Eshunna," *JSS* 8 (1963): 10–15.

228. McCarthy, *Treaty and Covenant*, 297–98.

229. *COS*, 1.158, l. 91.

230. Craigie, *Deuteronomy*, 139; for trans. see C. F. A. Schaeffer, *Le palais royal d'Ugarit*, par J. Naugayrol (Mission de Ras Shamra, Tome 9; Paris, 1956), 4:86; 17.338.4; 137; 17.365.6; M. Delcor, "Les attaches litteraries: L'origine et la signification de l'expression biblique 'prendre a témoin le ciel et la terre,'" *VT* 16 (1966): 8–25.

231. As given in L. Clapham, "Mythopoeic Antecedents of the Biblical World-View and Their Transformation in Early Israelite Thought," in *The Mighty Acts of God*, ed. F. Cross, W. Lemke, and P. Miller Jr. (New York: Doubleday, 1976), 115.

232. McCarthy, *Treaty and Covenant*, 123; *COS*, 2.17A, iv.32; 2.18, #25b; 2.82, 6–14a.

233. McCarthy, *Treaty and Covenant*, 192–93 for a discussion.

234. Kitchen, *Reliability*, 301–2.

235. Saggs, *Greatness*, 357; A. Berlejung, "Washing the Mouth: The Consecration of Divine Images in Mesopotamia," in *The Image and the Book*, ed. K. van der Toorn (Leuven: Peeters, 1997), 45–72.

236. Berlejung, "Washing the Mouth," 45–72.

237. Stephen Caesar, "The Prophets' Knowledge of Contemporary Idolatry," *Bible and Spade* 16/4 (2003): 111–15; Saggs, *Greatness*, 357; D. Rudman, "When Gods Go Hungry," *BR* 18/3 (2002): 37–39; M. B. Dick, "Worshipping Idols," *BR* 18/2 (2002): 30–37.

238. *CML*, 6:1:49; 3:10; see Weinfeld, *Deuteronomy 1–11*, 295.

239. McCarthy, *Treaty and Covenant*, 119; *ANET*, 294–98.

240. *COS*, 1.44.

241. Weinfeld, "Divine Intervention," 121–47; Kitchen, *Reliability*, 47–50, 115, 174, 224–25, 300.

242. *ANET*, 4, 29, 31, 415, 431–32, 495–96; 1.42, 7.1–2.

243. B. Couroyer, "Un Egyptianisme Biblique: 'Depuis La Foundateur de L'Egypte,' (Exode 9,18)," *RB* (1960): 42–48; K. A. Kitchen, *Pharaoh Triumphant: The Life and Times of Ramesses II* (Warminster: Aris & Phillips, 1982), 238; N. Grimal, *A History of Ancient Egypt*, trans. I. Shaw (Cambridge: Blackwell, 1992), 294–95, 298, 302.

244. J. Licht, "Biblical Historicism," *History, Historiography, and Interpretation*, 110–11, 118, nn. 8–9; see especially Lambert, "History and the Gods: A Review Article," *Or* 39 (1970): 170–77.

245. N. K. Sanders, *The Sea Peoples* (London: Thames & Hudson, 1978)—a fascinating account of the "Sea Peoples" and their impact on the Near East; for a short summary see Suano, "Trading Empires," 84–89.

246. Christensen, *Deuteronomy 1:1–21:9*, 97; *ANET*, 320, l. 29; Craigie, *Deuteronomy*, 145.

247. Weinfeld, *Deuteronomy 1–11*, 231.

248. See Rainey and Notley, *Sacred Bridge*, 162, 351, 358; Rasmussen, *NIV Atlas*, 18, 52, 102, 105, for all of these cities.

249. See discussion in Weinfeld, *Deuteronomy 1–11*, 250–57.

250. Westbrook, *HANEL*, 1–90; M. Weinfeld, *The Place of the Law in the Religion of Ancient Israel* (VTSup 100; Leiden: Brill, 2004); R. VerSteeg, *Law in Ancient Egypt* (Durham, N.C.: Univ. of Carolina Press, 2002).

251. K. A. Kitchen, "Egypt, Ugarit, Qatna and Covenant," *UF* 11 (1979): 453–64; D. R. Hillers, *Covenant: The History of a Biblical Idea* (Baltimore: Johns Hopkins Univ. Press, 1969); J. Sprinkle, *The Book of the Covenant* (JSOTSup 174; Sheffield: Sheffield Academic Press, 1994); T. D. Alexander, "The Composition of the Sinai Narrative in Exodus xix 1–xxiv 11," *VT* 49 (1999): 4–20.

252. Westbrook, *HANEL*, 978.

253. *COS*, 1.176, 28, 31, 34, 36, 42, 50, 154.

254. *COS*, 1.177, ll. 19–25.

255. B. Alster, *Wisdom of Ancient Sumer* (Bethesda, Md.: CDL, 2005), 245, ll. 76–7.

256. *COS*, 1.47, 2:7, 5:14, 6:11, 7:10.

257. D. E. Fleming, "Emar: On the Road from Haran to Hebron," in *Mesopotamia and the Bible*, ed. M. Chavalas and E. Younger Jr. (Grand Rapids: Baker, 2002), 237.

258. *ANET*, 538.

259. *COS*, 2.86, 7–14; Beyerlin, *Near Eastern Religious Texts*, 248.

260. *ANET*, 161. He pronounces a curse on anyone who erases his name and puts their name on it.

261. Hallo, "New Moons and Sabbaths," *HUCA* 48 (1977): 2–3.

262. M. Greenberg, "Some Postulates of Biblical Common Law," in *Essential Papers on Israel and the Ancient Near East*, ed. F. E. Greenspahn (New York: New York Univ. Press, 1991), 336–37.

263. Beckman, *Diplomatic Texts*, 37. See also McCarthy, *Treaty and Covenant*, 51.

264. J. H. Walton, *Ancient Near Eastern Thought in the Old Testament* (Grand Rapids: Baker, forthcoming); M. S. Heiser, "Deuteronomy 32:8 and the Sons of God," *BibSac* 158 (2001): 52–74.

265. Weinfeld, *Deuteronomy 1–11*, 288.

266. Kitchen, *Reliability*, 395–96; Edith Porada, "Understanding Ancient Near Eastern Art: A Personal Account," *CANE*, 2695–714.

267. M. I. Marcus, "Art and Ideology in Ancient Western Asia," *CANE*, 2487–505; G. Azarpay, "Proportions in Ancient Near Eastern Art," *CANE*, 2507; A. Caubet, "Art and Architecture in Canaan and Ancient Israel," *CANE*, 2671–91.

268. *COS*, 1.16, 2:25–28; 3:28–30; 4:21.

269. *COS*, 1.16, n. 3.

270. *ANET*, 661.

271. *ANET*, 312; Weinfeld, *Deuteronomy 1–11*, 296–97 (his refs. are incorrect, see *ANET*, 312, 661).

272. *ANET*, 207, 394–96.

273. Albrektson, *History and the Gods*, 106–7; T. de Roos, "Hittite Prayer," *CANE*, 2003.

274. Beyerlin, *Near Eastern Religious Texts*, 42–43; Text 42, "Religious Sentences and Maxims."

275. Ibid., 27, "Hymn of Mer-Sekhmet"; see also *ANET*, 371.

276. Ibid., 30.

277. Weinfeld, *Deuteromony 1–11*, 301.

278. COS, 1.22, "The Legend of Isis and the Name of Re"; J. Assmann, *The Search for God in Ancient Egypt* (Ithaca, N.Y.: Cornell Univ. Press, 2001), 83–84.

279. H. B. Huffmon, "The Fundamental Code Illustrated: The Third Commandment," in *Pomegranates and Golden Bells*, ed. D. P. Wright, D. N. Freedman, and A. Hurvitz (Winona Lake, Ind.: Eisenbrauns, 1995), 368–71, for texts and discussion.

280. COS, 1.22.

281. Weinfeld, *Deuteronomy 1–11*, 302–9; cf. Craigie, *Deuteronomy*, 157, n. 19.

282. W. W. Hallo, "New Moons and Sabbaths," *HUCA* 48 (1977): 8, 10–11.

283. Ibid., 12.

284. Ibid., 13, n. 67.

285. Ibid., 13, n. 68; 14–16; Weinfeld, *Deuteronomy 1–11*, 301.

286. Walton, *Ancient Near Eastern Thought* (forthcoming); Niels-Erik, A. Andreasen, *The Old Testament Sabbath: A Tradition-Historical Investigation* (SBLDS; Missoula, Mont.: Society of Biblical Literature, 1972), 182.

287. Olyan, "Honor, Shame, and Covenant Relations in Ancient Israel and Its Environment," *JBL* 115 (1996): 201–18.

288. Ibid., 204, 218.

289. Alster, *Wisdom of Sumer*, in "Counsels of Wisdom," 245, ll. 76–7.

290. R. Westbrook, "Emar and Vicinity," *HANEL*, 1:671.

291. I. M. Rowe, "Anatolia and the Levant: Alalakh," *HANEL*, 710.

292. R. Jasnow, "Egypt: New Kingdom," *HANEL*, 1:326.

293. R. Westbrook, "Old Babylonian Period," *HANEL*, 1:391.

294. K. R. Veenhof, "Old Assyrian Period," *HANEL*, 1:455.

295. C. Zacaagnini, "Nuzi," *HANEL*, 1:594.

296. *ANET*, 661.

297. *ANET*, 538.

298. COS, 2.36, ll. 15b–18; cf. 2.37, 15–17.

299. van der Toorn, *Family Religion in Babylonia, Syria, and Israel*, 48–52. Brichto, however, holds that Israel also was careful to care for their ancestral dead; see H. C. Brichto, "Kin, Cult, Land and Afterlife—A Biblical Complex," *HUCA* 44 (1974): 1–52.

300. A. Phillips, "Another Look at Adultery," *JSOT* 20 (1981): 3, 4, 19. Phillips argues for distinctive principles that operate in Israel's law.

301. R. Westbrook, "Adultery in Ancient Near Eastern Law," *RB* 97 (1990): 542–80; for the nature and function of these laws see Roth, *Law Collections*, 4–7.

302. Westbrook, *HANEL*, 77, 80; W. L. Moran, "The Scandal of the 'Great Sin' at Ugarit," *JNES* 18

(1959): 280–81; J. J. Rabinowitz, "The 'Great Sin' in Ancient Egyptian Marriage Contracts," *JNES* 18 (1959): 73.

303. H. J. Marsman, *Women in Ugarit* (OTS 49; Leiden: Brill, 2003), 168–91; Westbrook, *HANEL*, 538.

304. V. H. Matthews, "Marriage and Family in the Ancient Near East," in *Marriage and Family in the Biblical World*, ed. K. M. Campbell (Downers Grove, Ill.: InterVarsity Press, 2003), 27–30.

305. Marsman, *Women in Ugarit*, 169.

306. Westbrook, *HANEL*, 77.

307. Matthews, *Marriage and Family*, 27–30; see also "divorce" entries in Westbrook, *HANEL*, e.g., "Divorce," 325:5.1.4.

308. Greenberg, "Postulates," 337–38, nn. 14–15, for primary sources and bibliography.

309. Roth, *Law Collections*, 82–83, 85.

310. *ANET*, 166–67, 177; Roth, *Law Collections*, 85–86, 130; see discussion in Westbrook, *Biblical and Cuneiform Law*, 28, 38, 111–31.

311. *ANET*, 180; Roth, *Law Collections*, 155–56.

312. *ANET*, 192 (Laws 57–71); Roth, *Law Collections*, 226–27.

313. *ANET*, 192; Roth, *Law Collections*, 226–27.

314. ANET, 160, 162; Roth, *Law Collections*, 60–61.

315. COS, 1.174, l. 126.

316. COS, 1.174, l. 118.

317. *ANET*, 160; Roth, *Law Collections*, 29.

318. *ANET*, 166; Roth, *Law Collections*, 81, 83.

319. COS, 2.31; Weinfeld, *Deuteronomy 1–11*, 316, and refs.

320. W. L. Moran, "The Conclusion of the Decalogue (Ex. 20:17=Dt. 5:21)," *CBQ* 29 (1967): 543–44, 549–52; Weinfeld, *Deuteronomy 1–11*, 318–19, for additional refs.

321. COS, 1.47, Int.; 7:10–15; 11:5–9; 12:10–15.

322. COS, 1.43; *ANET*, 35, 413 (295), 415 (40), 409 (290).

323. COS, I.47, Int.; Prol., 1:9, n. 1.

324. COS, 2.131, Laws 6–9, 14, etc.

325. COS, 1.174, Sumerian Proberb Collection, ll. 15a, 175; other proberbs, 1.175, ll. 6–7, n. 44.

326. Craigie, *Deuteronomy*, 73, n. 3; McCarthy, *Treaty and Covenant*, 256–57.

327. McCarthy, *Treaty and Covenant*, 294.

328. Saggs, *Greatness*, 346–50.

329. Beyerlin, *Near Eastern Religious Texts*, 19, n. j.

330. McCarthy, *Treaty and Covenant*, 182; COS, 2.82.

331. *ANET*, 538 (34).

332. McCarthy, *Treaty and Covenant*, 102, n. 52; *ANET*, 206.

333. *ANET*, 140b; *UT*, 168; A. D. H. Mayes, *Deuteronomy* (NCBC; Grand Rapids: Eerdmans, 1979), 175.

334. Beyerlin, *Near Eastern Religious Texts*, 79.

335. Ibid., 36.

336. Christensen, *Deuteronomy 1:1–21:9*, 145.

337. N. MacDonald, *Deuteronomy and the Meaning of Monotheism* (Tübingen: Mohr Siebeck, 2003), esp. 218–21.

338. Cf. C. Gordon, "His Name is 'One,'" *JNES* 29 (1970): 198; M. Dahood, "Obey, Israel, Yahweh.

Yahweh Our God Is the Unique," *RSP* 1 (1972): 361.

339. Craigie, *Deuteronomy*, 169, n. 11.

340. A. Poebel, *Historical and Grammatical Texts*, vol. 5 (Philadelphia: Univ. of Pennsylvania, University Museum, 1914), no. 66 1.1–3.

341. Weinfeld, *Deuteronomy 1–11*, 338, for ref.; *CTA*, 4.7:49–50; Parker, *Ugaritic Poetry*, 1.4.7:49–52.

342. For a brief outline see Traunecker, *The Gods of Egypt*, 9–10.

343. J. L. Foster, *Hymns, Prayers and Songs*, ed. S. T. Hollis (SBLWAW 8; Atlanta: Society of Biblical Literature, 1995), 55–69, 73–74.

344. J. Baines, "Egyptian Deities in Context," in *One God or Many? Concepts of Divinity in the Ancient World*, ed. B. N. Porter (Bethesda, Md.: CDL, 2000), 61, 71; COS, 1.28.

345. Kitchen, *Reliability*, 330–33; esp. 572, nn. 58–59; W. H. C. Propp, "Monotheism and 'Moses,'" *UF* 31 (1999/2000): 532–75.

346. Assmann, *The Search for God in Ancient Egypt*, 199, 237.

347. Ibid., 56, 55–79; J. Assmann, *Egyptian Solar Religion in the New Kingdom*, trans. A. Alcock (SE; New York: Kegan Paul, 1995), 133–85.

348. *ANET*, 371; *DOTT*, 142; B. Watterson, *Amarna* (Charleston, S.C.: Tempus, 1999), 64–77.

349. COS, 1.47, Int.; Prol. 1:9, n. 1.

350. Beyerlin, *Near Eastern Religious Texts*, 36; cf. also 39.

351. Bryce, *Letters of the Great Kings of the Ancient Near East*, 11–41, 76–77.

352. McCarthy, *Treaty and Covenant*, 43, 81, 106; cf. 160–61, 168.

353. Parpola and Watanabe, *Neo-Assyrian Treaties and Loyalty Oaths*, 37, 39, 66, 72; *ANET*, 207.

354. Moran, "Love of God," 105, 112, nn. 21–22.

355. H. W. Wolff, *Anthropology of the Old Testament* (Philadelphia: Fortress, 1974), 40–58; D. G. Burke, "Heart," *ISBE*, 2:650–53.

356. Parker, *Ugaritic Poetry*, 108, ll. 25–27; cf. *CML*, 49, 3.B.ii, 25–27.

357. *CML*, 3.B.26; 5.vi.21; 6.ii.6:24.30.

358. COS, 1.15, 53–6.

359. Weinfeld, *Deuteronomy 1–11*, 340, for refs. and examples.

360. *ANET*, 421b; cf. Prov. 22:17–18a.

361. Beyerlin, *Near Eastern Religious Texts*, 35–36, 39–42, 54–60, 63–64; M. Lichtheim, *Ancient Egyptian Literature: A Book of Readings* (Berkeley: Univ. of Calif. Press, 1973), 1:54. The word occurs numerous times in every volume of her three vol. work.

362. *ANET*, 131b, n. 10; 1316; Ugaritica 5.3:5–7; Weinfeld, *Deuteronomy 1–11*, 335; *CML*, 2.iv.19–21.

363. COS, 1.97, The Recipe, ll. 29–31.

364. COS, 1.90, 49.

365. COS, 1.103, 17.ii.10.

366. COS, 1.8, CTII, 40c–43b, and n. 24; Hoffmeier, *Sinai*, 48, plus n. 6.

367. Weinfeld, *Deuteronomy 1–11*, 343.

368. Ibid., 335; *CAD*, M/1, 235.

369. G. Barkai, *Ketef Hinom: A Treasure Facing Jerusalem's Walls* (Jerusalem: Magnes, 1986), 29–31; Weinfeld, *Deuteronomy 1–11*, 342.

370. Weinfeld, *Deuteronomy 1–11*, 333–35, 342.

371. King and Stager, *Life in Biblical Israel*, 30–34, 304–10; A. Lemaire, "Writing and Writing Materials," *ABD*, 6:1001–4.

372. O. Keel, "Zeichen der Verbundenheit: Zur Vorgeschichte und Bedeutung von Deuteronomium 6:8f und Par," in *Mélanges Dominique Barthelemy* (OBO 38; Freiburg: Universitätsverlag Freiburg, 1981), 193–215.

373. A. J. Hoerth, *Archaeology and the Old Testament* (Grand Rapids: Baker, 1998), 388–403; Kitchen, *Reliability*, 301–2.

374. E. Merrill, *Kingdom of Priests* (Grand Rapids: Baker, 1987), 74, 110; King and Stager, *Life in Biblical Israel*, 28–29.

375. Stager, "Archaeology of Family," 11–22; King and Stager, *Life in Biblical Israel*, 123–27.

376. McCarthy, *Treaty and Covenant*, 77, 87, 89–105, 118–20; Parpola and Watanabe, *Neo-Assyrian Treaties*, 8, 11, 22, 44, etc.

377. *ANET*, 486 (256).

378. COS, 3.10.

379. F. C. Fensham, "Oath," *ISBE*, 3:572; for vows see T. Cartledge, *Vows in the Hebrew Bible and the Ancient Near East* (JSOTSup 147; Sheffield: Sheffield Academic Press, 1992).

380. COS, 2.33.

381. COS, 1.66, 67.

382. Hoffmeier, *Sinai*, 170; A. R. Millard, "Story, History, and Theology," in *Faith, Tradition and History*, ed. D. Baker, A. Millard, and J. K. Hoffmeier (Winona Lake, Ind.: Eisenbrauns, 1994), 37–64.

383. *ANET*, 378; COS, 2:41; Kitchen, *Reliability*, 496.

384. N. Grimal, *Ancient Egypt*, 84, 247.

385. Millard, *Treasures*, 60–63; H. G. Güterbock, "Resurrecting the Hittites," *CANE*, 2765–77.

386. H. A. Hoffner, "Hittites and Hurrians," in *POTT*, ed. D. J. Wiseman (Oxford: Clarendon, 1975), 130–31, 135–36, 152–53.

387. Chavalas and Adamthwaite, "Archaeological Light," 68–69.

388. K. Kitchen, *Ancient Orient and Old Testament* (Downers Grove, Ill.: InterVarsity Press, 1966), 51–52.

389. Cf. Weinfeld, *Deuteronomy 1–11*, 363.

390. *UT*, 3:381, no. 619.

391. D. W. Baker, "Girgeshites," *ABD*, 2:1028; cf. Weinfeld, *Deuteronomy 1–11*, 363.

392. R. S. Hess, "Non-Israelite Personal Names in the Book of Joshua," *CBQ* 58 (1996): 205–14; idem, *Joshua*, 27; H. A. Hoffner Jr., "Hittites," in *POTT*, 225.

393. Kitchen, *Reliability*, 175; EA 27 (El Amarna Letter).

394. D. W. Baker, "Hivites," *ABD*, 3:234; Weinfeld, *Deuteronomy 1–11*, 363.

395. S. A. Reed, "Jebus," *ABD*, 3:652–53; B. Obed, "The Table of Nations (Gen. 10)—A Socio-

cultural Approach," *ZAW* 98 (1986): 14–31; Weinfeld, *Deuteronomy 1–11*, 363–64.

396. Rainey, *Sacred Bridge*, 85, 89, 90, excurses 7.1, 7.2.

397. For a picture see Hoffmeier, *Sinai*, fig. 22; Kitchen, *Reliability*, 332, esp. n. 62; also 396, 402.

398. *ANEP*, 2:103, 104, 106.

399. *ANEP*, 2:105.

400. Kitchen, *Reliability*, 402–11.

401. J. Day, "Asherah," *ABD*, 1:483–87.

402. Ibid., 1:483.

403. *ANEP*, 203–4.

404. *ANEP*, 470–74.

405. *ANET*, 519; Day, "Asherah," *ABD*, 1:482.

406. COS, 2.47A, 47B; 2.52; Weinfeld, *Deuteronomy 1–11*, 367, for discussion and references; Dever, *What Did the Biblical Writers Know and When?* 183–87; for current discussion of topic, see King and Stager, *Life in Biblical Israel*, 343, 349, 350–52; Chavalas and Hostetter, "Epigraphic Light," 48–49; see full-scale study in J. Hadley, *The Cult of Asherah in Ancient Israel and Judah* (Cambridge: Cambridge Univ. Press, 2000), 4–11, 207–9.

407. Kitchen, *Reliability*, 294; E. Carpenter, "סְגֻלָּה," *NIDOTTE*, 3:224.

408. Weinfeld, *Deuteronomy 1–11*, 368; M. Greenberg, "Hebrew *segulla*: Akkadian *sikiltu*," *JAOS* 71 (1951): 172–74.

409. Machinist, "Distinctiveness," 434, n. 50; 429; COS, 1.111.

410. R. A. Oden Jr., "Cosmogony, Cosmology," *ABD*, 1:1162–71; E. E. Carpenter, "Cosmology," in *Contemporary Wesleyan Theology*, vol. 2 (Grand Rapids: Zondervan, 1982), 149–90.

411. *ANET*, 308–11.

412. *UT*, 126 III 13–15; *CML*, 4.iii.43; 16.iii, 1–16.

413. Mayes, *Deuteronomy*, 187 and refs.

414. R. D. Biggs, "Medicine, Surgery, and Public Health in Ancient Mesopotamia," *CANE*, 1911; Christensen, *Deuteronomy 1:1–21:9*, 164; Craigie, *Deuteronomy*, 181; F. Marti-Ibanez, ed., *A Pictorial History of Medicine* (New York: MD Publications, 1965), 33–51; Weinfeld, *Deuteronomy 1–11*, 374, for refs. to Pliny's relevant *Natural History*, 26.1.5.

415. K. R. Weeks, "Medicine, Surgery, and Public Health in Ancient Egypt," *CANE*, 1788, 1790; for ancient Mesopotamia see 1911–24.

416. O. Borowski, "The Identity of the Biblical *ṣirʿâ*," in *The Word Shall Go Forth*, ed C. Meyers and M. O'Connor (Winona Lake, Ind.: Eisenbrauns, 1983), 315–19; Christensen, *Deuteronomy 1:1–21:9*, 164; E. Ball, "Hornet," *ISBE*, 2:757; Weinfeld, *Deuteronomy 1–11*, 375.

417. G. Rendsburg, *The Bible and the Ancient Near East*, 4th ed. (New York: Norton, 1997), 169.

418. E. Neufeld, "Insects as Warfare Agents in the ANE," *Or* 49 (1980): 30–57.

419. B. Albrektson, *History and the Gods* (CB Series 1; Lund: Gleerup, 1967), 37–39.

420. Ibid., 37, n. 62; 39, n. 68; *ANET*, 354, n. 1; COS, 2.82, Face B21–45.

421. Ibid., 39–41, with text and trans.; COS, 1.60, 2d, Prayer, A 13–14; 2.16, passim; 2.122B, ii.16–31.

422. *ANET*, 378; COS, 2.6.

423. For discussion see Hoffmeier, *Sinai*, 711–13. Egyptian words may lie behind the expression; see M. Gorg, "Methodological Remarks on Comparative Studies of Egyptian and Biblical Words and Phrases," in *Pharonic Egypt: The Bible and Christianity*, ed. S. Israelite Groll (Jerusalem: Magnes, 1985), 61.

424. Kuhrt, *Ancient Near East*, 2:491, 577; cf. Christensen, *Deuteronomy 1:1–21:9*, 173–74, 491.

425. *ANET*, 96.

426. Weinfeld, *Deuteronomy 1–11*, 390.

427. Christensen, *Deuteronomy 1:1–21:9*, 176; Craigie, *Deuteronomy*, 186, n. 6: Weinfeld, *Deuteronomy and the Deuteronomic School*, 71–72.

428. McCarthy, *Treaty and Covenant*, 73.

429. Weinfeld, "The Covenant of Grant in the Old Testament and in the Ancient Near East," in *Essential Papers*, 69–70, 73–74.

430. Craigie, *Deuteronomy*, 186, n. 6.

431. COS, 1:99a; 151d, 314–15, 575–78; 3:214.

432. King and Stager, *Life in Biblical Israel*, 87.

433. *ANET*, 320.

434. *ANET*, 19–20; see esp. King and Stager, *Life in Biblical Israel*, 85–89.

435. For a discussion of metals in Mesopotamia see Moorey, *Mesopotamian Materials*, 242–96.

436. Craigie, *Deuteronomy*, 187; F. V. Winnett, "Mining," *ISBE*, 3:384–85; King and Stager, *Life in Biblical Israel*, 167–68.

437. King and Stager, *Life in Biblical Israel*, 164–65; Stager, "Archaeology of Family," 10–11.

438. King and Stager, *Life in Biblical Israel*, 164–69.

439. *ANET*, 325, n. 8; B. Conroyer, "Le Doigt de Dieu," *RB* 63 (1940): 481–95; J. Döller, "Zu Ex 8,15," *BZ* 10 (1912): 362. See Döller for texts and refs.

440. Kline, *Treaty*, 13–26; Christensen, *Deuteronomy 1:1–21:9*, 86.

441. Kitchen, *Reliability*, 272, 630.

442. Millard, *Treasures*, 73.

443. K. A. Kitchen, "The Tabernacle—A Bronze Age Artifact," *EI* 24 (1993): 119–29.

444. I. Jacob and W. Jacob, "Flora," *ABD*, 2:804; M. Zohary, *Plants of the Bible* (New York: Cambridge Univ. Press, 1982), 116; Weinfeld, *Deuteronomy 1–11*, 418.

445. Hoffmeier, *Sinai*, 209–11; cf. Z. Zevit, "Timber for the Tabernacle Tent: Text, Tradition, and Realia," *EI* 23 (1992): 137–43, whom Hoffmeier sufficiently refutes.

446. J. Hoffmeier, *Sinai*, 211–14.

447. Kitchen, "Egyptians and Hebrews," 96, n. 109.

448. King and Stager, *Life in Biblical Israel*, 25.

449. Rasmussen, *NIV Atlas*, 246.

450. G. I. Davies, "Gudgodah," *NBD*, 446; Craigie, *Deuteronomy*, 200.

451. Kitchen, *Reliability*, 631, 534, n. 93.

452. *ARAB*, 128–29; Weinfeld, *Deuteronomy 1–11*, 419–21.

453. G. I. Davies, "The Wilderness Wanderings: A Comparative Study," *TynBul* 25 (1974): 46–81.

454. W. W. Hallo, "The Road to Emar," *JCS* 18 (1964): 57–88.

455. Esp. C. Krahmalkov, "Exodus Itinerary Confimed by Egyptian Evidence," *BAR* 20 (1994): 54–62.

456. For daybooks see J. A. Spalinger, *Aspects of the Military Documents of the Ancient Egyptians* (New Haven, Conn.: Yale Univ. Press, 1982), 120–22.

457. Kitchen, *Reliability*, 198, has a full catalogue of such itineraries; 547, nn. 107–13 for bibliography.

458. *AEL*, 3, 14–15, 17, 19, 148, 154, 160, 162.

459. *ANET*, 326; Beyerlin, *Near Eastern Religious Texts*, 28.

460. King and Stager, *Life in Biblical Israel*, 43–4; R. G. Hall, "Circumcision," *ABD*, 1:1025.

461. J. Sasson, "Circumcision in the ANE," *JBL* (1966): 474.

462. See Weinfeld, *Deuteronomy 1–11*, 438 for references. (*CTA*, 64:11, 13, 26 = *KTU*, 3.1).

463. *ANET*, 164, 178; *CTA*, 17. v. 7–8; *RSP*, I, 47–48; II, 262–63; Weinfeld, *Deuteronomy 1–11*, 439–40.

464. M. H. Pope, "Seven, Seventh, Seventy," *IDB*, 4:294–95; *CML*, 4.vi. 46 notes the "seventy sons of Athirat"; 5.v.2; 6.i.18; 12.ii.49; *ARAB*, 242–43 for Mesopotamia.

465. *COS*, 2.37.

466. *COS*, 1.86; *CTA*, 6

467. *CML*, 63, 4. vi. 46.

468. Grimal, *Ancient Egypt*, 122, 138.

469. F. M. Labat, "Military Organization in Mesopotamia," *ABD*, 4:826–30.

470. King and Stager, *Life in Biblical Israel*, 86–87; Craigie, *Deuteronomy*, 210.

471. P. Monet, *Egypt and the Bible* (Philadelphia: Fortress, 1968), 83–84; Craigie, *Deuteronomy*, 210, n. 20.

472. *COS*, 1.48, 6.5; *ANET*, 433; C. J. Eyre, "The Agricultural Cycle, Farming, and Water Management," *CANE*, 177, 182–83.

473. *ANET*, 19.

474. Christensen, *Deuteronomy 1:1–21:9*, 214–15.

475. King and Stager, *Life in Biblical Israel*, 86–92, for description of rainy seasons and agricultural year.

476. Greenberg, "Postulates," 336–37.

477. *ANET*, 257c, n. 18; 471, n. 9.

478. See also Assyrian Treaties; *VTE*, 528–31, 538–39, 543–44; Weinfeld, *Deuteronomy 1–11*, 448.

479. *ANET*, 281b.

480. Weinfeld, *Deuteronomy 1–11*, 450; M. Weinfeld, "The Extent of the Promised Land—The Status of Transjordan," in *Das Land Israel in biblischer Zeit*, ed. G. Strecker (Göttingen: Vandenhoeck & Ruprecht, 1983), 59–75.

481. McCarthy, *Treaty and Covenant*, 169.

482. A. Zertal, "Has Joshua's Altar Been Found on Mt. Ebal?" *BAR* 11/1 (1985): 40–43.

483. Provan, Long, and Longman, *Biblical History*, 185–87.

484. A. Kempinski, "Joshua's Altar—An Iron Age I Watchtower," *BAR* 12/1 (1986): 42, 44–49; Dever, *What Did the Biblical Writers Know and When?* 114.

485. A. Zertal, "Ebal," *ABD*, 2:255–58; esp. see full bibliography, 258.

486. Mazar, *Archaeology of the Land of the Bible*, 349–50.

487. H. F. Vos, "Gerizim," *ISBE*, 2:448–49; R. G. Boling, *BA* 32 (1969): 82–103; Mazar, *Archaeology*, 178, 206, esp. 211–12, 376; R. Hess, "Shechem," *NIDOTTE*, 4:1214.

488. R. Westbrook, "Riddles in Deuteronomic Law," in *Bundesdokument und Gesetz* (New York: Herer, 1995), 4:159–62, 174.

489. *COS*, 1.80, 1, 25–35, 40.

490. Zevit, *Religions of Ancient Israel*, 252, n. 205.

491. See Craigie, *Deuteronomy*, 216, nn. 3–4.

492. *COS*, 1.158, 182.

493. *COS*, 1.57, A iii 28–34.

494. *COS*, 1.25, III.

495. S. Ackerman, *Under Every Green Tree* (Atlanta: Scholars Press, 1992), 189; Beyerlin, *Near Eastern Religious Texts*, 260–61, n. p.

496. E. C. LaRocca-Pitts, *Of Wood and Stone: The Significance of Israelite Cultic Items in the Bible and Its Early Interpreters* (HSM 61; Winona Lake, Ind.: Eisenbrauns, 2001), 180–83.

497. Del Olmo Lete, *Canaanite Religion*, 1–42; Larocca-Pitts, *Wood and Stone*, 180–83.

498. S. Richter, *The Deuteronomic History and the Name Theology* (BZAW 318; Berlin: de Gruyter, 2002), 41–42.

499. Ibid., 1–39, 207–17.

500. S. D. Sperling, "Blood," *ABD*, 1:761.

501. *UT*, 385.

502. *ANET*, 299b.

503. *ANET*, 102; T. H. Gaster, "Sacrifice," *IDB*, 4:149–50.

504. *COS*, 1.111, 6:5–9, 30–39; T. Abusch, "Blood in Israel and Mesopotamia," in *Emmanuel: Studies in Hebrew Bible, Septuagint, and Dead Sea Scrolls in Honor of Emmanuel Tov*, ed. S. M. Paul et al, (VTSup 94; Leiden: Brill, 2003), 680–94.

505. *COS*, 1.130, 205–14.

506. Abusch, "Blood in Israel and Mesopotamia," 675–84; E. E. Carpenter, "Sacrifice and Offering in the Old Testament," *ISBE*, 4:271–72; D. J. McCarthy, "The Symbolism of Blood and Sacrifice," *JBL* 88 (1969): 166–76; idem, "Further Notes on the Symbolism of Blood and Sacrifice," *JBL* 92 (1973): 205–10.

507. Green, *Role of Human Sacrifice*, 201–3.

508. Heider, *Cult of Molek*, 210, 222.

509. Ibid., 196–203.

510. Cross, "Some Old and New Texts Relating to Child Sacrifice," in *Scripture and Other Artifacts*, ed. M. D. Coogan, J. C. Exum, and L. E. Stager (Louisville: John Knox, 1994), 93–103.

511. van der Toorn, "Theology, Priests, Worship," *CANE*, 2054.

512. Heider, *Molek*, 210, 220–22.

513. *ANET*, 495.

514. Cf. Kitchen, *Reliability*, 387; Saggs, *Greatness*, 344–45, 364–65, 393–94.

515. Weinfeld, *Deuteronomy 1–11*, 101.

516. M. Weinfeld, "Ancient Near Eastern Patterns in Prophetic Literature," in *Prophecy in the Hebrew Bible*, ed. D. E. Orton (Leiden: Brill, 2000), 84.

517. *COS*, 2.36, 158.

518. Weinfeld, *Deuteronomic School*, 92–94.

519. B. Levinson, "But You Shall Surely Kill Him! The Text-Critical and Neo-Assyrian Evidence for MT Deuteronomy 13:10," in *Bundesdokument und Gesetz: Studien zum Deuteronomium*, ed. G. Braulik (Freiburg: Herder, 1995), 37–64.

520. Ibid., 38–40, 54–60, esp. 58–60.

521. *ANET*, 533–41.

522. COS, 1.72, Law 6.

523. COS, 1.166, l. 246.

524. COS, 2:28, I, A, 14b–35; aII, C, 15–17.

525. Parpola and Watanabe, *Neo-Assyrian Treaties*, 5.

526. Ibid., 12.

527. COS, 1.86, viii:1–32.

528. For a discussion of animals in this list see B. Hesse, "Animal Husbandry and Human Diet in the Ancient Near East," *CANE*, 203–22.

529. COS, 1.19; 1.20; *ANET*, 10.

530. COS, 1.33 (line 9/16).

531. Hoffmeier, *Sinai*, 230–33, suggests that the absence of pigs/pig bones in Israelite areas suggests an Egyptian origin for Israel.

532. E. Firmage, "Zoology," *ABD*, 6:1132.

533. J. C. Moyer, "Hittite and Israelite Cultic Practices: A Selected Comparison," in *Scripture in Context II: More Essays on the Comparative Method*, ed. W. W. Hallo, J. C. Moyer, and L. G. Perdue (Winona Lake, Ind.: Eisenbrauns, 1983), 29–33; J. Sasson, "Isaiah LXVI 3–4a," *VT* 26 (1976): 199–207.

534. B. J. Collins, "Animals in the Religions of Ancient Anatolia," in *History of the Animal World in the Ancient Near East*, ed B. J. Collins (Leiden: Brill, 2002), 323.

535. Firmage, "Zoology," 6:1132.

536. *ANET*, 351.

537. B. J. Collins, "Animal Sacrifice in Ancient Mesopotamian Religion," in *History of the Animal World in the Ancient Near East*, 392–93; W. G. Lambert, *Babylonian Wisdom Literature* (Oxford: Clarendon, 1960), 215.

538. *ANET*, 10, 351; Craigie, *Deuteronomy*, 231–32; Kitchen, *Reliability*, 230, 552, n. 165 and refs.

539. Kitchen, *Reliability*, 230; 552, n. 165; S. Ahituv, "The Origins of Ancient Israel—The Documentary Evidence," in *Origins of Early Israel*, 138; I. Finkelstein and N. A. Silberman, *The Bible Unearthed* (New York: Free Press, 2001), 72–168.

540. B. Hesse, "Animal Husbandry and Human Diet in the Ancient Near East," *CANE*, 215; Younger, "Early Israel," 195.

541. M. Maimonides, *The Guide for the Perplexed*, 2nd rev. ed., trans. M. Friedländer (New York: Dover, 1956), 371; P. Craigie, *Ugarit and the Old Testament* (Grand Rapids: Eerdmans, 1983), 74–76.

542. Craigie, *Deuteronomy*, 233, n. 19; cf. J. Milgrom, "An Archaeological Myth Destroyed," *BR* 1/3 (1985): 48–55; C. J. Labuschagne, "You Shall Not Boil a Kid in Its Mother's Milk," in *The Scriptures and the Scrolls*, ed. F. Garcia Martinez, A. Hilhorst, and C.J. Labuschagne (VTSup 49; Leiden: Brill, 1992): 6–17.

543. Milgrom, "An Archaeological Myth Destroyed," 48–55; Craigie, *Deuteronomy*, 232, nn. 17–18.

544. *ANET*, 19–20; J. Schäfers, "Zu Ex. 23, 19," *BZ* 7 (1909): 16.

545. Schäfers, "Zu Ex 23,19," 16.

546. *CML*, 23.14, plus n. 11.

547. Cf. Christensen, *Deuteronomy 1:1–21:9*, 293.

548. G. F. Hasel, "Sabbath," *ABD*, 5:850–51; C. J. H. Wright, "Sabbatical Year," *ABD*, 5:857.

549. Westbrook, *HANEL*, 1083.

550. Ibid.

551. Westbrook, *Biblical and Cuneiform Law*, 11–12.

552. *ANET*, 526.

553. M. Weinfeld, *Social Justice in Ancient Israel and in the Ancient Near East* (Minneapolis: Fortress, 1995), 30.

554. Greengus, "Bible and Ancient Near Eastern Law," *ABD*, 4:251.

555. R. Westbrook, *Property and the Family in Biblical Law* (Sheffield: Sheffield Academic Press, 1991), 45.

556. J. J. M. Roberts, "The Bible and the Literature of the Ancient Near East," in *The Bible and the Ancient Near East* (Winona Lake, Ind.: Eisenbrauns, 2002), 46; more cautiously on all of this see W. Hallo, "New Moons and Sabbaths," *HUCA* 48 (1977): 13–14, n. 68.

557. Hallo, "New Moons," 16–17.

558. Westbrook, *Biblical and Cuneiform Law*, 15.

559. COS, 1.162.

560. Weinfeld, *Social Justice*, 45–46.

561. Ibid., 47–49.

562. COS, 1.38, l. 273.

563. See esp. N. Lohfink, "Poverty in the Laws of the Ancient Near East and of the Bible," *TS* 52 (1991): 34–37, 49–50; F. C. Fensham, "Widow, Orphan, and the Poor in Ancient Near Eastern Legal and Wisdom Literature," *JNES* 21 (1962): 129–39.

564. *ANET*, 170–71.

565. *ANET*, 170–71b; cf. Coogan, Exum, and Stager, *Scripture and Other Artifacts*, 208.

566. Craigie, *Deuteronomy*, 239, n. 16.

567. R. Yaron, "The Middle Assyrian Laws and the Bible," *Bib* 51 (1970): 555.

568. Westbrook, *Property and the Family in Biblical Law*, 161; see also C. Chirichigno, *Debt-Slavery in Israel and the Ancient Near East* (Sheffield: Sheffield Academic Press, 1993).

569. V. Hurowitz, "'His Master Shall Pierce His Ear with an Awl' (Exodus 21:6)—Marking Slaves in the Bible in the Light of Akkadian Sources," *American Academy for Jewish Research* 58 (1992): 47–77.

570. Ibid., 68–77; for text and translation see E. Ebeling, "Eine assyrische Beschwörung, um einen entflohen Sklaven zurückzubringen," *Or* 23 (1954): 52–56; cf. R. Yaron, *The Laws of Eshnunna*, 2nd ed (Leiden: Brill, 1969), 162–65.

571. *ANET*, 177; Rendsburg, *Bible and the Ancient Near East*, 156–57.

572. COS, 2.15, Law 9.

573. COS, 2.131, Laws 280–81.

574. *ANET*, 331–33, 344.

575. F. Rochberg-Halton, "Calendars," *ABD*, 1:810, 817; B. M. Bokser, "Unleavened Bread and Passover," *ABD*, 6:755; J. C. Vanderkam, "Festival of

Weeks," *ABD*, 6:895; Chavalas and Younger, *Mesopotamia and the Bible*, 238.

576. E. Nordoni, *Rise Up, O Judge*, trans. S. C. Martin (Peabody, Mass.: Hendrickson, 2004), 17–18.

577. *ANET*, 35. In a negative confession of sins many of them are injustices that would be included in this discussion.

578. Nordoni, *Rise Up*, 7; cf. also Weinfeld, *Social Justice*, 45–56, 152–78, for all notes on Nordoni.

579. Ibid., 6–10.

580. Ibid., 11.

581. Ibid., 12.

582. Ibid., 23–24, 26.

583. Ibid., 27–36.

584. Ibid., 29.

585. Ibid., 37–38.

586. *ANET*, 151, 153.

587. Craigie, *Deuteronomy*, 249.

588. W. Horowitz and V. Hurowitz, "Urim and Thummim in Light of a Psephomancy Ritual from Assur (LKA 137)," *JNES* 24 (1992): 102, n. 22.

589. *COS*, 2.155, A.i.14.

590. Scurlock, "Animal Sacrifice," 391.

591. Ibid., 391.

592. *COS*, 1.103, *CTA*, 17, 5:3–33.

593. B. S. Easton, "Gate," *ISBE*, 2:408–9; Hoffmeier and Millard, eds., *Future of Biblical Archaeology*, 35–36.

594. R. de Vaux, *Ancient Israel* (New York: McGraw Hill, 1965), 1:152, 155–57; King and Stager, *Life in Biblical Israel*, 234–36.

595. Ibid., 234. See p. 235 for a picture of a gate at Gaza.

596. *COS*, 1.123.

597. E. A. Speiser, "Coming and Going at the City Gate," in *Oriental and Biblical Studies*, ed. J. J. Finkelstein and M. Greenberg (Philadelphia: Univ. of Pennsylvania Press, 1967), 83–88.

598. T. H. Blomquist, *Gates and Gods* (Stockholm: Almquist & Wiksell, 1999), 15–18.

599. R. Yaron, "The MA Laws and the Bible," *Bib* 51 (1970): 552–53; *ANET*, 180–81, 183, 190; cf. *COS*, 2.132, Law 41.

600. See esp. Kitchen, *Reliability*, 96, for a summary of the results of kingship at key cities and nations.

601. Kitchen, *Ancient Orient*, 158–59; idem, *Reliability*, 95–96.

602. P. Dutcher-Walls, "The Circumscription of the King: Deuteronomy 17:16–17 in Its Ancient Social Context," *JBL* 121 (2002): 601–16.

603. J. Baines, "Ancient Egyptian Kingship," in *King and Messiah in Israel and the Ancient Near East*, ed. J. Day (Sheffield: Sheffield Academic Press, 1998), 16–53; W. G. Lambert, "Kingship in Ancient Mesopotamia," in *King and Messiah*, 54–70, esp. 69.

604. *ANET*, 593, II A; Lambert, *Babylonian Wisdom Literature*, 163.

605. *ANET*, 617b, ll. 365–70; cf. COS, 1.166, Introd. n. 5.

606. R. J. Leprohon, "Royal Ideology/State Administration in Egypt," *CANE*, 274, 395.

607. J. N. Postgate, "Royal Ideology and State Administration in Sumer and Akkad," *CANE*, 2359.

608. M. Liverani, "The Deeds of Ancient Mesopotamian Kings," *CANE*, 2360.

609. Kuhrt, *The Ancient Near East*, 358–59, 507, 604, 676.

610. Ibid., 46, 112, 262–3; *ANET*, 298, 654.

611. Kuhrt, *Ancient Near East*, 175–76, 179–82.

612. Ibid., 372.

613. Ibid., 332–48, 374–80.

614. Ibid., 576–89. See table 31, 576.

615. Collins, *Animal World*, 291.

616. Ibid., 370.

617. King and Stager, *Life in Biblical Israel*, 186–87.

618. Firmage, "Zoology," 6:1136.

619. *COS*, 1.106.

620. B. J. Collins, "The Puppy in Hittite Ritual," *JCS* 42 (1990): 211–26.

621. D. F. Morgan, "Horse," *ISBE*, 2:760.

622. See Kitchen, *Reliability*, 115–16, for a discussion and further resources.

623. King and Stager, *Life in Biblical Israel*, 114–15.

624. Kuhrt, *Ancient Near East*, 251.

625. Ibid., 267–68.

626. Ibid., 293–95, 324.

627. Ibid., 352.

628. Ibid., 466, 482, 485, 526, 529, 543.

629. Kitchen, *Reliability*, 134.

630. Kuhrt, *Ancient Near East*, 69–70.

631. Millard, *Treasures*, 49.

632. Kuhrt, *Ancient Near East*, 68–69. See texts cited there.

633. Trevor Bryce, *Letters of the Great Kings of the Ancient Near East: The Royal Correspondence of the Late Bronze Age* (New York: Routledge, 2003).

634. R. S. Hess, "Literacy in Iron Age Israel," in *Windows*, 83–85; Hess establishes the widespread evidence of writing in pre-Israelite Canaan into Iron I-Iron II.

635. Ibid., 86–95; so also A. Millard, "Knowledge of Writing in Iron Age Palestine," *TynBul* 46 (1995): 207–17.

636. Hallo, "Compare and Contrast," 8, 17, n. 10.

637. Tadmor and Weinfeld, *History, Historiography and Interpretation*, 30–32; for literacy and writing in the ancient Near East, see H. Vanstiphout, "Memory and Literacy in Ancient Western Asia," *CANE*, 2183, 2211; Kitchen, *Reliability*, 295–99, 304–6; B. Sass, *The Genesis of the Alphabet and its Development in the Second Millennium B.C.* (Wiesbaden: Harrassowitz, 1988), 51–105.

638. *ANET*, 412–14.

639. *COS*, 1.47.

640. *COS*, 1.36; *ANET*, 418–19.

641. *COS*, 1.35; *ANET*, 414–18.

642. *COS*, 1.177.

643. For convenient summaries of theology, priests, and worship in Egypt, Mesopotamia, Hatti, Anatolia, Canaan, and Israel respectively, see *CANE*, 1731, 1857, 1981, 2034.

644. H. te Velde, "Theology, Priests, and Worship in Ancient Egypt," *CANE*, 1731–32.

645. Ibid., 1735; Hoffmeier, *Sinai*, 29–30, nn. 68–70.

646. D. Doxey, "Priesthood," *OEAE*, 373.

647. F. A. M. Wiggerman, "Theology, Priests, and Worship in Ancient Mesopotamia," *CANE*, 1864.

648. A. Berlejung, "Washing the Mouth," 45–72.
649. Wiggerman, "Worship in Ancient Mesopotamia," 1865.
650. G. McMahon, "Theology, Priests, and Worship in Ancient Mesopotamia," *CANE*, 1990; Kitchen, *Reliability*, 280–81. See notes for further discussion and information for priests in Hittite culture.
651. J. Milgrom, "The Shared Custody of the Tabernacle and a Hittite Analogy," *JAOS* 90 (1970): 204–9; cf. J. C. Moyer, "Hittite and Israelite Cultic Practices: A Selected Comparison," in *Scripture in Context* II, ed. W. W. Hallo, J. C. Moyer, and L. G. Perdue (Winona Lake, Ind.: Eisenbrauns, 1983), 19–38.
652. K. van der Toorn, "Theology, Priests, and Worship in Canaan and Ancient Israel," *CANE*, 2052; Saggs, *Greatness*, 345–58.
653. van der Toorn, "Theology, Priests, and Worship in Canaan and Ancient Israel," 2052.
654. Millard, "La prophétie," 139–41.
655. Kitchen, *Reliability*, 386. See n. 27 for sources.
656. *COS*, 1.45, 20–71; *AEL*, 1:140.
657. *AEL*, 1:217–20.
658. *AEL*, 1:211; Kitchen, *Reliability*, 387, 394. See 584 and notes for original sources.
659. P. Barmash, *Homicide in the Biblical World* (Cambridge: Cambridge Univ. Press, 2005), 44, 46, 50.
660. *COS*, 2:119, 409.
661. *COS*, 2.19, Laws 1–2.
662. R. Haase, "Hittite," *HANEL*, 644.
663. *COS*, 1.131, Law 153; see Westbrook, "Old Babylonian Period," *HANEL*, 414, for more examples (e.g., at Nippur murder trial; Rim Sin).
664. T. Frymer-Kenski, "Israel," *HANEL*, 1031; Craigie, *Deuteronomy*, 268.
665. A. L. Oppenheim, *Ancient Mesopotamia*, rev. ed. (Chicago: Univ. of Chicago Press, 1977), 123, 197; Kitchen, *Reliability*, 293–94; *COS*, 1:529.
666. *COS*, 2.119, Law 169.
667. *COS*, 2.135.
668. *ANET*, 422, ll. 11–17.
669. Hammurabi Law 3; Chavalas and Younger Jr., *Mesopotamia and the Bible*, 159; Roth, *Law Collections*, 81.
670. *COS*, 2.131, Law 1; 2.154, Law 17.
671. *COS*, 2.154, Law 28.
672. *ANET*, 175b, n. 134; Roth, *Law Collections*, 120–21.
673. Greengus, "Law," 4:248.
674. Ibid.; cf. *COS*, 2:348.
675. *COS*, 2.19, Law 7.
676. *COS*, 2:153, Law 18.
677. Kang, *Divine War*, 42–43.
678. *COS*, 3.2, 17.2; *ANET*, 476.
679. Kang, *Divine War*, 42–43, 108–10; for a "Hittite Ritual Before Battle," see *ANET*, 354–55; I. Eph'al, "On Warfare and Military Contol in the ANE Empires: A Research Outline," in *History and Historiography*, 88–106; see further A. C. Schulman, "Military Organization in Pharonic Egypt," *CANE*, 289–301, 413–22, 545–54; King and Stager, *Life in Biblical Israel*, 223–58; P. Craigie, "Idea of War," *ISBE*, 4:1018–19.
680. Kang, *Divine War*, 42–43, 108–10.
681. *ANET*, 48; Craigie, *Deuteronomy*, 273, n. 13.
682. *COS*, 1.171, 54.
683. R. H. Beal, "Hittite Military Organization," *CANE*, 545.
684. Ibid., 552.
685. *COS*, 1.88.
686. Ibid., 552.
687. Ibid., 553.
688. S. Dalley, "Ancient Mesopotamian Military Organization," *CANE*, 413, esp. 419–20; A. R. Schulman, "Military Organization in Pharonic Egypt," *CANE*, 289–99.
689. Dalley, "Military Organization," 419.
690. King and Stager, *Life in Biblical Israel*, 103–12.
691. *ANET*, 239–40; cf. *COS*, 2.2A, 90–94a; 2.2B, 8b–16a; 2.113C, 1–27.
692. M. Hasel, *Military Practice and Polemic: Israel's Laws of Warfare in Near Eastern Perspecive* (Berrien Springs, Mich.: Andrews Univ. Press, 2005), 112–13.
693. Ibid., 104–28.
694. *COS*, 2:267.
695. *COS*, 2:107.
696. *ANET*, 167b, Laws 23–24; *COS*, 2.19.
697. del Olmo Lete, *Canaanite Religion*, 335.
698. *CML*, 19.4.163–9; *UT*, 1 Aqht, 1148–68; Craigie, *Deuteronomy*, 278, n. 1.
699. C. Gordon, "Biblical Customs and the Nuzu Tablets," in *The Biblical Archaeological Reader*, ed. D. N. Freedman and E. F. Campbell (ASOR; Missoula, Mont.: Scholars Press, 1975), 31.
700. D. Wright, "Deuteronomy 21:1–9 as a Rite of Elimination," *CBQ* 49 (1987): 398, 401–2.
701. Ibid., 401–2.
702. See also N. Na'aman, "Amarna Letters," *ABD*, 2:177a.
703. Westbrook, *Biblical and Cuneiform Law*, 24, n. 75; J. Nougayrol et al., *Ugaritica* V, vol. 16, Text 27, 95–7, ll. 45–50, in *Mission of Ras Shamra* 80 (Paris: Imprimerie Nationale, 1968).
704. King and Stager, *Life in Biblical Israel*, 47–48 for discussion.
705. *COS*, 2.36, 30–32.
706. *COS*, 2.131, Laws 168–69.
707. J. Tigay, *Deuteronomy* (JPS Torah; Philadelphia: Jewish Publication Society, 1976), 196–97; for texts see D. Marcus, "Juvenile Delinquency in the Bible and the Ancient Near East," *JANESCU* 13 (1981): 31–52.
708. R. P. Carroll, "Rebellion and Dissent in Ancient Israelite Society," *ZAW* 89 (1977): 176–204; P. R. Calloway, "Deut. 21:18: Proverbial Wisdom and Law," *JBL* 103 (1984): 341–52.
709. *COS*, 1.167; 1.168.
710. *ANET*, 288d.
711. *ANET*, 662.
712. T. Abusch, "Ghost and God: Some Observations on a Babylonian Understanding of Human Nature," in *Self, Soul and Body in Religious Experience*, ed. A. I. Baumgarten (Leiden: Brill, 1998), 373–77.
713. van der Toorn, *Family Religion in Babylonia, Syria and Israel*, 55, 60–61.

714. Craigie, *Deuteronomy*, 285, n. 25; Fish, "War and Religion in Ancient Mesopotamia," *BJRL* 23 (1939): 397.

715. J. H. Tigay, "Archaeological Notes on Deuteronomy," in *Pomegranates and Golden Bells*, ed. D. P. Wright, D. N. Freedman, and A. Hurowitz (Winona Lake, Ind.: Eisenbrauns, 1995), 37–40.

716. COS, 2:113, Law 71.

717. *ANET*, 166d, n. 45; cf. Laws 6–13, 22–23, 25, 259–60, 265.

718. Parker, *Ugaritic Poetry*, 77; *CAT*, 1.19, 43–46.

719. R. Harris, "Inanna-Ishtar as Paradox and a Coincidence of Opposites," in *Gender and Aging in Mesopotamia* (Norman, Okla.: Univ. of Oklahoma Press, 2000), 160, 163.

720. Ibid., 166.

721. Moyer, "Cultic Practices," 27–29.

722. COS, 2.31, i.13–ii.9 for use of spindle as sign of womanhood.

723. COS, 1.86, *CTA*, 4, ii 3.

724. COS, 1.65, Law 8; 1.66, Law 9; Craigie, *Deuteronomy*, 288, nn. 5–6; for expanded bibliography see COS, 1, 232.

725. See King and Stager, *Life in Biblical Israel*, 272, for a description of women's dress.

726. Lambert, *Babylonian Wisdom Literature*, 226, 239.

727. COS, 2.130; *ANET*, 163.

728. Westbrook, *Biblical and Cuneiform Law*, 70–71.

729. COS, 2.19; *ANET*, 189; King and Stager, *Life in Biblical Israel*, 35.

730. King and Stager, *Life in Biblical Israel*, 66; L. E. Stager and S. R. Wolff, "Production and Commerce in Temple Courtyards: An Olive Press in the Sacred Precinct at Tel Dor," *BASOR* 243 (1981): 93–101, 243.

731. J. Milgrom, *Leviticus* (AB; New York: Doubleday, 2000), 3:1662–63.

732. COS, 2.19, Law 166.

733. COS, 2.152, also n. 12; Milgrom, *Leviticus*, 1662–63.

734. Milgrom, *Leviticus*, 1662.

735. King and Stager, *Life in Biblical Israel*, 147, 151.

736. Ibid., 151, n. 92; M. Haran, *Temples and Temple-Service in Ancient Israel* (Winona Lake, Ind.: Eisenbrauns, 1985), 160–62.

737. King and Stager, *Life in Biblical Israel*, 261 (pict.), 268–69.

738. COS, 3.119. See nn. 4–5 for a discussion of another way of reading the key line. The following references are helpful, but not directly relevant to the issue of virginity: COS, 1.98; 1.106, 2:5–6; 2.19, Law 188; 2.36, 20–34; 2.131, Law 141; 2.153, Law 22, 3.3, 23–26; H. A. Hoffner Jr., "Legal and Social Institutions of Hittite Anatolia," *CANE*, 555–69.

739. Roth, *Law Collections*, 33, Law 33.

740. J. S. Cooper, "Virginity in Ancient Mesopotamia," in *Sex and Gender in the Ancient Near East: Proceedings of the 47th Rencontre Assyriologique Internationale*, ed. S. Parpola and R. M. Whiting (Part 1; Helsinki: The Neo-Assyrian Text Corpus Project, 2002), 91–112.

741. M. Stol, "Private Life in Mesopotamia," *CANE*, 490.

742. See also Hammurabi Law 30; *ANET*, 162, 171; E. A. Goodfriend, "Adultery," *ABD*, 1:82–83.

743. Westbrook, *Biblical and Cuneiform Law*, 87–88.5, n. 3, and literature there.

744. J. Rabinowitz, "The 'Great Sin' in Ancient Egyptian Marriage Contracts," *JNES* 18 (1959): 73; W. Moran, "The Scandal of the 'Great Sin' at Ugarit," *JNES* 18 (1959): 280–81; Craigie, *Deuteronomy*, 305, n. 3.

745. Chavalas and Younger Jr., *Mesopotamia and the Bible*, 159; *ANET*, 171d, Law 129.

746. COS, 2.132, Laws 12–13; for a succinct summary of adultery in the Old Testament/ancient Near East, see Greengus, "Law," *ABD*, 4:247.

747. Hoffner, "Social Institutions," *CANE*, 557–58.

748. G. Pinch, "Private Life in Ancient Egypt," *CANE*, 376.

749. COS, 2.130, Law 28.

750. Phillips, "Adultery," 19; Greenberg, "Postulates," 337–38.

751. Marsman, *Women in Ugarit*, 168–77; 710–11; J. P. Vita, "The Society of Ugarit," in *Handbook of Ugaritic Studies*, ed. W. G. E. Watson and N. Wyatt (Leiden: Brill, 1999), 476–77.

752. *ANET*, 196–97; for discussion of rape in ancient Near East see Greengus, "Law," *ABD*, 4:247. See also Hoffner, "Social Institutions," *CANE*, 557–58.

753. COS, 2.131, Law 130.

754. COS, 2.131, Law 6.

755. *ANET*, 185; cf. relevant laws listed on 181b also.

756. COS, 2.130, Law 26.

757. COS, 2.131, Laws 130, 141; 2.132, Law 12; see also Middle Assyrian laws (ca. 15th century B.C.); see COS, 2.132, Law 55; *ANET*, 162.

758. COS, 2.19, Law 199.

759. V. P. Hamilton, "Marriage," *ABD*, 4:560–62; King and Stager, *Life in Biblical Israel*, 60.

760. COS, 3.59, n. 16; P. B. van Alfen, "Filthy Lucre," *Archaeology Odyssey* 7/5 (Sept/Oct 2004): 6–7.

761. See further *ANET*, 525–26; Greengus, "Law," *ABD*, 4:247.

762. Greengus, "Law," *ABD*, 4:250–51.

763. *ANET*, 172, Law 57; 196, Law 189.

764. *ANET*, 172, Law 190; but cf. COS, 2.158, Law 158.

765. H. A. Hoffner Jr., "Ancient Israel's Literary Heritage Compared with Hittite Textual Data," in *The Future of Biblical Archaeology*, ed. J. K. Hoffmeier and Alan Millard (Grand Rapids: Eerdmans, 2004), 188.

766. D. Christensen, *Deuteronomy 21:10–34:12* (WBC; Nashville: Nelson, 2002), 538, 543; also J. Tigay as noted, 538.

767. COS, 1.93, n. 17.

768. *ANET*, 167; Rendsburg, *Bible and the Ancient Near East*, 156; Greengus, "Law," 4:250–51.

769. COS, 2.82, 19b–20; *ANET*, 201, 204b.

770. *ANET*, 531, Law 3; Chavalas and Lawson, *Mesopotamia and the Bible*, 214; Richard Hess, "Alalakh Studies and the Bible: Obstacle or Contribution," in *Scripture and Other Artifacts*, ed. M. D. Coogan, J. C. Exum, and L. E. Stager (Louisville: John Knox, 1994), 201.

771. C. Tigay, *Deuteronomy*, 481, who holds that the prostitutes in vv. 17–18 are common prostitutes.
772. E. A. Goodfriend, "Prostitution (OT)," *ABD*, 5:506; *ANET*, 160, Law 27; 183–85, Laws 40, 49, 52; cf. *ANET*, 170, Law 117.
773. Goodfriend, "Prostitution," 5:507, 511.
774. Ibid., 511; K. van der Toorn, "Female Prostitution in Payment of Vows in Ancient Israel," *JBL* 108 (1989): 193–95, 199; cf. Marsman, *Women in Ugarit*, 598–99.
775. Marsman, *Women in Ugarit*, 497–501; Brenner, *The Israelite Woman* (Sheffield: JSOT, 1994).
776. P. Bird, "The End of The Male Cult Prostitute: A Literary Historical and Sociological Analysis of Hebrew *qādēš, qᵃdēšim*," in *Congress Volume: Cambridge 1995*, ed. J. A. Emerton (VTSup 65; Leiden: Brill, 1997), 37, 40, 43–44, 74–75.
777. Craigie, *Deuteronomy*, 301, n. 22.
778. Rendsburg, *Bible and the Ancient Near East*, 160.
779. King and Stager, *Life in Biblical Israel*, 83.
780. Goodfriend, "Prostitution," 5:506.
781. P. Maloney, "Usury and Restrictions on Interest-Taking in the Ancient Near East," *CBQ* 36 (1974): 1; King and Stager, *Life in Biblical Israel*, 20; R. J. Williams, "Interest," *ISBE*, 2:860–61.
782. Maloney, "Usury and Restrictions," 2; see 6–10 for laws (18A, 19–21).
783. Ibid., 12.
784. Ibid., 3.
785. *ANET*, 162, 168–70, Law 90.
786. Maloney, "Usury and Restrictions," 12–20, 22.
787. *ANET*, 168, Law 48.
788. H. Gamoran, "The Biblical Law against Loans on Interest," *JNES* 30 (1971): 127–34, esp. 30–31.
789. *COS*, 3.56; 3.57.
790. *ANET*, 629a, n. 73.
791. *COS*, 3.116.
792. R. Westbrook and R. Jasnow, eds., *Security and Debt in Ancient Near Eastern Law* (CHANE 9; Leiden: Brill, 2001), 1–5.
793. *COS*, 2.143.
794. Cartledge, *Vows in the Hebrew Bible and the Ancient Near East*, 73. See 73–136 for the ancient Near Eastern context of vows.
795. Cartledge, *Vows*, 134–36.
796. King and Stager, *Life in Biblical Israel*, 37; *ANET*, 48b.
797. Craigie, *Deuteronomy*, 306, n. 5.
798. *CML*, 84, ll. 100–102.
799. Westbrook, *Biblical and Cuneiform Law*, 21.
800. K. van der Toorn, "Mill, Millstone," *ABD*, 4:831; King and Stager, *Life in Biblical Israel*, 94–95; R. Amiran, "The Millstone and the Potter's Wheel," *EI* 4 (1956): 46–49 (Heb).
801. Westbrook, *HANEL*, 650; Christensen, *Deuteronomy 21:10–34:12*, 573; Craigie, *Deuteronomy*, 307.
802. Westbrook, *HANEL*, 421.
803. *COS*, 2.19, Laws 19–21.
804. Tigay, *Deuteronomy*, 224.
805. E. V. Hulse, "The Nature of Biblical 'Leprosy' and the Use of Alternative Medical Terms in Modern Translations of the Bible," *PEQ* 107 (1975): 87;

however, see W. Westendorf, *Handbuch der Altägyptischen Medizin* (HOS 630.1; Leiden: Brill, 1999), 311, for possible words used for it.
806. Ibid., 91; see also Milgrom, *Leviticus 1–16*, 817.
807. Hulse, "Biblical Leprosy," 104; Tigay, *Deuteronomy*, 224,
808. J. Scurlock and B. Andersen, *Diagnoses in Assyrian and Babylonian Medicine* (Urbana, Ill.: Univ. of Illinois Press, 2005), 70–73.
809. King and Stager, *Life in Biblical Israel*, 77–78 and nn. 75–78.
810. Craigie, *Deuteronomy*, 308, n. 15.
811. King and Stager, *Life in Biblical Israel*, 315; cf. 269; for text see *COS*, 3.41, 12–15; Baker and Arnold, *Face of Old Testament Studies*, 53.
812. A. Lemaire, *Textbook of Syrian Semitic Inscriptions* (Oxford: Clarendon, 1973), 1:29.
813. *COS*, 2.131, 273–74; M. A. Powell, "Weights and Measures," *ABD*, 6:897; A. E. Berriman, *Historical Metrology* (New York: Greenwood, 1969).
814. M. A. Powell Jr. and R. H. Sack, "Ancient Mesopotamia Weight Metrology: Methods, Problems and Perspectives," in *Studies in Honor of Tom B. Jones* (AOAT 203; Kevelaer: Neukirchen-Vluyn, 1999), 106, Table A.
815. Ibid., 83, 88.
816. *COS*, 2.131, Laws 273–274.
817. Westbrook, *Bible and Cuneiform Law*, 20, and n. 55.
818. *ANET*, 180, Law 1; *COS*, 2.19.
819. *ANET*, 182, Law 32; *COS*, 2.19; Yaron, "The Middle Assyrian Laws and the Bible," 551.
820. Greenberg, "Postulates," 344–45; Greengus, "Law," 4:249.
821. *KTU*, 1:40:18, 35–36; *RS*, 18.115; *PRU*, 4.158–59; Weinfeld, *Deuteronomy 1–11*, 308.
822. C. Van Houten, *The Alien in Israelite Law* (Sheffield: Sheffield Academic Press, 1991), 25.
823. *ANET*, 151a, 178a, 408d, 415c, 425c; in general see J. R. Spencer, "Sojourner," *ABD*, 4:250–51.
824. *COS*, 1.181, 45–50.
825. Van Houten, *The Alien*, 35.
826. Spencer, "Sojourner," 103; *COS*, 2.23, 14–18.
827. W. Fields, *Sodom and Gomorrah* (Sheffield: Sheffield Academic Press, 1997), 27–53.
828. Beyerlin, *Near Eastern Religious Texts*, 26.
829. *ANET*, 175; Roth, *Law Collections*, 121.
830. *ANET*, 183, 185–88; Roth, *Law Collections*, 167–69, 175, 178–81, 183–91.
831. *ANET*, 185; Roth, *Law Collections*, 175.
832. *COS*, 2.132, Law 40.
833. Craigie, *Deuteronomy*, 313, n. 5.
834. E. Firmage, "Zoology," 6:1136, 1129; B. J. Collins, *Animal World*, 105, 446.
835. *COS*, 2.152.
836. *COS*, 2.131.
837. Code of Hammurabi Laws 241–49; see *COS*, 2.131; cf. also 2.131, Laws 268–71.
838. *COS*, 3.121.
839. *ANEP*, 2nd ed., 89, 122, row 6; M. S. and J. L. Miller, *Encyclopedia of Bible Life* (New York: Harper, 1955), 19 (pictures 7–8); O. Borowski, *Agriculture in Iron Age Israel* (Winona Lake, Ind.: Eisenbrauns, 1987), 63–65.

840. J. M. Myers, "Sandals and Shoes," *IDB*, 4:213–14.

841. de Vaux, *Ancient Israel*, 1:169; cf. D. W. Manor, "A Brief History," 133; for refs. see E. A. Speiser, "Of Shoes and Shekels," *BASOR* 77 (1940): 15–17.

842. S. M. Olyan, "Honor, Shame, Covenant," *JBL* 115 (1996): 204, 207, 210, 218.

843. Craigie, *Deuteronomy*, 315–16, nn. 12–15.

844. *ANET*, 181; cf. 525, n. 24; the text for "eyes" or "nipples" is missing and must be restored. Cf. *COS*, 2.132, A#8.

845. In general see *COS*, 2.153, 135–49; King and Stager, *Life in Biblical Israel*, 195–98.

846. *COS*, 2.153, 135.

847. *ANET*, 423, Law 16.

848. *COS*, 2.12, col. 6, p. 60.

849. *COS*, 1.43, 2:104–10.

850. Saggs, *Greatness*, 292.

851. *COS*, 2.131, gap #x; Roth, *Law Collections*, 98.

852. *COS*, 1.117; cf. *COS*, 1.162, 140–44; *ANET*, 388b.

853. *COS*, 2.6, n. 5.

854. Kitchen, *Reliability*, 438; also H. Sader, *Les états araméens de Syrie* (Wiesbaden: Steiner, 1987).

855. K. A. Kitchen, "Arameans," *NBD*, 67–68; Chavalas and Younger, *Mesopotamia and the Bible*, 227, 230, 283; *POTW*, 207–30; *ANET*, 258–59; A. R. Millard, "Arameans," *ABD*, 1:348.

856. D. E. Fleming, "Genesis in History and Tradition: The Syrian Background of Israel's Ancestors, Reprise," in *The Future of Biblical Archaeology*, ed. J. K. Hoffmeier and A. Millard (Grand Rapids: Eerdmans, 2004), 229–30.

857. Ibid., 231.

858. G. Barkay, "A Bowl with the Hebrew Inscription קדש," *IEJ* 40 (1990): 124–29; cf. *COS*, 1.125, 31–52; Kitchen, *Reliability*, 416–17.

859. D. W. Thomas, *Documents from Old Testament Times* (New York: Harper & Row, 1958), 271.

860. *CML*, "Baal and Mot," 14–19, 68–81; *COS*, 1.86, 5.v.–6.ii. 1–21.

861. B. Schmidt, *Israel's Beneficent Dead* (FAT 11; Tübingen: Mohr, 1994), 26, 41, 121, 130; T. Lewis, *Cults of the Dead in Ancient Israel and Ugarit* (HSM 39; Atlanta: Scholars Press, 1989), 95–98.

862. *ANET*, 34–35.

863. *ANET*, 533–41.

864. McCarthy, *Treaty and Covenant*, 161–62, n. 54; see Hittite treaties further in *ANET*, 199–201.

865. Cf. McCarthy, *Treaty and Covenant*, 186.

866. *COS*, 1.169, 13–32.

867. T. Crawford, *Blessings and Curses in Syro-Palestinian Inscriptions of the Iron Age* (New York: Peter Lang, 1992), 2, 231.

868. Coogan, Exum, and Stager, *Scripture and Other Artifacts*, 117; King and Stager, *Life in Biblical Israel*, 304–5.

869. King and Stager, *Life in Biblical Israel*, 204–5.

870. J. R. Branton, "Writing," *IDB*, 4:915, 918–19.

871. Zertal, "Joshua's Altar," 26–43.

872. See Provan, Long, Longman III, *Biblical History of Israel*, 186, for discussion and evaluation.

873. Kempinski, "Iron Age I Watchtower," 42.

874. Kitchen, *Reliability*, 284; see also McCarthy for the flexibility of the ancient Near Eastern treaty/covenantal forms, *Treaty and Covenant*, chs. 7 (basic unity) and 8 (diversity).

875. H. F. Vos, "Ebal," "Gerizim," *ISBE*, 2:8, 448; Rasmussen, *NIV Atlas*, 18, 38.

876. M. Weinfeld, "Covenant Terminology in the Ancient Near East and Its Influence on the West," *JAOS* 93 (1973): 190–99; D. R. Hillers, *Treaty Curses and Old Testament Prophets* (Rome: Pontifical Biblical Institute, 1964); Beckman, *Diplomatic Texts*, 11–124; Kitchen, *Reliability*, 292–93, plus supporting notes on 563–64.

877. *COS*, 1.87, n. 20.

878. Beyerlin, *Near Eastern Religious Texts*, 37, n. o.

879. *COS*, 1.159, ll. 63–64.

880. *COS*, 2.131; *ANET*, 173b, Laws 154–58.

881. *ANET*, 196b; *COS*, 2.19, Law 189.

882. *ANET*, 196, Law 195; *COS*, 2.19.

883. *ANET*, 181, AL.A10; 185, B2.

884. H. A. Hoffner, "Legal and Social Institutions of Hittite Anatolia," *CANE*, 556.

885. Greengus, "Law," 4:29; see *ANET*, 189, 542 (homicide), 547 (homicide).

886. Christensen, *Deuteronomy 21:10–34:12*, 663.

887. *ANET*, 388b, "Hymn to the Sun God."

888. *COS*, 2.154, 36–48; *ANET*, 161.

889. *COS*, 2.131, 47–79; *ANET*, 201, 204–6.

890. For English translations of all of the ancient Near Eastern texts utilized in these notes see Kitchen, *Reliability*, 562, n. 104; cf. also McCarthy, *Treaty and Covenant*, 172–87, 301–8.

891. Kitchen, *Reliability*, 283–86; for color presentations see Kitchen, *BAR* 21/2 (1995): 54–55.

892. *ANET*, 201, 205–6.

893. Roberts, "Bible and Literature of ANE," 49.

894. *COS*, 1.99, xvii.

895. *ANET*, 539.

896. Craigie, *Deuteronomy*, 344 and nn. 20–24.

897. Ibid., 344, n. 24; *CML*, 119 (Aqhat 19:167); Fitzmeyer, *Aramaic Inscriptions*, 47 (I.A.39); *COS*, 1:1103, 151–68.

898. *ANET*, 179, vv. 26–27.

899. *COS*, 1.88.

900. *COS*, 1.166, 225–40, 260–64; 3.45X, 22–39.

901. *ANET*, 105; Craigie, *Deuteronomy*, 350, n. 33.

902. *ANET*, 538 (46–48); Craigie, *Deuteronomy*, 350, n. 33 and refs.

903. *COS*, 2.135, iv. 35-vi.16.

904. *COS*, 2.86, ll. 1–14.

905. *COS*, 2.86, *ANET*, 658; F. M. Cross and A. J. Saley, "Phoenician Incantations on a Plaque of the Seventh Century B.C. from Arslan Tash in Upper Syria," *BASOR* 197 (1970): 42–49.

906. *COS*, 1.15, 53–56.

907. *ANET*, 4; *COS*, 1.15, 53–56.

908. *ANET*, 538. Emphasis mine.

909. *COS*, 2.82, 35b–42; E. P. Deatrick, "Salt, Soil, Savior," *BA* 25 (1962): 45.

910. S. Gevirtz, "Jericho and Shechem: A Religio-Literary Aspect of City Destruction," *VT* 13 (1963): 52–62.

911. *ANET*, 294b–95.

912. *ANET*, 300.

913. *ANET*, 91b, 92d, 716, 726.

914. *ANET*, 926, ll. 2–6, xxiv.

915. *ANET*, 48c.

916. *COS*, 1.153, 2; *ANET*, 604a.

917. *COS*, 1.154.

918. *ANET*, 438d.

919. *ANET*, 93a, l. 10. Cf. Dan. 2 and 5.

920. *ANET*, 93a, ll. 25–26; 93, l. 4; *COS*, 1.132

921. *ANET*, 371; *COS*, 1.27; 1.28.

922. Ibid.

923. *COS*, 2,59, 2–6, Aramaic inscription (ca. 690 B.C.).

924. According to Memphite Theology; see *ANET*, 56; *COS*, 1.15, 57.

925. *COS*, 2.17A, 1v. 30–32; 2.17B, D iii. 5–6; 2.18, 25; 2.82, 6b–14a; Beyerlin, *Near Eastern Texts*, 248.

926. *COS*, 2.17B, A iv. 4–20.

927. *COS*, 1.56.

928. *COS*, 1.27, Prayers, 44b.

929. *ANET*, 265.

930. *ANET*, 414; A. Malamat, "Longevity: Biblical Concepts and Some ANE Parallels," *AfO* 19 (1982): 215–18.

931. *ANET*, 414b.

932. J. Klein, "The 'Bane' of Humanity: A Lifespan of One Hundred and Twenty Years," *Acta Sumerologica* 12 (1990): 57–70.

933. For general discussion, see J. G. Harris, "Old Age," *ABD*, 5:10–12.

934. Ibid., 10.

935. *ANET*, 312a.

936. *COS*, 2.123B, ii. 3–31. The kings before the flood in the Sumerian King List were attributed lives of thousands of years by the author.

937. R. E. Friedman, "The Tabernacle in the Temple," *BA* 43 (1980): 241–48; in support, M. Holman, *To Your Tents, O Israel! The Terminology, Function, Form, and Symbolism of Tents in the Hebrew Bible and the Ancient Near East* (Leiden: Brill, 2002), 170–77; *COS*, 1.135, 1st section.

938. V. A. Hurowitz, "The Form and Fate of the Tabernacle: Reflections on a Recent Proposal," *JQR* 86 (1995): 127–51; discussion in Hoffmeier, *Sinai*, 198–201.

939. R. Clifford, "The Tent of El and the Israelite Tent of Meeting," *CBQ* 33 (1971): 221–27; see n. 22 at Deut. 1:2; Smith, *The Early History of God*, 2–4.

940. J. Wilson, "The Assembly of the Phoenician City," *JNES* 4 (1945): 244–45.

941. Hoffmeier, *Sinai*, 208; M. Homan, "The Divine Warrior in His Tent: A Military Model for Yahweh's Tabernacle," *BR* 16 (2000): 22–33.

942. D. E. Fleming, "Mari's Large Public Tent and the Priestly Tent Sanctuary," *VT* 50 (2000): 484–94.

943. Weinfeld, *Social Justice*, 75–96, 175–79.

944. Coogan, Exum, and Stager, *Scripture and Other Artifacts*, 87–90.

945. van der Toorn, *Family Religion*, 48.

946. Ibid., 49–50.

947. Ibid., 55–58.

948. E. Bloch-Smith, *Judahite Burial Practices and Beliefs about the Dead* (Sheffield: Sheffield Academic Press, 1992), 149–51.

949. Foster, *Hymns, Prayers, and Songs*.

950. Beckman, *Diplomatic Texts*, 108, 114; Kitchen, *Reliability*, 288.

951. See further McCarthy's discussion of the basic unity of treaties compared to their evident diversity, *Treaty and Covenant*, chs. 7–8; see also chs. 3–6 for illustrations.

952. So S. Niditch, *Oral World and Written Word* (Louisville: Westminster John Knox, 1996), 86–87, 99–107, 104.

953. Ibid., 68.

954. Ibid., 166, for list of sources; for a cogent critique of her helpful but excessive claims see Hess, "Literacy in Iron Age Israel," 83.

955. Kitchen, *Reliability*, 304–5.

956. McCarthy, *Treaty and Covenant*, 102.

957. Ibid., 102–3 and n. 55.

958. Kramer, as quoted in D. R. Tasker, *Ancient Near Eastern Literature and the Hebrew Scriptures About The Fatherhood of God* (New York: Peter Lang, 2004), 28; emphasis mine.

959. For a thorough review of this fascinating topic see ibid., 28, 32, 48, 67, 86, 107, 204.

960. *COS*, 1.86, ii, n. 13.

961. *COS*, 2.21, 1–75, nn. 10–13; 2.31.

962. *COS*, 1:25, 149.

963. *COS*, 1:434, 436.

964. See M. S. Heiser, "Deuteronomy 32:8 and the Sons of God," *BibSac* 158 (2001): 54–74.

965. Ibid., 63, 69–70.

966. *ANET*, 134c; 1336; *UT*, 51 IV:50–1; VI:46; cf. D. Block, *The Gods of the Nations: Studies in ANE National Theology* (Winona Lake, Ind.: Eisenbrauns, 1988), 21–22; Machinist, "Distinctiveness," 434, n. 30; Craigie, *Deuteronomy*, 378, n. 18; Heiser, "Deuteronomy 32:8 and the Sons of God," 54.

967. Heiser, "Deuteronomy 32:8 and the Sons of God," 59–73.

968. *COS*, 1.123, ll. 35–36.

969. *COS*, 1.24; E. T. Mullen Jr., *The Divine Council in Canaanite and Early Hebrew Literature* (HSM 24; Missoula, Mont.: Scholars Press, 1980).

970. A. R. Millard, *Atrahasis: The Babylonian Story of the Flood* (Oxford: Clarendon, 1969), 43.

971. *COS*, 1.102, 123–36; *ANET*, "The Deluge," 34d, ll. 90–100.

972. Baal dies at Ugarit; Qingu dies in Babylon, both gods; see *COS*, 1.111, 6:30–39; *COS*, 1.86, 5:14–15.

973. *COS*, 1.22; 1.24.

974. *COS*, 1.111, 5.124–30; *ANET*, 502.

975. Beyerlin, *Near Eastern Religious Texts*, 267.

976. Christensen, *Deuteronomy 21:10–34:12*, 797; C. Wilcke, *Das Lugalbandae Epos* (Wiesbaden: Harrassowitz, 1969), 94–95; H. Vanstiphout, *Epics of Sumerian Kings* (Atlanta: Society of Biblical Literature, 2003).

977. *COS*, 1.131.

978. See Walton, Smith, and Chavalas, *IVPBBC-OT*, 205–6.

979. *COS*, 1.131, 2:140; 3:16.

980. *COS*, 1.131, 3:457a.

981. O. Keel, *Symbolism and the Bible* (New York: Seabury, 1978), 190–92; cf. Hoffmeier, *Sinai*, 213, 312; P. Houlihan and S. Goodman, *The Birds*

of Ancient Egypt (Cairo: American Univ. Press, 1986).

982. Saggs, Greatness, 487.

983. Von Soden, Ancient Orient, 199–200; COS 1.168.

984. Chavalas and Adamthwaite, "Archaeological Light," 93–94.

985. For protective spirits see F. A. M. Wiggerman, Mesopotamian Protective Spirits (Cuneiform Monographs 1; Groningen: Styx, 1992), 105–88, The Shedu is listed also as an evil demon represented by a human-headed bull in the Neo-Assyrian period, 219; Tigay, Deuteronomy, 306.

986. Oppenheim, Ancient Mesopotamia, rev. ed., 201.

987. J. Hoftizger and G. van der Kooij, Aramaic Texts from Deir ʿAlla (Leiden: Brill, 1976), 179–82; A. Lemaire, "Fragments from the Book of Balaam Found at Deir ʿAlla," BAR 11/5 (1985): 33–34.

988. Chavalas and Adamthwaite, "Archaeological Light," 92–94; Chavalas and Hostetter, "Epigraphic Light on the Old Testament," 46–47.

989. COS, 1.18, col. b, 28.

990. COS, 1.34.

991. COS, 1.113, 5:1–2.

992. Beyerlin, Near Eastern Religious Texts, 160–64; see COS, 2.82, Face C, ll. 23b–27 for additional example.

993. W. G. Lambert, "Three Unpublished Fragments of the Tukulti Ninurta Epic," AfO 18 (1957–58): 42–45; P. Machinist, "Literature as Politics: The Tukulti Ninurta Epic and the Bible," CBQ 38 (1976): 458; Niehaus, God at Sinai, 136–41.

994. Josephus, Against Apion I, trans. H. J. Thackeray (Cambridge, Mass.: Harvard Univ. Press, 1926), 65–79.

995. ANET, 305–7, 315–16; L. F. Hartman, The Book of Daniel (AB; Garden City, N.Y.: Doubleday, 1978), 190–92.

996. COS, 2:20.

997. Craigie, Deuteronomy, 384, nn. 44, 47.

998. COS, 2:156 (ca. 750 B.C.).

999. COS, 1.166, 260–64.

1000. McCarthy, Treaty and Covenant, 111.

1001. Rasmussen, NIV Atlas, 18, 24, 224, 246.

1002. A. J. Ferch, "Avarim," ABD, 1:6–7.

1003. ANET, 320; M. Piccirillo, "Mount Nebo," ABD, 4:1057.

1004. Rasmussen, NIV Atlas, 92; Aharoni and Avi-Yonah, Macmillan Bible Atlas, 46.

1005. R. L. Roth, "Hor," ABD, 3:287; Coogan, Exum, and Stager, Scripture and Other Artifacts, 90.

1006. G. I. Davies, "Wilderness Wanderings," ABD, 6:913; Rasmussen, NIV Atlas, 17, 18, 89.

1007. Green, Storm-God in the Ancient Near East, 258–59.

1008. Ibid., 266–69; cf. Craigie, Deuteronomy, 396, plus nn.

1009. Craigie, Deuteronomy, 393, n. 7; Rasmussen, NIV Atlas, 84, 89.

1010. Greenberg, "Ezekiel's Vision," in History, Historiography, and Interpretation, 162–63; ANEP, 536.

1011. COS, 2.47D, 1–2.

1012. CML, 64; Green, Storm-God in the Ancient Near East, 268.

1013. COS, 1.57, A iii 28–34; Green, Storm-God in the Ancient Near East, 268, for this and nn. 200–201.

1014. Beyerlin, Near Eastern Religious Texts, 166; I. Mendelsohn, "Urim and Thummim," IDB, 4:739–40; H. G. May, "Ephod and Ariel," AJSL 56 (1939): 44–69.

1015. Hallo, "Before Tea Leaves," 34, 37.

1016. C. Van Dam, The Urim and Thummim (Winona Lake, Ind.: Eisenbrauns, 1997), 45–80.

1017. Kitchen, Reliability, 294, plus n. 116; M. Weinfeld, "Covenant vs. Obligation," Bib 56 (1975): 120–28; cf. CAD N/2, 43, 44; CAD R, 353.

1018. Beyerlin, Near Eastern Religious Texts, 250–51; cf. COS, 1:306.

1019. COS, 2.4B; for a grammatical tie to "the loins of …" see Gibson, CML, 150.

1020. Green, Storm-God in the Ancient Near East, 267–68, n. 197.

1021. COS, 1.94, plus n. 2.

1022. Craigie, Deuteronomy, 397, n. 27; COS, 1.73.

1023. COS, 1.88, 26–36; King and Stager, Life in Biblical Israel, 32–33.

1024. COS, 2.4D.

1025. Craigie, Deuteronomy, 402, n. 47; Beyerlin, Near Eastern Religious Texts, 198, 210.

1026. CML, 43, 2:iv:6–10; COS, 1.86, iv. 7–20; 2:iv. 28–30.

1027. COS, 1.86, n. 56; 3:ii, 5.

1028. COS, 1.160, iv; Beyerlin, Near Eastern Religious Texts, 78–79.

1029. Christensen, Deuteronomy 21:10–34:12, prefers to read this as "their backs" (858, n. 29dd).

1030. J. T. Whitney, "Bamoth in the Old Testament," TynBul 30 (1979): 125–47; M. D. Fowler, "The Israelite bāmâ: A Question of Interpretation," ZAW 94 (1982): 203–13.

1031. Zevit, Religions, 262.

1032. J. M. Grintz, "Some Observations on the 'High Place' in the History of Israel," VT 27 (1977): 111–13; COS, 2.23, l. 3.

1033. King and Stager, Life in Biblical Israel, 320–21.

1034. Millard, Treasures, 96–97; T. A. Holland and Ehud Netzer, "Jericho," ABD, 3:723–40.

1035. ANET, 143–45, ll. 40, 153, 155, 299; COS, 1.102.

1036. Niehaus, God at Sinai, 228.

1037. Ibid., 120–24.

1038. W. F. Albright, "The 'Natural Force' of Moses in the Light of Ugaritic," BASOR 12 (1944): 32–35.

1039. D. P. Wright, "The Gesture of Hand Placement in the Hebrew Bible and in Hittite Literature," JAOS 106 (1986): 433–46.

1040. Ibid., 436, 446.

1041. Niehaus, God at Sinai, 123–24, nn. 43–44, for CAD refs. & detail (CAD Q, 320).

Sidebar and Chart Notes

A-1. I. Beit-Arieh and R. Gophna, "The Early Bronze Age II Settlement at ʿAin el-Quiderat (1980–1981)," Tel Aviv 8 (1981): 12–35; idem, "Early Bronze Age II Sites in Wadi el-

Qudeirat (Kadesh-Barnea)," *Tel Aviv* 3 (1976): 142–50.

A-2. A. Mazar, *Archaeology of the Land of the Bible* (New York: Doubleday, 1992), 444–46; Y. Aharoni, "Kadesh Barnea and Mount Sinai," in *God's Wilderness Discoveries in Sinai*, ed. B. Rothenberg (New York: Nelson, 1961), 137.

A-3. For a discussion of the options, see Hoffmeier, *Sinai*, 123–24.

A-4. Ibid., 153–59, for an up-to-date discussion of the number of Israelites in the Exodus.

A-5. Kitchen, *Reliability*, 190–93.

A-6. For tents in the ancient Near East and in Egypt see Hoffmeier, *Sinai*, 196–98; D. Wiseman, "They Lived in Tents," in *Biblical and Near Eastern Studies: Essays in Honor of William Sanford LaSor*, ed. Gary Tuttle (Grand Rapids: Eerdmans, 1978), 195–200; A Poebel, "The Khorsabad King List," *JNES* 1 (1942): 251.

A-7. Kitchen, *Reliability*, 191, see 545, n. 86, for up-to-date resources.

A-8. For full discussion and literature see Rainey and Notley, *Sacred Bridge*, 33–36, with map on 34; P. J. King and L. E. Stager, *Life in Biblical Israel* (Louisville: Westminster John Knox, 2001), 302, 352.

A-9. L. Grabbe, "Ugaritic and 'Canaanite': Some Methodological Observations," in *Ugarit and the Bible*, ed. G. J. Brooke, A. H. W. Curtis, and J. F. Healey (UBL 11; Münster: Ugarit-Verlag, 1994), 116–17.

A-10. King and Stager, *Life in Biblical Israel*, 302, 352.

A-11. W. G. Dever, *What Did the Biblical Writers Know and When Did They Know It?* (Grand Rapids: Eerdmans, 2001), 114–18.

A-12. K. Schoville, "Canaanites and Amorites," in *POTW*, 166–67.

A-13. Millard, *Treasures*, 88–89.

A-14. Rainey and Notley, *Sacred Bridge*, 59, 426, discusses the West Semitic alphabet; A. Lemaire, "Writing and Writing Materials," *ABD*, 6:1000. The details of the formation and development of the alphabet are still not entirely clear; it may be as early as 2100 B.C. per J. Darnell, "Journey to the Valley of Terror," *Chicago House Bulletin, Epigraphic Survey of the Oriental Institute 2* (April 1994): 1–2. For some discussion see Hoffmeier, *Sinai*, 179–81.

A-15. The following books are helpful: J. M. Miller and J. H. Hayes, *A History of Ancient Israel and Judah* (Philadelphia: Westminster, 1986), 40–53; P. J. King and L. Stager, *Life in Biblical Israel* (Louisville: Westminster John Knox, 2001), 85–112; R. P. Martin, "Food," *NBD*, 383–87; Rasmussen, *NIV Atlas of the Bible*, 25–26; H. T. Frank, *Atlas of the Bible Lands* (Maplewood, N.J.: Hammond, 1997), 7.

A-16. J. Kelso, "Agriculture," *NBD*, 20–21; King and Stager, *Life in Biblical Israel*, 86–101.

A-17. Miller and Hayes, *History of Ancient Israel and Judah*, 51.

A-18. King and Stager, *Life in Biblical Israel*, 94.

A-19. Ibid., 112–22.

A-20. Gerald Mattingly, "Moabites," *POTW*, 323–24.

A-21. Kitchen, *Reliability*, 195.

A-22. R. R. Stieglitz, "Ebla and the Gods of Canaan," in *Eblaitica: Essays on the Ebla Archives and Eblaite Language*, ed. C. H. Gordon and G. A. Rendsburg (Winona Lake, Ind.: Eisenbrauns, 1990), 2:83, 85–86.

A-23. Mattingly, "Moabites," 325.

A-24. LaBianca and Younker, "The Kingdoms of Ammon, Moab and Edom," 403, 405, 407, 411.

A-25. Weinfeld, *Deuteronomy 1–11*, 161–62.

A-26. Peter Craigie, *Deuteronomy* (Grand Rapids: Eerdmans, 1976), 110.

A-27. G. Mattingly, "Ar," *ABD*, 1:131; Rainey and Notley, *Sacred Bridge*, 123, 203.

A-28. For a helpful discussion see M. Suano, "The First Trading Empires: Prehistory to c. 1000 B.C.," in *The Mediterranean in History*, ed. D. Abulafia (Los Angeles: Getty, 2003), 70–71, 82–83, 303; 71 with picture.

A-29. E. C. Stone, "The Development of Cities in 'Ancient Mesopotamia,'" *CANE*, 236, 241, 1524.

A-30. D. Oredsson, *Moats in Ancient Palestine* (ConBOT 48; Stockholm: Almquist & Wiksell, 2000), an excellent resource.

A-31. Ibid., 175–83.

A-32. Z. Herzog, "Cities," *ABD*, 1:1035.

A-33. Tina Haettner Blomquist, *Gates and Gods* (CBOTS 46; Stockholm: Almquist & Wiksell, 1999), 11–21; Dever, *What Did the Biblical Writers Know and When?* 198–200.

A-34. R. Gonen, "Urban Canaan in the Late Bronze Period," *BASOR* 253 (Winter 1984): 61–73.

A-35. Stone, *CANE*, 244–45.

A-36. Herzog, "Cities," 1036–38.

A-37. S. Bunimovitz, "On the Edge of Empires—Late Bronze Age (1500–1200 B.C.)," in *The Archaeology of Society in the Holy Land*, ed. T. Levy (New York: Facts on File, 1995), 324–29; M. W. Chavalas and M. R. Adamthwaite, "Archaeological Light on the Old Testament," in *Face of Old Testament Studies*, 81; K. Kochavi, "The Israelite Settlement in Canaan in the Light of Archaeological Surveys," in *Biblical Archaeology Today*, ed. J. Aviram (Jerusalem: Israel Exploration Society, 1985), 54–60; J. M. Miller, "Archaeology and the Israelite Conquest of Canaan: Some Methodological Observations," *PEQ* 109 (1977): 87–93.

A-38. Gonen, "Urban Canaan," 70; Walton, "Exodus, Date of," 269.

A-39. McCarthy, *Treaty and Covenant*, esp. 1–24, 37–85, 106–21; see Beckman, *Diplomatic Texts*, 16–114 for translation of all texts; Kitchen, *Reliability*, 284–89.

A-40. *ANET*, 277–301.

A-41. G. E. Mendenhall and G. A. Herion, "Covenant," *ABD*, 1:1187; E. Merrill, "Archaeology and Biblical History," in *Giving the Sense*, 94–95.

A-42. So A. F. Campbell in his review of Paul Kalluveettil in *Declaration and Covenant: A Comprehensive Review of Covenant Formulas from the O.T. and the ANE* (AnBib 88; Rome:

Biblical Institute, 1982), 134. He sees the Ten Commandments as "summarizing the stipulations"; cf. Kitchen, *Reliability*, 284.

A-43. Kitchen, *Reliability*, 284–89.

A-44. Provan, Long, and Longman III, *Biblical History*, 134.

A-45. H. Güterbock, "Hittite Historiography," in *History, Historiography and Interpretation*, ed. H. Tadmor and M. Weinfeld (Jerusalem/ Leiden: Magnes/Brill, 1986), 29.

A-46. See Christensen, *Deuteronomy 1:1–21:9*, 87; H. W. F. Saggs, *The Greatness That Was Babylon* (New York: Hawthorne, 1962), 314–29; Millard, *Treasures*, 50–53; del Olmo Lete, *Canaanite Religion*, 43–44, 87, 213, 324–25.

A-47. Millard, *Treasures*, 50–53.

A-48. Machinist, "Distinctiveness," 429.

A-49. For a recent discussion of magic and divination see L. Ciraolo and J. Seidel, eds., *Magic and Divination in the Ancient World* (Ancient Magic and Divination 2; Leiden: Brill, 2002), esp. 7, 41, 47–49, 57–59, 83–84.

A-50. J. Lindsay, *Origins of Astrology* (New York: Barnes & Noble, 1971), 42; see esp. H. Hunger, ed., *Astrological Reports to Assyrian Kings* (SAA 8; Helsinki: Helsinki Univ. Press, 1992).

A-51. Ciraolo and Seifel, *Divination*, 45–49.

A-52. W. Farber, "Witchcraft, Magic, and Divination in Ancient Mesopotamia," *CANE*, 1907–8.

A-53. F. Rochberg, "Astronomy and Calendars in Ancient Mesopotamia," *CANE*, 1925–40.

A-54. Lindsay, *Astrology*, 42; Hunger, *Astrological Reports*, passim.

A-55. H. W. F. Saggs, "The Divine in History," in *Essential Papers on Israel and the Ancient Near East*, ed. F. Greenspahn (New York: New York Univ. Press, 1991), 41–42.

A-56. Christensen, *Deuteronomy 1:1–21:9*, 111–12.

A-57. U. Avner, "Sacred Stones in the Desert," *BAR* 27/3 (2001): 39.

A-58. T. Mettinger, *No Graven Image* (CBOTS 42; Stockholm: Almquist & Wiksell, 1995), 55–56.

A-59. See discussion in Hoffmeier, *Sinai*, 239–40.

A-60. U. Avner, "Sacred Stones," 40; idem, "Ancient Cult Sites in the Negev and Sinai Deserts," *Tel Aviv* 11 (1984): 115–31.

A-61. Craigie, *Deuteronomy*, 154–55.

A-62. *COS*, 2.29; 2.30; for more examples see Weinfeld, *Deuteronomy 1–11*, 285.

A-63. C. Teaunecker, *The Gods of Egypt* (Ithaca, N.Y.: Cornell Univ. Press, 2001), 96–99.

A-64. J. Assman, *The Search for God in Ancient Egypt*, trans. D. Lorton (Ithaca, N.Y.: Cornell Univ. Press, 2001), 141.

A-65. *ANET*, 251.

A-66. Craigie, *Deuteronomy*, 162.

A-67. Weinfeld, *Deuteronomy 1–11*, 340–41.

A-68. *ANET*, 412–20, 921–25; *COS*, 1:115–22.

A-69. R. E. Murphy, "Wisdom in the Old Testament," *ABD*, 6:929.

A-70. *ANET*, 589–91, 600–604.

A-71. J. Vanderkam, "Ahiqar," *ABD*, 1:113–14; 6:929–30; *ANET*, 427–30.

A-72. M. Civil, "Education," *ABD*, 2:301–12; G. Pinch, "Private Life in Ancient Egypt," *CANE*, 379, 492, 644.

A-73. *ANET*, 538 (34).

A-74. In general see M. Smith, *The Early History of God: Yahweh and the Other Deities in Ancient Israel* (San Francisco: HarperCollins, 1990); R. M. Seltzer, *Religions of Antiquity*, ed. R. M. Seltzer (New York: Macmillan, 1989).

A-75. See Merrill, *Kingdom of Priests*, 159–61, for a brief summary of Canaanite religion; for detail see del Olmo Lete, *Canaanite Religion*, 1–388; Smith, *The Early History of God*; essays in Seltzer, *Religions of Antiquity*.

A-76. M. S. Smith, "Myth and Mythmaking in Canaan and Ancient Israel," *CANE*, 2034, and chart; see Deut. 32:9; e.g., *COS*, 2.29, ll. 1–3.

A-77. Millard, *Treasures*, 181–83.

A-78. Rendsburg, *Bible and Ancient Near East*, 153–61; see also Eckart Otto, "Town and Rural Countryside in Ancient Israelite Law: Reception and Redaction in Cuneiform and Israelite Law," *JSOT* 57 (1993): 3–22. Otto concludes that the literary form of ancient Near Eastern and biblical laws and even content to a lesser degree show a dependency on common features of ancient Near Eastern laws (esp. 20–22).

A-79. Ibid., 153–61.

A-80. Westbrook, *Biblical and Cuneiform Law*, 133–35.

A-81. Greengus, "Law," *ABD*, 4:245b; see 242–51 for a helpful overview of comparisons *and* contrasts between Israel's laws and the legal tradition of the rest of the ancient Near East.

A-82. K. van der Toorn, "Theology, Priests, and Worship in Canaan and Ancient Israel," *CANE*, 2053.

A-83. Del Olmo Lete, *Canaanite Religion*, 28–29, has a description of both.

A-84. Ibid., 32. For the Ugaritic pantheon see 43–86; Hill and Walton, *A Survey of the Old Testament*, 470, for a helpful chart.

A-85. Kitchen, *Reliability*, 403.

A-86. J. Day, "Religion of Canaan," *ABD*, 1:831.

A-87. *COS*, 1.86, *CTA*, 4.V. 64–73.

A-88. Ibid., 1:831–32.

A-89. Kitchen, *Reliability*, 404.

A-90. Ibid., 405.

A-91. Del Olmo Lete, *Canaanite Religion*, 37; W. G. E. Watson and N. Wyatt, eds., *Handbook of Ugaritic Studies* (Leiden: Brill, 1999), 564–65.

A-92. Ibid., 38–39.

A-93. *COS*, 1.122.

A-94. J. Day, "Religion of Canaan," *ABD*, 1:834.

A-95. See discussion in Marsman, *Women in Ugarit*, esp. 415–19, 433–35, 497–99, 570, 598–99, 728.

A-96. *COS*, 1.90; 1.91; 1.92; 1.93; cf. 1.94; 1.96.

A-97. *COS*, 1.90, Introd; 1.120, 8–15; P. Xella, "The Omen Texts," in *Handbook of Ugaritic Studies*, ed. W. G. E. Watson and N. Wyatt (Leiden: Brill, 1999), 353–54; also 56, 163–64; M. Dietrich, O. Loretz, and J. Sammartin, *The*

Cuniform Alphabetic Texts, 2nd ed. (Münster: Ugarit-Verlag, 1995), 117–20, 136, 143; *KTU*, 1.103; 1.145; 1.140; 1.124.

A-98. *COS*, "Divination," 1:421–22; 1.120; W. W. Hallo, "Before Tea Leaves: Divination in Ancient Babylonia," *BAR* 31.2 (March/April 2005): 33–39.

A-99. Day, "Canaanite Religion," *ADB*, 1:834; Hallo, "Before Tea Leaves," 35–36.

A-100. See Kitchen, *Reliability*, 406–7, for a full description of the Lachish temple, its contents, and its rituals.

A-101. Ibid., 409.

A-102. For a review of the current knowledge in this area see ibid., esp. 403–9.

A-103. G. C. Heider, *The Cult of Molek* (JSOTSup 43; Sheffield: Sheffield Academic Press, 1985), 101, 113, 146, 164–68, 200, 222; see also A. R. W. Green, *The Role of Human Sacrifice in the Ancient Near East* (ASOR Dissertation 1; Missoula, Mont.: Scholars Press, 1975).

A-104. Del Olmo Lete, *Canaanite Religion*, 39; Day, "Canaanite Religion," 1:834.

A-105. Day, "Canaanite Religion," 1:833–36.

A-106. Watson and Wyatt, *Handbook*, 560–64, 576–78, 580.

A-107. *ANET*, 417; *COS*, 1.35, 129; Hallo, "Compare and Contrast," 12–13; A. Malamat, "A Forerunner of Biblical Prophecy," in *Essential Papers on Israel and the Ancient Near East*, ed. F. Greenspahn (New York: New York Univ. Press, 1991), 153, 156–69; Greene, *Role of Messenger*, 232–66, compares the Heb. prophet with ancient Near Eastern and Hebrew messengers.

A-108. Most of what follows is illustrated well in Kitchen, *Reliability*, 383–93; H. B. Huffmon, "Prophecy (ANE)," *ABD*, 5:477–81, for a succinct summary of ancient Near Eastern prophecy.

A-109. R. K. Ritner, "Ecstatic Episode from 'The Report of Wenamon,'" in *Prophets and Prophecy in the ANE*, ed. M. Nissinen (SBLWAW 12; Atlanta: Scholars Press, 2005), 220.

A-110. B. Uffenheimer, "Hamath in Northern Syria," in *Early Prophecy in Israel* (Jerusalem: Magnes, 1999), 32–38.

A-111. M. Nissinen, *References to Prophecy in Neo-Assyrian Sources* (SAAS 7; Helsinki: Univ. of Helsinki, 1998), 96.

A-112. Weinfeld, *Prophecy*, 90–91.

A-113. Nissinen, *References to Prophecy*, 166–67.

A-114. Weinfeld, "Patterns," 84–101; Kitchen, *Reliability*, 389–93.

A-115. A. R. Millard, "La prophétie et l'écriture Israël, Aram, Assyrie," *RHR 202* (1985): 125–45.

A-116. See Roberts, "Ancient Near Eastern Environment," 19, for discussion and references.

A-117. Cf. also Craigie, *Deuteronomy*, 227, and Additional Note; Weinfeld, *Deuteronomic School*, 100, claims "proof" for the seventh-century date of the biblical laws, which is certainly not the case.

A-118. *COS*, 1.126, The Consecration Day, ll 9–10; D. Fleming, "The Etymological Origins of the Hebrew 'nabi'," *CBQ* 55 (1993): 220–24.

A-119. J. Huehnergard, "On the Etymology and Meaning of Hebrew 'navi,'" *EI* 26 (1999): 89, 88–93.

A-120. Nissinen, *References to Prophecy*, 93–94.

A-121. Lemaire, "Mari," 102.

A-122. D. Baker, "Israelite Prophets and Prophecy," in *The Face of Old Testament Studies* (Grand Rapids: Baker, 1999), 274–75.

A-123. M. Pope, "The Cult of the Dead at Ugarit," in *Ugarit in Retrospect*, ed. G. D. Young (Winona Lake, Ind.: Eisenbrauns, 1981), 159–79.

A-124. D. Pardee, *Ritual and Cult at Ugarit* (SBLWAW 10; Atlanta: Society of Biblical Literature, 2002), 195–210.

A-125. H. A. Hoffner Jr., "Second Millennium Antecedents to the Hebrew *bôr*," *JBL* 86 (1967): 385–401.

A-126. C. A. Kennedy, "Cult of the Dead," *ABD*, 2:106; B. S. Levine and J.-M. de Terragon, "Dead Kings and Rephaim: The Patrons of the Ugaritic Dynasty," *JAOS* 104 (1984): 649–59; P. Xella, "Death and Afterlife in Canaanite and Hebrew Thought," *CANE*, 2060–66; *COS*, 1.105.

A-127. Beyerlin, *Near Eastern Religious Texts*, 215.

A-128. T. J. Lewis, *Cults of the Dead in Ancient Israel and Ugarit* (Atlanta: Scholars Press, 1989), 100; cf. *CML*, 73, 5:18–20; 19:169–79.

A-129. *COS*, 1.103; Lewis, *Cults of the Dead*, 100–101.

A-130. Lewis, *Cults of the Dead*, 101.

A-131. *ANET*, 98.

A-132. *CANE*, 888–89.

A-133. B. Arnold, "Religion in Ancient Israel," in *The Face of Old Testament Studies*, ed. D. W. Baker and B. T. Arnold (Grand Rapids: Baker, 1999), 414–15. See for a brief summary and bibliography.

A-134. B. R. Schmidt, *Israel's Beneficent Dead* (Winona Lake, Ind.: Eisenbrauns, 1996), 27–41.

A-135. *COS*, 2.36, ll. 15b–18; 2.37, ll. 17–19.

A-136. Rendsburg, *Bible and Ancient Near East*, 55–56.

A-137. King and Stager, *Life in Biblical Israel*, 376.

A-138. Craigie, *Deuteronomy*, 230–31; he refers esp. to *CTA*, 5.VI.14–18 (=*UT* 67); *CTA*, 19.IV.173, 184 (=*UT* 1 Aqht); Parker, *Ugaritic Poetry*, 149; *CML*, 19.4.184–87; J. Nougoyrol, "Textes suméro-accadiens des archives et bibliothèques privées d'Ugarit," *Ugaritica* 5 (1968): 265–73; Driver, *Deuteronomy*, 156.

A-139. Westbrook, *HANEL*, 264–65; *COS*, 1.38, 1.248–50; 1.43, ll. 183–85.

A-140. Ibid., 302–6.

A-141. Ibid., 439.

A-142. Ibid., 489–90, 572–74, 569–71.

A-143. Ibid., 628–30, 658–61, 695–97, 720–22, respectively.

A-144. Greengus, "Legal and Social Institutions," *CANE*, 621–27; H. Reviv, *The Elders in Ancient Israel* (Jerusalem: Magnes, 1989), 146–47.

A-145. Westbrook, *HANEL*, 143–44.

A-146. Ibid., 145.

A-147. Ibid., 159–60, 161–91.

A-148. Greengus, "Legal and Social Institutions," 622.

A-149. S. D. Spealing, "Avenger of Blood," *ABD*, 1:764; EA 8:26–29.

A-150. *COS*, 1.76, Law 49.

A-151. For the development of these cities in biblical perspective, see Barmash, *Homicide*, 71–93.

A-152. P. Barmash, "Blood Feud and State Control: Differing Legal Institutions for the Remedy of Homicide during the Second and First Millennia B.C.E.," *JNES* 63 (2004): 183–99.

A-153. F. E. Greenspahn, "Primogeniture in Ancient Israel," in *Go to the Land I Will Show You*, ed. J. Coleson and V. Matthews (Winona Lake, Ind.: Eisenbrauns, 1996), 72–73.

A-154. *ANET*, 160; Roth, *Law Collections*, 112.

A-155. Cf. *ANET*, 546.

A-156. *ANET*, 220a; Roth, *Law Collections*, 113.

A-157. Westbrook, *HANEL*, 710, 712.

A-158. Ibid., 678.

A-159. Ibid., 544.

A-160. Westbrook, *HANEL*, 276–77.

A-161. Ibid., 333–34.

A-162. Cf. *ANET*, 185d; Craigie, *Deuteronomy*, 283, n. 19; *COS*, 1.38, 235–45; cf. in general 3.63, 17–37.

A-163. Kitchen, *Reliability*, 326, 570, nn. 41–43.

A-164. *ANET*, 185d; Westbrook, *HANEL*, 58.

A-165. Cf. *COS*, 3.63, 17–54.

A-166. Roth, *Law Collections*, 158, 160, Laws 15, 20; *ANET*, 181, would also include Laws 18–19 in this category by castration; COS and Roth translate as "cut off their beard/hair."

A-167. J. S. Hawkins, "Eunuchs Among the Hittites," in *Sex and Gender in the Ancient Near East*, ed. S. Parpola and R. M. Whiting (Part 1; Helsinki: The Neo-Assyrian Text Corpus Project, 2002), 229, 231–33.

A-168. K. Deller, "The Assyrian Eunuchs and Their Predecessors," in *Priests and Officials in the Ancient Near East*, ed. K. Watanabe (Heidelberg: Universitätsverlag C. Winter, 1999), 303–12.

A-169. *COS*, 1.70, Law 32.

A-170. Ibid., 309–11.

A-171. H. Tadmor, "Rab-saris and Rab-shakeh in 2 Kings 18," in *The Word of the Lord Shall Go Forth: Essays in Honor of D. N. Freedman*, ed. C. L. Meyers and M. O'Connor (Winona Lake, Ind.: Eisenbrauns, 1983), 279–82, nn. 10, 17. These were titles of the Chief Eunuch.

A-172. A. K. Grayson, "Eunuchs in Power: Their Role in the Assyrian Bureaucracy," in *Vom Alten Orient zum Alten Testament: Festschriften für Wolfram Freiherrn von Soden zum 85 Geburtstag am 19 Juni 1993*, ed. M. Dietrich and O. Loretz (AOAT 240; Kevalaer/Neukirchen-Vluyn: Butzon & Bercker/Neukirchener Verlag, 1995), 93–94.

A-173. Ibid., 95.

A-174. *COS*, 1.159, ll. 75–9.

A-175. *ANET*, 497.

A-176. K. M. Campbell, ed., *Marriage and Family in the Biblical World* (Downers Grove, Ill.: InterVarsity Press, 2003), 24–25.

A-177. Saggs, *Greatness*, 26–27.

A-178. *ANET*, 107 (138–40).

A-179. Campbell, *Marriage and Family*, 26.

A-180. *COS*, 22.19, Law 26b.

A-181. *COS*, 3.101B.

A-182. A. Rofé, *Deuteronomy* (New York: T. & T. Clark, 2002), 185, n. 49.

A-183. Craigie, *Deuteronomy*, 305.

A-184. R. Westbrook, "The Prohibition on Restoration of Marriage in Deuteronomy 24:1–4," in *Studies in Bible*, ed. S. Japhet (Jerusalem: Magnes, 1986), 404.

A-185. J. Walton, "The Place of the Hutqattel within the D-Stem Group and its Implications in Deuteronomy 24:4," *Hebrew Studies* 32 (1991): 12–15.

A-186. Rofé, *Deuteronomy*, 222–23.

A-187. K. van der Toorn, *From the Cradle to Her Grave*, trans. S. J. Denning-Bolle (Sheffield: Sheffield Academic Press, 1994), 135, 139–40; King and Stager, *Life in Biblical Israel*, 55.

A-188. *COS*, 3.46; Westbrook, *Biblical and Cuneiform Law*, 21.

A-189. Westbrook, *Biblical and Cuneiform Law*, 11–12, nn. 9–13.

A-190. F. Fensham, "Widow, Orphan, and the Poor in ANE and Wisdom Literature," *JNES* 21 (1962): 138.

A-191. *COS*, 1.43, 62–71.

A-192. Fensham, "Widow, Orphan," 133.

A-193. Ibid.; see entire article, 129–39.

A-194. Ibid., 135; cf. also H. Lohfink, "Poverty in the Laws of the Ancient Near East and of the Bible," *TS* 52 (1991): 34–50.

A-195. Tigay, *Deuteronomy*, 482–83, excursus 23; D. W. Manor, "A Brief History of Levirate Marriage as It Relates to the Bible," *RQ* 27 (1984): 129–42; Westbrook, *HANEL*, 49, 538, 637.

A-196. V. P. Hamilton, "Marriage (OT & ANE)," *ABD*, 4:560.

A-197. Ibid., 4:567.

A-198. *ANET*, 196, Law 193; Roth, *Law Collections*, 236; Marsman, *Women in Ugarit*, 301–2.

A-199. Tigay, *Deuteronomy*, 483.

A-200. J. Huehnergard, "Biblical Notes on Some Akkadian Texts from Emar," *CBQ* 47 (1985): 431–33; for other examples see *COS*, 2:118, 356; cf. also 3:86, "The Widow's Plea."

A-201. Beyerlin, *Near Eastern Religious Texts*, 232; see also M. Tsevat, "Marriage and Monarchical Legitimacy in Ugarit and Israel," *JSS* 3 (1958): 237–43.

A-202. *ANET*, 182b, Laws A30, 33, A43; Marsman, *Women in Ugarit*, 300–301; Roth, *Law Collections*, 164–65, 169.

A-203. *ANET*, 205; Beckman, *Diplomatic Texts*, 46.

A-204. For text see *COS*, 1.123.

A-205. See *COS*, 1.123.

A-206. Beyerlin, *Near Eastern Religious Texts*, 219.

A-207. Kitchen, *Reliability*, 282, 562, n. 102.

A-208. Ibid., 234.

A-209. Ibid., 237, 244.

A-210. J. N. Lawson, *The Concept of Fate in Ancient Mesopotamia of the First Millennium* (OBC 7; Wiesbaden: Harrassowitz, 1994), 19–41.

A-211. Ibid., 130–34.

A-212. COS, 1.111, ll. 60–70, and passim; *ANET*, 502a.

A-213. COS, 1.113, Tablet IV (413a).

A-214. *ANET*, 438.

A-215. *ANET*, 111, esp. 112b–113, 502, 515–16; COS, 3.147, ll. 65–87.

A-216. *ANET*, 541.

A-217. A. R. George, "Sennacherib and the Tablet of Destinies," *Iraq* 48 (1986): 134, 138–39.

A-218. *ANET*, 575, 577.

A-219. COS, 1.47, 19:10–15.

A-220. COS, 1.27, esp. n. 1.

A-221. See W. Horowitz and V. Hurowitz, "Urim and Thummim in Light of a Psephomanacy Ritual from Assur (LKA 137)," *JANESCU* 24 (1992): 95–115.

A-222. Horowitz and Hurowitz, "Urim and Thummim," 104.

A-223. Ibid., 104–5; F. Nötscher, "Die Omen-Serie *šuma âluina mêlê šakin*," *Or* 51 (1930): 218–20.

A-224. Horowitz and Hurowitz, "Urim and Thummim," 104–15.

This is an index to all of the pictures used in the five volumes of *Zondervan Illustrated Bible Background Commentary—Old Testament*. This index does not list the page number for the appropriate entry in each volume; rather, it lists the approximate location of each picture by Bible book and chapter. Each entry should be easy to locate within a page or two of where the comments on each Bible chapter begin.

Ibex, 1 Sam. 24

Jackal, Judg. 15; Job 30; Jer. 8

Lamb, Ex. 12; 2 Sam. 12

Leopard, Jer. 13

Lion, Gen. 6; Judg. 2; 14; 1 Kings 12;
   2 Kings 17; Ezra 7; Ps. 15; Isa. 11; Jer. 2;
   Ezek. 22; Dan. 6; Amos 3; Zeph. 3

Lion Attack, 1 Kings 13; Isa. 31; Jer. 16;
   Ezek. 19

Lion Attacking Bull, Isa. 5

Lion Hunting, Gen. 10; 1 Sam. 17;
   2 Sam. 23; 1 Chron. 11; Ps. 45; Jer. 22;
   27; Nah. 2

Lion Scepter, Gen. 49

Lions after Hunt, 2 Kings 21

Locusts, Ex. 10; Isa. 33; Joel 1

Lord of Animals, Gen. 2

Mollusk, Ex. 25

Monkeys, Jer. 24

Murex Snail, Isa. 1; Ezek. 26

Ostrich, Job 39; Mic. 1

Ostrich Eggs, Lam. 4

Ox Butchering, Gen. 9

Oxen, 2 Kings 6

Pig Remains, Deut. 14; Neh. 10; Isa. 66

Quail, Ex. 16

Ram, Gen. 22; 30; 2 Chron. 32

Sheep, Gen. 12; 30; 1 Sam. 16; Isa. 32;
   Amos 1; Mic. 2

Snail, Gen. 49

Snake, Serpent, Gen. 3; Ex. 4; Num. 21;
   2 Kings 18; Ps. 58; 140; Eccl. 10;
   Isa.22; 30; 37; Jer. 7; Jon. 2

Vulture, Ex. 19; Job 15; Ezek. 17; Mic. 1

Anointing

Anointing of Pharaoh, 1 Sam. 2; 10;
   1 Kings 1; 1 Chron. 11; Isa. 45

Anointing Vessel, Lev. 8; 1 Sam. 10; 16

Banquet

Ashurbanipal Banquet, Est. 5; Ps. 23

Banquet, 1 Sam. 25; Isa. 5; Obad.; Job 21;
   Ps. 110

Beer Drinking, Prov. 20

Standard of Ur, Gen. Introduction;
   1 Kings 10; 2 Chron. 1; Job 1

Boundary Stones

Astral Symbols, Deut. 4

Babylonian Land Grant (Nabu-apla-
   iddina), Gen. 13; Josh. Introduction;
   1 Sam 22

Chaos Creature, Gen. 1; Ps. 75

Eanna-shum-iddina, Prov. 23

Gezer, Ruth 2

Marduk, Isa. 46

Marduk Temple, Deut. 19

Marduk-zakir-shumi, 2 Chron. 24

Melishihu, Dan. 8

Meli-shipak, Num. 28; Ps. 84; Isa. 13

Merodach-baladan, 2 Kings 20; Isa. 39

Michaux Stone, Job 24

Nabu-apla-iddina, 1 Sam. 22

Nature Gods, Isa. 43

Senusret III's Boundary Marker, Isa. 19

Setting Up Boundary Stone, Hos. 5

Shamash, Judg. 13

Sippar, 2 Kings 9

Unfinished Kudurru, Job 9; Ps. 104;
   Jonah 2

Bowing/Lifted Hands

Ashkelon relief (Merneptah), Lev. 9;
   Judg. Introduction; 2 Sam. 1; 2 Kings 3

Bowing backwards, Lev. 9

Bowing before Ruler, 1 Sam. 16; Est. 3

Bowing Captives, Deut. 20

Bowing in Lachish, 2 Sam. 10; Neh. 8;
   Ps. 95; Isa. 66

Bowing Servant, Isa. 60

Elamite Captive Bowing, Ps. 2

Hands Raised, Isa. 1; Job 11

Hazor Stone, 1 Kings 8

Kneeling Man, Jer. 7

Kneeling Pharaoh, 2 Chron. 6

Lady Taperet, Ps. 28

Praying Priest, 1 Kings 8; Ps. 44

Shalmaneser III's Black Obelisk, 1 Sam. 24

Worshiper Seal, Amos 5

Burial

Abraham's Tomb, Gen. 25

Absalom's Tomb, 2 Sam. 18

Achaemenid Tombs, Ezra 4

Offerings

Pedestal

Plants

Pottery

Reconstructions

Reliefs, Mesopotamian

We want to hear from you. Please send your comments about this
book to us in care of zreview@zondervan.com. Thank you.

ZONDERVAN.com/
AUTHORTRACKER
follow your favorite authors